Artists' Things

Artists' Things

Rediscovering Lost Property from Eighteenth-Century France

Katie Scott & Hannah Williams

GETTY RESEARCH INSTITUTE, LOS ANGELES

This publication was created using Quire™, a multiformat publishing tool from Getty.

The free online edition of this open-access publication is available at getty.edu/publications/artists-things/ and includes zoomable illustrations. Free PDF and EPUB downloads of the book are also available.

First edition 2024

Any revisions or corrections made to this publication after the first edition date will be listed here and in the project repository at github.com/thegetty/artists-things/, where a more detailed version history is available. The revisions branch of the project repository, when present, will show any changes currently under consideration but not yet published here.

Getty Research Institute Publications Program
Mary E. Miller, *Director, Getty Research Institute*

Published by the Getty Research Institute, Los Angeles
Getty Publications
1200 Getty Center Drive, Suite 500
Los Angeles, California 90049-1682
getty.edu/publications/

Lauren Edson, *Project Editor*
Mary Christian, *Manuscript Editor*
Greg Albers, *Digital Publications Manager*
Picnic Design, *Design*
Molly McGeehan, *Production*
Karen Ehrmann and Pauline Lopez, *Image and Rights Acquisition*

Distributed in the United States and Canada by the University of Chicago Press

Distributed outside the United States and Canada by Yale University Press, London

Printed and bound by CPI Group (UK) Ltd, Croydon, CR0 4YY

Library of Congress Cataloging-in-Publication Data
Names: Scott, Katie, 1958– author. | Williams, Hannah, 1980– author.
Title: Artists' things : rediscovering lost property from eighteenth-century France / Katie Scott and Hannah Williams.
Description: First edition. | Los Angeles : Getty Research Institute, 2024. | Includes bibliographical references. | Summary: "This innovative book looks at objects that once belonged to artists, revealing not only the fabric of the eighteenth-century art world in France but also unfamiliar—and sometimes unexpected—insights into the individuals who populated it, including Jean-Antoine Watteau, François Boucher, Jean-Baptiste Greuze, and Elisabeth Vigée-LeBrun"— Provided by publisher.
Identifiers: LCCN 2023024679 | ISBN 9781606068632 (paperback) | ISBN 9781606068649 | ISBN 9781606068656 (adobe pdf) | ISBN 9781606068663 (epub)
Subjects: LCSH: Artists—France—History—18th century. | Personal belongings—France—History—18th century. | Material culture—France—History—18th century. | Art, French—18th century.
Classification: LCC N6846 .S36 2024 | DDC 709.44/09033-dc23/eng/20230602 LC record available at https://lccn.loc.gov/2023024679

This publication was peer reviewed through a single-masked process in which the reviewers remained anonymous.

Front cover: Double-hinged wig spectacles, ca. 1795. White metal frame and glass lenses, 38 mm (eye). London, British Optical Association Museum, College of Optometrists, inv. 1998.235.

Contents

List of Owners

Bouchardon, Edme (model)

Boucher, François (shell)

Chardin, Jean-Siméon (lantern, water fountain)

Cochin, Charles-Nicolas (handkerchief, lantern)

Collot, Marie-Anne (nightingale)

Concierge of the Académie Royale (funeral book)

Coypel, Charles-Antoine (bed, watch)

David, Jacques-Louis (table)

Desportes, Claude-François (lantern)

Drevet, Pierre-Imbert (votive)

Drouais, François-Hubert (sugar spoon)

Duplessis, Joseph-Siffred (bath, dog, red lake)

Falconet, Étienne-Maurice (quill)

Fragonard, Jean-Honoré (armchair, color box)

Giroust, Marie-Suzanne (pastels)

Greuze, Jean-Baptiste (marriage contract)

Grimou, Alexis (wine)

Houdon, Jean-Antoine (écorché, modeling stand)

Huët, Jean-Baptiste (*crayon*)

Jacquemin, Pierre-André (lantern)

Janinet, Jean-François (hot-air balloon)

Lagrenée, Louis-Jean-François (order book)

Largillière, Nicolas de (picture)

Le Bas, Jacques-Philippe (umbrella)

Le Prince, Jean-Baptiste (mannequin)

Lemoyne, François (sword)

Lemoyne, Jean-Baptiste (lantern)

Liotard, Jean-Étienne (gaming set)

Marlié, Renée-Elisabeth (burin)

Massé, Jean-Baptiste (will)

Moreau the Younger, Jean-Michel (sketchbook)

Natoire, Charles-Joseph (intaglio)

Nattier, Jean-Marc (harpsichord, teacup)

Oppenord, Gilles-Marie (book)

Oudry, Jean-Baptiste (snuffbox)

Parrocel, Charles (camera obscura)

Perronneau, Jean-Baptiste (*porte-crayon*)

Peyron, Pierre (key)

Pigalle, Jean-Baptiste (carriage, lantern)

Rigaud, Hyacinthe (letters, relic)

Robert, Hubert (baptism certificate)

Saint-Aubin, Gabriel de (book)

Secretaries of the Académie Royale (document box)

Tocqué, Louis (harpsichord)

Van Loo, Louis-Michel (*robe de chambre*)

Vernet, Claude-Joseph (almanac, lantern, wig)

Vien, Joseph-Marie (decoration, lantern)

Vigée-Lebrun, Elisabeth (palette)

Vincent, François-André (glasses)

Watteau, Jean-Antoine (dressing-up box)

Wille, Johann Georg (journal)

Abbreviations & Symbols

ABBREVIATIONS

AAF	*Archives de l'art français*
AN	Archives Nationales de France
BJHS	*British Journal for the History of Science*
BM	*The Burlington Magazine*
BnF	Bibliothèque Nationale de France
BSHAF	*Bulletin de la Société de l'histoire de l'art français*
CDR	*Correspondance des directeurs de l'Académie de France à Rome avec les surintendants des bâtiments*, ed. Anatole de Montaiglon and Jules Guiffrey, 18 vols. Paris: Charavay Frères, 1887–1908
ECL	*Eighteenth-Century Literature*
ECS	*Eighteenth-Century Studies*
Encyclopédie	*Encyclopédie, ou dictionnaire raisonné des sciences, des arts et des métiers, etc.* (1751–72), ed. Denis Diderot and Jean Le Rond d'Alembert. University of Chicago: ARTFL Encyclopédie Project (Autumn 2017 edition), ed. Robert Morrissey and Glenn Roe, http://encyclopedie.uchicago.edu/
ENSBA	École Nationale Supérieure des Beaux-Arts, Paris
GBA	*Gazette des beaux-arts*
INHA	Institut National d'Histoire de l'Art, Paris
MC	Minutier Central, Paris
Mémoires inédits	*Mémoires inédits sur la vie et les ouvrages des membres de l'Académie royale de peinture et de sculpture*, ed. Louis Dussieux, 2 vols. Paris: J.-B. Dumoulin, 1853–54
NAAF	*Nouvelles archives de l'art français*. Paris: J. Baur, 1873

PV	*Procès-verbaux de l'Académie royale de peinture et de sculpture, 1648–1793*, ed. Anatole de Montaiglon, 10 vols. Paris: Charavay Frères, 1875–92
SVEC	*Studies in Voltaire and the Eighteenth Century* (Oxford University Studies in the Enlightenment)

AUTHOR SYMBOLS

§	Katie Scott
‡	Hannah Williams

Introduction

Artists are makers of things. Yet it is a measure of the disembodied manner in which we generally think about artists that we rarely consider the everyday things artists themselves owned. And not for lack of evidence. Though most eighteenth-century artists' Lives are reticent about their subjects' belongings and refer only briefly to, for example, a lute, or a dressing gown, or a wine glass, wittily to figure some aspect of personality or character,[1] the painters, sculptors, and printmakers of early modern Europe were in fact generally sufficiently rich in stuff to warrant, on death, the drawing up of estate inventories that run, in some cases, to tens of pages listing hundreds of items.[2] Since the 1980s, such notarized lists—which survive in great number for the early modern period—have been the focus of studies of consumption by economic and social historians,[3] but they have mostly not commanded the same level of critical attention from art historians.[4] Although no longer regarded as transparently factual because bound by legal convention and by local practices of expertise, inventories nevertheless afford a detailed picture of things—their material, size, condition, value, location—the critical reading of which has the potential to yield a richer understanding of artists' relations to their work and their world.[5] This book thus begins in paradox. We know things about artists the knowing of which is often discounted in advance as irrelevant by normative art-historical discourses on the artist, then and now.[6] Does it matter, in other words, that the portraitist Maurice-Quentin de La Tour had a passion for telescopes, that history painter Jean-Baptiste-Marie Pierre kept chickens, and that sculptor Clodion owned a clyster for administering enemas?[7]

Our aim in this book has not been to write a definitive history of the material culture of painters, sculptors, and printmakers in eighteenth-century France, but, less ambitiously, to open up a line of investigation into things overlooked by, which is to say effectively lost to, the discipline of art history, and to see where it leads. Though we have been inspired by a range of interdisciplinary work, none provided a genre with which our project seemed entirely to fit. It is not, for example, in the tradition of studies of the artist-as-collector, because we do not confine our investigations to the art object.[8] Neither does it follow in the footsteps of Pierre Bourdieu's sociology of taste, because things are not for us exclusively, or even always primarily, indexes of social stratification—that is, of class.[9] Nor does it sit neatly alongside studies of commodity chains, which attend to the "career" of specific objects as they move in and out of exchange, because not all our things behaved like commodities.[10] And while we share Daniel Miller's concern with the affect of things, our own microhistorical studies of the relationships between owner and possession are driven by a more art-historical attention to the materiality of the thing itself.[11]

For lack of an obvious model for our hybrid inquiry, we turn to Johnnie Gratton and Michael Sheringham's *The Art of the Project* (2005).[12] The "art" of the title of this collection of essays is both denotative and sly. It indexes contemporary art practice, or project art, as a distinct field of study, and it alludes to the skills of experimentation and exploration on which projects in the conventional sense generally depend. Gratton and Sheringham identify the following characteristics of projects. First, the procedures that enact projects are at least as important as, if not ultimately more significant than, the findings they generate. Second, projecting often involves a conscious act of re-siting, that is to say, projects relocate the field of operation outside and beyond habitual places of research and study. Third, projects unfold within and are shaped by self-imposed and self-consciously acknowledged constraints. And lastly, lacking respect for disciplinary boundaries, projects are often the work of "amateurs"—investigators moving and operating beyond their professional expertise.

To begin with the last feature, we are both art historians. By vocation and training we are specialists in the history and critical analysis of the visual arts of eighteenth-century France. This project has turned us into would-be ethnographers—participant observers, so to speak, of eighteenth-century artists and their stuff. We have collected, compared, listed, and classified things as we found them. It has led us beyond the sensory dimension privileged by our discipline. The scope of artists' things encompasses the whole sensorium—taste, hearing, touch, smell, as well as sight—and has encouraged us to work across the subdivisions of history and material culture studies that enclose books, fashion, food, musical instruments, natural history objects, tools, vehicles, etc. into their particular scholarly specialisms.[13] Our lack of expertise in these fields has been turned to critical advantage, we hope, and has produced the kind of "inter-in-disciplinarity"—the stepping forward unprejudiced into the unknown—advocated so compellingly by Gratton and Sheringham.

In terms of procedure, our project consisted initially of no more than the simple injunction to search and find things of undisputed artist provenance. Whatever surfaced from museum and library displays, stores, stacks, and databases, or came to light in response to the questionnaire we sent to museum professionals, would be included in the corpus.[14] In short, we put aside the conventions of the artist monograph and its often grand narratives of artistic self-realization in order to gather *sans* prejudice, and without preconception of value, what things had survived: curious or mundane, useful or symbolic, affective or trivial, learned or dumb. None was ruled out in advance so long as it had once belonged to an artist active in eighteenth-century France. One might, following Ursula Le Guin, call the result a "carrier bag" history of art and artists, one held together, that is, by unanticipated, contingent, yet often powerful threads, which variously connected things, and artists through things.[15]

With stuff surfacing—the remnant of a **hot-air balloon**, a couple of annotated **books**, the Académie's **document box**, a **gaming set** in a fancy lacquer case, a sculptor's **modeling**

stand, a **sketchbook**, an antique-style **table**, etc.—we moved to the second phase of the project: imposing constraints and order on the rising number of discoveries. An obvious limit could have been number: twenty-five, fifty, or even one hundred. But round numbers imply unity, an internally coherent collection. In Neil MacGregor's *History of the World in 100 Objects* (2010) that logic was supplied by time: cultural millennia reduced and condensed to one hundred significant moments embodied in specific objects.[16] We, however, were less concerned to reduce history to a collection than to open up our research practice of collecting to history. Our things were self-selecting by virtue of survival alone; they were not picked to exemplify "the advent of bureaucracy" at the Académie in the early 1700s (**document box**), or "the birth of bourgeois leisure" in the 1770s (**gaming set**), or "the triumph of science" in the 1780s (**hot-air balloon**). We therefore opted for the arbitrary and value-neutral order of the alphabet. A dictionary, we thought, would accommodate the potentially random nature of the items yielded by our fieldwork, and we embraced its textual form as peculiarly apt for a project set in the great age of dictionaries and encyclopedias.[17] Denis Diderot and Jean Le Rond d'Alembert gave their *Encyclopédie* dictionary-form in order, among other reasons, to attract the general reader; dictionaries meet their readers halfway, providing a locus where their curiosity, their need to know, can come into first focus.[18] Understanding in the *Encyclopédie* is supplied later, on second encounter, by analysis within each autonomous entry, which likewise aimed for openness, eased by the simple layout of the text in columns, uninterrupted by commentary and unencumbered by excessive scholarly apparatus.[19] We intend similar advantages for our project, though without Diderot and d'Alembert's additional ambition for synthesis. There is no "tree of knowledge" to which the individual artist items can be referred for classification and further context.[20] Our things are gathered but not collectively explained. As such, dispute, competition, conquest, struggle, the conflict implicit in history conceived as "progress" (toward enlightenment, empire, and modernity) is absent from the modest narrative of this whole, though matters of desire and discord, of difference (in class, gender, and ethnicity) do arise in relation to specific things and therein lie the histories of things larger.[21]

The choice of alphabetical order, once made, suggested limits of its own: one thing for each letter, we thought initially, for twenty-six in all. However, that constraint soon began to chafe, not least because the things emerging were not, we realized, evenly distributed across the alphabet. Some letters were oversubscribed: How could we decide between a **camera obscura**, a **carriage**, and a **color box** to figure C? Others proved unexpectedly elusive: How to find any relevant thing beginning with N?[22] Moreover, it had become clear that records of ownership (visual and textual) were far more numerous and just as fascinating as actual things. Why exclude François Lemoyne's **sword**, the instrument of his death, depicted so vividly in the city's police reports, simply because the object itself survived only in words? We changed our rules. We opted to include those items of secure artist provenance for which we had good documentary and/or visual evidence.[23] And to improve our chances of filling A to Z, we increased the total number to fifty. In the end, that total was exceeded, and the alphabet not quite completed (no X, Y, or Z). The book's final form is thus unfinished. The numerical oddity of fifty-something things—neither a round number, nor exact, but random—recalls the project's original purpose of open, continuing process.

To touch briefly on site, the feature of the art of projecting that remains still to be discussed, our project's dedication to surviving artists' things compelled us to re-orient our activities, where it did not oblige us fully to re-site them. We were forced to expand the scope of our object research, to look, that is, beyond the habitual *art* gallery to museums of all kinds, to auction houses, libraries, archives, repositories, etc., and to inquire about things as disparate as weapons and military regalia, umbrellas and copper cisterns. The priority of provenance led us to ask curators questions that none, it sometimes seemed, had thought it relevant to ask before: whether, for example, that watch (in a museum of science and technology), or that pair of glasses (in a museum of optical instruments), or any of those devotional objects (in a museum housed in a former convent) had once belonged to an artist? Systems of museum classification and the relevant histories of technology, medicine, and religion narrated by the museum displays in these cases foreclosed our concerns.[24] In some instances we discovered our things repurposed for the needs of today: for example, we found Houdon's **modeling stand** functioning as a pedestal at the Musée Carnavalet in Paris, its original function as tool obscured by the imposing classical bust of Antoine Barnave placed upon it to tell a story not of studio practices in the capital during the 1780s and 1790s but of political culture.[25] In other cases, our things were not on display at all but in store. If the environment of the storeroom can often seem dead, without the least historical resonance, it has this advantage: stores are places where one is allowed to handle things. At the History of Science Museum at the University of Oxford we picked up drawing instruments, experienced how they fit into the hand, and were able to imagine the effect of the weight and balance of an eighteenth-century brass ***porte-crayon*** on the pressure and velocity of lines drawn by it. We became aware of the intimate sounds made by the folding and working of these pocket instruments, and we even caught the faint whiff of leather from the case in which they were kept. Likewise, at the Musée d'Art et d'Histoire's subterranean storage facility in Geneva, we unpacked the nesting boxes of Jean-Étienne Liotard's Chinese **gaming set**, removed their lacquer lids, and rehearsed the gesture of a bet placed, gently tossing mother-of-pearl counters onto an unfurled silk cloth and hearing the quiet clatter as the pile grew. Such multisensory experiences enabled us to understand our things in action better.

In summary, the rules and practices of our experiment with the scholarly monograph has involved a denaturalization of the mimetic design of the "life," individual or collective. It has diverted attention from understanding the exceptional individual via the narrative of biographical events and the history of works, to carrying out repeated investigations into possessions and things. Repetition of procedure according to the alphabetical protocol and chance's role in our discoveries have together led to a modest but creative remapping of art's history in eighteenth-century France. No one thing is here emblematic of the artist, not even the **palette**. Instead, our gathering proposed multiple oblique views of the artist from the refracted perspectives of the everyday.

Turning our art-historical attention to artists' things has required definitions of both and a reckoning with the nature of the possessive relation between them. What is a thing? Who are these artists? And what do their relationships tell us about each? Most of the things in this book might also be described as objects (an **armchair**, a **teacup**, an **umbrella**), but others are less amenable to that classification (a **dog** is a sentient being, but still belongs to its owner; **red lake** is a substance, but also a recipe to which a claim of intellectual property might be made). This book also contains many things that *are* objects but tend not to get treated as such. **Books** and documents (**baptism certificates** or **wills**), for instance, are often detached in historical analysis from their thingness and examined for what they relate in words rather than for what they are (materially) and where they have circulated (spatially). Artworks too, especially in relation to artists, normally reside in the aesthetic and the discursive realms of objecthood, but are more rarely explored through dynamics of function and use, were they decorative (a **picture** to enliven a room), educational (a sculpted **écorché** to teach anatomy), or spiritual (a **votive** to save the soul). Connecting all these things is their status as both property and material culture. They are all things that were once owned by an artist, either legally as property or in a more subjective sense as a belonging. And they are all traces of the stuff that once filled people's homes and workplaces, the elements that composed the material environments of the eighteenth-century art world.[26]

Artists have in some ways been easier to define, by borrowing the delineation established by the Académie Royale de Peinture et de Sculpture—France's definitive early modern art institution—whose membership was restricted to painters, sculptors, and engravers.[27] While the owners of our things thus shared a set of trades, their experiences as artists were inflected by differences in institutional affiliation, gender, nationality, wealth, religion, and generation, to name but some of the factors distinguishing this book's community of roughly fifty artists, whose collective life spans stretch from the mid-seventeenth into the mid-nineteenth century. The Académie's dominance, both in eighteenth-century Paris and in the subsequent narratives of French art history, persists in the existence of sources: surviving things and archival documents tend to privilege academicians. Wherever possible, however, this book attends to those who worked elsewhere, often as members of Paris's guild, the Académie's abiding rival.[28] Artists outside the Académie figure both as owners of things (Marie-Anne Collot, Alexis Grimou, Renée-Elisabeth Marlié, Jean-Étienne Liotard) and as agents in others' stories (as suppliers of **mannequins**, **pastels**, or ***crayons***), emphasizing the often-overlooked connections between the city's art worlds. Diversity of experience surfaces similarly in the narratives of women, whose professional lives we have foregrounded in working objects (Marlié's **burin**, Elisabeth Vigée-Lebrun's **palette**), alongside the less visible roles they played as wives or daughters (see **harpsichord**, **marriage contract**, or **umbrella**). Mobility and transcultural exchange also emerge as crucial dynamics at a historical moment when technology and infrastructure, as well as interest and opportunity, increased movement and relocation. Most artists gathered here were French (some Parisian, like Jacques-Louis David, others provincial, like Joseph-Siffred Duplessis), but some were immigrants, either short-term (Liotard from Switzerland) or long-term (Johann Georg Wille from Germany). Many others traveled internationally as tourist, envoy, or emigrant (Jean-Baptiste Le Prince to Finland, Marie-Anne Collot to Russia, Charles-Joseph Natoire to Italy), as did many of their things, some made or acquired abroad (a Chinese **gaming set**, South Pacific **shells**), others designed to voyage (a traveling **color box**, a **hot-air balloon**). While we have thus emphasized circuits of movement and intersecting networks, most of the possessive relationships in this book reside with the individual. There are, however, a handful of exceptions that directly explore the dynamics of collective ownership, whether institutionally within the Académie (the secretary's **document box**, the concierge's **funeral book**), or privately, between family members (the **harpsichord**) or a group of artist-neighbors (the **lantern**).

Tension can arise between histories of things and of artists. The importance we attribute to the role of things in making individuals into persons has led us to emphasize the horizontal social networks connecting artists, their things, and the immediate court and urban societies in which they lived and worked. Things, however, also invite a vertical reading, because the material flows they instantiate are often extensive in both time (production, distribution, consumption, destruction) and space (local, regional, national, global).[29] In prioritizing artists' consumption and use of things over vertical commodity chains, we sometimes risk becoming victims to the same commodity fetishism (meaning, oblivious to the interests and rights of producers of goods) that Madeleine Dobie describes as characterizing eighteenth-century commercial and colonial discourse.[30] We risk, to put it another way, not seeing the sugar for the **sugar spoon**, the snuff for the **snuffbox**, or the tea for the **teacup**.[31] If we have, in some instances, added an outsider perspective to mitigate that danger, our concern remains to understand artists' relations to their stuff from the inside. This is not to say that the provenance of things was without significance. That Jean-Marc Nattier's **teacup** was imported from Japan, that Jean-Baptiste Perronneau's ***porte-crayon*** was made in England, and that Natoire's **intaglio** was excavated in Rome contributed appreciably to the value and meaning they had for those to whom they belonged. But these things are not studied here in the context of Arita's porcelain industry and Dutch East Indian trade in the 1720s, or London science and precision instrument making in the 1760s, or, again, Rome's archaeology and antiquarianism in the 1760s to 1770s. Ours is, in that sense, not a multisited art history.

France is the spatial unit of our study, more particularly Paris. Art history's European eighteenth century has usually taken for granted Paris's position as center of the arts, birthplace of the Enlightenment, and capital of the consumer revolution. Though we do not conspicuously challenge this view, some of our artists' things do contest the assumption implicit in it, that the arts could only have developed as they did in Paris. For example, Perronneau's peregrinations to Lyon, Orléans, and, notably for this book, to Bordeaux (where he lost his ***porte-crayon***) suggest that for this portraitist France afforded alternative centers for the progress of his art, ones bustling with industry and international trade, the ports on the Atlantic coast especially. Moreover, the Paris that materializes from this alphabet of things is one closer, we think, to the urban experience of eighteenth-century artists than the reified category "Paris" sometimes becomes when serving as "context" or container for histories of eighteenth-century French art. The scale and heterogeneity of the city is made apparent: Jean-Baptiste Pigalle's **carriage** was necessary to him, a luxury to get him to the monthly meetings of the Académie at the Louvre from his house in Montmartre. In part for the lack of one, Charles Parrocel felt isolated and marginalized at the Gobelins, located on the other side of the river and at a similar distance from the center. Paris consisted, moreover, of multiple artistic centers: those of the print trade in and around the rue Saint-Jacques (**burin**, **journal**, **umbrella**), and of the Roule (**écorché**, **model**), where sculptors' studios and foundries took root from the late seventeenth century, as well as that of the Louvre and other privileged, princely enclaves, such as the Temple in the Marais, which, for instance, gave Nattier shelter for the better part of his career. Thus, while **books** and some luxury goods such as ***robes de chambre*** and **watches** uphold Paris's premier status in learning and fashionability, other things (**handkerchief**, **intaglio**, **nightingale**, **wine**) complicate this narrative and suggest that artists were sometimes equivocal in their attachment to the capital and its material culture.

As spatial entities spanning scales from body to globe, things must reside somewhere. Place therefore emerges vividly in this book, coproduced with things as its encompassing horizon. Some things, like **snuffboxes** and **watches**, scaled experience down to the intimate reaches of the pocket and the confidence of a drawer; others (**carriage**, **hot-air balloon**, **quill**) scaled it up, actually or in imagination, to sometimes dizzying distances through the city, around the kingdom, across the world, or up in the air. The "placial" setting of the bulk of our things was, however, the median zones of rooms, apartments, houses.[32] Broached from the perspective of things, our research reinforces what historians of material culture have long known, that division of architectural space in the eighteenth century did not correspond neatly to the distinctions we are apt as scholars to draw between social functions: production and consumption, work and play, public and private.[33] Making and collecting, for example, were sometimes imbricated activities in François Boucher's studio (**shell**), and apparently private spaces—Jean-Baptiste Lemoyne's bedroom (**sword**), Jean-Siméon Chardin's kitchen (**water fountain**), a Louvre corridor (**lantern**)—were the setting for public, or at any rate extra-domestic, as well as intimate behaviors, for both short and extended social relations. Common to all these experiences with and through things was the body, its comportments and its gestures. The focus of our thing-history of eighteenth-century French art is therefore phenomenological rather than psychoanalytical, trained not on interiority but on corporeal gesture and activity.[34] How did artists engage with the places they inhabited? What relationships did they form with (and through) the material things in their possession?

The in-placeness of things and the exhibition they necessarily make of their spatiality through the obtrusiveness of their material forms positions this book as a contribution to the recent spatial turn of eighteenth-century studies.[35] Chronology is not abandoned, but as a structuring force it becomes secondary. To be sure, individual entries trace historical narratives about specific artist's things, some of them in consciously biographical terms (like **harpsichord**, **journal**, or **order book**). But, as already noted, the alphabetization of the corpus breaks up emergent grand narratives, even at the level of the individual, in spite of suggestive sequences such as **B**(aptism certificate)—**M**(arriage contract)—**W**(ill), where by chance the **marriage contract** pinpoints the midpoint of the book and the other two help contain its edges. The writings of Michel Foucault inaugurated study of the Enlightenment as the patterned configuration of emergent spaces—those notably of the asylum, the clinic, and the prison—in place of a chronological measuring of the temporal unfolding of the Enlightenment's liberalist ideas.[36] To these spaces of modernity, art historians have added the Salon (the Académie's biennial art exhibition at the Louvre) and also the museum.[37] The things in this book make a compelling case for another place—the studio—to join this schema.

As a place, the studio emerges as pervasive yet elusive. A reading of **votive** with **hot-air balloon** *might* look like a desacralization of the studio and a secularization of its practices in between the 1730s, when Pierre-Imbert Drevet engraved the first, and the 1780s, when Jean-François Janinet fabricated the second. Likewise, reading **bed** with **bath** *could* imply substitution of commodities for symbolic goods and, by extension, the transformation of rank and status by money, in between the lived experience of Charles-Antoine Coypel, who commissioned the first, and Joseph-Siffred Duplessis, who owned the second. However, this book's spatial orientation more forcefully reveals the instability of the studio in the eighteenth century, literally as physical space and figuratively as an artistic institution. Duplessis's problems with his **bath**, a thing essential to safeguard his sight (so he claimed) and therefore to the fulfillment of his vocation, arose partly from the forced removal of his studio from place to place. In that regard his studio can, arguably should, be read as of a piece with the discourse of an earlier generation of artist's lives—that of Coypel's (**bed**), in fact—in which the space of artistic creation was not only a dedicated *place* but knotted in a network of social relations with patrons, assistants, family, and students that constituted art production prior to the marketization of the art world.[38] Likewise, Janinet's repurposing of his innovative skills in printmaking to the lacquering of balloon envelopes, though absolutely unique, nevertheless speaks of the multifunctional practices of eighteenth-century studios, a multifunctionality more usually associated with the Renaissance workshop than the dedicated offices of the modern studio.

If there is a story to be told about the enclosure and specialization of the studio in the eighteenth century, it is seemingly not one that can be told as a straight linear progression. The pattern of its emergence was more complex and demands tracing across multiple sites: the home, the street, the city, as well as the Académie and the Salon. Crucial also was the power of the state. The Bâtiments du Roi, the royal division responsible for cultural production (buildings, artworks, tapestries, porcelain, etc.) looms large throughout the book's narratives, often in the form of its directors-general and their multifaceted relationships with artists that encompassed official affairs (like the administrative rigmarole involved in securing a chivalric **decoration** for Joseph-Marie Vien) and more unexpectedly intimate interactions (like Duplessis's vulnerable exchanges with the director concerning the death of a pet **dog**). The Bâtiments was also in charge of assigning *logements* at the Louvre, studio-lodgings for artists and their families that became, over the course of the eighteenth century, increasingly central to the city's art world, geographically, socially, and symbolically.[39] Since the seventeenth century, successive royal administrations had strategically used the granting of *logements* to shape and discipline production to meet the material and ideological needs of the Crown.[40] For artists, in turn, the bestowal of this royal privilege became an object of professional ambition and an external marker of their success once attained, a dynamic evident in different ways in the stories of the **almanac** and the **order book**, among others. Perhaps most significant to the experience of the studio, however, was the inextricable entwining of individual and collective afforded by this palace neighborhood of artists living and working side by side. Traces of communal life were borne in the material environment of the *logements*, both in architectural transformations to the building (see **Bed**) and in the accumulation of objects that responded to its exigencies, whether demarcating shared space from private (**key**), negotiating community responsibilities (**lantern**), or managing neighborly jealousies (**bath**).

The prominence of the studio in this book—in all its centrality and permeability—was not necessarily intended at the outset. Our search for things was certainly concerned with the paraphernalia of making (**burin**/printmaking, **modeling stand**/sculpture, **palette**/painting), but it was also premised on expanding the art-historical consideration of artists' "working lives" to retrieve the myriad intersections therein with other realms of experience: leisure (**gaming set**, **wine**); domestic labor (**lantern**, **water fountain**); family relationships (**journal**, **marriage contract**); animal interactions (**dog**, **nightingale**); religious inclinations (**picture**, **relic**); sartorial pleasures (***robe de chambre***, **watch**); or even alternative professional aspirations (**armchair**, **quill**). But like people, things do not live their lives statically. Constantly on the move between already shifting spaces, these things have stories that rarely limit themselves to a single focus and sometimes careen in unexpected directions. The **watch**, for instance, leads to a parish church, while the **relic** ventures toward luxury boutiques. The **marriage contract** calls attention to the finances of the studio, while the **burin** directs us to the conjugal hearth. Despite the range of our selection, however, nearly every thing, by dint of ownership no doubt, situates us in some aspect of the art world, revealing something about its owner's artistic practices, professional networks, or acts of making (**glasses** that facilitated an artist's vision; **letters** that expose institutional hierarchies; or a **table** that was needed to make a painting).

In our consideration of the professional, the personal, and everything in between, this retrieval of lost property has been a conscious effort to push against art history's often uncomfortable relationship with the artist's life. While far from advocating a revival of

Vasarian *Lives*, this book does seek a re-engagement with the biographical, both as subject and mode of inquiry, to restore the agency of the artist as a historical actor and to reorient the social history of art toward an anthropology of experience.[41] To answer "yes," in other words, to the question posed at the beginning of this introduction, it *does* matter to art history that these artists owned these things. Tuning in to the meaningfulness of objects for their owners, our approach also recognizes agency in the thing itself, via the particular actions, behaviors, or relationships it affords for those around it. Written as a series of object biographies, this is a book about the lives of things, which (with a nod to the eighteenth-century literary genre of the it-narrative) can be called upon as intermediaries to relate the lives of their owners.[42] These lives are by necessity partial—no artist can be represented by a single possession—in fact some owners appear more than once, each of their things granting access to a different dimension of experience. Crucially, however, our take on the biographical is also set against the monographical, that focus on individual artists that has persisted through art history's critical interventions. Dispersing that spotlight on the individual to encompass instead networks and communities, our book's multiple entries might indeed be described as together forming an object prosopography—a collective biography-by-thing of an eighteenth-century art world.

How, then, to read this book of things? First and foremost, it is not designed to be read from A to Z. The order of things here does not relate a sequential narrative but rather that arbitrary arrangement owed simply to the initial letter of the signified's signifier (A for **almanac**). Of course, the reader is free to choose an alphabetical approach, mobilizing it for a random path through non sequiturs (from **gaming set** to **glasses**; from **handkerchief** to **harpsichord**) and unexpected connections (***porte-crayon*** to **quill**, both implements of mark-making; **key** to **lantern**, two items granting access to the infra-ordinary materiality of the Louvre's corridors; **snuffbox** to **sugar spoon**, two European commodities implicated in the circulation of colonial commodities). Choice, however, is the operative action. The reader of this book is envisaged as an active participant in a process of use in which reading becomes a project in its own right, with its own procedures, constraints, re-sitings, and interdisciplinary risks. In place of the habitual cover-to-cover journey, this book invites a trajectory traced at the reader's desire, following paths of interest and curiosity, whether pre-existing (a penchant for **dogs**, an obsession with **wigs**, a scholarly concern with **wills**), or ones that emerge extemporaneously through the reading project.

To facilitate the reader's wanderings, the book is equipped with a range of wayfinding mechanisms. First, it deploys a system of cross-references. Every thing with its own entry appears in bold (as throughout this introduction) whenever it makes an appearance somewhere else in the book, drawing attention to the connections between these objects and the connectedness of their owners' lives within the eighteenth-century art world. Like the "renvois" of the *Encyclopédie*, these cross-references provide alternative paths of discovery, sometimes no less random than the alphabetized route, but sometimes providing a thematic train of thought (a musing on studio props perhaps, from **écorché**, to

mannequin, to **dressing-up box**). Next, in the book's contents, along with the alphabetical inventory of things there is also a "List of Owners," providing a differently inflected arrangement of this stuff, each thing restored as property to its erstwhile possessor. A reader interested in a specific artist might go directly to retrieve their belongings (Coypel, for instance, with his **bed** and **watch**; Van Loo via his ***robe de chambre***; Giroust for her **pastels**). Finally, at the end of the book, there is a set of taxonomies that offer further re-orderings of these things to accommodate navigation by chronology (according to its owner's birthdate), type (the category of thing it was, from studio tool to family heirloom), theme (the discursive realms it encompasses), and material (the substances from which it was made). These taxonomies provide summative encapsulations of the book's historical scope (from the birth of Nicolas de Largillière in 1656 to the death of Vigée-Lebrun in 1842) and its thematic scope (from global commerce to religion, from death to travel). They also tabulate the material composition of the eighteenth-century art world (its animal, vegetable, and mineral forms) and the range of dynamics, agencies, relationships, and functions that its inanimate inhabitants were required to enact (whether tool, gift, souvenir, or weapon). While serving as navigational apparatus, these taxonomies are also offered as sets of analytical data (some empirical, some more subjective) that the reader is invited to interrogate, perhaps to disagree with our interpretations, and ideally to devise alternative classifications and re-orderings of these lost things of the Paris art world.

---

1. For some exceptions, see Antoine-Joseph Dézallier d'Argenville, *Abrégé de la vie des plus fameux peintres* (Paris: De Bure, 1745–52) 2:370–71 ("Elizabeth Chéron"—musical instruments: refinement); 287 ("Joseph Vivien"—*robe de chambre*: fashionability); 243 ("Jean-Baptiste Blin de Fontenay"—wine glass; *bon viveur*).

2. For an introduction to the inventory in early modern Europe, see Giorgio Riello, "'Things Seen and Unseen': The Material Culture of Early Modern Inventories and Their Representation of Domestic Interiors," in *Early Modern Things: Objects and Their Histories, 1500–1800*, ed. Paula Findlen (New York: Routledge, 2013), 124–50.

3. Annik Pardailhé-Galabrun, *The Birth of Intimacy: Privacy and Domestic Life in Early Modern Paris* (Oxford: Polity, 1992). A corpus of 2,306 Paris inventories formed the basis of her study of the eighteenth century. See also Daniel Roche, *A History of Everyday Things: The Birth of Consumption in France, 1600–1800* (Cambridge: Cambridge University Press, 2000).

4. The notable exception is the history of collecting. See especially Krzysztof Pomian, *Collectors and Curiosities: Paris and Venice 1500–1800* (Oxford: Polity, 1991); Colin B. Bailey, *Patriotic Taste: Collecting Modern Art in Pre-Revolutionary Paris* (New Haven: Yale University Press, 2002); and Rochelle Ziskin, *Sheltering Art: Collecting and Social Identity in Early Eighteenth-Century Paris* (University Park: Penn State University Press, 2012). The periodicals *Archives de l'art français* and *Bulletin de la Société de l'histoire de l'art français* prioritize the publication of artists' inventories.

5. On the inventory as a "representation" of wealth, and on the "art" of appraising, see Donald Spaeth, "'Orderly Made': Re-Appraising Household Inventories in Seventeenth-Century England," *Social History* 41, no. 4 (2016): 417–35.

6. For a classic critical analysis of eighteenth-century attitudes to wealth and the artist, see Mary Sheriff, "Love or Money? Rethinking Fragonard," *ECS* 19, no. 3 (1986): 333–54.

7. According to La Tour's will of 9–20 February 1784, he owned two telescopes by the London instrument maker Peter Dollond. See Neil Jeffares, "Chronological Table of Documents Relating to de La Tour," *Pastels and Pastellists*, 67, http://www.pastellists.com/Misc/LaTour_chronology.pdf. According to Jean-Baptiste Marie Pierre's *inventaire après décès*, AN, MC/ET/XXXI/253, 25 May 1789, a hen hutch with fourteen hens and a cock were to be found in the courtyard of his house at the Louvre, rue Fromenteau. In Clodion's study, after his death, were inventoried a tin clyster and five water jars, along with a "bad" razor, razor blades, and the conventional furniture for such a room. See Jules-Joseph Guiffrey, "Inventaire après décès de Clodion (30 avril 1814)," *AAF* 6 (1912): 223.

8. Michael Yonan, in his review of the relations between art history and material culture studies, notes that the two come closest to one another in the field of collecting. See Yonan, "Toward a Fusion of Art History and Material Culture Studies," *West 86th: A Journal of Decorative Art* 18, no. 2 (2011): 236.

9. Pierre Bourdieu, *Distinction: A Social Critique of the Judgement of Taste*, trans. Richard Nice (Cambridge: Harvard University Press, 1984).

10. See Arjun Appadurai, *The Social Life of Things: Commodities in Cultural Perspective* (Cambridge: Cambridge University Press, 1986).

11. Daniel Miller, *The Comfort of Things* (Cambridge: Polity, 2008).
12. Johnnie Gratton and Michael Sheringham, eds., *The Art of the Project: Projects and Experiments in Modern French Culture* (New York: Berghan, 2005).
13. On the multisensory study of material culture, see David Howes, "Scent, Sound, and Synaesthesia: Intersensoriality and Material Culture Theory," in *Handbook of Material Culture*, ed. Chris Tilley et al. (Los Angeles: Sage, 2006), 161–72; specifically in relation to France, see Alain Corbin, *The Foul and the Fragrant: Odor and the French Social Imagination*, trans. Miriam Kochan, Roy Porter, and Christopher Prendergast (Cambridge: Harvard University Press, 1986); and Corbin, *Village Bells: Sound and Meaning in the Nineteenth-Century French Countryside*, trans. Martin Thom (New York: Columbia University Press, 2000).
14. We sent a questionnaire to national, municipal, and other related museums in France. It asked conservators to indicate whether they had in their collections objects of professional use (palette, easel, paintbrush, modeling stand, chisel, copperplate, burin, etc.) or domestic use (furniture, musical or scientific instruments, silver, jewelry, dress, etc.). We received few replies.
15. See Ursula K. Le Guin, *The Carrier Bag Theory of Fiction*, with an introduction by Donna Haraway (London: Ignota, 2019), 25–37. Our warm thanks to Harvey Shepherd for this reference. For an anthropological study of the narratives of and on the carrier bag, see Janet Hoskins, *Biographical Objects: How Things Tell Stories of People's Lives* (London and New York: Routledge, 1998), chapter 2, "The Betel Bag: A Sack of Souls and Stories," 25–58.
16. Neil MacGregor, *A History of the World in 100 Objects*, BBC Radio 4 broadcast in 2010; published as a book under the same title by Penguin Books, 2010.
17. See Richard Yeo, *Encyclopaedic Visions: Scientific Dictionaries and Enlightenment Culture* (Cambridge: Cambridge University Press, 2001); special issue, "Dictionnaires en Europe" in *Dixhuitième siècle* 38, no. 1 (2006).
18. See Jean Le Rond d'Alembert, "Discours préliminaire," in *Encyclopédie*, https://encyclopedie.uchicago.edu/node/88, 1:ix, xviii, in particular. See also Judith Flanders, *A Place for Everything: The Curious History of the Alphabetical Order* (London: Picador, 2020), on the alphabet as a navigator for readers.
19. The design of the *Encyclopédie* was in marked contrast to Pierre Bayle's multilayered dictionary, *Dictionnaire historique et critique*, 2 vols. (Rotterdam: Reinier Leers, 1697).
20. The "Système figuré des connoissances humaines" (Figurative system of human knowledge), the taxonomic tree is included in the *Encyclopédie*'s front matter.
21. Thus, following Le Guin, our book more nearly resembles the novel than the "killer stories" of much conventional history. See Le Guin, *The Carrier Bag Theory of Fiction*, 35.
22. We are very grateful to all our friends and colleagues who have generously proposed things for our attention. "N" is a particular case in point. Thank you, Melissa Hyde.
23. On working with documentary traces of lost things, see Glenn Adamson, "The Case of the Missing Footstool: Reading the Absent Object," in *History and Material Culture*, ed. Karen Harvey, 2nd ed. (London and New York: Routledge, 2009), 192–207.
24. Curators frequently mentioned, however, that their response would have been different had we been inquiring about the nineteenth century, by which time things were invested with value as souvenirs of people as well as places. See Susan Stewart, *On Longing: Narratives of the Miniature, the Gigantic, the Souvenir, the Collection* (Durham, NC: Duke University Press, 1992).
25. Antoine Barnave (1761–93) was a lawyer and a member of the parlement of Grenoble who promoted the cause of constitutional monarchy in the early years of the Revolution.
26. Daniel Miller, *Stuff* (Cambridge: Polity, 2010).
27. On the history of the Académie and its development, see Christian Michel, *The Académie Royale de Peinture et de Sculpture: The Birth of the French School*, trans. Chris Miller (Los Angeles: Getty Research Institute, 2018); and Hannah Williams, *Académie Royale: A History in Portraits* (New York: Routledge, 2015).
28. On relations between the Académie and the guild, see Charlotte Guichard, "Arts libéraux et arts libres à Paris au XVIIIe siècle: Peintres et sculpteurs entre corporation et Académie Royale," *Revue d'histoire moderne et contemporaine* 49, no. 3 (2002–3): 54–68; and Katie Scott, "Hierarchy, Liberty, and Order: Languages of Art and Institutional Conflict in Paris (1766–1776)," *Oxford Art Journal* 12, no. 2 (1989): 59–70.
29. See, for example, Anne Gerritsen and Giorgio Riello, eds., *The Global Lives of Things: The Material Culture of Connections in the Early Modern World* (London: Routledge, 2016).
30. Madeleine Dobie, *Trading Places: Colonization and Slavery in Eighteenth-Century French Culture* (Ithaca: Cornell University Press, 2010). Dobie does not, however, mobilize the Marxist concept of fetishism but rather the Freudian notion of displacement for her interpretation.
31. On not seeing the "fingerprints of exploitation" on the surfaces of things, see David Harvey, "Between Space and Time: Reflections on the Geographical Imagination," *Annals of the Association of American Geographers* 80, no. 3 (1990): 423. On the particular methodological challenges presented by substances as opposed to things, see Hans Peter Hahn and Jens Soentgen, "Acknowledging Substances: Looking at the Hidden Side of the Material World," *Philosophy and Technology* 24 (2011): 19–33.
32. The term is Edward Casey's. See Edward S. Casey, "How to Get from Space to Place in a Fairly Short Stretch of Time: A Phenomenological Prolegomena," in *Senses of Place*, ed. Steven Feld and Keith H. Basso (Santa Fe: School of American Research Press, 1996), 13–52.
33. See Pardailhé-Galabrun, *The Birth of Intimacy*; and the essays in *Everyday Objects: Medieval and Early Modern Material Culture and Its Meanings*, ed. Tara Hamling and Catherine Richardson (London and New York: Routledge, 2016).
34. See Julian Thomas, "Phenomenology and Material Culture," in *Handbook of Material Culture*, ed. Chris Tilley et al. (Los Angeles: Sage, 2006), 43–59.
35. For a review of this reorientation see Daniel Brewer, "Lights in Space," *ECS* 37, no. 2 (2004): 171–86; as an example, see Charles W. J. Withers, *Placing the Enlightenment: Thinking Geographically about the Age of Reason* (Chicago: University of Chicago Press, 2007).
36. Michel Foucault, *Madness and Civilization: A History of Insanity in the Age of Reason* ([1961] New York: Vintage, 1988); *The Birth of the Clinic: An Archaeology of Medical Perception* ([1963] New York: Pantheon, 1973); and *Discipline and Punish: The Birth of the Prison* ([1975] New York: Pantheon, 1977).

37. See, for example, Thomas Crow, *Painters and Public Life in Eighteenth-Century Paris* (New Haven: Yale University Press, 1985); Richard Wrigley, *The Origins of French Art Criticism: From the Ancien Régime to the Restoration* (Oxford: Clarendon, 1994); and Andrew McClellan, *Inventing the Louvre: Art, Politics, and the Origins of the Modern Museum in Eighteenth-Century Paris* (Berkeley: University of California Press, 1994).
38. At greater length, see Katie Scott, "Parade's End: On Charles-Antoine's bed and the origins of inwardness," in *Interiors and Interiority*, ed. Ewa Lajer-Burcharth and Beate Söntgen (Berlin: De Gruyter, 2016) 17–48.
39. On the shifting geography of artistic communities, see Hannah Williams, "Artists and the City: Mapping the Art Worlds of Eighteenth-Century Paris," *Urban History* 46, no. 1 (2019): 106–31.
40. On the history of the *logements* see Jules Guiffrey, "Logements d'artistes au Louvre," *NAAF*.
41. Giorgio Vasari, *Lives of the Artists* (1550), 2 vols. (London: Penguin, 1987). Historiographically this tradition continued through eighteenth-century works like: Antoine-Joseph Dézallier d'Argenville, *Abrégé de la vie des plus fameux peintres*, 4 vols. (Paris: De Bure, 1745); François Bernard Lépicié, *Vies des premiers peintres du Roi, depuis M. Le Brun jusqu'à présent* (Paris: Durand & Pissot, 1752); [Pierre-Jean Mariette], *Abecedario de P.-J. Mariette*, ed. Philippe de Chennevières and Anatole de Montaiglon, 6 vols. (Paris: Dumoulin, 1851–60). On experience as a subject and object of social and historical analysis see, for example, Victor W. Turner and Edward M. Bruner, eds., *The Anthropology of Experience* (Champaign: University of Illinois Press, 1986); and David Carr, *Experience and History: Phenomenological Perspectives on the Historical World* (Oxford: Oxford University Press, 2014).
42. Our invocation of object biographies acknowledges Kopytoff but describes narratives more embedded in experience than abstracted from economies. Igor Kopytoff, "The Cultural Biography of Things: Commoditization as Process," in Arjun Appadurai, ed., *The Social Life of Things: Commodities in Cultural Perspective* (Cambridge: Cambridge University Press, 1986), 64–91. See also Janet Hoskins, "Agency, Biography and Objects," in *Handbook of Material Culture*, ed. Chris Tilley et al. (London: Sage, 2006), 74–84. On it-narratives (such as Claude Crébillon fils's *Le sopha, conte moral* [1742]) and objects in French literature, see Jonathan Lamb, *The Things Things Say* (Princeton: Princeton University Press, 2016); Rori Bloom, "'Un Sopha rose brodé d'argent': Crébillon *fils* and the Rococo," *Eighteenth-Century* 51, nos. 1–2 (2010): 87–102; and *Esthétique & poétique de l'object au XVIIIe siècle*, ed. Christophe Martin and Catherine Ramond, special issue of *Lumière* 5 (Bordeaux: Presses Universitaires de Bordeaux, 2005).

Things

ALMANAC

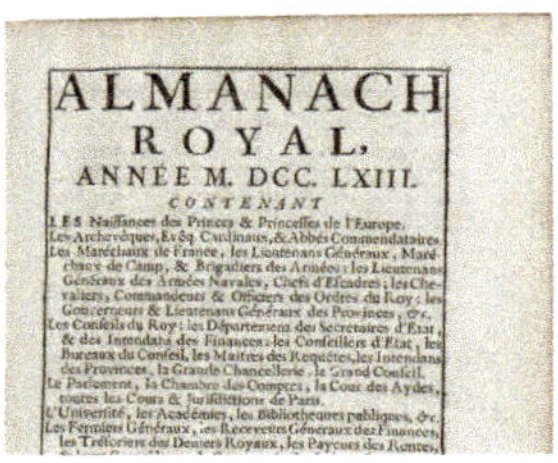

ARMCHAIR

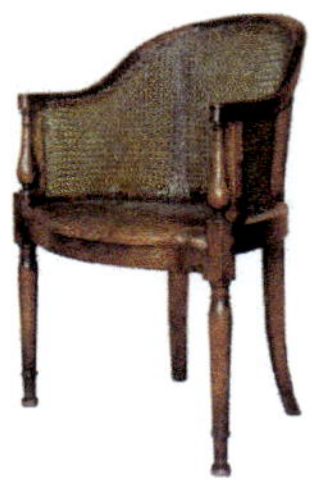

BAPTISM CERTIFICATE

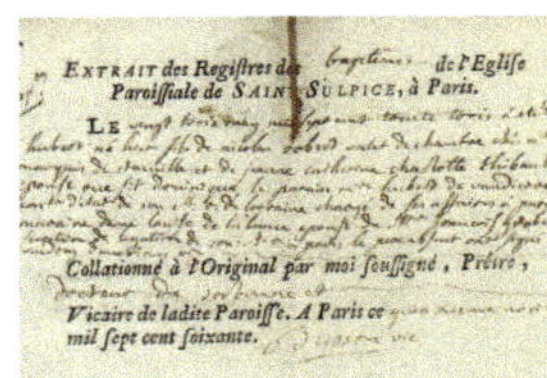

BATH

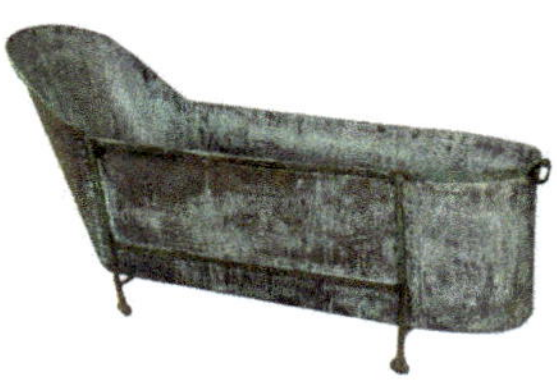

BED

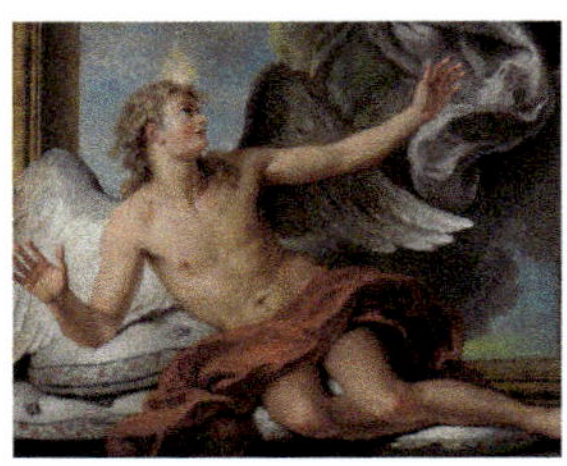

BOOK

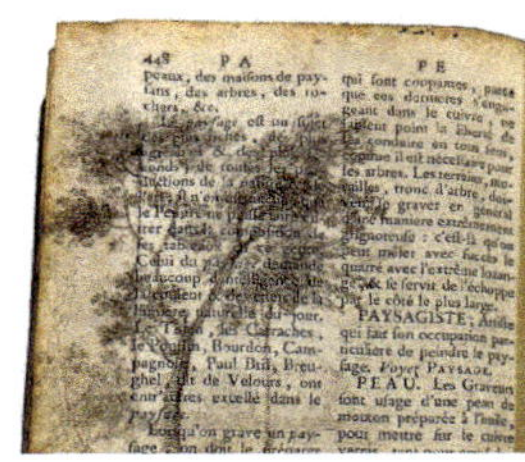

BURIN

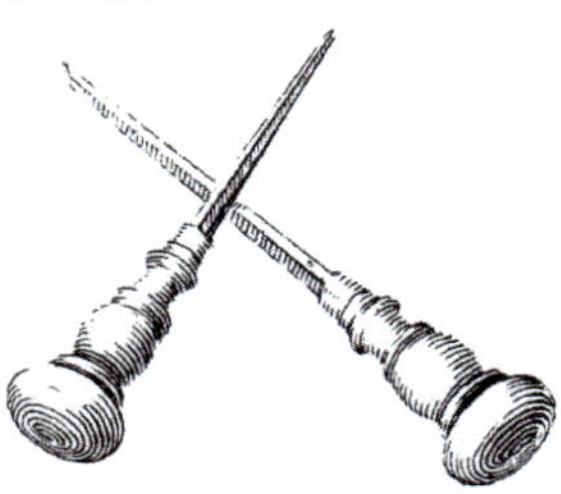

CAMERA OBSCURA

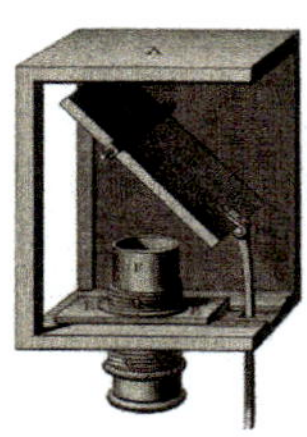

CARRIAGE

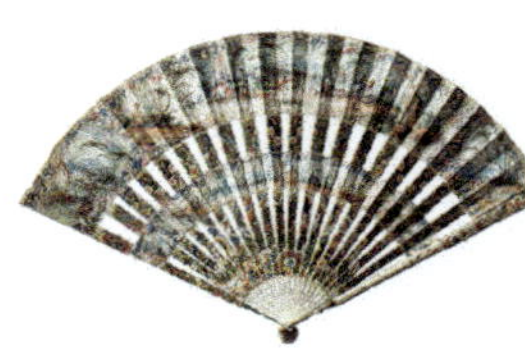

COLOR BOX

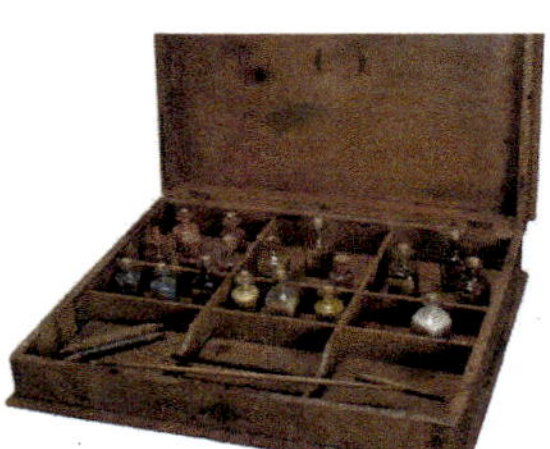

CRAYON

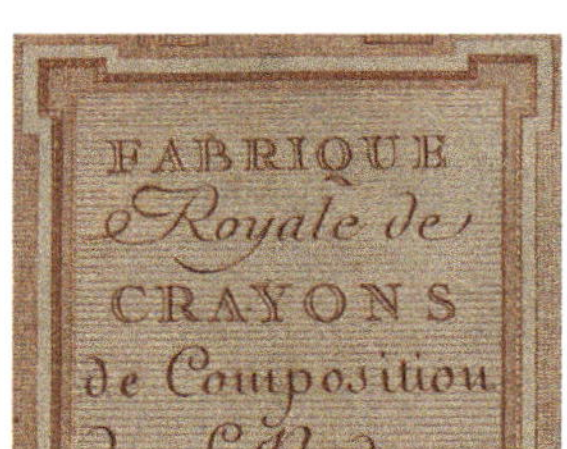

DECORATION

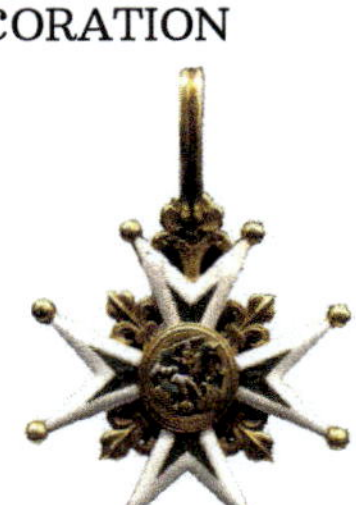

DOCUMENT BOX

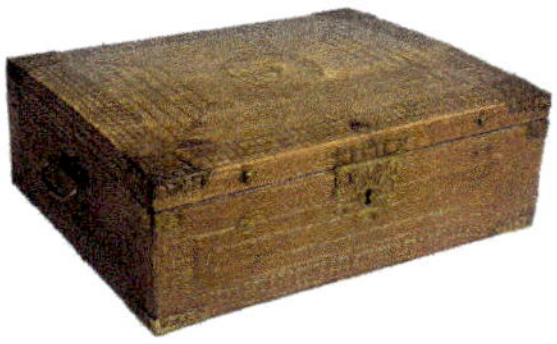

DOG

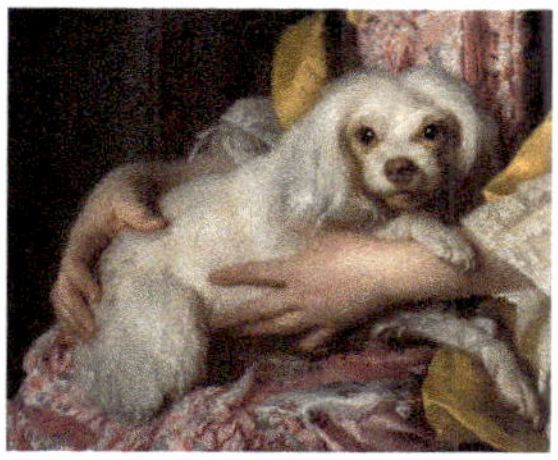

DRESSING-UP BOX

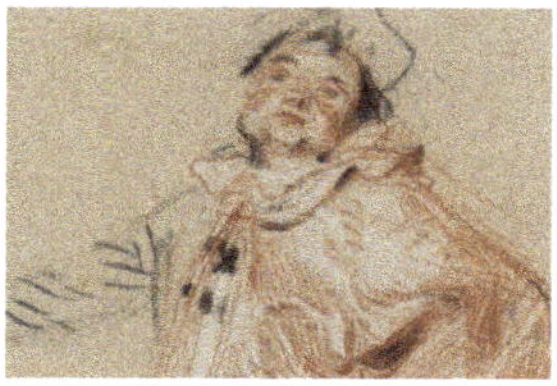

ÉCORCHÉ

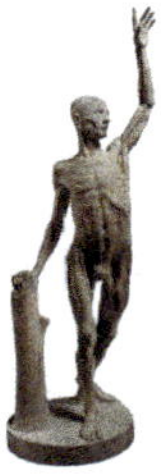

FUNERAL BOOK

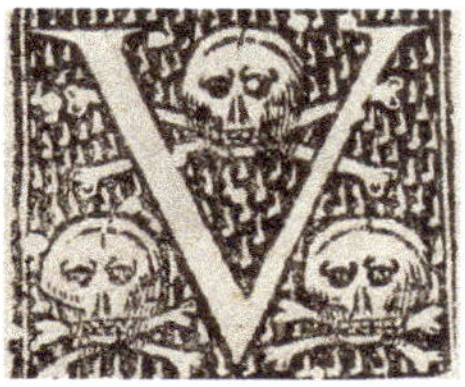

GAMING SET

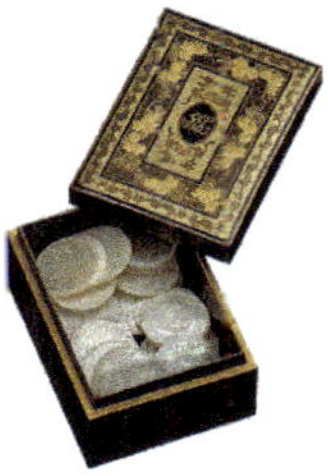

GLASSES

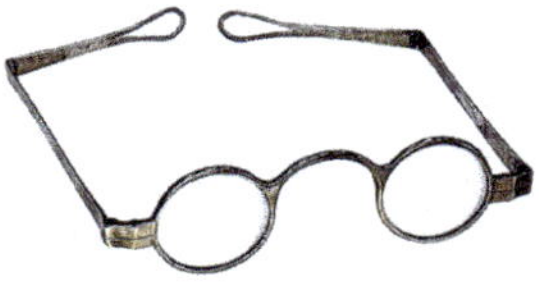

HANDKERCHIEF

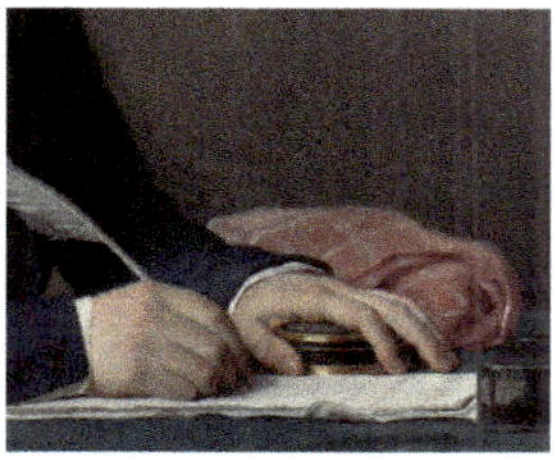

HARPSICHORD

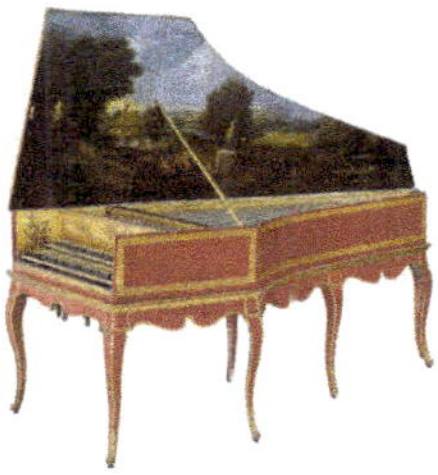

HOT-AIR BALLOON

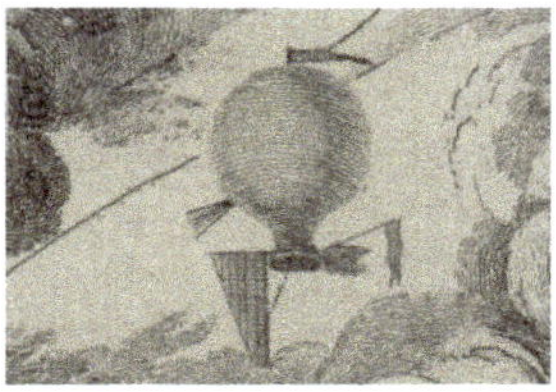

INTAGLIO

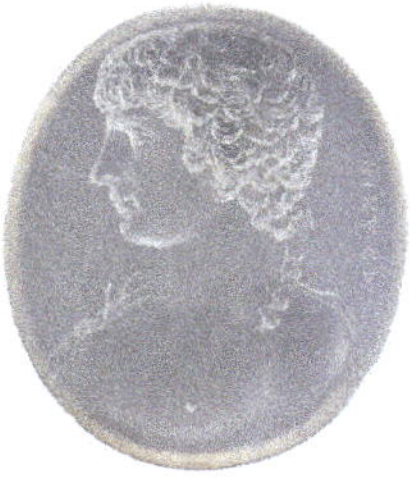

JOURNAL

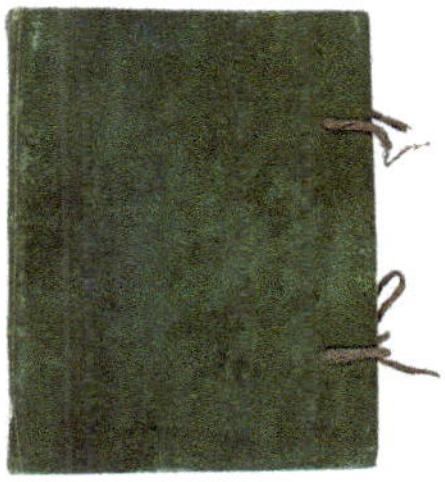

KEY

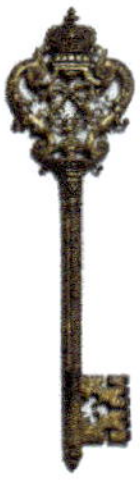

LANTERN

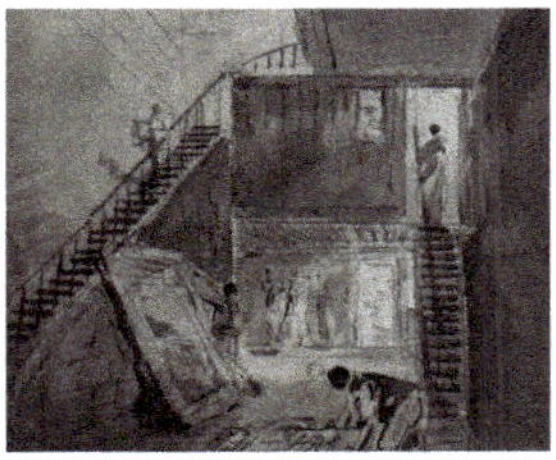

LETTERS

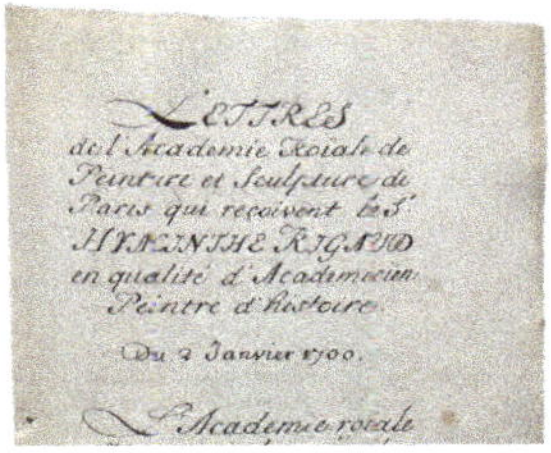

LETTRES
de l'Academie Roiale de
Peinture et Sculpture de
Paris qui reçoivent le S.
HYACINTHE RIGAUD
en qualité d'Academicien
Peintre d'histoire.

Du 2 Janvier 1700.

L'Academie roiale

MANNEQUIN

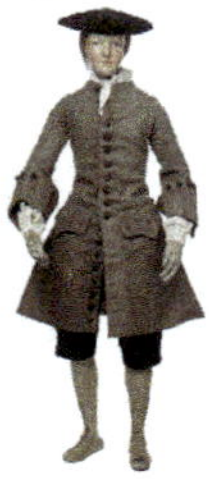

MARRIAGE CONTRACT

MODEL

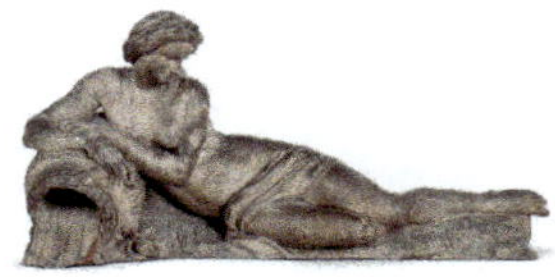

MODELING STAND

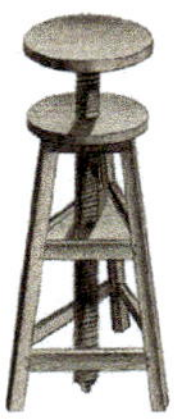

NIGHTINGALE

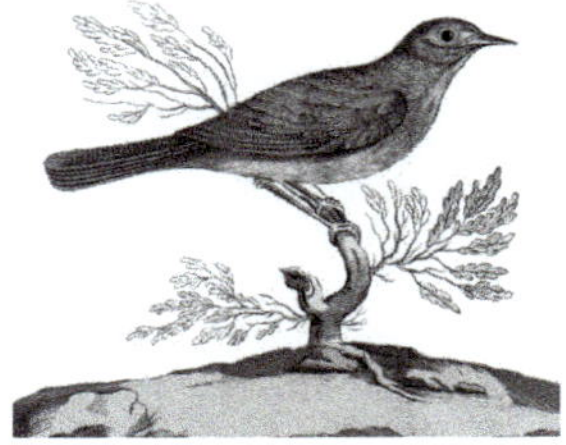

ORDER BOOK

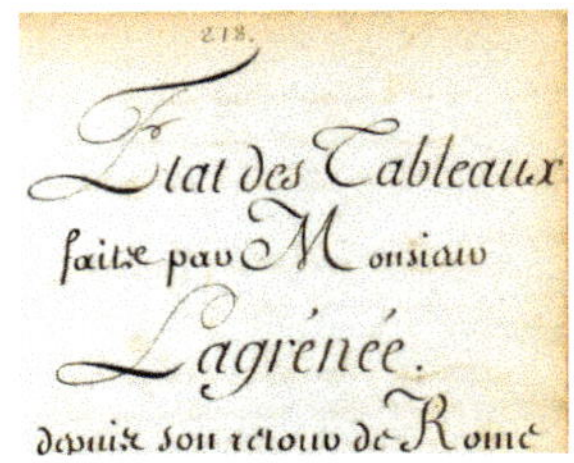

PALETTE

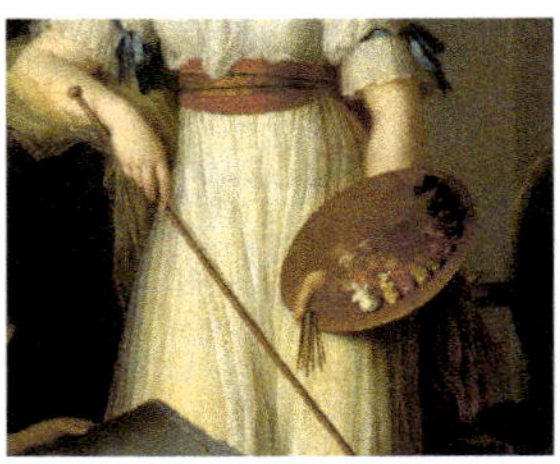

PASTELS

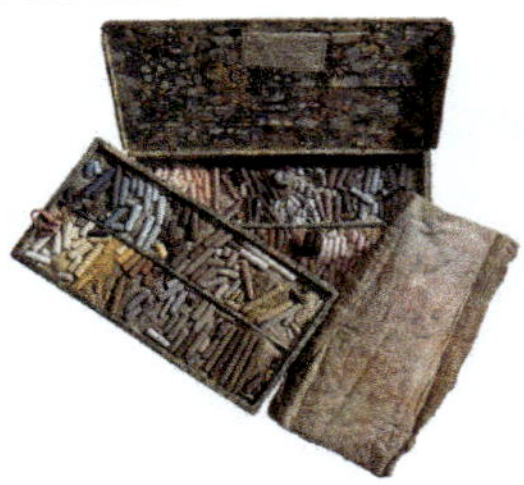

PICTURE

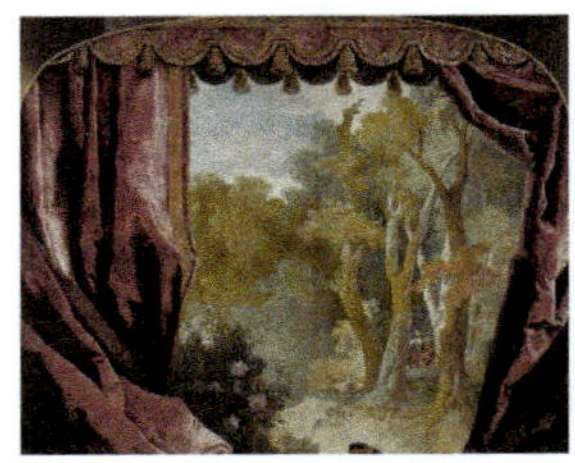

PORTE-CRAYON

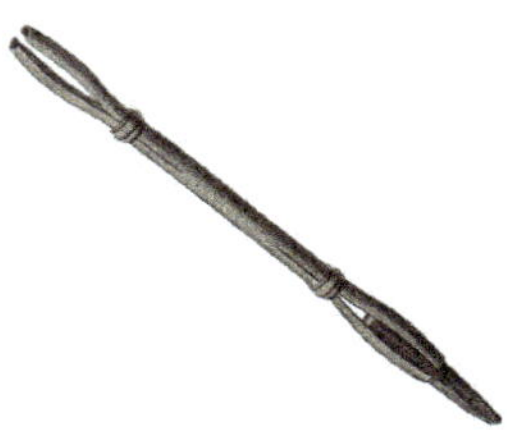

QUILL

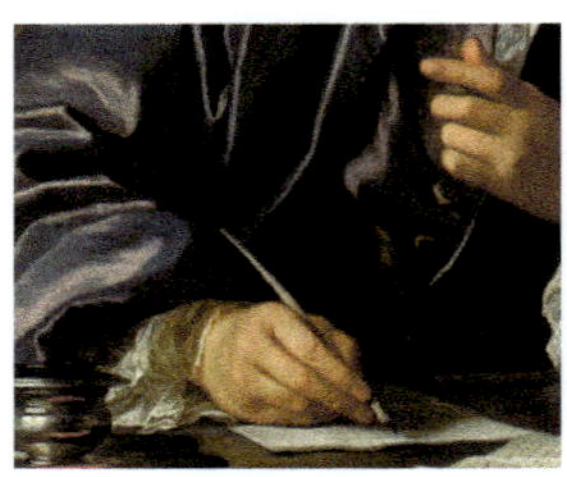

RED LAKE

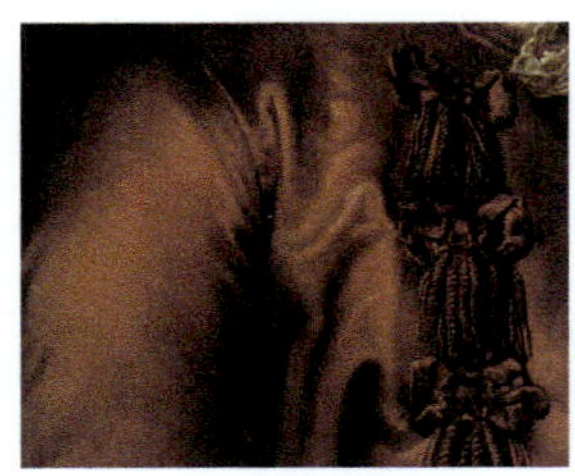

RELIC

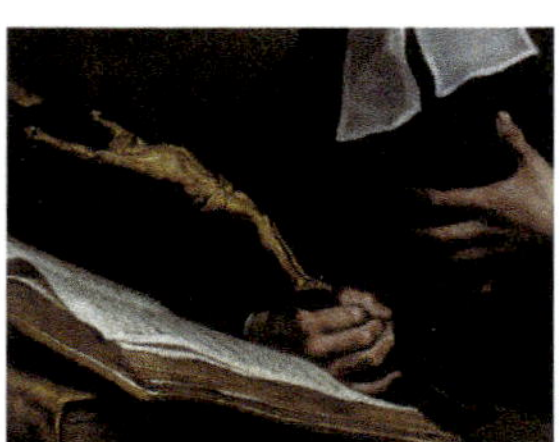

ROBE DE CHAMBRE

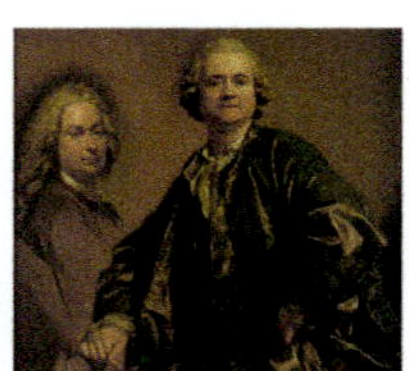

SHELL

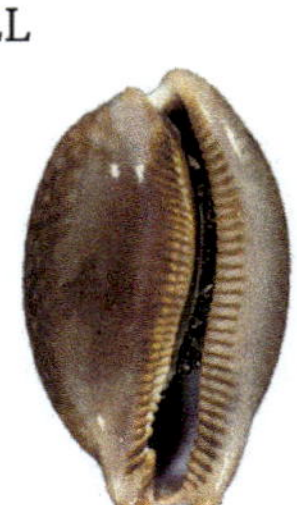

SKETCHBOOK

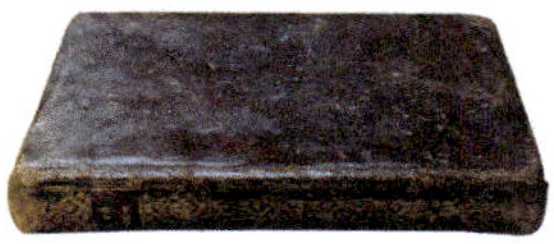

SNUFFBOX

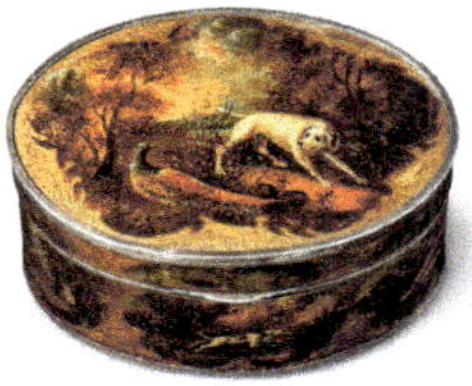

SUGAR SPOON

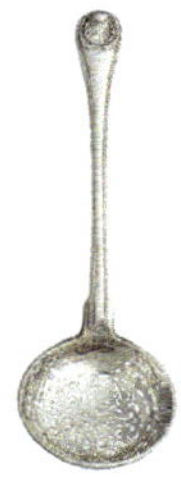

SWORD

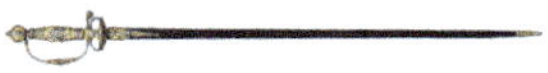

TABLE

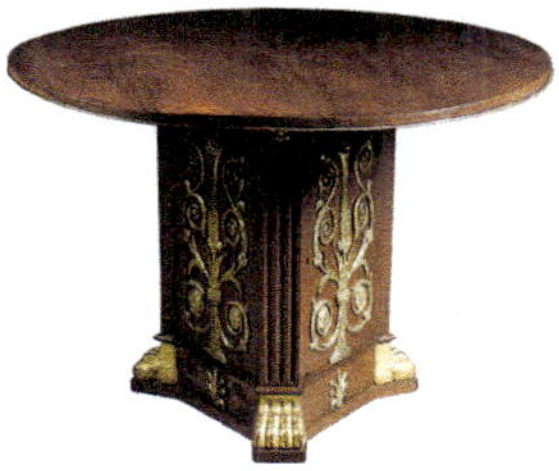

TEACUP

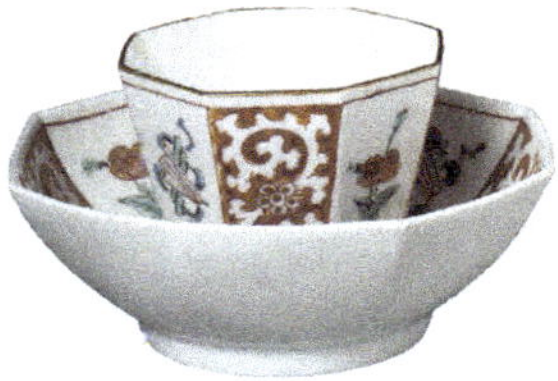

UMBRELLA

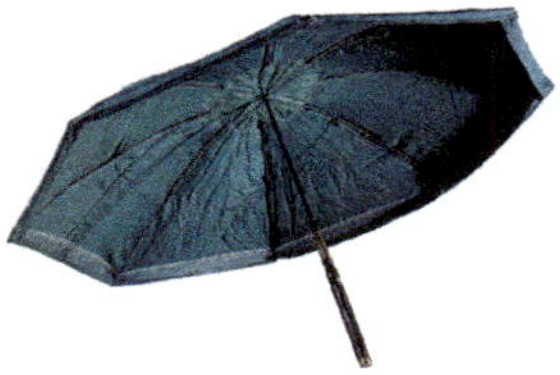

VOTIVE

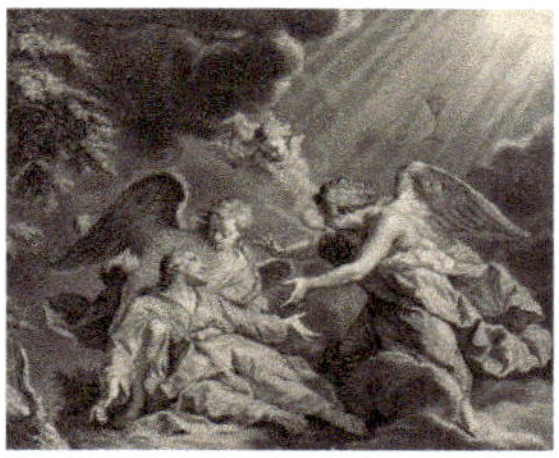

WATCH

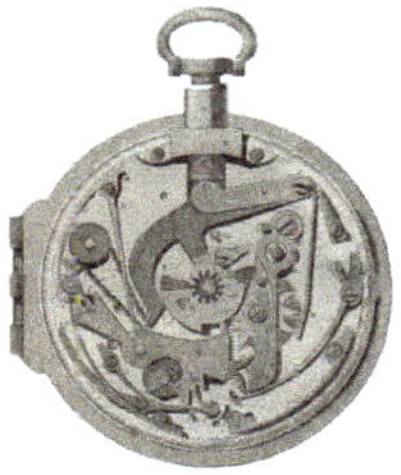

WATER FOUNTAIN

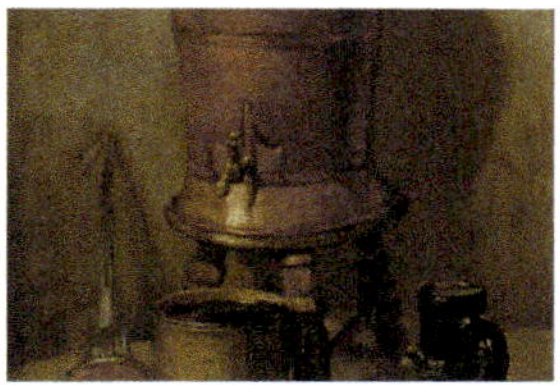

WIG

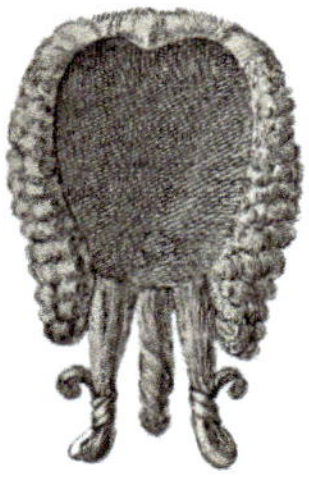

WILL

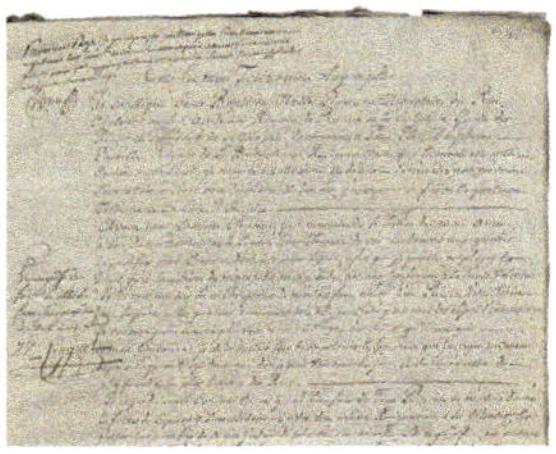

WINE

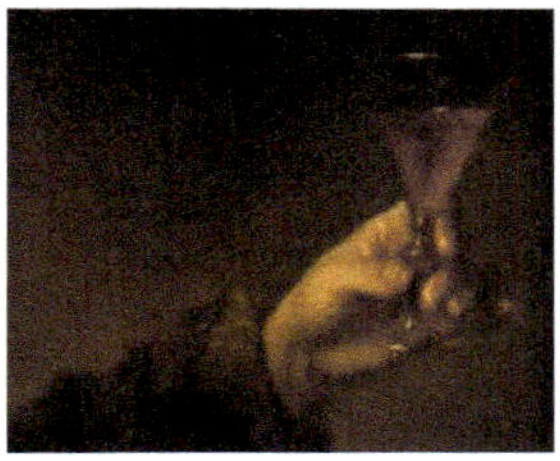

Almanac

Claude-Joseph Vernet (1714–89)

TYPE OF OBJECT	THEME	MATERIAL
Instrument	Everyday, Louvre, Travel	Synthetic Materials | Paper

Almanacs are calendars, first and foremost. According to an eighteenth-century dictionary definition, *calendar* was in fact a synonym of *almanac* because the almanac invariably begins with a table of the days of the year, arranged in rows and gathered into weeks and months, no matter what else it also contained.[1] The almanac proper condensed an impressive amount of astronomical, theological, meteorological, and astrological knowledge (solar and lunar orbits, Catholic feasts and saints' days, weather warnings, and signs of the zodiac), embedding it in the typographical design by use of columns, variations in type, signs, symbols, and figures, in addition, of course, to numerals. Although the result was a dense, consolidated matrix of abstruse information, almanacs nevertheless remained easy to understand and simple to use. Their purpose was to measure time, not by the hour, like clocks and **watches**, but by the day.

On Saturday, 1 January 1763, the marine and landscape painter Claude-Joseph Vernet bought a copy of the *Almanach royal* (fig. 1) for 5 livres at the offices of the Maison du Roi and recorded his purchase in his journal-cum-**order book**.[2] This particular Paris almanac was published by Antoine Le Bretton, the publisher, with others, of Diderot and d'Alembert's *Encyclopédie*.[3] It enjoyed the status of a semiofficial publication because as an appendix to the calendar the *Almanach royal* listed, in order of rank and office, the names of appointees to the king's household and government, and of members of royal and corporate institutions, including the Académie Royale de Peinture et de Sculpture, to which Vernet had been elected a member in 1746. It was a list that by 1763 ran to several hundred pages. Updated annually, the *Almanach royal* was reputed for its accuracy: the solar and lunar calendars were calculated by the astronomers of the Académie royale des sciences, and the who's who of the kingdom's bureaucracy and corporate bodies was scrupulously checked by the editor.[4] Every year, it went on sale on 31 December to coincide with the celebration of the New Year. According to Vernet's accounts, 1763 was the first year he bought such a thing. His purchase is itemized midpoint in his list of expenses on New Year gifts; it was a novelty he apparently afforded himself.[5]

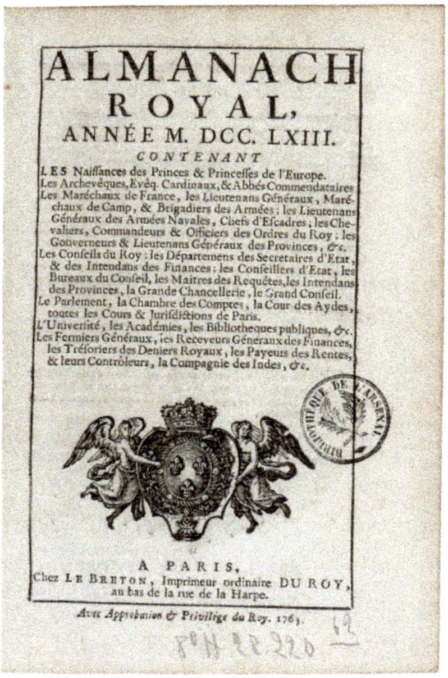
ALMANACH
ROYAL,
ANNÉE M. DCC. LXIII.
CONTENANT
LES Naiſſances des Princes & Princeſſes de l'Europe.
Les Archevêques, Evêq. Cardinaux, & Abbés Commendataires
Les Maréchaux de France, les Lieutenans Généraux, Maréchaux de Camp, & Brigadiers des Armées; les Lieutenans Généraux des Armées Navales, Chefs d'Eſcadres; les Chevaliers, Commandeurs & Officiers des Ordres du Roy; les Gouverneurs & Lieutenans Généraux des Provinces, *&c.*
Les Conſeils du Roy; les Départemens des Secretaires d'Etat, & des Intendans des Finances; les Conſeillers d'Etat, les Bureaux du Conſeil, les Maîtres des Requêtes, les Intendans des Provinces, la Grande Chancellerie, le Grand Conſeil.
Le Parlement, la Chambre des Comptes, la Cour des Aydes, toutes les Cours & Juriſdictions de Paris.
L'Univerſité, les Académies, les Bibliotheques publiques, *&c.*
Les Fermiers Généraux, les Receveurs Généraux des Finances, les Tréſoriers des Deniers Royaux, les Payeurs des Rentes, & leurs Contrôleurs, la Compagnie des Indes, *&c.*

A PARIS,
Chez LE BRETON, Imprimeur ordinaire DU ROY, au bas de la rue de la Harpe.
Avec Approbation & Privilège du Roy. 1763.

FIG. 1 *Almanach royal*, 1763, title page. Paris, Bibliothèque Nationale de France. (Image source: Gallica, BnF.)

Why did Vernet buy an almanac in 1763, having not bought one before? How did he use it? Or, should we be asking, how did it use him? There are no simple answers because the questions relate to a heterogeneity of different temporalities: to the time of the body, the individual, the family, and the social, to the time also of biography and of history. They concern the synchronization of some of these temporalities and the discontinuation of others.

Vernet's copy of the 1763 *Almanach royal* is lost. It was almost certainly lost during Vernet's lifetime, because it is not among the possessions inventoried at his death.[6] Given the yearly obsolescence of calendars, it is even possible that Vernet threw it away.[7] Nevertheless, its particular form provides some clues about why he wanted it and how he might have used his copy. Like others of its day, the *Almanach royal* was routinely bound with extra blank sheets of paper interleaved between the pages of the calendar, to facilitate annotation and enable its use as a diary or **journal**. Marked almanacs that survive from the period indicate that eighteenth-century owners employed them to record events (meteorological, political, economic, financial, and so on) and to schedule activities (jobs, meetings, transactions).[8] Since the beginning of his career, Vernet had kept his own daily record of commissions, engagements, letters written and received, and sundry shopping in medium-size vellum-covered ledgers, but between the end of 1762 and the beginning of 1764, that record is, as Léon Lagrange has observed, remarkably thin.[9] Entries relating to commissions drop off, and those few recorded warrant only brief mention and rough dating.[10] By contrast, his notation of his domestic expenses remains relatively detailed and exact. He noted, for instance, the expenses incurred for hangings, lighting, and fireworks to celebrate the Fête Dieu, a capital-letter day in the *Almanach royal*.[11] It seems possible, therefore, that in 1763 Vernet used his copy to manage and record his professional activity, and in so doing, that he was led to reckon and organize his work-time separately from the time of other daily matters.

To suggest such a division is to ask whether Vernet's experience of time, the way he lived it, was "modern," since our current definitions of Western modernity presuppose the disaggregation of work and leisure and the separation of the spaces of work and the home. E. P. Thompson famously argued that modern temporality, that of work discipline, emerged with the advent of capitalism and the factory during the second half of the eighteenth century.[12] Intermittent and uneven task-related and seasonal works were replaced by the industrial labor of workers contracted to work continuously for the duration of a set number of hours in the day and a fixed number of days in the week. The proliferation of public clocks in cities like Paris, and the dissemination of pocket **watches** and paper instruments of time measurement, such as almanacs, fostered the internalization of this new experience and perception of time by society at large, among those, that is, not themselves dominated by industrial schedules.[13] Arguably, the straight-lined frames that parcel out the months in the *Almanach royal*, and the lines of assembled type, regularly spaced, that conjugate the different days of the week, participated in this transformation: together they served to articulate a more abstract image of time as the equal flow of temporal units in contrast to that afforded by the sensual impact of sounded time emitted by the city's turret clocks and church bells.[14]

Insofar as art has traditionally been defined as task oriented, historians presume that artists were spared the pain of the temporal transformation brought about by modernity's disciplines. We rarely question the time *of* painting in the early modern period, as opposed to time represented *in* paintings, subject matter that Vernet made his own: at the Salon of 1763 he exhibited *Four Times of Day*, four overdoors painted the previous year for the dauphin's library at Versailles. Of *Night* (fig. 2) Diderot marveled, "everywhere it is night-time and everywhere it is day."[15] He continued: the moonlight "illuminates and colors the world" like sunlight, and "blends with the firelight" that clarifies the daily tasks of night. Across all four paintings time is flexible; the moments of the day stretch and extend into one another, creating, through modulated light, patterns of repetition and renewal at odds with the unidirectional, dark linearity of the almanac and its continuous sequence of rigidly plotted points. It is rather in the participation of artists in print culture and their exploitation of reproduction in all its forms that art historians recognize the modernity of eighteenth-century art: modernity as commoditization and commercialization, not industrialization.[16] Such a view fits neatly with alternative theories of modern time. According to Jan de Vries, the eighteenth century experienced not an industrial revolution but an industrious one.[17] He identifies change not in the regularity of work time but in its intensity. He argues that increases in work discipline were not imposed by capitalists but self-imposed by workers motivated to work more competitively in order to be able to buy from an expanding range of consumer goods: in Vernet's case in the year 1763, prints à la grecque, a guitar, a cushion for his sedan chair, and a world of goods that at his death encompassed also a **snuffbox**, a **sword**, an **umbrella**, and a **wig**, all things in this book. By such an argument Vernet bought his almanac in order to enjoy a sophisticated, expert timepiece (in place of his plain, generic ledgers), and to delight in its ornaments.

To propose such an interpretation presumes the correlation of historical change and individual time. However, the exact timing of Vernet's purchase perhaps indicates something else. In July 1762, Vernet and his family arrived in Paris to take up lodgings at the Louvre after a decade of moving from point to point along France's Mediterranean and Atlantic seaboards following the prescribed itinerary of the painter's royal commission of 1753: to paint twenty ports of France. Vernet had first broached the matter of a Louvre

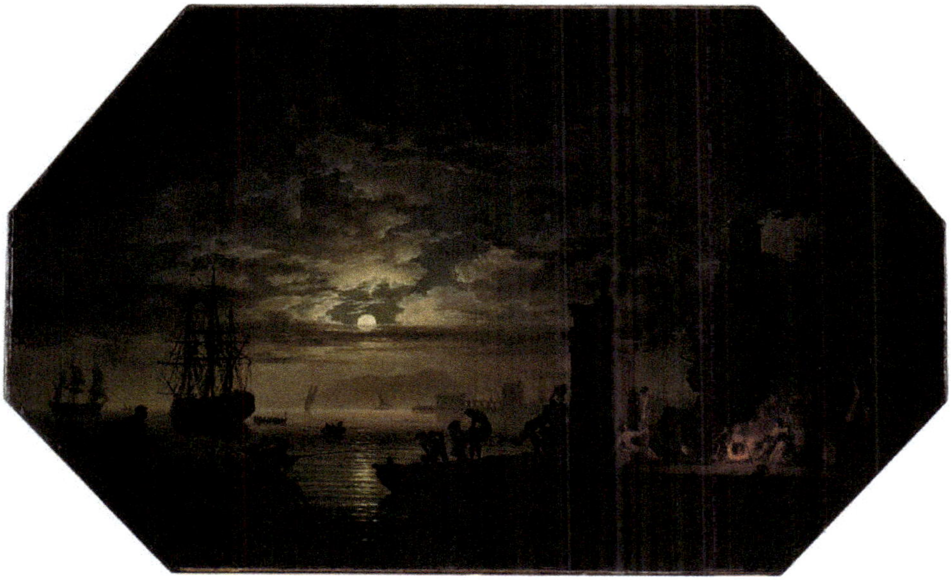

FIG. 2 Claude-Joseph Vernet (French, 1714–89), *Night*, from the series *Four Times of the Day*, 1762. Oil on canvas, 83.5 × 135 cm. Châteaux de Versailles et de Trianon, MV5927. (© RMN-Grand Palais / photo: Christophe Fouin / Art Resource, NY.)

logement (lodgings) in December 1759, after six years of "traveling for the king" and shortly after the birth of his second son, Carle.[18] The father Vernet wanted to synchronize the family clock, shaped by socially constructed expectations of settled domesticity, with the external meter of work time. He was initially rebuffed by the marquis de Marigny, the *directeur des bâtiments du roi* (director of the king's buildings), in whose gift a *logement* rested, and in whose view the end of migration and the end of the job were necessarily temporally related.[19] It was not until April 1762 that Marigny relented and allowed the claims of Vernet's family and his children's education to override the king's command.[20] It is possible that the delay and frustration Vernet suffered in setting up a permanent home made the painter especially conscious of his late transition to fatherhood, and that he marked this turning point in his life's course by purchase of an almanac for the year in which he moved into the Louvre and had his name painted on the door.[21]

Did Vernet perceive this turning point as a new beginning not only personally but professionally? Did he intend, with the almanac's help, to find a different way, a more disciplined way, of working and thinking about work, one in which time was reckoned in standard units, regularly performed and coordinated with the actions of others—one, in short, that calendars facilitate? The exchange of letters between Vernet and Marigny during the course of the execution of the *Ports of France* provides some provisional answers.

On 1 August 1763 Vernet wrote to Marigny for his orders on which port to paint next, pressing him for a decision because of "the lateness of the season in regard to the things [*opérations*] I must undertake."[22] There was a season to landscape and a time to the purpose of depicting it: the "beautiful" days of summer, stretching into early autumn.[23] In the *Port of Dieppe* (fig. 3), the modest Normandy port proposed as the subject by Vernet and accepted by Marigny, the time of painting coincides with the time depicted. Vernet arrived in September 1763 and portrayed the quayside at dawn decked with the night's catch of skate, rays, herring, and conger eel, fish harvested with lines and nets in late summer and early autumn.[24] Moreover, the sharp observation of the patterns of light and shadow cast by the sun, rising off-stage to the right, and captured seemingly in the dawn moment, suggests a natural synchrony between the diurnal rhythms of fishing and painting. But if Vernet's reference to the time of painting in the letters is couched in the vocabulary of nature, the temporal categories he used to articulate his "operations," and to report on his progress, was much more calculating and abstract. When estimating the time needed to rough out, paint, and finish one of his ports, he reckoned in days and working weeks, measurements of time that in the letters chime with the schedules of the postal system that delivered his canvases to Paris, rather than the order of nature.[25]

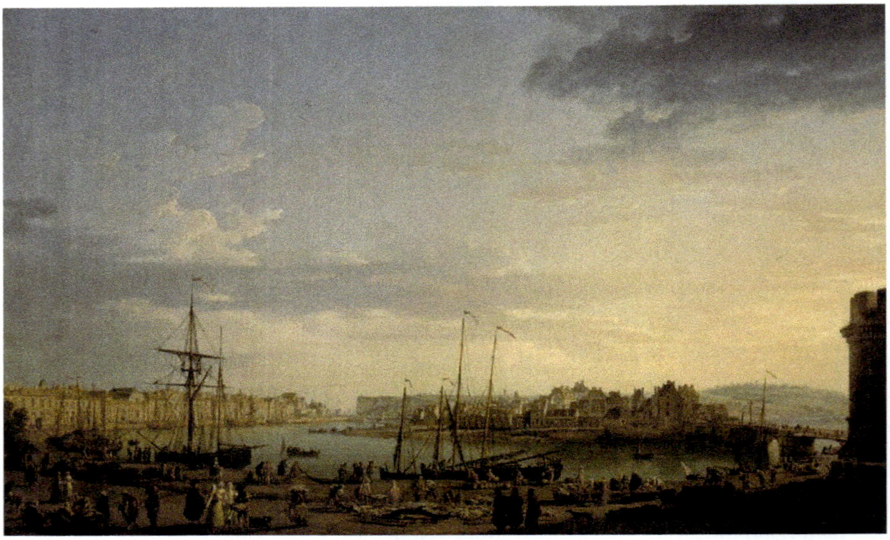

FIG. 3 Claude-Joseph Vernet (French, 1714–89), *Port of Dieppe*, 1765. Oil on canvas, 165.5 × 264 cm. Paris, Musée de la Marine, 5OA13. (© RMN-Grand Palais / Art Resource, NY.)

There is a case for saying that Vernet was compelled so to reckon time more abstractly by Marigny's micromanagement of the project through the continuous flow of his letters enjoining the painter to keep to his task and deliver to schedule.[26] Marigny met with some resistance. Vernet reminded the director of the constraints on speed that the frailties of the body and the materiality of paint imposes: the body must rest to recover from illness, paint must dry.[27] Ultimately, however, Marigny's ability to impose time discipline on Vernet was frustrated not by fever or the tackiness of black but by the exchequer.[28] With the outbreak of the Seven Years' War in 1757, regular payments for the *Ports* in cash and on receipt ended.[29] Vernet asked permission to take on private work to mitigate the effects of delayed payment.[30] Marigny initially refused. He argued that the *Ports of France* was a "collection," that is, an indivisible entity, and as such, Vernet having accepted the commission, he was bound to its continuous serial production.[31] Vernet, on the other hand, considered the *Ports* piecework, like any other commission—that is, a discontinuous series, production of which stopped and restarted with receipt of payment. Thus, where patron and painter were as one in reckoning time in more or less standard units, and on concentrating work by efficiencies of organization,[32] they were at odds over regularity in production.

The evidence of the letters indicates that Vernet was using abstract measures of time and value sometime before he bought his calendar in 1763. Moreover, he was prompted to adopt a modern orientation to work time by the disciplines of government bureaucracy, not those of industry. His clock was royal; metaphorically solar. Moreover, he experienced the pressure of it, an experience he shared with Marigny, in the terms and the discourse of deference, not efficiency: Vernet was "anxious" to serve; Marigny was "impatient" to admire, praise, and reward.

However, Vernet's purchase of an almanac in 1763 is less likely the response of identification with the linearity and rigidity of its tabulated sovereign time than it was the answer to his need to synchronize effectively and blend the rhythms of multiple overlapping commissions necessitated by the breakdown in royal patronage. The appendix of the *Almanach royal* afforded him, moreover, the names and addresses of those from whom future commissions might come. In September 1764 Vernet was still writing to Marigny for the settlement of his account for the *Ports* dating back to 1761, a commission that had ended although the "collection" was not complete.[33] In the letter, Vernet underscored his right to payment by the pressing needs of his family. He was not given to "mad extravagance"; he was not inflamed by consumer desire.[34] His expenditure of 20,000 livres, a huge sum, to establish his "house" at the Louvre was an obligation he owed to rank, and it was the only "extraordinary payment" that he had made since entering the king's service.[35] For Vernet, it seems, the almanac was a hybrid object whose meaning and uses were both backward and forward facing. Its date, "année MDCCLXIII," was a red-number year in his family's life and also marked the moment when he fully acceded to his title of academician by his presence in Paris and at the Louvre. These symbolic and collectively determined meanings of family and status time, which the *Alamanch royal* embodied for him, cohabited irregularly, however, with the calendar's utility, its force potentially to organize future time for profit and to free the spending of profit on things for pleasure. §

---

1. See *Dictionnaire de l'Académie française*, 4th ed. (1762; reprint, Chicago: University of Chicago ARTFL Project, 1998), https://artfl-project.uchicago.edu/content/dictionnaires-dautrefois, s.v. "almanach," 1:56. See also Véronique Sarrazin-Cani, "Formes et usages du calendrier dans les almanachs parisiens au XVIIIe siècle," *Bibliothèque de l'École des chartes* 157 (1999): 417–46.

2. Léon Lagrange, *Joseph Vernet et la peinture française au XVIIIe siècle* (Paris: Didier, 1864), 390.

3. On the *Almanach royal*, see Nicole Brondel, "*L'almanach royal, national, impérial*: Quelle verité, quelle transparence?

(1699–1840)," *Bibliothèque de l'École des chartes* 166, no. 1 (2008): 15–87.

4. See *Almanach royal pour l'année MDCCLXIII* (Paris: Le Breton, 1763), 2.

5. Lagrange, *Vernet*, 390. On the almanac as a New Year present, see *Mémoires et journal de J. G. Wille, graveur du roi*, ed. Georges Duplessis (Paris: Renouard, 1857), 2:82.

6. Claude-Joseph Vernet, "Inventaire après décès," 2 March 1790, AN, MC/ET/LXV/369.

7. Almanacs retained their value as directories; Vernet renewed his in 1771. See Lagrange, *Vernet*, 398.

8. For an annotated almanac, see "Sur mon *Almanach royal* de 1750," in *Lyon et l'Europe, hommes et sociétée: Mélanges offerts à Richard Gascon* (Lyon: Pul, 1980), 1:230–35; and Nicolas Lemas, "Les 'pages jaunes' du bâtiment au XVIIIe siècle: Sur une source méconnue de l'histoire du bâtiment parisien," *Histoire urbaine* 12 (2015): 175–82.

9. Lagrange, *Vernet*, 342.

10. On Vernet's journal, see Charlotte Guichard, "Les écritures ordinaires de Claude-Joseph Vernet: Commandes et sociabilité d'un peintre au XVIIIe siècle," in *Les écrits du for privé: Objects matériels, objects édités*, ed. Jean-Pierre Bardet et al. (Limoges: CTHS, 2007), 231–44.

11. Lagrange, *Vernet*, 390.

12. E. P. Thompson, "Time, Work-Discipline, and Industrial Capitalism," *Past and Present* 38, no. 1 (1967): 56–97.

13. See David S. Landes, *Revolution in Time*, rev. ed. (Cambridge: Harvard University Press, 2000).

14. The carillon of the clock on the Samaritaine on the Pont Neuf was a case in point.

15. Denis Diderot, *Salons*, ed. Jean Seznec and Jean Adhémar, 2nd ed. (Oxford: Clarendon, 1975), 1:228.

16. See Ewa Lajer-Burcharth, *The Painter's Touch* (Princeton: Princeton University Press, 2018), 13–32, on François Boucher.

17. Jan de Vries, "The Industrial Revolution and the Industrious Revolution," *Journal of Economic History* 54, no. 2 (1994): 249–70.

18. Jules Guiffrey, "Correspondance de Joseph Vernet avec le directeur des bâtiments du roi sur la collection des *Ports de France*, 1756–1787," *Revue de l'art ancien et moderne* 9 (1893): 34–36.

19. Guiffrey, "Correspondance," 36–37.

20. Guiffrey, "Correspondance," 49–50.

21. Lagrange, *Vernet*, 392. Biologically, Vernet was a father long before he moved into the Louvre. The argument here is that the social and moral experience of fatherhood was closely connected to a settled existence. See Jean-Joseph Expilly, *Dictionnaire géographique, historique et politique des Gaules et de la France* (Paris: Desaint & Saillant, 1762–70), 5:432 for record of names on doors. Under "things to do" in 1763 Vernet listed fitting a doorbell, getting a key to the outer door of the Louvre, and putting "Mon nom sur la porte." See Lagrange, *Vernet*, 392.

22. Guiffrey, "Correspondance," 55.

23. Guiffrey, "Correspondance," 21–22, 55.

24. See A. R. Michell, "The European Fisheries in the Early Modern Period," in *The Cambridge Economic History of Europe*, ed. E. E. Rich and C. H. Wilson (Cambridge: Cambridge University Press, 1977), 5:134–84, esp. 139–40, 153–54.

25. On the post, see Guiffrey, "Correspondance," 10, 21, 28, 31.

26. Guiffrey, "Correspondance," 5, 12, 13, 32.

27. Guiffrey, "Correspondance," 29–30 (illness); 13, 50 (paint).

28. Guiffrey, "Correspondance," 50: his overdoor *Night* required an extra forty days "étant fait de couleurs difficiles à sécher."

29. See Lagrange, *Vernet*, 114–15.

30. Guiffrey, "Correspondance," 26, 30.

31. Guiffrey, "Correspondance," 32.

32. On not wasting time waiting for the necessary permissions to draw the ports, see Guiffrey, "Correspondance," 12, 14, 15, 43–44.

33. Guiffrey, "Correspondance," 61–63.

34. See the same point in an earlier letter. Guiffrey, "Correspondance," 34–36.

35. Guiffrey, "Correspondance," 62. Adding up items of expenditure in Vernet's accounts related to the *logement*, Lagrange estimates that Vernet only actually spent 3,000 livres. See Lagrange, *Vernet*, 118.

Armchair

Jean-Honoré Fragonard (1732–1806)

TYPE OF OBJECT	THEME	MATERIAL
Furniture	Administration, Louvre, Studio	Animal | Leather/Parchment, Plant Matter | Cane, Plant Matter | Wood

In the 1790s, Jean-Honoré Fragonard stopped painting. By this point in his life, he had enjoyed a long and successful career as an artist spanning three decades, scores of clients, and hundreds of artworks (paintings and drawings), and he had established a name with his distinctively bravura take on the rococo mode. Indeed, the only thing he had not achieved was admission to the Académie.[1] But at the age of sixty, he made a career change and became a bureaucrat.[2]

Fragonard's professional pivot from painter to arts administrator kept him in the same cultural sector—working for the Commission du Muséum Central to establish France's first national museums—but involved a dramatic change in daily activities: from the tasks of the studio (grinding pigments, preparing canvases, sketching compositions, charging and cleaning **palettes**, creating works of art); to the tasks of the cabinet (reading and writing, and more reading and writing). As human activity exists in an inextricable relationship with things, Fragonard's career change also necessitated a shift in his material environs: a redelineation of his space, a demotion (perhaps even discarding) of previously essential tools, acquisition of new items to enable new activities, and a changing relationship with the old. Among the many things in Fragonard's possession involved in this moment of transition was his armchair (fig. 4).[3]

A cane *fauteuil* with a continuous back and armrests and an upholstered leather seat, Fragonard's armchair has certain decorative details (like its turned front legs), but other aspects suggest a privileging of functionality over aesthetics (like the single cane layer that makes it somewhat less elegant from behind). In an effort to define chairs, Denis Diderot described them rather self-evidently as "an article of furniture upon which one sits," but the furniture makers of eighteenth-century Paris assured far more specification of use and activity within this generic category of object.[4] There exists, as Mimi Hellman has articulated, a mutually defining relationship between bodies and furniture.[5] Every chair allows its user to sit, but each chair accommodates that operation differently, ensuring a particular corporeal position, subtly directing comportment and behavior, and physically delimiting a range of actions and gestures. Any given chair will facilitate some activities, but in turn make others more challenging. In the increasingly literate world of Enlightenment Paris, furniture designed specifically for reading and writing became an important business. Chairs could be optimized for the physical actions of intellectual labor,

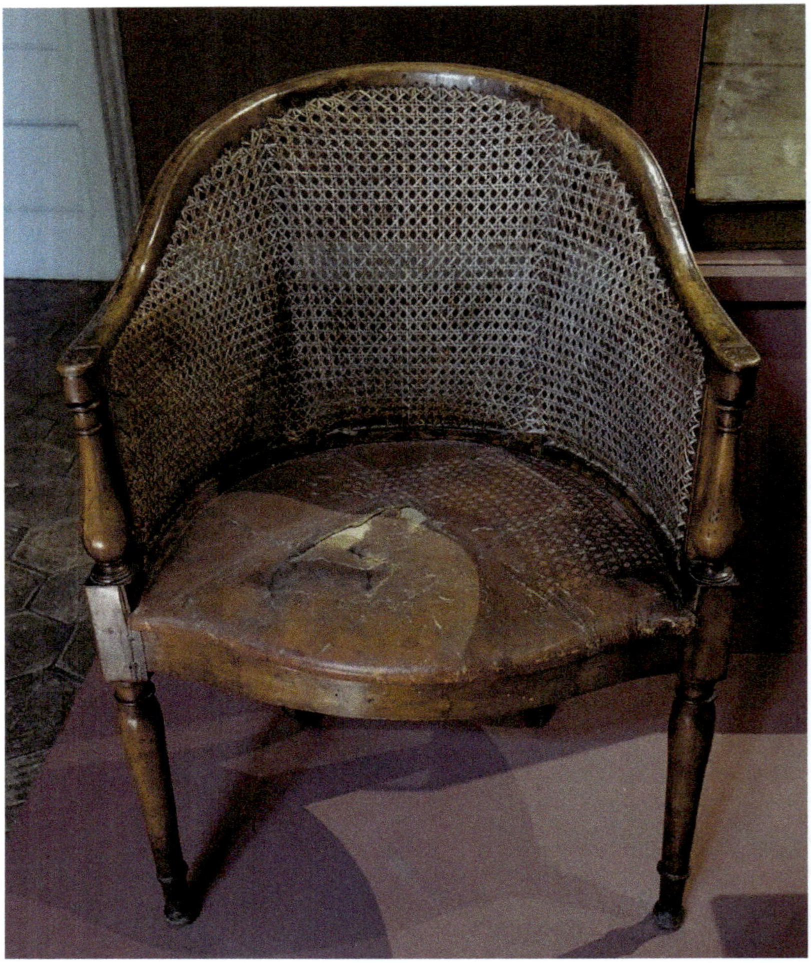

FIG. 4 Unknown maker, *Fauteuil*, last quarter of the eighteenth century. Wood, cane, and leather, 89 × 59 cm. Paris, Musée du Louvre, OA 7879, on loan to Grasse, Villa-Musée Fragonard. (© 2022 Musée du Louvre / Objets d'art du Moyen Age, de la Renaissance et des temps modernes.)

like, at the more customized end of the spectrum, the *fauteuil* designed for Voltaire by the *menuisier* Charles-François Normand (fig. 5): on one side, an adjustable stand for books or papers to read; on the other, a flat surface for writing (if left-handed) that doubled as a container for storage; and casters on the feet so the chair could be wheeled at whim to a more amenable position.[6] For other readers and writers, who unlike Voltaire were less averse to stationary deskwork, the chair of choice might be a *fauteuil de cabinet* (fig. 6), with its central leg at the front and its rounded seat cut away at the sides to ease pressure on the thighs. According to the *menuisier* André-Jacob Roubo, this assured a commodious experience for those required to sit for long periods leaning forward, "as all those who write do."[7] As a desk-dwelling administrator, Fragonard would have shared such requirements, but his armchair was not designed with quite the same degree of specification.

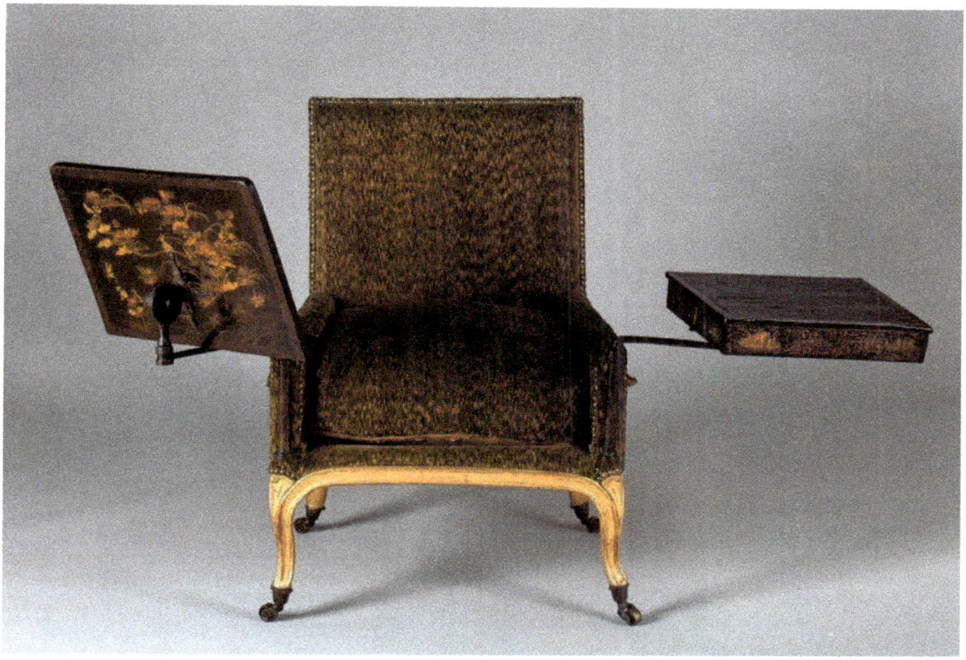

FIG. 5 Charles-François Normand, Voltaire's *fauteuil*, ca. 1775. Gilded beech, velvet, lacquer, and iron, 91 × 66 × 55 cm. Paris, Musée Carnavalet.

Nevertheless, its features would have qualified it well for the role of a bureaucrat's desk chair. Its seat height would elevate the user to the appropriate level for writing, while allowing the feet to remain ergonomically on the floor; the curved front edge of the seat would alleviate some pressure on the legs; and the height of the armrests would offer support to the elbow of the writing hand. While amenable to the deskwork required in his new administrative life, Fragonard's chair was not so specialized in its design as to preclude alternative uses or to imply that it was acquired expressly for this purpose. Its style and materials certainly suggest it was made in the last quarter of the century, so it may well have been bought new by Fragonard in the 1790s to mark his career change, but it could also have been a slightly older purchase re-appropriated for new service.[8] Indeed, it is not impossible that it had already served as a work chair in a different space, in the studio of the erstwhile painter. Though the bodily comportment and gestures of deskwork and easel work are completely different, it seems, from the evidence of artists' portraits, that *fauteuils* were also frequently the chairs of choice for painting (see, for instance, figs. 36, 38, and 65). With the artist's active brush hand raised to the canvas, the armrests of an armchair were not an impediment to painterly action and, for the palette hand, they would provide welcome relief for a tired arm.

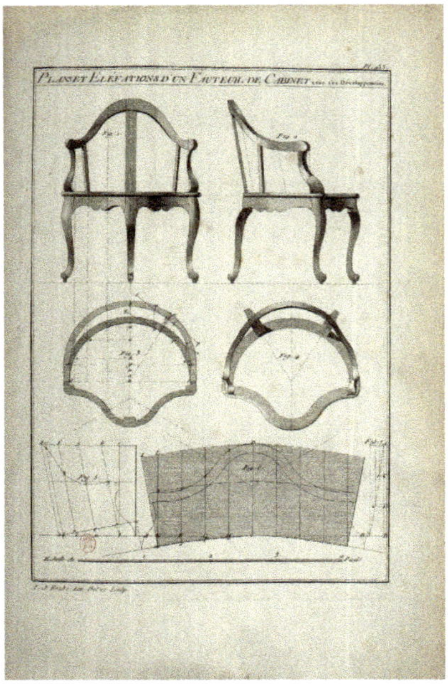

FIG. 6 André-Jacob Roubo (French, 1739–91), Design of a *fauteuil de cabinet*, 1772, from André-Jacob Roubo, *L'art du menuisier en meubles* (Paris, 1772), no. 233. Paris, Bibiliothèque Nationale de France. (Image source: Gallica.)

Fragonard's armchair, with its amenable versatility and potential for re-appropriation, thus invites an alternative way of thinking about the painter's late career change. The timing of Fragonard's decision has always made it ripe for dramatic speculation, even while his exact reasons remain unknown. In many ways, with the events of the French Revolution, this was a moment of collective transformation. From the civil unrest of 1789 to the increasing violence and disruptions of the 1790s, life in France changed significantly in a few short years. Yet in other ways, normal life continued through it all, not least in the form of the relentless litany of loss and ill health that besets every family. For Fragonard, indeed, this extraordinary moment of French history was marked by some very ordinary tragedies, which themselves have been seen as climactic points in his narrative of transition. In 1788 his beloved daughter Rosalie died when only eighteen and, not long afterward, Fragonard himself became seriously ill with a gastrointestinal condition known as cholera morbus.[9] In 1790 he traveled to his native Grasse in the south of France to recuperate over the following year, and it was after this, upon his return to Paris, that Fragonard gave up painting. Whether correlation or causation, Fragonard's trip and the events around it have come to stand as a watershed. His career change looks tantalizingly like a decision provoked by poor health or grief (like that rupture marked in Wille's **journal** after his wife's death) or like a reaction to the tumultuous events of the day (a new job for this new world). But what if this choice was, like Fragonard's chair selection, less dramatic change than pragmatic readjustment, less a renunciation of his former life than a reconfiguration of it?

When considered from the perspective of his armchair, there was certainly as much continuity as change in this shift. From the vantage of its leather seat, Fragonard would be working in the same professional field, in the same building, with the same colleagues, albeit performing quite different tasks. Along with several other artists, including, at different times, Jacques-Louis David, François-André Vincent, Augustin Pajou, and Hubert Robert, Fragonard's role on the Commission du Muséum Central was to oversee the Louvre's transformation into France's first public museum. When the monarchy fell on 10 August 1792, the Louvre and its collections transitioned from royal to national property, and the existing plan to establish a museum was adopted by the new regime, as Andrew McClellan has shown, as a matter of political urgency.[10] Delivering this crucial goal would be an enormous administrative feat, from the loftiest acts of selecting and curating artworks for display to the more mundane tasks of managing wages and arranging the transport of objects.[11] Fragonard's work in this endeavor was simplified by living onsite, for, like so many of the artists and objects in this book, Fragonard and his chair were residents of the Louvre, despite this being a privilege usually only accorded to academicians, that title Fragonard had never achieved.[12] But in this respect, his new role actually proved a valuable opportunity for closure. Not only did this key administrative post bring him an institutional legitimation that had always been lacking, it also resolved an unsettled relationship with the Louvre itself. For Fragonard's failure to become an academician stemmed from his failure to paint the reception piece requested of him: a ceiling painting to complete the decoration of the Louvre's Apollo Gallery.[13] Joining the commission was then a chance to tie off the loose threads still left from his artistic career. David certainly saw it as a natural progression—a way for Fragonard to devote "his old age to preserving the masterpieces whose numbers, in his youth, he succeeded in increasing"—but perhaps in that moment, it was actually the masterpiece he had failed to complete that proved more decisive.[14] Whatever the case, from his desk chair, Fragonard was certainly able to make a mark on Paris's art-world institutions—and on the Louvre—that he had never quite managed with his brush. ‡

---

1. Fragonard was *agréé* in 1766 but never completed the admission process.

2. On Fragonard's career change, see Pierre Rosenberg, "Fragonard: Functionnaire at the Louvre," in *Fragonard*, exh. cat. (New York: Metropolitan Museum of Art, 1987), 581–82.

3. Part of the Louvre's collection, the chair is now at the Villa-Musée Fragonard, Grasse. Curators have traced its provenance back to Fragonard's apartments in the Louvre; see *Jean-Honoré Fragonard, peintre de Grasse*, exh. cat. (Grasse: Villa-Musée Fragonard, 2006), 13.

4. "Chaise," *Encyclopédie*, https://encyclopedie.uchicago.edu/, 3:13.

5. Mimi Hellman, "Furniture, Sociability, and the Work of Leisure in Eighteenth-Century France," *ECS* 32, no. 4 (1999): 415–45.

6. Anne Forray-Carlier, *Le mobilier du Musée Carnavalet* (Dijon: Faton, 2000), 300.

7. André-Jacob Roubo, *L'art du menuisier en meubles*, part 3, section 2 (Paris: Saillant & Nyon, 1772), 643.

8. With thanks to Mia Jackson and Ulrich Leben for the dating of this chair.

9. Pierre Rosenberg, ed., *Fragonard*, exh. cat. (New York: Metropolitan Museum of Art, 1987), 417–19.

10. Andrew McClellan, *Inventing the Louvre: Art, Politics, and the Origins of the Modern Museum in Eighteenth-Century Paris* (Berkeley: University of California Press, 1999), 91.

11. McClellan, *Inventing the Louvre*, 91–123; and Rosenberg, "Fragonard," 581–82.

12. Fragonard seems to have been living in the Louvre before he left for Grasse, as his name is included in a description from 1790: "État des logemens," transcribed in Jules Guiffrey, *NAAF*, 1873, 147. He then remained in the Louvre until the general eviction of all artists in 1805.

13. The request of a ceiling painting for the Apollo Gallery was made following Fragonard's *agrément* in 1766 (*PV*, 7:330–31). Ten years later, Fragonard wrote to the Académie seeking to be relieved of the obligation, and it was agreed that he could submit an ordinary easel painting instead (*PV*, 8:242), but Fragonard never did that either.

14. Jacques-Louis David, *Rapport sur la suppression de la commission du Muséum* (Paris: Imprimerie Nationale, 1973), 5.

Baptism Certificate

Hubert Robert (1733–1808)

TYPE OF OBJECT	THEME	MATERIAL
Document	Family, Identity, Money, Religion	Synthetic Materials | Ink, Synthetic Materials | Paper

A small piece of paper, around the size of a postcard, contains enough information in its printed and handwritten lines to paint a rich picture of Hubert Robert's earliest days (fig. 7). A baptism certificate is, indeed, a fairly meta thing about which to write an object biography, given that such documents are a conventional source of biographical facts, at least in the Catholic culture of eighteenth-century France, where an *acte de baptême* was a near universal marker of the beginning of a life. But as a thing with its own life, this piece of paper reveals far more than the factual information it contains about Robert's origins, providing insights into religious customs and legal procedures, as well as a father-son relationship and some savvy financial dealings.

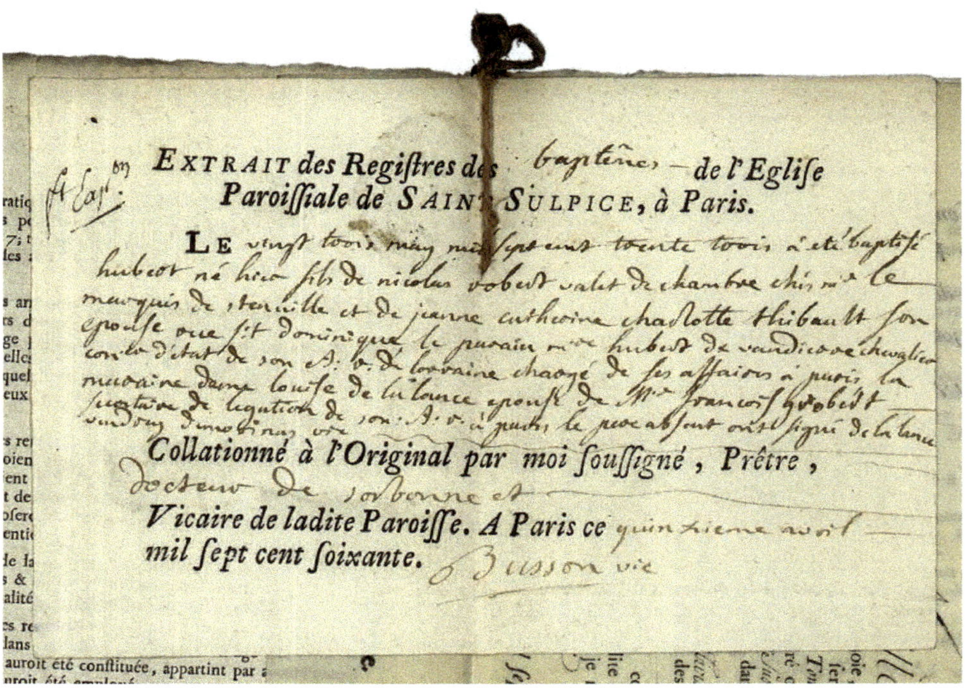
EXTRAIT des Regiſtres des baptêmes de l'Egliſe Paroiſſiale de SAINT SULPICE, à Paris.

LE vingt trois may mil sept cent trente trois a été baptisé hubert né hier fils de nicolas robert valet de chambre chez mr le marquis de stainville et de jeanne catherine charlotte thibault son epouse …

Collationné à l'Original par moi ſouſſigné, Prêtre, docteur de sorbonne et Vicaire de ladite Paroiſſe. A Paris ce quinzieme avril mil ſept cent ſoixante. Busson vic

FIG. 7 Baptism certificate of Hubert Robert (baptism 1733, certificate issued 1760). Paris, Archives Nationales, MC/ET/LXXXIII/490.

Recording details about his family, his social background, and the urban neighborhood in which he was born, Robert's baptism certificate tells us, quite directly, who this artist was and where he came from before he became an artist. We discover that Robert was born on 22 May 1733 and was baptized the next day, following the convention of baptizing babies as soon as possible after birth (sometimes even later the same day), in order to reduce the likelihood of the infant dying without receiving the sacrament. We also meet Robert's parents—his mother, Jeanne-Catherine-Charlotte Thibault, and his father Nicolas Robert—and learn that the latter was in the service of a noble household, as *valet de chambre* to François-Joseph de Choiseul, marquis de Stainville, a courtier to the dukes of Lorraine.[1] This, we find, was the social milieu into which Robert was born, for both his godparents were in the service of the Paris household of the duke of Lorraine, François III (who would later become Holy Roman Emperor). Robert's godfather, Hubert de Venvières, was *chevalier conseiller d'État* to the duke, and his godmother was Louise de La Lance, wife of François Gobert, the duke's *secrétaire de légation*. Robert's godparents thus offered an elite social network for their charge, but his godfather specifically had a more immediate role in shaping the infant's identity. Robert was christened Hubert following the custom of naming the child after the godparent of the same gender (a custom that, for instance, saw the painter Hyacinthe Collin de Vermont named after his godfather and future colleague Hyacinthe Rigaud). Finally, we also encounter some of the urban spaces in which Robert began his life. The family address is recorded as Rue Saint-Dominique, a street running parallel to the Seine on Paris's Left Bank, starting near the abbey of Saint-Germain-des-Prés and ending near Les Invalides. This street was located in the parish of Saint-Sulpice, which, as the certificate states, was the church in which Robert was baptized and where this telling piece of paper was produced.

Robert's baptism certificate is thus a treasure trove of personal details for the biographer, but at the time, its significance lay more in its value as a material vestige of a religious rite and as an important legal document. Baptism is the first of the Catholic Church's seven sacraments, those outward and visible signs of God's grace that sanctify the faithful. According to the tenets of that faith, as elaborated in eighteenth-century catechisms, the rite of baptism served to wash away original sin, allowing for rebirth through Christ, and making the recipient a child of God and the Church.[2] It was, in other words, the sacrament by which one was initiated into the Christian faith and without which one would be denied eternal salvation. An *acte de baptême* was proof that the sacrament had been received, a record that Robert had been held at the font by his godparents while a priest had enacted this solemn rite to make him a child of God. Yet as was often the case in ancien régime society, where lay laws and customs were structured around religious beliefs and practices, the sacrament of baptism also had a legal dimension. A baptism certificate might seem a fundamentally religious thing—a material trace of a sacrament, signed by a priest and issued by a parish church—but it was as much, if not more, or inextricably both, a legal document, serving to register the birth and record the existence of a new member of society.

For the most part, this legal registering of baptisms actually took a different material form. Unlike Robert, most people did not own a certificate, but rather simply had the record of their baptism written into the baptismal register of their parish church. While the vast majority of Paris's eighteenth-century parish registers were sadly destroyed in the nineteenth century, a rare volume remains from the church of Saint-Roch (fig. 8).[3] Covering the year 1790, the ledger offers a sense of the materiality of these records, in which each baptism was entered by the priest who performed the rite—usually the *curé* (parish priest) or the *vicaire* (curate)—and signed beneath by the parents and godparents after the service. On page 78, for instance, we find three entries, two of them children of painters—Jean-Henry, son of Nicolas Frémont; and Catherine-Pierrette, daughter of Louis-Nicolas Vincent—their surnames written in the left margin for ease of retrieval.[4] Such communal ledgers (listing all children, born of painters, nobles, and servants alike) were the standard material records of baptisms. But on occasion, proof was needed in a more mobile form. As Robert's certificate states at the top, this was an "extrait des registres" (an extract from the registers) of Saint-Sulpice, that is, a transposition of Robert's entry in the ledger to create a readily transportable individualized version. From the text printed on the certificate, it is also clear that it was an adaptable pro forma, allowing the *vicaire* to supply details from any of the parish's registers (baptisms, marriages, or funerals) as and when required.

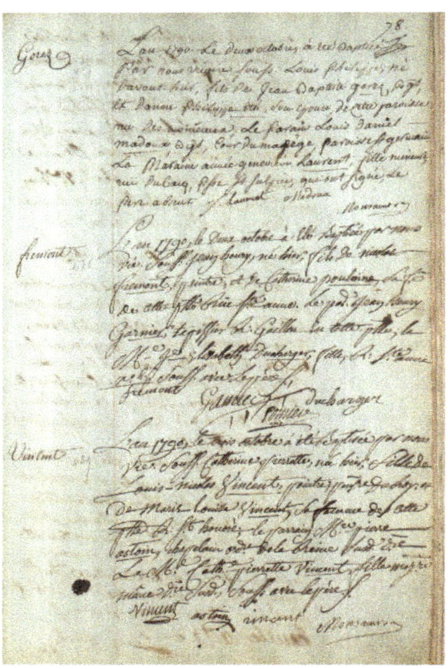

FIG. 8 *Registre des baptêmes*, parish of Saint-Roch, 1790, page 78. Archives de Paris, V.6E 1.

Robert's requirements for a baptism certificate occurred, as the document reveals in its issue date, on 15 April 1760, about a month before his twenty-seventh birthday. As a material thing, Robert's baptism certificate thus has little connection with his actual baptism. The document was produced nearly three decades after the sacrament was administered, by a priest who performed no role in the rite. Its current location (in the Archives Nationales) reveals why it was sought in the first place, for it is to be found attached with a piece of notary's string to a contract outlining a *tontine* (fig. 9).[5] This was an early modern speculative investment scheme in which subscribers would pay an initial amount and then receive a life income via an annuity. Participants in the *tontine* were divided into age groups, and over time, as others died, shares were redistributed to surviving members, leaving the last one standing as the recipient of a substantial fortune.[6] Hubert Robert was a *pensionnaire* at the Académie de France in Rome when this *tontine* was drawn up, but his share was purchased by his father, Nicolas, who seems to have made this investment in his son's favor as a paternal gesture to assure a financial income for the young painter.[7] Nicolas paid 1,000 livres in order for Hubert to receive a *rente viagère* (life annuity) with a principal of 80 livres plus interest, which, for a twenty-six-year-old man with a normal life expectancy, would have looked like a secure and profitable investment. Given the importance of age to a *tontine*, baptism certificates were required to provide proof of a participant's date of birth.[8] Thus, on the final page of the contract, the notary confirmed that the extract from the baptismal register of Saint-Sulpice had been supplied; a note was added to the back of that certificate indicating that it had been "certifié véritable" (certified as true); and the small piece of paper was tied in perpetuity to this financial deal.

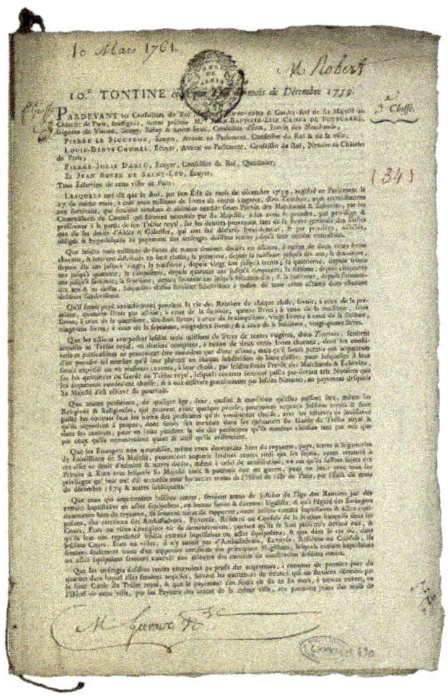

FIG. 9 Nicolas Robert's contract for a "Tontine créée par Édit du mois de Décembre 1759," signed 10 March 1761. Paris, Archives Nationales, MC/ET/LXXXIII/490.

Through the baptism certificate's passage from parish register to investment contract we not only encounter two distinct moments of Robert's life—the infant of 1733 and the young artist of 1760—we also find a connection between the seemingly disparate spaces of religion and finance. Given the moral qualms about speculative financial ventures, especially for a scheme in which participants benefited from the deaths of others, one might envisage an uncomfortable discord between what this piece of paper represented and how it was used: that is, between the holy sacrament that turned Hubert Robert into a child of God, and the worldly business deal that brought him fiscal return. Yet this document proffers a material trace of the more symbiotic relationships between religion, law, and finance that existed in the lived experience of eighteenth-century France. ‡

---

1. Though not mentioned on the certificate, Robert's mother was also in service in the marquis's household as a *femme de chambre*. See *Hubert Robert, 1733–1808: Un peintre visionnaire*, exh. cat. (Paris: Musée du Louvre, 2016), 29.

2. *Catéchisme, ou exposition de la doctrine chrétienne* (Soissons: Ponce Courtons, 1756), 197–203.

3. Copies of Paris's parish registers were kept in the Tuileries Palace and were destroyed in 1871, when the building was burned during the Paris Commune.

4. Neither painter was ever admitted to the guild (which was disbanded in 1776) or the Académie, but Louis-Nicolas Vincent exhibited works at the Académie's open Salon of 1791: *Collection des livrets des anciennes expositions depuis 1673 jusqu'en 1800* (Paris: Liepmannssohn, 1870), 20, 32.

5. AN, MC/ET/LXXXIII/490.

6. John Dunkley, "Bourbons on the Rocks: Tontines and Early Public Lotteries in France," *ECS* 30, no. 3 (2007): 311. See also David R. Weir, "Tontines, Public Finance, and Revolution in France and England, 1688–1789," *Journal of Economic History* 49, no. 1 (1989): 95–124.

7. Robert was in Rome from 1754 to 1765.

8. Dunkley, "Bourbons," 312.

Bath

Joseph-Siffred Duplessis (1725–1802)

TYPE OF OBJECT	THEME	MATERIAL
Commodity, Furniture, Instrument	Everyday, Health/Medicine, Invention, Louvre, Luxury	Metal | Copper

What does it mean to own a thing but not have the power to command its functions? More importantly, perhaps, how does it feel? These questions arise in the case of Joseph-Siffred Duplessis's bath. In 1788 Duplessis, Louis XVI's official portrait painter, had been in possession of a bathtub for some time, but in that particular year he sought to install it at his *logement* (lodgings) at the Galerie du Louvre. To that end he wrote to the comte d'Angiviller, the *directeur des bâtiments du roi*, for permission to do so. His request was denied. An argument ensued, the progress of which was first recounted by Jules Belleudy in his yet-to-be bettered monograph on the painter.[1] From the summary description of the bath given during the exchanges between Duplessis and d'Angiviller, we learn that it was a common or garden bath, an infraordinary thing that for most of its life existed below the level of conscious notice, but as a result of the men's disagreement about the practical and social values of bathing, and of bathing in relation to art and royal service, became momentarily contentious and thereby conspicuous.

By 1788 Duplessis had been living at the Louvre for over a decade. Unlike artists such as the Coypels and the Silvestres, that is, families of artists who had worked for the Crown for generations, whose members held and inherited offices in the Maison du Roi and the lodgings at the Louvre attached to those offices, Duplessis was a newcomer.[2] He was born in Carpentras in the south of France. He arrived in Paris in his mid- to late twenties following a trip to Rome at his own expense. He was without either connections or introductions. Initially he joined the painters' and sculptors' guild, the Académie de Saint-Luc;[3] it was not until 1774, more than twenty years after stepping foot in the capital, that he was admitted a full member of the Académie. In that year he was commissioned by d'Angiviller to paint the king's portrait, and the following year he was awarded a studio at the Louvre to enable him to do so.[4]

The year 1774 had also been the year of d'Angiviller's appointment as *directeur* of the king's works.[5] He inherited an office that was a shambles and critically in debt. Within two years he had instituted new rules and regulations for the structure and running of his department.[6] The allocation of studios and *logements* was largely unaffected; it continued to proceed on the mixed basis of seniority, talent, utility, and connections (see **key**). However, reforms were introduced to the maintenance and repair of the royal buildings. The 1776 regulation established a clear division in law between the responsibilities of the

Bâtiments to maintain the structure of the building, specifically the load-bearing walls, beams, and roofs, thereby ensuring its safety, and the liability of the "concessionaires," or occupants, for the cost of the decoration undertaken to make their accommodations pleasant and commodious.[7] To that end, artists were required to seek permission from the director for any works they intended to carry out; moreover, those works had to be approved by one of the Bâtiments' architects and realized by its workmen.[8] The clarity of that dividing line was not, however, absolutely crystal. When Duplessis moved from the Cour Carré to a new *logement* in the Galerie du Louvre in 1781 he wrote to d'Angiviller: "[W]hen you gave me this *logement* I thought that you had also given me tacit permission to secure it with doors and windows, but I have made it a law unto myself not to employ a mason for even the simplest things, without the approbation of M. [Maximilien] Brébion [the Louvre's architect]."[9] The note of irony in Duplessis's request to enclose his living space was lacking in the letters of May 1788 about the installation of his bath, but they nevertheless parade Duplessis's confidence that permission was a formality, since a bath was "such a small thing of no consequence and of which there are [already] other examples at the Galerie."[10]

D'Angiviller's refusal came as a surprise to Duplessis and prompted him to write an unusually long and detailed reply.[11] In it he sought to strengthen his case by addressing the points that had motivated the director's decision. The bath is disclosed in the process as not one thing, but two: an unprepossessing, tin-lined copper vessel of average dimension (see fig. 179) and a hazardous object of administration.[12] D'Angiviller had argued that the bath, with its water tank and heater, put the Louvre at risk of both fire and flood. By implication, he categorized it with other objects, notably stoves, that had engrossed the attention of successive directors. In 1754 a stove fire had broken out in the *logement* of the engraver Claude Drevet, from which the Louvre was saved only by the prompt action of the police.[13] Moreover, such was the continuing concern of the comte d'Angiviller's predecessor, the marquis de Marigny, about the unlicensed proliferation of such stoves, that in 1773 he ordered the inspection and review of those in all artists' studios and *logements* and the removal of any judged defective or unsafe.[14] By more closely regulating permissions to improve, maintain, and repair the accommodations granted to concessionaires, d'Angiviller had hoped to preempt the risk of disaster, but in June 1787 a fire broke out at the Tuileries that virtually destroyed the Pavillon de Flore.[15] Duplessis could not have made his request at a more inopportune moment, nor in more inappropriate terms: "a small thing of no consequence."

D'Angiviller's objection had not, however, been limited to questions of safety. In his opinion, apparently, Duplessis's bath was both a novelty and a luxury, one to which neither the portraitist's order nor his estate entitled him. Baths were rare "amenities" even in the houses of the elite, he had observed.[16] In this respect, d'Angiviller perhaps also classed the bath with another category of administrative object: the status symbol. Article 4 of the 1776 regulations legally reserved the distinction of a doorbell installed and maintained at the Bâtiments' expense, for office holders only.[17] The doorbells of simple concessionaires, or the bulk of the artists lodged at the Louvre, would be tolerated, but no claims on the royal purse could be made for them. In summary, d'Angiviller's objections to Duplessis's bath were based, sight unseen, on a perception of it as a luxury and a technological novelty that threatened both the physical building and the social order at the Louvre.

Duplessis dispatched d'Angiviller's objections on grounds of safety, reluctantly but swiftly by renouncing his *chaudière* and offering to conform to the normal practice of heating (bath) water in the hearth.[18] However, he actively challenged d'Angiviller's perception of the bath as a luxury. It was not, he insisted, in his case "a sensual object," and he was not "a petit bourgeois" tormented by desire to possess one and appear *grand*.[19] Rather, it was a medical object: the means to relieve his suffering and necessary to the preservation of his health, specifically his eyesight.[20] Duplessis was, that is to say, reminding d'Angiviller that his painting skills were embodied. Unlike the administrative personnel in d'Angiviller's department, whose knowledge and bureaucratic competences were transferable, the talent of the artist was *in* his hands and eyes, and Duplessis's royal service thus depended directly on the health of them both. He did also point out that if indeed few bourgeois homes could pretend to bathrooms, many contained bathtubs on doctors' orders.

In response to d'Angiviller's advice that he bathe not at home but in one of the capital's many public baths, Duplessis noted not only that he was often too ill to venture out, but also the inconvenience, when well, of wasting time for art waiting in line. Moreover, he observed, that a home bath was cheap, little more than the price of coal to heat the water, unlike a bath chez a wigmaker-cum-steambather (*perruquier-étuviste*), or one taken at one of the newer bathhouses on the Seine.[21] In place of d'Angiviller's discourse on the bath as contrived object with both material and symbolic effects for the corps of artists at the Louvre, Duplessis's proposed arguments grounded in the natural body and the benefits to it of bathing, on the one hand, and on his thrift in domestic economy, on the other.

During the course of Duplessis and d'Angiviller's correspondence, the bath, use of which the painter had initially thought so small and trivial a matter that he had almost forgotten to mention it, grew dramatically in importance to the point of requiring a full account of Duplessis's medical history and an informal portrait of his temperament. At stake was not just the thing itself but the terms of the relationship between the director and the painter. That relationship was repeatedly construed by Duplessis as one of patronage, which is to say, a relationship in which the exercise of power was personal and not derived from bureaucratic rules and regulations. He referred to his request as a "prayer" (*prière*) a word from the vocabulary of eighteenth-century civility that denoted the reciprocal obligations between friends.[22] Structured by asymmetries of rank and power, patronage was, of course, a lopsided form of friendship. Duplessis offered his obedience and his unstinting and profound "respect," immaterial assets in return for the more immediate and tangible fruits he hoped to elicit from d'Angiviller's "goodness."[23] The detail of his letter, which alluded to his professional sufferings—his lack of work and his financial losses—in addition to his many health problems, aimed to oblige d'Angiviller to treat him as a person and not a case. He regretted not being able to entreat d'Angiviller face to face, that he might press his need by exhibition of his suffering body. His excessive elaboration of his theme, his endless repetition of salient points, and his generous deployment of emphatic adjectives and particles was substitution by missive for the physical affect of presence. Even the unsaid in Duplessis's letter is enrolled to his plea. Nowhere does he state, but everywhere he implies, that d'Angiviller was his only source of succor and comfort. Such was his health and melancholy temperament that he was alone, isolated, and without other resources.[24] He was not, like Hubert Robert and Anne Vallayer-Coster, the painters already enjoying baths at the Louvre, blessed with powerful connections at court.[25]

There is no evidence in the Bâtiments papers to suggest that d'Angiviller was moved by Duplessis's anguish to change his mind. Seemingly, he did not relent from his "measured refusal." He replied to Duplessis's entreaty in the calm, controlled, and depersonalized language of the nobleman and the royal office holder enforcing bureaucratic regulations by his rational and objective decision making. In order to bathe, Duplessis was forced to keep additional rented lodgings outside the Louvre, a cost he had hoped to save himself by fully installing himself at the Galerie. However, the painter seems not to have borne d'Angiviller any ill will for his perceived betrayal of the trust. In 1791 Duplessis publicly defended d'Angiviller and his administration against accusations of corruption leveled by revolutionaries.[26] §

---

1. See Jules Belleudy, *J. S. Duplessis, peintre du roi (1725–1802)* (Chartres: Durand, 1913), 101–7.

2. See Jules-Joseph Guiffrey, "Logements d'artistes au Louvre," *NAAF*, 1873, 1–221. For Coypel, see also **Bed**. For the Silvestres, see Dena Goodman and Emily Talbot, "Documenting Art, Writing Biography: Construction of the Silvestre Family History 1660–1868," *Journal of Family History* 40, no. 3 (2015): 277–304. When Jacques-Augustin Silvestre wrote to Marigny in 1766 formally to request the succession of his father's *logement*, he observed, "for more than one hundred years it has been our honor, inherited from father to son, to teach the king and the royal family to draw. For almost the same amount of time our ancestors have enjoyed possession of a *logement* at the Louvre" ("il y a plus de cent ans que de père en fils nous avons l'honneur d'enseigner à dessiner au Roy et à la famille Royale. Il y a à peu près le même temps que nos ancestres ont l'avantage de posséder un logement aux galleries du Louvre"). See AN, O[1]/1673/24: Silvestre to Marigny, 30 April 1766.

3. See Jules Guiffrey, "Histoire de l'Académie de Saint-Luc," *NAAF*, 1915, 277–78.

4. The portrait was exhibited at the Salon of 1775. On the portrait, see Belleudy, *Duplessis*, 53–74.

5. See Jacques Silvestre de Sacy, *Le comte d'Angiviller dernier directeur des bâtiments du roi* (Paris: Plon, 1953), 49–65.

6. *Bâtiments du roi: Règlements pour leur administration par déclaration du Roi 1er septembre 1776; Edit de règlement, donné au mois de septembre 1776* (Paris: Hérissant, 1776).

7. *Bâtiments du roi: Règlements*, art. 1 and 3. See, for example, the correspondence relating to the fitting out of Ménageot's and Vincent's studios in 1784: AN, O[1]/1674/230, 232, 239.

8. The *bâtiments* regulations by the *Arrêts du conseil du roi* of 30 January 1672, 16 March 1757, and 30 January 1774 required the use of Bâtiments agents for works at the royal palaces; they had not been enforced. In July 1781 d'Angiviller pursued a case against a mason (Guérin) and a joiner (Bellanger) for works on the *logement* of the comtesse de Salles. The workmen were fined 300 livres but avoided imprisonment. For the *Judgement de police*, see AN, O[1]/1674/24.

9. Belleudy, *Duplessis*, 95–107.

10. Belleudy, *Duplessis*, 102.

11. D'Angiviller's letter to Duplessis has not survived, however its content is summarized in Duplessis's reply; see Belleudy, *Duplessis*, 102.

12. Contemporary descriptions of bathtubs suggest they were standardized. See *Encyclopédie*, https://encyclopedie.uchicago.edu/, 2:15–16. See also François-Alexandre-Pierre de Garsault, *L'art du perruquier* (Paris: n.p., 1767), 33 and plate 5; and André-Jacob Roubo, *L'art du menuisier en meubles*, 4 parts in 5 vols. (Paris: Saillant & Nyon, 1772), 3, pt. 2:660–61 and plate 240.

13. AN, O[1]/1672/293: Garnier d'Isle to Marigny, 28 November 1754.

14. AN, O[1]/1673/273: [Jacques-Germain Soufflot], *Rapport à Monsieur le Directeur général faite par ses ordres les 29 janvier et 5 février 1773* (15 February 1773).

15. Silvestre de Sacy, *D'Angiviller*, 65.

16. D'Angiviller's assertion is confirmed in Georges Vigarello, *Concepts of Cleanliness: Changing Attitudes in France since the Middle Ages* (Cambridge, England: Cambridge University Press, 1988), 96. See also Mimi Hellman, "Staging Retreat: Designs for Bathing in Eighteenth-Century France," in *Interiors and Interiority*, ed. Ewa Lajer-Burcharth and Beate Söntgen (Berlin: De Gruyter, 2016), 49–72.

17. *Bâtiments du roi: Règlements*, art. 4.

18. Belleudy, *Duplessis*, 103.

19. Belleudy, *Duplessis*, 104. Suggestively, bath follows *chaise longue* in Roubo's *L'art du menuisier en meubles*.

20. On Duplessis's health problems, see Guiffrey, "Logements d'artistes au Louvre," 189; and Belleudy, *Duplessis*, 96–97. See also **Glasses**.

21. Belleudy, *Duplessis*, 103–4. For the cost of baths in the 1770s, see *Almanach parisien en faveur des étrangers et personnes curieuses*, ed. Daniel Roche (Saint-Étienne: Presse Universitaire de Saint-Étienne, 2000), 117–18. On the bath boats on the Seine, see Reed Benhamou, "The Public Baths and the Press: Changing Behaviors in Eighteenth-Century Paris," *SVEC* 371 (1999): 275–303.

22. See Antoine Furetière, *Dictionnaire universelle*, 3 vols. (The Hague: Husson, Johnson & Swart 1727), s.v. "Prière": "se dit . . . par civilité des devoirs réciproques qu'on ne refuses point aux amis, aux voisins quand ils les demandent."

23. Belleudy, *Duplessis*, 103–6.

24. See Belleudy, *Duplessis*, 97.

25. Robert and Vallayer-Coster were protected by Marie Antoinette, whose influence secured Vallayer-Coster a *logement*. See Marianne Roland Michel, *Anne Vallayer-Coster (1744–1818)* (Paris: C.I.L., 1970), 260–64.

26. See Silvestre de Sacy, *D'Angiviller*, 225–26.

Bed

Charles-Antoine Coypel (1694–1752)

TYPE OF OBJECT	THEME	MATERIAL
Furniture, Ritual Thing	Family, Identity, Memory, Louvre, Luxury	Plant Matter | Wood, Synthetic Materials | Paint/Pigment, Textile | Cotton, Textile | Silk, Textile | Wool

Charles-Antoine Coypel's bed does not survive, or not as a bed. What remains is a picture (fig. 10), oil on canvas, 190 by 135 centimeters, which originally served as the backboard for a *lit à la Polonaise.*[1] Such beds stood sideways against the wall and were distinguished by two *chevets*, or bed ends. Rarely did they incorporate large decorative paintings. However, a preparatory drawing by Coypel (fig. 11), a history painter and a royal academician, establishes *Painting Awakening Genius* in its original function as furniture. Information about the dimensions, materials, and exact form of the bed to supplement the evidence of the drawing, alas, is not to be had because, by the time of the painter's death, bed and picture had parted company; this bed is not the one inventoried with his effects.[2]

At some point before 1752, the painting had been relegated to the studio, where it was itemized unframed with a miscellany of other paintings, plaster casts, prints, drawings, and other paraphernalia. Meanwhile, Coypel's bed had returned to the norm.[3] It was, according to his inventory, dressed with a base valence of old, jonquil-colored damask and hung with yellow serge curtains. On the frame were three differently stuffed mattresses piled with bolsters, cushions, and horsehair pillows. Coverlets and various fur foot warmers were scattered upon it. It was valued for probate at 300 livres and was the most expensive single item in the room, which was otherwise furnished with armchairs, a settee, assorted tables, a chest of drawers, two corner cupboards, and a desk, and was decorated with seven mirrors and over fifty pieces of Chinese and European porcelain, some of them mounted on gilded sconces.[4] The beds had, nevertheless, dominated the scene.

Henri Havard, in *Dictionnaire de l'ammeublement et de la décoration* (1894), assembled a vast primary literature on the bed, culled from inventories, letters, **journals**, plays, novels, and the first newspapers, which testify to the cultural and social significance of beds in France from the thirteenth century to the end of the ancien régime. He notes not only that beds hosted the most important moments in the lives of their owners, he establishes also that, in the seventeenth and eighteenth centuries, beds were exchanged to commemorate those events. His examples are mostly drawn from the history of the king and his court, but he cites, from the history of art, a four-poster bed with gray serge curtains that the painter Pierre Mignard brought to his marriage in 1656, and a bed with curtains and a counterpane in "yellow tabby," or silk taffeta, that Nicolas Fouquet provided for Charles Le Brun to seal his contract for work at Vaux-le-Vicomte.[5] This suggests that the history of

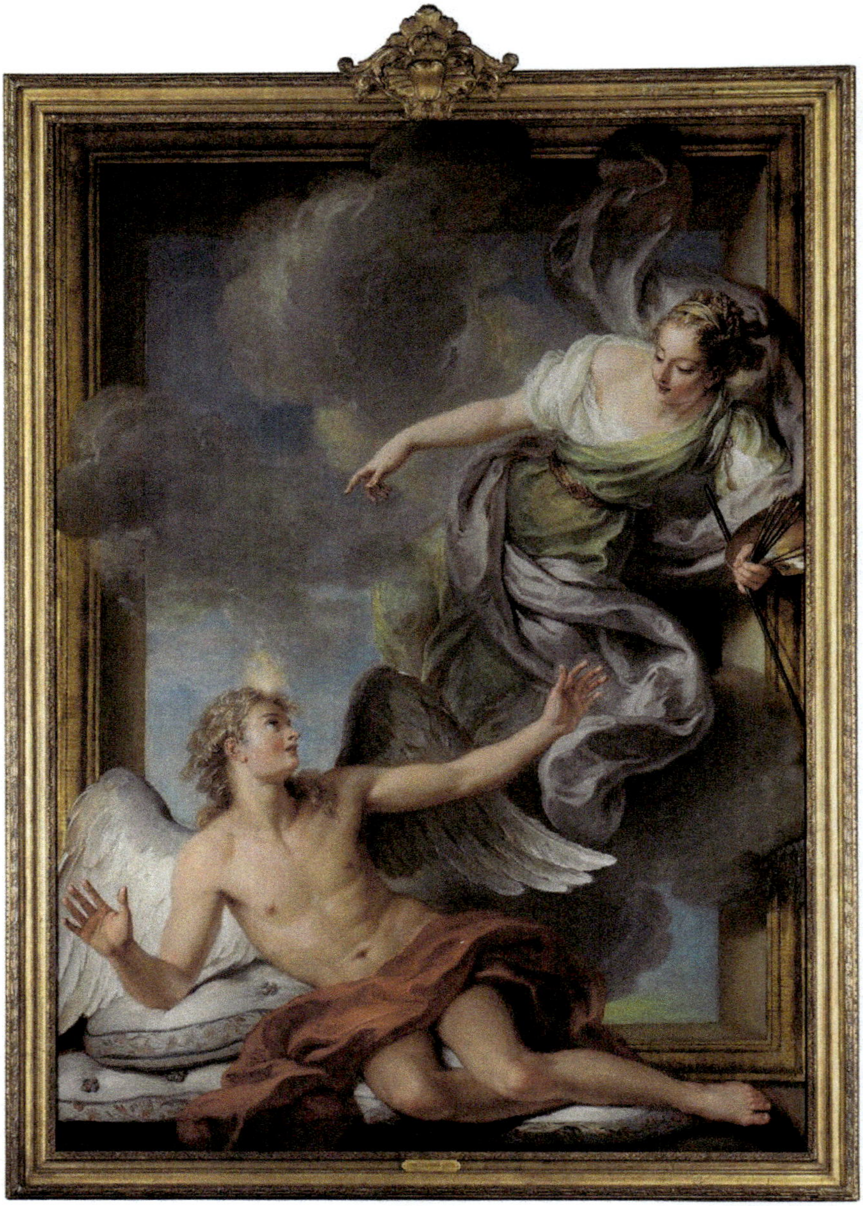

FIG. 10 Charles-Antoine Coypel (French, 1694–1752), *Painting Awakening Genius*, ca. 1723. Oil on canvas, 190 × 135 cm. Private collection. Image source: Christie's/Bridgeman Images. (Photo © Christie's Images/Bridgeman Images.)

Coypel's bed was closely entangled with the story of his life and in ways, moreover, not all envisaged by Havard, because Coypel invented as well as owned and used his bed.

Havard attends only superficially to the material history of the bed, or *lit*. For information about its forms, materials, and the techniques of its manufacture we turn instead to the monumental *L'art du menuisier en meubles*, written by the furniture maker

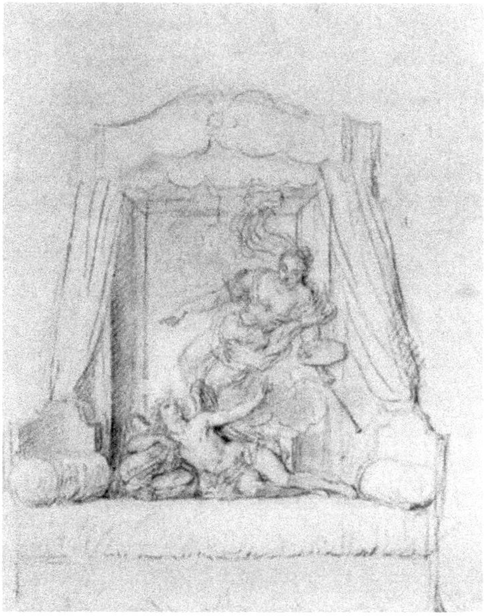

FIG. 11 Charles-Antoine Coypel (French, 1694–1752), Preparatory drawing for *Painting Awakening Genius*, ca. 1723. Black chalk. Location unknown. (Image source: Christie's catalogue.)

André-Jacob Roubo and published by the Académie Royale des Sciences fifty years after Coypel designed his bed. In it, Roubo divides beds into two basic types: the French bed that stands out in the room, has four posts and a tester, or canopy, that mirrors the size and rectangularity of the base, and the "Polish" bed and its variants (*à l'italienne*, *à la turque*, etc.), which hugs the wall and whose tester, smaller than the base and variously shaped, sits on two rather than four posts.[6] Roubo favored the French. He singled out for particular praise examples where the woodwork—in oak or walnut—was glossy and apparent, and not hidden by the curtains or incorporated in the upholstery.[7] Coypel's bed appears at first glance to have belonged to the second of Roubo's categories, to the modern "fashionable" bed, made with a cheaper structure—which, Roubo argued, broke not only with the traditions of furniture making but also with the customs of the *chambre de parade*, the formal bedroom.[8] Interpretation of *Painting Awakening Genius* rests not simply on recognizing its decorative function and its provenance, but also on determining the kind of bed the picture embellished and the physical and social space it occupied in Coypel's house.

The bed and its headboard were made sometime shortly after 1722.[9] Coypel was twenty-eight years old and a bachelor. In that year his father, Antoine Coypel, formerly the director of the Académie Royale de Peinture et de Sculpture, died. From him Charles-Antoine inherited the twin offices of first painter to the duc d'Orléans and keeper of the King's Cabinet of drawings. Title to the Coypel lodgings at the Louvre, in part a perquisite of the second of Antoine's offices, also passed to him, along with a studio in the Cour Carré of the old Louvre that had originally belonged to his grandfather, the history painter Noël.[10] Coypel marked this prodigious legacy and his social and professional coming of age by embarking on a reorganization and renovation of his estate.

Artists had been awarded *logements* (lodgings) at the Louvre by the kings of France since the reign of Henri IV, in recognition of their service to the Crown.[11] The *logements* were located below the Grande Galerie that until 1871 ran along the embankment of the Seine and linked the Louvre with the Tuileries palace. Behind the magnificent seventeenth-century river and court facades, artists were provided with apartments, more like terraced houses, rising the full height of the building. Charles-Antoine had grown up there, his father having moved in when his son was only three. The family lived in a total of some fifteen rooms distributed over three floors and entresols.[12] Comparison of Charles-Antoine's 1752 inventory and the inventory taken at his father's death reveals that Charles-Antoine redistributed the rooms in his father's house along lines that more closely resemble those of an aristocratic *hôtel* than a bourgeois home.[13] He removed the bedroom to the first floor, or piano nobile, and assigned it the role of principal reception room in the vertically articulated enfilade of his accommodations. The bed was placed in the depth of the room, between two *garderobes*, or closets, and facing the windows onto the courtyard.

Roubo's dismissal of Polish, or niche, beds as suitable only for private, domestic apartments, where comfort is the priority, was based on a number of counts. First, such beds disrupt the orientation of the bedroom by sidelining the bed.[14] Decorum dictated the bed to be the axis of the room. Secondly, enclosed on three sides, the alcove bed restricts opportunities for social intercourse between the seigneur on the bed and those in attendance in the room.[15] On both counts such beds undermined the identity of the bedchamber as the prime locus of display and public reception.[16] The design for Coypel's bed (see fig. 11) suggests that the painter was not unaware of the issues. The verticality of *Painting Awakening Genius* and the high art of its allegory corrected the lateral and self-marginalizing drift of the niche bed. In effect, the picture turned the bed's side into the front. Moreover, Coypel used the illusion of Painting flying into the room through a window, opposite the real windows, to allude to the double aspect of the grand Bourbon gallery above, famed for its heroic decoration tragically left incomplete by Nicolas Poussin. According to Roubo, the distinguishing mark of the seigneurial bed was its size, not, of course, he acknowledged, because the nobleman is built bigger but because in the houses of the nobility the proportions of the furniture are in keeping with the architecture, that is, with the nobility's symbolic, not physical, body.[17] By internalizing the aspect, form, and proportions of the Louvre's architecture into the fiction of the painting, Coypel reoriented his niche bed and represented its modest structure as nevertheless *de parade*.

Roubo blamed the demise of the parade bed on fashion and society's apparently insatiable desire for novelty.[18] In the 1770s Paris upholsterers sourced a dizzying range of cloth suitable for bed hangings, from heavy and expensive silk brocades and velvets to cheaper and lighter printed cottons.[19] Coypel's summer hangings for his second bed were exactly of this pretty kind of thing: cotton, with sprigged flowers.[20] But in the case of his first, more consequential bed, we can ask whether his painting was intended rather as an alternative to tapestry, that most prestigious stuff of European court cultures, and a genre that readily combined ornament and figure.[21] The *Mercure galant*, according to Havard, reported that the bed that the comte de Toulouse had made to receive the dauphin during the latter's stay at Rambouillet in July 1707 was "extremely beautiful" because it was hung with the finest tapestry that incorporated "portraits" into its design, meaning pictures as opposed to pattern.[22] Moreover, to Toulouse himself belonged a bed in Paris that, according to one of the city's guidebooks, was "a masterpiece of tapestry pictures" embellished with gold embroidery of a delicacy to match "the grace of the figures."[23] Tapestry, it seems, offered itself to the decoration of beds as a figurative and narrative art of noble substance, in contrast to the ephemerality that Roubo identified with fashion. *Painting Awakening Genius* does not imitate tapestry in any formal sense—it has not the touch of textile, so to speak—but it did, arguably, model its place as picture in the composition of the bed on tapestry's artistic achievements. Thus, in structure, stuff, and figuration, Coypel's bed emulated the parade of the seigneur and fitted its form to the decorum of the palace in which it stood. It did so with the means at Coypel's disposal and within the constraints imposed by his *logement*: by substitution, that is, of cheaper materials for more expensive ones and by adjustment of the axiality of the bed by the illusion of the picture.

Coypel's drawing of the bed (see fig. 11) represents it as a stage, curtains raised, in the depths of which we see depicted not Morpheus quiet with his poppy crown, but Genius quickened, flames dawning on his brow (see fig. 10). Genius awakened by Painting represents, you could say, the painter's *levée*, his morning call to rise to art. It is an image and it was an occasion that presumed an audience. To judge by the other furniture inventoried in Coypel's bedroom, that audience was potentially at once large and socially mixed. Its needs and expectations were to be variously met by twelve armchairs as well as the large settee, an assortment of tables for writing and playing games, as well as the desk, a coffee grinder, and seven tobacco jars. Charles-Antoine owed his *logement* not only to the accumulated talents of generations of Coypels but also, as noted, to his office of the king's keeper of drawings; he would no doubt have received visitors to the Cabinet first in his bedroom. The bureau in the room suggests that he conducted professional business there. On the other hand, the games table, boxes of cards, and ivory counters for playing quadrille; the coffee grinder and **teacups**; and the tobacco jars all mark the bedroom as a space of sociability:[24] for receiving friends, patrons, and neighbors from other *logements* at the Louvre. The bedroom was an imbricated space: both public and private, for both the performance of status and the related exercises of business, and for pleasure.

Bed and bedroom, object and space are not as idiosyncratic as they perhaps at first appeared. They marked Charles-Antoine's accession to his hereditary titles and his determination to honor and equal his father's success and reputation in the language of distinction. Antoine's triumph had been lent symbolic expression by the **carriage** and pair of horses given to him toward the end of his life as a reward for the decoration of the Aeneas Gallery at the Palais Royal by the regent in 1717.[25] Coypel's achievements, by contrast, were only anticipated—anticipated, moreover, in a thing of the expectant son's own devising. That its parade was not absolutely conventional, that it "modernized," in

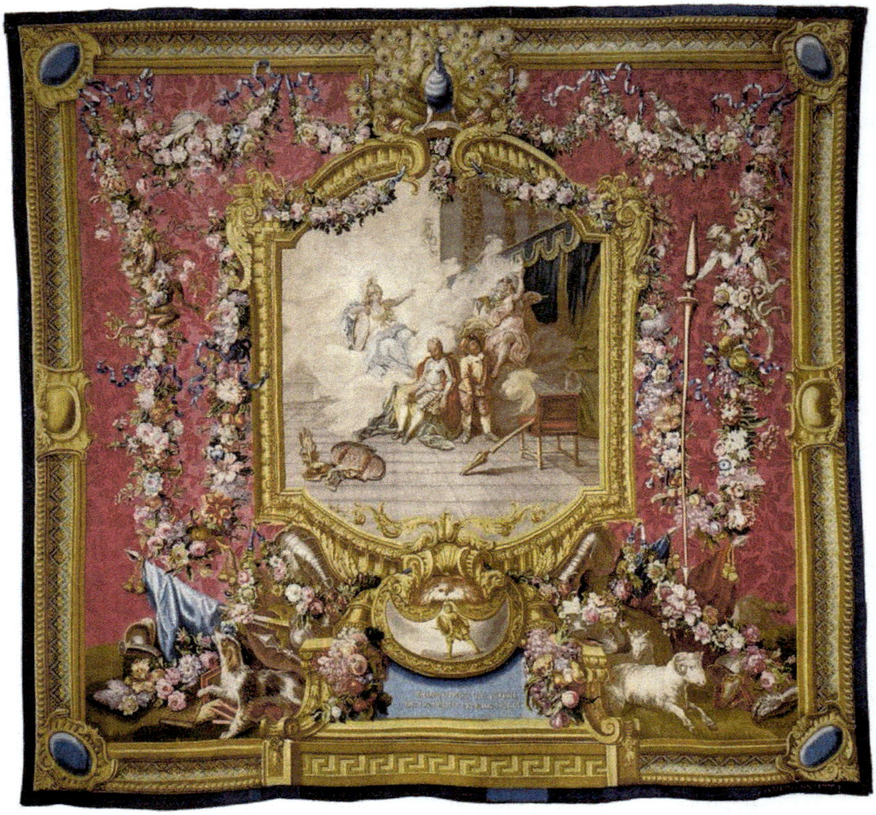

FIG. 12 After Charles-Antoine Coypel (French, 1694–1752), *Don Quixote Dreams*, from the series *HIstory of Don Quixote*, ca. 1727. Gobelins high-warp tapestry, silk and wool, 370.8 × 386.1 cm. Los Angeles, The J. Paul Getty Museum.

Roubo's terms, both the forms and the materials of the bed, raises questions about Coypel's conviction.

It invites us to compare *Painting Awakening Genius* not with the father's scenes of Aeneas's tragedy but rather with its travesty: the son's Don Quixote series. In 1727 Charles-Antoine painted for the Gobelins the cartoon for the last scene in his set of *The Adventures of Don Quixote* (fig. 12), in which Quixote, asleep in his bedroom, is visited in his dreams by Minerva, who by her wisdom cures him of his chivalric illusions embodied by Folly, who beguilingly flutters by the bed, her drapery merging with the bed hangings.[26] The same model appears to have served Coypel for the blonde female figures of Folly and Painting. Insofar as Painting is also Folly's familiar, we can consider the possibility that the parade of the bedchamber was semiseriously and semiconsciously staged by Coypel as a fantasy—that his bed was his castle in the air.

Among Coypel's high-born friends was the marquis de Calvière, an aristocrat and courtier, for whom Coypel wrote an epistle, published in the *Mercure de France* in 1724.[27] A lyrical letter on the subject of friendship and the importance of truth in the commerce between true friends, the poem betrays Coypel's fear of ridicule for aspiring to mix in company socially and in virtue above his own. The not-quite-rightness of Coypel's bed, its artistic misprision of noble design, manifests the difficulty of steering a social course that balances prerogatives of distinction while politely appearing not to believe oneself deserving of them. That Coypel eventually dismantled his bed and put the painting into storage in the studio suggests he came later to regret his *levée* as an overreach of the claims of his talent. §

---

1. See Thierry Lefrançois, *Charles Coypel: Peintre du roi (1694–1752)* (Geneva: Arthena 1994), P 115. The terminology of bed types is in André-Jacob Roubo, *L'art du menuisier en meubles*, 4 parts in 5 vols. (Paris: Delatour, 1769–75), 3, pt. 2:665–85.

2. Charles Coypel, "Inventaire après décès," 25 September 1752, AN, MC/ET/LXXVI/337.

3. The phrasing is ambiguous because the documentary evidence does not indicate whether the picture alone was detached or whether the whole bed was replaced.

4. AN, MC/ET/LXXVI/337, 25 September 1752: only the cost of the mirrors approximated the cost of the bed.

5. Henri Havard, *Dictionnaire de l'ammeublement et de la décoration* (Paris: Quantin, 1894), 3:424. Havard mistakenly gives the date of Mignard's marriage as 1660.

6. Roubo, *L'art du menuisier*, 3, pt. 2:665–85.

7. Roubo, *L'art du menuisier*, 3, pt. 2:671.

8. Roubo, *L'art du menuisier*, 3, pt. 2:681.

9. Thierry Lefrançois dates it on stylistic ground to circa 1730. See Lefrançois, *Charles Coypel*, P 115. For alternative dating to ca. 1724–25, see Katie Scott, "Parade's End: On Charles-Antoine's Bed and the Origins of Inwardness," in *Interiors and Interiority*, ed. Ewa Lajer-Burcharth and Beate Söntgen (Berlin: De Gruyter, 2016), 17–47.

10. On the Coypel studios, see Nicole Garnier, *Antoine Coypel (1661–1722)* (Paris: Arthena, 1989), 171–72; and Lefrançois, *Charles Coypel*, 42.

11. Jules-Joseph Guiffrey, "Logements d'artistes au Louvre," *NAAF*, 1873, 1–221.

12. See Coypel's "Inventaire après décès."

13. For Antoine Coypel's inventory, see Garnier, *Antoine Coypel*, 249–55. For further comparison of the Louvre lodgings, see Scott, "Parade's End," 23–37.

14. Roubo, *L'art du menuisier*, 3, pt. 2:681.

15. Roubo notes the impossibility of servants waiting on their masters in such beds.

16. On the enfilade and bedchamber, see Katie Scott, *The Rococo Interior* (London: Yale University Press, 1995), 106–7.

17. Roubo, *L'art du menuisier*, 3, pt. 2:668.

18. Roubo, *L'art du menuisier*, 3, pt. 2:681.

19. For the silks available in the second half of the eighteenth century, see Lesley Ellis Miller, *Selling Silks: A Merchant's Sample Book 1764* (New York: V&A, 2014).

20. AN, MC/ET/LXXVI/337, 25 September 1752: hangings "de cotton à fleurs."

21. Thomas P. Campbell, "Collectors and Connoisseurs: The Status and Perception of Tapestry, 1600–1660," in *Tapestry in the Baroque: Threads of Splendor*, exh. cat. (New Haven: Yale University Press; and New York: Metropolitan Museum of Art, 2007), 325–39. Tapestry was used also in nonelite housing; see Annik Pardailhé-Galabrun, *La naissance de l'intime* (Paris: Presses Universitaires de France, 1988), 363–76.

22. Havard, *Dictionnaire*, 3:421–22; and *Mercure gallant*, September 1707, 153. They are identified by Charissa Bremer-David with a set of four tapestries at the Metropolitan Museum of Art (MMA46.43.1–4). See Bremer-David, "The Tapestry Patronage of Mme de Montespan and Her Family," in *Tapestry in the Baroque: New Aspects of Production and Patronage*, ed. Thomas P. Campbell and Elizabeth A. H. Cleland (New Haven: Yale University Press, 2010), 324–25.

23. Havard, *Dictionnaire*, 3:421–22; and Jean Aimar Piganiol de La Force, *Description de Paris, de Versailles, de Marly, de Meudon, de S.-Cloud* (Paris: Poiron, 1745), 3:87.

24. AN, MC/ET/LXXVI/337, 25 September 1752: sixty-nine different porcelain teacups, saucers, and *pots pouri*, valued collectively at just 8 livres, indicating useful wares. On Coypel's sociability, see Jean-Baptiste Massé, "Lettre de M. Massé, Peintre du roi et conseiller en son Académie Royale de Peinture et de Sculpture," *Mercure de France*, August 1752, 147–48.

25. See Garnier, *Antoine Coypel*, 250. Antoine Coypel's carriage, which was upholstered in red velvet and taffeta curtains, was valued at 300 livres.

26. On the series, see Charissa Bremer-David, *French Tapestries and Textile in the J. Paul Getty Museum* (Los Angeles: J. Paul Getty Museum, 1997), 40–53.

27. Charles-Antoine Coypel, "Épître sur l'amitié," *Mercure de France*, December 1724, 2550–52.

Book

Gilles-Marie Oppenord (1672–1742)
Gabriel de Saint-Aubin (1724–80)

TYPE OF OBJECT	THEME	MATERIAL
Companion	Education, Leisure, Studio	Synthetic Materials | Ink, Synthetic Materials | Paper

Cesare Ripa, *Iconologie; ou Explication nouvelle de plusieurs images* (Paris, 1636) and Antoine-Joseph Pernéty, *Dictionnaire portatif de peinture, sculpture et gravure* (1757). Gilles-Marie Oppenord, architect, and Gabriel de Saint-Aubin, draftsman. Two books and two owners. How can we understand the relationship between these artists and the books they owned? That early modern artists were deeply invested in books as a sign of their status as liberal artists is to state the obvious. For Oppenord and Saint-Aubin it was perhaps particularly so since neither were academicians and thus beneficiaries of the reputation for learning that academic membership conferred. A better question is, how did artists read their books? The question is the more pertinent because reading habits were changing. Oppenord and Saint-Aubin belonged to different generations, the architect having grown up and established his career in the last decades of Louis XIV's reign, while the draftsman came of age professionally at the time Louis XV began his personal rule, in 1742, coincidentally also the year when Oppenord died. Comparison of the two artists' relations with their books expressed in the marginalia they added to them provides material for thought on how such relations evolved.

To emphasize reading is to set aside approaches to marginalia that construe doodling as an opportunistic colonization of the virgin spaces of the printed page. Instances of "not reading" but drawing often feature in artists' lives. They serve as tropes of genius, of the irrepressible and defiant exultations of artistic will. According to Charles-Nicolas Cochin, the schoolboy Jean-Baptiste Massé thus crammed his copies of the classics, until his father relented and allowed him to take up art, and not finish the courses in humanities in which he had had him enrolled.[1] Doodling as a mode of reading returns drawing to the shores of the text. To interpret it, we should first note than a revolution in European reading practices occurred in the eighteenth century.[2] A world in which individuals owned few books and related to them in a manner Rolf Engelsing describes as "intensive"—that is, characterized by close, sustained reading, rereading, and memorization—was disappearing, and in its place, a new world characterized by extensive reading was taking shape, one in which readers browsed, casting their attention lightly and widely over a constellation of different texts. Roger Chartier has since proposed a more nuanced understanding of this "great transformation," one that also takes into account classes of readers and genres of texts.[3] From the work of Engelsing and Chartier the following questions arise: Were artists a particular kind of reader? How did such readers read their chosen texts?

The editors of *The Artist as Reader* (2013) propose three distinct modes of specifically artistic reading: (1) "following," or copying; (2) "independent reading," where the artist's interpretation competes with the text, and (3) "critical reading," where reading subverts the discourse of the original.[4] We can position these practices as points between the intensive/extensive poles as follows: "following" at the intensive end, and "independent" and "critical" reading toward the extensive end. Modes of reading are, of course, not independent of the specifics of texts. Both *Iconologie* and *Dictionnaire portatif* are types of dictionaries, the self-confessed product by collation of extensive reading. Dictionaries surely invite reading of the same extensive kind. Roger de Piles certainly distinguished between such manuals of occasional, dispersed reference, and the proper, concentrated reading elicited by books of poetry and ancient and modern history.[5] Yet the material evidence of Oppenord's and Saint-Aubin's marginalia suggests the very opposite. The very fact of it, inscribed in both cases throughout the books, from beginning to end, suggests sustained and thoughtful readerly attention. Moreover, Saint-Aubin's dated annotations (from 1761 to 1770) indicate repeated use of and engagement with his book over the best part of a decade. With these contradictions in mind, "following," "independent," and "critical" reading are, nevertheless, helpful categories with which to study the intercourse between artists and books and to trace the shifts in relations of power between reader and author, person and book.

Evidence of "following" in its simplest form is to be found in the scattered tracks left by Saint-Aubin as he sprinted through Pernéty's introduction, "Traité des différentes manières de peindre," at the front of the dictionary. He checkmarked passages of note with a cross. He underlined points to remember.[6] Saint-Aubin modestly submits to the authority of the text; he reads to annex the other's knowledge, repeating it with emphasis in order to incorporate it better. This culture of following, or of the copy, is one particularly associated with academic training, and Saint-Aubin gave it visual echo in the nudes he drew, as if from the model, to decorate "A" for "Académie" (2). The education of architects, no less than that of painters, was based on a regimen of exact copying and verbatim transcription. Antoine Desgodets's courses on architecture given at the Académie Royale d'Architecture in the 1720s have come down to us through the transcripts and copies of his students. Jean Pinard's copy of Desgodets's *Traité de la commodité de l'architecture* was, for instance, made more or less at the same time that Oppenord was "reading" his Ripa.[7] Oppenord, however, unlike Pinard, was not a teenager. At the moment the books here in question were being read, both he and Saint-Aubin were in their forties and established artists; moreover, the context of their study was the studio not the classroom. Were acts of copying always also instances of following?

Jean-François Bédard's analysis of Oppenord's use of Ripa as a source of ornament shows how the architect extracted motifs from Ripa's emblems and built them up into ornamental trophies—the zodiac hoops of Agriculture, the dolphin from Courtesy, the star from Reason, the laurels from Patriotism, and the flame from Love of God.[8] In the copying process, Ripa was abandoned. His symbolic forms were prized from the text, recycled and gathered as ornamental flotsam and jetsam. They were transformed into detail with pictorial effect but no meaning. Bédard argues that this playful combinatory practice of ornament is best understood in the context of late seventeenth-century *honnêteté* and demonstrates an aping of the extensive ludic reading and learning practices of the elite, for whom Oppenord created such arabesques, rather than close fellowship with Ripa's text.[9]

Saint-Aubin also copied. Below Claude-Alphonse Dufresnoy's advice, "never a day without a line," paraphrased by Pernéty in his entry "Ligne" (392), Saint-Aubin chorused "nulla dies sine linea," chasing the citation back to its source.[10] Floating in the margin without context, the phrase, like Oppenord's ornaments, is insubstantial for all its antique gravity. Though lexically full, parroted mechanically it appears threadbare. It drifts away from trope and toward cliché.[11] The effect of *déjà dit* or *déjà vu* that characterizes cliché is present also in Saint-Aubin's response to Pernéty's definition of pastoral landscape as a stand of trees (447–48). He draws between "*arbres*" at the top of the page and "*paysage*" at the bottom, to link the two, a line of saplings (fig. 13) willfully unoriginal in the extreme.

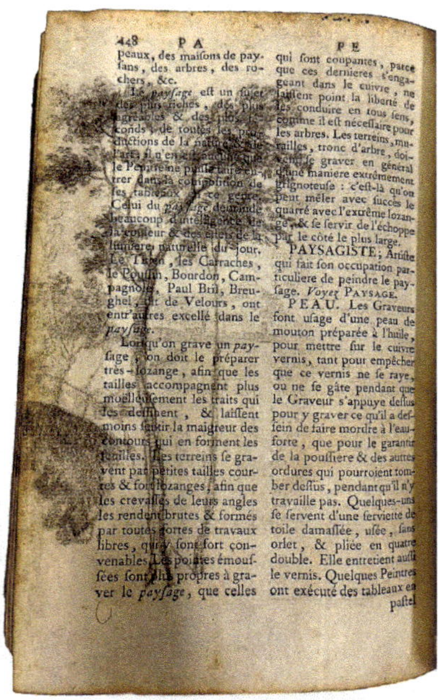

FIG. 13 Antoine-Joseph Pernéty, *Dictionnaire portatif de peinture, sculpture et gravure* (1757), annotated by Gabriel de Saint-Aubin (French, 1724–80), ca. 1757–67. Graphite. Paris, Petit Palais. (CCØ Paris Musées / Petit Palais, Musée des Beaux-Arts de la Ville de Paris.)

These examples call into question the notion of copying as imitation in the classical sense, which is to say, as the faithful rendition of an original by one who submits to its authority as exemplar. Oppenord's and Saint-Aubin's copying, though authentic in its way, is conspicuously lacking in seriousness. It is light. There are, however, differences as well as similarities in the spirit of their copies. For Oppenord, lightness was actively and repeatedly sought as a property of grace and energy. The delicacy and liveliness of his lines is consistent with an intimate, if not always respectful, relationship with Ripa's emblems. By comparison, Saint-Aubin's text touching seems automatic and glancing, an engagement that turns outward and extends onto other texts: Pliny by way of Dufresnoy, the landscapes of Bourdon, Campagnola, Brill, Breughel de Velours, whose names as exponents of the genre we discern through the branches of his trees. In the case of both, a more flexible concept of following is required to capture their engagement with their books.

The distinction between following and independent reading is clearly subtle. Independent reading competes with the text but always on the terms of the original. It seems significant that Oppenord's attention in reading *Iconologie* was most intense at the beginning and the end: he drew at least two alternative frontispieces (fig. 14) and provided two to three possible endings. It is significant because Oppenord's repetitions seem to respond to a contradiction inherent in the *Iconologie*, which simultaneously promotes itself as a compendium of universal knowledge of "moral things" while simultaneously disaggregating that knowledge by distributing it alphabetically. In other words, the *Iconologie* promotes itself as a full account of affirmative or symbolic signs yet denies the reader the ability to grasp its unity by scattering that knowledge under the arbitrary signs of the alphabet in a way that precludes reasoned articulation of the ethical connections that make sense of its multiple parts. Ripa's *Iconologie* is without hierarchy or system; it is, in this epistemological sense, an unmapped continent. It seems possible that Oppenord's alternative paratexts were an attempt to rescue the *Iconologie* as a circle of knowledge with the help of allegory and narrative. In one of the alternative frontispieces (see fig. 14) he places the text under the sign of Mercury, god of sense and communication. In place of *Zèle* (Zeal), that most intense feeling of active agency, of being alive, which paradoxically brings the text of *Iconologie* to its end, he substitutes a tomb. Marsyas swaps place with Mercury (fig. 15) and silence falls.

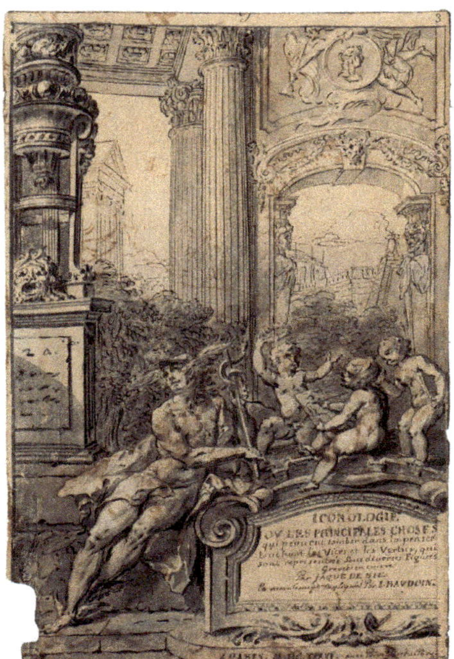

FIG. 14 Gilles-Marie Oppenord (French, 1672–1742), Alternative title page or frontispiece for Cesare Ripa and Jean Baudouin, *Iconologie; ou, Explication nouvelle de plusieurs emblemes* (Paris, 1636). Pen and brown ink, brush in brown and gray ink over a pencil sketch, 32.5 × 21.5 cm. Montreal, Canadian Centre for Architecture.

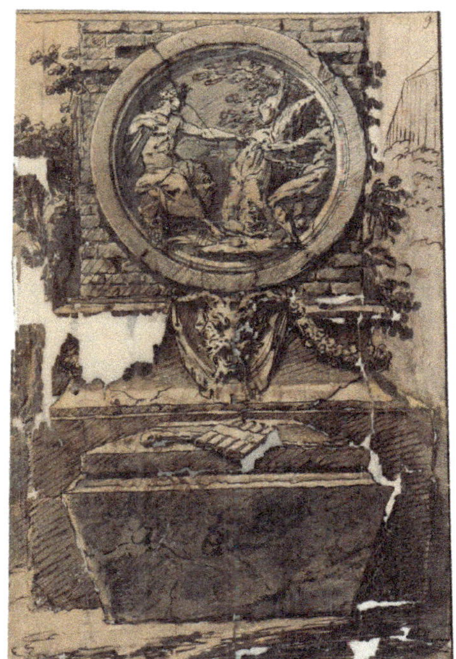

FIG. 15 Gilles-Marie Oppenord (French, 1672–1742), Design for a funeral monument for the 1636 French edition of Cesare Ripa and Jean Baudouin, *Iconologie; ou, Explication nouvelle de plusieurs emblemes* (Paris, 1636). Pen and brown ink with brown and gray wash, 32.6 × 21.3 cm. Montreal, Canadian Centre for Architecture.

Saint-Aubin read with a different kind of independence. His most consistent and conspicuous marginal additions are in connection with artists' pigments. Pernéty's dictionary provides basic scientific definitions of them in terms of their organic and mineral sources and rates them for their stability, permanence, and safety. He refers his readers to the *Mémoires* of the Académie Royal des Sciences and cites such scientific authorities as the chemist Johann von Löwenstern-Kunckel.[12] Saint-Aubin's response seems, at first, to amount to no more than following: he supplements Pernéty's definitions by using the line ends of the dictionary as so many drawers in which to lodge specimens, like filling up a **color box.**[13]

However, in the accompanying annotations, Saint-Aubin's reading urges him beyond illustrative repetition. It prompts in him the recollection and articulation of another discourse on color—everyday, concrete, retail talk of suppliers and prices. He takes a virtual tour of Paris to the best shops for **red lake**, orpiment, ultramarine, umber, and ivory black.[14] He measures the rise and fall in prices over time. If we can assume that the paintbrush preceded the pen in this independent reading, we can infer that Saint-Aubin's autonomy was secured above all by the materiality of the text: by the layout of the page, by the gutter and margins. It was these physical properties that led to samples, and from samples to geography and accountancy. The marbled endpapers were further grist to Saint-Aubin's private milling of the text (fig. 16). At the front, easy to overlook, is a figure of a boatman curled into a landscape.

Oppenord and Saint-Aubin responded quite differently to the circle. Oppenord works around the circles of Ripa's emblems (fig. 17), treating them as fixed features of the page, as monuments in a paper setting. He does not frame them, in the sense of setting them off with more of the same; he offsets them, throwing into relief their difference. Insofar as they are appropriated, it is as found objects, not designs or signs. Saint-Aubin, by contrast, invades the page; his filling figure recasts the marbled paper as background. His is the reading response advocated by Leonardo (and I paraphrase):

> *[L]ook upon an old wall covered with dirt, or the odd appearance of some streaked stones and in them you will discover landscapes, battles, clouds, uncommon attitudes, funny faces, draperies, etc. Out of this confused mass of objects, the mind will be furnished with an abundance of designs and subjects perfectly new.*[15]

Where Oppenord's independent reading pursues and demonstrates learning, erudition, and intellect in the same humanist terms as Ripa's *Iconologie*, Saint-Aubin's strategies of reading and response reveal objectives quite at odds with those of Pernéty. They were at once more banal (the price of paint and canvas) and more inspired.

To turn finally to critical reading: critical reading involves challenge: furious skirmishes against authority of the text. There are, perhaps, few unambiguous signs of it in Oppenord's apostils. But perhaps we can suggest one. Aurora and Avarice, or dawn and greed, have nothing in common; they are not even entities of the same ethical kind. Their

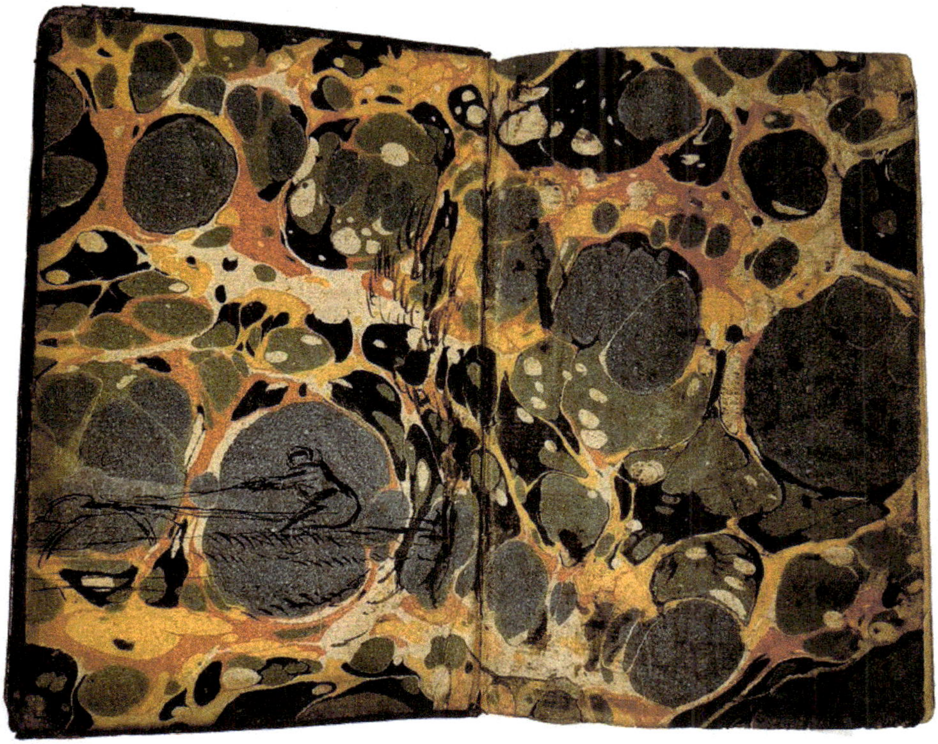

FIG. 16 Antoine-Joseph Pernéty, *Dictionnaire portatif de peinture, sculpture et gravure* (1757), annotated by Gabriel de Saint-Aubin (French, 1724–80), ca. 1757–67. Pen and black ink on endpaper. Paris, Petit Palais. (CCØ Paris Musées / Petit Palais, Musée des Beaux-Arts de la Ville de Paris.)

adjacency in the *Iconologie* is an accident of language. Oppenord, however, portrays them as mirror images of one another, virtually counterproofing them across the opening of facing pages.[16] They appear materially, and therefore causally, linked: both on chariots, both with torches, neither with their attributes—respectively wings and wolves. Their resemblance at Oppenord's hand undermines, one could say, the transparency and legibility of Ripa's icons, and, if deliberate, transforms them into enigmas such that bright Aurora gestures toward Avarice as the dark, hidden side of herself. Did Oppenord understand that every sign has something enfolded within it, something other, and that in order to learn not its explicit and conventional meaning but its more profound and unsettling truth, it has to be unfolded?

Saint-Aubin's critical approach is more direct. Inserted between the black lines of Pernéty's definitions of *ébauche* (sketch) and *ébaucher* (to sketch) (152–53) Saint-Aubin writes, in tiny letters, alternative definitions—gleaned from Jean-Baptiste Oudry, whose "Discourse on the Practice of Painting" he had attended in December 1752—that run like a red thread of dissonance through the established truths of the text.[17] On another occasion he directly contradicts Pernéty. In a discussion of artistic temperament, Pernéty had asserted that painters portray themselves (343): the lighthearted and jocular artist, for

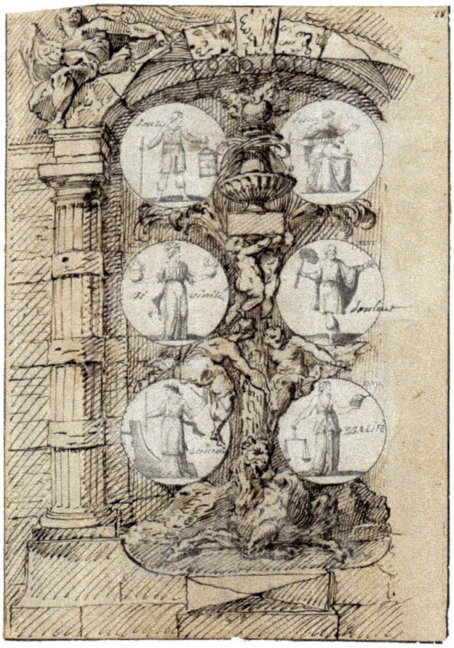

FIG. 17 Gilles-Marie Oppenord (French, 1672–1742), Design for a portal with ornamentation drawn on a printed folio, with medalions of Doute, Discretion, Divinité, Douleur, Economie, and Égalité, for Cesare Ripa and Jean Baudouin, *Iconologie, ou Explication nouvelle de plusieurs emblemes* (Paris, 1636). Pen and brown ink over engraving, 32.8 × 22.3 cm. Montreal, Canadian Centre for Architecture.

example, paints comic scenes and the grotesque. Thus, led to connect his family's taste for jokes, famously recorded by them in *The Book of Bums*, and his own propensity for melancholy, Saint-Aubin retorts: "this is not always true."[18] And, on top of critique and contradiction, he also piled irony. Next to the orderly column of Pernéty's definition of *composition* (75), he scrawled a collapsing tower, a decomposition, citing as counter-evidence of Pernéty's fine principles of unity and integrity the tragicomic example of collapse on Rue de la Huchette on 9 February 1767.[19]

The different modes of reading—imitative and independent, sympathetic and critical—blend into one another and provide through these examples complexity and refinement to the rough binary intensive/extensive. They indicate a smoother, more graduated evolution from one practice to the other, a bloodless revolution, not least because those different modes were, it seems, not mutually exclusive and often exercised together in response to one text. That said, change is surely discernable. On the basis of the marginalia, Oppenord's reading appears to have been more intense. He cleft to Ripa and to the moralized universe that the *Iconologie* represented. Saint-Aubin's reading, on the other hand, erred from the text, jeopardizing its authority and putting its integrity at risk by opening it onto the world of everyday commerce and to the conflicting opinions of other texts. Though idiosyncratic in so many ways, the reading habits of Oppenord and Saint-Aubin were, by this analysis, structured by more general shifts in social and cultural practices brought about by expansion of the book trade and development of new literary products, such as cheap pocket dictionaries.

What do Oppenord and Saint-Aubin and their books tell us about artistic identity in the eighteenth century? The answer is not simple because reading was a focus for anxiety. For Roger de Piles, whose opinions were influential for much of the eighteenth century, learning was essential to the artist, and he lamented the decline of reading among the painters of his day.[20] Antoine-Joseph Dézallier d'Argenville was perhaps less categorical. He reported Charles de La Fosse's view that reading distracted attention from the practice of painting, inhibiting the formation of skill, and he noted with favor painters such as Claude Lorraine and Rembrandt, nonreaders both, whose genius was fed on nature alone.[21] Oppenord and Saint-Aubin appear to have subscribed to the first view. They identified themselves in and with their books. In one of his title pages Oppenord added his name at the bottom of the page, beneath the name of Ripa's translator, Jean Baudouin. In an extra illustration, he framed his monogram "GMO" in a massive cartel toward which a putto, balanced on the upper rim, gestures unnecessarily. Saint-Aubin's monogram "GDSA" appears in his copy of the *Dictionnaire portatif*, not on the flyleaf or title page but in the body of the text.[22] In the opening page of the introductory "Treatise," he drew figures of Oil Painting and Encaustic, and inscribed the plinths on which they stand with his initials. There are differences, however. Oppenord's presence in his copy of Ripa seems to be that of an owner: the cartouche for his monogram resembles those used in the design of bookplates. Oppenord's Ripa was one book among others. He possessed a library.[23] Books, we can infer, were important to the professional and social identity he fashioned for himself. According to the guidebook writer Germain Brice, Oppenord's house, on Rue Saint-Thomas-du-Louvre, was "filled and decorated with many beautiful things,"[24] which at his death included rosewood and purplewood bookcases with marble tops and gilt-bronze fittings in which his books were shelved.[25] His acquired knowledge, praised by Brice, may not have been as deep and thorough as connoisseurs like de Piles desired, but Oppenord's intensive reading and the material display of his learning secured his title as a gentleman and *honnête* companion to princes and the elite.

By contrast, such was the dirt and chaos of Saint-Aubin's lodgings, Rue de Beauvais, at his death in 1780 that the inventory of his possessions was delayed.[26] Neither his studio nor his stuff, nor in fact his extensive mode of reading, conformed to the classic humanist ideal of *doctus Artifex*, nor to standards of gentility. By signing his name not on Pernéty's book but on the fictions conjured up within it by his marginalia, Saint-Aubin realized a profoundly different entanglement with textual things. His annotations display not a rational and ethical self-fashioning, rather they express a more modern subjectivity based on interiority, an interiority not always easily read. On the page facing Saint-Aubin's inoffensive drawing of trees is a neat inscription in ink at the top (449). It reads, with an insertion mark: "Pédéraste ou Sodomite" (Pederast or Sodomite). What made him write it? What does it mean? Where the inscription "nulla dies . . ." was and is for the researcher a commonplace, a repetition whose voicing fades to echo and into insignificance, "Pederast or Sodomite" explodes on the page, reverberates like the strike of a malediction. According to what eighteenth-century logic did the homosexual man belong to a dictionary of art? By what experience of life, by what inner feeling did the dictionary's rule of ordered Ps invite, provoke, and apparently require the insertion of "Pederast" between "Péché" (sin), defined metaphorically in relation to art, and "Peintre"? We have no answer: such findings are not only dramatic evidence of breaking rank in the ancien régime—infraction of its criminal laws and transgression of social laws of polite speech—they also confound the researcher's frameworks for interpreting the past, put her "hors du rang" as a scholar of the eighteenth century. §

---

1. Charles-Nicolas Cochin, "Éloge de J.-B. Massé," in Émile Compardon, *Un artiste oublié: J.-B. Massé peintre de Louis XV, dessinateur graveur* (Paris: Charavay, 1880), 31.

2. See Rolf Engelsing, "Die Perioden der lesergeschichte in der Neuzeit: Das statistische Aumass und die soziokulturelle Bedeutung des Lektüre," *Archiv für Geschichte des Buchwesens* 10 (1970): 944–1002.

3. Roger Chartier, "Commerce in the Novel: Damilaville's Tears and the Impatient Reader," *Inscription and Erasure*, trans. Arthur Goldhammer (Philadelphia: University of Pennsylvania Press, 2017), 104–25.

4. Heiko Damm, Michael Thimann, and Claus Zittel, eds., *The Artist as Reader: On Education and Non-Education of Early Modern Artists* (Leyden: Brill, 2013), 22–23.

5. Charles-Alphonse Duquesnoy, *De la peinture traduit par Roger de Piles* (Paris: Nicolas Langlois, 1668), 79–83.

6. His marks begin with the section on oil painting, xciii. Saint-Aubin put a cross by the statement that yellow and red orpiment should be used pure and not mixed, and on xcxvi, by the statement that retouches should be made with darks, not lights. "Particularly" is underlined on cii for mixing vegetable colors with eel bile. Page numbers to the *Dictionnaire portatif* will hereafter be given in brackets in the text.

7. See *Oeuvres de Desgodets, Traité de la commodité de l'architecture*, copied by Jean Pinard, BnF, Département des Estampes et de la Photographie, Pet Fol-HA-23.

8. Jean-François Bédard, *Decorative Games: Ornament, Rhetoric and Noble Culture in the Work of Gilles-Marie Oppenord (1672–1742)* (Newark: Associate University Presses, 2011), 18–19, 21.

9. Bédard, *Decorative Games*, 26.

10. Pliny, *Natural History* 35.

11. See Ruth Amossy and Terese Lyons, "The Cliché in the Reading Process," *SubStance* 11, no. 2 (1982): 34–45.

12. Antoine-Joseph Pernéty, *Dictionnaire portatif de peinture, sculpture et gravure* (Paris: Bauche, 1757), s.v.,"Johann von Löwenstern-Kunckel."

13. Pernéty, *Dictionnaire*, see "Bleu de lavis," 31; "Cendre bleue," 51; "Noir," 421; "Orpiment," 436; "Outremer," 437; and "Verd," 547.

14. Pernéty, *Dictionnaire*, see "Bleu de Prusse," 31; "Carmin," 47; "Outremer," 437; "Stile de grin," 521; "Terre d'Italie," 531; "Terre verte," 532; and "Vert," 547.

15. Leonardo as quoted in Roger de Piles, *L'Idée du peintre parfait* (1699), ed. Xavier Carrère (Paris: Gallimard, 1993), 30.

16. Bédard, *Decorative Games*, 102–3.

17. See Jean-Baptiste Oudry, "Discourse on the Practice of Painting and Its Main Processes" (1752), trans. Steve Stella, https://www.getty.edu/conservation/our_projects/science/coll_res/discours_en.pdf.

18. See Colin Jones, Juliet Carey, and Emily Richardson, eds., *The Saint-Aubin "Livre de caricatures"* (Oxford: Voltaire Foundation, 2012).

19. See Siméon-Prosper Hardy, *Mes loisirs (1753–1789), Volume 1, 1753–1770,* ed. Pascal Bastien and Daniel Roche (Quebec: Presses de l'Université Laval, 2008), "9 February 1767," 205–6.

20. Duquesnoy, *De la peinture*, 79–83.

21. Antoine-Joseph Dézallier d'Argenville, *Abrégé de la vie des peintres* (Paris: De Bure, 1752), 3:192, 54.

22. The portrait sketch on the title page is of the publisher, Jean-Baptiste-Claude Bauche.

23. Gilles-Marie Oppenord, "Inventaire après décès," 9 May 1742, AN, MC/ET/IV/517. His 234 volumes included dictionaries (Bayle, Moreri, Richelet, Furetière, Bruzen de la Martinière), history (Anselme, Mezeray, Fleury, Rollin), and literature (Fénelon, Corneille, Molière, and Swift).

24. Germain Brice, *Description de la ville de Paris* (Paris: Fournier, 1713), 1:127.

25. Mireille Rambaud, *Documents du Minutier Central concernant l'histoire de l'art (1700–1750)*, 2 vols (Paris: Imprimerie Nationale, 1964–71), 2:146.

26. See Jules Guiffrey, "Scellés et inventaires d'artistes, 1771–1790," *NAAF*, 1885, 3:105–7.

Burin

Renée-Elisabeth Marlié (1714–73)

TYPE OF OBJECT	THEME	MATERIAL
Tool	Family, Gender, Making, Studio	Metal | Steel, Plant Matter | Wood, Synthetic Materials | Paper

"A burin is a steel instrument for engraving on metal."[1] The best kind, according to this anonymous writer of the entry "Burin" in volume 2 of Diderot and d'Alembert's *Encyclopédie*, were those made from German or British steel: "its virtue is its fine grain and its ash gray color."[2] We have no way of knowing whether Renée-Elisabeth Marlié was fortunate enough to have a German burin, but we do learn from her "life," briefly told by the collector and connoisseur Pierre-Jean Mariette, that a burin of some kind was "put in her hand" by the engraver and royal academician François-Bernard Lépicié, whom she married in 1731 at the age of sixteen.[3]

Burins consist of a square shaft that tapers toward a diamond- or lozenge-shaped cutting face (fig. 18). They were supplied in a variety of sizes by the capital's master needlemakers and were later fitted with wooden handles furnished by its master turners.[4] These were not generic tools. Rather, they were made to the engraver's specification, in relation to hand size and with regard to habits of practice. Some engravers favored long burins, others short, some diamond-tipped, others lozenge.[5] Of whatever kind, a burin did not become a tool, properly speaking, however, until it had been remade in the printmaker's workshop.[6] The handle was cut away and flattened in a line perpendicular to the cutting face, and the point was further shaped, sharpened, and refined on an oil stone. The burin was therefore a highly individualized thing that belonged to its owner not only as property but as an extension of the body (hand and lower arm) and of thought: it prefigured the character of the line—bold, fine, etc.—that she envisaged and intended to cut.[7]

The burin was put to work on a copper plate bought ready-made from a master coppersmith.[8] Figures 1 and 2 of plate 11 of Charles-Nicolas Cochin's 1745 revised edition of *De la manière de graver à l'eau-forte et au burin* (see fig. 18) depicts how to hold the burin and put it to the plate: not grasped like a **quill** or ***crayon***, but rather with thumb and forefinger on the belly of the tool to guide the point, and the other fingers tucked up so that none come between the burin and the cutting surface. Cochin admitted that plates and description were not alone sufficient to understand fully the techniques of engraving, such was the range of pressure and the manifold subtleties in manipulation of the angle of the point to produce a flowing line to the desired width and depth.[9] A tacit form of knowledge, engraving was only fully revealed in the workshop.[10] Learned by doing, that is,

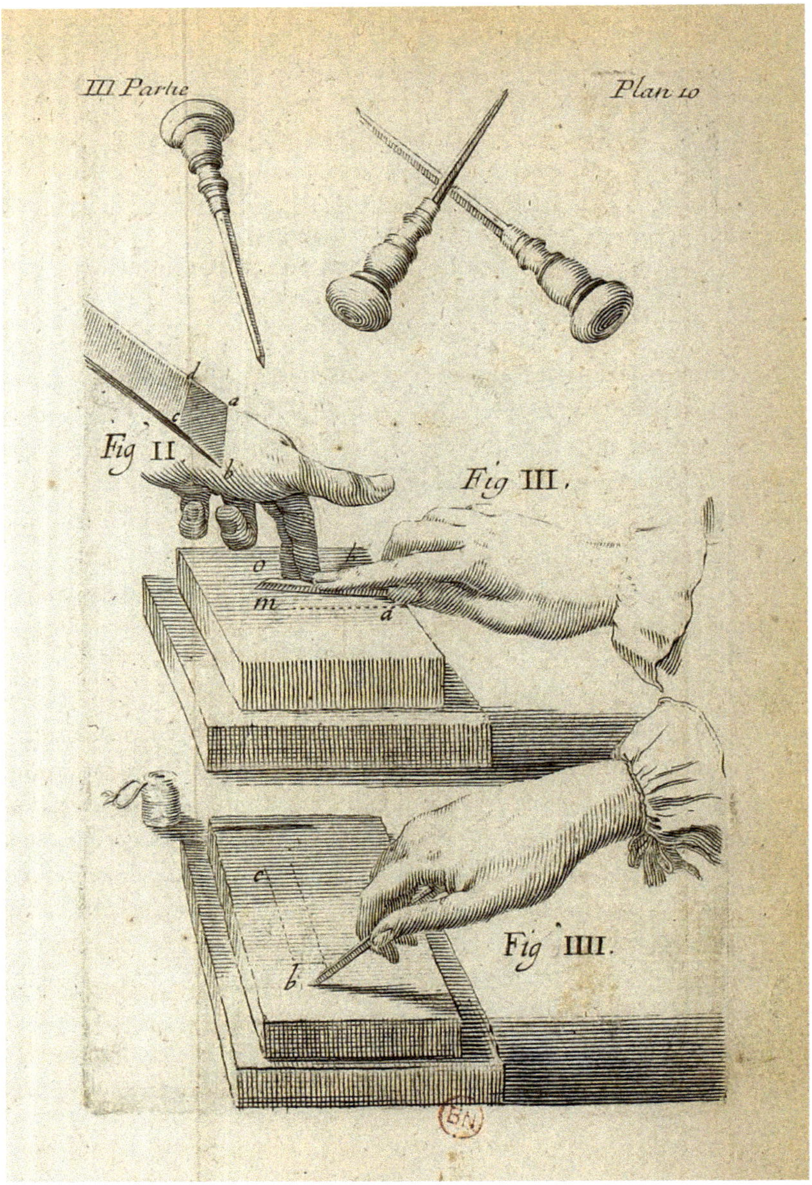

FIG. 18 Charles-Nicolas Cochin (French, 1715–90), *De la manière de graver à l'eau-forte et au burin*, 1745. Etching and engraving. Paris, Bibliothèque Nationale de France. (Image source: Gallica, BnF.)

by watching the master work and replicating his efforts in the presence of his example, engraving was a skill acquired slowly, through practice over time.[11]

Marlié's entitlement to such training and to exercise her burin professionally was secured by the Edict of Saint-Jean-de-Luz, signed by Louis XIV in May 1660, which confirmed intaglio printmaking as a liberal art.[12] There was no formal requirement of apprenticeship, journeymanship, and trial by masterpiece for printmaking, and no formal prohibition of women's participation, in contrast to needlemaking, turning, and coppersmithing, the trades that supplied the engraver's tools and medium, whose regulations proscribed access by women other than the widows of masters.[13] In law, printmaking was thus gender neutral. Women like Marlié could and did pick up the tools of printmaking in increasing numbers in the eighteenth century.[14] In addition to a professional tool, the burin, therefore, was potentially an agent and sign of independence.

The image we inherit of women in the eighteenth-century print trade is personified not by Marlié, that is, a print*maker*, however, but by Elisabeth Duret, Mme Le Bas, a workshop manager. In the portrait that Charles Joullain *fils* draws of her in his life and oeuvre of Jacques-Philippe Le Bas, her womanly work is portrayed as the perfect counterpart to her husband's art and industry.[15] She kept the books, and by her thrift safeguarded the success of his business. She compensated Le Bas's students and assistants for his exacting demands by her loving kindness and solicitude in hard times, ensuring the smooth and efficient running of his shop. Marlié's burin tells a different story, not of bourgeois feminine virtue and companionate marriage but of the starker economic conditions of women's work.

Her husband, Lépicié, was not a publisher and printseller with a large commercial enterprise like Le Bas. He had trained as a reproductive engraver, and by the late 1720s or early 1730s was making his reputation as the interpreter of modern French masters, first Charles-Antoine Coypel and later, in the 1740s, Jean-Siméon Chardin. He envisaged marriage, arguably, not as a partnership in which the moral, social, and economic assets each invested in the marriage's joint stock (*communauté de biens*) are shared and distinct,[16] but as an opportunity to recruit free labor and mitigate some of the economic risks of small-scale art reproduction. The lack of examples of Marlié's work before her marriage suggest that Mariette's quip that Lépicié put the burin in his bride's hand was actually a statement of fact and not the figure of speech it appears on the page. The **marriage contract**, from this perspective, looks not a little like an apprenticeship agreement: Lépicié to provide trade know-how and board, lodging, and laundry, Marlié to contribute dowry and labor. The known dates of Marlié's prints indicate that her training lasted five to six years,[17] the average, in fact, for engravers on metal.[18]

Her first commercial efforts in the mid-1730s were portraits for the printseller Michel Odieuvre's down-market series *Les portraits des personnes illustres* (1735). Next, she published with her husband's publisher, Louis Surugue, engravings of *Sight* (fig. 19), *Taste*, and *Smell* for a set of *The Five Senses* (ca. 1741), which resemble more-or-less formal demonstrations of skill—chefs-d'oeuvre in the guild sense. Her prints, produced alongside those of *Touch* and *Hearing* by her exact contemporary Pierre-Louis Surugue *fils*, are literal copies of Jan Saenredam's engravings after Henrick Goltzius (ca. 1595), and sought to rival the originals in that beauty and softness for which Goltzius's burin was renowned.[19] Three years later, in 1744, she replicated her husband's engraving after Chardin's *Le Bénédicité* (1740), the work that sealed Lépicié's reputation as an engraver, matching it faithfully line for line.[20] Surugue *fils* had meanwhile been made an *agréé* (provisional member) of the Académie in 1742, where he exhibited another print after Goltzius at the Salon. In 1744 he also engraved a Chardin: *The Card Game*, after the original painting (now lost), however, not another's print. In 1747 he was elected a full academician. Marlié's talent brought her no comparable independent public recognition. In 1737 Lépicié had been appointed the secretary of the Académie. His elevation can only have deepened her burdens as helpmeet in the studio.

Her comparative invisibility as an engraver-wife, compared to Surugue's prominence as *fils* of a lineage of engravers, is partly explained by cultural notions of appropriate womanly work. The burin's line was associated with masculine values of strength, precision, and boldness.[21] The resistance of the tool on the plate, metal to metal, required that the lines, swelling with the push, and tapering with the release of controlled and skillfully directed muscle power, were laid in systematically and evenly, creating a "net of rationality" not, it was generally thought, afforded by womanly work.[22] Contra such prejudice, in *Sight* (see fig. 19) Marlié reproduces the almost geometric precision of Saenredam's lines: the faces of the protagonists are rendered in swinging parallel arcs (the woman's cheek) and in contrary motions of curves and counter-curves (the man's jaw and brow) whose flat abstraction is relieved just enough with dots and cross-hatching to render the effect representational. In praising Saenredam's engraving for its "softness," François Basan applauded not his feminine sensibility but his virtuosic mastery of the manual challenges presented by the burin and the hard obduracy of the engraver's medium.[23] Though the amateur Claude-Henri Watelet acknowledged that engraving was not as physically demanding as received wisdom supposed, his account did nothing to overturn the general presumption that engraving is an art unfit for a woman.[24] Women like Marlié challenged the idea of the burin and the category of woman; the meaning of one or the other had to change when she picked up her tool and engraved a line.

By the end of the seventeenth century the status of engraving was under assault. According to the publisher Charles-Antoine Jombert, the engraved line expressed, in the eyes of the modern viewer, not strength but "rigidity," not clarity but "coldness."[25] Cochin alleged that engravers like Goltzius had turned virtuoso performance with the burin into an end in itself. Such self-reflexive displays of facility, he argued, undermined the proper purpose of engraving: to imitate the expressiveness, chiaroscuro, and *coloris* of drawings and paintings.[26] For reproduction he promoted the more flexible technique of etching. Cochin's criticism could well have been leveled at Marlié's 1756 engraving after Carle Van Loo's *The Marriage Contract* (1736) (fig. 20), a painting in Ange-Laurent de La Live de Jully's collection, and described in the collection's catalog as "in the taste of Rembrandt," a "pastiche" of the Dutchman's art.[27] Only the really attentive viewer appreciates Marlié's efforts to find with her burin a cut to correspond to the loose, broken paintwork of Van Loo's brush and the rich tenebrism of his glazes. Even so, "Rembrandesque," it is not. For such failings Cochin downgraded engraving to the secondary role of reinforcing etching's finer line work, of adding mere accent and finish. Arduousness, in the sense of drudgery

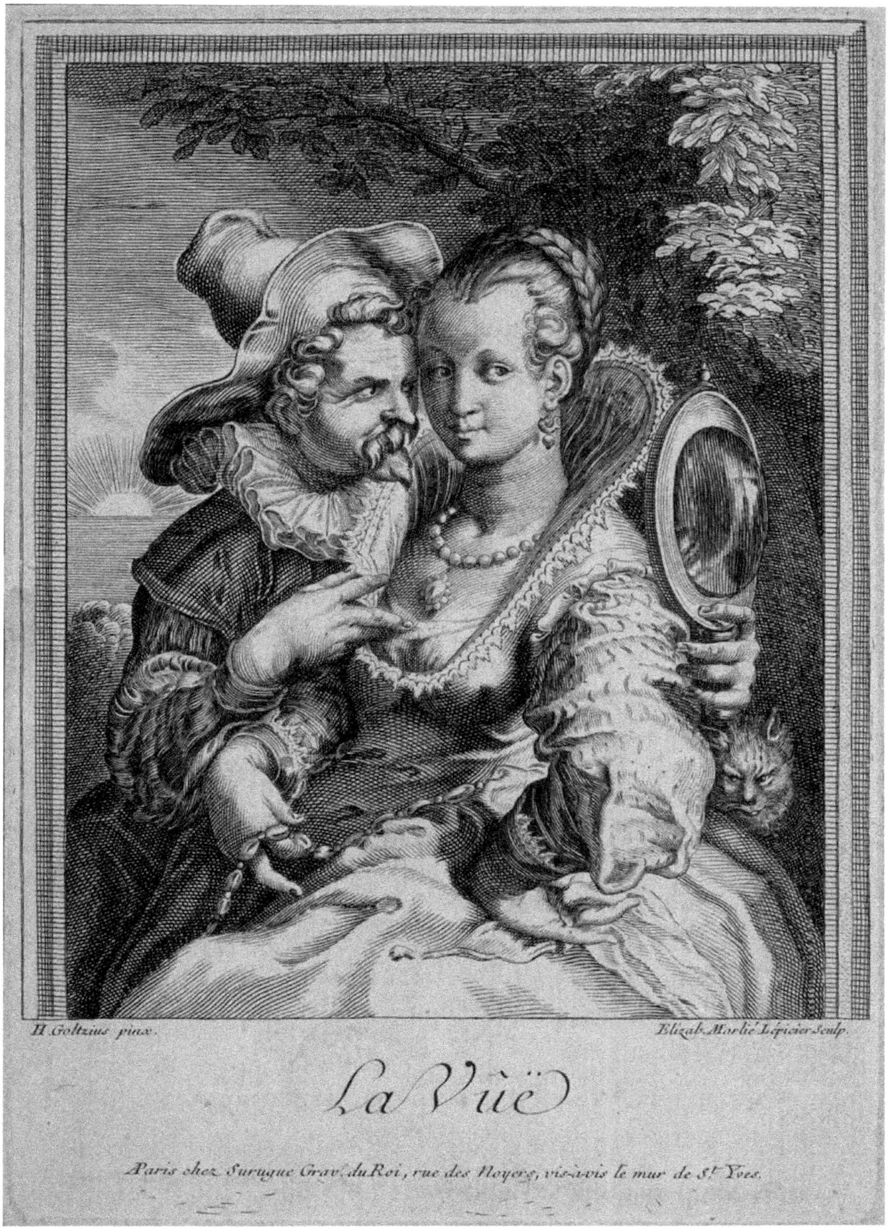

FIG. 19 Renée-Elisabeth Marlié (French, 1714–73), after Jan Saenredam (Dutch, 1565–1607), after Henrick Goltzius (Dutch, 1558–1617), *Sight* from *The Five Senses*, ca. 1741. Engraving, 22 × 15.2 cm. London, British Museum. (© The Trustees of the British Museum / Art Resource, NY.)

and routine, was the salient feature of engraving in this redefined role, a value that the woman might embody, but without artistic credit.

Marlié's print was advertised in the *Mercure de France* in November 1756.[28] Having praised the print in generic terms for capturing the "beauties" of Van Loo's "Drawing" and

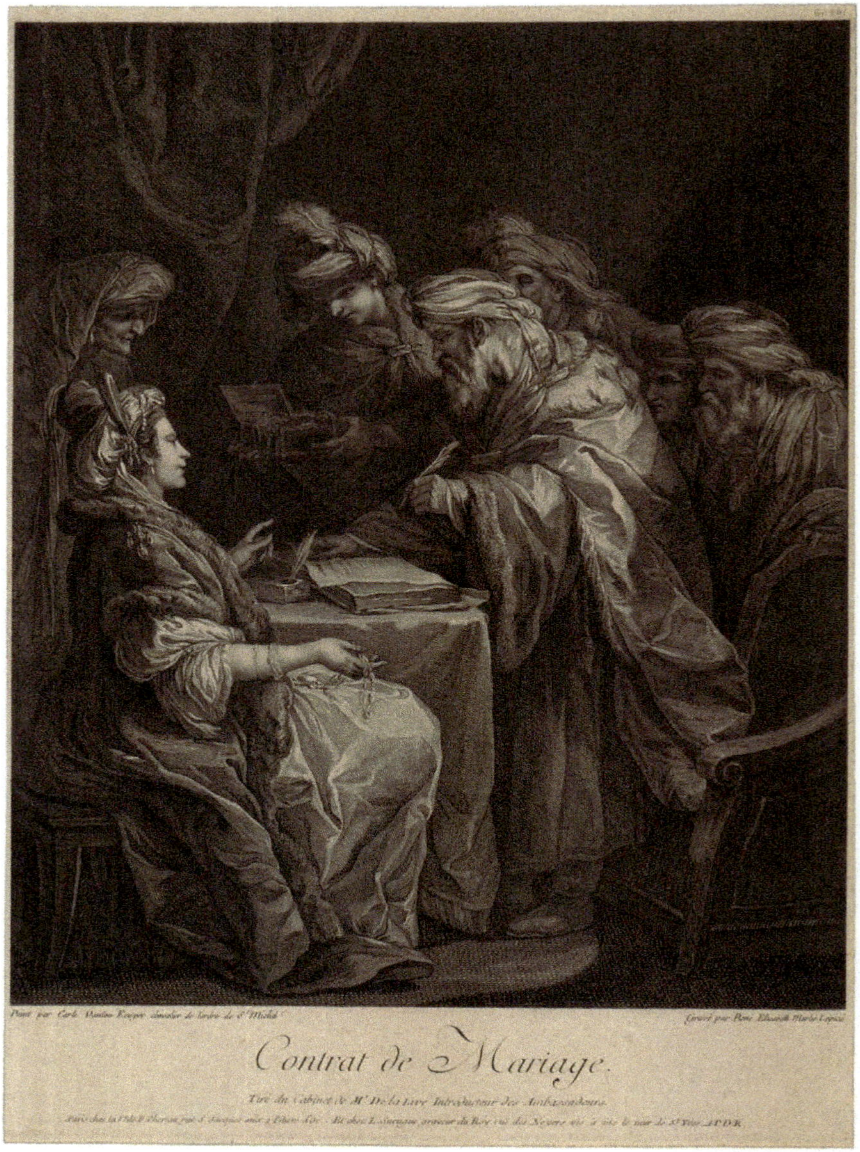

FIG. 20 Renée-Elisabeth Marlié (French, 1714–73), after Carle Van Loo (French, 1705–65), *The Marriage Contract*, 1756. Engraving. Paris, Bibliothèque National de France.

the "vigor" of his "*coloris*," the writer of the ad concluded by saying that the print "pays tribute also to M. L'Epicié, deceased, who knew how to leave us a second self . . . by resurrecting his talents" in his wife. The compliment was backhanded. It implied that although Marlié signed her work in her own name, nevertheless, under Lépicié's training, she had not developed an independent artistic voice.[29] Not a compliment, it was, in Lépicié's case, also not a figure of speech. His purpose had indeed been to create a second, indistinguishable self, to share the labor of printmaking by "finishing" his work to preserve by her burin his etched *disegno* from the wear and tear of printing, thus increasing the size of the edition that could be pulled from the workshop's copper plates and consequently the profitability of the business. In an invoice in the form of a poetic writ, addressed by Lépicié to the Fermiers généraux in June 1738, the engraver observed that the print they had commissioned from him after Hyacinthe Rigaud's *Portrait of Philibert Orry*, had taken two years of "painful and continuous labor," during which "Patience" had been his soul's only condition and "Migraine" his only companion.[30] Marlié was that patience personified. So close is her technique to his that connoisseurs find it impossible to untangle their work.

The *Marriage Contract* is Marlié's last known engraving. Shortly after Lépicié's death in 1755 she put her burin down. Released from a contract of drudgery and artistic nonentity, she retired at his lodging at the Louvre. §

---

1. "Burin" in *Encyclopedie,* 2:465, https://encyclopedie.uchicago.edu/.

2. Johann Georg Wille sourced his steel burins from London—four dozen in 1763. See *Mémoires et journal de J. G. Wille*, ed. Georges Duplessis (Paris: Veuve Jules Renouard, 1857), 1:238.

3. Pierre-Jean Mariette, *Abecedario de P. J. Mariette*, ed. Philippe de Chennevières and Anatole de Montaiglon (Paris: J. B. Dumoulin, 1853–62), 3:192. For Lépicié and Marlié's marriage contract, see Mireille Rambaud, *Documents du Minutier Central concernant l'histoire de l'art (1700–1750)*, 2 vols. (Paris: Imprimerie Nationale, 1964–71), 1:188–89.

4. See Jacques de Savary des Bruslons, *Dictonnaire universel du commerce* (Paris: Estienne, 1723–30), 1: s.v. "Aiguillers," 3: s.v. "Tour."

5. Charles-Nicolas Cochin refused to discuss the physical properties of burins in detail in *De la manière de graver à l'eau-forte et au burin* (Paris: Jombert, 1745), 100, because each engraver choses what suits them best. See also Claude-Henri Watelet's article "Gravure" in *Encyclopédie*, 7:888.

6. See Cochin, *De la manière*, 100–101. After Gérard Edelinck's death in 1707 students fought over his burins in the hope that his art was his tool. See Cousin de Constamine, "Vie d'Edelinck," in *Mémoires inédits*, 2:58; and Antony Griffiths, *Print before Photography* (New Haven: Yale University Press, 2016), 471.

7. Watelet noted that the hilt of the burin sits in the palm of the hand such that its blade aligns directly with the bones of the forearm. See Watelet, "Gravure" in *Encyclopédie*, 7:888.

8. Savary des Bruslons, *Dictionnaire universel*, 2: s.v. "Chaudronnier."

9. Cochin, *De la manière*, 104.

10. On tacit knowledge, see Michael Polanyi, *The Tacit Dimension* (1966; reprint, Chicago: University of Chicago Press, 2009).

11. See Abraham Bosse's "preface" (1645), republished in Cochin, *De la manière*, xvii. See also Cousin de Constamine, "Vie d'Edelinck," in *Mémoires inédits*, 2:57, on Edelinck as a teacher: "son trait ne fut ni précédé, ni suivit d'aucun discours"; cf. Jean-Gérard Castex, "Réduire la gravure en art et en principes: Lecture et réception du *Traité des manières de graver à l'eau-forte* d'Abraham Bosse," in *Réduire en art: La technologie de la Renaissance aux Lumières*, ed. Pascal Dubourg and Hélène Vérin (Paris: Maison des sciences de l'homme, 2014), 235–48.

12. See Marianne Grivel, *Le commerce de l'estampe à Paris au XVIIe siècle* (Geneva: Droz, 1987), 96–99.

13. On gender and the guilds, see Clare Crowston, "Women, Gender, and Guilds in Early Modern Europe: An Overview of Recent Research," *International Review of Social History* 53 (2008): 19–44.

14. See Delia Gaze, ed., *Dictionary of Women Artists* (London: Routledge, 1997), 1:62.

15. See Charles Joullain *fils*, *Oeuvre de Jacques-Philippe Le Bas*, 5 vols. (BnF, Ee11–Ee11d fol), 1.

16. On the marriage contract in the ancien régime, see Claude-Joseph de Ferrière, *La science parfaite des notaires*, updated by François-Benoît Visme (Paris: Saugrain, 1752), 1, pt. 4, esp. 256–63.

17. She started producing portrait engraving for Michel Odieuvre's series *Portraits des Grands Hommes et Personnes Illustres*. Four were advertised in the *Mercure de France* in 1736 (June, July, September, and October), including the portrait of the engraver Claude Mellan.

18. The apprenticeship documents for engravers on metal shows that the average training contract was six years. See Rambaud, *Documents du Minutier Central*, 1: xliv–xlvi.

19. François Basan, *Dictionnaire des graveurs* (Paris: Prault, 1789), 2:147. The Saenredam originals almost certainly belonged to the publisher of the copies, Louis Surugue the Elder, in whose collection Goltzius's work was prominent both in the original and reproduced by Saenredam, among others. See François Basan, *Catalogue d'estampes des plus grands maîtres italiens, flamands et françois du cabinet de feu Louis de Surugue* (Paris: Pierres, 1769), lots 47, 134, 195, 315, 387, 434, 435–36, and 500.

20. Close comparison of their prints reveals that Marlié did simplify her husband's work, reducing the number of lines especially in the rendering of the ground.

21. See Cochin, *De la manière*, xxiii; *Encyclopédie*, 7:284 ("Franchise de pinceau ou de burin").

22. The phrase is from William M. Ivins Jr. See Ivins, *Prints and Visual Communication* (Cambridge: MIT Press, 1969), 70, 73.

23. Basan, *Dictionnaire*, 2:147–48.

24. *Encyclopédie*, 7:887.

25. Charles-Antoine Jombert, "Préface de l'éditeur," in Cochin, *De la manière*, xix.

26. Cochin, *De la manière*, 106.

27. See *Catalogue historique du Cabinet de peinture et de sculpture françoise de M. de La Live* (Paris: Le Prieur, 1764), 79.
28. *Mercure de France,* November 1756, 169–70.
29. She signed, seemingly at random, Marlier, Lépicié, and Marlié-Lépicier. To contrast Marlié's situation with Marguerite Gérard's relationship with Jean-Honoré Fragonard at the end of the century, see Rena M. Hoisington and Perrin Stein, "'Sous les yeux de Fragonard': The prints of Marguerite Gérard," *Print Quarterly* 29, no. 2 (2012): 142–62.
30. See *Placet à Messieurs les Fermiers généraux sur le portrait de Monseigneur le Contrôleur général gravé par ordre de la Compagnie* (n.p., 1738), 2.

Camera Obscura

Charles Parrocel (1688–1752)

TYPE OF OBJECT	THEME	MATERIAL
Instrument	Making, Studio	Plant Matter | Wood, Synthetic Materials | Glass

A *chambre noire*, or camera obscura, in a case was inventoried in the studio of the battle painter and academician Charles Parrocel at his death in 1752.[1] The camera obscura is an optical instrument that by alignment of a biconvex lens with a mirror projects a righted image of objects in the sunlit world onto a two-dimensional surface in a darkened "room." Parrocel's camera was itemized as "for drawing," and it was very likely of the desktop variety illustrated as figure 2 in plate V of "Drawing," in Diderot and d'Alembert's *Encyclopédie* (fig. 21).[2] The text of the plate itemized the components of the instrument but provided no instructions for use, observing only that, contrary to the reader's expectation, the view seen by the projectionist lies behind and not in front of them. The surprise that the writer anticipated this revelation would provoke suggests that although the camera obscura was a familiar object in scientific circles in mid-eighteenth-century France, it was still something of a novelty in the art world.[3]

The camera obscura is not, it is true, generally associated with the French school and with traditions of academic art. Rather, art historians have researched the origins of its use as an instrument for perfecting the exact imitation of nature in Renaissance Italy and seventeenth-century Holland.[4] It is no surprise to learn from the abbé Gougenot's Life of Jean-Baptiste Oudry, an artist whose work was profoundly informed by northern practices of painting, that this still-life and landscape painter used a camera obscura.[5] By contrast, Parrocel's ownership of one poses a dilemma. The camera is not mentioned in any other contemporary source on Parrocel. His biographers unite, in fact, in characterizing his talent in terms of imagination, invention, and genius, skills that notionally render the resources of the camera obsolete.[6] How do we explain this omission and make sense of the camera's presence in Parrocel's studio? Is the inborn secretiveness of artists about their methods to blame, as David Hockney alleges?[7] Did Parrocel use it only exceptionally, for specific works? Or was the utility of the camera obscura not what we think it was, that is, not just a machine for copying? Answers to these questions in the context of things inevitably directs us to focus less on the newness of the technology and more on its significance in relation to alternatives embodied in the old tools of the early modern workshop.[8]

Estate inventories cannot tell us when things were acquired, but they do tell us where they were kept, from which we can infer use and significance. Parrocel's studio was at the

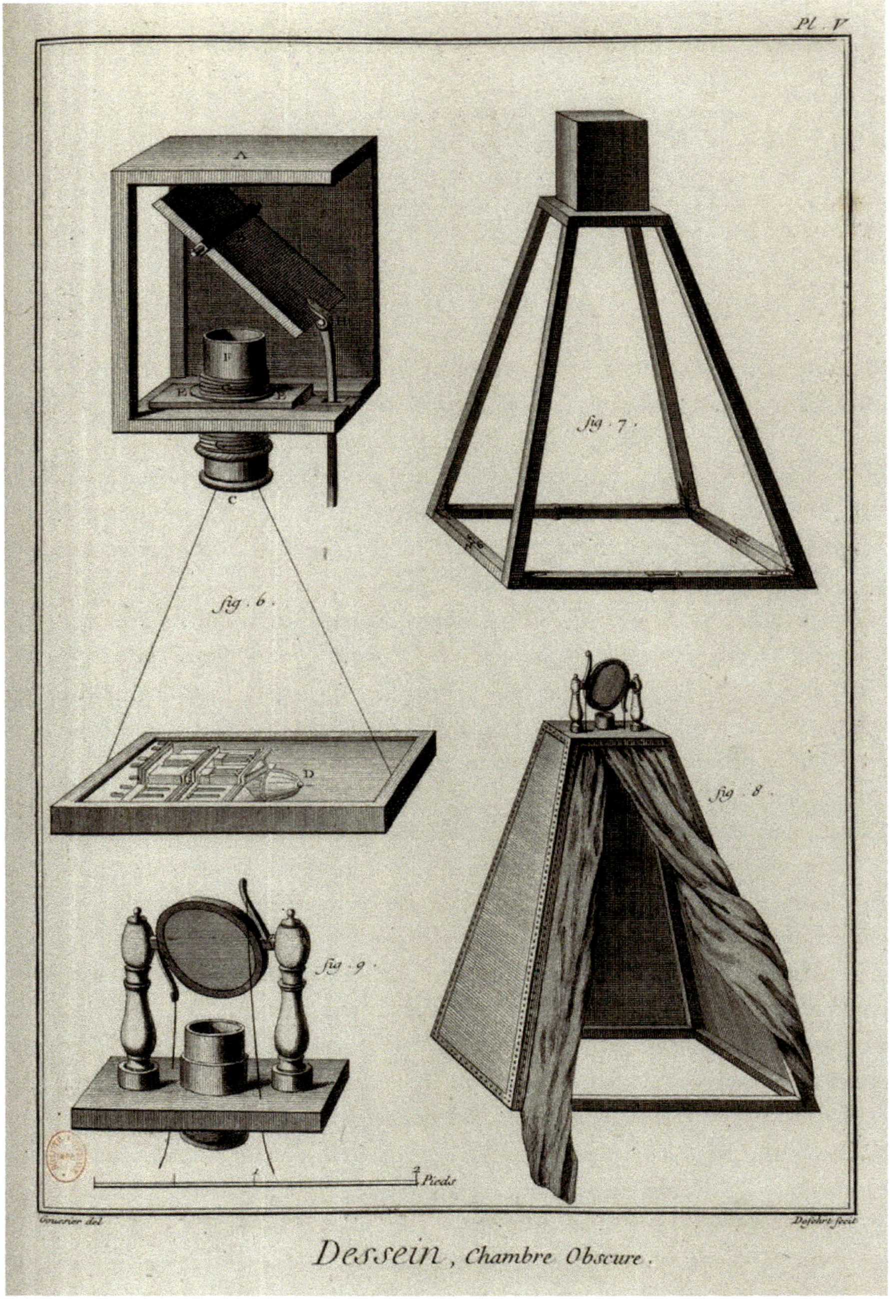

FIG. 21 Camera obscura, "Dessein" from *Recueil de planches sur les sciences, les arts libéraux et les arts mécaniques* (1765), plate V. (Paris, Bibliothèque Nationale de France.)

Gobelins on the outskirts of Paris.[9] It was off the inner courtyard of the tapestry manufactory and looked out onto the gardens of the art collector and textile manufacturer Jean de Julienne.[10] Above the studio, his living space was distributed in six rooms, including a "room" serving as a *cabinet* that was north facing, like the studio.[11] Parrocel's tools were itemized in both his domestic and his work spaces, suggesting that he divided his time between the two: his drawing implements (***porte-crayon***, **quill**, and geometry set) were listed in a walnut cupboard in the *cabinet*, while the record of the studio stuff (easels and other working surfaces, **color-boxes**, and props) indicates that it was equipped for painting.[12] Classified as "for drawing" yet located in the painting workshop, the camera obscura was seemingly an instrument operating between zones: between drawing and painting and also between indoor and outdoor. (Listed immediately after the camera was a tent of cotton drill and assorted tent pegs.)

A preparatory drawing for the *Reception of the Turkish Ambassadors at the Tuileries* (fig. 22), a work commissioned from Parrocel by the crown in 1727, exhibits the technique of perspectival construction using the conventional tools of geometry (compass, ruler, and setsquare).[13] The drawing is divided by color into black-chalk figures and sanguine setting. The disjunction between the even and exactly measured red space, mapped from a point of central perspective by a compass and ruler, and the mottled and mobile impression of events unfolding in that gridded locale under the differential pressure of black chalk's painterly point, could not be more apparent. The perspective and the figures belong to different worlds. It appears, moreover, that the Turkish envoys and the Parisian crowds were drawn first, in space minimally ordered by a vanishing point, on which perspective's rigid order was later imposed (red over black, in the lines of the steps) and into which the sharply foreshortened architecture was inserted, very possibly by another hand. That Parrocel struggled with the perspective is evident in the corrected positioning of the vanishing point: the eye from which black orthogonals tentatively radiate was removed by the red hand to a lower position.[14] The clash between the propositional statements of geometry about space in the abstract, and the gestural marks provoked by concrete things—the sheen of a skirt, the curved rump of a horse, the assorted pitches of rifles on shoulders and swords on hips—are irreconcilable, and pull the image in opposite directions, breaking it apart.[15]

The projection of the camera obscura healed that rift. It enabled the artist to transpose the relative position and size of objects in a scene, freehand, onto the two-dimensional surface.[16] The locus of scientific knowledge shifted from paper work to camera work; focused projection relied on exact calculation of the optimum distance between the lens and its objects, and on the informed choice of aperture in relation to light conditions.[17] On the page, meanwhile, figure and ground, objects and space were created in a single gestural practice, paradoxically closer to the sketch than the mechanical copy. In *Cavalry Engagement*, for instance, a pen-and-brown-ink drawing with brown and gray wash (fig. 23), the energetic, almost continuous flow of Parrocel's inky line feels its way with squiggles and accents toward the "real" of a scene of conflict, working with wash to create space both on the material surface of the drawing and in the picture plane. A camera obscura was obviously not used to make this drawing; rather, the drawing helps us see how the camera afforded a new experiential understanding of perception, one that enabled artists to work in practice back and forth across drawing and painting, or *disegno* and

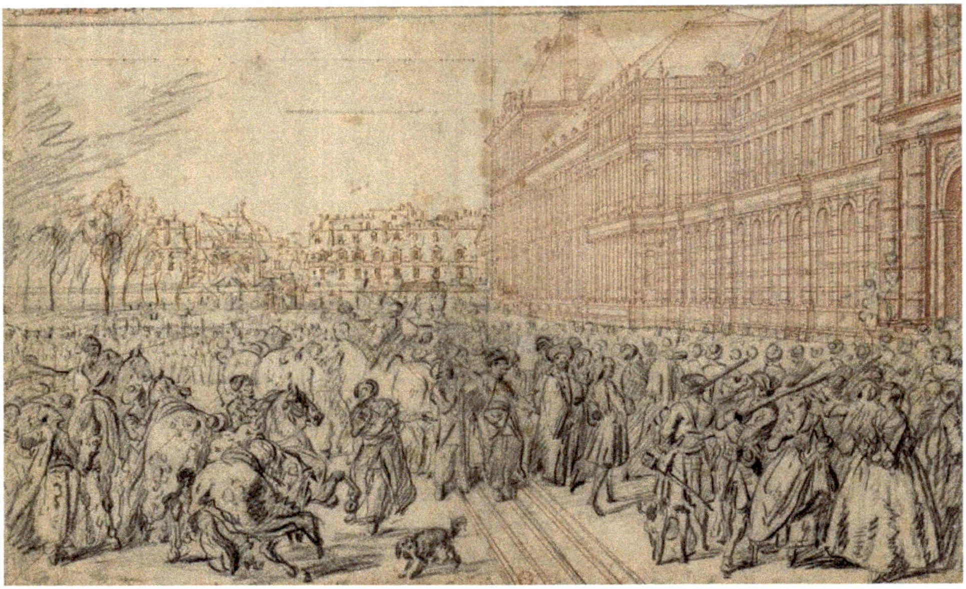

FIG. 22 Charles Parrocel (French, 1688–1752), *Reception of the Turkish Ambassadors at the Tuileries*, ca. 1727. Red and black chalk. Paris, Bibliothèque Nationale de France.

colore, domains that academic art theory had enshrined in the seventeenth century as cognitively distinct.

The Académie in 1700 was not, however, the same institution it had been at the height of Charles Le Brun's influence, when a rationalist order of painting, based in line and narrative, was dominant. Camilla Pietrabissa has shown that, by the turn of the century, a more empirical approach was developing at the Académie school. Louis Joblot, the professor of perspective, introduced the camera obscura to teaching.[18] Students, of which Parrocel was almost certainly one, were given a comprehensive course in optics, starting with the anatomy of the eye, followed by lessons in the science of light and color, and ending with instruction on how to build basic optical instruments.[19] But, though Joblot encouraged students to take the camera obscura into the countryside to draw, there is no evidence that he promoted it as a means to achieve a heightened form of naturalism. A tiny ornamental dragon (fig. 24) is the object of the eye's attention in his design for a magnifying glass published in 1718 in his book on microscopy.[20]

In the years Joblot was teaching, the art theorist Roger de Piles was giving lectures on art theory, published in 1708. In his *Cours*, de Piles advocated use of optical instruments, specifically mirrors, not in the context of imitation but as an aid to composition—in relation, that is, to invention. He argued that by looking in a convex mirror, which increases the force of central focus, the painter can understand better how to order his or her composition to achieve the "unity of effect" that is, he argues, crucial to satisfying the eye at a single glance, and thus to fulfilling the primary purpose of painting: the illusion of perception.[21] The camera obscura is no different. Its lens only brings into view that which

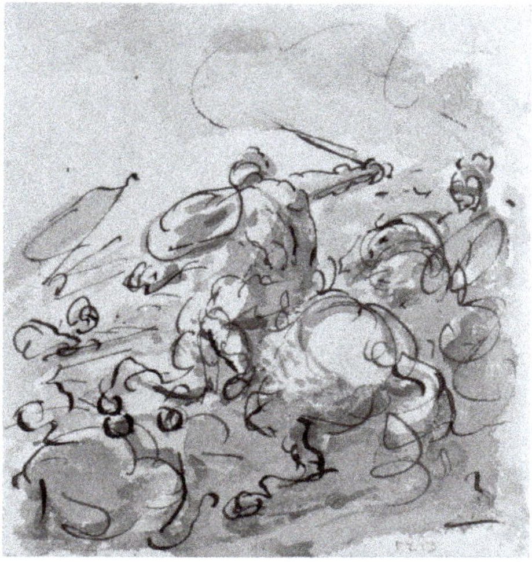

FIG. 23 Charles Parrocel (French, 1688–1752), *Cavalry Engagement*, ca. 1745. Pen and brown ink with brown and gray wash, 35.7 × 18.2 cm. Stockholm, Nationalmuseum, NMH 2892/1863. (Photo: Nationalmuseum.)

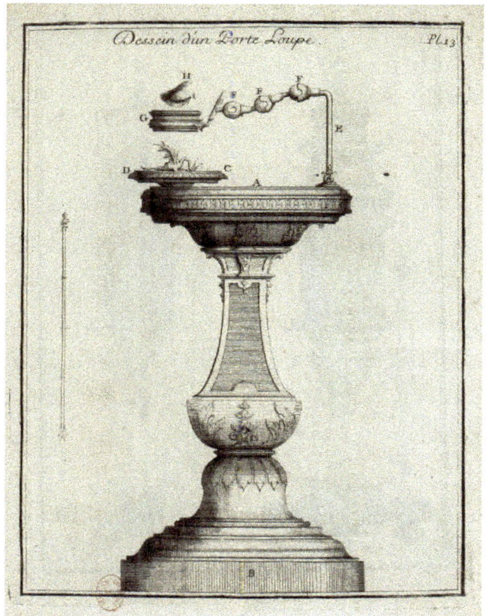

FIG. 24 Louis Joblot (French, 1645–1723), *Dessin d'une porte loupe*, 1718. Paris, Bibliothèque Nationale de France.

is directly in its line of sight and upon which it is focused; that which is not is registered is seen, if at all, with the progressively diminishing sharpness of peripheral vision. Unless the camera is refocused for each object in a scene, it will impose, like the history painter, an order on the world by the honor of its attention, and by consigning lesser things to the indistinctness of the edge.[22] Joblot's innovative teaching with the camera obscura did not of itself revolutionize the paradigms of pictorial representation at the Académie. Indeed, so natural seeming was ideal nature that the camera's projections appeared artificial to some. Fifty years later, in *Méthode pour apprendre le dessein*, Charles-Antoine Jombert criticized as unnatural and exaggerated the contrast of light and shadow and the brightness of color projected by the camera.[23] He cautioned restraint in the imitation of its "piquant" illusions and advised artists to check them against the "real" of unaided vision.

In light of this review of early eighteenth-century academic theory and pedagogy, the presence of a camera obscura in Parrocel's studio appears less odd, less contradictory. Optical instruments were not reserved for imitation, they were also tools of invention and imagination. A reading, thus contextualized, of the Lives of Charles Parrocel for what they say about his art in relation to the tradition of battle painting and to the manner of his masters—his father the battle painter Joseph Parrocel, and the history painters Charles de La Fosse and Bon de Boullogne—may now indicate some material impacts of the technology on his practice.

Charles-Nicolas Cochin emphasized the bold liveliness of his friend Parrocel's battle scenes by comparison to the small, detailed precision of the figures and settings in the work of the celebrated Adam Frans Van der Meulen, Louis XIV's official war artist.[24] He explained the forcefulness of their illusion of presence by reference to Parrocel's lifelong study of the physiognomy and movement of the horse. Though he notes the importance of memory to the process, his characterization of Parrocel's habitual manner of drawing as "square" and "flat" (see fig. 23), by which he meant that Parrocel privileged a single plane, parallel to the picture surface, invokes a haptic process of making in which the horse is introduced into the studio as an object for examination and manipulation, like a specimen on paper, though the gestures of representation remain open and sketchlike.[25] Of Parrocel's color, Cochin notes that it was compared unfavorably by some with that of his father and the generation of La Fosse. Antoine-Joseph Dézallier d'Argenville, for one, lamented its blueish, silvered tone, compared to the hot, red **palette** of the earlier colorists.[26] In the difference introduced by Parrocel *fils* to Parrocel *père*'s pictorial heritage, Cochin saw, by contrast, a willingness to recognize the faults of the venerated father, whose works surrounded Parrocel in the studio, and to revise "convention" in the light of nature, a "piquant" nature—the adjective also used to describe the effects of the camera obscura.[27]

We can infer from the Lives that the camera obscura did graft a new mode of perception onto Parrocel's body, one that via the technical actions of a lens enabled him to imagine and execute a bold and vivid representation of man and the natural world. This fits with the weak thesis of the impact of optical instruments on early modern Western art, according to which naturalism was stimulated by the look of objects and scenarios reflected in mirrors or projected through a lens, not manufactured with specific projections and reflections. It does not, however, rule out the stronger, instrumentalist argument. At the time of his death Parrocel was working on a set of battle paintings depicting Louis XV's campaigns in Flanders (1744–48) during the War of the Austrian Succession in preparation for which he was despatched in the spring of 1746 to "reconnoitre" the environs of Ypres, Tournai, and Fontenay, very likely taking his tent and his camera with him.[28] What both strong and weak theses register is the contribution made by the camera to the interiorization of practice brilliantly analyzed by Svetlana Alpers: to its becoming, as she puts it, *the* place "where the world as it gets into painting is experienced."[29]

Light was a precondition of that experience, of which the camera, by the difference of its optical values to the steady, diffuse, ideal light of the north-facing studio, made the artist more acutely aware. They were consequently encouraged to control and manipulate those conditions, with optical instruments and with furniture: there was a green curtain on the window in Parrocel's studio and a mirror on the wall.[30] Interiorization led also to a re-visioning of the subjects of representation, reframing and refocusing history thematically, with the means of portraiture and still life.[31] Parrocel was famed for his speed of execution and for his depiction of movement, qualities contrary, no doubt, to the slow-worked stillness of the descriptive genres generally favored by the camera obscura. However, for the Choisy commission, Parrocel was certainly concerned with the quiddity of things, and not just their narrative potential. He wrote to the *directeur des bâtiments du roi*, Le Normand de Tournehem, for loan of the king's and the dauphin's clothes at the Battle of Fontenay, hats and gloves included, which he described at length.[32] Models of the horse and of ordnance, and examples of weaponry filled his studio.[33] The studio, not the battlefield, was for Parrocel the place of encounter between history and painting.

One of the problems created by this shift to the interior was, as Alpers notes, the isolation of the artist.[34] Parrocel's natural melancholy was, according to Cochin, exacerbated by his distance from the center of Paris and his friends at the Louvre.[35] Of course, melancholy had been a literary trope in the discourse on the artist since Vasari at least.[36] In Cochin's "Vie de Charles Parrocel," however, it is not a sign of genius but a symptom of psychosis. What he describes as melancholy we term paranoia. Believing that the superiority of his talent was insufficiently recognized, Parrocel felt persecuted; imagined hostile motives in the behavior of brother academicians; became progressively self-absorbed, secretive, and aloof. Relevant here is that neither the privilege of a royal studio nor access to modern optical instruments appear to have given Parrocel a sense of agency; on the contrary, he believed himself to be the victim of forces beyond his control. The painter Nicolas Lancret was, apparently, the embodiment of those forces.[37] Parrocel experienced Lancret's commercial and popular success with domestic genre, with subjects native to the studio as interior, as a humiliating injustice. We catch a glimpse here of the dark side of the Enlightenment and the progress of commercial culture, or the distorted images that mirrors and lenses can produce.[38] §

---

1. Charles Parrocel, "Inventaire après décès," 3 June 1752, AN, MC/ET/CXXII/684.

2. Plate V, "Dessein," *Encyclopédie*, https://encyclopedie.uchicago.edu/, 22:7.

3. On the use of the camera obscura in science and art, see Wolfgang Lefèvre, ed., *Inside the Camera Obscura: Optics and Art under the Spell of the Projected Image* (Berlin: Max-Planck-Institut für Wissenschaftsgeschichte, 2007).

4. See Martin Kemp, *The Science of Art* (London: Yale University Press 1990), chapter 4.

5. Louis Gougenot, "Vie de Jean-Baptiste Oudry," in *Mémoires inédits*, 2:377–78.

6. Charles-Nicolas Cochin, "Vie de Charles Parrocel," *Mémoires inédits,* 404–27; Antoine-Joseph Dézallier d'Argenville, *Abrégé de la vie des plus fameux peintres* (Paris: De Bure, 1762), 4:429–34; and Pierre-Jean Mariette, *Abecedario de P.-J. Mariette*, ed. Philippe de Chennevières and Anatole de Montaiglon (Paris: J. B. Dumoulin, 1853–62), 4:82–83.

7. David Hockney, *Secret Knowledge: Rediscovering the Lost Techniques of the Old Masters* (Harmonsworth: Thames and Hudson, 2001).

8. David Egerton, *The Shock of the Old: Technology and Global History since 1900* (London: Profile, 2006).

9. Parrocel moved to the Gobelins in 1728. See Hannah Williams and Chris Sparks, *Artists in Paris: Mapping the 18th-Century Art World,* www.artistsinparis.org.

10. Parrocel's *inventaire* does not support the studio on Jacques-François Blondel's ground plan in *Architecture françoise* (Paris: Jombert, 1752–54), 3: plate 19.

11. The room is called a "salle" in the *inventaire.*

12. AN, MC/ET/CXXII/684, 3 June 1752.

13. Only two of the three commissioned works recorded in Charles-Nicolas Cochin's biography of Parrocel were executed. This scene did not progress beyond the preparatory stage. See Cochin, "Vie de Charles Parrocel," 409. On record of the commission in the Bâtiments's accounts, see Fernand Engerand, *Inventaire des tableaux commendés et achetés par la direction des bâtiments du roi (1709–1792,* (Paris: E. Leroux, 1900), 381–82.

14. The first vanishing point is represented as an eye; the second vanishing point in red chalk is a point.

15. On these modes of drawing, see Tim Ingold, *Making: Anthropology, Archaeology, Art and Architecture* (Abington, Routledge, 2013), 125–41.

16. For such tracings in the case of landscape, see Christoph Löthy, "Hockney's Secret Knowledge: Vanvitelli's Camera Obscura," *Early Science and Medicine* 10, no. 2 (2009): 315–39.

17. See Willem Jacob 's Gravesande, *Essai sur la perspective: Usage de la chambre obscure pour le dessein* (The Hague: Troyel, 1711), 1–35.

18. See Camilla Pietrabissa, "From Perspective to Place: The Landscape Tableau in Paris, c. 1680–c. 1750," PhD diss., Courtauld Institute of Art (London, 2018), 22–26.

19. According to Dézallier d'Argenville, Parrocel won several student prizes at the Académie. See *Abrégé de la vie*, 4:429.
20. Parrocel owned two magnifying glasses.
21. Roger de Piles, *Cours de peinture par principes* (1708; reprint, Paris: Gallimard, 1989), 65–68.
22. 's Gravesande, *Essai sur la perspective*, 5–24.
23. Charles-Antoine Jombert, *Méthode pour apprendre le dessein* (Paris: Jombert, 1759), 139.
24. Cochin, "Vie de Charles Parrocel," 408, 423.
25. Cochin, "Vie de Charles Parrocel," 421–22.
26. Dézallier d'Argenville, *Abrégé sur la vie*, 432.
27. Cochin, "Vie de Charles Parrocel," 420–21.
28. Engerand, *Inventaire des tableaux*, 383.
29. Svetlana Alpers, "The Studio, the Laboratory and the Vexations of Art," in *Picturing Science, Producing Art*, ed. Caroline A. Jones and Peter Galison (New York: Routledge, 1998), 401–17.
30. AN, MC/ET/CXXII/684, 3 June 1752.
31. Alpers, "The Studio," 410.
32. Engerand, *Inventaire des tableaux*, 384–85, ft. 5.
33. AN, MC/ET/CXXII/684, 3 June 1752.
34. Alpers, "The Studio," 411.
35. Cochin, "Vie de Charles Parrocel," 423–24. Mariette attributes Parrocel's ills to idleness and alcoholism. Mariette, *Abecedario*, 4:83. See **wine**.
36. See the classic account in Margot and Rudolf Wittkower, *Born under Saturn: The Character and Conduct of Artists* (New York: Random House, 1963), 98–132.
37. Cochin, "Vie de Charles Parrocel," 417.
38. On paranoia as a modern ill, see John Farrell, *Paranoia and Modernity: Cervantes to Rousseau* (Ithaca, NY: Cornell University Press, 2006).

Carriage

Jean-Baptiste Pigalle (1714–85)

TYPE OF OBJECT	THEME	MATERIAL
Vehicle	Travel	Plant Matter | Wood, Synthetic Materials | Glass, Synthetic Materials | Paint/Pigment, Textile | Silk

Prompted to consider carriages *and* artists in the eighteenth century, we think perhaps first of specialist trades, those of the coach painter and the ornamental carver.[1] Or, in the context of metaphors of modernity, we think of the image of the extravagantly decorated coach used by critics and satirists to figure the rise of luxury consumption and the corresponding degradation of art.[2] We do not, generally, think of carriages as things owned and used by artists. The fine art sculptor and academician Jean-Baptiste Pigalle, who lived at the end of his life on the outskirts of Paris in the semirural district of Montmartre, compels us to think again. Parked at the stable of his house, 12 Rue de La Rochefoucault, in 1785 were a cart and a carriage and a cabriolet. In the stable were a pair of bays to drive the carriage and a black mare for the cabriolet.[3] Pigalle's vehicles contributed to the enormous increase in the number of carriages on the streets of the capital, which had risen from 310 in 1658 to over 15,000 by 1750.[4] Growth in vehicular transport occurred in tandem with the gradual improvement of the country's roads.[5] The combination transformed travel, multiplying and speeding up connections between people and places, technological progress regarded as crucial to the modernization of the western world, according to historians.

Was this simultaneous opening up of geographical space and collapse of distance in the seventeenth century experienced professionally, socially, and culturally by artists like Pigalle? Was it reason enough to keep a carriage? Answering these questions begins with knowing more about Pigalle's vehicles. None survive, but the words used by the notaries to denote them in his postmortem inventory are telling. Of the three types, the cart and the cabriolet mark extremes: of slowness in the case of the cart, a heavy, unsprung, and open vehicle used to transport goods, and of speed and maneuverability in the case of the cabriolet, a light two-seater with a collapsible hood, for expeditions locally. Between the two stands the carriage, specifically a Berline, a four-wheel enclosed vehicle with suspension, for both short- and long-distance travel. Pigalle probably used his cart to ferry materials to and from his studio, and the cabriolet for the short trip to the center of town. The only reference to Pigalle's travel choices in a contemporary source describes the sculptor leaving the Louvre after a difficult meeting of the Académie's membership in September 1768; according to Charles-Nicolas Cochin, the Académie's secretary, Pigalle got into a "chaise," a cabriolet-style vehicle, and amid heckling from students, made his escape.[6] The larger, sturdier, and less nimble Berline was, meanwhile, very possibly his choice for the journeys he made to Reims, Ferney, and Strasbourg in relation to his commissions, respectively, in 1765 for the monument to Louis XV, in 1770 for *Voltaire nu*, and in 1776 for the mausoleum of the maréchal de Saxe, always assuming he did not opt for public transport.

Although, as Nicolas Clément has noted, Pigalle's journeys all date from the latter part of his career, they don't coincide neatly with his purchase of a house with a stable.[7] When the monument to Louis XV took him to Reims, and the Voltaire commission to Ferney on the Swiss border, he was living at the Louvre. What were his alternatives? Pigalle's exact contemporary, the pastel painter Jean-Baptiste Perronneau, traveled by *diligence*, or public stagecoach, as he crisscrossed France in pursuit of commissions for portraits in the 1760s and 1770s.[8] Stagecoaches for Reims left Paris from the Rue Saint-Martin every Saturday at 4 o'clock in the morning, and for Lyon—the first stage of the route to Ferney—at dawn every three days from Quai des Célestins.[9] The *Almanac royal* would have provided Pigalle with all the necessary information to plan his journeys and calculate the cost. Alternatively, he might have borrowed a carriage. In 1767 Cochin borrowed one from the wealthy art publisher Charles-Antoine Jombert to make his regular summer visit to the marquis de Marigny at his country house, Ménars.[10] It is possible that Pigalle's generous friend the abbé Gougenot made one available to him.[11]

Perronneau and Cochin, though they were using different kinds of transport—public and private, scheduled and unscheduled—both traveled in an open-ended manner, one that Tim Ingold calls "going along."[12] As they drove or were driven, both were alert, it seems, to the opportunities of the road, living it as they moved along. Perronneau, as Francesca Whitlum-Cooper has shown, scanned the markets at Lyon, Bordeaux, and Orléans for openings to paint, matching his movements to the economics of his environment, and Cochin, at leisure, looked for occasions to renew acquaintances and to visit places of interest.[13] Pigalle's journeys, whether undertaken by *diligence* or in his own carriage, were, by contrast, almost always determined in advance.[14] They were oriented toward a precise destination in fulfillment of a specific goal; with few exceptions, immediate return followed.

Travel for Pigalle was a matter of itinerary, not geography. An itinerary is a list of points or places through which to pass in order to reach your destination.[15] By the mid-eighteenth century, such itineraries could be bought as single sheets for a few sous from book and map sellers. Some were no more than a sequence of place names in geographical sequence, but by the mid-eighteenth century the cartographers Claude Sidone Michel and Louis-Charles Denos were publishing *L'Indicateur fidèle*, strip maps that outlined itineraries along a single route.[16] Sheet number 4, the route from Paris to Lyon (fig. 25), depicts two roads, the older, slower road for goods and local traffic along the Loire, and the new, fast, metaled "Route de la Diligence," for quick transit across the Île-de-France and the Nivernais to the Burgundy capital. The topography of the wider landscape is reduced to a minimum—just enough for the traveler "to see all the places through which

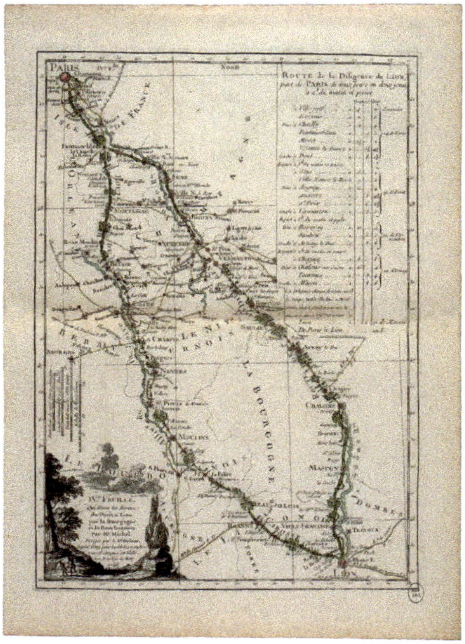

FIG. 25 Claude Sidone Michel and Louis-Charles Denos, "Route from Paris to Lyon," from *L'indicateur fidèle, ou guide des voyageurs* (Paris, 1767). Paris, Bibliothèque Nationale de France.

he must pass."[17] It represents, in a sense, the view from the carriage window.[18] Such was the speed of traveling by post, according to Arthur Young in 1787–89, that one saw "nothing"[19]—nothing, that is, but the "milestones," or rather the *toise*-stones that, with a fleur-de-lis, punctuated the distance traveled from Paris in units of a thousand *toises* (fig. 26). Carriage and itinerary isolated travelers perceptually and socially from the environment: it enabled them, as Michel and Denos proudly noted, to journey from point to point without having to scan the horizon for landmarks or stop and ask the way,[20] just follow their map with a finger.

Both carriage and map were agents of speed and mobility. Speed is also a leitmotif of contemporary accounts of Pigalle's journey to Ferney. According to baron Grimm, the sculptor promised to leave for the environs of Geneva "immediately" after the famous dinner chez Mme Necker in April 1770, at which the specifics of the Voltaire monument were decided, and the Swiss artist Jean Huber described with astonishment the speed with which the sculptor modeled Voltaire's likeness and then left, according to Grimm, without stopping to say goodbye.[21] Such accounts not only gloss over the practical difficulties that Pigalle must have faced on this trip, especially on the last leg from Lyon to Ferney, off the *grands chemins*, they also imply that the time of travel between points was dead time. Only destination mattered.

Can we conclude that Pigalle embraced a modern mode of travel, one structured by ends and made efficient by the *routes royales* built by the king's engineers at the Ponts et Chaussées, and by carriages designed for speed and long distance? In the case of *Voltaire nu*, such a conclusion would align developments in infrastructure with the expansion of

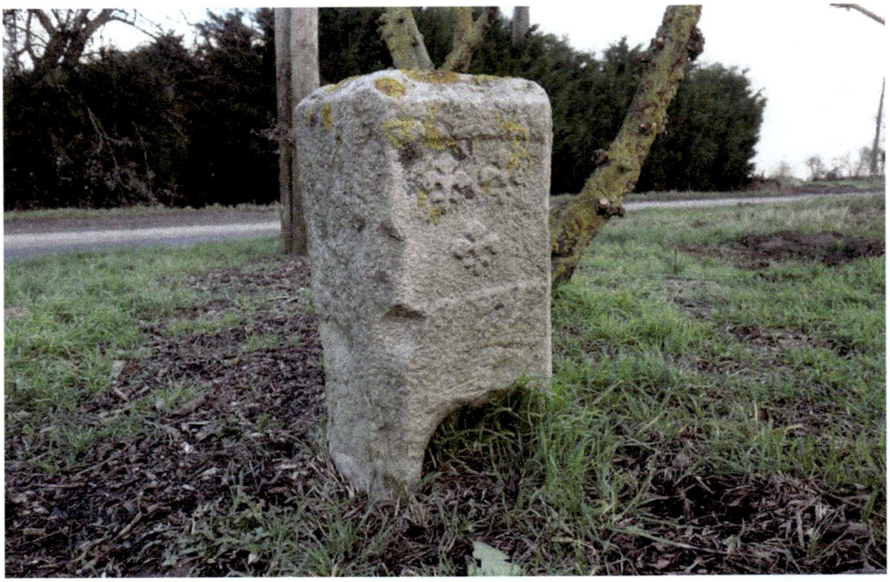

FIG. 26 French milestone with fleur-de-lis, eighteenth century. (Photo: Jpcuvelier, CC BY SA 4.0.)

the public sphere through the increased circulation of people, objects, and enlightened ideas.[22] However, the history of the maréchal de Saxe monument tells a different story. Commissioned in 1753 by the king, it was ready for installation by 1771. Saxe, the hero of Fontenay and victor of Louis XV's campaigns in Flanders during the War of the Austrian Succession (1744–48), was Protestant and could not be interred in a Catholic church, and therefore not in Paris. The mausoleum was destined for the church of Saint-Thomas at Strasbourg, part of the Alsatian lands conquered by France at the end of the seventeenth century and still predominantly Lutheran. The logistics of the tomb's transfer from Paris to Strasbourg were hugely complex. From the sources published by Jules Guiffrey in 1891 emerges a picture of energetic, efficient administration headed by the *directeur des bâtiments du roi*, the comte d'Angiviller, who between March 1775 and July 1776 secured the preparation of the site and the safe delivery and installation of the mausoleum.[23] He contracted hauliers for the medium-weight packing cases,[24] commissioned the design of special wagons for the heaviest from the king's mechanic, Antoine-Joseph Loriot,[25] organized passports for the convoys to exempt their loads from entry duties as they crossed into Alsace,[26] and generally coordinated the arrival of information, works, and personnel in good order and at the right time.[27] In d'Angiviller's bureaucratic imagination, space was abstract extension, and executive power radiated from its nodal point, Paris, along geometric lines to its destination.

Pigalle's centrism was quite different from both Enlightenment circulation and the lines of royal rule. In 1771 and again in 1774 he had attempted to overturn the decision to send the mausoleum to Strasbourg and to keep it instead in Paris.[28] For him, Paris was not a capital node at the center of a power grid but a locality, a place in itself, home of the arts, and, therefore, where the mausoleum properly belonged. He was unable to envisage Strasbourg as having any cultural resources. He sent a wooden hoist and other equipment in the packing cases, as if, the outraged *préteur royal*, baron d'Antigny, remarked, wood was in short supply at Strasbourg and the city had no carpenters.[29] His eagerness to travel to Ferney for the sake of a sitting, the better to execute a commission for Paris, turned to reluctance when the work was to be alienated: he visited Strasbourg for the first time in July 1776, arriving with the last of the dispatches from his studio.[30] The itinerary was for him less an invitation to travel—Michel's and Denos's *L'indicateur fidèle* is prefaced with a map of Paris in the form of a *patte d'oie* enticingly labeled with final destinations—than it was security for a rapid and safe homecoming.

If Pigalle did make use of his carriage for work *extra-muros*, he more likely actively enjoyed it, we can suppose, for excursions *intra-muros*. Public transport was again available, in the form of the *fiacre*, or taxicab; there were ranks in Pigalle's neighborhood at Montmartre du Mail and Porte Saint-Denis.[31] But, as Perronneau discovered to his cost when returning from petite Charône, a village in the northeast of Paris, a *fiacre* was not always on hand when you wanted one.[32] According to the *Dictionnaire de l'Académie française*, carriages were by definition things of convenience.[33] They were also, of course, always much more: a thing as well as means. From the moment the carriage was introduced to France in the early seventeenth century it was regarded as a luxury and was subject to sumptuary law.[34] In the early eighteenth century, the rule of ownership and of the decoration of vehicles was still a matter for the courts. Though enforcement lapsed in the 1720s, carriages continued to signify illegitimate and scandalous fortune in the luxury debate.[35] Thus, in the physical, social, and moral space of the eighteenth century, the carriage, as Daniel Vaillancourt has noted, polarized distinctions between the entitled and the not, between those forced to walk or hire, like Perronneau, and those able to drive.[36] In the second half of the eighteenth century, the boulevards in the west and northwest of Paris attracted those who wanted to be seen in their cars, transforming the road into a space of spectacle. Pigalle had been decorated with the Order of Saint Michel in 1769, reward for the Reims monument. According to Louis Réau, his escutcheon, by its choice of tools for charges—gold modeling tool and riffler rasp on an azure field—confirms Pigalle's natural modesty, though a nobleman.[37] Did his carriages, perhaps, say differently?

Pigalle's carriage was valued at 800 livres, his cabriolet at 300 livres, the harness and horses at 72 and 1,000 livres, respectively—valuations that exceeded most other things he owned, except his own sculpture.[38] The vehicles were well kept. The carriage had metal springs, a technological novelty, and the cabriolet was elegantly decorated: blue and white Utrecht velvet upholstery on the inside and green coachwork on the outside, the color of fashion in the 1770s, according to the *vernisseur* Jean-Félix Watin.[39] For a final flash of brilliance: silver buckles and ornaments decorated the harness.

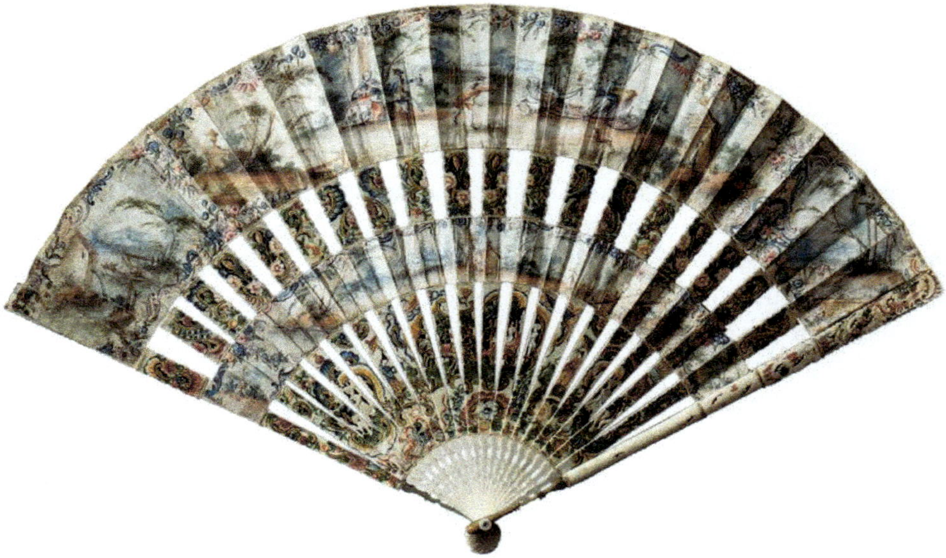

FIG. 27 Cabriolet fan, ca. 1755. Paper leaves, carved ivory guards, backed with mother-of-pearl, 28.5 cm (guardstick). London, Royal Collection, RCIN 25380. (Royal Collection Trust / © Her Majesty Queen Elizabeth II 2021.)

In contrast to fiction and satire, which in the eighteenth century often featured carriages, sometimes prominently as engines of narrative and foci of scorn, the carriage is largely inconspicuous in the pictorial record of the city. We grasp its ubiquity, luxury, and fashion only indirectly, from its regular appearance as a motif on luxury goods. On a so-called cabriolet fan in the Royal Collection (fig. 27), the cabriolet appears twice: in the scene of accident on the upper fan leaf and across the carved ivory sticks at the bottom. A pair of mandarins with parasols frame the carved cabriolet and its occupants. They, and the materials from which the fan is made—ivory, tortoiseshell, and mother-of-pearl—represented and embodied luxury in motifs and stuffs arriving in Paris from outside France: from China, India, the Caribbean, and the South Seas. What is remarkable about Pigalle's domestic luxe is, by contrast, the almost complete absence of the exotic: the Utrecht velvet of the cabriolet was produced at Amiens; Mme Pigalle's porcelain **teacups** were Sèvres, not Chinese; Pigalle did not collect **shells** and minerals; and his furniture was not made of *bois des Indes* but solid oak, walnut, and pine, and, moreover, it was upholstered in wool *moquette*, not silk.[40] His luxury was local, sometimes literally as well as metaphorically so. The house on Rue de La Rochefoucault was wallpapered throughout. In 1779 the firm Arthur and Grenard had established their wallpaper factory on the corner of Boulevard des Capucines and Rue Louis-le-Grand, a stone's throw south of Pigalle's dwelling. §

1. See, for example, Carl Nordenfalk, "The Stockholm Watteaus and Their Secret," *Nationalmuseum Bulletin Stockholm* 3, no. 3 (1979): 105–39; and Georg J. Kugler, *The Golden Carriage of Prince Joseph Wenzel von Liechtenstein* (New York: Metropolitan Museum of Art, 1985).

2. See Étienne La Font de Saint-Yenne, *Réflexions sur quelques causes de l'état présent de la peinture en France* (The Hague: Neaulme, 1747), 17–18; and Jean-Jacques Rousseau, "Discours sur les sciences et les arts," trans. Lowell Blair, in *The Essential Rousseau* (New York: New American Library, 1974), 220.

3. Nicolas Clément, *Sculpter au XVIIIe siècle: Jean-Baptiste Pigalle (1714–1785)* (Paris: Honoré Champion, 2014), 328.

4. "Carrosse," *Encyclopédie*, https://encyclopedie.uchicago.edu/, 2:705.

5. Guy Arbellot, "La grande mutation des routes de France au XVIIIe siècle," *Annales economies, sociétés, civilisations* 3 (1973): 765–91.

6. See "Correspondance de M. de Marigny avec Coypel, Lépicié et Cochin," ed. Marc Furcy-Raynaud, *NAAF*, 1904, 155–56.

7. Clément, *Sculpter*, 24–25.

8. See Francesca Whitlum-Cooper, "Itinerant Pastellists: Circuits of Movement in Eighteenth-Century Europe," PhD diss., Courtauld Institute of Art (London, 2015), 197–231.

9. See *Almanach royal* (Paris: Breton, 1764), 486 (Reims); and *Almanach royal* (Paris: Le Breton, 1770), 514 (Lyon).

10. See Paul Ratouis de Limay, *Un amateur orléanais au XVIIIe siècle: Aignan-Thomas Desfriches* (Paris: Champion 1907), 66–70.

11. On abbé Gougenot, see Hélène Guicharriaud, "Un collectionneur parisien, ami de Greuze et de Pigalle, l'abbé Gougenot, 1724–1767," *GBA* 134 (1999): 1–74.

12. Tim Ingold, *Lines: A Brief History* (London: Routledge, 2007), 72–103.

13. Whitlum-Cooper, "Itinerant Pastellists," 197–231.

14. See Samuel Rocheblave, *Jean-Baptiste Pigalle* (Paris: Lévy, 1919), 112–23.

15. On the itinerary see, Catherine Delano-Smith, "Milieus of Mobility: Itineraries, Route Maps, and Road Maps," in *Cartographies of Travel and Navigation*, ed. James Ackerman (Chicago: University of Chicago Press, 2006), 16–68.

16. *L'Indicateur fidèle, ou guide des voyageurs* (Paris: n.p., 1767). The sheets were regularly updated and reissued.

17. *L'indicateur fidèle*, "Prospectus du guide des voyageurs," unpaginated.

18. On the enclosure of carriages and the introduction of windows necessitating flat doors to lower them, see André-Jacob Roubo, *L'art du menuisier*, 4 parts in 5 vols. (Paris: Delatour, 1769–75), 3:496–509.

19. Patrick Marchand, *Le Maître de poste et le messager: Les transport publiques en France au temps des chevaux* (Paris: Belin, 2006), 87.

20. *L'indicateur fidèle*, "Prospectus."

21. See Louis Réau, *J-B Pigalle* (Paris: Tisne, 1950), 61–63.

22. See Dena Goodman, "Pigalle's *Voltaire nu*: The Republic of Letters Represents Itself to the World," *Representations* 16 (1986): 86–109.

23. See Jules Guiffrey, "Le Tombeau du maréchal de Saxe par Jean-Baptiste Pigalle: Correspondance relative à ce monument (1752–1783)," *Revue de l'art ancien et moderne* 7 (1891): 161–234. See also Clément, *Sculpter*, 154.

24. Guiffrey, "Le Tombeau," 204. See also AN, O^1/1905/2:125, an invoice for transportation submitted by the hauler Bricard, representing twenty-two days out and eighteen days return with the loss of three horses, total cost 7,200 livres.

25. Guiffrey, "Le Tombeau," 203, 213, 218.

26. Guiffrey, "Le Tombeau," 206–7. See also AN, O^1/1905/2:113, "Passavant en exemption des droits," 13/04/1775; and AN, O^1/1905/2:132, Memorandum by the *Fermiers générals* in defense of their rights to levy dues, 12 November 1776.

27. Guiffrey, "Le Tombeau."

28. Guiffrey, "Le Tombeau," 174–76, 184–87.

29. Guiffrey, "Le Tombeau," 215, 217.

30. Guiffrey, "Le Tombeau," 224.

31. See Bernard Causse, *Les Fiacres de Paris au XVIIIe siècle* (Paris: Presses Universitaires de France, 1972): map of the fiacre ranks in Paris.

32. Whitlum-Cooper, "Itinerant Pastellists," 220.

33. *Dictionnaire de l'Académie française*, 4th ed. (Paris: Brunet 1762), 1: s.v. "Carrosse."

34. See *Edit du roy pour le retranchement du luxe*, March 1700, in Nicolas De La Mare, *Traité de police*, 4 vols. (Paris: Brunet 1705–38), 1:419–23.

35. See Antoine Hatzenberger, "Luxe d'ostentation et luxe de mollesse: La critique rousseauiste des carosses," in *Architecture, Cultural History, Autobiography*, ed. Jonathan Mallinson, *SVEC* (Oxford: Voltaire Foundation, 2003): 227–42.

36. Daniel Vaillancourt, "Faire rouler la carosse, ou comment le XVIIIe siècle ne marche pas," in *Classical Unities: Place, Time, Action*, Acts of the 32nd Annual Congress of the North American Society for Seventeenth-Century French Literature, Tulane University, 13–15 April 2000, ed. Erec Koch, Biblio 17 (Tübingen: Narr, 2001), 45–55.

37. Réau, *J-B Pigalle*, 23.

38. AN, MC/ET/LVII/574, Jean-Baptiste Pigalle, "Inventaire après décès," 29 August 1785.

39. Jean-Félix Watin, *L'art du peintre, doreur, vernisseur* [1773], ed. Thierry Verdier (Montpellier: Pulm, 2005), 101–2.

40. Jean-Baptiste Pigalle, "Inventaire après décès," 29 August 1785, AN, MC/ET/LVII/574.

Color Box

Jean-Honoré Fragonard (1732–1806)

TYPE OF OBJECT	THEME	MATERIAL
Container, Tool	Global Commerce, Making, Studio, Travel	Plant Matter | Cork, Plant Matter | Wood, Synthetic Materials | Glass, Synthetic Materials | Paint/Pigment

Upstairs in the Villa-Musée Fragonard, in the southern French town of Grasse, where Jean-Honoré Fragonard was born, there is a shallow wooden box (fig. 28). Inside, its colorful contents immediately convey its function. Divided into nine compartments, the box is home to eighteen cork-stoppered glass bottles, slightly varied in shape, each filled with a different ground pigment and labeled by hand: Prussian blue, burnt sienna, carmine, etc. Along with the colors, the three compartments at the front are designed to house tools, with central dividers carved to a curve, so utensils can rest without rolling away. The bits and pieces left include an ebony stick, some well-worn blending stumps, and a fine brush darkened at the tip. Covered in marks and stains, this unassuming box is thought to have belonged to one of the best- and least-known painters of eighteenth-century France.[1] Celebrated for the distinctive painterly canvases that have secured his place in the canon of European art, Fragonard is nevertheless still surprisingly enigmatic as a person.[2] The color box thus presents a compelling material trace, promising a personal connection otherwise limited by archival sources. Now residing in a museum installed in the house of Fragonard's cousin, where the painter lived for a year in the 1790s, the color box offers vivid insights into the practicalities and economics of eighteenth-century art making and an alternative view of the materiality of Fragonard's painterly practice.

Of all the painter's tools, the **palette** might be the most symbolically recognizable, but color boxes were just as ubiquitous amid the paraphernalia of the eighteenth-century studio. In the imagined composite studio offered as initial vignette to the *Encyclopédie*'s plates on "Painting" (fig. 29), color boxes indeed become a defining feature of the space. Most evident is the *grande boîte à couleurs* in the foreground near the history painter's steps. More elaborate than a mere container, this genre of color box was a piece of furniture, with additional drawers for storage, and legs that made it a commodious height for use in the studio (handy for placing a brush or hanging a **handkerchief**). Fragonard's box, meanwhile, was a simpler kit, closer in form to that on the far left beside the portraitist, or that in the center beside the copyist scaling down a canvas. Without legs or drawers, this type was less furniture than storage case, not as capacious but eminently more transportable than its cumbersome legged relative. The *Encyclopédie*'s vignette suggests a taxonomy of color boxes in which size was related to specialization, as though painters of lesser genres required lesser tools. But the form of the box was actually more related to specification, that is, the context of its use. As a history painter Fragonard likely

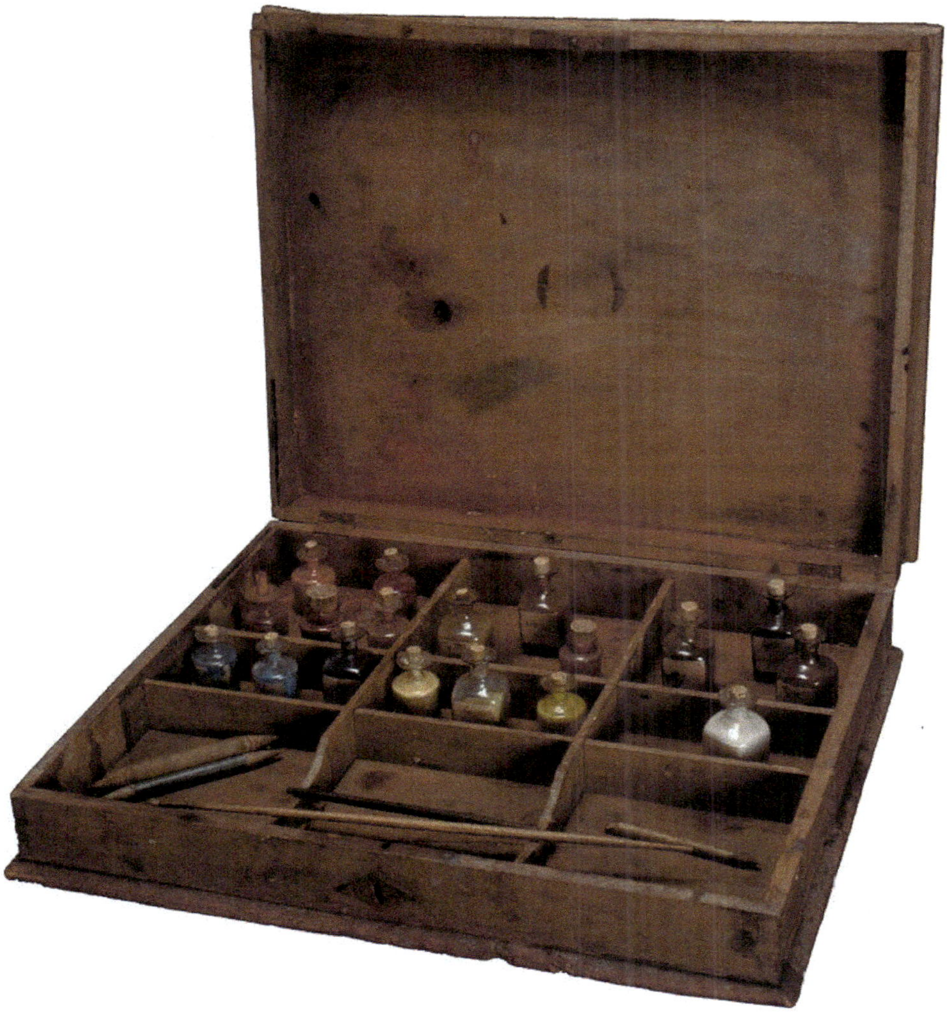

FIG. 28 Color box, eighteenth century. Wood, metal, glass, and various pigments, 10 × 46 × 37 cm. Grasse, Villa-Musée Fragonard. (Courtesy of Villa-Musée Fragonard, Grasse.)

kept a *grande boîte à couleurs* in his studio, but this smaller version was a tool customized for use outside that space.

The eighteenth century was not yet the era of plein-air painting, but it was a period when artists traveled. Whether on the short cross-town trip of a portraitist visiting an important client for a sitting, or longer journeys for out-of-town commissions or a European grand tour, artists often needed to transport their tools. From the physical evidence of use, Fragonard's box certainly did not lead a life confined to the studio. Punched through the lid are two metal clips or fasteners that once attached a leather handle (now perished) so it could be carried without upsetting the contents. Nevertheless, traces of bright-red pigment indelibly staining the wood inside the lid betray a mishap, perhaps a jostled explosion of vermilion. Another accident of transit is recalled in the

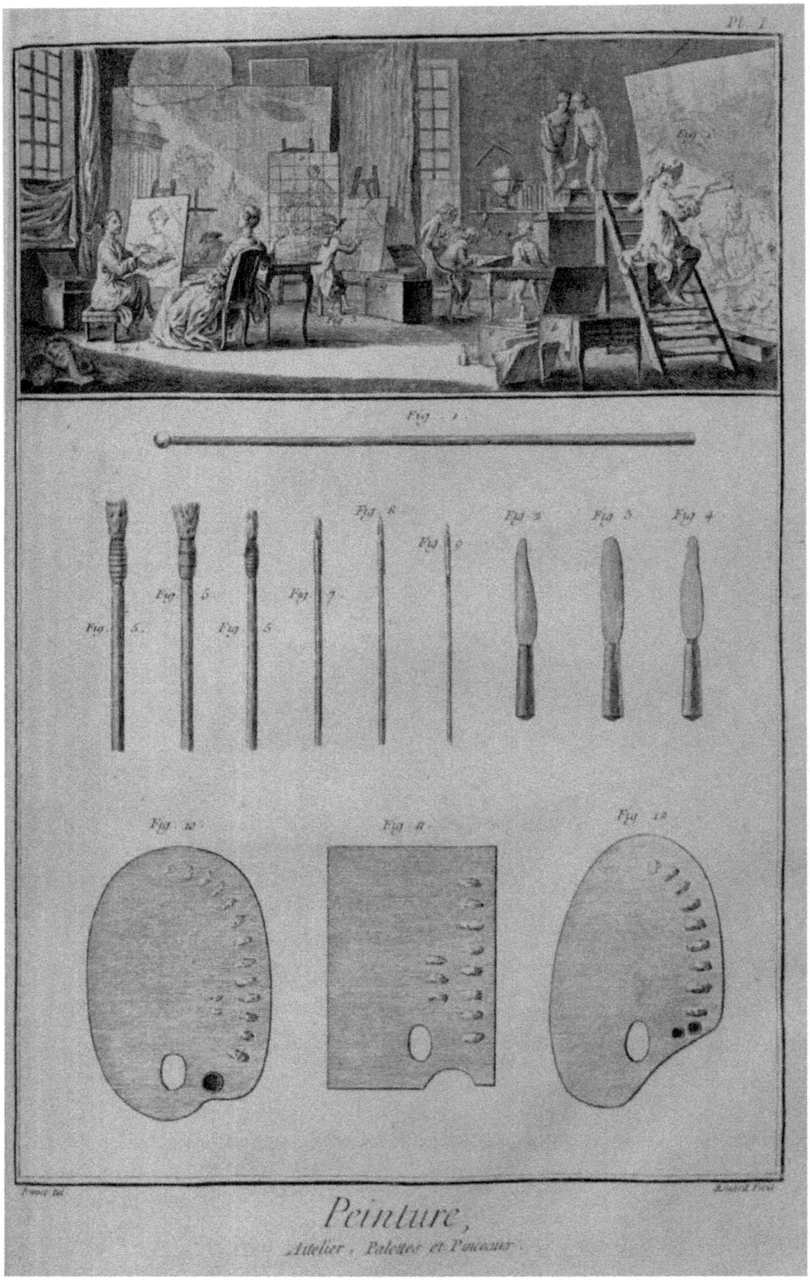

FIG. 29 "Painting" from *Recueil de planches sur les sciences, les arts libéraux et les arts mécaniques* (1765), plate I. (Image courtesy of the ARTFL Encyclopédie Project, University of Chicago.)

splintered wood and detached joint at one corner of the lid, while chips and scratches all over the exterior bear witness to a peripatetic life.

During his career, Fragonard undertook two substantial periods of travel.[3] His first journey began in 1756, when at the age of twenty-four he was sent to Italy as a *pensionnaire* to finish his training at the Académie's school in Rome.[4] It is even possible that this was when Fragonard acquired his color box. According to regulations issued later under Joseph-Marie Vien's directorship (which were quite possibly ratifications of already established customs), all new *pensionnaires* were supplied upon arrival with a color box and two palettes.[5] As they were encouraged to travel as part of their artistic formation, it is likely that this institutional color box was of the transportable variety. Fragonard returned to France in 1761 and then made his second grand tour between 1773 and 1774, this time under the patronage of Pierre-Jacques-Onésyme Bergeret de Grancourt, an *associé libre* of the Académie. Bergeret's journal records the extent of the trip's itinerary and its numerous participants: Bergeret, his son, a cook, two coachmen, and other servants, along with Fragonard and his wife, traveled from Paris, through France's Massif Central, along the Mediterranean coast into Italy, then north through Slovenia, followed by Vienna and Prague, and finally into Germany before heading home via Strasbourg.[6] The majority of works that survive from these trips, particularly the second, are drawings, but despite his focus on chalk and ink during the journeys, it is unlikely that Fragonard would have been without his colors for such a long period, making a traveling color box an essential piece of equipment.

If the box as container indicates the mobility in Fragonard's artistic practice, the contents attest to its persistent economies and labors, both to the complex commercial ecosystem of eighteenth-century colors and to the artist's physical activities in the studio. Color making in this period involved specialized materials, techniques, and supply chains, some of which stretched to a truly global scale. Inside the bottles in Fragonard's box, there are substances from at least three continents. From Europe, burnt sienna, Italian terra, and Naples yellow all came from Italy; from Africa, mummy brown was made from the ground remains of Egyptian mummies; and from Central America, carmine was made from cochineal beetles imported from Mexico or Honduras.[7] Other pigments were known as regional specialties: Prussian blue was derived from a chemical synthesis invented around 1706 in Berlin, where it was produced exclusively until the 1720s, when the secret of the recipe was published; lead white, meanwhile, was the product of an industrial process that was mastered particularly effectively by English manufacturers.[8] Interactions between artists, scientists, and entrepreneurs were crucial to the color industry's development. This is evident in Joseph-Siffred Duplessis's collaborations with chemists to perfect his **red lake**, but also in the regular occurrences in the Académie's minutes of new pigments being eagerly presented by their discoverers. In 1771 new ochers found on the estate of Baron de La Lézardière were tested by a group of academicians including Vien, Jean-Baptiste-Marie Pierre, Alexander Roslin, Jean-Siméon Chardin, and Joseph Vernet (notably a heterogenous sample of history, portrait, still-life, and landscape painters). Proving successful, the new ochers were certified by the Académie, but not all were so fortunate.[9] In 1781 the chemist Louis-Bernard Guyton de Morveau proposed a new zinc white as a safer alternative to lead white (which smelled foul and caused serious health problems with long-term exposure).[10]

Despite its benefits, the academicians who tested the zinc alternative reported a litany of faults: it was difficult to grind finely and so less tractable on the brush; it was too transparent; it took a long time to dry and stayed tacky on the fingers; and the resulting color was "sad."[11] No surprise, then, that the white of choice in Fragonard's box remained "blanc de plomb" (lead white).

When it comes to the question of procurement, we do not know where exactly Fragonard bought his colors. But eighteenth-century Paris had no shortage of suppliers from which to choose. This was the period when the specialized trade of *marchands de couleurs* (color merchants) began to develop, emerging on one side through the *épicier* (grocery) trade and on the other through guild artists, who were more able than academicians to supplement their incomes through commercial ventures. One grocer-cum-color merchant from the beginning of the century, Louis Picard, referred to himself generically as a *marchand épicier*, but his trade card shows that his shop—*Au Mortier d'Or* (At the Golden Mortar)—specialized in artists' supplies (fig. 30). The trade card evokes a shop counter adorned with a garland of palettes, brushes, and pig-bladder pouches (used for preserving premixed paints) hung over the eponymous golden mortar in which the pigments were ground. Behind are dozens of drawers where the raw pigments were stored, many with legible labels familiar from Fragonard's box ("blanc de plomb," "cendre bleu," etc.). Located near the Châtelet, Picard's shop was in one of the areas of Paris's Right Bank that became something of a color quarter. Along with numerous shops on or around Rue Saint-Denis—including *À la Momie* (named after the Egyptian brown pigment), *Le Bon Broyeur* (The Good Grinder), and *Le Gros Mailletz* (The Big Mallet)—this area extended up to the Porte Saint-Martin, a part of the city dense with both guild artists and color merchants (who were sometimes both).[12]

Expansion of the color trade offered artists a greater range of materials, and also a change in the practicalities of their own profession. A price list published by Jean-Félix Watin, a color merchant in the 1770s, suggests the choices between labor and economy now open to painters.[13] Take yellow, Fragonard's signature color: stil de grain was 2 livres per pound if bought "en pierre" (as stones or fragments), but double if bought finely preground; a cheaper option was yellow ocher, which was only 2 sols per pound "en pierre," and 4 sols when ground. Some pigments could even be bought already suspended in a binder, prepared for different uses: "blanc de céruse" mixed for laying undercoats, or "blanc de plomb" mixed for finishing. Many artists still preferred to grind and mix their own pigments, giving them more control over quality. But the process was labor intensive. To prepare the pigments found in Fragonard's color box, the basic tools required were a *molette* (muller) and a marble or porphyry slab (both visible in the *Encyclopédie* vignette near the *grande boîte à couleur*, see fig. 29). Raw materials had to be ground on the slab using the *molette* with small amounts of solvent (water, oil, or turpentine) to limit the dust. Once ground, the residue was left to dry on paper while all the equipment was thoroughly cleaned before the next color to avoid contamination.[14] Dried pigments could be stored in airtight containers, like Fragonard's cork-stoppered bottles, until needed, when they would

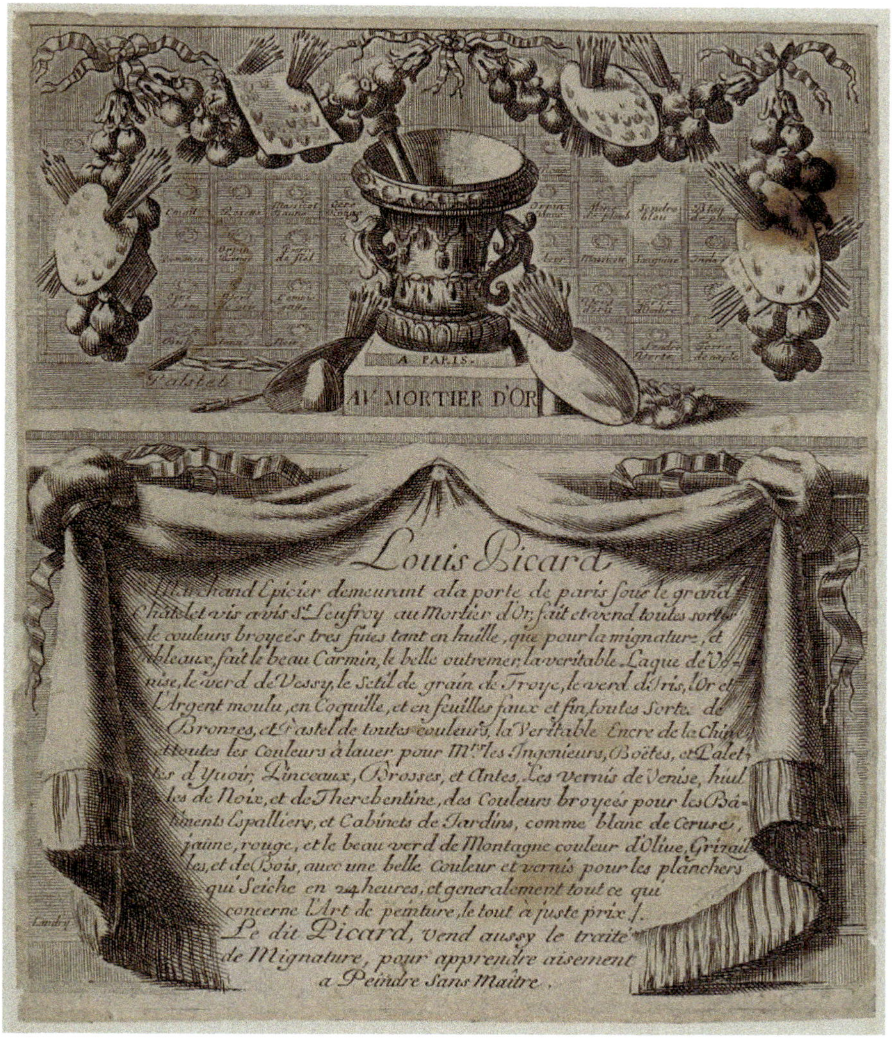

FIG. 30 Pierre Landry (French, 1630–1701), *Trade Card of Louis Picard, Marchand Épicier, Au Mortier d'Or*, ca. 1695. Etching and engraving, 24 × 20 cm. Waddesdon Manor. (Waddesdon Image Library.)

be mixed with oil (usually linseed or walnut). But mixed pigments had a limited life, so all these operations were being performed constantly, sometimes with the aid of apprentices or assistants. As each pigment had its own properties and peculiarities, this required a complex body of tacit knowledge, secret recipes, and jealously guarded procedures, passed from master to student in that alternative pedagogic space of the studio. Fragonard's training with François Boucher is frequently acknowledged, but we seldom envisage that relationship in terms of a transfer of practical know-how, instead focusing on a more creative lineage of style and subject matter, as though the two were not inherently linked.

Oily stains inside the lid of Fragonard's box draw attention to this less abstract, more applied side of eighteenth-century color. Upon encountering this material object, familiar art-theoretical debates seem to fade; discourses about color and line, harmony and resemblance give way to the practicalities of messy, volatile substances that required scientific knowledge to produce, money to buy, and labor to prepare.[15] For an artist who, more than any of his contemporaries, produced an oeuvre defined by the rich materiality of paint, such a realization is arresting. In the textured surface of a work like *Head of an Old Man* (fig. 31), paint is treated almost sculpturally, as the viscous liquid is modeled into forms (the scroll of an ear; the curl of a moustache). Fragonard does not delineate features and fill them with color, nor does he imitate hair and skin by layering wispy strokes over smooth; instead, he builds the man's face with paint, forming his features through gestures of the brush. Scholars have interpreted Fragonard's approach (especially in his so-called fantasy portraits) through a history of ideas that explains them alternatively via cultural traditions of the imaginary, Enlightenment "sensationist" philosophy, or art-theoretical adaptations of courtly aesthetics.[16] For Mary Sheriff, those paintings are an artistic encapsulation of *sprezzatura*—that nonchalance that makes effort appear effortlessness.[17] But Fragonard's color box is a reminder of precisely the opposite. Like a before and after, the pigments in those little bottles recall the hours of physical labor required to transform raw materials into usable colors, not to mention the cost of procuring them. In that light, Fragonard's heavily laden canvases take on a sense of artistic generosity, a material trace of his investment of time, labor, and expense, as though each artwork places us in the presence of a munificent host.

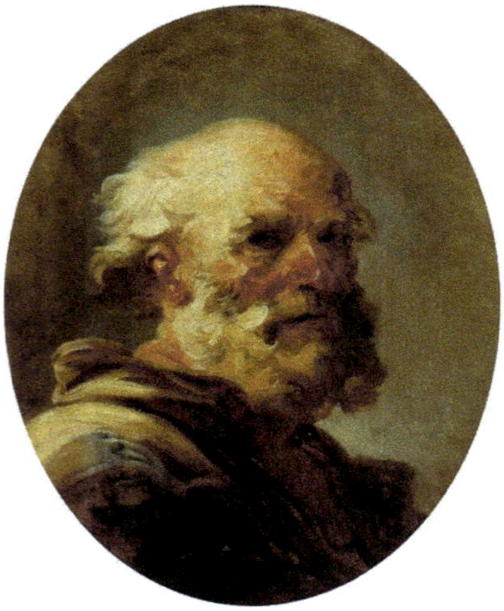

FIG. 31 Jean-Honoré Fragonard (French, 1732–1806), *Head of an Old Man*, detail, ca. 1765. Oil on canvas, 54 × 45 cm. Amiens, Musée de Picardie, inv. M.P.Lav.1894-144. (Photo Marc Jeanneteau /Musée de Picardie.)

On the outside of the box, across its lid, there is a final trace of ownership in a curious inscription, just visible amid the scratches and stains. Rather than a description of the box's contents or the name of its owner, someone at some point instead wrote the word *L'amour* (Love), a floating signifier claiming some affective relationship to something. Now at the Villa Fragonard, the box's inscription calls attention to the erstwhile presence there of Fragonard's most famous commission—*Les progrès de l'amour* (*The Progress of Love*, The Frick Collection, New York)—which, in an unexpected way, leads to the end of Fragonard's career and a possible explanation for the box's survival. In 1790, amid the events of the Revolution and the death of his daughter, Fragonard fell ill and left Paris for the warmer climes of Grasse, bringing his wife, his sister-in-law (the painter Marguerite Gérard), and his young son (the future artist Alexandre-Évariste).[18] For some reason, he also brought the four rolled canvases of *The Progress of Love*, a series notoriously rejected by Madame du Barry in the 1770s.[19] In Grasse, Fragonard sold them to Alexandre Maubert, his first cousin once removed, from whom he was renting the villa, and they were installed in the salon on the ground floor until they were sold a hundred years later by Maubert's descendants.[20] Like the paintings, the color box also ended up in Maubert's possession, perhaps left behind after Fragonard returned to Paris the following year. As the story of his **armchair** relates, Fragonard stopped painting around this time. But his color box bears evidence of continued use, one of its bottles containing chrome yellow, a pigment derived from chromium, which was not discovered until 1797.[21] Far from being preserved as a relic of Fragonard's practice, the box was evidently adopted by another (possibly Gérard or Alexandre-Évariste), who gave this useful thing at least a few more years of valuable service. ‡

---

1. Attribution rests on its provenance through Fragonard's family and chemical analysis of the contents. François Delamarre and Bernard Guineau, "La boîte de couleurs dite 'de Fragonard': Analyse du contenu des flacons," in *Jean-Honoré Fragonard, peintre de Grasse*, exh. cat. (Grasse: Villa-Musée Fragonard, 2006), 25–31.

2. *Fragonard*, exh. cat. (New York: Metropolitan Museum of Art, 1987), 15.

3. *Fragonard*, 61–71, 361–70.

4. Fragonard was awarded the Académie's *grand prix* in 1752, then entered the École des Élèves Protégés from 1753 to prepare for Rome. On the Académie de France in Rome during this period, see Reed Benhamou, *Charles Natoire and the Académie de France à Rome: A Re-evaluation* (Oxford: Voltaire Foundation, 2015).

5. Vien was director in Rome from 1775 to 1781. Article IV, "Règlemens qui doivent être observés par les pensionnaires de l'Académie de France à Rome," in *CDR*, 13:159.

6. *Bergeret et Fragonard: Journal inédit d'un voyage en Italie, 1773–1774* (Paris: May et Motteroz, 1895). See also Pierre de Nolhac, "Fragonard en Italie d'après le journal de Bergeret de Grancourt," *Revue des deux mondes* 41 (1917): 613–29.

7. For the colors in Fragonard's box, see Delamarre and Guineau, "La boîte de couleurs," 27–28. On the composition of eighteenth-century colors, see Le Pileur d'Apligny, *Traité des couleurs matérielles, et de la manière de colorer, relativement aux différens arts et métiers* (Paris: Saugain & Lamy, 1779).

8. Alexander Kraft, "On the Discovery and History of Prussian Blue," *Bulletin of the History of Chemistry* 33, no. 2 (2008): 61–67; and R. D. Harley, *Artists' Pigments c. 1600–1835: A Study in English Documentary Sources*, 2nd ed. (London: Butterworth, 1982), 70–74, 166–72.

9. 23 August 1771, *PV*, 8:82.

10. 29 September 1781, *PV*, 9:80. In 1783, the Royal Society of Arts in London offered a prize for a harmless method of preparing lead white, without much success. Harley, *Artists' Pigments*, 168–69.

11. 22 June 1782, *PV*, 9:114; and 6 July 1782, *PV*, 9:116.

12. Martine Jaoul et al., *Des teintes et des couleurs* (Paris: RMN, 1988), 52–53; and Hannah Williams, "Artists and the City: Mapping the Art Worlds of Eighteenth-Century Paris," *Urban History* 46, no. 1 (2019): 106–31.

13. Jean-Félix Watin, *L'art du peintre, doreur, vernisseur*, 2nd ed. (Paris: Grangé, 1773), n.p.

14. Watin, *L'art du peintre*, 58–60.

15. On color in art theory, see Jacqueline Lichtenstein, *The Eloquence of Color: Rhetoric and Painting in the French Classical Age*, trans. Emily McVarish (Berkeley: University of California Press, 1993).

16. See Mary D. Sheriff, *Fragonard: Art and Eroticism* (Chicago: Chicago University Press, 1990); and Melissa Percival, *Fragonard and the Fantasy Figure: Painting the Imagination* (Farnham: Ashgate, 2012).

17. Sheriff, *Fragonard*, 120–23

18. Pierre Cuzin, "Fragonard, un Grassois à Paris," in *Jean-Honoré Fragonard, peintre de Grasse*, exh. cat. (Grasse: Villa-Musée Jean-Honoré Fragonard, 2006), 19.

19. Colin B. Bailey, *Fragonard's Progress of Love at the Frick Collection* (London: D Giles, 2011).

20. Cuzin, "Fragonard," 20.

21. Robert L. Feller, ed., *Artists' Pigments: A Handbook of their History and Characteristics* (Washington: National Gallery of Art, 1986), 1:187–217.

Crayon

Jean-Baptiste Huët (1745–1811)

TYPE OF OBJECT	THEME	MATERIAL
Tool	Education, Invention, Making, Studio	Mineral | Chalk, Synthetic Materials | Paper

***Crayon* is a generic term for a commonplace object** found in every eighteenth-century studio.[1] In spite of its ubiquity, we know little about it. We grasp the *crayon* only indirectly, through its products: the mass of sketches, studies, and drawings it drew forth. However, a set of four chalk head studies by the painter Jean-Baptiste Huët, reproduced by Louis-Marin Bonnet sometime after 1780 (fig. 32), allows us to begin to understand the *crayon* from the other end. The prints inform the viewer that the specific *crayons* used by Huët had been manufactured by André Nadaux, whose shop was located on the Rue de la Vieille Draperie, Île de la Cité.[2] They were sold in packets of a dozen, wrapped in blue paper and sealed with wax stamped with a fleur-de-lis.

Nadaux, a printmaker, draftsman, and natural scientist, was also a shopkeeper and specialist supplier of artists' *crayons*.[3] In 1780 he bought the exclusive rights to the "secret" of his *crayons de composition* from Gabriel Dumarest, a "draftsman" on the Pont Notre-Dame. From the contract of sale between the two tradesmen we learn that for an annuity of 200 livres, Dumarest agreed to provide Nadaux with recipes for assorted *crayons* and a written explanation of the techniques necessary to their production.[4] In addition, he consented to assist Nadaux practically in mastering the "secret," time and inclination permitting. Before Conté, it seems, therefore, *crayons* were produced on a small scale and that the integrated process could only be fully transferred by demonstration.[5]

Dumarest had built up his business in the 1750s supplying the Académie and its members, a market that Nadaux hoped to take over, notwithstanding the fact that in the deed of sale Dumarest expressly declined to recommend Nadaux's *crayons* to his former clients. Undaunted, Nadaux presented a copy of the notarized contract to the Académie in April 1780 in order to obtain its imprimatur and formal recognition of himself as Dumarest's legitimate successor.[6] In October, he successfully petitioned the Maison du Roi for the title of *Fabrique Royale de crayons de composition*, and at the very end of the year he published an account of his success together with a full description of his products in a pamphlet for which he designed an ostentatious frontispiece (fig. 33).[7] Where, as Charlotte Guichard has argued, Bonnet's prints after Huët sought to attract the attention of amateurs, Nadaux's pamphlet strongly suggests that his *crayons* were primarily things for professional use.[8] Indeed, such allegedly was his concern for the Académie and its members that he promised to discount the price of his *crayons* for its students.[9]

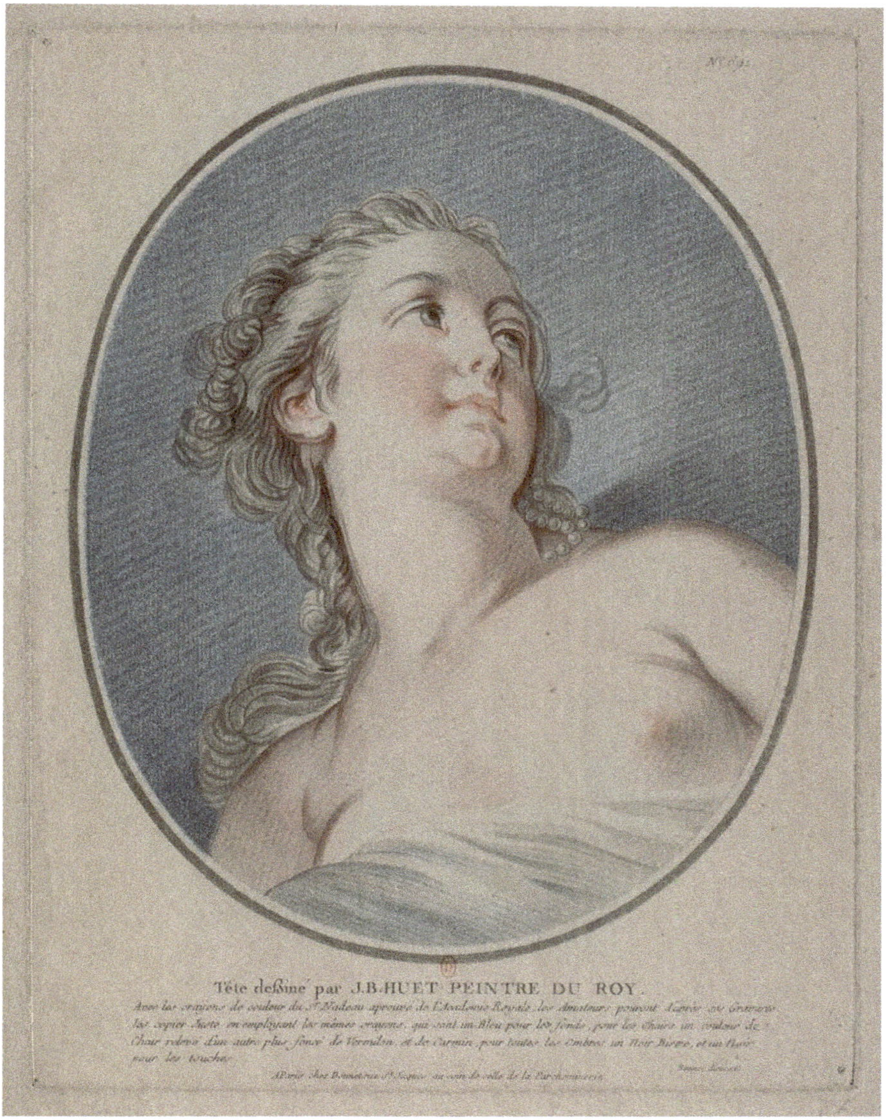

FIG. 32 Louis-Marin Bonnet (French, 1736–93), after Jean-Baptiste Huët (French, 1745–1811), *Head of a Woman*, after 1780. Crayon-manner etching, 47.4 × 36.5 cm. Paris, Institut National d'Histoire de l'Art.

Intimately associated with the conceptual dimension of art, with the contours of thought, how can we understand the thingness of this thing, that which emerges only in practice? Nadaux was not willing to divulge his secret; the matter and composition of his *crayons* remains unknown.[10] However, if we divert our attention from the mystifications of his publicity and redirect it at his critique of conventional drawing materials, his *crayon* will become historically present to us in new ways. Nadaux stressed the flaws in naturally occurring red and black chalk and in charcoal. He described the ways in which impurities interrupt the flow of the drawing line and how the frangibility of some minerals compromised both the permanence and price of the *disegno*. When natural sanguine is too

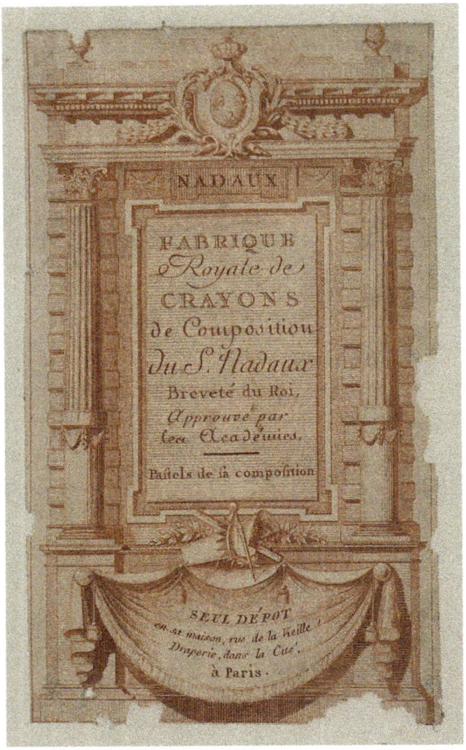

FIG. 33 André Nadaux, Frontispiece, 1780. Crayon-manner etching. Paris, Archives Nationales. (Waddesdon Image Library, University of Central England Digital Services.)

soft, the pencil point breaks; when it is too dry and hard, it "skins" the support.[11] Dry charcoal is, he notes, unstable, and lines drawn using it often detach themselves from the paper; meanwhile, the vitriol in oiled charcoal attacks the paper, and the linseed oil with which it is infused can turn black lines a brassy yellow.[12] In these instances of breakdown, we momentarily glimpse the thingness of *crayon*;[13] simultaneously, we are also made aware of the socially and culturally encoded values attributed to the properly functioning object. That is to say, that the qualities that Nadaux singled out as virtues of his alternative, "chemically" produced compounds were those that, metaphorically speaking, were also said to define properties of rational thinking: firmness, clarity, integrity, coherence, stability, and permanence. The challenge is to find the materiality in this (drawing) instrument, which seems precisely to disavow it.

Nowhere was the conceptual thinking associated with drawing made more explicit than in the teaching at the life school, and in so-called *académies*, drawings of the nude (fig. 34).[14] The male nude was its focus because, according to tradition, the complexity of man's body was such that study of it encompassed all others for shape and shading, line, and light. The uncompromising, categorical division that the "firm" line contours between figure and ground coupled with the complications of the human body led Charles-Antoine Jombert to propose problem-solving techniques: an ocular compass for the perceptual measurement of symmetries and alignments of the body's parts, and for calculation of their relative proportions, or an abstract, mental grid of perpendicular lines to net the body and allow the draftsman to grasp the angles of deviations of the body's curves.[15] Such strategies of process predate, of course, the invention of Dumarest-Nadaux's *crayons* but what these *crayons*, offered in terms of improved flow, evenness, and firmness very likely promoted further the role of perception and strategic thinking over motor control of the medium as the defining art of drawing.

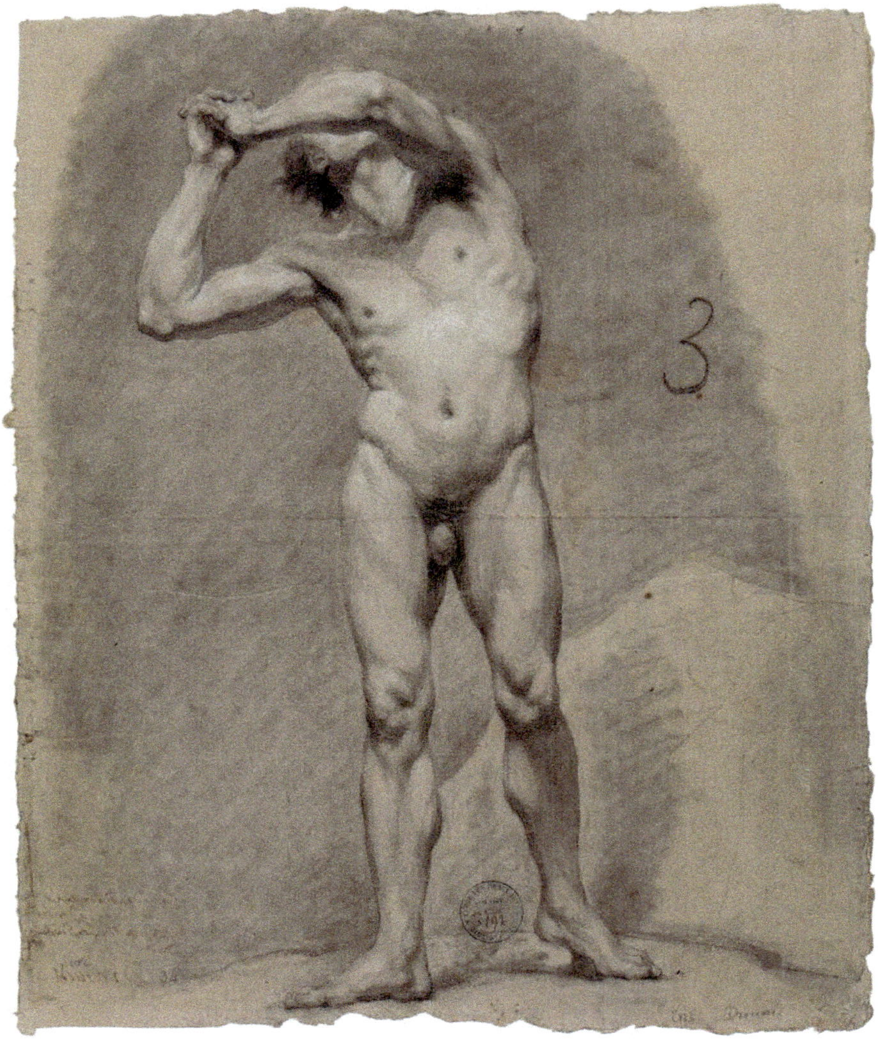

FIG. 34 Jean-Germain Drouais (French, 1763–88), *Academy Study*, 1778–79. Black chalk on paper, 54.6 × 44.5 cm. Paris, École Nationale Supérieure des Beaux-Arts, EBA2883. (Art Resource / NY.)

If we can say that the material properties of drawing media enabled and furthered the development of cognitive thinking, that thinking nevertheless returns to the body, both the physical and the social body. Not just in the anecdotal, everyday sense that *crayons* were often pocket objects for artists,[16] doubly intimate, by physical proximity and by association with bread (*crayon*'s eraser), but also because in terms of art's objects, the body was not only its greatest challenge, it was also its most familiar and intimate subject: experienced and known from the inside. Calculation of shape and size were made in relation to the artist's own (generally male) body, and in relation to the drawing tools that did its duty.[17] In Charles Natoire's depiction of the life school (fig. 35), a student in a black hat, on the far right, raises his pencil to measure the proportions of the models before him. *Crayon* holders (***porte-crayons***) were, according to Claude-Henri Watelet, a standard size: a demi-pied (half foot).[18] Units of measure in the eighteenth century were based on the body: thumbs, hands, feet, stride. For the eighteenth-century artist, the body was by default the site of skilled perception, or what Jombert termed "*justesse*" (accuracy).[19]

That mathematical and geometrical sensibility was not developed in isolation and alone but in the thick of the drawing school: with others. The arrangement of the benches and desks in tiers and in a semicircle around the model, as shown in Natoire's watercolor, served to activate the young draftsman's proprioception and allowed him to learn from his awareness of his own body's position in relation to those of others, as well as from the object of his task. Above–below, near–far, greater–smaller, before–behind were experienced as the material conditions of perception as well as the syntax of visual representation.

Natoire's image depicts not only the arrangement of persons and things in his narrative of learning, it also encodes social values. The beginners are positioned unchaired and below the more advanced students, and the professor sits before, enthroned in the foreground. He, possibly Natoire himself, holds his students to order, a discipline he enacted not only formally by his rank but also by his posing of the model and through the matter of *crayon*. According to Jombert, professors often forbade students to sharpen their pencils more than once during a drawing session, and in so doing compelled them to reproduce the hierarchies of sharp outline (*trait*) and blunt shading, representation and illusion, that were the foundation of the humanistic theory of art.[20]

At the time that Huët had bought and was using Nadaux's *crayons*, he had long since left the classroom. For him, as no doubt for the purchasers of Bonnet's prints after his *Têtes de femmes*, the attraction and value of Nadaux's products lay in their colors—red, blue, and green.[21] Arguably that freedom to cherish *crayons* on grounds other than line was won by the prior internalization of linear values to the point that habituation pushed them below the level of conscious notice. §

---

1. We have chosen the French *crayon* over the English *pencil* because a pencil refers to a drawing tool with a graphite core, whereas *crayon* is an inclusive noun whose meaning included charcoal, black and red chalk, and pastel, in addition to graphite. For contemporary definitions, see Jacques Lacombe, *Dictionnaire portatif des beaux-arts* (Paris: Hérissant & Estienne, 1752), s.vv. "Crayon," "Crayons," "Crayonner"; Antoine-Joseph Pernéty, *Dictionnaire portatif de peinture, de sculpture et de gravure* (Paris: Bauche, 1757), s.vv. "Crayon," "Crayonner." For the evolution of *crayons* into modern pencils, see Henry Petroski, *The Pencil: A History of Design and Circumstance* (London: Faber & Faber, 1989).

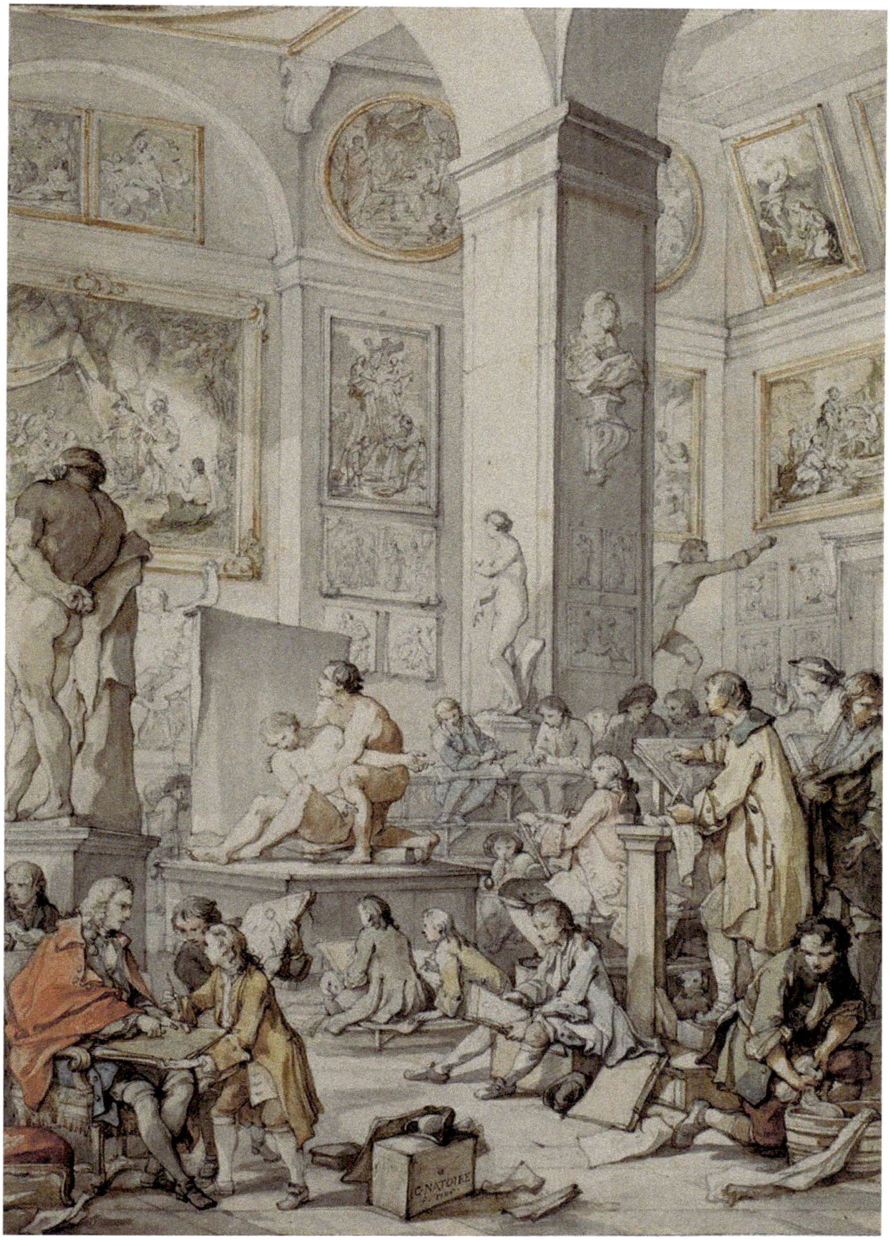

FIG. 35 Charles Natoire (French, 1700–1777), *Life Drawing Class*, 1746. Pen, black and brown ink, gray wash, and watercolor, 45.3 × 32.2 cm. London, Courtauld Institute of Art. (The Courtauld, London [Samuel Courtauld Trust], photo © The Courtauld.)

---

2. On the prints, see Jacques Hérold, *Louis-Marin Bonnet (1736–1793): Catalogue de l'oeuvre gravée* (Paris: Société pour l'Étude de la Gravure Française, 1935).

3. On André Nadaux (1726–1800), see Neil Jeffares, *Dictionary of Pastellists before 1800*, http://www.pastellists.com/Articles/Nadaux.pdf.

4. *Constitution viagère*, 12 February 1780, AN, MC/ET/CIX/751.

5. On the transformations in manufacturing brought about by Nicholas-Jacques Conté, see Petroski, *The Pencil*, 70–78.

6. *PV*, 9:19.

7. For the correspondence between Antoine-Jean Amelot and the comte d'Angiviller on this matter, see AN, O^1/1916:1780/345, 355, 356.

8. Charlotte Guichard, *Les Amateurs d'art aux XVIIIe siècle* (Seyssel: Champ Vallon, 2005), 244–45.

9. André Nadaux, *Fabrique royale: Description et analyse des crayons de composition* (Paris: Nadaux, 1780). See AN, O^1/1674/171, 174, 175 on Charrier, former laboratory assistant to Claude de Bernières at the Ponts et Chaussées, who lived at the Louvre and claimed to have invented "crayons de composition" that he sold to Académie students in the 1780s.

10. Nadaux refused to reveal his secret and forfeited a medal awarded him by the Société d'émulation for its invention; see Lilianne Hilaire-Perez, *Invention technique au siècle des Lumières* (Paris: Albin Michel, 2000), 214–15.

11. Nadaux, *Fabrique royale*, 9–10.

12. Nadaux, *Fabrique royale*, 28–30.

13. On "thingness," see Bill Brown, "Thing Theory," *Critical Inquiry* 28, no. 1 (2001): 1–22.

14. See *L'Académie mise à nu*, exh. cat. (Paris: ENSBA, 2009), especially cat. no. 26.

15. Charles-Antoine Jombert, *Méthode pour apprendre le dessein* (Paris: Jombert, 1755), 59–60. See also Trevor Marchand, "Towards an Anthropology of Mathematizing," *Interdisciplinary Science Reviews* 43, nos. 3–4 (2018): 295–316.

16. Charles-Antoine Jombert, following de Piles, warned students against pocketing *crayons* because body heat dried them out. See Jombert, *Élémens de peinture pratique par M. de Piles* (Paris: Jombert, 1766), 39.

17. On mathematizing in the arts, see Marchand, "Towards an Anthropology of Mathematizing," 295–316.

18. "Dessein," *Encyclopédie*, https://encyclopedie.uchicago.edu/, 4:890.

19. Jombert, *Méthode*, 59–60.

20. Jombert, *Méthode*, 64.

21. Nadaux, *Fabrique royale*, 33–34.

Decoration

Joseph-Marie Vien (1716–1809)

TYPE OF OBJECT	THEME	MATERIAL
Apparel, Ritual Thing, Symbolic Thing	Identity, Memory	Metal | Gold/Gilding, Synthetic Materials | Paint/Pigment, Textile | Silk

It is not often that we know the exact moment an artist acquired a possession. At the end of January 1776, three months after Joseph-Marie Vien moved to Rome to become director of the Académie de France, a courier arrived from Paris bearing a package.[1] Inside was an item that Vien had been anticipating for months—his official regalia as a *chevalier* in the Order of Saint Michel—an honor he had been granted before he left for Italy. Proudly displayed in his portrait by Duplessis painted a decade later (fig. 36), the decoration that Vien received in that package consisted of the usual two parts: a black riband to be worn as a sash across the body and, hanging from it, a gold badge with the insignia of the order. The insignia's design dated from the 1660s, when this late medieval chivalric order had been revived by Louis XIV, and consisted of a Maltese cross outlined in white enamel, with four gold fleurs-de-lis at the angles, and a central gold oval with a partially enameled relief of Saint Michel, or the Archangel Michael (fig. 37).[2]

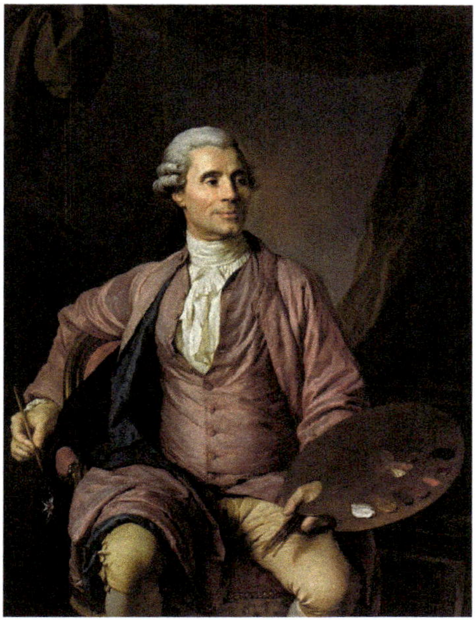

FIG. 36 Joseph-Siffred Duplessis (French, 1725–1802), *Joseph-Marie Vien*, 1785. Oil on canvas, 133 × 100 cm. Paris, Musée du Louvre, INV4306. (© RMN-Grand Palais / photo: Michel Urtado. / Art Resource, NY.)

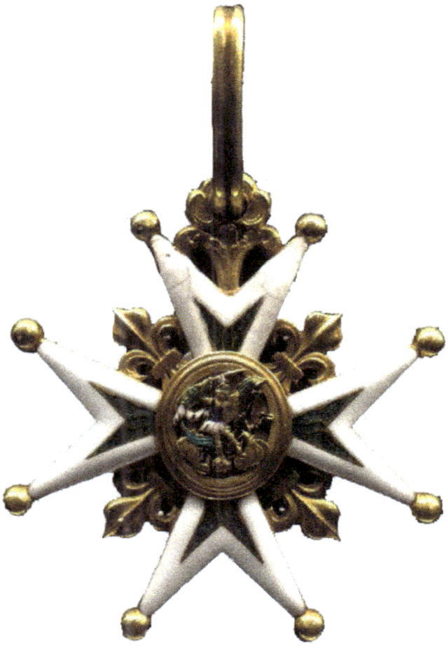

FIG. 37 Decoration of the Order of Saint Michel, eighteenth century. Gold and enamel. Paris, Musée de la Légion d'Honneur et des Ordres de Chevalerie, Gift of the marquis de Champreux, 1912, inv. 0160.

In a book filled with tools and other active objects busily working, enabling, and creating, Vien's chivalric decoration might seem like a thing that *did* very little. Even as an item of clothing, it was more accessory than garment, an auxiliary addition that performed no protective or practical service and was, perhaps not surprisingly, usually categorized as an item of *bijoux* (jewelry) in estate inventories.[3] But for some things, purpose lies more in meaning than action. And it would be difficult to find in these pages a more semantically charged item than this wearable insignia, whose principal function was, after all, significance itself.

The semantic operations of Vien's decoration reside in its very name. *Décoration* was a word that, as Katie Scott has argued, carried two distinct but entwined meanings in eighteenth-century France: a "mark of honor" indicating rank or title, and an "embellishment [or] ornament" that enhanced a space or, in this case, a person.[4] As a mark of honor, Vien's decoration conveyed his specific chivalric title through the insignia's symbolic details, from the fleur-de-lis of the House of Bourbon to the iconography of Michael slaying Satan in the form of a dragon. But when worn on the person as an embellishing accessory, this decoration served as a marker of elite status long before such specific detail could be appreciated. Its functionality in this regard stemmed precisely from its lack of function. As an ornamental addition, it was an item of apparel designed for a socially restricted sartorial circuit, where superfluity was both affordable and necessary. In other words, only someone with a status to convey required an item whose sole purpose was to convey status.

While a decoration's raison d'être was to signify, exactly what Vien's own decoration signified was ironically somewhat ambiguous, partly because of what the Order of Saint Michel had become, and partly because of Vien's specific position within it. In 1665, when Louis XIV revived the order, the decoration had been an irrefutable sign of noble status. According to the original statutes, the requirements for becoming a *chevalier* were (along with being Catholic and over thirty) hereditary nobility through at least two branches, and ten years' service in the military or law, the two spheres represented by the nobility of the "**sword**" and of the "robe."[5] But by the time Vien received his, things had shifted. Nobility was still a requirement, but according to Benoît de Fauconpret's demographic analysis of membership, 69 percent overall were actually *anoblis*—individuals granted noble status, usually specifically so they could be admitted to the order—while only 11 percent were hereditary nobles.[6] Moreover, from 1701, very few traditional members of the nobility were admitted at all, with *chevaliers* instead being drawn from the professions, among them doctors, merchants, manufacturers, architects, and, of course, artists.[7] Along with Vien, other painters who received this ennobling honor included Hyacinthe Rigaud, Carle and Louis-Michel Van Loo, Jean-François de Troy, Charles-Joseph Natoire, Noël Hallé, and Jean-Baptiste Pigalle (who wears his decoration in Giroust's portrait, see fig. 130).[8] Thus, while the decoration continued to signify membership of a chivalric order, the order itself had subtly but surely evolved: from one honoring hereditary noble status to one lauding professional merit. Indeed, when the comte d'Angiviller wrote to Vien confirming his title, he described it as "a reward for your talents" and "an object of emulation for everyone pursuing the same career as you."[9] Given its steady evolution into an award for professional achievement, the Order of Saint Michel is now even perceived as a forerunner to Napoleon's Légion d'honneur, the imperial order of merit that replaced the old orders of chivalry.[10]

The decoration delivered to Vien in 1776 was thus potentially an empty signifier, floating without a clear referent, and certainly no longer meaning what it had a century earlier. But for Vien, this was no concern whatsoever. However it might have shifted, the Order of Saint Michel was still the preeminent honor an artist could attain, a highly sought and much cherished sign of success. More urgently still, in Vien's new role as director of the Académie de France in Rome, the decoration was also to serve as a crucial accoutrement for navigating the Italian city's appearance-conscious society, in which, as d'Angiviller described it, a hefty weight was placed on "external marks" of status.[11] By the 1770s, following the long directorships of de Troy and Natoire, both of whom were admitted as *chevaliers* during their tenure, the decoration had essentially become part of the Rome package. As soon as Vien was appointed, d'Angiviller immediately set about acquiring the chivalric order for his new director, as though it were simply part of the administrative process.[12] Yet in this context, as the decoration edged from sign of nobility to professional award, and then seemingly to requisite tool of office, the distance between signifier and signified slipped even further. This was particularly so in the case of Vien. For at the moment the courier arrived with his decoration—that ostensible marker of noble status and membership of the Order of Saint Michel—Vien was in fact technically neither.

Though Vien's admission to the order had been approved in September 1775, he had to leave for Rome before the next stages of the process could occur.[13] Unable to attend a chapter meeting in Paris for the official ritual of reception, Vien was left in the liminal state of *admis et non reçu* (admitted but not received) and not yet entitled to wear the order's regalia.[14] Indeed, it was not until seven years later, after Vien had returned to Paris, that he would eventually be ennobled by Louis XVI (via the **letters** patent issued on 13 March 1782) and soon after officially received as a *chevalier* of Saint Michel.[15] For Vien's mission to Rome, d'Angiviller had to solicit special permission from the king authorizing the painter to wear the order's sash and cross before he had the right to do so, a process of administrative negotiation that took some time, which is why the decoration had to be sent by courier months after Vien's departure.[16]

With so much semantic ambiguity in every direction, one might imagine some reticence on Vien's part when it came to his status as a *chevalier*, at least during his time in Rome before the honor had been fully conferred. But that would be to underestimate the power of the object. For while Vien was certainly quick to ratify his status upon returning to Paris, it seems that, for the painter, the real moment of achieving that status occurred seven years earlier, when the courier arrived with his parcel. From the letter that Vien wrote to d'Angiviller immediately afterward, it is evident that this was the day he felt he became a *chevalier*. With the decoration finally in his possession, he offered heartfelt thanks to the minister for "the honor, which you obtained for me and which I have just received," as though the medal itself had just conferred his new title.[17] This is not to suggest that Vien was superficially privileging appearance over substance, valuing the external marker of status more highly than the status itself, but rather that the two were inseparable from each other: to acquire the decoration was to become the thing it represented. Such an understanding was perhaps even more persistent for someone like Vien, the son of a locksmith, who was made noble rather born it, who achieved his title through success rather than blood. After all, for the *anoblis*, nobility could only ever be legitimated by a "thing" (whether a chivalric decoration or letters patent), an object whose materiality could manifest the very substance they lacked.

Whatever Vien lacked in noble blood, he certainly made up for in the eighteenth-century's emergent metric of success, and given the political events to come soon after his ennoblement, success would certainly prove the more valuable currency. It would actually be difficult to imagine a more successful artistic career than Vien's, with his ascent to the top steadily passing every rank and role in the art world. Admitted by the Académie in 1754, he was elected *adjoint à professeur* only three months later and then *professeur* in 1759, thus reaching career grade by the age of forty-three.[18] After that he began climbing his way through prestigious administrative posts, first securing the directorship of the Académie's École des Élèves Protégés (1771) and then the directorship of the Académie de France in Rome (1775).[19] Even from Italy, he managed to continue his promotion in absentia through the Académie's internal ranks, being elected *Adjoint à recteur* (1778) and then *recteur* (1781) so that upon his return from Rome he was poised to make his final ascent.[20] Named *chancelier* of the Académie in 1785, he eventually reached the peak in 1789, when he was elected *directeur* of the Académie and made *premier peintre* (first painter) to the king.[21]

Vien's was undoubtedly a superlative career, but timing could have been his downfall, for he claimed the summit of those institutional structures right as they were about to crumble, only two months, in fact, before the storming of the Bastille. Yet though Vien remained the king's man, leading the Académie Royale until its final demise in 1793, the Revolution did not mark the end of Vien's success.[22] Indeed, Vien's greatest skill of all perhaps was his ability to work a system, and once a system was reestablished in Napoleon's First Empire, Vien found himself redecorated in the regalia of a new regime. Like the counterpoint to Duplessis's portrait of 1785 (see fig. 36), Gabrielle Capet's group portrait of 1808 shows Vien in this fresh guise (fig. 38), dressed as a member of France's new order of nobility—an imperial count—and on his chest, where he once wore his Order of Saint Michel, a flash of red ribbon draws the eye to his new decoration: *commandeur* in Napoleon's Légion d'honneur.[23] What is perhaps most interesting in this coda is not that Vien survived the rupture, but rather that—as these decorations suggest—rupture is not always the best way to understand this moment of French history. After all, the Order of Saint Michel had become an order of merit long before the Légion d'honneur, and despite

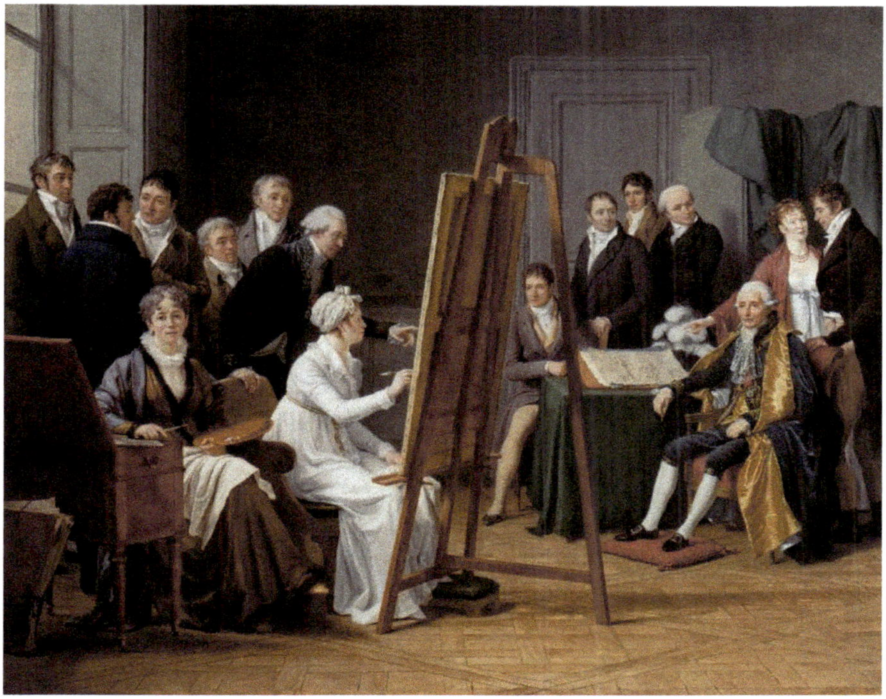

FIG. 38 Gabrielle Capet (French, 1761–1818), *Adélaïde Labille-Guiard Painting the Portrait of Joseph-Marie Vien*, 1808. Oil on canvas, 69 × 83.5 cm. Munich, Neue Pinakothek, Inv. FV 9. (bpk Bildagentur / Neue Pinakothek/Bayerische Staatsgemaeldesammlungen/ Munich / Art Resource, NY.)

the different systems they represented, an ancien régime *chevalier* and an imperial *commandeur* might have more in common than their accessories. ‡

---

1. Joseph-Marie Vien to comte d'Angiviller, 31 January 1776. *CDR*, 13:188. Vien recounts the moment in his memoirs, but he misremembers it happening only a fortnight after his arrival: Thomas Gaehtgens and Jacques Lugand, *Joseph-Marie Vien: Peintre du roi, 1716–1809* (Paris: Arthena, 1988), 313.

2. Founded in 1469 by Louis XI, the Order of Saint Michel was the oldest (though not the most senior) of the French chivalric orders. The insignia is described in the 1665 statutes: *Statuts de l'Ordre de Saint Michel: Ordonnances et règlements rendus en conséquence* (Paris: Imprimerie Royale, 1728), 11.

3. For example, Louis-Michel Van Loo, "Inventaire après décès," 22 April 1771, AN, MC/ET/LVI/166.

4. "Décoration," *Dictonnaire de l'Académie française*, fourth edition (1762). The importance of this relationship in architecture is elaborated in part two of Katie Scott, *The Rococo Interior: Decoration and Social Spaces in Early Eighteenth-Century Paris* (London and New Haven: Yale University Press, 1995).

5. Article IV, *Statuts de l'Ordre* (1728), 8.

6. These are percentages for all members from 1660 to 1790 with traceable biographies. Benoît de Fauconpret, *Les chevaliers de Saint-Michel, 1665–1790: Le premier ordre de mérite civil* (Paris: P. du Puy, 2007), 47.

7. Fauconpret, *Les chevaliers*, 91.

8. On artists who were made *chevaliers* of the order, see [Jules Guiffrey], *Lettres de noblesse accordées aux artistes français (XVIIe et XVIIIe siècles)* (Paris: Dumoulin, 1873), 40–44. On artists who were ennobled, see Louis de Grandmaison, "Essai d'armorial des artistes français," *Réunion des sociétés des Beaux-Arts des départements*, part 1 (Paris: Plon-Nourrit, 1903), 296–403; part 2 (Paris: Plon-Nourrit, 1904), 589–687.

9. D'Angiviller to Vien, 26 September 1775. *CDR*, 13:135.

10. Fauconpret, *Les chevaliers*, 97–100.

11. D'Angiviller to Charles de Vergennes, 18 September 1775. *CDR*, 13:131.

12. Beginning with his letter to Vergennes, 18 September 1775. *CDR*, 13:131.

13. Vien's admission was approved in Vergennes to d'Angiviller, 23 September 1775. *CDR*, 13:134.

14. Natoire experienced the same state of limbo and actually remained in it because he did not return to Paris between his admission to the order in 1756 and his death in 1777.

15. On Vien's ennoblement and reception into the order, see Grandmaison, "Essai d'armorial" (1904), 660–62; and [Guiffrey], *Lettres de noblesse*, 38–39.

16. D'Angiviller to Vergennes, 4 December 1775. *CDR*, 13:169.

17. Vien to d'Angiviller, 31 January 1776. *CDR*, 13:188.

18. *PV*, 6:383, 391; and *PV*, 7:95.

19. *PV*, 8:70, 200.

20. *PV*, 8:341; and *PV*, 9:69.

21. *PV*, 9:255; and *PV*, 10:12.

22. On Vien's role in the revolutionary politics of the Académie, see Nicolas Mirzoeff, "Revolution, Representation, Equality: Gender, Genre, and Emulation in the Académie Royale de Peinture et de Sculpture, 1785–1793," *ECS* 31, no. 2 (1997–98): 153–69.

23. On Vien's post-revolutionary career, see François Aubert, "Joseph-Marie Vien (sixième article)," *GBA* 23 (November 1867): 475–82.

Document Box

Secretaries of the Académie Royale (1650–1793)

TYPE OF OBJECT	THEME	MATERIAL
Container, Document, Ritual Thing	Administration, Community, Louvre	Animal | Leather/Parchment, Metal | Bronze, Metal | Gold/Gilding, Plant Matter | Wood

Still residing today in the archives of the Académie at the École Nationale Supérieure des Beaux-Arts, there is a leather chest that witnessed a century and a half of institutional life (fig. 39). Like the other things in this book that once occupied the Académie's rooms—the concierge's **funeral book** or Jean-Antoine Houdon's **écorché**—the *secrétaire*'s document box is one of those rare traces that restores a sense of materiality to an institution that is often largely dematerialized in the narratives of art history, abstracted into ideas of cultural ideology, art theory, and pedagogy. By contrast, the long life of this well-used object reveals aspects of the lived experience of its members, from administrative practicalities and habitual customs to singular dramatic events and divisive community conflicts.

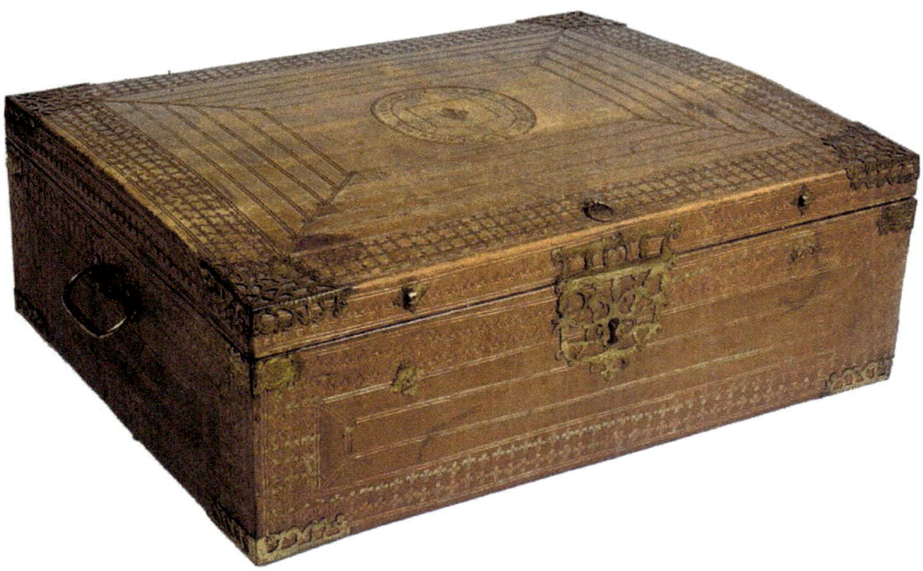

FIG. 39 The Académie's document box, ca. 1655. Paris, École Nationale Supérieure des Beaux-Arts, MU 12579. Gilding, brass, Morocco leather. 19.8 × 54.3 × 43 cm. (© Beaux-Arts de Paris, Dist. RMN–Grand Palais / Art Resource, NY.)

As an item of property, the document box has a complex status that draws attention to the personal in the professional in this art-world space. Legally it belonged to the

Académie, serving as the vessel for the very documents that constituted that institution as an entity in ancien régime law. In practice, however, it was possessed by a succession of individuals, in the form of the Académie's secretaries, each of whom became the box's temporary custodian during his long term in office, usually held from nomination until death. Thus, while the box belonged in some sense to every member of the Académie—and thus to nearly every artist in this book—it had a much closer connection to the tenures of the six artists who served as *secrétaire* and keeper of the box's **key**: Henri Testelin (1650–81), Nicolas Guérin (1681–1714), François Tavernier (1714–25), Bernard Lépicié (1737–55), Charles-Nicolas II Cochin (1755–90), and Antoine Renou (1790–93).[1] While most of these artists would have known only the secretary who came before or after, the box created a material link between them all. Passing from hand to hand—kept but never owned—it was not only a container for legal documents but a repository of shared institutional heritage, recalled in the thing itself and in the ritualized practices that its keepers performed.

Those ritualized practices developed over the box's long and fairly mundane professional career as an item of administrative equipment. Along with its sedentary daily charge of preserving the Académie's official papers, the box performed a more active annual rite. Every January, at the first meeting of the year, the *secrétaire* carried the box into the assembly room, opened it, took out the *Statuts*, and read aloud the articles that the assembled members had all sworn to uphold.[2] This little annual ceremony was never written down as an official regulatory practice, but the company's minutes reveal that it began somewhat organically at the end of the 1670s and continued right through the eighteenth century, with every *secrétaire*—from Testelin to Renou—participating in this habitual rite to mark the start of the year and reiterate the collective aims and ideals of this community.

The box's working life thus unfolded quietly and rhythmically, but it started very differently. Indeed, the origins of those ritualized practices actually took shape two decades earlier, during its incredibly dramatic entry into the world as the ceremonial focus of a pivotal event. The box's beginnings are inextricably linked with a founding legend of the Académie as it was recorded by Testelin and retold in the eighteenth century in the official *Mémoires pour servir à l'histoire de l'Académie*.[3] At its formation in 1648, the Académie had notoriously set itself in direct opposition to the Guild of Painters and Sculptors. But in 1651 the rival institutions attempted a reconciling *jonction* (union) to serve their mutual ends: the guild masters looking to profit from the Académie's privileges; and the academicians seeking to secure the *lettres patentes* (letters patent) that the guild had hitherto been opposing.[4] Not surprisingly, the *jonction* was a disaster. Remaining loyal to the supremacy of the guild, the masters persistently threatened the Académie's stability with their large numbers, disrupting meetings and inciting discord.[5] By 1654, the academicians were fed up and started planning an elaborate coup to oust the obstreperous masters once and for all.[6] Led by Charles Le Brun and with the patronage of Antoine de Ratabon, they began meeting in secret to arrange three crucial documents: a new set of

Statuts; a *brevet* from the king ensuring royal support; and the long-awaited *lettres patentes* that would grant legal legitimacy. When all three had been passed by the Paris Parlement in June 1655, the academicians set about preparing for a ceremonial showdown, in which the document box would make its début performance.[7]

Calling a general assembly, the plotting academicians set the stage the night before, secretly decorating the meeting room. Its walls were hung with rich tapestries and, at the far end, a table was installed along with three **armchairs**, all covered in sumptuous red velvet and gold trim.[8] When the masters arrived the next morning, they realized something was up, but before they could react, three coaches drew up outside, and the senior academicians descended, with Testelin, as *secrétaire*, carrying the new ceremonial box acquired for this moment. Processing the full length of the room, Testelin placed the box upon the table. Ratabon, as *directeur*, took his place on one of the armchairs, leaving the others symbolically empty for the absent *protecteur* and *vice-protecteur*, positions recently accepted by two of the most powerful men in France, Cardinal Mazarin and Chancellor Séguier. With the power and patronage of the court established, Ratabon declared that he spoke at the command of the king to bring the Académie new graces and privileges from its bountiful monarch. At this point, he turned to the *secrétaire* and ordered the opening of the chest.

Testelin rose and took from the box the three precious documents for which it had been made, and which would in turn "make" the Académie. Unfurling them over the table, he began to read aloud. First, the *brevet du roi*, granting the Académie privileges including an annual income and new lodgings in a royal building. Next, the *lettres patentes*, legally ratifying these privileges and granting others, in particular that the Académie had the sole right to conduct life drawing classes. Finally, the new *Statuts*, whose twenty-one articles Testelin turned to last. When he reached Article IX—decreeing that only elected officers would now hold voting rights—the impact of the coup started to resonate; an indignant rumble emanated from the masters as they realized their majority numbers were now worthless.[9] As Testelin concluded his reading, the masters rose, remonstrating passionately and, in a dramatic flurry, gathered their retinue and exited the meeting, never again to return to the Académie.[10] That was the end of the *jonction*. But that moment reinforced a bitter institutional rivalry that would continue for over a century, until the guild was eventually disbanded in the 1770s.

Although its leather has discolored from blue to brown and much of its gilding has worn away, the box is still recognizable from its description in the *Mémoires* as the ritual object borne by Testelin: "a small chest of blue leather covered with gold fleur-de-lis, decorated with gilt silver . . . and adorned on top with the arms of the Académie."[11] The box's materiality reveals the functionality—both practical and symbolic—for which it was always intended. This "small chest" is actually a fairly large box (around 20 by 54 by 43 centimeters—the size of a small suitcase): sizeable enough to accommodate the grand format of the legal parchments (when folded) (fig. 40), but still comfortably carried by a single person, grasping the handles at each short end. Decorative gilt-metal mounts on every corner provide reinforcement where contact and pressure were most likely for an object designed to be moved around, while the hinges and rings permit ease of opening for contents that needed to be accessed. The lock fitted for security suggests the considerable value ascribed to the contents, but with its single closure mechanism (the simplest kind of chest lock available), it seems no imminent threat of theft was anticipated.[12] The box's design also addressed its symbolic functions. Ownership was inscribed directly in the words on the lid, ACADEMIE ROYALE DE PEMTVRE ET SCVLPTVRE, while the arms—a fleur-de-lis in a shield—made clear the extent of the institution's elite and powerful patronage. A symbol of the French crown, the fleur-de-lis is actually repeated all over, as the shape of the tooled pattern bordering each face of the chest, thus ensuring that the Académie's royal connections were established from every angle. In short, the institution's document box was entirely fit for purpose: a bespoke, transportable, lockable, and ideologically decorated container, with administrative functionality and ceremonial gravitas.

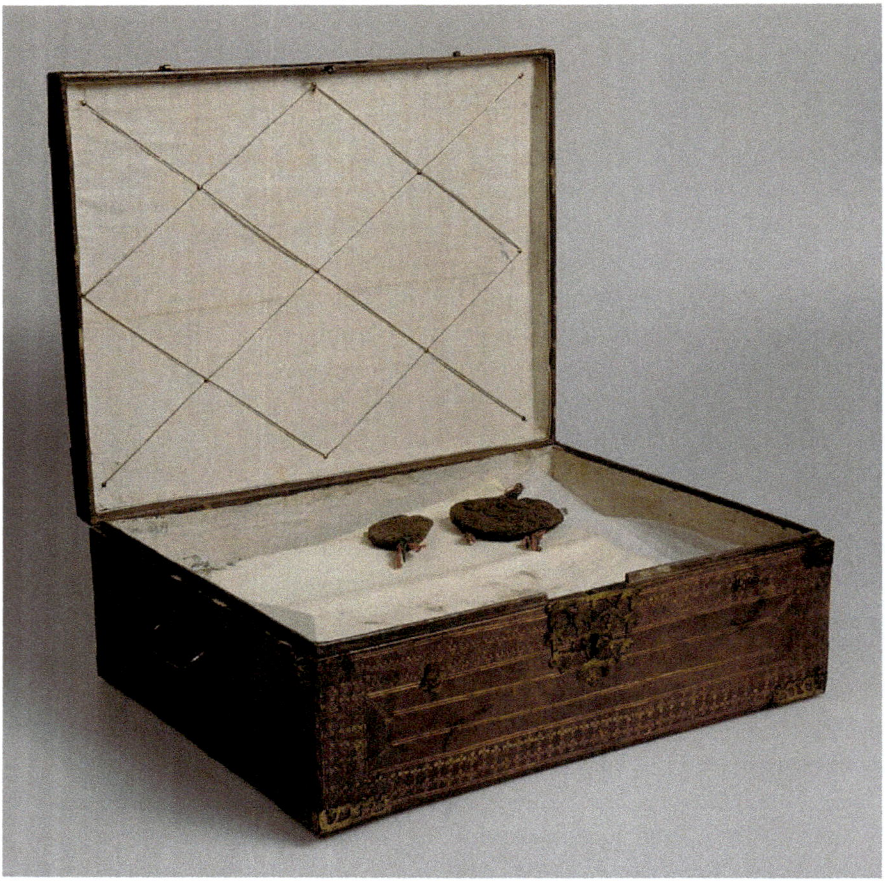

FIG. 40 The Académie's document box (open), ca. 1655. Paris, École Nationale Supérieure des Beaux-Arts, MU 12579. Gilding, brass, Morocco leather. 19.8 × 54.3 × 43 cm. (© Beaux-Arts de Paris, Dist. RMN-Grand Palais / Art Resource, NY.)

Despite the contrast between the box's dramatic beginnings and its quieter subsequent career, as an object, its function changed very little. From start to finish, it served as the receptacle for the Académie's official documents and as a vehicle for institutional rituals. What did change, however, after that inaugural entry, was its mode of being, as it transitioned from theatrical prop to everyday equipment. In the academicians' coup, the document box was an indispensable part of a staged performance, captivating attention and orchestrating the climax. The documents could have been carried on their own, but inside the box they were kept intriguingly hidden until the crucial moment of their reveal. At the same time, the box elevated the status of those pieces of parchment, conveying that their symbolic value far exceeded their material worth. But, for the box, this was a one-time performance. While there were always echoes of its past in those later ritualized annual practices, the box would never again perform its task in the guise of a prop, in such a ceremonial manner, on such a theatrical stage, or with such a riveted audience.

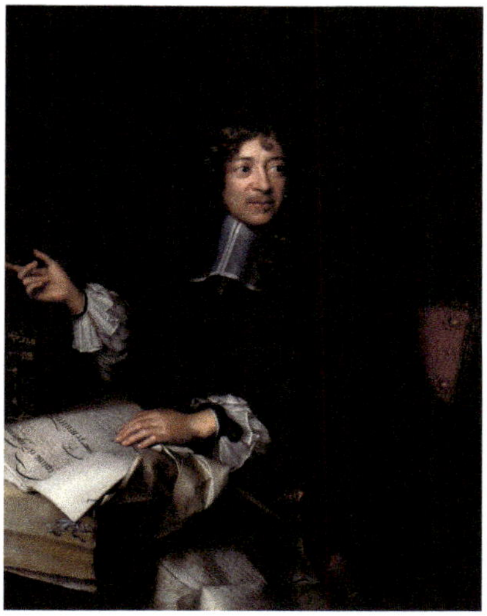

FIG. 41 Jean Tiger, *Henri Testelin*, 1675. Oil on canvas. 116 × 89 cm. Châteaux de Versailles et de Trianon, MV3585. (© RMN-Grand Palais / photo: Gérard Blot / Art Resource, NY.)

Whatever the relationship between the box and its eighteenth-century keepers—Guérin, Tavernier, Lépicié, Cochin, and Renou—theirs was a slightly different lived experience from that of Testelin, its original guardian, with whom it had that additional poignant history. It is perhaps no coincidence then that only Testelin ever had himself painted with the box (fig. 41). Recognizable from its original description and from its current state, the blue leather box with gilt metal mounts sits quietly under the elegant gesture of Testelin's pointing hand in his official Académie portrait, thus serving as his defining professional attribute. His other hand rests on the box's precious contents, pressing down the central fold of the *Statuts* as though he were about to launch into the annual recital of the institution's rules and regulations. Hanging in the Académie, this portrait immortalized not only its sitter but also the box and its ritualized customs, giving them an iconic status in the institution's past, even as the material thing itself continued to exist and operate in the present. Indeed, for the *secrétaires* that followed, this painted representation of the box may have proved a self-reflexive presence in their own working lives. Installed in the Académie's Salle des Portraits, the portrait was not only next door to the company's meeting room but hung such that Testelin was perpetually pointing to its door.[13] Thus, every January, as the current *secrétaire* brought the box for the customary reading of the statutes, it would be carried past its official portrait, in a passage that instilled that annual rite with the symbolic echoes of its original foundational act. ‡

1. The role was also held by Louis-François Dubois de Saint-Gelais (1725–37), an amateur but not an artist. On the Académie's *secrétaires*, see Hannah Williams, *Académie Royale: A History in Portraits* (New York: Routledge, 2015), 46, 57–61.

2. The first new-year reading of the *Statuts* took place on 7 January 1679. *PV*, 2:142. On that occasion, it was noted that the practice would be repeated on the last Saturday of every quarter, so it is possible that the box served in more regular rituals than the annual reading.

3. *Mémoires pour servir à l'histoire de l'Académie royale de peinture et de sculpture*, ed. Anatole de Montaiglon, 2 vols. (Paris: P. Jannet, 1853). This text was described in a meeting on 1 February 1772 as "Mémoires de M. Testelin, rédigés par feu M. Hulst, Honoraire Amateur." *PV*, 8:94.

4. *Mémoires pour servir*, 1:95–96.

5. *Mémoires pour servir*, 1:111–31. On the history of the Académie and the period known as the *jonction*, see Christian Michel, *The Académie Royale de Peinture et de Sculpture: The Birth of the French School, 1648–1793*, trans. Chris Miller (Los Angeles: Getty Publications, 2018), 18–20.

6. *Mémoires pour servir*, 1:162–64.

7. *Mémoires pour servir*, 1:173, 179–80.

8. *Mémoires pour servir*, 1:181.

9. "Articles que le roi veut être augmentés et ajoutés aux premiers statuts et règlements de l'Académie Royale de Peinture et de Sculpture." 24 December 1654, ratified by Parlement on 23 June 1655. Léon Aucoc, *Loi, statuts et règlements concernant les anciennes Académies et l'Institut de 1635 à 1889* (Paris: Imprimerie Nationale, 1889), cxiii–cxviii.

10. *Mémoires pour servir*, 1:183–87. Proceedings were recorded much more prosaically in the official minutes of the meeting on 3 July 1655. *PV*, 1:101.

11. *Mémoires pour servir*, 1:182.

12. On lock types, see plate XXVII, "Serrurier" in *Encyclopédie*, http://encyclopedie.uchicago.edu/, 26:4:1.

13. In 1781 the portrait was described as hanging "above the door to the Gallery of Apollo," in Antoine-Nicolas Dézallier d'Argenville, *Description sommaire des ouvrages de peinture, sculpture et gravure exposé dans les salles de l'Académie royale* (Paris: De Bure, 1781), 46. On the Académie's Salle des Portraits, see Williams, *Académie Royale*, 144–51.

Dog

Joseph-Siffred Duplessis (1725–1802)

TYPE OF OBJECT	THEME	MATERIAL
Companion, Gift	Animal, Family, Friendship, Louvre	Animal

What is a dog doing in a book about things? Like many artists before and since, Joseph-Siffred Duplessis lived with a dog. On the one hand, Duplessis's pet was a possession, something that belonged to him, like any other item of property in his Louvre *logement* (his **bath**, for instance, discussed elsewhere in this book). On the other hand, as an animate being rather than an inanimate object, the dog was unlike anything else in his home and unlike nearly everything else in this book. Like Collot's **nightingale**, the only other animal in this collection of things, Duplessis's dog holds an ambiguous place in these pages: it is a thing with value (both monetary and sentimental) and material properties, which Duplessis acquired, owned, maintained, and eventually disposed of; but also, it is a living creature who could behave independently of its owner and with whom Duplessis could interact and relate in very different ways. Pondering the "thingness" of Duplessis's dog draws us into distinctly Enlightenment debates about the subjectivity of animals, a subject that many philosophers, naturalists, and theologians explored at length, usually as terrain for understanding the human condition. Were animals, following Descartes, simply automata, machines without thought, language, or feeling?[1] Or were they, as the abbé de Condillac argued, sentient beings capable of reflection, sociability, and emotion?[2] Modern perceptions of animals incline firmly to the latter, but Duplessis's dog invites us to consider the nature of the pet in the eighteenth century.[3] What role did the dog play in this artist's life? And what was the affective relationship between this particular master and hound?

Ironically, the only surviving trace of Duplessis's dog comes from the day she died. On 15 August 1788, Duplessis wrote an extremely long letter to the comte d'Angiviller, the *directeur général des bâtiments du roi* (director general of the king's buildings), seeking permission to make changes to his Louvre apartments for the sake of his health and his working conditions. At the very end, the painter made a final, much more personal request, and in doing so divulged the tragedy of his very recent loss. "Permit me, Monsieur le comte, to remind you that over a year ago you once promised me a little dog that I might raise myself, from a breed of which you have both males and females, namely small Braques. Not wanting to add torments of jealousy to the existing infirmities of my old dog, I prayed that you might reserve me this favor for another time. Today she died and finding myself in such solitude following the marriage of my ward, I feel the need more than ever for that kind of company."[4]

While we never discover the name or even the breed of Duplessis's dog, the letter reveals many insights into his feelings for his pet, along with some salient details about her. For instance, we learn that she was a "chienne" (a bitch); that she was old—suggesting Duplessis had had her for a long time; that she had been sick or infirm for over a year; and that Duplessis had kept looking after her until she died. Caring for the hound through her frailty is already an indication of Duplessis's attachment to his pet, but there is a sense of an even more complex affective relationship in the painter's concern for her mental well-being as well as her physical health. Duplessis projects upon her the very human emotion of jealousy when he imagines how she might have felt should he have disloyally introduced a new dog into the home. While this might tell us something about the dog's personality, it is probably more suggestive of Duplessis's anxieties than hers, and of his dependence on her canine devotion for staving off that "solitude" that he now found descending following her death.

For an artist who never married or had children, and who lacked an extensive social circle, Duplessis's dog had become an alternative source of companionship, upon which, it would seem, he had come to rely quite desperately. The painter lived with servants and, until she married, his ward, but loneliness was a pressing issue for Duplessis, one compounded by both physical conditions and personality traits. Duplessis suffered from numerous health complaints (of which we discover many through the story of his **bath**), but it was his deafness that proved most detrimental to his social life. Hearing problems, he once claimed, made conversation so difficult that they had forced him to withdraw from society, instead spending long evenings miserably alone.[5] Despite being so often at home, he seems not to have socialized much with his Louvre neighbors (with the possible exception of Vernet) and was apt to assume cantankerously that his colleagues were being granted privileges that he was being denied.[6] With human society proving such a challenge, Duplessis's dog became a stand-in to satisfy the artist's needs for social interaction. Indeed, the extent to which Duplessis seems to have replaced human with canine companionship is suggested in both the crisis of loneliness prompted by her death and the solution he finds for it, namely the acquisition of a new dog. After all, *that* was the kind of "société" (company) that he found himself craving.

Duplessis's brief mention of his dog in the letter is full of tantalizing insights, but it does not offer an actual encounter between master and hound, written, as it was, in the pain of her absence. We do, however, find occasional glimpses of the painter's canine interactions in his portraits, like the exquisite *Madame Fréret d'Héricourt and Her Dog* (fig. 42). If a portrait is the trace of an encounter between artist and sitter, then this painting is as much a record of Duplessis's encounter with the lap dog as it is with the lady. Certainly it is a painting that demands to be read as a double portrait. The little spaniel might be a possession like the luxurious vase behind, or an accessory like the fur-lined *mantelet* over her shoulders, but it is also a living being, interacting socially with both its owner and the stranger looking at it. Even if we did not know that Duplessis was a dog person, his acute attunement to the dog's behavior in this portrait would seem enough to out him as a follower of Condillac rather than Descartes. Not only does the work bring center stage the affective relationship between a woman and her dog—their affectionate gestures of hand and paw, reaching to hold each other—but it can also be read as an articulation of canine consciousness. The spaniel's gaze is as direct and as attentive to the artist-viewer's presence as its owner's, but with those heightened white highlights, the dog's eyes become the dominant pair. Whether it was a trace of the experience or an imagined conceit, Duplessis gives the lap dog a penetrative and knowing stare with which to observe its interlocutor.

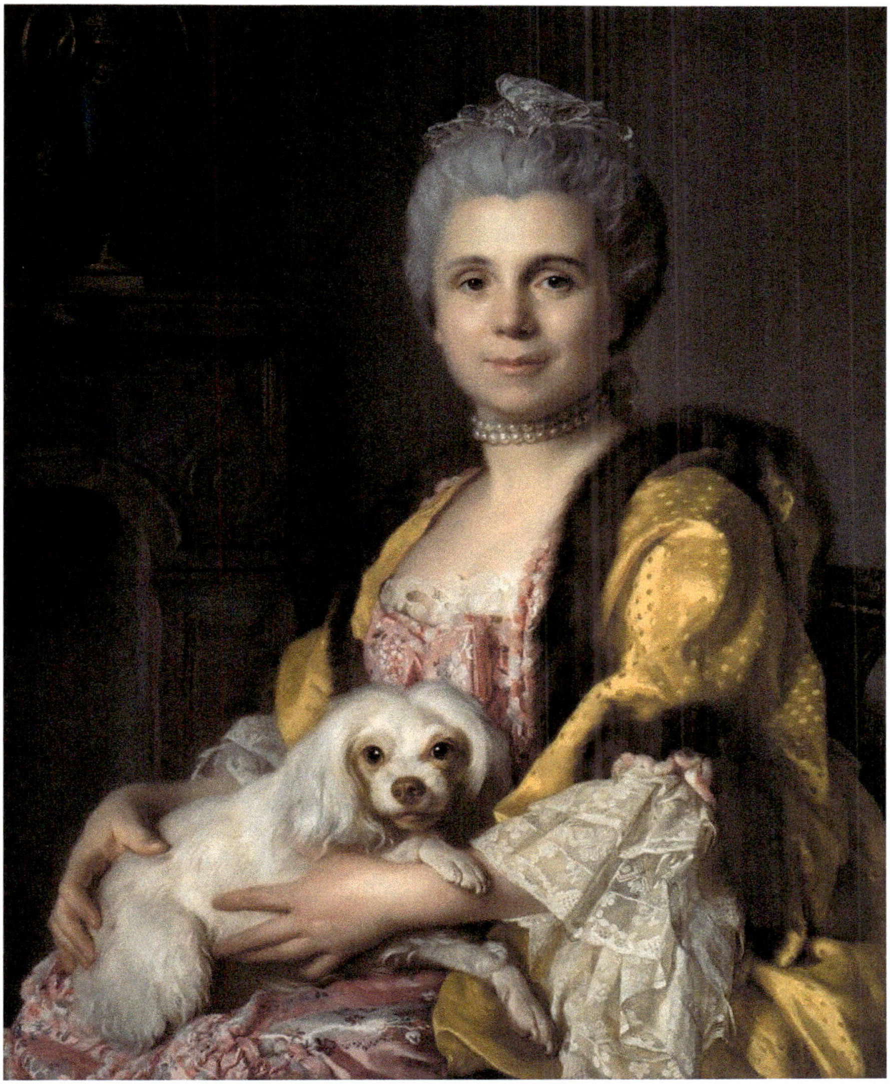

FIG. 42 Joseph-Siffred Duplessis (French, 1725–1802), *Madame Fréret d'Héricourt and Her Dog*, 1769. Oil on canvas, 81.3 × 64.8 cm. Kansas City, The Nelson-Atkins Museum of Art, Purchase of William Rockhill Nelson Trust, 53-80. (Photo: Michael Lamy.)

Be it in representations of endearing cognizant spaniels or in epistolary revelations about the depth of his emotional attachment to his own dog, Duplessis's canine interactions appear strikingly familiar to the modern mindset. This is perhaps most resonant in his reaction to her death, for any pet owner who has experienced the loss of a long-term companion would recognize the infinite emptiness of a home bereft of its presence. At the same time, however, there is an unsettling disjunction in Duplessis's reaction: between, on one hand, his distress at the loss of his beloved old dog and, on the other, the ease and immediacy with which he decides to fill the void by getting a new one. Mere hours after her death, the painter was already setting plans in motion to replace her. Duplessis's response thus looks less like grief at the death of a particular hound—an individual with whom the painter had a unique relationship—and more like generalized anxiety at finding himself alone in his home. Nevertheless, this reaction underscores Duplessis's feelings toward his dog, very different than those toward any other thing in his apartments, and the distinct role the pet played in his life. There may have been some sense of interchangeability (any dog would do), but no other material object in his Louvre *logement* could stave off loneliness and become a replacement for human company.

Duplessis may have been more dependent on his dog than some people, but he was far from alone in his canine preferences. Dogs were, according to the naturalist Louis-Jean-Marie Daubenton, the most popular pets in eighteenth-century France because they were the animals that attached themselves most easily to humans.[7] It is difficult to discern quite how many of Duplessis's colleagues were fellow dog owners, because the animals seldom appear in archival records: there was no paperwork associated with dog ownership (no licenses or permits), and unlike inanimate objects, they do not feature in after-death inventories. But if family portraits are evidence to go by, then other dog-owning artists certainly emerge. Nicolas de Largillière appears to have been the proud owner of a charming doguin, or pug, who springs into the foreground of the painter's *Portrait of the Artist and His Family* (fig. 43). Jean-Baptiste Isabey, meanwhile, is shown with a larger dog—an early pinscher or terrier, or a mixed breed, known at the time as a "chien des rues" (street dog)—who bounds up the steps in his collar to join his master in François Gérard's *Jean-Baptiste Isabey and His Daughter, Alexandrine* (fig. 44).[8] Choice of breed, as ever, reveals something about the owner, even if merely a suggestion of lifestyle.[9] Largillière's pug—a favored lap dog of noble ladies—conjures urbane and aristocratic connotations, while Isabey's seems a more practical choice, both pinschers and terriers being bred to chase vermin (particularly useful for any artist living in the Louvre, which was known to have a rat problem).[10] While the breed of Duplessis's beloved old dog remains unknown, the breed of his potential new dog is mentioned explicitly as a Braque, a type of French hunting dog, usually white with brown or black markings, and distinguished by its large, hanging ears.[11] Rather than indicating any inclination on Duplessis's part to engage in sporting activities, his choice seems to have been entirely determined by the fact that this was the type of dog that d'Angiviller bred. Indeed, Duplessis specifies that he wanted a Braque "de petite espèce" (of a small size), suggesting he was aware that this was not the most appropriate breed for an urban lifestyle and ensuring he got a small one that would be content living in his Louvre lodgings.

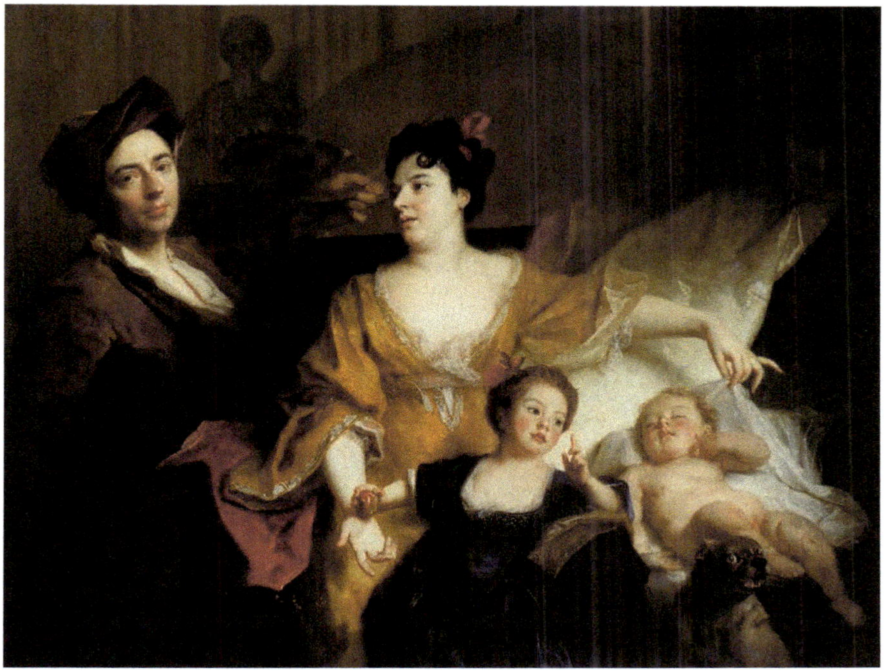

FIG. 43 Nicolas de Largillière (French, 1656–1746), *Portrait of the Artist and His Family*, ca. 1704. Oil on canvas, 128 × 167 cm. Kunsthalle Bremen. (© Kunsthalle Bremen–Lars Lohrisch–ARTOTHEK.)

As source proved more important than suitability for Duplessis, in this instance, choice of breed reveals less about the painter's lifestyle and more about his relationship with the *directeur général des bâtiments*. For as much as this is a story about a man and his dog, it is also a story about an artist and his patron. At the very end of his letter, Duplessis makes quite overt how entwined the two relationships were, adding a final rhetorical flourish to drive home his request: "If I got it [the dog] from you, I would love it even more, and I could say in truth that I do not possess anything—not even my dog—that was not a kindness from you."[12]

In a deft display of professional bargaining (or emotional manipulation, depending how you read it), Duplessis made a plea that would have been difficult to refuse. Not only did he solicit the dog as a gift, he also established the terms upon which that gift would be given, namely a "bienfait"—an act of kindness. Like any other academician living in the Louvre, Duplessis was dependent on the *directeur général des bâtiments* as both employer and landlord. Wielding power over an artist's professional success and their quotidian comforts, it was d'Angiviller who distributed the commissions for royal portraits that had made Duplessis's name, and d'Angiviller who made every decision about lodgings in the Louvre (including the drama of Duplessis's **bath**). In the context of that dynamic, the

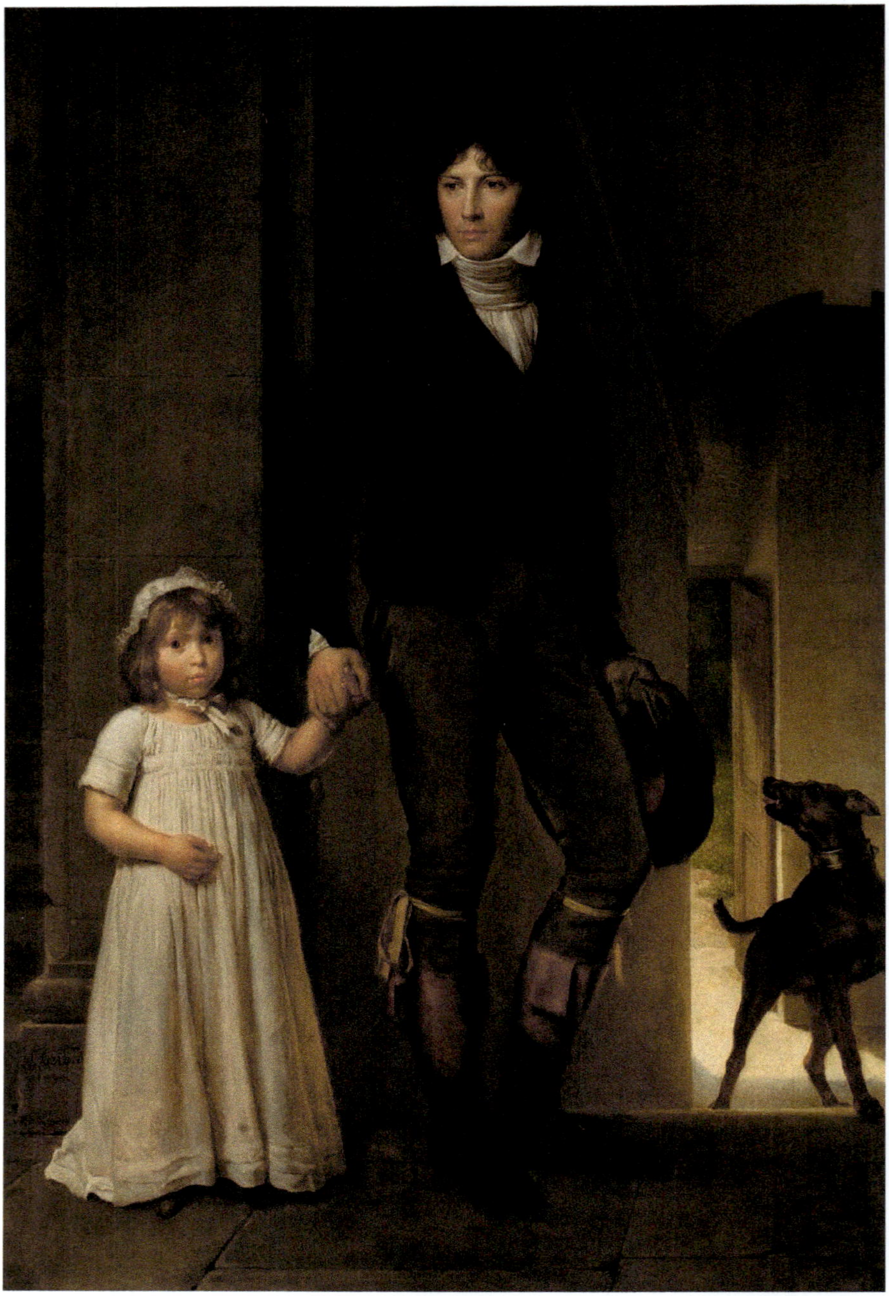

FIG. 44 François Gérard (French, 1770–1837), *Jean-Baptiste Isabey and His Daughter, Alexandrine*, 1795. Oil on canvas, 195 × 130 cm. Paris, Musée du Louvre, INV4764. (© Musée du Louvre, Dist. RMN-Grand Palais / Angele Dequier / Art Resource, NY. Photo: Angele Dequier.)

painter's request for a dog was a dexterous ploy to push their professional relationship firmly into the personal: this particular "kindness" would be a gift from the man (d'Angiviller), rather than the role (the *directeur général des bâtiments*). Indeed, it is hard to imagine any other inanimate object being quite as effective in this regard as the dog. Not only did Duplessis connect with d'Angiviller's own penchant for dogs (and his preferred breed), but even more compellingly, Duplessis's affective relationship with the dog became a proxy for tacitly expressing an affective relationship with the comte: were it a gift from *you*, "I would love it even more." Sadly, there is no surviving response to Duplessis's letter, so we may never know the outcome of his impassioned canine gambit. ‡

---

1. Peter Harrison, "Descartes on Animals," *Philosophical Quarterly* 42, no. 167 (April 1992): 219–27.

2. Étienne Bonnot de Condillac, *Traité des animaux* (1755) (Paris: Librairie Philosophique, 2004), 150–87.

3. On modern relationships between dogs and humans, see Majorie Garber, *Dog Love* (New York: Touchstone, 1996).

4. Letter from Duplessis to d'Angiviller, 15 August 1788, AN, $O^1$1674. Jules Belleudy, *J-S Duplessis, peintre du roi, 1725–1802* (Chartres: Durand, 1908), 106.

5. Duplessis made these remarks in another letter to d'Angiviller. Belleudy, *Duplessis*, 97.

6. See **Bath** for instances of Duplessis claiming that other artists were allowed what he was being denied. On another occasion, Duplessis complained that he had been forced to take in a royal officer as a lodger when his neighbors—Hubert Robert, Alexander Roslin, and Anne Vallayer-Coster—had been exempt from this service. Belleudy, *Duplessis*, 97, 106–7.

7. "Chien," *Encyclopédie*, http://encyclopedie.uchicago.edu/, 3:327–28. Cats have since taken over in popularity in France, but in the eighteenth century cats held a much more ambiguous place, as fascinatingly discussed in Amy Freund and Michael Yonan, "Cats: The Soft Underbelly of the Enlightenment," *Journal18* 7 (Spring 2019), http://www.journal18.org/3778.

8. Georges-Louis Leclerc, comte de Buffon, "Le Chien," *Histoire naturelle, générale et particulière*, 36 vols. (Paris: L'Imprimerie Royale, 1755), 5:229. With thanks to Rebecca McAuley and her colleagues for assistance identifying the breed of Isabey's dog.

9. On common dog breeds in eighteenth-century France, see Buffon, "Le Chien," 5:239–63.

10. Mercier describes "a multitude of rats" making their home in the Louvre. Louis-Sébastien Mercier, *Tableau de Paris*, 12 vols. (Amsterdam: n.p., 1783), 5:239.

11. On dogs and hunting in this period, see Amy Freund, "Sexy Beasts: The Politics of Hunting Portraiture in Eighteenth-Century France," *Art History* 42, no. 1 (2019): 40–67.

12. Duplessis to d'Angiviller, 15 August 1788, AN, $O^1$1674. Belleudy, *Duplessis*, 106.

Dressing-Up Box

Jean-Antoine Watteau (1684–1721)

TYPE OF OBJECT	THEME	MATERIAL
Container, Prop, Tool	Education, Making, Studio	Textile | Canvas, Textile | Silk

Antoine Watteau was celebrated in his own day as the inventor of a new genre of subject painting, the fête galante (fig. 45), a defining feature of which is the mix of costume—theatrical and actual, fashionable, dated, and everyday—in which the figures populating his landscapes are dressed. According to the comte de Caylus, a longtime friend of the painter and author of one of the Lives of the artist, Watteau owned a collection of clothes specific to that purpose.[1] Watteau scholars have followed Caylus in linking it to the prominence of dress in the *fêtes*.[2] Can this book's focus on things add anything to the considerable knowledge we already have of Watteau's passion for the theater, dressing up, and fashion? To account historically for the costumes, rather than the images that index them, foregrounds the when, where, and why of Watteau's collecting, and the how of his use of them.

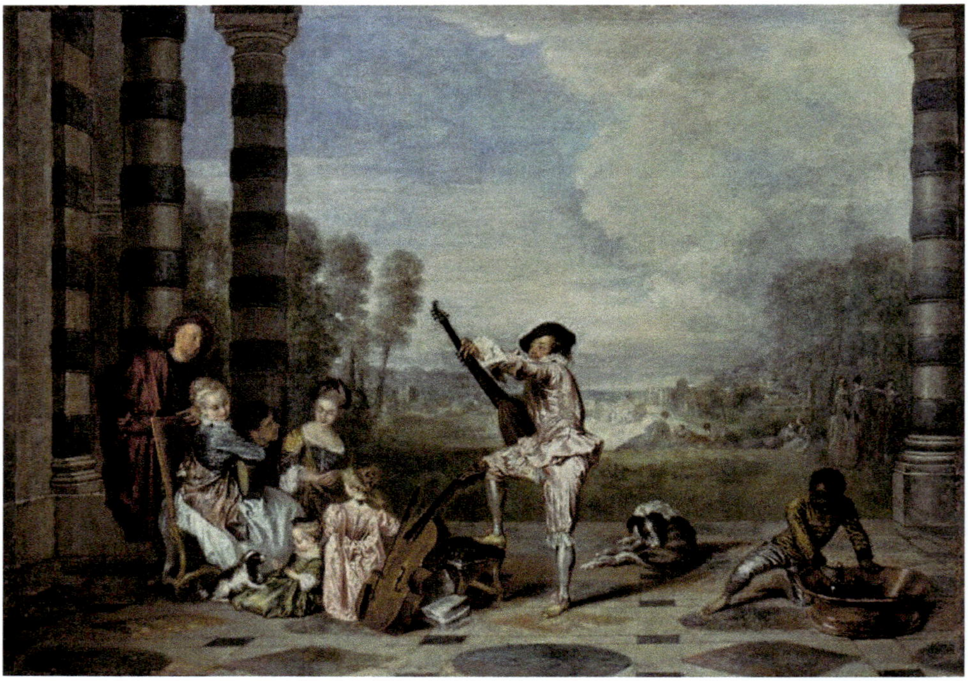

FIG. 45 Jean-Antoine Watteau (French, 1684–1721), *Les charmes de la vie*, ca. 1718–19. Oil on canvas, 67.3 × 92.5 cm. London, Wallace Collection. (By kind permission of the Trustees of the Wallace Collection, London / Art Resource, NY.)

Neither costumes nor container has survived. In none of the other Lives of Watteau is the costume collection mentioned. Description of the painter's goods and chattels in the documents concerning his estate is so limited that it adds little to our knowledge of his things, not even confirmation that the costumes were still in his possession at the time of his death.[3] In short, direct evidence about the collection is in limited supply.

Guillaume Glorieux has suggested that Watteau sought out commedia dell'arte and other theatrical dress to borrow, hire, or purchase at the shop of theatrical costumier Michel-Joseph Ducreux, on the Pont Notre-Dame, the bridge whose merchants gave Watteau his first job as a copyist when he arrived in Paris from his native Valenciennes as a teenager around 1702.[4] Three years later Watteau had moved on to the studio of the painter Claude Gillot, an aficionado of the capital's theaters, for some of which he worked as a costume and set designer.[5] As an artist Gillot made something of a specialty also from painting genre scenes inspired by the fair companies and their plays. Scholars agree that Watteau's interest in the theater dates from this time.[6] Did he, perhaps, begin acquiring costumes and other dress items when he set up independently, circa 1710, and no longer had immediate access to the resources of the Pont Notre-Dame and Gillot's studio? All Watteau's biographers underscore working "after nature" as Watteau's only practice—practice, that is, supported by the presence of things, not memory and imagination.

That Caylus thought to make note of Watteau's costume collection—though he, like Watteau's other biographers, made a point of remarking the painter's contempt for things in general—is explained by the purpose of his biography.[7] Written as a lecture for the Académie and its students, Caylus believed it incumbent on him "to connect" the events of Watteau's Life to "reflections" on the painter's "manner" and "*faire*," that is, to his artistic practice.[8] Reference to the costume box occurs toward the end of the life in the wake of Caylus's description of Watteau's drawing habits, ones that involved working not only after life but with no objective in mind.[9] Earlier in the biography Caylus offered a critique of Watteau's artistic process that, he argued, had been produced negatively: by lack of that precious academic training that anchored and shaped his audience's artistic experience. Caylus related both that Watteau had had little exposure to the life class and that he did not use a **mannequin**. That is to say, the nude was an unfamiliar practice to him, and the dressed body was a study in observation after nature, and not for him a contrived event using studio equipment.[10] Reference to the **mannequin** and model derived its significance from the "operational sequence" of academic practice and its staging of costume at a particular point in that sequence.[11]

The history painter worked with a project in mind in a five-stage sequence. A rough and inspired "première pensée" (initial idea) was followed in stage two by, on the one hand, its careful elaboration as a coherent composition and by, on the other, detailed studies of its parts (single figures and figure groups). Stage three was that of the finished drawing, all the problems relating to the arrangement, pose, gesture, and dress of the figures having been resolved. This drawing was then scaled and prepared for transfer in stage four, and in stage five the transferred design was realized with brush, medium, and pigments on a canvas. Jean Restout's *Dedication of the Temple of Solomon* (1743, Paris, Musée du Louvre) for the Abbey of Chaalis was produced in this manner.[12] A drawing at Rouen (fig. 46) records the painter's evolving solutions to the complexities of multiple-figure arrangement to the right of the temple steps in designs redrawn on successive flaps of paper pasted onto that side of the composition.[13] To help him, Restout very likely used small-scale **mannequins** to model the groups of draped figures.[14] A clean, finished drawing—with drapery rendered in finest detail, squared for transfer, and now in the Musée des Beaux-Arts at Orléans (fig. 47)—marks the end of the preparatory stages.[15]

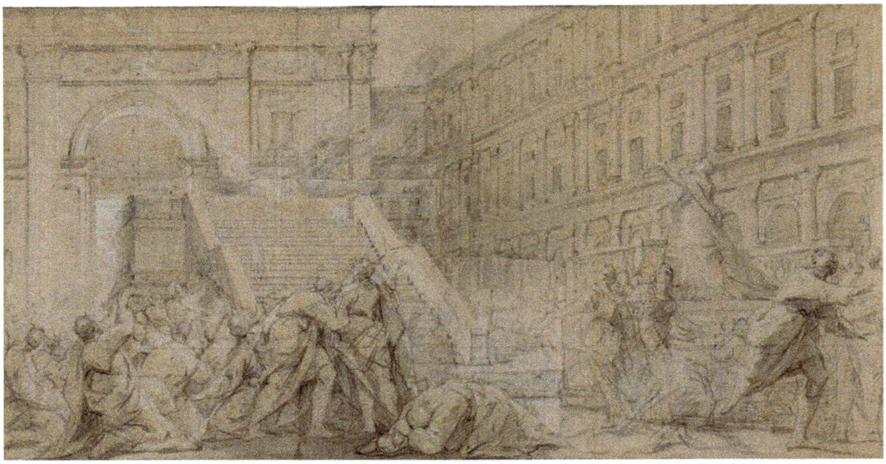

FIG. 46 Jean Restout (French, 1692–1768), *Dedication of the Temple of Solomon*, 1743. Black and white chalk on paper, 35.8 × 67.5 cm. Rouen, Musée des Beaux-Arts, inv. AG 1909.34.63. (© Agence Albatros /Réunion des Musées Métropolitains Rouen Normandie, Rouen, Musée des Beaux-Arts.)

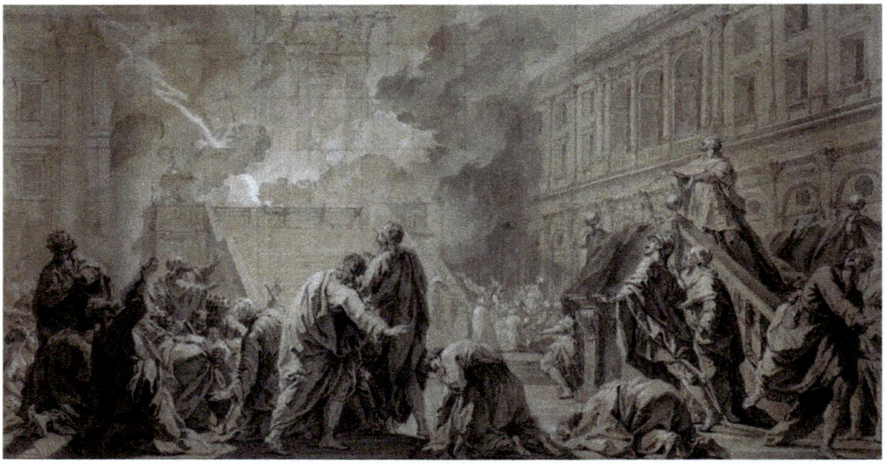

FIG. 47 Jean Restout (French, 1692–1768), *Dedication of the Temple of Solomon*, 1743. Black chalk with white highlights on blue paper, 56 × 88 cm. Orléans, Musée des Beaux-Arts.

Watteau's practice, according to Caylus, was by comparison compressed and inverted. As a general rule, Watteau drew only studies—studies that, having no end or purpose, were therefore not intentionally part of operational sequences in the production of pictures.[16] His process began, rather, with painting; according to Caylus, with rubbing the canvas surface all over with oil, so it would be ready in stage two to receive the flow of figures and figure groups randomly culled and transposed from his **sketchbooks** and recycled from earlier paintings.[17] Composition was not for him a sequenced and reasoned formation, stage by stage or point to point, but rather a looser process of essaying and improvisation.[18] It comprised not just painting but repainting, moving forward and doubling back. The chaos of it was replicated in the mess of his **palette**.[19] The X-ray of, for example, *Les charmes de la vie* (see fig. 45) reveals that work had begun on the foundation of Watteau's earlier composition *The Concert* (ca. 1717–18, Charlottenburg Palace, Berlin).[20] The distribution of the three principal elements—theorbo player, foreground group left, and background group right—were copied onto the new canvas and then reworked.[21] A nest of figures, middle distance right, in *The Concert* becomes in *Les charmes* a looser horizontal line of distant, almost ghostly human forms. A woman in yellow standing on the left facing right is repainted, following a drawing, to represent a man in red facing forward, leaning over the guitar player.

Watteau's painting process—(1) covering, (2) transposing, (3) repainting—not only condensed the production method advocated at the Académie; by putting painting before drawing, it also muddled media as operational tools. With the removal of drawing from the preparatory to the executive stage, the study of costume becomes difficult to locate. For the history painter it belonged without doubt to stage two, and to drawing. Selected for specific narrative purpose, according to social norms of decorum and literary rules of verisimilitude, costume was modeled on the **mannequin** or copied from visual sources.[22] In Watteau's case the figure is always already dressed. Several biographers recorded that Watteau drew people while out walking—as found objects, you could say.[23] Caylus recollected that visitors to Watteau's studio were encouraged to use the dressing-up box and improvise poses and identities for the painter to draw.[24] Hats and cloaks are, arguably, the things most versatile for the quick and easy transformation of selves.[25] The man in red in *Les charmes de la vie* has been identified as the painter Nicolas Vleughels, with whom Watteau was sharing a studio around the time he painted the picture.[26] A drawing by Watteau at Frankfurt (fig. 48) shows Vleughels in a cloak and a beret. The way these items are worn, not residing on the body but rather the cloak draped over one shoulder, the hat perched on the back of the head, seem to register the impromptu, momentary nature of the posing sessions. Was the sketch drawn before the painting or after the painting had begun, with no view in mind or in train with *Les charmes*?

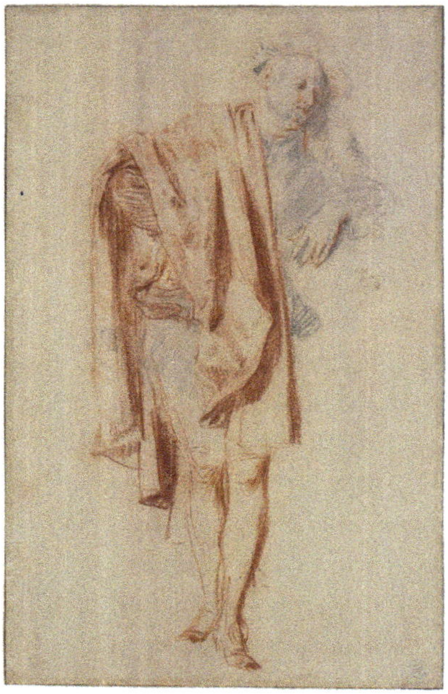

FIG. 48 Jean-Antoine Watteau (French, 1684–1721), *Study of Nicolas Vleughels*, ca. 1718–19. Red and black chalk on paper, 29.4 × 18.4 cm. Frankfurt am Main, Städel Museum, Graphische Sammlung, 1040. (bpk Bildagentur / Graphische Sammlung im Städelschen Kunstinstitut, Frankfurt / Art Resource, NY.)

We have no way of telling. What we do know is that Watteau's process was open, both in the sense that it had no fixed beginning or end, and because he invited the creative participation of others in the choice and modeling of dress. Staging the composition of the *fêtes* independently of the dressing-up sessions, and transposing sketched figures on the basis of pose as much as costume, may account for the absence of unity in the *fêtes*' costuming, a heterogeneity of dressing that surprised and delighted Watteau's contemporaries.[27] Caylus did not, of course, read Watteau's practice this way. He saw in it the groping of an artist handicapped by lack of that academic schooling on which depended the mastery of art as a sequence of discrete operational techniques combined with a body of rational knowledge. That Watteau produced masterpieces in spite of his disadvantages was precisely the point revealed by Caylus's biography.[28]

The methodology of "operational sequences" (*chaînes opératoires*) has the considerable advantage of enabling close comparison of technical practices (as above). However, defining technology exclusively as sets of operations in the transformation of "matter" by "human beings," to paraphrase Pierre Lemonnier, separates object and subject categorically.[29] It allows "matter," in this case cloth, no agency, thus limiting our understanding of cloth's uses to painting. When Caylus praised Watteau's imitation of material, he remarked that Watteau "seldom painted stuff other than silk, *which always tends to produce small folds*."[30] *Silk* folds. It is self-altering—delicately so, in Caylus's manner of speaking. His observation raises the following question for us: was Watteau transformed in his practice by the surface "operations" of the stuffs in his collection?

Contemporary sources described Watteau's manner of painting in terms of touch, a gesture uniquely oriented to the surface.[31] According to Caylus, he first "rubbed" his blank canvases all over "haphazardly" with oil, before, according to the amateur Antoine-Joseph Dézallier d'Argenville, applying "a flowing brush and the finest and lightest touch" to paint them.[32] "Rubbing" and "flowing" denote the contact of one surface with another under different degrees of pressure. "Haphazardly" and "light" suggests free and untargeted movements of the hand and arm that cover the surface without necessarily delineating or circumscribing it. This is to suggest that Watteau responded to the affordances of canvas and rag paper as infinitely extendable surfaces, rather than viewing them as objects, or "windows," defined by their edges. In *Les charmes de la vie* (see fig. 45) he painted, to be sure, an elaborate architectural frame for the musical *fête*, the polychrome marble squares of the terrace serving as a checkerboard on which to locate his foreground figures in space, in a manner consistent, at first glance, with the boxlike perspective that Jean Restout later constructed for *Dedication of the Temple of Solomon* (see fig. 46). On closer inspection, the lines of recession in the terrace and the landscape do not align exactly. The narrow strip of empty middle distance appears to bank upward. Afar is confused with above. Space becomes backdrop.

Directly transposing figure and figure groups from sketchbook to canvas and working them into scenes by painting around them tended to produce spatial ambiguities of this kind in complex, multifigure compositions. The treatment of the empty space below and above the guitarist and the embracing couple in another work, the smaller and simpler *La surprise* (fig. 49), suggests, however, that flatness was actively sought by Watteau; it was not simply an accident of method. Light touches of paint in the areas of foreground, foliage, and sky of *La surprise* describe edges of grass, leaf, and cloud without obscuring the continuous and amorphous colored surface they accent.[33] Moreover, by combining fine and precise signifying brush marks with fluid passages of indistinctness—for example, the blending of landscape and figures in the background of *Les charmes* and the blurring of built forms on the horizon of *La surprise*—Watteau's handling disrupts illusion and allows such qualities as smoothness and evenness to surface—qualities of touch, that is, not sight.

Meanwhile, what of the behaviors of cloth, the folding noticed by Caylus? Watteau was, his works suggest, fascinated by the myriad creases, crumples, wrinkles, rumples, tucks, pleats, and gathers "expressed" by cloth, his attention trapped by the curious, often complex shapes it folded and wrapped.[34] An unexplained rumple in Vleughels's cloak (see fig. 48) creates a puzzling trapezoid shape across the lower body. The cloak-rifle-man assemblage sketched on a sheet of studies of a soldier (Courtauld Institute of Art, London), configures, through the cloak's wrapping action, a strange polygonal shape comprised of two unequal triangles, the bases of which sit and hang on the diagonal of the gun.[35] A later study of a man in a cape (fig. 50), likewise withholds information about the body beneath the wrap and gather of silk. It tells, rather, of the folds the silk itself knots, folds that, like the damp patches on walls, invite imaginative projection: here, the features perhaps of a grotesque face.[36]

This focus on the collection of apparel, a collection that Watteau began to assemble at the beginning of his career and very likely kept to the end, has revealed when, where, and how it oriented his artistic practice, how it anchored his knowledge of the dressed body (like the **écorché** grounded knowledge of the nude), and how it stimulated his imagination. License so to reconstruct the collection's functions is given by the sources, the works, and also recent scholarship that emphasizes the lack of conventional fit between the costumes and the social identities of the persons wearing them in the fêtes galantes. What was so transgressive about Watteau's portrayal of the dressed figure is that, whatever the figure is

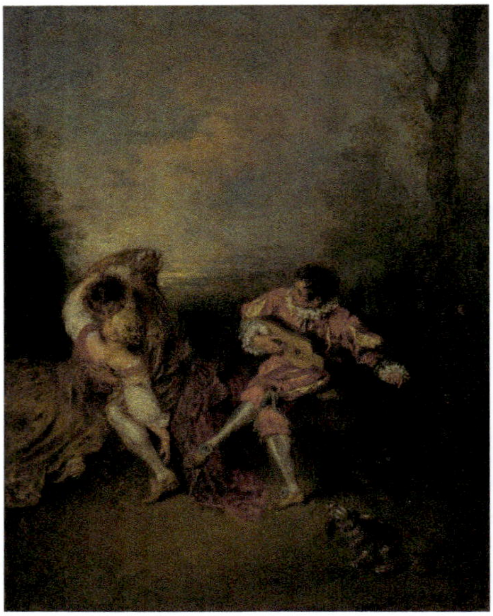

FIG. 49 Jean-Antoine Watteau (French, 1684–1721), *La surprise*, ca. 1718–19. Oil on panel, 36.4 × 28.2 cm. Los Angeles, The J. Paul Getty Museum.

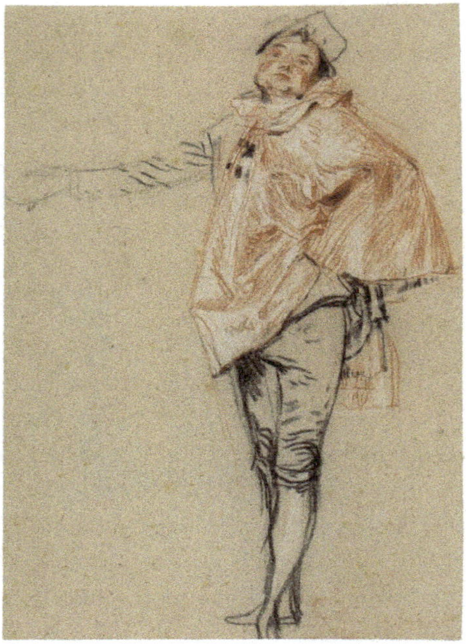

FIG. 50 Jean-Antoine Watteau (French, 1684–1721), *Man in a Cape*, ca. 1718–19. Red and black chalk with white heightening on paper, 27.2 × 18.9 cm. Rotterdam, Museum Boijmans van Beuningen. (HIP / Art Resource, NY.)

wearing—haute couture, yesterday's fashions, theatrical dress, rustic rags—they appear to be no one other than themselves, though themselves dressed up almost to the point of disguise. Identity, by this account, was constructed on the surface, through artifice, and not conferred by blood, birth, or sensibility. According to Caylus, Watteau was once bewitched by a **wig**. Brought to his studio by a barber client, Watteau was enchanted by its perfect "imitation of nature."[37] Apparel was to him, apparently, no less natural than the body. §

---

1. Anne-Claude-Philippe de Tubières, comte de Caylus, "La vie d'Antoine Watteau," in Pierre Rosenberg, ed., *Vies anciennes de Watteau* (Paris: Honoré Champion, 1984), 78.

2. See especially François Moureau, "Theatre Costumes in the Work of Watteau," in *Antoine Watteau (1684–1721): The Painter, His Time and the Legend*, ed. Margaret Morgan Grasselli and Pierre Rosenberg, exh. cat. (Washington: National Gallery of Art, 1987); and Suzanne Pucci, "Watteau and the Theatre: Movable Fêtes," in *Antoine Watteau: Perspectives on the Artist and the Culture of His Time*, ed. Mary Sheriff (Newark: Universtity of Delaware Press, 2006), 106–22.

3. See François Mandaret, "Jean-Antoine Watteau: The First Documents," *BM* 153, no. 1298 (2011): 312–13.

4. Guillaume Glorieux, "Michel-Joseph Ducreux (1665–1715), marchand de masques de théâtre et d'habits de carnaval au temps de Watteau," *BSHAF 2006* (2007): 119–29; and Glorieux, "Les débuts de Watteau à Paris: Le Pont Notre-Dame en 1702," *GBA* 139 (2002): 251–62.

5. See Jennifer Tonkovitch, "Claude Gillot's Costume Designs for the Paris Opera: Some New Sources," *BM* 147, no. 1225 (2005): 248–52; and Tonkovitch, "A New Album of Theatre Drawings by Claude Gillot," *Master Drawings* 44, no. 4 (2006): 464–86.

6. Donald Posner, *Antoine Watteau* (London: Weidenfeld & Nicholson, 1984), 47–58; Marianne Roland Michel, *Watteau: An Artist of the Eighteenth Century* (New York: Trefoil, 1984), 17–22; and Julie Anne Plax, *Watteau and the Cultural Politics of Eighteenth-Century France* (Cambridge, England: Cambridge University Press, 2000), 7–52.

7. Edmé Gersaint, "Abrégé de la vie de Watteau," in Rosenberg, *Vies*, 29–40 at 36; and Caylus, "Vie," in Rosenberg, *Vies*, 67.

8. Caylus, "Vie," in Rosenberg, *Vies*, 55.

9. Caylus, "Vie," in Rosenberg, *Vies*, 78.

10. Caylus, "Vie," in Rosenberg, *Vies*, 70–72. Some scholars, such as Roland Michel, have disputed Caylus's claims. She argues that Watteau drew the nude regularly if infrequently; see *Watteau*, 135.

11. The notion of "operational sequences" is a descriptive tool developed in the anthropology and archaeology of technology. See Pierre Lemonnier, *Elements of an Anthropology of Technology* (Ann Arbor: University of Michigan Press, 1992).

12. See Christine Gouzi, *Jean Restout (1692–1768): Peintre d'histoire à Paris* (Paris: Arthena, 2000), P115.

13. Gouzi, *Restout*, D79 and 141–49.

14. **Mannequins** were listed among Restout's studio paraphernalia in 1753. See AN, O^1/1671/133–35.

15. Gouzi, *Restout*, D81.

16. On Watteau's studies, see Roland Michel, *Watteau*, 93–111; and JoLynn Edwards, "Watteau Drawings: Artful and Natural," in Sheriff, *Antoine Watteau: Perspectives*, 41–62, esp. 43–50. See also Alan Wintermute, *Watteau and His World: French Drawings from 1700 to 1750*, exh. cat., The Frick Collection, New York (London: Merrell Holberton, 2000).

17. Caylus, "Vie," in Rosenberg, *Vies*, 76. See Élizabeth Martin and Claudia Sindaco-Domas, "Le Technique picturale des peintres de fêtes galantes dans le contexte du XVIIIe siècle," *Technè* 30–31 (2009–10): 25–36.

18. See Tim Ingold, *Lines: A Brief History* (London: Routledge, 2007) on different modalities of mark making, esp. 39–71.

19. Caylus, "Vie," in Rosenberg, *Vies*, 77.

20. See John Ingamells, *Wallace Collection: Catalogue of Pictures*, vol. 3: *French before 1815* (London: Wallace Collection, 1999), P410.

21. See Christoph Vogtherr, "Fêtes Galantes in London and Potsdam: Different Versions of the Same Theme in Watteau's Work," *Technè* 30–31 (2009–10): 179–84.

22. As an example of the mannequins used by history painters, see Charles-Antoine Coypel, *Catalogue des tableaux, desseins, marbres, bronzes, modèles, estampes* (Paris: n.p., 1753), lot 492 (miniature armor), lot 493 (mannequins), lots 494–96 (miniature theaters for staging scenes).

23. See Jean de Julienne, "Abrégé de la vie d'Antoine Watteau," in Rosenberg, *Vies*, 17; and Antoine-Joseph Dézallier d'Argenville, "Abrégé de la vie d'Antoine Watteau," in Rosenberg, *Vies*, 49.

24. Caylus, "Vie," in Rosenberg, *Vies*, 78.

25. Certain models recur in Watteau's drawings—for instance, a man with heavy brows, an aquiline nose, and dimples. Watteau draws him alternatively in a cap, beret, tricorn, and straw hat, and essaying a range of corresponding metropolitan and pastoral identities. See Pierre Rosenberg and Louis-Antoine Prat, *Antoine Watteau (1684–1721): Catalogue raisonné des dessins*, 3 vols. (Milan: Arte, 1996), no. 56. Cloaks conferred on models the cast of the soldier, the hurdy-gurdy player, the friar, or the Italian comedian (the Doctor).

26. See Ingamells, *French before 1815*, P410.

27. See Antoine de La Roque in Rosenberg, *Vies*, 5; and Dézallier d'Argenville, "Abrégé," in Rosenberg, *Vies*, 50.

28. See Caylus's statement of purpose, "Vie," in Rosenberg, *Vies*, 55.

29. Lemonnier, *Elements*, 26.

30. Caylus, "Vie," in Rosenberg, *Vies*, 72.

31. The discussion below is indebted to Tim Ingold, "Surface Visions," *Theory, Culture, and Society* 34, nos. 7–8 (2017): 99–108.

32. Caylus, "Vie," in Rosenberg, *Vies*, 76; and Dézallier d'Argenville, "Abrégé," in Rosenberg, *Vies*, 50.

33. On what Étienne Jollet calls the "peu visible" in Watteau, see Jollet, "Analyse technique et poétique de l'oeuvre: le cas des 'fêtes galantes' d'Antoine Watteau," *Technè* 30–31 (2009): 229–36.

34. Caylus uses the word *express* rather than *depict* for Watteau's representation of cloth. See Caylus, "Vie," in Rosenberg, *Vies*, 72.

35. See Rosenberg and Prat, *Watteau: Catalogue raisonné*, 1:cat 59.

36. See Roger de Piles's endorsement of Leonardo's commendation of the damp wall in *L'idée du peintre parfait* (Paris: Gallimard, 1993), 30–31.

37. Caylus, "Vie," in Rosenberg, *Vies*, 67–68.

Écorché

Jean-Antoine Houdon (1741–1828)

TYPE OF OBJECT	THEME	MATERIAL
Artwork, Tool	Death, Education, Health/Medicine, Louvre, Luxury, Making, Studio, Travel	Metal | Bronze, Mineral | Clay, Synthetic Materials | Plaster

Houdon's écorché is a thing with many stories, not least because the thing known as "Houdon's écorché" is actually many things existing in many forms.[1] This anatomical **model** of a flayed human figure exists in two distinct versions: one with arm extended, one with arm raised. Both versions exist in life-size and reduced-scale formats. Each version and format were executed in different materials, mostly plaster or bronze, but also terracotta. And the dates of production extend from 1767 right into the nineteenth century, with Houdon producing numerous casts throughout his life, and copies continuing to be made after his death in 1828. In fact, versions of Houdon's écorché are still being sold today, such is its enduring appeal as an aesthetic object and its value as an educational tool for artists: the two qualities for which it was prized from the very moment of its creation.[2]

The écorché's story begins in the 1760s in Rome, where it was created almost by accident. At the age of twenty-three, having won the Académie's *grand prix* for sculpture, Houdon traveled to Italy to complete his training at the Rome branch of the institution (then in the Palazzo Mancini).[3] Embarking on the life of a *pensionnaire*, Houdon spent his days attending drawing classes, copying great works of art, and creating his own. He was also one of only two students in his cohort who took anatomy classes, setting out at dawn with his colleague, Johann Christian von Mannlich, for the hospital of Saint-Louis-des-Français, where the professor of surgery, Monsieur Séguier, taught them human anatomy by dissecting fresh cadavers.[4] It was amid these encounters with corpses that Houdon's first écorché (fig. 51) began to take shape. At the time, he was working on a sculpture of Saint John the Baptist and, according to Mannlich, "had the idea to make the model in clay, first in the form of an écorché, and each day used our anatomy lessons . . . to make a thorough study of the muscular system."[5] The young sculptor's experimental plan was to create a life-size model for his sculpture, building it up from the inside out, to produce an anatomically correct figure.[6]

Houdon's teachers and fellow students in Rome were so struck by the model that they encouraged him to take a mold of the skinless body before making any further additions, and this incidental object became the first version of the écorché. Its extended-arm pose was thus not chosen for any scientific reason, but rather determined by the baptizing gesture of the saint. Charles Natoire, the Rome Académie's director at the time, was so taken with Houdon's anatomical model that he requested a plaster cast for the school,

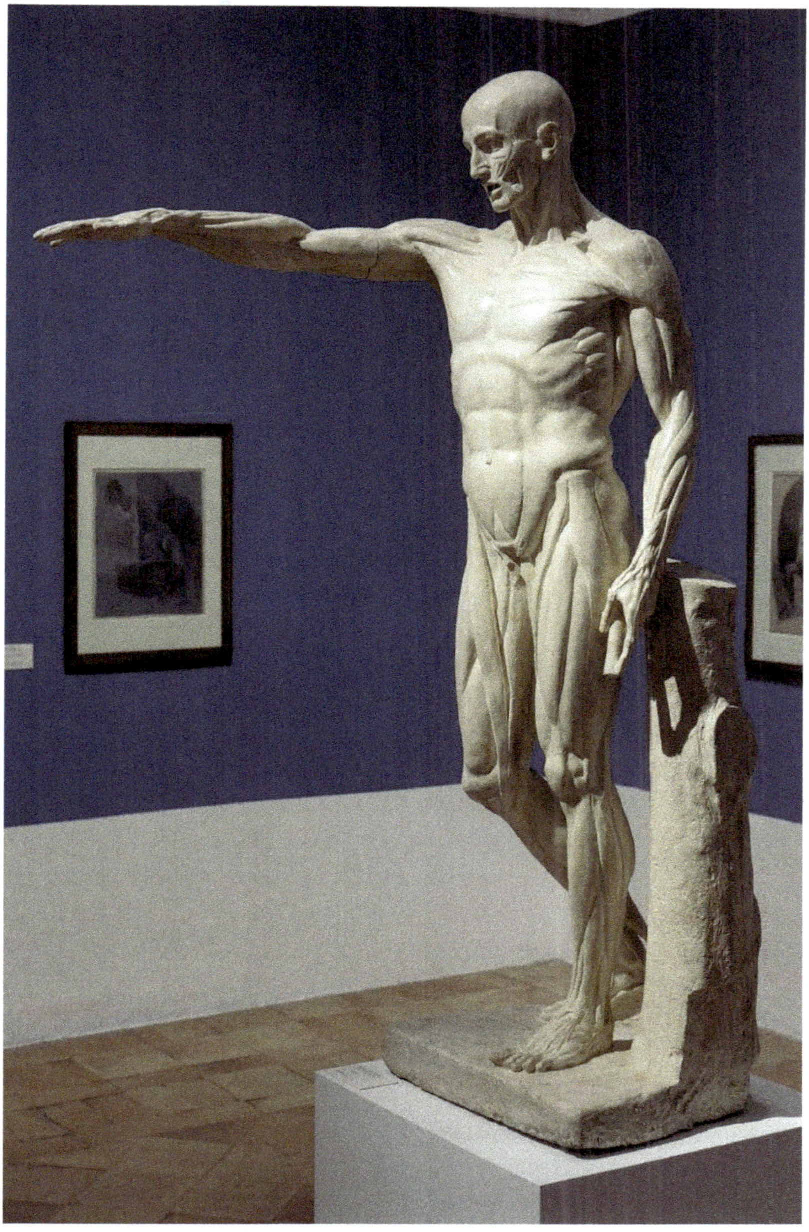

FIG. 51 Jean-Antoine Houdon (French, 1741–1828), Écorché, 1767. Plaster, 181 cm. Rome, Villa Medici, 2015.0.136. (Collections of the Académie de France in Rome–Villa Medici. Photo: © Daniele Molajoli.)

declaring that the *squelette* (skeleton) would be an invaluable tool for instructing students.[7] Houdon obliged, and the cast remains at the Rome Académie today (now in the Villa Medici) (see fig. 51). Perhaps the most intriguing point to note from the écorché's origins (other than the fact that Natoire clearly did not have a word for it, calling it a "skeleton" despite the complete absence of any bones) is that this object, which would go on to become such a fundamental tool in academic teaching, was made neither as a tool nor by a teacher. Rather, it was made by a student and began life as the experimental preparatory stage of an artwork. The écorché's accidental making and enthusiastic reception also reveal a great deal about the role of anatomy in art education at this moment. Indeed, it is telling that when Houdon took his Roman anatomy classes, he was very much in the minority. But less than a decade later, anatomy had become a compulsory part of the *pensionnaire* curriculum, in part thanks to Houdon's écorché. When Joseph-Marie Vien, as the new director, rewrote the school's regulations in 1775, anatomy classes were fixed in the rules, and so too was their principal object of instruction: "Article 2: Among the studies that student painters and sculptors must follow in Rome are anatomy and perspective. . . . Anatomy will be taught using the écorché that M. Houdon made for the Académie."[8]

Back in Paris, anatomy had been nominally part of the Académie's curriculum since its founding in 1648, with a professor of anatomy employed especially for the purpose. Nearly always a surgeon (with the exception of the history painter Jacques-Antoine Friquet de Vauroze), these medical men were something of an incursion of science into the arts.[9] This was evident in the things they used to teach, which included an actual human skeleton, casts of body parts taken from skinned cadavers, and medical treatises.[10] While anatomical knowledge was generally accepted as an important skill for history painters and sculptors, science and art did not coexist without friction. There was a disconnect between the surgeons' interest in the human body (a pathologized machine to be healed) and the artists' interest in the human form (an aesthetic object to be represented). Houdon understood this disjunction implicitly, as he explained in a letter written in 1772, a few years after his return to Paris: "Surgeons, as skilled as they may be, are not draftsmen, and draftsmen are not surgeons. In my view, the skilled surgeon must study nature, as defective as one may find it, in order to be able to treat every infirmity. But we must study it differently. It is nature in all her nobility, her perfect state of health, that we are seeking."[11]

Houdon was not the first to articulate this problem, and his écorché was not the first attempt at a solution.[12] Already a hundred years earlier, Roger de Piles and François Tortebat had produced their *Abrégé d'anatomie accommodé aux arts de peinture et de sculpture* (1667). Made in the tradition of Vesalius, this was a medical textbook for artists, complete with straightforward tables and illustrative engravings of skinless bodies set incongruously in Italianate landscapes (fig. 52).[13] According to de Piles, its intention was to provide the detailed knowledge of the body required by artists, without the "infinity of useless things" that normally cluttered medical books.[14] Yet despite such efforts to tailor anatomy for artists, there remained an ambivalence in the early eighteenth century.[15] Scientific interests in observing the human body still seemed anathema to the aesthetic goals of perfecting the human form. In the second half of the century, however, anatomy made an academic comeback.

Soon after his return to Paris, in August 1769, Houdon presented himself at the Académie for his *agrément* (provisional admission).[16] That he included the écorché in his

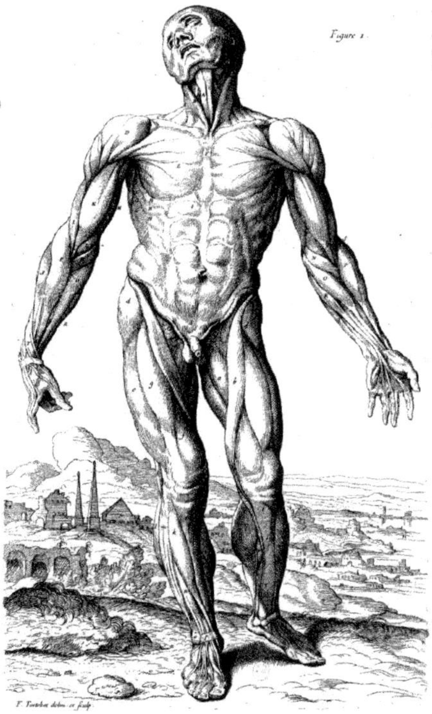

FIG. 52 François Tortebat, from *Abrégé d'anatomie accommodé aux arts de peinture et de sculpture* (Paris: Jean Mariette, 1733), fig. 1. Paris, Bibliothèque Nationale de France

portfolio of works for this ritual examination suggests the extent to which Houdon considered it an aesthetic achievement, given that artistic skill and quality were the key criteria for acceptance. But that a month later, the sculptor offered to donate a plaster cast of the écorché to the Académie, "as it might be of use to the students," also suggests the educational value he attached to his model.[17] For the Académie's part, Houdon's gift came at the right moment. After decades of dwindling interest and even resistance, anatomical study was having a resurgence under the new professor of anatomy, the surgeon Jean-Joseph Sue, who had devised a bespoke curriculum for his artistic students.[18] Combined with the shifting stylistic approach to the human body emerging with the neoclassical revival in the 1760s, the climate of reception for Houdon's écorché was ideal.[19]

This was entirely different from the lack of fanfare that had greeted an earlier écorché by Edme Bouchardon in 1741 (fig. 53), when the Académie had been at its most resistant to anatomical study. But Houdon's success and Bouchardon's lack of it were also due to the defining differences between these objects, whatever their superficial similarities. Bouchardon's écorché was a cast taken directly from a cadaver. Houdon's, meanwhile, was a cast taken from a clay model that was made by observing cadavers. The distinction was crucial. Both sculptors took actual human bodies as their source, but only Houdon had that vital artistic remove from nature, which allowed him to bridge the problematic divide between art and science. Houdon's écorché was not an index of an imperfect real body (like Bouchardon's), nor an artistic scientific diagram (like Tortebat's), but rather an

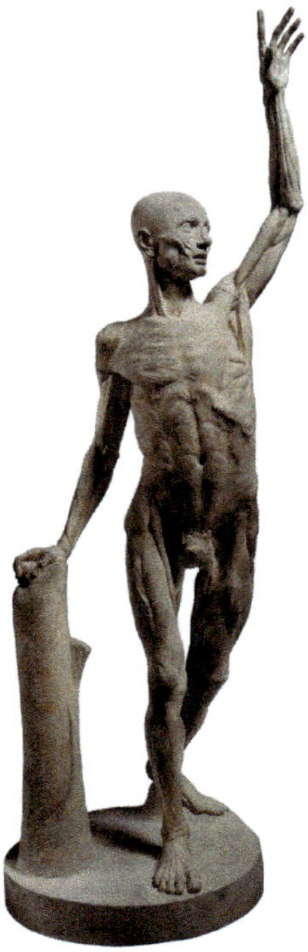

FIG. 53 After Edme Bouchardon (French, 1698–1762), Écorché, nineteenth-century cast of 1741 original. Plaster and metal, 208 × 70 × 60 cm. Paris, École Nationale Supérieure des Beaux-Arts, MU12201. (Art Resource, NY.)

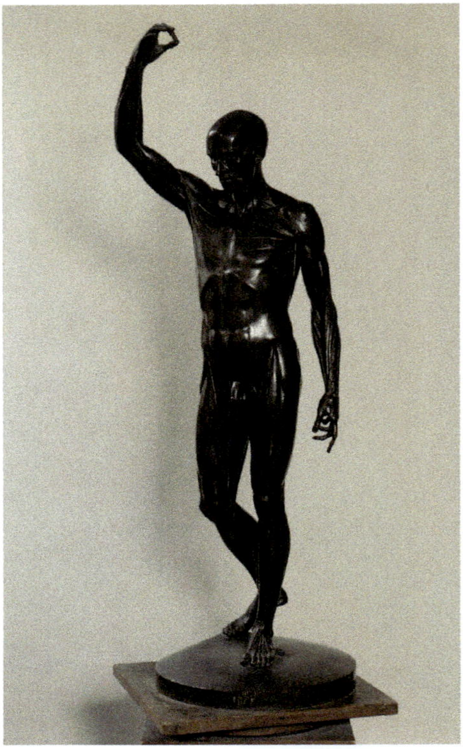

FIG. 54 Jean-Antoine Houdon (French, 1741–1828), Écorché, 1790. Bronze, 194 × 70 cm. Paris, École Nationale Supérieure des Beaux-Arts, MU11974. (© Beaux-Arts de Paris, Dist. RMN-Grand Palais / Art Resource, NY.)

anatomical *sculpture*. This was not the natural anatomy of a single dead man, but an art-made muscular system, derived from numerous bodies to create a universally ideal form. Like the *Doryphoros* or the *Apollo Belvedere*, Houdon's écorché was an invention of bodily perfection, just in this case, it was a perfection of the corporeality beneath the skin.

Simultaneously tool and artwork, the écorché's distinctive scientific and artistic qualities gave it broad appeal. By the 1770s plaster copies had been acquired not only by the Paris and Rome academies, but also by those of Toulouse, Bordeaux, and Flanders. At the same time, it was beginning a life beyond institutional bounds, becoming a sought-after object of curiosity at foreign courts in Poland, Parma, Russia, and Gotha.[20] Its appeal was so great that Houdon's fellow academicians soon wanted copies for themselves. But a life-size sculpture is a difficult thing to accommodate in most domestic spaces, so Houdon was encouraged by his colleagues to create smaller copies that would be both "less expensive" and "more convenient" for individual ownership.[21] In its new reduced format, Houdon's écorché became an object for personal use, to be found standing on the desks of amateurs, residing on the shelves of collectors, and taking on practical roles in artists' studios, as a tool to be used alongside live models and **mannequins** to guide the composition of human forms.[22]

With increasing demand and expanding production in the 1770s, Houdon created his second version of the écorché: its right arm raised overhead, thumb and finger pressed together, and mouth closed (fig. 54). The sculptor never recorded a definitive explanation for the changed pose, but it was likely in pursuit of both scientific value and economic potential. Unlike the first version, originating as a study for a specific artwork, the second was an anatomical model from the outset. Free of compositional constraint, the new pose demonstrated a more complete range of muscle movement across the body, from fully flexed to entirely relaxed. On the practical front, it was also more compact and less vulnerable to accidental breakages, crucial for the friable plaster versions, and more straightforward to fire in bronze. As bronze casts could travel more easily, while also attracting a higher price, the second écorché thus greatly increased the potential for circulation and commercial revenue.

Over time, Houdon certainly found ingenious ways to profit from his écorché's success. In 1790 he announced that he wanted to donate a new écorché to the Académie so the school could possess one in each pose.[23] Casting a life-size version in bronze was a tricky business, so when the planning was complete, he decided to turn the firing into a promotional gathering. The event was by invitation only, with those lucky enough to receive *billets* (tickets) making their way on a Sunday evening out to Houdon's studio and foundry at the Roule, on Rue du Faubourg Saint-Honoré.[24] One attendee declared that the crowds were so intense that "truth be told, one could not see much of the founding at all," but no matter, for there was other entertainment.[25] Upon arrival, Paris's high society was met with a vast room where Houdon had installed an exhibition of his sculptures, all lit strikingly from above. It seems this one-man showcase was the real purpose of the event, with the écorché merely serving as headline act to fill the house.

Houdon's écorché survived its firing, and the sculptor eventually presented one to the Académie in 1792 (see fig. 54).[26] It is this life-size bronze incarnation that is most associated with Houdon's mature years, not least due to its appearances in Louis-Léopold Boilly's well-known paintings of Houdon's studio from the early 1800s (see fig. 113). Like the **modeling stand**, the écorché becomes a ubiquitous resident of Houdon's studio in these interiors. But unlike the modeling stand, which is resolutely *used*—a piece of furniture with utilitarian functionality (like Fragonard's **armchair**), rather than aesthetic value (like David's **table**)—the écorché remains decisively both. As tool and artwork, it is as much part of the artist's paraphernalia strewn about the studio (at home with the portfolios, rags, saucers of water, and modeling tools), as it is one of the many sculptures displayed around the room. For an object that gained its reputation precisely because of its ability to inhabit the roles of both tool and artwork, the sculptor's studio was perhaps its most natural habitat. Notwithstanding all the places that Houdon's écorchés ended up, this was where it deployed itself most authentically, just as it does in Boilly's vision. Looming to the left, it bookends the scene, becoming the art-made instrument that oversees the sculptor's work, its commanding gesture conducting the artistic endeavors undertaken in this space. ‡

1. For comprehensive examinations of the two versions and their associated works, see Anne L. Poulet's entries in *Jean-Antoine Houdon, Sculptor of the Enlightenment*, exh. cat. (Washington: National Gallery of Art; Los Angeles: J. Paul Getty Museum; and Musée National du Château de Versailles, 2004), 63–71.

2. An updated version of Houdon's original écorché is, for instance, sold by the Eaton London sculpture studio.

3. Houdon won the prize in 1761 but did not travel until 1764. *PV*, 7:175.

4. *Histoire de ma vie: Mémoires de Johann Christian von Mannlich (1741–1822)*, ed. Karl-Heinz Bender et Hermann Kleber, 2 vols. (Trier: Spee, 1989–93), 1:260, cited in *Jean-Antoine Houdon*, 63.

5. *Histoire de ma vie*, 1:260, cited in *Jean-Antoine Houdon*, 63.

6. On the écorché's origins, see Louis Réau and Pierre Vallery-Radot, "Les deux écorchés de Houdon," *Æsculape* 28, no. 1 (January 1938): 174–76.

7. Charles Natoire to the marquis de Marigny, 18 February 1767, in *CDR*, 12:140.

8. "Règlements qui doivent être observes par les pensionnaires de l'Académie de France à Rome" (1775), in *CDR*, 13:158.

9. A contrast to the professor of perspective, who was usually an artist (e.g., Abraham Bosse, Michel-Ange Challe, Sébastien Leclerc, Pierre-Antoine Demachy).

10. Anatole de Montaiglon, ed., *Mémoires pour servir à l'histoire de l'Académie royale de peinture et de sculpture depuis 1648 jusqu'en 1664* (Paris: P. Jannet, 1853), 1:56; and Philippe Comar, "Une leçon d'anatomie à l'École des Beaux-Arts," *Une leçon d'anatomie: Figures du corps à l'École des Beaux-Arts*, exh. cat. (Paris: ENSBA, 2008–9), 19.

11. "État des choses renfermées dans les caisses envoyées à son Altesse Monseigneur le duc de Saxe-Gotha," July 1772, cited in *Jean-Antoine Houdon*, 356.

12. See Mechthild Fend, *Fleshing Out Surfaces: Skin in French Art and Medicine, 1650–1850* (Manchester: Manchester University Press, 2017), especially 193–234.

13. Andreas Vesalius, *De humani corporis fabrica* (n.p., 1555).

14. Roger de Piles, "Préface," *Abrégé d'anatomie accommodé aux arts de peinture et de sculpture* (Paris: Jombert, 1765), i.

15. In 1737, the professorship in anatomy was actually defunded and made into a nominal post. Comar, "Une leçon," 21.

16. Houdon returned to Paris in 1768. He was *agréé* (provisionally admitted) at the Académie on 23 August 1769, in the same meeting as Jean-Baptiste Greuze's infamous *réception*. *PV*, 8:19.

17. 30 September 1769. *PV*, 8:24.

18. The Académie approved Sue's classes, but set conditions for entry. Before enrolling, students had to pass a life drawing test. *PV*, 6:43–44.

19. In 1764 the comte de Caylus even proposed a slightly bizarre new Osteology Prize, with students competing to draw the best skeleton in "an interesting attitude." The prize did not really take off. *PV*, 7:249.

20. Jean-Antoine Houdon, 13 February 1776. Bibliothèque Municipal de Versailles, F946, no. 229, cited in *Jean-Antoine Houdon*, 64.

21. Houdon, 13 February 1776, cited in *Jean-Antoine Houdon*, 65.

22. Reduced-scale versions of Houdon's écorché can be seen in paintings like Guillaume Voiriot's *Portrait of Jean-Joseph Sue* (1789, Châteaux de Versailles et de Trianon) and Louis-Léopold Boilly's *A Painter's Studio* (ca. 1800, Washington, National Gallery of Art).

23. *PV*, 10:58, 187.

24. Geneviève Bresc-Bautier, "Fonderie et ateliers du Roule," *La Rue du Faubourg Saint-Honoré* (Paris: 1994), 373.

25. Gerhard Anton Von Halem, *Blicke auf einen Theil Deutschlands, der Schweiz und Frankreichs bey einer Reise vom Jahre 1790* (Hamburg: Carl Ernst Bohn: 1791), 1:84.

26. *PV*, 10:187.

Funeral Book

Concierge of the Académie Royale

TYPE OF OBJECT	THEME	MATERIAL
Heirloom	Administration, Community, Death, Louvre, Memory	Animal | Leather/Parchment, Synthetic Materials | Paper

In 1879 Étienne Arago, playwright, journalist, and militant republican, wrote a short article on the Le Nain brothers for the magazine *L'art.*[1] His purpose was to establish the dates of each of the three brothers—Antoine, Louis, and Mathieu—whose lives and works were, at that time, often confused in the historiography of art. More or less by chance, he had discovered a book of the funeral and burial notices of academicians since the beginnings of the Académie in 1648. The opening page of the "Billets d'enterrement & de service de Messrs de l'Académie Royale de Peinture & Sculpture qui sont morts, depuis l'etablissement d'icelle en 1648 jusqu'à l'année courante," in the library of the École Nationale Supérieure des Beaux-Arts, contains notices for Antoine's and Louis's funerals, held two days apart at the end of May 1648 at the church of Saint-Sulpice in Paris.[2] Following Arago's lead, the book has been mined for the evidence of the civil status of academicians in the seventeenth and eighteenth centuries. It is an object of research also for scholars of Le Vieux Papier, a society founded in 1900 for the study of "old" paper ephemera such as wall **almanacs**, games, trade cards, and funeral notices.[3] Art historians, however, have rarely noticed the book.[4] For good reasons, perhaps: long lost among the former Académie's "useless paperwork," it is not a symbolic and ritual object like the Académie's **document box**, in which the company's articles of foundation were kept, nor is it an attribute of membership in group or individual Académie portraits, like, for instance, the Order of Saint Michel. When considered at all, it has been in the historical context of administration and bureaucracy. We claim it for this book because, as we demonstrate, it was an unauthorized product of the bureaucracy that historians argue played so vital a role in the formation of "modern" art institutions and it thereby affords a different perspective on academic culture.[5]

As a thing, the funeral book is a collage of printed and written texts and decorated papers gathered together between the covers of a register that opens with a cut-and-pasted ornamental title page (fig. 55). It is not a book in any conventional sense; it is not a text published in an edition of identical printed copies. Rather, it is what one might call a scrapbook, a uniquely fabricated collection of recycled things, many of them standard products retailed by the print and paper trades in the eighteenth century. The register is of the kind supplied by Paris stationers, but it was almost certainly secondhand, because, at points where the infrastructure of the book is visible, the pages shows signs of use: marks of writing, possibly even drawing. The register's boards were bound in vellum: a surplus copy of the Académie's 1655 statutes was purloined for the purpose. Meanwhile, out-of-date copies of the annual printed lists of members supplied the endpapers smoothing the transition between cover and contents. In the pages proper, the funeral notices are glued three, sometimes four to a page (fig. 56), laid out using black-and-white marbled paper to contain and level the surface. The resulting folios are stiff and substantial, like placards.

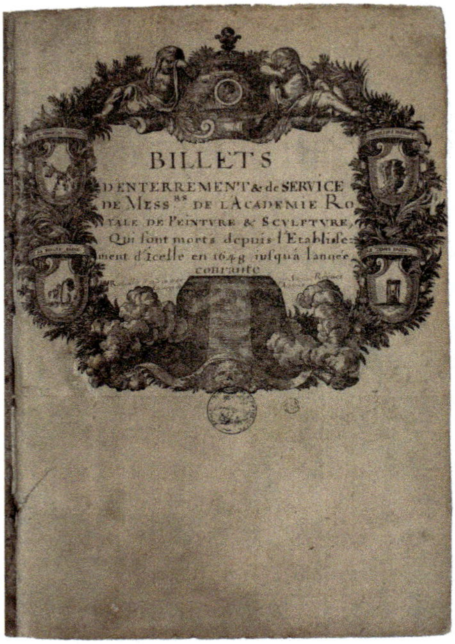

FIG. 55 Title page, "Billets d'Enterrement & de Service de Messrs d l'Académie Royale de Peinture et de Sculpture," ca. 1703–13. Ink on parchment, 50 × 36 × 9 cm. Paris, École Nationale Supérieure des Beaux-Arts, Archives 137-01. (© Beaux-Arts de Paris, Dist. RMN-Grand Palais / Art Resource, NY.)

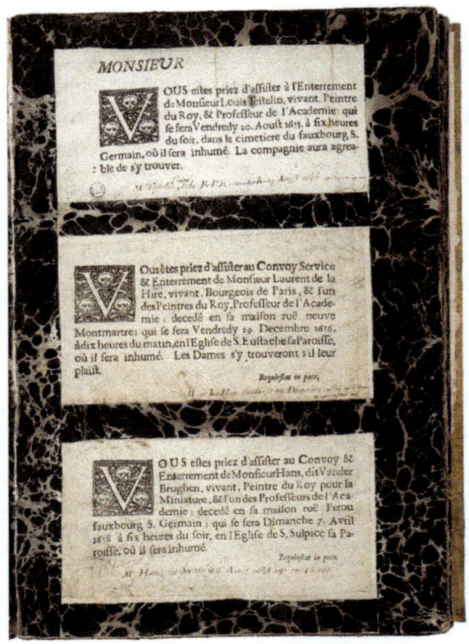

FIG. 56 Page from "Billets d'Enterrement & de Service de Messrs d l'Académie Royale de Peinture et de Sculpture," ca. 1703–13. Woodcut decorated letter and marbled paper. Paris, École Nationale Supérieure des Beaux-Arts. (© Beaux-Arts de Paris, Dist. RMN-Grand Palais / Art Resource, NY.)

Inscribed under the title but within the cartouche (see fig. 55), we learn it was "gathered and arranged in order by Antoine Reynès, Concièrge of the Académie." Reynès was only appointed to the post of concierge or porter in 1701, providing a terminus ante quem for the making of the book.[6] He stepped into the shoes of Pierre Pérou, whom he had served first informally as an office boy and then in 1697 by appointment as second *huissier* (usher).[7] The functions of the ushers and the porter were defined in the Académie's statutes, and indeed, those relating to the former are, by coincidence, legible on the upper right corner of the book's front cover. Those duties were elaborated and supplemented by decisions made at the institution's assemblies and recorded in the minutes. The primary task of the ushers was to clean and provision. That of the porter was to maintain order in the school,[8] and to safeguard the Académie's collections, tasks facilitated by the distribution of the rooms that, from 1721, located the porter's lodge at the top of the main stairs and on an axis with the life class.[9]

Nowhere in either the legal or the bureaucratic literatures relating to the Académie were scribal tasks assigned to either *huissiers* or concierges, although the supply of candles and heating fuel, equipment for the life class, and liveries for the models presupposes invoicing and record keeping. The point being that the existence of the *recueil* is not explained by the role of its "author." On the contrary, his functions denied him access both to some of the stuffs of the book, notably the statutes—locked in the **document box**—and to the time to make it. The roughness of the finish—the marbled paper often inexpertly trimmed to fit around the notices, the notices themselves sometimes disfigured by sloppy cutting—and the occasional errors of sequence that required hinged additions to reinstate order suggest interrupted thought to add to the scattered materials. In terms of the comparison famously drawn by Claude Lévi-Strauss between the modus operandi of the engineer and the *bricoleur* (handyman), Reynès acted like the handyman he actually was, generating something new from materials and ideas not made for the purpose but to hand.[10]

Lévi-Strauss's technological metaphor—*bricolage*—for the savage mind lacks context. It is not related as a cognitive and creative process to specific structures of power: economic, political, symbolic, bureaucratic. More apt in the current context is Michel de Certeau's critique of modern practices of everyday life, in which he identifies "making do" as one of the tactics of resistance practiced by the weak in the face of that "legal-rational" form of domination that authority assumes under capitalism.[11] He argues that "making do" is an active form of poaching that generates a more or less conscious and subversive counterculture. Does this model of deviant production fit the precapitalist world of early eighteenth-century France and the culture of deference at the Académie? Can we make a historical case for Reynès as disaffected and observe him finding within its bureaucratic grip both the time out and the débris from which creatively to assemble something other?

Although the book was assembled from old ends (the printed *billets*), which became in Reynès's hands the means to a new purpose (the *Recueil*), Reynès's *découpage* was not extempore, like Lévi-Strauss's *bricolage*. On the contrary, the book was conceived and planned in advance, closer to engineering, *bricolage*'s opposite. It was "engineered," moreover, with tools specific to the purpose: scissors and glue. The notices were trimmed of excess paper (that excess originally required to post them on walls and doors about the parish before the funeral) in order to adjust them to the pages of the register in a densely spaced chronological list (see fig. 56). In place of the dispersed spatial order created by the town criers responsible for distributing the *billets* in multiple copies to sites and mourners across the city, Reynès substituted a rigid timeline of events represented by single copies of the notices of individual deaths.[12]

His objective to gather a complete series from the Académie's foundation to "the present day" drove him to create substitute *billets* when burial notices were unavailable, rather than make do with the fragments at hand.[13] The portrait of the Académie he constructed was an ideal one, not just in material terms and consequent to filling gaps, but also in terms of formal composition: Reynès included in the collection notices of the Académie's first, elite protectors and directors, for example cardinal Mazarin and Martin de Charmois, even though the Académie received no invitation to their obsequies.[14] Likewise, he excluded notices of models, concierges, and concierges' wives; their *billets* were set aside because they were not of academicians, not agents in its grand narrative.[15] Finally, Reynès's choice of a marbled paper that simulated the particular variety of breccia often used for tombs (fig. 57) proposed the book as a monument upon which the names of the exalted were in the process of being inscribed.

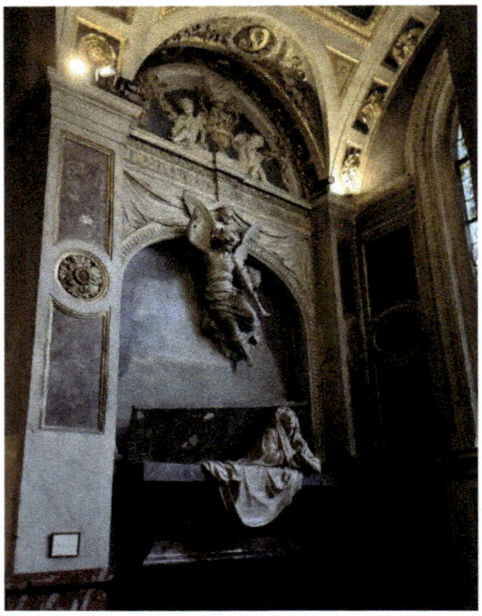

FIG. 57 Jean-Baptiste Tuby, Funerary monument to Charles Le Brun's mother, 1669–84. Marble. Paris, Church of Saint-Nicolas-du-Chardonnet. (SiefkinDR / Wikipedia.)

Reynès was not a *bricoleur* in the strict sense. Lévi-Strauss's theorization of *bricolage* and engineering as typological modes of thinking and making precludes, in fact, the practice of either one in a pure form. To make sense of Reynès's particular blend of the two we need to compare his recycling of funeral notices with other notices, and to consider the funeral book in light of the range of jobs he performed. Lawyers and notaries used surplus funeral notices as covers or folders for paperwork, but their reuse was confined to the paper; it does not extend to recycling the text.[16] A comparable dossier of notices announcing the funerals of the capital's publishers and printers was, however, assembled later in the century by the police inspector Joseph d'Hémery.[17] D'Hémery's files on men of letters are well known. Robert Darnton argues that the inspector's systematic collection of printed and other data and his filing of it alphabetically by name represents "an early phase in the evolution of the modern bureaucrat," a phase of state rationality he sees as beginning with Colbert and Vauban in the 1670s and stretching to Turgot and Necker a century later.[18] D'Hémery's perspective on his subject—the book trade—was that of an outsider, and the scope of his information gathering was more comprehensive that Reynès's, but comparison of the two projects is suggestive. It encourages connecting the funeral book to a second register in the Académie's archives, identical in size to the *Recueil*, also bound in vellum, and also with a title page by Reynès.[19] It contains the annual lists of members of the Académie (fig. 58), each one trimmed and pasted onto a page and each one annotated over the course of the year with the names of new or departed members. Comparison underscores the largely secular nature of the annotations in the funeral book: Reynès supplemented the notices with dates of death where they were not the same as the dates of burial, noting age at time of death, changes of name, and the name of his informant when his source was not a funeral notice.[20] The collector and amateur Pierre-Jean Mariette regarded Reynès as the embodiment of accuracy and precision.[21]

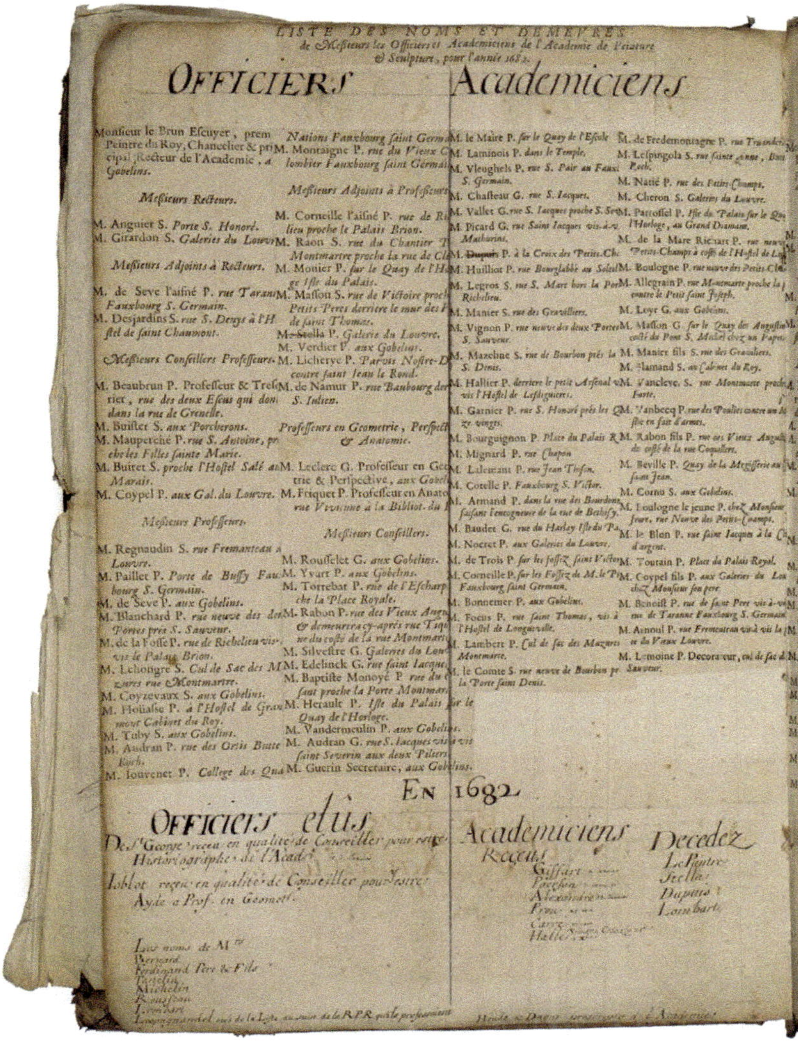

FIG. 58 Page from the register of lists of members of the Académie royale, 1675–1735. Letterpress annotated in pen and ink, 45 × 30 cm. Paris, École Nationale Supérieure des Beaux-Arts, Ms 22. (© Beaux-Arts de Paris, Dist. RMN-Grand Palais / Art Resource, NY.)

However, Reynès's position within the Académie inflected his administrative work in ways quite different from d'Hémery. His writing was not about mapping networks of patronage, locating sources of slander, and identifying dangerous subjects in need of police surveillance; it was an unsolicited, unacknowledged, perhaps even unwanted attempt by the concierge to participate in writing the Académie's history, the task that had officially fallen to Nicolas Guérin, appointed the Académie's secretary in 1705.[22] He highlighted by annotation the status of some of the twelve *anciens* (founder members), and he recorded the genealogies of descendants of academicians, occasionally noting works executed by the deceased.[23] Instead of drawing attention to religious dissent, he included without comment burial notices of Huguenots expelled after the revocation of the Edict of Nantes

(1685).[24] By the simple act of reclaiming by notice of death those who had left France rather than abjure their religion, he disguised the rent in the Académie's fabric caused by Colbert's instruction to expel Protestant members in October 1681.[25] Though methodical, systematic, and concerned with the reliability of evidence, Reynès's collection of data was neither impersonal nor unprejudiced. It exhibits loyalty, reverence even, for the Académie, and it bears the marks of Reynès's artistic sensibility in its layout and decoration.

What, then, was the purpose of the book? To whom was it addressed? The answer lies not so much in the book itself as in its contribution to the corpus of Reynès's writings. In addition to the two bound *recueils* of funeral notices and lists, Reynès made a fair copy of the Académie's minutes (*procès-verbaux*) from its foundation to 1722, and he wrote what he called a collection of "historical descriptions" of the *morceaux de réception* (reception pieces) of which he was the keeper.[26] This is an extraordinary body of writing for a porter. The last of these includes an open letter to the "Messrs of the Académie," seeking their permission to publish his text and to dedicate it to them.[27] The letter suggests that all Reynès's works were at some level addressed to the officers of the Académie. Written after his promotion to concierge, they were intended perhaps to demonstrate his potential for further advancement: his secretary's hand, his accuracy in virtual minute-taking, and his intellectual promise in two of the genres of *conférence* writing that the secretary Guillet de Saint-Georges had inaugurated in the 1680s—the "explanations" of the *morceaux de réception* and the obituary notice.[28] Reynès was attempting to engineer his own advancement not so much by poaching the Académie's property as by trespassing on the territory of its secretary and historiographer. Although the Académie had established a fairly complex administration for its smooth running, one in which power was exercised through formally defined, quasi-legal offices, it seems that personnel like Reynès lived that domination by identifying with its elders and seeking to participate in its symbolic body.

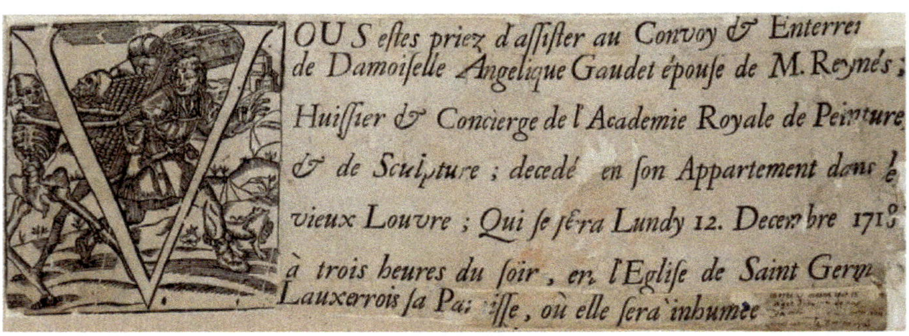

FIG. 59 Funeral notice for Angélique Gaudet, 1718. Woodcut. Paris, École Nationale Supérieure des Beaux-Arts. (© Beaux-Arts de Paris, Dist. RMN-Grand Palais / Art Resource, NY.)

Why did it not work? Reynès was not considered when a new secretary and historiographer was appointed after Nicolas Guérin's death in 1715. In the case of the funeral book, the answer may have been, at a formal level, because sophisticated marbled frame notwithstanding, Reynès's re-presentation of the funeral notices failed to repress the noisy popular tradition of the danse macabre manifest in the decorated initial "V[ous]" (You) (fig. 59), by which mourners were simultaneously interpolated, and also forewarned, of death.[29] At an institutional level, it was perhaps because death is more than the departure of the physical body, it is also a dissolution of the social being and as such constitutes a blow to the social order. Both the social status of individuals and the social order of the community must adjust in order to survive the loss. If registration of the death of ordinary members was sometimes neglected in the Académie's minutes, that of an officer was not. The void was immediately filled.[30] Funeral notices were privately commissioned. They registered the rite by which the person passed over, but not the rite of representation by which the social body was repaired through the affirmation of its offices and statutes. The collection of notices, however complete, accurate, and appropriately presented, could not represent the Académie as an institution nor develop its ideology. However, if by making the book Reynès was not contributing to the "governmentality" of the Académie, neither was his *bricolage* a crafty manipulation of academic resources for his own purposes. It was rather the product of mishap and misjudgment, partly because the *billets*' overdetermined symbolic and semantic value distorted Reynès's intentions and partly because the opportunities for advancement that he thought he saw and that prompted his secretarial work were not really there. §

---

1. Étienne Arago, "Les frères Le Nain: À propos d'un recueil mortuaire," *L'art* (1879): 301–9.

2. "Billets d'enterrement & de service de Messrs de l'Académie Royale de Peinture & Sculpture qui sont morts, depuis l'etablissement d'icelle en 1648 jusqu'à l'année courante," ENSBA.

3. See Octave Fidière, *État civil des peintres et sculpteurs de l'Académie royale: Billets d'enterrement de 1648 à 1713 publiés d'après le registre conservé à l'École des Beaux-Arts* (Paris: Charavay, 1883); and Lucien Raulet, "Billets d'enterrement et pièces funéraires," *Le vieux papier* 40 (1907): 19–35.

4. Notable exceptions are Maxime Préaud, "On ne meurt qu'une fois: Note sur l'initiale V des billets d'enterrement aux XVIIe et XVIIIe siècles," *Revue de la Bibliothèque nationale de France* 10 (2002): 73–76; and Christian Michel, *The Académie Royale de Peinture et de Sculpture: The Birth of the French School 1648–1793*, trans. Chris Miller (Los Angeles: Getty Research Institute, 2018), 2–3.

5. Classically, by Nikolaus Pevsner, who describes the regime at the Académie as an "ingeniously adapted civil-servantdom" in *Academies of Art Past and Present* (London: Cambridge University Press, 1940), 101. This approach is challenged by Michel in *Académie Royale*.

6. "Fait en 1703" in Reynès's hand on the billet for Denis Parmentier appears to confirm this. On Reynès's appointment to the post of concierge, see *PV*, 3:212. On the duties of the concierge, see article XII of the 1655 statutes and article XVII of the 1664 statutes.

7. On the usher's role, see article XVI of the 1655 statutes and article XX of the 1664 statutes; *PV*, 1:255. According to the *Procès-verbaux*, the ushers derived part of their income from payment of a fee of 6 livres for summons to funerals. *PV*, 2:81.

8. See *PV*, 4:41, 134.

9. See the ground plan of the first floor of the Louvre, in Jacques-François Blondel, *Architecture Françoise*, 4 vols. (Paris: Jombert, 1752–56), 4:38–39 (PE).

10. Claude Lévi-Strauss, *The Savage Mind* (Oxford: Oxford University Press, 1996), 8–13, 16–22.

11. Michel de Certeau, *The Practices of Everyday Life* (Berkeley: University of California Press, 1984), 29–42.

12. The notices were printed in three sizes of poster (small, medium, and large). The *jurés-crieurs* were organized in a guild. They enjoyed a monopoly on the publication and distribution of burial notices. Small posters were priced by the *Tarif des droits, salaires et vacations attribuez aux jurés-crieurs de Paris* (1671) at 40 sous; medium were priced at 50 sous, and large at 3 livres. The distributor was paid 30 sous per day. For an example of funeral costs later in the century, see "Mémoire des fournitures de deuil" for the sculptor Edme Bouchardon, 28/07/1762 (AN, AB/XIX/4220) 400 billets were printed and posted at a cost of 32 livres.

13. Thirty-two of the 184 notices were written, not printed.

14. See Fidière, *État civil*, nos. 15 and 17. Other such manuscript notices concern academicians who died outside Paris.

15. Those of Pérou, his predecessor; Germain Gobin, a model; and of Angélique Gaudet, his wife, were folded in at the back.

16. Those used by notaries are now at the Archives Nationales de France: ADXX^C^/78–89. A further collection from the files of the Châtelet are at the Archives de Paris.

17. BnF, Ms. f.f. 22155.

18. Robert Darnton, "Policing Writers in Paris c. 1750," *Representations* 5 (1984): 1–31.

19. ENSBA, Ms. 22.

20. Fidière, *État civil*, nos. 4, 5, 11, 23, 26, 42, 58, 127.

21. See Georges Duplessis, "Académie de peinture et de sculpture: Liste des members par Reynès," *Revue universelle des arts*, 4 (1856): 313–26 at 314.

22. On the role of the secretary, see Christian Michel, *Charles-Nicolas Cochin et l'art des lumières* (Rome: Ecole Française de Rome, 1993), 81.

23. See Fidière, *État civil*, nos. 1, 2, 11, 48 (founder members); nos. 82, 107, 168, 171 (son/daughter of an academician); no. 58 (painted the altarpiece in the church where he was buried).

24. See Fidière, *État civil*, nos. 5, 7, 12, 16, 37, 38, 47, 53, 72, 87, 97, 112, 177. The last four (Samuel Bernard, Louis Elle Ferdinand, Jacques Rousseau, and Jean Forest) converted to Catholicism and were reintegrated into the Académie. See also Lucien Raulet, "Les billets d'enterrement d'artistes huguenots de l'ancienne Académie royale de peinture et de sculpture (1653–1712)," *Bulletin de la Société de l'histoire du protestantisme,* 1907, 53–69.

25. *PV*, 3:197–98 (10 October 1681).

26. ENSBA, Ms. 475.

27. ENSBA, Ms. 475, 39–40.

28. See Jacqueline Lichtenstein and Christian Michel, *Conférences de l'Académie royale de peinture et de sculpture* (Paris: ENSBA, 2008), 2, pt. 1:31–387.

29. See Préaud, "On ne meurt qu'une fois."

30. See, for example, during the first decade of the eighteenth century: *PV*, 3:319 (death of Antoine Paillet, recteur); 4:30 (death of Thomas Regnaudin, adjoint recteur, and Nicolas de Plattemontagne, professeur); 4:54 (death of Noël Coypel, recteur); 4:129 (death of Étienne Baudet, conseiller).

Gaming Set

Jean-Étienne Liotard (1702–89)

TYPE OF OBJECT	THEME	MATERIAL
Commodity, Container, Gift	Global Commerce, Leisure, Luxury, Travel	Animal | Shell, Plant Matter | Wood, Synthetic Materials | Lacquer, Synthetic Materials | Paper, Textile | Silk

Jean-Étienne Liotard's gaming set is an exquisite Chinese box, by origin and operation: an exotic luxury object that entices at every layer of its unboxing (fig. 60).[1] Kept in storage in the Musée d'Art et d'Histoire in Liotard's hometown of Geneva, the set still resides in its original traveling box, made to measure from rough wooden boards, painted black on the outside, with the artist's initials, JEL, still legible on a handwritten label in the corner. Protected inside is the set's principal container: a sumptuous black and gold lacquer box, decorated all over with botanical designs and Liotard's initials again, this time more formally painted in a cartouche on the lid. Opening that lid, the unpacker is greeted by five smaller lacquer boxes nestled perfectly within, decorated in a similar fashion to the main box, complete with initialed cartouches, but each one slightly individualized by the form or placement of a leaf or stem. With the final layer of boxes reached, the next mystery is their contents. Two of the small boxes are empty, presumably left so in order to accommodate two decks of cards, which would fit comfortably in their confines. The other three together contain the ultimate treasure trove: 140 mother-of-pearl counters—20 oval, 40 round, and 80 shuttle-shaped—each incised with more decorative designs, and every single one bearing the artist's initials in the center (fig. 61).

Accepting this object's ineluctable invitation to open, touch, and admire, a close encounter with its materiality reveals much about the gaming set's function but somewhat less about its actual use, because its pristine condition points more to inactivity than vigorous play—a gaming set that did not see much gaming. Yet it is perhaps more accurate to think of this as an object whose history of use merely differed from its intended function, for even unused things are functional in other ways. And Liotard's gaming set certainly served many purposes in its far-from-sedentary life, as an item of international trade, a munificent gift, and a luxurious thing of beauty.

Liotard's gaming box may not suffer the telltale scuffs and chips of a well-worn set, but it definitely bears traces of playful interaction. Sets like this were not games in their own right (like chess or backgammon sets), but rather counters that facilitated a variety of card games. Card playing took off dramatically in the eighteenth century at every social level, from the bawdy gambling spaces of taverns and fairs to the decadent salons and *soirées* of the aristocracy, where games of whist, piquet, réversis, or quadrille could bring hours of amusement. Liotard's set belonged to the latter world, even if Liotard himself did not.

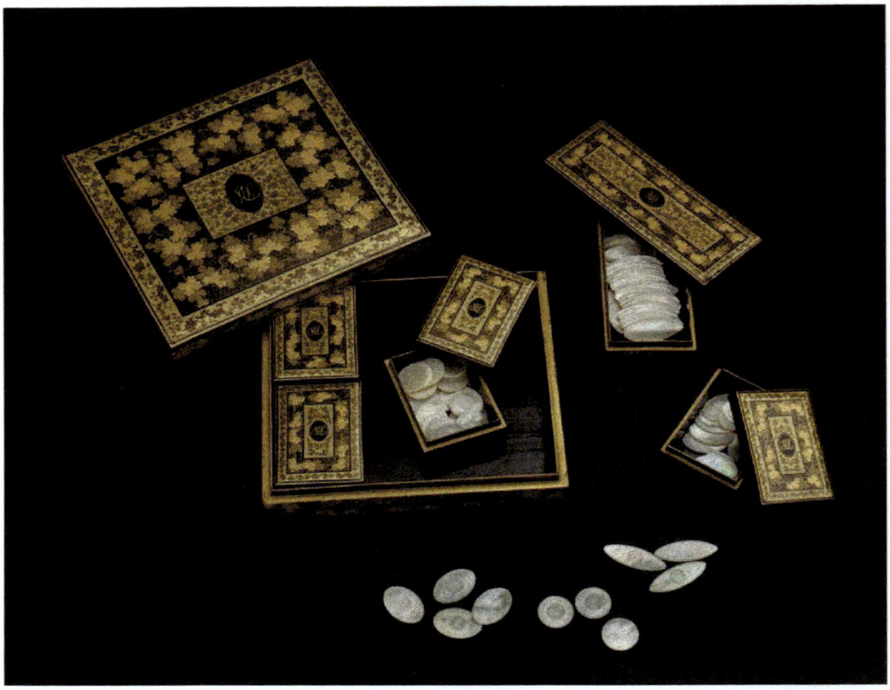

FIG. 60 Jean-Étienne Liotard's Chinese lacquer gaming set, ca. 1770–80. Main box: 6.5 × 29 × 27 cm. Wood, black lacquer, gilding, mother-of-pearl, and silk. Geneva, Musée d'Art et d'Histoire, Don de Marie-Margereta Liotard-Hülsche r, 1975. (Photo © Musées d'art et d'histoire, Ville de Genève, photo: Flora Bevilacqua.)

Tucked into the box, there are two additional items that bear witness to the set's ludic activities. One is a hemmed square of silk—red on one side, blue on the other—large enough to be thrown over a table to ready it instantly for gaming purposes, providing a soft, silky surface to lay cards and toss counters. The other is a scoring card for a game called *Boston russe* (fig. 62).

Devised in France in the 1770s, Boston was a trick-taking game (similar to whist or quadrille) in which players placed bids for the number of tricks they could win. The highest bidder then sought to achieve their tally, either alone or in a pair, while the others thwarted the mission.[2] Named after the American Revolutionary War (1775–83), Boston had a specific terminology inspired by transatlantic events, like bids known as a "Philadélphie" or an "Indépendence." *Boston russe* (Russian Boston) was not a Russian version but rather a variant in which diamonds were the top suit (as opposed to the usual hearts), and it had its own quite complicated scoring system, detailed in the two tables pasted to either side of Liotard's scoring card. Upon successful fulfillment of a bid, this card would be used to determine the player's reward, to be then paid out in those mother-of-pearl counters, each shape representing a different amount. Boston may have been Liotard's game of choice or merely a new fad that passed his way, but the presence of the card suggests it was certainly a game enjoyed at some point by the artist, in a leisurely moment with friends or family.

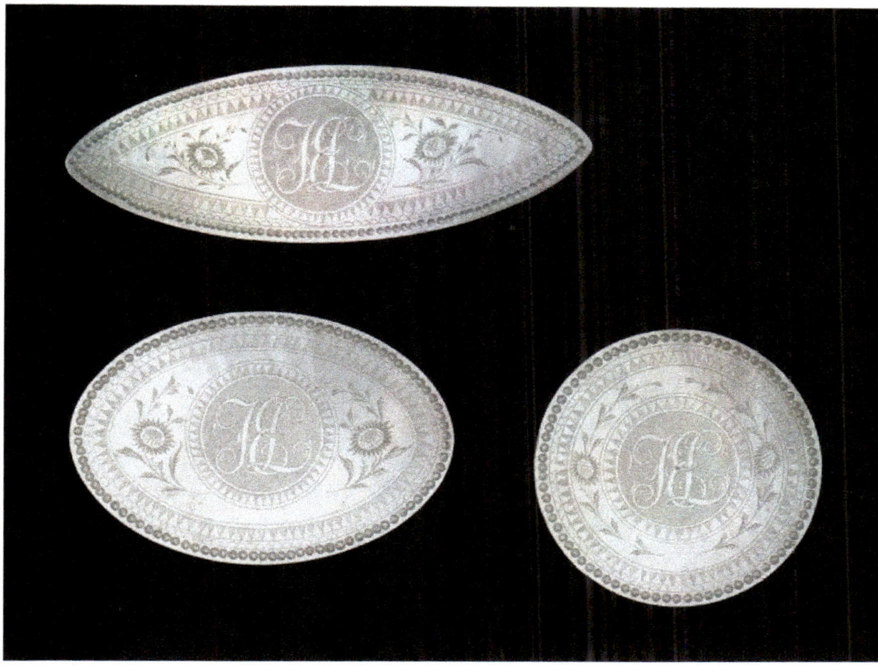

FIG. 61 Three counters from Liotard's Chinese lacquer gaming set, ca. 1770–80. Mother-of-pearl. Geneva, Musée d'Art et d'Histoire, Don de Marie-Margereta Liotard-Hülsche r, 1975. (Photo © Musée d'art et d'histoire, Ville de Genève, photo: Flora Bevilacqua.)

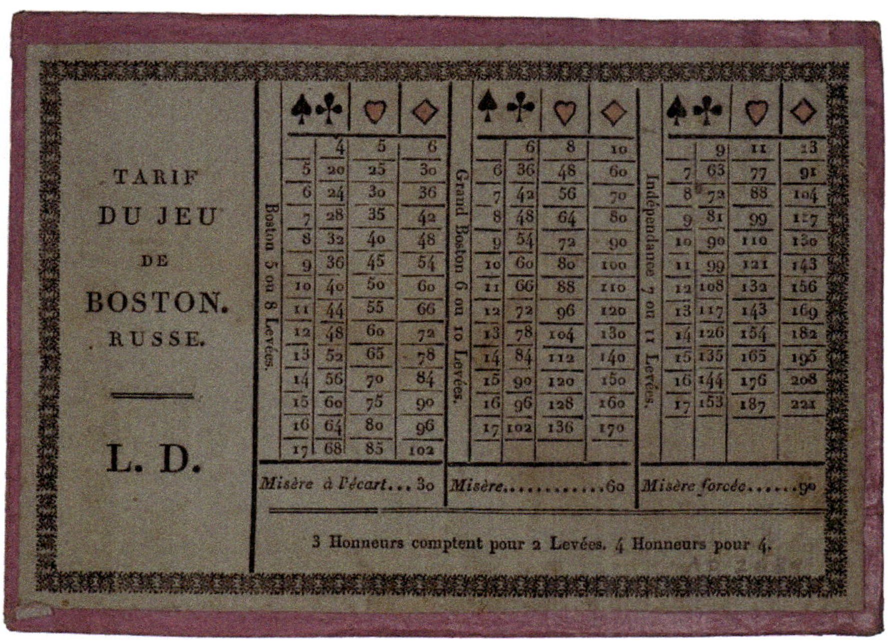

TARIF DU JEU DE BOSTON. RUSSE.

L. D.

Boston 5 ou 8 Levées.

	♠♣	♥	♦
	4	5	6
5	20	25	30
6	24	30	36
7	28	35	42
8	32	40	48
9	36	45	54
10	40	50	60
11	44	55	66
12	48	60	72
13	52	65	78
14	56	70	84
15	60	75	90
16	64	80	96
17	68	85	102

Misère à l'écart... 30

Grand Boston 6 ou 10 Levées.

	♠♣	♥	♦
	6	8	10
6	36	48	60
7	42	56	70
8	48	64	80
9	54	72	90
10	60	80	100
11	66	88	110
12	72	96	120
13	78	104	130
14	84	112	140
15	90	120	150
16	96	128	160
17	102	136	170

Misère..............60

Indépendance 7 ou 11 Levées.

	♠♣	♥	♦
	9	11	13
7	63	77	91
8	72	88	104
9	81	99	117
10	90	110	130
11	99	121	143
12	108	132	156
13	117	143	169
14	126	154	182
15	135	165	195
16	144	176	208
17	153	187	221

Misère forcée......90

3 Honneurs comptent pour 2 Levées. 4 Honneurs pour 4.

FIG. 62 Scoring card for *Boston russe* in Liotard's gaming set. Printed paper on card. Geneva, Musée d'Art et d'Histoire, Don de Marie-Margereta Liotard-Hülsche r, 1975. (Photo: © Musée d'art et d'histoire, Ville de Genève, photo: Flora Bevilacqua.)

Like most eighteenth-century artists, Liotard, the son of a tailor, was not born to the leisured classes.[3] But painting was a profession that could grant its practitioners access to the most elite circles. As a portraitist active throughout the royal courts and high societies of Europe, Liotard had a wide experience of these social worlds, their luxurious materials, and their entertainments.[4] Indeed, while the precise origins of Liotard's gaming set are somewhat obscure, tradition has it that the box was a gift from none other than Maria Theresa, Hapsburg empress and mother of the French queen Marie-Antoinette.[5] Liotard developed a certain professional intimacy with Maria Theresa over many years, visiting Vienna several times (1743–45, 1762, and 1777–78), becoming an acquaintance of the court, and painting numerous, sometimes quite informal portraits of the empress and her family. When his second daughter was born in 1763, he named her Marie-Thérèse and asked the empress to be her godmother.[6] If the gaming set was a gift from his most powerful patron (eminently plausible given the significant cost of such an object, and given the empress's penchant for lacquer), it was probably made in 1778.[7] When Liotard was leaving the court at the end of that visit, Maria Theresa is known to have presented him with a boxed porcelain coffee service (fig. 63) as a gift for his wife.[8] Given the formal synergies of these two boxed luxuries, it is certainly tempting to envisage the porcelain service and the gaming set as an elegant (and readily transportable) pair of gifts—for husband and wife—in recognition of Liotard's artistic services to the court.

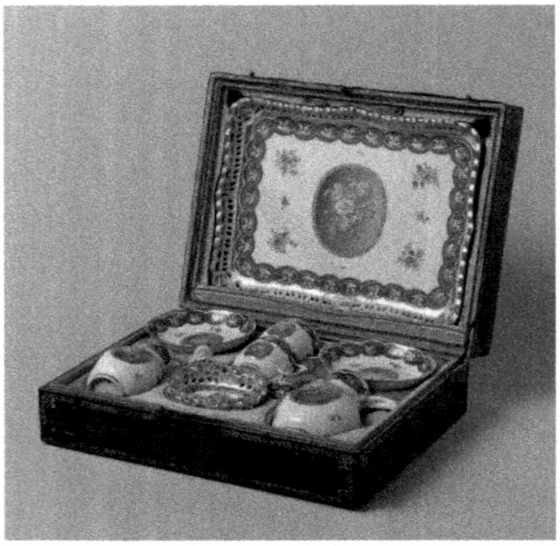

FIG. 63 Kaiserliche Porzellanmanufaktur, Coffee service for two people (Tête-à-Tête) given to Liotard by Empress Maria Theresa, ca. 1775–78. Porcelain, gold, leather, wood. Amsterdam, Rijksmuseum, Gift of L. Haase Scheltema, BK-1960-35.

While the coffee service was a local production, made in Vienna's Kaiserliche Porzellanmanufaktur, the Chinese gaming set had more global origins.[9] Of all the things in this book, Liotard's lacquer box is among those that traveled the farthest to reach the European home it would come to inhabit, though some of Boucher's Pacific **shells** and Nattier's Japanese porcelain **teacup** also vie for that accolade. Liotard's gaming set found its way to Geneva, via Vienna, from the city of Canton (now Guangzhou), which from 1757 was the only Chinese port permitted by the Qing court to trade with Europeans.[10] Like most things traded in Canton, the set would have been produced expressly for the export market and procured by a European trader from one of the many shops on Old or New China Street selling lacquerware, porcelain, silk, paintings, carved ivory, tortoiseshell, and mother-of-pearl.[11] A watercolor depicting a lacquerware shop in Canton (fig. 64) that is showing numerous lacquer boxes displayed on open shelves suggests that many of the wares sold here were made speculatively for immediate sale. But Liotard's set would have been custom ordered, with a lacquerware maker and a mother-of-pearl carver employed to paint and incise the artist's initials—JEL—on every element of the set. Creating personalized objects with initials or crests was a common practice in Canton, with empty cartouches waiting to be filled when traders arrived, but it added to the cost and required more time to prepare the commission.[12] Liotard's gaming set was thus not only an expensive gift but one planned well in advance.

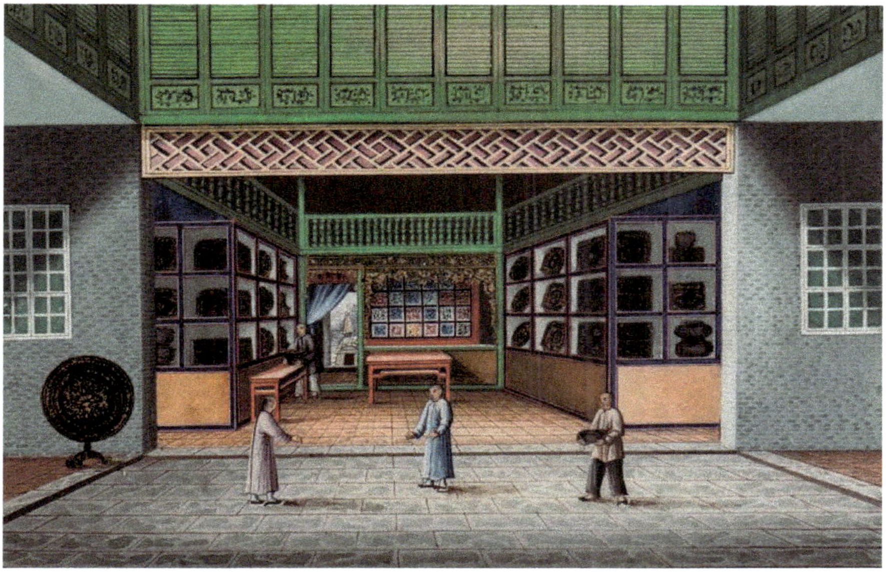

FIG. 64 Unknown artist, *Interior of a Lacquerware Shop, Canton, Old or New China Street*, 1840. Watercolor on paper, 11.5 × 17.2 cm. Collection of Edward G. Tiedemann, Jr., Ph.D. (Photograph by Kathy Tarantola.)

As a Chinese product imported into Europe via international trade routes, given to a Swiss-born artist by an Austrian empress, and used to play a French game called *Boston russe*, named after an American war, this was a thoroughly global object connecting three continents materially and conceptually. It is strangely appropriate, and probably not coincidental, that a thing with such global reach should have been owned by the eighteenth century's most notoriously cosmopolitan artist. Across his peripatetic career, Liotard lived in cities throughout Europe and its Asian borders, spending his working life (in descending order of duration) in Geneva, Paris, Vienna, Amsterdam, London, Constantinople, Rome, Florence, and Iaşi in Moldavia, plus visiting many others, but rarely staying anywhere longer than a few years. After he returned from Constantinople in the 1740s, he famously styled himself the "Turkish painter" and dressed accordingly, promoting his orientalist art through that intentionally exoticized persona.[13] Though his days of cultural cross-dressing were over by the 1770s, when he acquired the gaming set, his exotic reputation remained, no doubt making Far Eastern lacquerware seem like an ideal gift for the most adventurous artist-traveler of the day.

Though created to fulfil a specific leisurely purpose, Liotard's Chinese lacquer box was never a practical container in the vein of Fragonard's **color box** or the Académie's **document box**. That evident disjunction between its intended function (a gaming set to be played with) and its actual use (a beautiful thing to be given and admired) was always inherent in its materiality. Lacquer, gold, and mother-of-pearl made the set a luxury, an exotic commodity, a worthy gift from a powerful monarch, but they also made this thing's functionality secondary to all its aesthetic charms. ‡

---

1. Thanks to Bénédicte De Donker, Noémie Étienne, and David Pullins for discussions about this object.

2. *Règles raisonnées du jeu de Boston* (Paris: Defrelle, 1808).

3. On Liotard's biography, see Neil Jeffares, *Dictionary of Pastellists before 1800*, www.pastellists.com/Articles/LIOTARD.pdf.

4. William Hauptman, "British Royal and Society Portraits" and "Continental Royal and Society Portraits," in *Jean-Étienne Liotard, 1702–1789*, exh. cat. (Royal Académie of Arts, London; Scottish National Gallery, Edinburgh: 2015–16), 91–101, 127–33.

5. This legend of the imperial gift is recorded as the probable provenance by the Musée d'Art et d'Histoire.

6. Marcel Roethlisberger and Renée Loche, *Liotard: Catalogue, sources, et correspondence*, 2 vols. (Doornspijk: Davaco, 2008), 1:45.

7. On the empress's interest in lacquer, see Michael Yonan, "Veneers of Authority: Chinese Lacquers in Maria Theresa's Vienna," *ECS* 37, no. 4 (2004): 652–72.

8. This timing corresponds both with the dating of the object and the period in which Boston was first being played. On the gift of the coffee service, see Jean-Étienne Liotard to his son, Jean-Étienne Liotard, 27 May 1783, in Roethlisberger and Loche, *Liotard*, 2:767.

9. Maria Theresa also had interests in local production of lacquer (see Yonan, "Veneers of Authority"), but Liotard's gaming set has been firmly attributed as a product of China by curators at Geneva's Musée d'Art et d'Histoire.

10. Paul A. Van Dyke, *Merchants of Canton and Macao: Success and Failure in Eighteenth-Century Chinese Trade* (Hong Kong: Hong Kong University Press, 2016), 2.

11. On Canton's shopping streets, see Patrick Conner, *The Hongs of Canton: Western Merchants in South China 1700–1900* (London: English Art Books, 2009), 75–88.

12. On lacquerware and mother-of-pearl exports, see Carl L. Crossman, *The Decorative Arts of the China Trade: Paintings, Furnishings and Exotic Curiosities* (Woodbridge: Antique Collectors' Club, 1991), 263–88, 289–96.

13. On the "peintre turc," see Mary D. Sheriff, "The Dislocations of Jean-Étienne Liotard, Called the Turkish Painter," in *Cultural Contact and the Making of European Art since the Age of Exploration* (Chapel Hill: University of North Carolina Press, 2010), 97–121.

Glasses

François-André Vincent (1746–1816)

TYPE OF OBJECT	THEME	MATERIAL
Apparel, Instrument	Health/Medicine, Invention, Making, Studio	Metal | Bronze, Metal | Steel, Synthetic Materials | Glass

It is difficult to take one's eyes off François-André Vincent's glasses. In his portrait, at forty-nine, painted by Adélaïde Labille-Guiard—a lifelong acquaintance who would become his wife five years later—Vincent's glasses are a conspicuous accessory (fig. 65).[1] They occupy only a fraction of the canvas's surface area, but their location over the eyes of the sitter—where the beholder's own eyes are inevitably drawn and redrawn—ensure that this optical device becomes the focus of everyone's gaze. Yet what is perhaps most distracting about Vincent's glasses is less their lenses than their arms. Compositionally and formally, these insistent appendages demand attention, with their sudden stark linearity amid the soft contours of his face, with the darkness of the metal against his pale skin and gray hair, and with the quietly observed detail of their engineered construction. The lug and hinge at the front, where the arm meets the frame, is a regular feature of spectacles to this day; but far less familiar to the modern eye is the other end, where instead of curving gently around the ear, the arm bends abruptly at a sharp angle behind Vincent's head. This tiny detail may also have caught the attention of Vincent's contemporaries, though for entirely different reasons. For what appears today as a cumbersome, outmoded feature was, in the eighteenth-century, the height of optometric technology.

By the time Vincent was sporting his spectacles in the 1790s, lens technology was long-established (dating back at least to the thirteenth century), but the development of the arm had been one of the eighteenth century's major design innovations.[2] For an artist like Vincent, or indeed anyone who required glasses in their work, the invention of the arm as a means of securing lenses to the face had been a liberating convenience. Before these lateral appendages, lenses either had to be attached to headwear—like Anna-Dorothea Therbusch's reading monocle in her *Self-Portrait* (fig. 66)—strapped to the head with cords or ribbons, or clamped to the nose—like Jean-Siméon Chardin's precarious *besicles*, worn in his *Self-Portrait* (fig. 67), which pinched so tightly that they restricted breathing. But at midcentury, a renowned Parisian *lunetier*, or eyeglass maker, Marc Mitouflet Thomin, advertised for sale in his shop "glasses with silver or steel arms," whose major selling points were that they "cling to the temples" and "do not impede respiration"[3] A pair of this first generation of armed spectacles were sketched by Vincent in Rome, clasped to the head of his fellow *pensionnaire* Pierre-Charles Jombert (fig. 68), revealing their rounded ends, which were sometimes padded with velvet to alleviate pressure on the side of the head.

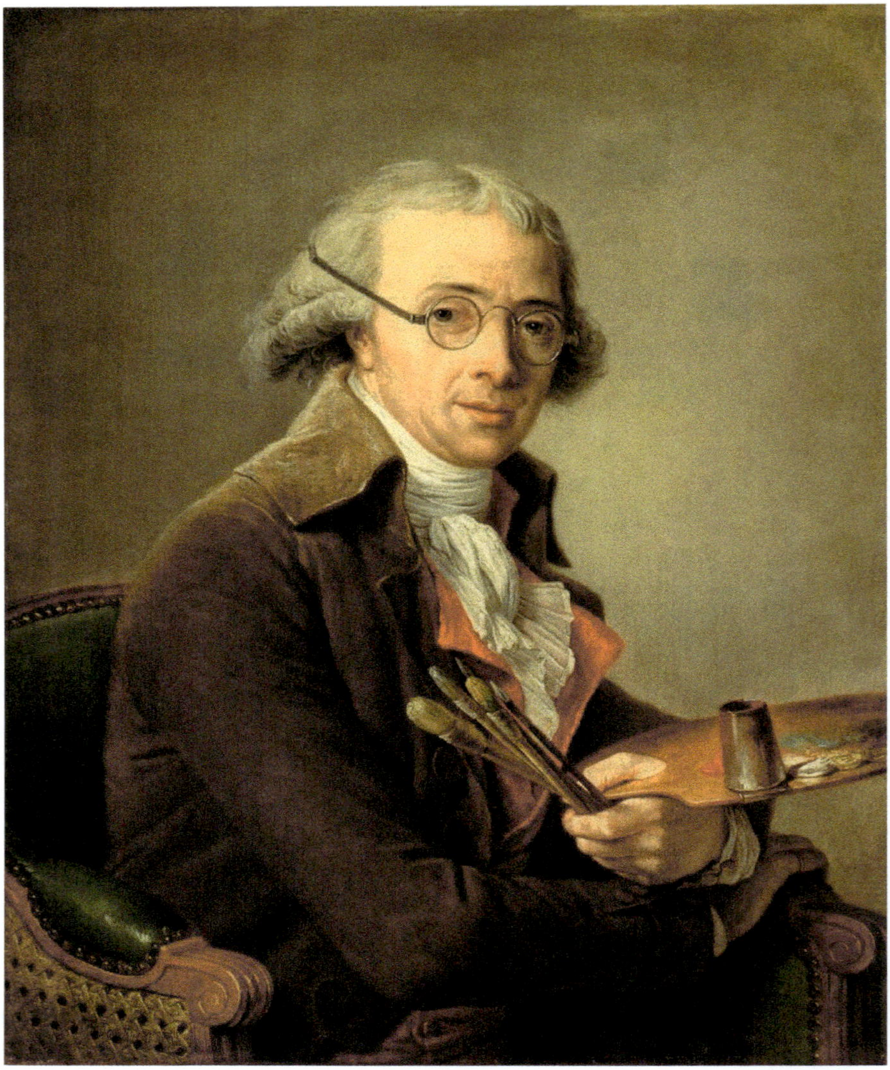

FIG. 65 Adélaïde Labille-Guiard (French, 1749–1803), *Portrait of François-André Vincent*, 1795. Oil on canvas, 73 × 59 cm. Paris, Musée du Louvre. (© RMN-Grand Palais / Photo: Hervé Lewandowski / Art Resource, NY.)

But Vincent's glasses were an example of the next advancement—the double-hinged side (fig. 69). No longer constraining breathing or pressing on the temples, these modern spectacles were specially designed with elongated and articulated arms to wrap neatly and lightly around the wigged head of the wearer.[4]

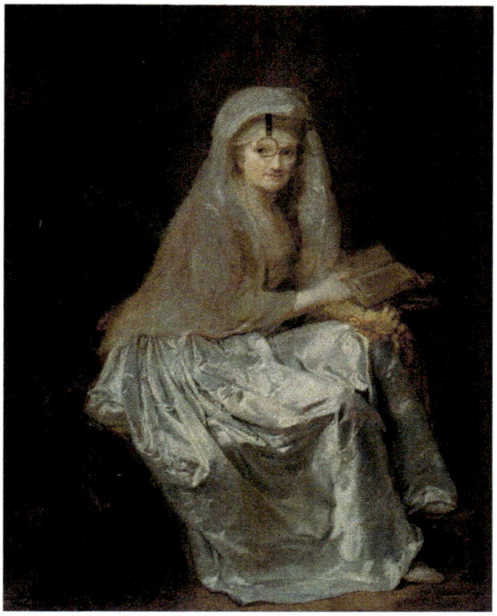

FIG. 66 Anna-Dorothea Therbusch (German, 1721/22–82), *Self-Portrait*, 1777. Oil on canvas, 154 × 118 cm. Berlin, Staatliche Museen, Inv. 1925. (bpk Bildagentur / Gemäldegalerie/Staatliche Museen/Berlin/Germany /Photo: Jörg P. Anders/ Art Resource, NY.)

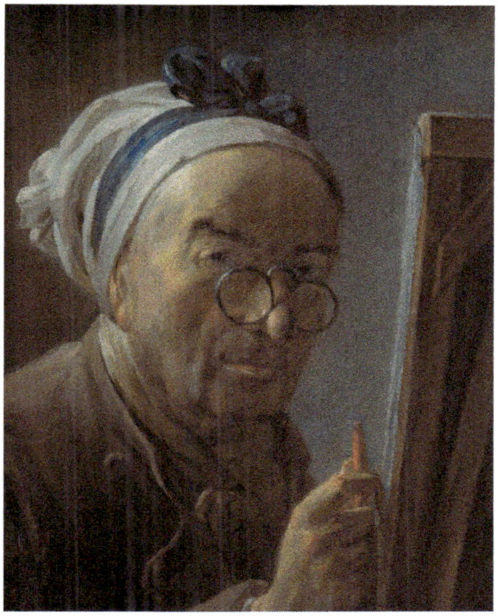

FIG. 67 Jean-Siméon Chardin (French, 1699–1779), *Self-Portrait*, 1776. Pastel on blue paper, 40.7 × 32.5 cm. Paris, Musée du Louvre, Département des Arts Graphiques, RF31748-recto. (© RMN-Grand Palais / photo: Michel Urtado / Art Resource, NY.)

Technologies of design no doubt influenced Vincent's decision in his acquisition of this latest development in eyewear. But while arms were important, it was the lenses that were crucial; remaining comfortably attached to the face was a desirable quality for a pair of glasses, but their principal function was correcting vision. As sight was an indispensable sense for an eighteenth-century painter, correcting its deterioration or dysfunction was essential for continued professional activity. Indeed, the *lunetier* Mitouflet Thomin considered artists among those "who have the greatest need to spare and fortify their sight with the aid of . . . glasses," and he described many items in his shop as being of particular use to the artistic professions.[5] Most of these instruments were made using lenses ground precisely from glass into one of three main types: concave lenses for correcting shortsightedness; convex lenses for correcting longsightedness; and double-sided convex lenses for the intense magnification required in items like telescopes and microscopes.[6] Aside from spectacles, these were the kinds of optical devices that Mitouflet Thomin envisaged for his artist customers: magnifying glasses and handheld microscopes for painters and engravers; lenses that shrunk objects, for the use of miniature painters; glass prisms with which painters could learn about color; and **camera obscuras** for "drawing with no master."[7]

Vincent did not purchase his glasses from the shop of Mitouflet Thomin, who died many years before the history painter's vision required correcting.[8] While Vincent's particular spectacle maker is not known, it is quite likely that he acquired this pair from a *lunetier* somewhere on the Île de la Cité. In 1798, when the *Almanach du Commerce* began its annual record of the trades of Paris, there were still only fifteen *lunetiers* in the city, and all but four of them were on the island.[9] The greatest concentration was on Quai de l'Horloge, where its seven spectacle shops helped earn the street its nickname, "Quai des Lunettes."[10] Vincent was living in the Louvre in the 1790s (remaining there until 1802, when he moved across the river to the Palais des Beaux-Arts in the Institut), so the Quai de l'Horloge was certainly a convenient shopping destination for a man who would have crossed Pont-Neuf with regularity.[11] And given the number of optical aids in Vincent's possession, he must have been a keen and frequent customer of the *lunetiers* of Paris.

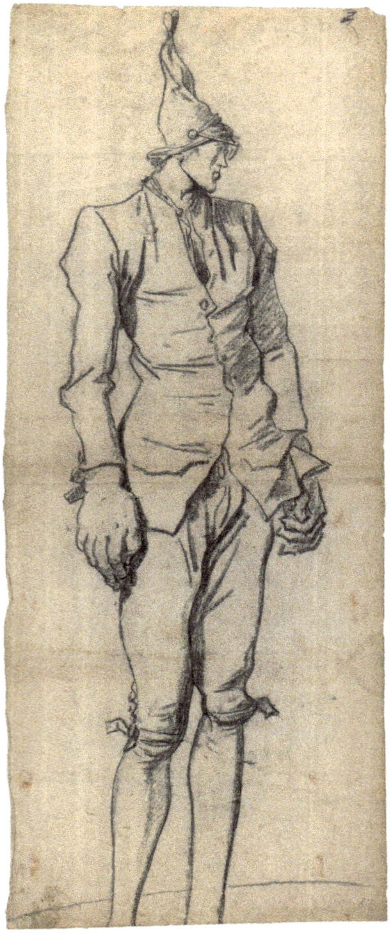

FIG. 68 François-André Vincent (French, 1746–1816), *Caricature of Pierre-Charles Jombert*, detail, 1773–75. Black chalk, 107 × 43 cm. New York, Metropolitan Museum of Art, The Elisha Whittelsey Collection, The Elisha Whittelsey Fund, 1967. (Image copyright © The Metropolitan Museum of Art. Image source: Art Resource, NY.)

When the inventory was taken of Vincent's apartments in the Palais des Beaux-Arts after his death in 1816, there were at least seven devices for correcting or enhancing the artist's vision.[12] This optical haul included three pairs of glasses: two pairs of *lunettes* with steel frames (like those depicted in Labille-Guiard's portrait), and one more glamorous pair with gold arms, which was kept in a bespoke shagreen case with silver decoration (this pair alone was valued at 60 francs). In addition, Vincent also owned a *loupe* (a magnifying glass); two *lorgnettes de spectacle* (opera glasses with handles), one ivory, one tortoiseshell; and a *lunette à longue vue* (a spyglass or small telescope). Despite this extensive list of optical instruments, it is difficult to determine the kind of vision problems that afflicted Vincent.[13] His magnifying glass would have been used for close work; his opera glasses and spyglass for viewing at distance; and his pairs of *lunettes* could have corrected either myopia or hyperopia, depending on the shape of the lenses. While lens type can sometimes be deduced by seeing the eye behind its lens (the convex lenses correcting hyperopia making eyes appear larger and the concave lenses for myopia making them smaller), even Labille-Guiard's portrait cannot assist in a definitive diagnosis, for neither eye looks particularly enlarged or reduced. However, the fact that Vincent gazes *through* the lenses, as he looks over at his companion painting the portrait, would seem to tip the scales in favor of myopia. In contrast to the apparently hyperopic Chardin (see fig. 67), who looks over his *besicles* to see himself in the mirror, and Therbusch (see fig. 66), who has donned her monocle to read her book, Vincent seems to require his *lunettes* to focus on something farther away.[14]

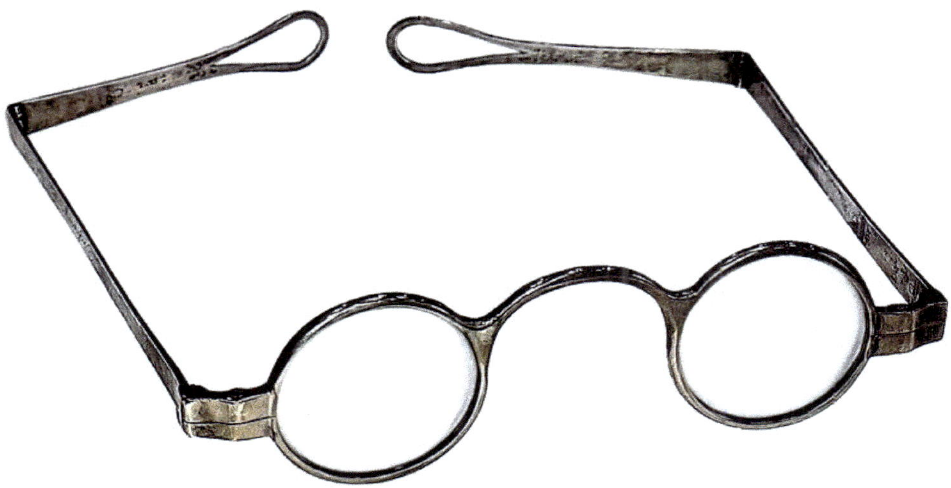

FIG. 69 Double-hinged wig spectacles, ca. 1795. White metal frame and glass lenses, 38 mm (eye). London, British Optical Association Museum, College of Optometrists, inv. 1998.235. (© College of Optometrists British Optical Association Museum.)

For a history painter, distance vision was more important than it was for many other artists. While miniature painters and engravers worked in close proximity to both their subjects and their supports, history painters were often pushed back: looking at posed models across a room, studying spaces for settings, and forming compositions on large canvases. Among the Académie's genres, perhaps only the landscapist required a longer gaze. In a period when painting was still necessarily an art of visual representation, failing eyesight was a dire affliction for a painter, threatening the ability to continue professional practice. For Chardin, visual impairment is commonly attributed as the cause of his shift from oils to pastels in his later years. Writing to the comte d'Angiviller only of his "infirmities," Chardin did not blame his eyesight specifically, but clearly some aspect of his health forced him to alter his approach in order to keep on painting.[15] For his part, Vincent made no drastic changes to his practice and recorded no complaints about his eyesight.[16] It would appear, therefore, that by relying on his corrective lenses, Vincent's visual health remained professionally robust.

Vincent's glasses were thus an indispensable tool for the middle-aged artist, as essential a workday item as his palette and brushes, as Labille-Guiard's portrait suggests.

Yet while their presence was a professional necessity, Vincent seems also to have been adept at deploying their absence for strategic gain. One evening he was invited to the home of his neighbor, the artist Adélaïde-Marie-Anne Castellas, wife of the sculptor Jean-Guillaume Moitte. When he arrived, she was showing her latest drawings to a friend, and she invited Vincent to join them and offer his thoughts on her work. But somewhat conveniently, so Madame Moitte thought, Vincent made excuses, claiming that he was "completely blind in the evenings," and was thus tactfully relieved of having to make any commentaries at all.[17] Clearly on that occasion, Vincent found it more professionally and socially expedient to leave his glasses at home. ‡

---

1. The Louvre portrait is an autograph version of the original, which remained in the collection of Labille-Guiard and Vincent until their deaths. Anne-Marie Passez, *Adélaïde Labille-Guiard: Biographie et catalogue raisonné* (Paris: Arts et Métiers graphiques, 1973), 266.

2. Astrid Vitols, *Dictionnaire des lunettes: Historique et symbolique d'un objet culturel* (Paris: Christine Bonneton, 1994), 45–48.

3. Marc Mitouflet Thomin, *Instruction sur l'usage des lunettes ou conserves pour toutes sortes de vues* (Paris: Claude Lamesle, 1746), 128.

4. The evolution of eighteenth-century glasses can be seen in the historical collections held at the Musée des Lunettes et Lorgnettes–Pierre Marly, Paris, or the Museum of the College of Optometrists, London.

5. Mitouflet Thomin, *Instruction*, 16.

6. Plate I, "Lunetier," *Encyclopédie*, http://encyclopedie.uchicago.edu/, 22:13:1. See also "Myope" and "Presbyte," *Encyclopédie,* http://encyclopedie.uchicago.edu/, 10:913 and 13:309.

7. Mitouflet Thomin, *Instruction*, 126–27.

8. Mitouflet Thomin died in 1752.

9. There were also five "opticiens," two of whom were based on the Île de la Cité, and one on Quai de l'Horloge. *Almanach du Commerce et de toutes les addresses de la ville de Paris* (Paris: Favre, Year VII [1798]), 238–39, 361.

10. Vitols, *Dictionnaire des lunettes*, 116.

11. Vincent was first granted apartments in the Louvre in 1784; he and Labille-Guiard moved to the former College des Quatre Nations in 1802. Jules-Joseph Guiffrey, "Brevets de logements dans la galerie du Louvre," *NAAF*, 1873, 101; and Jean-Pierre Cuzin, *François-André Vincent, 1746–1816* (Paris: Arthena, 2013), 322–23.

12. François-André Vincent, "Inventaire après décès," 9 August 1816, AN, MC/ET/LXIV/577. The inventory also mentions "trois paires de ciseaux," which may have been either scissors or *binocles ciseaux* (pairs of corrective lenses with a single central handle). For Vincent's inventory, see also Cuzin, *François-André Vincent*, 524–31.

13. Mansfield and Cuzin both discuss Vincent's health problems, recorded in various primary sources. These mostly relate to a delicate constitution in his youth (due to which he suffered in the heat and sun of Rome) and nervous attacks in his later years. Elizabeth C. Mansfield, *The Perfect Foil: François-André Vincent and the Revolution in French Painting* (Minneapolis: University of Minnesota Press, 2012), 5, 56–57; and Cuzin, *François-André Vincent*, 61.

14. Chardin made three different self-portraits in the 1770s (in numerous versions); in two he looks at himself over his *besicles*, while in the other he looks through the lenses with his eyes shaded by a visor. On the multiple versions, see Neil Jeffares, *Dictionary of Pastellists before 1800*, http://www.pastellists.com/Articles/Chardin.pdf.

15. Jean-Siméon Chardin to comte d'Angiviller, 21 July 1778. Marc Furcy-Raynaud, *Chardin et M. d'Angiviller: Correspondance inédite de l'artiste et de sa femme avec le directeur général des bâtiments du roi* (Paris: Chamerot et Renouard, 1900), 31.

16. Once he mentioned being sick and unable to read, but he did not specify eyesight as the problem. François-André Vincent to Pierre-Narcisse Guérin, 5 November 1804. Cuzin, *François-André Vincent*, 542–43.

17. *Journal inédit de Madame Moitte, femme de Jean-Guillaume Moitte, statuaire*, ed. Paul Cottin (Paris: Plon, 1932), 62.

Handkerchief

Charles-Nicolas Cochin (1715–90)

TYPE OF OBJECT	THEME	MATERIAL
Apparel, Commodity, Companion, Gift, Tool	Death, Everyday, Friendship, Health/ Medicine	Textile | Cotton, Textile | Linen

On 30 June 1782, the draftsman and printmaker Charles-Nicolas Cochin the Younger, formerly secretary of the Académie and responsible for the day-to-day royal administration of the arts during the ministry of the marquis de Marigny, wrote from Paris to his friend and fellow academician, the painter Jean-Baptiste Descamps at Rouen, with a "small commission": purchase on his behalf of a dozen pocket handkerchiefs.[1] The handkerchiefs do not survive, but Cochin's letters do. Carefully kept by the Rouennais artist, they were ceded at Descamps's death along with the rest of his papers to the Académie de Rouen and are now at the Bibliothèque Municipale. Indirectly these letters afford evidence of the penetration of a relatively new and apparently elite thing into the consumer lives of artists. They unfold, at this one level, a practical narrative of getting in all its particular historical complexity and associated anxiety. At another, however, the handkerchief opened up a discursive space for the correspondents, supplying them with an anchor, reassuring in its banal materiality, for reflection on transcendental matters of art and death.

Of the importance of the commission to Cochin there can be no doubt. He was embarrassed, in fact, by the length and detail with which he set out his instructions and apologized for his long-winded chat on so trivial a matter in the letter of 30 June. A month later, he wrote again and began by shamefacedly admitting to "pestering you and ruining you in postal charges" for the sake of his petty haberdashery wants, before giving equally detailed instructions for the delivery of the handkerchiefs to his *logement* (lodgings) at the Louvre.[2] In August, two additional letters on the subject followed in which Cochin warmly thanked his friend and arranged payment.[3] From the letters we learn that Cochin didn't know where to shop for such items in Paris and that he had lately been in the habit of buying his handkerchiefs at Orléans, through which he passed once a year en route to the marquis de Marigny's country estate, Ménars.[4] However, Marigny's death in May 1781 had robbed him of the opportunity of shopping in person on Orléans's Rue Royale. His friend Aignan-Thomas Desfriches, amateur artist, sugar trader, and native of Orléans, had tried to make good the handicap.[5] He had sent Cochin samples of stuff from which to choose, but the handkerchiefs that had arrived from Orléans in April had disappointed, in spite of Desfriches's precautions.[6]

Cochin was not wrong in thinking that Rouen was better placed than Orléans to meet his needs. Cloth had been an important industry in that city and its hinterland since the seventeenth century. In 1737, when Louis-François-Armand Du Plessis, duc de Richelieu, was collecting samples of French stuffs for his library scrapbooks, Rouen's weavers were producing handkerchiefs in a range of stuffs, some cotton, others mixes (notably of cotton and linen) and in a range of colors and patterns, at prices starting at 36 livres and rising to 39 livres per dozen (fig. 70). Annual output from the city's workshops in 1737–38 was, according to the Richelieu albums, in excess of 30,000 pieces: the smallest were 18 centimeters square, the largest 860 centimeters.[7] Fifty years later, a memorandum on Rouen's cloth industry drawn up for the Bureau of Trade and Industry estimated that the 1,250 master weavers of Rouen and its environs were producing cotton goods to the value of 50 million livres per annum, of which handkerchiefs continued to form a significant proportion.[8]

Cochin told Descamps he was prepared to pay top price for such "beautiful" handkerchiefs as were to be had at Rouen: 36 livres for a dozen small ones and 48 livres for large ones.[9] He was evidently not too particular about size, but he was exigent about stuff and color. His preference, against general consumer trend, was for linen not cotton, for a robust handkerchief whose softness was countered by stoutness and absorbency. As to color, his first choice was for red ones, but he also countenanced brown. By the 1780s, so-called Turkey red, a saturated hue, had successfully been introduced at Rouen's dyeworks and was replacing the traditional darker, duller madder.[10] It provided precisely the strong color of handkerchief that Cochin was after and that is depicted in Jacques-Louis David's portrait of Jacobus Blauw (fig. 71).

In spite of the references to price and payment, the status of Cochin's handkerchiefs as either commodities or gifts is not certain. They stand apart from the gifts of food (sweets and cherries), the small coin of social bonding, that Descamps sent Cochin from time to time, and from the drawings, prints, and texts that Cochin, for his part, gave his friend.[11] The services required to unite Cochin with his new handkerchiefs involved, however, investments of time, attention, and personal care that are generally associated with gifts, the more so since, in order to avoid the custom duties of the *Grande Ferme*, Descamps had had to oversee the hemming and laundering of the handkerchiefs before their dispatch to Paris.[12] When Cochin requested a final invoice from his friend, he was sensitive to say that had this hemming and washing been done by Descamps's daughters, he would not insult them by offering wages, gallantly promising instead to send them an equal number of pairs of bedsheets in return.[13] Thus, Cochin's "small commission" for *petit linge* commodities was in its execution giftwrapped by the mutual regard of the parties for each other's feelings; it was the occasion and site of shared intimacy.

Why did handkerchiefs—objects of little intrinsic value and short lived—give rise to such feelings? The advent of handkerchiefs as items of dress in the seventeenth century has generally been linked to rising standards of polite comportment and personal

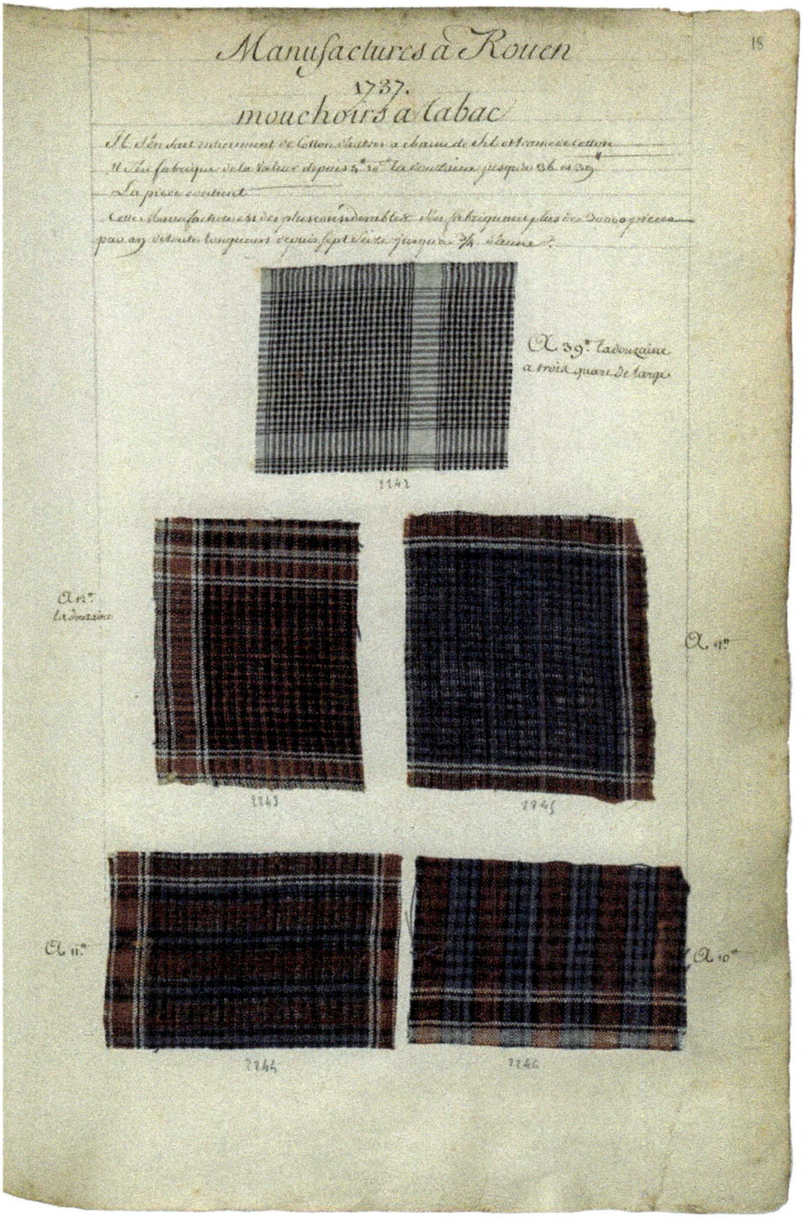

FIG. 70 Handkerchief samples from Rouen, 1737. Linen and cotton on paper. Paris, Bibliothèque Nationale de France.

hygiene.[14] Cochin acknowledged to Descamps that he felt obliged to keep up the appearance of nobility, given his **decoration** in 1757 with the cross of the Order of Saint Michel, though he was often short of the ready means for doing so.[15] The inventory of his clothes taken after his death in May 1790 confirms that commitment.[16] In the pair of wardrobes in his *cabinet*, notaries found twelve three-piece suits, five pairs of britches, seven frocks, eighteen waistcoats, and two redingotes. Most of the items were sober and of

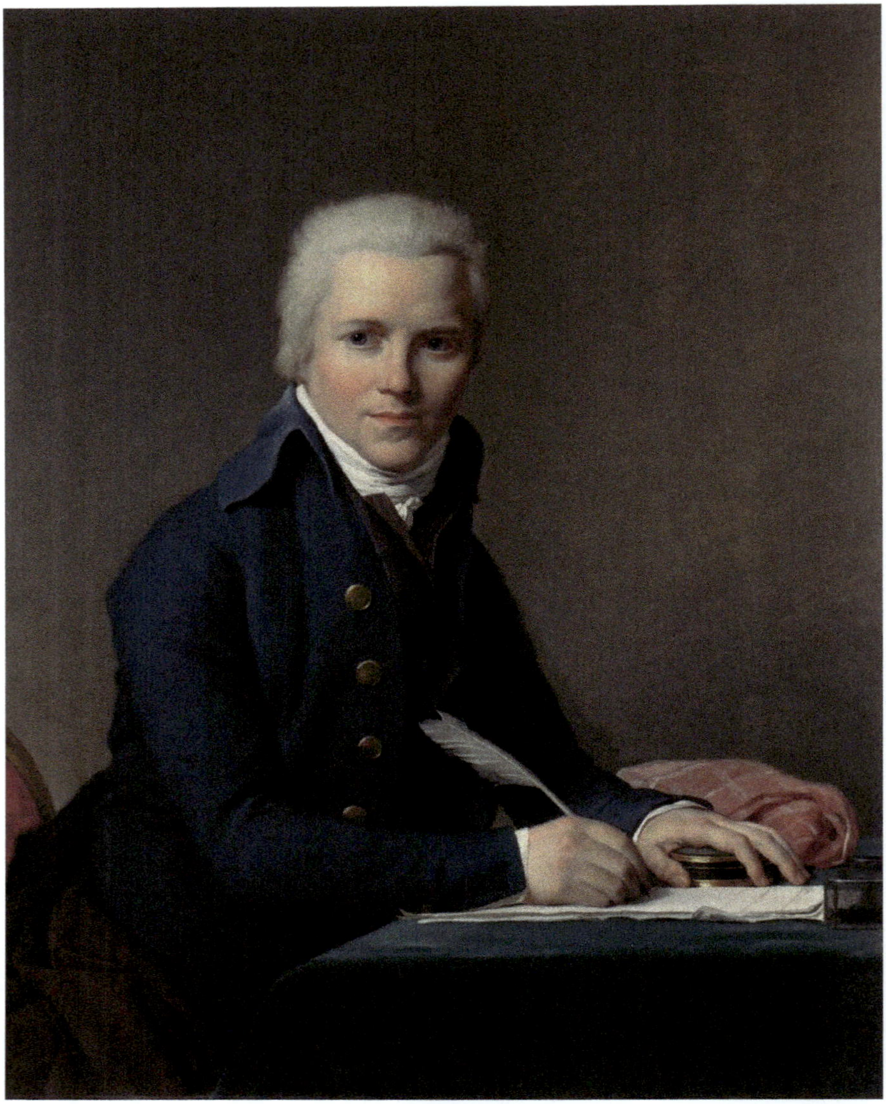

FIG. 71 Jacques-Louis David (French, 1748–1825), *Jacobus Blauw*, 1795. Oil on canvas, 92 × 73 cm. London, National Gallery, NG6495. (© National Gallery, London / Art Resource, NY.)

good woollen broadcloth: blacks, browns, and grays predominate. But there was luxury too: a brown suit with gold embroidery, another of "spring" or silk velvet with gold buttons. There were silk and satin breeches and, stunningly, a scarlet waistcoat embroidered with gold. His linen was likewise generous and included thirty-two shirts, four camisoles, five caps, thirteen collars, and six pairs of variously colored stockings, as well as twenty-six handkerchiefs.[17] The handkerchiefs Cochin was after were not, however, of the kind held by the *surintendent des bâtiments du roi* Antoine de Ratabon in Pierre Rabon's 1660 portrait, its finely woven folds glowing white in Ratabon's casually elegant grasp (fig. 72). Though handkerchiefs, Cochin's ideal corresponded more to *mouchoirs de col*, the large colored kerchiefs worn for work around the neck and head. Cochin's friend Jean-Siméon Chardin represented himself with two such in his 1771 self-portrait (Paris, Musée du Louvre) and in so doing voiced painting's connection with the trades because *mouchoirs de col* were items of the occupational dress of artisans, tradesmen, coachmen, and sailors.[18]

The contradictory evidence of the inventory of Cochin's wardrobe and the request expressed in his letters forestalls interpretation of his *mouchoirs à moucher* as signs of upward social mobility and increased bodily propriety. Cochin did, to be sure, emphasize to Descamps his need of thick, dark hankies, thick enough to prevent the unhappy feeling of blowing one's nose in one's hands, and dark enough to camouflage the shaming ocher stains of snot and phlegm discharged by snuff takers like himself and diplomat Blauw; Blauw's handkerchief is coupled with a **snuffbox** (see fig. 71).[19] But as mere pieces of unstructured cloth, handkerchiefs were close relatives of cleaning cloths and rags used in the studio. Their ambiguous status as both high—like fine linen collars and cuffs or cotton veils—and defiled was registered in history painting. In Nicolas Vleughels's *Apelles and Campaspe* (fig. 73), a scrap of white fabric smeared with yellow ocher lies on the floor. We might mistake it for a handkerchief, given its proximity to Apelles in yellow ***robe de chambre*** and to Campaspe cushioned and veiled in white and gold, were it not for the fallen paintbrush that has rolled away to the right.[20] Stuff played a significant role in the daily toilette of art—cleaning brushes and **palettes**, wiping copperplates—just as it did in the grooming and comfort of artists.[21]

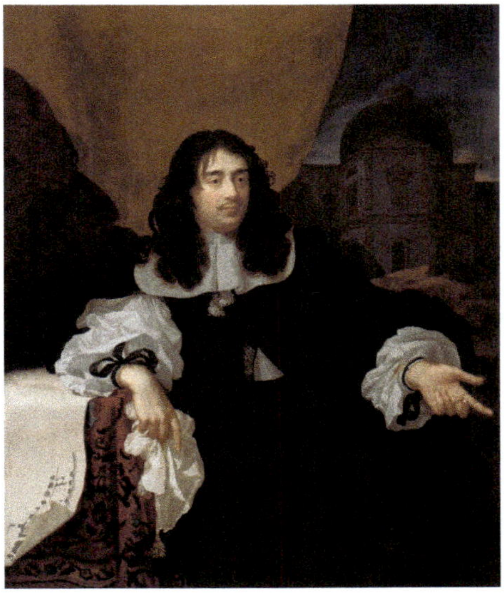

FIG. 72 Pierre Rabon (French, 1619–84), *Antoine de Ratabon*, 1660. Oil on canvas, 152 × 126 cm. Châteaux de Versailles et de Trianon, MV4346. (© RMN-Grand Palais / photo: Gerard Blot / Art Resource, NY.)

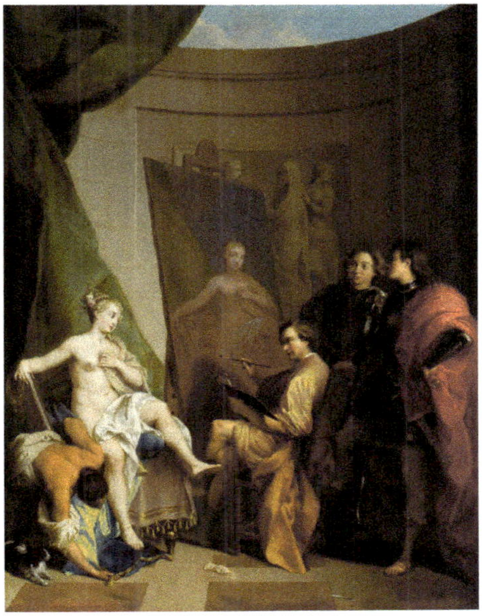

FIG. 73 Nicolas Vleughels (French, 1668–1737), *Apelles and Campaspe*, 1717. Oil on canvas, 125 × 97 cm. Paris, Musée du Louvre, Inv8482. (© RMN-Grand Palais / photo: Stéphane Maréchalle / Art Resource, NY.)

In light of the continuities in materiality, functionality, and signification across cloths as items of dress and as artistic tools, is there more to be said about Cochin's quest for handkerchiefs in 1782? Is the meaning of the handkerchief exhausted by reconstruction of the historical contexts of production and consumption and of the social connotation of handkerchiefs, high and low? If so, how do we account for the exceptional emotional investment of both parties in the exchange of words and things? More was surely at stake.

Cochin's request for handkerchiefs followed in the wake of regular news bulletins about his health in which he alluded to the messes and wastes of his aging body: he was sixty-six years old. He was plagued, apparently, by incurable sores and heavy colds that made his eyes weep.[22] The handkerchief, in this sense, indirectly denoted his failing body, itself the ultimate example, surely, of Bill Brown's reasoning that we are most aware of the thingness of things, of our mortality, when things and bodies break down.[23] Notwithstanding his ailments, Cochin continued to work; the state of his finances apparently left him no choice. The anxiety about his infirmities that Cochin projected onto his worry about the getting of handkerchiefs was, professionally speaking, not, however, an anxiety about practice and did not focus on sight or touch. The aged artist's shaky hand was virtually a trope in the narrative of artists' lives, but not one mobilized here.[24] Rather, Cochin worried, in a letter to Descamps in July 1781, about the cooling of his imagination, that is, of mental atrophy. He didn't think his talents were declining but couldn't be sure.[25] Three years earlier he had written at greater length about getting old and on the falling off of his genius, something he sought to remedy with a regimen of copying the Old Masters to nurture the embers of his remaining talent in the comforting knowledge that "should genius fail entirely no one will notice and it will save me the humiliation that befalls old men who work beyond their time."[26]

In theories of everyday life, repetition is often equated with commoditization, with the standardization of modern, industrially produced goods and with the homogenization of consumption.[27] It is tempting to interpret the copies that Cochin confessed to making, and indeed his late reprises of his earlier compositions, as analogues in art to the increasingly stock handkerchiefs offered for sale by industry and produced in the deregulated market that followed the suppression of the guilds in 1776. In such a picture, the natural bodily cycles of the artist-become-ancient-automaton are in harmony with the increasingly regimented cycles of modern, protoindustrial production. But by linking repetition with the highest standards of quality, the Old Masters, Cochin assigned a positive value to repetition. Moreover, as his comments to Descamps about the printmaker Jean-Baptiste Le Bas indicate, he was critical of precisely the routinization of practice and the cheapening of product that was becoming increasingly widespread in the printshops of late eighteenth-century Paris.[28] Cochin equated repetition with tradition. He understood it as a buttress (in art and in haberdashery) against the erosions of time and progress. In begging Descamps's help in the getting of "beautiful" handkerchiefs, he was asking not only for an apparently limited kind of thing but also for the rare values that such kinds embodied. Good handkerchiefs—thick, color-permanent, and square—made good artists.

They not only helped to articulate artistic identity and to secure, by cleaning, sharp lines and pure color respectively in printmaking and painting, they also perpetuated beauty and the dignity of artistic and artisanal work.

This portrait of Cochin's handkerchiefs accounts, we think, for the intensity of his concern for them. It describes how, as a material thing, a handkerchief could tether ideals of the aesthetic, and how, as a sign, it resonated with meaning about the pain of suffering and the fear of death. Moreover, the close identification of the handkerchief with tears in eighteenth-century literature suggests that it not only served to ground Cochin's anxieties about mortality in the material everyday, but reference to it also helped to mobilize Descamps's sympathy and kindness.[29] Cochin had observed to Descamps in 1778, during a bout of illness, that he was not afraid of dying, only of suffering. He would, he said, have wanted the upright death of the young man—the good, clean cannon shot on the battlefield (he was writing during the War of American Independence)—not the mess and misery of the old man's portion,[30] not, that is, the pathetic, out-of-breath death, prone between the sheets, hand on hanky, bed curtains closed. Loss of Descamps's letters deprives us of the comfortable words that the Rouennais surely sent his friend in reply; we know them only in the handkerchiefs and in the pains he evidently took to secure and send them. §

---

1. Christian Michel, "Lettres adressées par Charles-Nicolas fils à Jean-Baptiste Descamps, 1757–1790," *AAF* 28 (1986): Letter LXXVI, 68.

2. Michel, "Lettres," Letter LXXVIII, 69. Postage was paid by the recipient rather than the sender of a letter.

3. Michel, "Lettres," Letters LXXX and LXXXI, 70–71.

4. Michel, "Lettres," Letter LXXVI, 68.

5. On Desfriches's involvement with the sugar trade, see Patrick Villiers, "Quelques influences atlantiques à Orléans au XVIIIe siècle," in *Villes atlantiques dans l'Europe occidentale du Moyen Âge au XXe siècle*, ed. Guy Saupin (Rennes: Presses Universitaires de Rennes, 2006), 89–100.

6. See Paul Ratouis de Limay, *Aignan-Thomas Desfriches (1715–1800)* (Paris: Honoré Champion, 1907), 81–82; and a second letter on the subject on 18 May 1782, 82–84.

7. *Echantillons d'étoffes et toiles des manufactures de France recueillis par le maréchal de Richelieu* (n.p.: n.p., 1736–37), 4:fol. 18, BnF, Département des Arts Graphiques, Réserve LH-45 (B) folio), published in Roger-Armand Weigert, *Textiles en Europe sous Louis XV: Les plus beaux spécimens de la collection Richelieu* (Fribourg: Office du Livre, 1964), 86. See also François-Alexandre-Pierre Garsault, *L'art de la lingerie* (Paris: Delatour, 1771), 20.

8. "Mémoire général sur les bureaux de visite et de marque établis dans la ville et généralité de Rouen, sur les différentes fabriques, et sur les principaux établissements de commerce" (1787), AN, F12/1365, 2–3.

9. Michel, "Lettres," Letter LXXVIII, 69.

10. Rouen was home to ninety-six dyers, among them two Englishmen who had brought a superior method of indigo dying to the town, and Sr. Osmont, who introduced red dyes, so-called *façon rouge d'Andrinople*, or Turkey red. See "Mémoire général," 8. On madder see also **Red Lake**.

11. Michel, "Lettres," Letters XIII and LXX, 19, 63. Desfriches regularly sent Cochin wine, vinegar, and pâté. See Ratouis de Limay, *Desfriches*, 63, 73, 75, 79, 81, 83, 85.

12. Michel, "Lettres," Letter LXXVIII, 69.

13. Michel, "Lettres," Letter LXXX, 70.

14. See Daniel Roche, *The Culture of Clothing: Dress and Fashion in the Ancien Régime* (Cambridge: Cambridge University Press, 1996), 184–220.

15. Michel, "Lettres," Letter LXXII, 65.

16. Charles-Nicolas Cochin, "Inventaire après décès," 4 May 1790, AN, MC/ET/CXV/967.

17. On linen as an index of class, see Roche, *Culture of Clothing*, 151–83.

18. See Françoise Bayard, "Le mouchoir à Lyon, en Lyonnais et en Beaujolais au XVIIe et XVIIIe siècles," in *Le mouchoir dans tous ses états* (Cholet: Musée du Textile de Cholet, 2000), 91–104.

19. Oddly, there are no snuffboxes among the "jewels" listed in Cochin's inventory, AN, MC/ET/CXV/967, 4 May 1790.

20. If not yellow ocher, the pigment may be Naples yellow, one of the first synthetic pigments on the market.

21. Specifically in relation to Cochin's art, printmaking, see Charles-Nicolas Cochin, *De la manière de graver à l'eau forte* (Paris: Jombert, 1745), 145–48 and plate 19. For painting, see Elisabeth Lavezzi, "La peinture au supplice," *Cycnos* 11, no. 1 (1994), http://revel.unice.fr/cycnos/index.html?id=1368, 29 August 2019.

22. Michel, "Lettres," Letters LVII and LX, 51, 54.

23. Bill Brown, "Thing Theory," *Critical Inquiry* 28, no. 1 (2001): 1–22.

24. See René Démoris, "Les enjeux de la main en peinture au siècle Classique," in *La main* (Orléans: Presses universitaires François-Rabelais, 1986), 243–58.

25. Michel, "Lettres," Letter LXXII, 66.

26. Michel, "Lettres," Letter XXXVIII, 40. See also Christian Michel, *Charles-Nicolas Cochin et l'art des lumières* (Rome: École française de Rome, 1993), 149–62.

27. See Henri Lefebvre, "The Everyday and Everydayness," *Yale French Studies* 73 (1987): 7–11.

28. See Michel, "Lettres," Letter XXXVII, 38, in which Cochin relates to Descamps how he rebuked Le Bas approaching printmaking "comme un vray marchand d'images" rather than "un Artiste distingué"; Michel, *Cochin*, 443.

29. See Anne Vincent-Buffault, *The History of Tears: Sensibility and Sentimentality in France* (Basingstoke: Palgrave Macmillan, 1986), 3–76.

30. Michel, "Lettres," Letter LVII, 51.

Harpsichord

Jean-Marc Nattier (1685–1766)
Louis Tocqué (1696–1772)

TYPE OF OBJECT	THEME	MATERIAL
Heirloom, Instrument, Prop	Family, Gender	Animal | Feather, Plant Matter | Wood, Synthetic Materials | Paint/Pigment

Though it resided at different times in the homes of two painters—Jean-Marc Nattier and, later, Louis Tocqué—this harpsichord was never really owned by either. Instead, it belonged to their wives and daughters. Originally, it was the possession of Madame Nattier, Marie-Madeleine Delaroche (1698–1742), who acquired it before her marriage to Nattier in 1724 or quite soon thereafter. It had evidently become a treasured possession by the time she died in 1742, at the age of only forty-four, because she bequeathed it to her eldest daughter, Marie-Catherine-Pauline Nattier (1725–75).[1] Still a teenager living in her father's home when she inherited the instrument, Marie-Catherine-Pauline would take it with her at the age of twenty-one, when in 1747 she became the wife of Tocqué, her father's former student. The harpsichord even played a role in the marriage proceedings as part of her dowry, a fact that would have a lasting impact on its subsequent journey. According to the legal arrangements laid out in the couple's **marriage contract**, the harpsichord was entailed "en préciput," meaning that it was kept separate from her husband's estate when Tocqué died in 1772.[2] The harpsichord remained with Madame Tocqué through her short widowhood, and she was ultimately able to bequeath it as she desired. When she died just three years later, it passed to her only daughter, Catherine-Pauline Tocqué, who became the third generation of Nattier-Tocqué women to own this musical instrument.[3]

When the harpsichord was constructed in the workshop of Nicolas Dumont, a Paris instrument maker, it had been designed with one purpose in mind: to make music.[4] Made before 1710, when Dumont died, the Nattier-Tocqué harpsichord was a product of the instrument's golden age.[5] By this point, the harpsichord had developed its familiar form and mechanism: a lidded triangular case containing sets of metal strings (copper for base notes, steel for the higher range), which were plucked (rather than hammered) by jacks with a **quill** plectrum (often from a crow feather), each one activated when its corresponding key was pressed by the player's finger.[6] While instrument makers had been perfecting its physical structure, French composers had created a tradition of music specifically attuned to its sonorous qualities—the *pièce de clavecin*—firmly established in the late seventeenth century by the likes of Jacques Champion de Chambonnière and Jean-Henry d'Anglebert, and reaching its apex in the early eighteenth century with François Couperin and Jean-Philippe Rameau (the latter's *Premier livre de pièces de clavecin* appearing in 1706).[7] Thus, in its construction the Nattier-Tocqué harpsichord had been optimized as a thing to play a certain kind of music. But whatever its maker's intention, as is often the case, once the instrument acquired an owner, its function as an object expanded beyond that calling.

It is not that the harpsichord ever stopped being played, but rather that, as a family possession, its life demanded it take on new roles and acquire new meanings. So while its affordances as an object—those physical features that invite use—never changed, the instrument ended up doing things beyond its designed specifications. On its trajectory through the hands of the Nattier-Tocqué women, for instance, the harpsichord was called upon several times to perform more legal services. As property—a thing owned—it acted as an item of inheritance (twice) and as a dowry. Bequeathed and transferred, it circulated between people, tying them together (mothers and daughters; husbands and wives), and leaving a documentary trail through wills and contracts that now allow its life to be traced, at least for a while, in notarial archives. What is more difficult to trace is what it meant on these occasions. For each of these legal acts was also a major event in the life of this family, at which the harpsichord was incongruously present. Through each death and marriage, this object became connected with moments of irreparable loss and change, charged with the emotions of these experiences, from grief and despair to hope and joy. Of course, in between, the harpsichord had more quotidian services to fulfil, being used, as it was intended, for musical entertainments. We might imagine its *pièces de clavecin* providing the soundtrack to the varied experiences of family life, on dull afternoons or special occasions, for lively gatherings or moments of melancholy. But every now and then, it had more poignant roles to play as a material witness to significant episodes in the lives of the Nattier-Tocqués.

Looking back, those particular events that the harpsichord witnessed—wives and mothers dying, children leaving home—must have felt like the ends of chapters, moments when family life as it had been would forever cease to be so. "Looking back" is certainly what Nattier seems to have done when he painted the harpsichord as part of his *Self-Portrait with His Family* (fig. 74), a painting whose unusual production involved multiple stages of remembering and revisiting. Nattier began it in 1730, a few years after his marriage to Delaroche and the birth of his children, but then he stopped, putting the work aside unfinished for thirty years, before finally completing it in 1762. By this point, everything had changed. Delaroche was dead. So too was Nattier's son, Jean-Frédéric, who had drowned tragically while studying in Rome in 1754. Nattier's three daughters were still alive, but, far from infant children, they were now women in their thirties, all married or about to become so.[8] Like everyone else in the scene, the harpsichord had gone too, now residing in the home of Marie-Catherine-Pauline and her husband, Tocqué, as it had done for fifteen years. Yet in his portrait, a nostalgic act of reimagining, Nattier reassembled everything as it once had been.

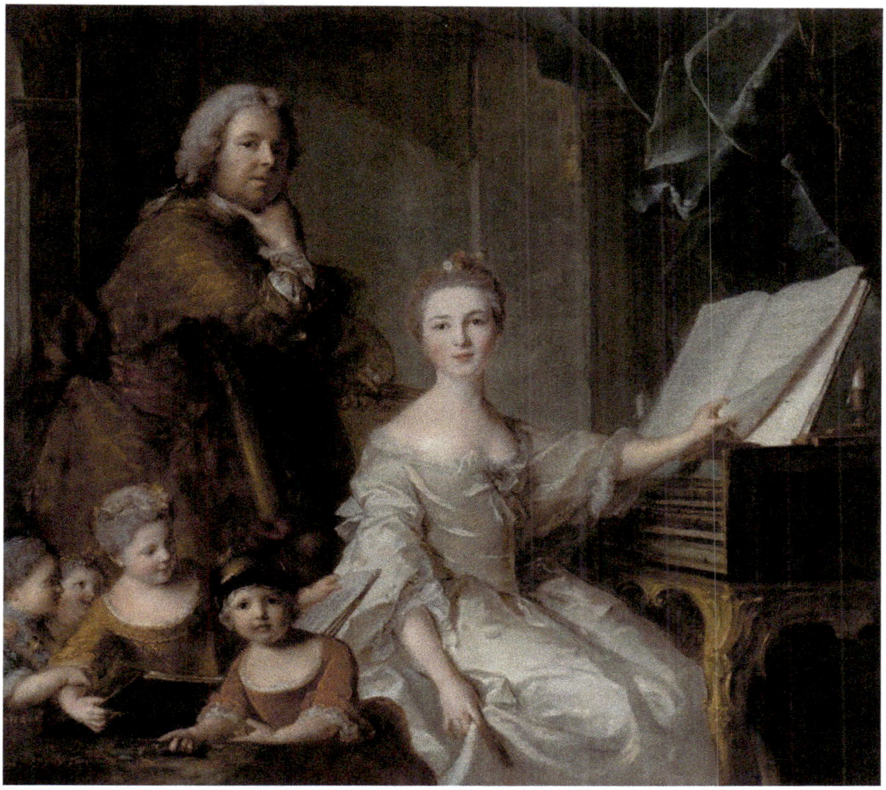

FIG. 74 Jean-Marc Nattier (French, 1685–1766), *Self-Portrait with His Family*, 1730–62. Oil on canvas, 149 × 165 cm. Châteaux de Versailles et de Trianon, MV4419. (© RMN-Grand Palais / photo: Gerard Blot / Art Resource, NY.)

Nattier's depiction of the family harpsichord is arresting, not least because eighteenth-century artists did not usually paint their possessions. Despite how it may appear in this book, with its many images of personal objects, the representation of ordinary things was actually quite controlled by the Académie's hierarchy of genres and restrictions around subject matter. For the most part, everyday objects remained the preserve of still-life or genre painters, like Chardin, who painted his **water fountain** (see fig. 180). Far fewer, for obvious reasons, crept into history paintings—David's **table** being an exception (see fig. 163). And while certain items did find their ways into portraits, these were usually sartorial accessories, like Vincent's **glasses** (see fig. 65), or professional tools, like Houdon's **modeling stand** (see fig. 113). Beyond its mere inclusion, however, what makes Nattier's harpsichord even more striking is the prominence it is given. Compositionally, the instrument pushes into the foreground, demanding attention as part of the row of figures assembled before Nattier, almost like another member of the family in this lineup of his nearest and dearest. In its treatment too, it is painted more like the figures than the rest of the setting, with more detail and resolution than the chair or table. Moreover, it is given a commanding role, actively orchestrating both the fiction of the image and the reality beyond the object. The harpsichord is the ostensible focus of this gathering, as the erstwhile household enjoys Madame Nattier's musical entertainments. But it is also the narrator of the family's history, relating the deaths of the departed members in its two snuffed-out candles and telling the story of the painting itself in the inscription on its cheek: "painting from the studio of Jean-Marc Nattier . . . begun in 1730 and finished in 1762."[9] It might be going too far to describe this image as a portrait of the harpsichord, but the instrument has certainly become the voice of the painting. Imbued with so many memories, this thing seems to have been, for Nattier at least, a material reminder of the past in the present.

It is possible that the harpsichord loomed so large in the Nattier-Tocqué family because it did so literally *and* figuratively, as significant in sheer size as it was in poignant associations. Nattier's painting shows a double-manual harpsichord—with two keyboards and two choirs of strings—but it only reveals the tip of the iceberg in terms of the instrument's dimensions. Some sense of its physical presence can be gleaned from an encounter with one of the only remaining Dumont double-manual harpsichords (fig. 75), now at the Philharmonie de Paris.[10] At over two meters long, the instrument would have occupied the better part of all but the largest rooms in the Paris homes inhabited by the Nattier and Tocqué households, whether in the complex of the Templars in the Marais (where Nattier lived in the 1740s), or in Tocqué's apartments on Rue du Mail, Rue de Cléry, and off Rue Saint-Honoré, or even in the Louvre *logement* he was granted in 1760.[11] Though numerous, most of these moves did not involve great distances, and certainly there would have been larger items to manage (like **beds** or chests of drawers) and more fragile items to protect (anything made from porcelain or glass). But the harpsichord's particular combination of size and delicacy would have made it a logistical challenge on every one of its moves, perhaps never more so than during its relocation after Tocqué's death. Forced to leave her late husband's Louvre *logement*, the widowed Madame Tocqué found first-floor rooms in the convent of Notre-Dame de Bon-Secours, which meant transporting her harpsichord all the way across Paris, right out to the Faubourg Saint-Antoine.[12]

Moving the harpsichord was facilitated by the instrument's practical detachability from its stand. Though acquired as a complete item, a harpsichord was in fact composed of parts and created by a team of specialized trades. Within the restrictions of Paris's guild system, the instrument makers, who made and sold harpsichords, were actually only responsible for constructing the case and musical mechanism, while all other elements and decorations were contracted out. A decorative painter was employed to paint the case (most commonly red or, as in this case, a green known as *merde d'oie*), to adorn the soundboard with floral designs, and sometimes to paint the lid with an Italianate landscape or pastoral scene (as in fig. 75).[13] Meanwhile, a *menuisier* (cabinetmaker) was commissioned to make the legs and frame of the instrument. While the instrument maker determined the harpsichord's sound, these other agents were responsible for its look, giving it a visual aesthetic that resonated with its musical qualities and harmonized with contemporary domestic interiors.

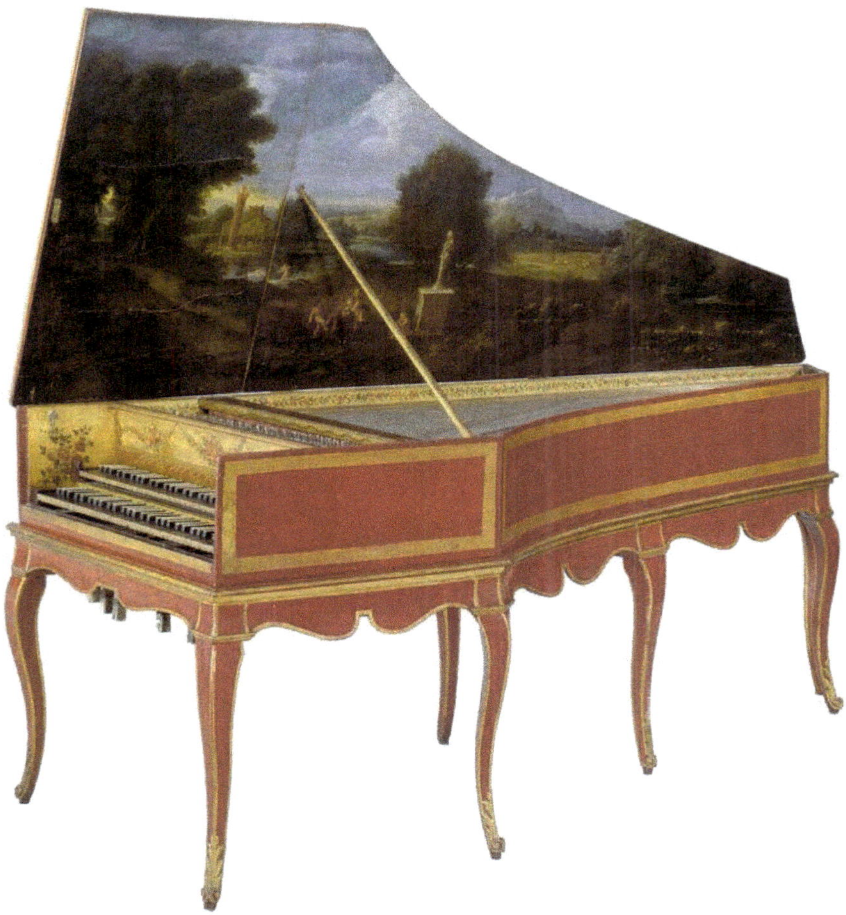

FIG. 75 Nicolas Dumont, modified by Pascal-Joseph Taskin in 1789, Two-manual harpsichord, 1697. Length 226 cm. Paris, Philharmonie de Paris, Cité de la Musique, Collections Musée de la musique. (Photo: Jean-Marc Anglès.)

Design aesthetics were, however, less stable than musical ones. Mechanisms might need repair or tuning (the miniaturist Charles Boit once paid a *raccomodeur de clavecins* [harpsichord repairer] 8 livres for a service), but the look could be revamped entirely.[14] The Nattier-Tocqué family seemingly did this on two occasions, finding yet another practical application for the detachability of the base. If accurately described, the gilded rococo legs in Nattier's portrait are too modern to be the originals of an instrument made before 1710, suggesting a new stand was commissioned—presumably by Madame Nattier—to keep the object up to date. This vested interest in the fashions of home furnishings may have been inherited by the next generation, for in Madame Tocqué's inventory of 1775, the harpsichord is described as having "wooden legs painted black and gilded," indicative of another possible change, perhaps after one of its many relocations.[15] Beyond suggesting a certain taste consciousness on the part of its owners (and a ready enough income to satisfy such cosmetic desires), these design modifications also highlight something of the harpsichord's ambiguous categorization. Unlike smaller musical instruments—say, a guitar (an instrument owned by both Oudry and Vernet)[16]—the harpsichord's size and form made it more like a piece of furniture. It was not a thing that could be put away or stored in a case but a thing that had to be accommodated at all times by its setting.

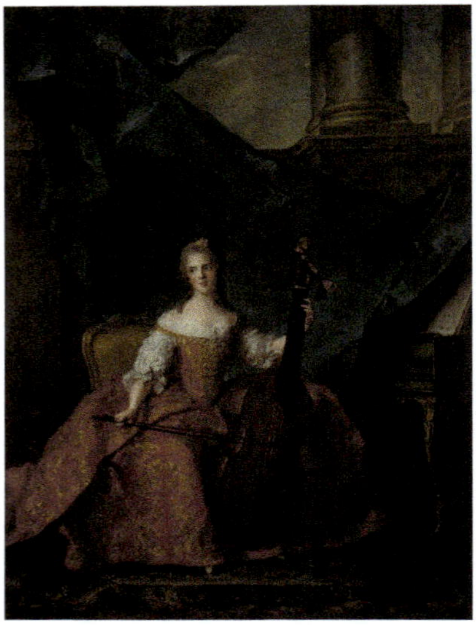

FIG. 76 Jean-Marc Nattier (French, 1685–1766), *Madame Henriette Playing a Bass Viol*, 1754. Oil on canvas, 249 × 184 cm. Châteaux de Versailles et de Trianon. MV3800. (© RMN-Grand Palais / Art Resource, NY.)

On at least one occasion, however, the harpsichord broke free of its domestic interior, not through a physical relocation, but via a fictional performance. Among the many roles the object played in its long life—musical instrument, item of inheritance, dowry, heirloom, piece of furniture—in 1754 it also became a studio prop for one of Nattier's most important commissions: his portrait of the king's daughter, *Madame Henriette Playing a Bass Viol* (fig. 76).[17] By this time, the instrument itself was residing in Tocqué's home, so Nattier presumably used his unfinished self-portrait as a model, as suggested in the striking similarities not only between the objects (a double manual with a green case, dark cheek, and gilded scalloped legs) but also in their depictions (cut off at the left edge of the canvas, with music on the stand, and a blue curtain overhead). Yet the differences between the family portrait and the royal portrait underscore its different roles in each work: from its dominant foreground position as narrator or quasi member of the family, to an incidental bit part in the mid-ground as a thematically appropriate compositional device. Like David's **table** in his painting of *Brutus*, this was a real thing playing a fictional part—the family harpsichord masquerading as the princess's harpsichord. But unlike the table, designed expressly for that purpose, the harpsichord's performance was more of a cameo appearance, fifteen minutes of fame before returning to everyday life. ‡

---

1. It is described as "provenant de la succession de sa mère" in the marriage contract of Marie-Catherine-Pauline Nattier and Louis Tocqué, 6 February 1747, AN, MC/ET/LIX/238. The contract is transcribed in Philippe Renard, *Jean-Marc Nattier (1685–1766)* (Saint-Rémy-en-l'Eau: Monelle Hayot, 1999), 194.

2. Marriage contract, Louis Tocqué and Marie-Catherine-Pauline Nattier, 6 February 1747, AN, MC/ET/LIX/238.

3. The harpsichord is not mentioned separately in Marie-Catherine-Pauline Nattier's will, but Catherine-Pauline Tocqué was designated as her mother's principal heir, inheriting everything apart from a small number of specific items bequeathed to family members and servants. Will, Marie-Catherine-Pauline Nattier (Madame Tocqué), 27 March 1775, AN, MC/ET/CXIII/477. See also Renard, *Jean-Marc Nattier*, 205.

4. It is described as a Dumont harpsicord in the estate inventory of Marie-Catherine-Pauline Nattier (Madame Tocqué), 10 April 1775, AN, MC/ET/CXIII/477.

5. Nicolas Dumont (1673–ca. 1710) was a Parisian harpsichord maker, received into the Guild of Instrument Makers in 1675. Donald H. Boalch, *Makers of the Harpsichord and Clavichord,*

1440–1840, 3rd ed. (Oxford: Clarendon, 1995), 52, 305–6. On the form of the harpsichord, see Edward L. Kottick, *A History of the Harpsichord* (Bloomington: Indiana University Press, 2003). Thanks to Julie Anne Sadie Goode and Jenny Nex for assistance with research on eighteenth-century French harpsichords.

6. On the materials used in eighteenth-century French harpsichords, see "Clavecin," *Encyclopédie*, http://encyclopedie.uchicago.edu/), 3:509.

7. On the early evolution of harpsichord music, see Carol Henry Bates, "French Harpsichord Music in the First Decade of the Eighteenth Century," *Early Music* 18, no. 2 (May 1989): 184–96.

8. The youngest, Madeleine-Sophie, would marry the painter Charles-Michelange Challe the following year. For a more extensive analysis of this family portrait, see Hannah Williams, *Académie Royale: A History in Portraits* (New York: Routledge, 2015), 189–92, 198–99.

9. The full inscription is: "Tableau de lattelier de M. / Jean-Marc Nattier trésorier / de Lacademie Royale de Peinture / et de Sculpture / commencé en 1730. et fini / par Le dit S. en 1762."

10. Physical comparisons are difficult because the Philharmonie de Paris instrument was modified by Pascal-Joseph Taskin in 1789.

11. For Nattier's and Tocqué's addresses during their careers, see Hannah Williams and Chris Sparks, *Artists in Paris: Mapping the 18th-Century Art World*, www.artistsinparis.org.

12. Marie-Catherine-Pauline Nattier (Madame Tocqué), "Inventaire après décès,"10 April 1775, AN, MC/ET/CXIII/477. See also Renard, *Jean-Marc Nattier*, 148.

13. On the decoration of harpsichords, see Sheridan Germann, "Monsieur Doublet and His Confrères: The Harpsichord Decorators of Paris," *Early Music* 8, no. 4 (1980): 435–53; and Kottick, *A History of the Harpsichord*, 263–64.

14. An *opposition* by Jean Desnoue, *raccommodeur de clavecins*, was made in the *Scellé* of Charles Boit on 6 February 1727. AN, Y/15767.

15. Marie-Catherine-Pauline Nattier (Madame Tocqué), "Inventaire après décès," 10 April 1775, AN, MC/ET/CXIII/477.

16. Louis Gougenot, "Vie de M. Oudry," in L. Dussieux et al., eds., *Mémoires inédits*, 2:379; and Léon Lagrange, *Joseph Vernet et la peinture au XVIIIe siècle, avec le texte des livres de raison et un grand nombre de documents inédits* (Paris: Didier, 1864), 392.

17. The harpsichord would appear in several versions and studio copies of this important commission.

Hot-Air Balloon

Jean-François Janinet (1752–1814)

TYPE OF OBJECT	THEME	MATERIAL
Vehicle	Invention, Leisure, Studio, Travel	Textile | Canvas

According to Denis Diderot, the material conditions for something to be called "balloon" are that it is round and hollow, no matter how it is made, or what it is for.[1] A balloon is an envelope, casing, or wrapper that encompasses something other. Does it qualify as a thing, specifically an artist's thing? Should we not, rather, be indexing it by its contents? At the time of the *Encyclopédie*'s publication (1751–77) "balloon" was generally a glass object, a component in a scientific apparatus used in chemical and physical experiments to produce compound substances such as the pigments verdigris and orpiment.[2] The printmaker Janinet's balloon was, however, a different, inflatable type of thing, a hot-air balloon, the invention of which in 1783 was the by-product of the seventeenth century's discovery of the materiality, that is the weight, of air. We have a scrap of the cerulean balloon that Janinet and the abbé Laurent-Antoine Miollan were primed to launch from the Luxembourg gardens on 11 July 1784 (fig. 77).

Janinet and Miollan were not, of course, the inventors of the hot-air balloon. That honor goes to the Montgolfier brothers, who had successfully launched the first balloon at Annonay in June 1783 and had repeated the performance in front of Louis XVI and the court at Versailles in September of the same year.[3] Their success in rendering "navigable the air" detonated an explosion of ballooning in Paris, which attracted huge crowds of curious onlookers from all ranks and professions, including artists.[4] The German engraver Johann Georg Wille attended the Montgolfier launch at the Réveillon wallpaper factory in the Faubourg Saint-Antoine in October 1783 and the first manned assent in Paris at the Tuileries gardens in December, from which he returned home stunned, dizzy and unable to think of anything else, according to the late-night entry in his **journal**.[5] Ten days later he bought a silver medal to commemorate the Montgolfier invention (fig. 78), whose obverse bore the double profiles of genius, designed by the sculptor Jean-Antoine Houdon. Wille added it to his collection of European medals illustrating the monuments of the modern age.[6] Janinet, however, was not content to be a spectator, nor even an amateur scientist, for whom the market soon produced balloon kits for making and flying miniature model balloons.[7] Hot-air balloons were not entertainment or toys to him; rather, the balloon was his thing, in the sense of his *métier*, in 1784.

Janinet styled himself an artist-physicist. How, when, and where he acquired his science is uncertain; he may have attended the abbé Miollan's public lectures on physics.[8] Whatever the case, by February 1784 the two men were embarked on a joint venture to

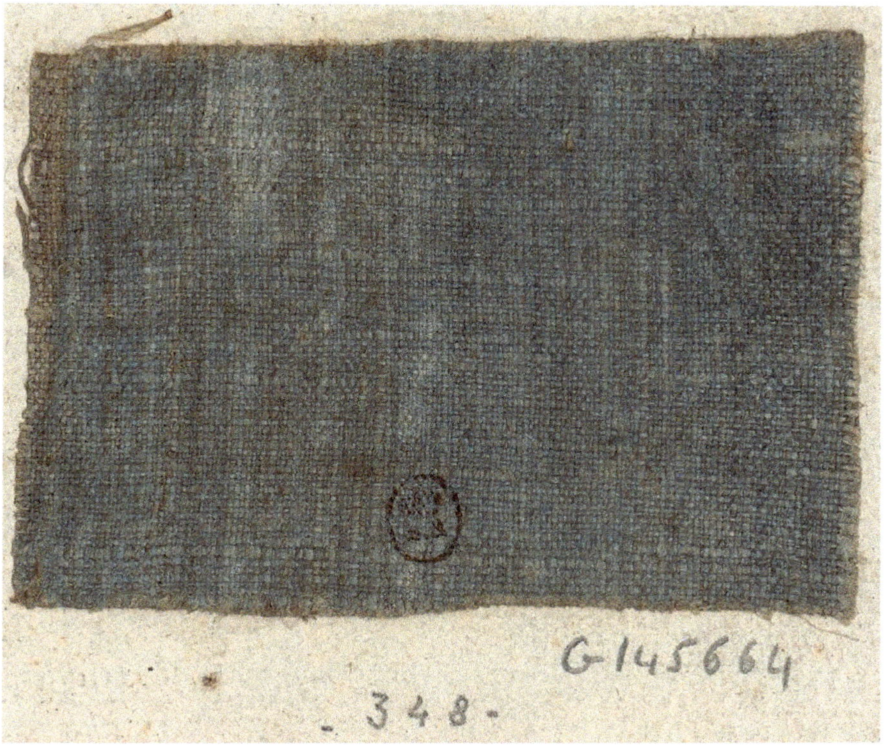

FIG. 77 Hot-air balloon fragment, 1784. Hemp. Paris, Bibliothèque Nationale de France.

send up their own *montgolfière*, as the hot-air balloon was popularly called, and to that end they opened a subscription to finance the project and sold tickets.[9] From the ticket etched by the "artist" Janinet (see fig. 79), the purchaser learned that the Miollan–Janinet flying machine was to consist of not one but three balloons, loosely tied together with string, and that an aerial rudder would be attached to the gondola. The authors explained in the prospectus that their prime objective was to be useful. Their balloon would be a flying laboratory, in which observations and demonstrations of "the density and qualities of the different layers of the atmosphere" could be made. The small upper balloon would rise above the other two because it was filled with hydrogen. The lowest balloon would sink below the two others because it was filled with cold air—a lesson for all to see in the relative densities of gasses and in the effects of heat upon them.[10] The rudder and lateral vent in the big balloon, inferable from the ticket by the burst of radiating lines Janinet etched to represent escaping air, would demonstrate a combination of means to pilot the flying ship: by leverage and by propulsion. To date, no one had successfully devised a technology to steer balloons, which severely compromised the balloon's perceived utility.[11]

In the immense space of the heavens and relative to the globe, the balloon, blown by "long laughing winds" (*quousque iudibria ventis*), looks small and delicate, and yet it was then the largest balloon to have been launched aloft, a gigantic azure machine 100 feet high and 80 feet in diameter, on a scale and of a color, in fact, to equal the hue and

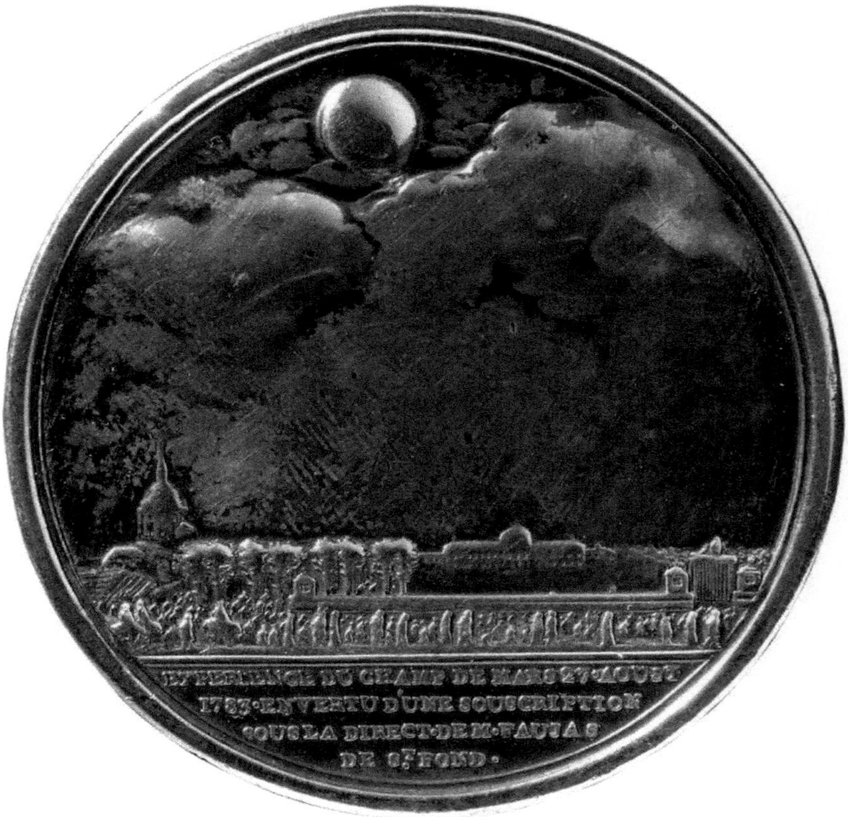

FIG. 78 Nicolas-Marie Gatteaux (French, 1751–1832), Medal commemorating the ascent of Joseph and Etienne Montgolfier, balloonists at the Champ de Mars, 1784. Silver, diam. 4.1 cm. London, Science Museum. (SSPL/Science Museum / Art Resource, NY.)

cumuliform of Janinet's skyscape. The creation of so large a thing apparently demanded an approach to production liberated from the traditional mindset of craft; Miollan and Janinet emphasized the modernity of their balloon's technology in the press releases they regularly made to the newspapers.[12] The design of the burner, for example, would be informed by Antoine Quinquet's improvements to the oil lamp; the gondola would be built in the lightest of materials, a reinforced paper invented by the model maker Montfort and already in use for **baths** and **carriages**.[13] The most expensive tickets bought not only the best seats for the launch but access also to the workshops in which the new technologies were being developed, and entry to the exhibition of the 1:10 maquette or **model** of the balloon at the Grands Augustins on 31 March 1784, coincidentally at the same time and in the same place that Jean-Joseph Sue was giving a lecture to Académie students on the importance of the study of human anatomy to the practice of art.[14]

After successful test flights of the full-scale balloon at the Observatoire in June and July, the "physicists" fixed the day of the official public launch for Sunday, 11 July 1784, at noon. Wille, who almost certainly knew Janinet, was eager to go.[15] He proposed buying

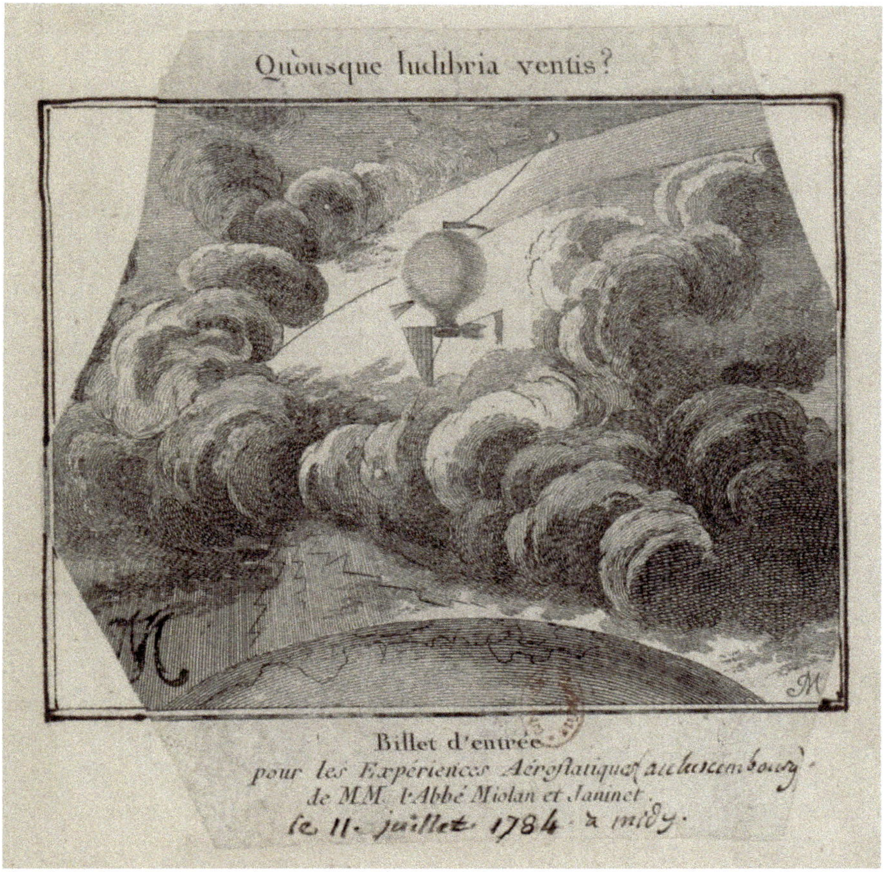

FIG. 79 Jean-François Janinet (French, 1752–1814), Entry ticket to Janinet and Miollan's balloon flight, 1784. Etching. Paris, Bibliothèque Nationale de France.

tickets for the enclosure at the Luxembourg (see fig. 79), but his wife could not face the crowds; they made their way instead to a convenient viewing spot on the boulevard.[16] About two o'clock they saw rising in the sky not the balloon but a pall of smoke. Miollan and Janinet had repeatedly tried to inflate the envelope and failed.[17] Instead, it caught fire, though whether by accident or torched by the disappointed crowd is not clear. According to draftsman and printmaker Charles-Nicolas Cochin, the moment the would-be aviators accepted defeat, the crowd of angry, non-ticket holders outside the enclosure broke in, ripped up the stands, and fed the fire with chairs and fencing. What they did not set alight they tore up and took as trophies (see fig. 77).[18] His account of the day's events was written in a letter to the painter Jean-Baptiste Descamps, to whom in bafflement Cochin remarked of Janinet: "What was he thinking?"

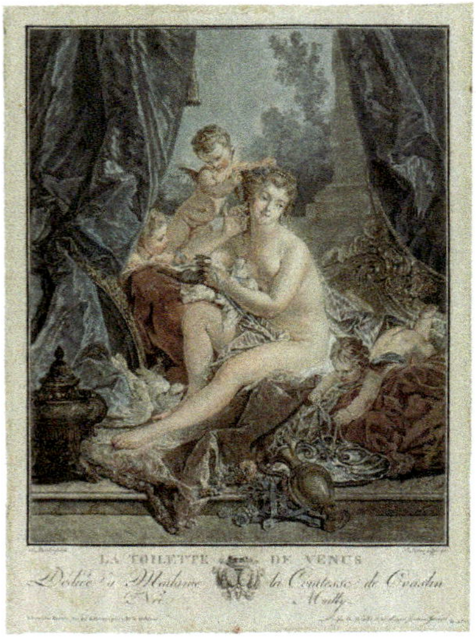

FIG. 80 Jean-François Janinet (French, 1752–1814), after François Boucher (French, 1703–70), *Toilette of Venus*, 1784. Color aquatint and crayon-manner etching, 37.5 × 29.5 cm. Paris, Bibliothèque Nationale de France.

Had Janinet perhaps felt himself interpolated by Gudin de Brenellière's rousing imperatives in the wake of the first balloon ascent,[19] and published in the *Journal de Paris*, to "Follow Montgolfier . . . ," to "Leave, fly, and discover air less even, purer horizons in these, our cerulean planes"? Had he thought that his practical knowledge specifically marked him out? He certainly saw no contradiction in principle between scientific and artistic ambition: in March 1784 he put an advertisement in *Annonce, affiches et avis divers* with news scrambled in a single paragraph both of his print after François Boucher's *Toilette of Venus* (fig. 80) and of the subscription to launch the balloon.[20]

The relic of his and Miollan's attempted flight indicates a dense inner envelope of linen, possibly hemp, tough but not woven tightly enough to contain air. It was almost certainly covered with outer layers of paper and varnish, materials common to the printmaker's studio, in order to seal it properly. Moreover, Janinet had brought experimentation to his art. He had adapted the process of color printing using multiple plates, learned in the workshop of the pastel-manner etcher Jean-Claude Bonnet to the technique of acquatint, a development that had required experimental manipulation of varnishes (to protect the copperplate), acids (to bite the design), and inks, including indigo (to print the image). He could legitimately lay claim to a practical knowledge of chemistry that was there to be mobilized for the science as well as the arts of ballooning, including perhaps the making of hydrogen by the chemical reaction of acid on metal.[21]

The thrust of the caricatures, satirical songs, and critiques that flooded the market in the immediate aftermath of the Luxembourg gardens fiasco was deflationary—an assault, that is, on the puffed and false science of Miollan and Janinet. Janinet was routinely portrayed as an ass. In *Les deux Midas* (fig. 81) his ears identify him as the left caryatid, tangled up with Miollan the cat, on the right, by a skein running along the top of the frame, their pursuit of scientific knowledge exposed as half-assed, as a pseudo, alchemical art that licenced renaming them "Midas." Furthermore, the recorders (*flutes à bec*) that the two men have in their mouths by the wrong end illustrate the idiocy of those who pretend to experimentation without knowledge of scientific principles.[22] This was satire by the elite against the pretentions of outsiders and against the opening up of science to a wider public of artisans and amateurs. In the middle of the bottom rail of the frame, the caricaturist had drawn a medal, "Project of a Monument," around which runs the proverb: "To each his craft, and the cows will be well guarded." Both the turn of events and such

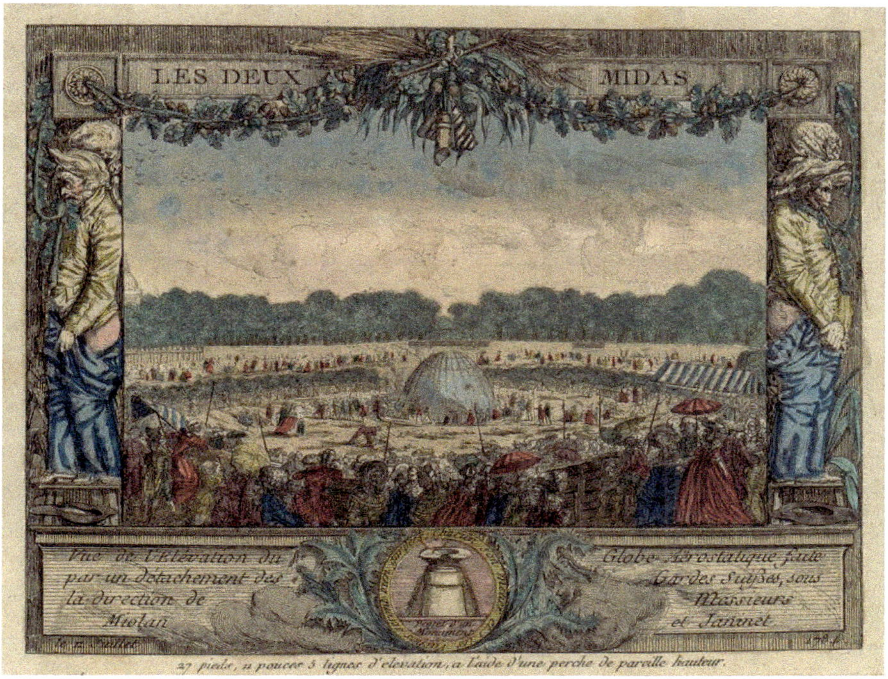

FIG. 81 Unknown maker, *Les deux Midas*, 1784. Etching and engraving, 18.7 × 24.1 cm.
Paris, Bibliothèque Nationale de France.

caricatures punctured Janinet's sublime ambition, stayed his willingness to risk in order to be "king of the elements," master of air. Provenance of the balloon fragment at the Bibliothèque Nationale de France is unknown, but we can be sure it was no souvenir of Janinet's. Humiliated, both by public ridicule and, no doubt, by the pity of academic colleagues, this heaven-headed printmaker forgot the dreams that had inspired the design of his ticket and returned to the everyday, earth-bound business of earning a living.[23] §

---

1. "Ballon," *Encyclopédie*, http://encyclopedie.uchicago.edu/, 2:47.

2. "Orpiment, ou Orpin" and "Verd-de-gris, ou Verdet," *Encyclopédie*, http://encyclopedie.uchicago.edu/, 11:665, 17:58.

3. There is a vast secondary literature on ballooning in the eighteenth century. See, among others, Charles Coulson Gillispie, *The Montgolfier Brothers and the Invention of Aviation, 1783–1784* (Princeton: Princeton University Press, 1984); and Marie Thébaud-Sorger, *L'aerostation au temps des lumières* (Rennes: Presses Universitaires de Rennes, 2009).

4. Michael Lynn estimates that approximately 400,000 people, or half the population of Paris, watched the first assent at the Tuileries in 1783. See Lynn, *Popular Science and Public Opinion in Eighteenth-Century France* (Manchester: Manchester University Press, 2006), 136.

5. *Mémoires et journal de J-G Wille*, ed. Georges Duplessis (Paris: Renouard, 1857), 2:65 (6 October 1783); 2:76–78 (2 December 1783). Setting off for the Tuileries on 2 December, Wille had been too impatient to write a proper letter to Jean-Baptiste Descamps. On his return he met up with others who had also been at the launch: "Nous dînâmes chez nous, et ne parlâmes que de ce que nous avons vu et n'en parlâmes qu'avec feu."

6. Wille, *Mémoires*, 2:81.

7. See, for example, those sold by Blondy, cul-de-sac de Rouen, advertised in the *Journal de Paris*, 17 September 1783; also, Marie Thébaud-Sorger, *Une Histoire des ballons: Invention, culture matérielle et imaginaire, 1783–1909* (Paris: Editions du Patrimoine Centre des Monuments Nationaux, 2010), 88–101.

8. See *Journal de Paris*, 11 April and 4 December 1783.

9. *Journal de Paris*, 26 February 1784.

10. "Observatoire volant" was in the same year the title of a poem by Arnaud de Saint-Maurice: *L'Observatoire volant et le triomphe héroïque de la navigation aérienne* (Paris: Cussac & Samson, 1784).

11. See the debate in the *Journal de Paris*, 30 August 1783.

12. *Journal de Paris*, 29 March 1784. Jean Sgard argues in "Les philosophes montgolfères," *SVEC*, 303 (1992): 105, that ballooning was the occasion for putting into practice the enlightened principles of the *Encyclopédie*.

13. *Journal de Paris*, 21 March 1784, 29 March 1784. Montfort is identified as "ancien officier d'artilerie" and "Directeur des plans en relief des fortifications du Royaume."

14. *Journal de Paris*, 29 March 1784.

15. Janinet had reproduced two of Wille *fils*'s early genre paintings, *Le Repas des moissonneurs* (1774) and *La Noce de Village* (1775). See *Inventaire du fonds français: graveurs du XVIIIe siècle* (Paris: Bibliothèque nationale de France, 1973), 12:9-10.

16. Wille, *Mémoires*, 2:94–95 (11 September 1784).

17. This was almost certainly because of the midday heat. Generally, hot-air ballooning takes place at first light when the differential in the temperatures inside and outside the balloon is especially marked.

18. See Charles-Nicolas Cochin *fils* to Jean-Baptiste Descamps, 2 June 1784, published in Christian Michel, "Lettres adressées par Charles-Nicolas fils à Jean-Baptiste Descamps, 1757–1790," *AAF* 28 (1986), Letter LXXXVI, 75–76. See also *Correspondance littéraire*, ed. Maurice Tourneux (Paris: Garnier, 1877–82), 14:9–11.

19. *Journal de Paris*, 28 August 1783.

20. *Annonce, affiches et avis divers*, 23 March 1784.

21. On "practical knowledge" and ballooning, see Marie Thébaud-Sorger, "Capturing the Invisible: Heat, Steam, and Gases in France and Great Britain, 1750–1800," in Lisa Roberts and Simon Werret, eds., *Compound Histories: Materials, Governance and Production, 1760–1840* (Leiden: Brill, 2018), 85–106.

22. The joke was informed by the connection that Antoine Rivarol made between the technologies of air used, respectively, in ballooning and in the abbé Mical's "Talking Heads," the first successful reproduction of the human voice. See Rivarol, *Lettre à M. le Président de *** sur le globe airostatique, les têtes parlantes et l'état present de l'opinion publique à Paris* (London: Cailleau, 1784), 20–22, 29–30.

23. According to Portalis and Béraldi, Janinet produced his best prints in the immediate aftermath of this failure. See *Inventaire du fonds français: graveurs du XVIIIe siècle*, vol. 3.

Intaglio

Charles-Joseph Natoire (1700–77)

TYPE OF OBJECT	THEME	MATERIAL
Apparel, Collectible, Souvenir	Antiquity, Death, Friendship, Memory, Travel	Mineral Gem

On 14 December 1778, the collection of the history painter and director of the Académie de France à Rome, Charles-Joseph Natoire, was auctioned at the hôtel d'Aligre, Rue Saint-Honoré. Natoire had died in Italy after more than twenty-five years as director at the Palazzo Mancini, but his heirs decided that the collection would sell better in Paris than in Rome.[1] Shipped back to France and cataloged by the auctioneer Alexandre Paillet, Natoire's "*cabinet*" had contained, in addition to examples of his own paintings and drawings, "choice and distinguished works" by "Pierre Subleyras, Jean-Paul Panini, and other Masters."[2] Among those who attended the sale was the artist Gabriel de Saint-Aubin, whose marginal drawings in his copy of the sale catalog capture in quick, black, accented chalk strokes the salient features of many of the paintings, drawings, and sculptors' **models** for sale—a sale that ended with a handful of ancient and modern gems, and a crop of red wax sulphur pastes, cast from gems.[3] We sense the ebbing of Saint-Aubin's interest with the gems (fig. 82); his sketches become perfunctory, in some cases no more than the oval ghost of a form, and his record of the winning bids erodes as he grows distracted. Since that brief moment of his glancing attention, total silence has befallen the gems, as no art historian has reflected on their presence.[4]

Intaglios and cameos are gems, usually no larger than 1 inch (2.5 cm) in diameter, on which a design is recessed, embossed, engraved, or carved. Intaglios were used as seals; cameos were worn as jewelry. According to eighteenth-century antiquarians, both originated in ancient Egypt, from where the art of gem engraving spread throughout the Mediterranean, reaching a high point of noble simplicity and refinement in fifth- and fourth-century BCE Greece.[5] In the Renaissance, examples of antique gems were collected by princes, nobles, and scholars alongside classical sculpture and antique medals, but by the early eighteenth century the taste for antiquities in France, particularly medals, was in decline. Krzysztof Pomian's quantitative analysis of the contents of Paris auctions shows that, after 1750, antiquities were surpassed by **shells** and natural history, as objects of desire.[6] In partial explanation of this shift in taste, Pomian mapped its gradient onto changes in the social makeup of collectors: the market share of the nobility and clergy, who had dominated the art market to 1750, declined after midcentury in direct proportion to the rise in collecting by new money, that is, by financiers, merchant capitalists, and other professional classes, of which artists were by no means the least significant. In this context, important though Natoire's *cabinet* is as an instance of the new economy of collecting, his intaglios appear to strike a false note, to be out of tune with modern trends.

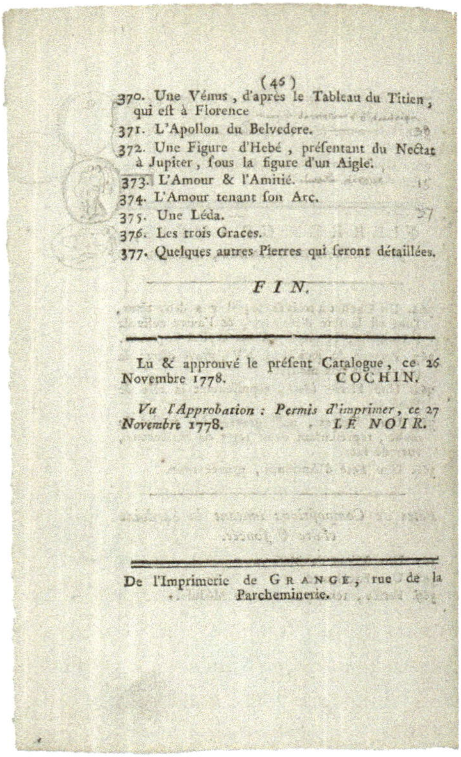

(46)

370. Une Vénus, d'après le Tableau du Titien, qui eſt à Florence

371. L'Apollon du Belvedere.

372. Une Figure d'Hebé, préſentant du Nectar à Jupiter, ſous la figure d'un Aigle.

373. L'Amour & l'Amitié.

374. L'Amour tenant ſon Arc.

375. Une Léda.

376. Les trois Graces.

377. Quelques autres Pierres qui ſeront détaillées.

FIN.

Lu & approuvé le préſent Catalogue, ce 26 Novembre 1778. COCHIN.

Vu l'Approbation: Permis d'imprimer, ce 27 Novembre 1778. LE NOIR.

De l'Imprimerie de GRANGE, rue de la Parcheminerie.

FIG. 82 Gabriel de Saint-Aubin's pencil annotations in *Catalogue des tableaux et dessins originaux des plus grands maîtres . . . qui composoient le cabinet de feu Charles Natoire* (1778). Paris, Bibliothèque Nationale de France.

Was this, as Georges Brunel has suggested in relation to Natoire's taste in paintings and drawings, because the painter was isolated in Rome, unaware of or unresponsive to developments in contemporary art and to fashions in curiosity? Should we interpret his intaglios as evidence of a reactionary taste in contrast to his contemporary François Boucher's radical appetite for both contemporary Italian art (he owned 137 works by or after Giovanni Battista Tiepolo)[7] and for **shells**?

The answers may perhaps be found in Natoire's collecting, not in his collection. This is to acknowledge that Natoire's "collection" was at least partly the retrospective construct of Paillet's cataloging. The dealer's classification of the gems in the 1778 Paris sale implied that the painter had responded to them not individually as things but as examples of types of things: original or reproduction, ancient (fig. 83) or modern, and, if the latter, by Giovanni or Luigi Pichler (fig. 84) or Alessandro Cades.[8] The fifteen engraved gems and ten sulphur pastes assume, in the catalog, the appearance of a bounded system whose meanings emerge from the relations between the different examples: by connecting and comparing a paste of an ancient gem of *Leda and the Swan* with Pichler's carnelian intaglio, or contrasting Cades's two versions of the bust of Antinous, or alternatively—for a study of youth and age—of reading the one *Antinous* mounted on a multifaceted seal (*cachet*) against a head of Homer, also by Cades, with which it was paired and with which it had been set for Natoire in a three-sided jewel.[9]

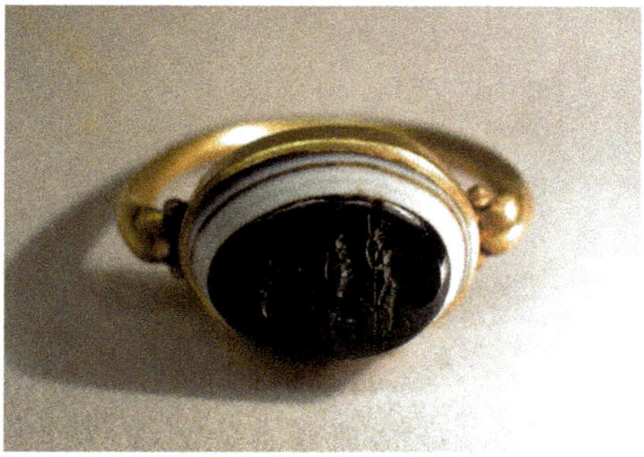

FIG. 83 Roman engraved gem with a group of soldiers, late second–early third century CE. Gold ring and onyx intaglio, 1.6 cm. New York, Metropolitan Museum of Art, Bequest of Rupert L. Joseph, 1959, 60.55.80.

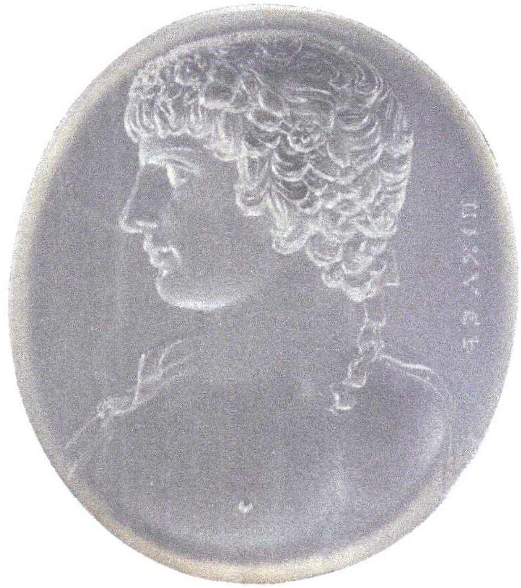

FIG. 84 Giovanni Pichler (Italian, 1734–91) or Luigi Pichler (Italian, 1773–1854), *Antinous*, ca. 1750–1850. Engraved gem, chalcedony. Los Angeles, The J. Paul Getty Museum, 83.AL.257.17.

Paillet's description of the gems focuses primarily on the subject matter, but insofar as he identifies the minerals of which the gems were made, he also invokes their color—red (cornelian), brown (sardonyx), white (chalcedony), and the pure clarity of rock crystal (quartz). Moreover, in the case of the antique gems, he intersperses his description with observations—"one sees . . . ," "one notices . . ."—observations that prioritize the experience of looking over the value of knowing.[10] Paillet's address to sight and his deft erudition removed Natoire's gems from the domain of antiquarianism and aligned them with the paintings and drawings in the collection as instances of art and beauty. The reason for Paillet's appeal to the senses may have been his lack of classical learning, but its effect was to assign autonomy to Natoire's "collection," to detach his gems from both their actual uses in antiquity and from their latent function as concrete witnesses of history. Parallels can be drawn with the new historiography of gems generated by connoisseurs like the comte de Caylus and Pierre-Jean Mariette in the 1720s and 1730s, and which culminated in 1750 with the publication of the catalog of the king's gem cabinet, introduced by a *Traité des pierres gravées*, written by Mariette.[11] Mariette's *Traité* reinvented gems as objects of desire, by forgetting or largely ignoring questions of historical and local context in favor of properties of authorship and authenticity, that is, characteristics directly relevant to the exchange economy and the market for art.

Disengaging Natoire's collecting from Paillet's collection is tricky. Alternative primary sources are scant. However, by analyzing what little we can extract from his letters to his friend Antoine Duchesne, and by comparing his choices with those of other artists, among them those directly involved in the illustration of Caylus's and Mariette's successive cataloging projects of the royal gems—Charles-Antoine Coypel, Jean-François De Troy, and

Edme Bouchardon—we may be able to shed some light on it.[12] The material, phenomenological, and symbolic factors at play in gem collecting will serve as a focus.

Before leaving Paris, Natoire organized a sale of things not for Rome. A manuscript list of the sale indicates that before his departure he had owned engraved views of Roman ruins and prints after antique sculpture, but no gems, nor any pastes, prints, or books related to them.[13] Thus, in spite of his connections with the Caylus-Mariette circle in the 1730s and 1740s, he was not apparently infected with the love of gems—"monuments in miniature" Mariette called them.[14] A letter to Duchesne posted *en route*, in October 1751, suggests that his interest in antique things was sparked by the journey. He remarked on the abundance of medals and other antiquities he had seen for sale at Nîmes,[15] and, after arriving in Rome, he sent more news: he alluded briefly to participation in hunting parties for "curiosities and antiquities" (*antiquailles*). Looking, he seems to imply, had given way to possessing.[16] The use of the verb "roder" (to roam) to describe his mode of quest indicates a spontaneous, nonsystematic, and nonserial manner of acquisition, one in which chance and whim played a part, in contrast to the planned and ordered collection by type and set practiced by numismatists and antiquarians like the abbé de Rothelin, by whom Coypel was given a collection of 1,680 glass pastes, cast from the gems in the royal collection and arranged "symmetrically" in red leather–lined trays, inside a pair of olivewood and brass boxes that Coypel kept in his *cabinet*.[17] Natoire's gems, though mostly originals, not reproductions, were unworthy of such containers for lack of the unity, totality, and coherence that buying for collection confers.

Antiquailles was the word Natoire used to describe the treasures he hunted, translated above as "antiquities" for lack of an equivalent word in English. Unlike *antiquities*, the meaning of *antiquailles* is loaded.[18] It is unlikely that Natoire intended it to convey contempt for his discoveries; more likely he meant Duchesne to understand the worn agedness, even grubbiness, of his modest finds: wastes of an earlier civilization. His were not gems like De Troy's, whose "*bijoux*" (jewels) Pierre Rémy cataloged as rings, not *pierres gravées*, because they were precious: an amethyst intaglio of a sea horse, an extraordinary onyx and agate cameo carved with the head of a "négresse" (black woman) that "exploited the different accidents in the stone to great effect."[19] If Natoire selected his gems individually, without thought of collection, it was not on the basis of nature's strange accidents, or the curious exoticism of the design, or the total novelty of the commodity; their subjects were arguably hackneyed: Venus, Leda, the Bacchantes.

Not collected by genre, author, or theme, and not worn as luxuries of dress, Natoire's gems seemingly formed a more private and personal relationship with their owner than did Coypel's and De Troy's. Natoire confessed to Duchesne that it was close bodily experience of the ancient past at Nîmes, on visiting Jacques-Philippe Mareschal's excavations of the Roman "fountain," that had made him, instantly—that is, without the mediation of learning—an "antiquaire."[20] On the day of his arrival in Rome, he wrote to his friend that such had been the impact, we might even say the shock, of the city and of his reception there, that he experienced his “landing” almost as a “dream.”[21] Not only do his letters register his aesthetic and emotional response to specific changes of scene, they also suggest a more general temporal disorientation. Born at Nîmes, at seventeen Natoire left to finish his training in Paris. Having obtained the Prix de Rome, he spent 1723 to 1729 at the Palazzo Mancini as a *pensionnaire*. His journey south in 1751 was therefore a much longed-for return, to judge by his bid at the directorship of the school as early as 1737. He remembered the Maison Carrée, “that monument that would not be the least of Rome's,” but did not recognize his brothers, not seen since he had left as a lad. He was greeted in Rome by “old acquaintances” whom he had forgotten, but he knew again the beautiful “curiosities” of the city studied in his youth.[22] Antique things anchored his memory; they marked his place in and passage through life, transforming ancient history into private time. Natoire's gems were his souvenirs.[23]

Susan Stewart says of the souvenir, in contrast to the collection, that it prompts narrative, storytelling not about the objects but about the persons to whom the specific things belonged. To categorize Natoire's gems with souvenirs distinguishes them further from those collected and classified by Coypel and consumed for show by De Troy. It also sets them apart from Bouchardon's antique gems, with which, on grounds of biography, we could have expected greater affinity. Natoire and Bouchardon had studied together in Rome, and the connection they formed there survived the return to France. In Paris they worked alongside each other on projects for Pierre-Jean Mariette, Natoire making copies of the collector's drawings, Bouchardon drawing the king's gems for Mariette's *Traité*. In François-Hubert Drouais's portrait of Bouchardon (1758, Paris, Musée du Louvre), the sculptor holds a volume entitled “Monum[ents] antiq[ues]” with his right hand. On his little finger sits a gem set in a gold ring that we can identify with one of the antique cameos inventoried among the sculptor's possessions at his death in 1762.[24] In the narrative of the portrait, the gem, though closely attached to Bouchardon, signifies across him, connecting along a diagonal “ancient monuments” in the foreground with the **models** of Bouchardon's modern ones in the background. Insofar as the cameo speaks of Bouchardon, it tells of his participation in the epic transmission of ideal form across time and place, and of his identity in the history of the classical tradition.

For Natoire, antiquity was a matter first of his own origins at Nîmes, a place he experienced as another Rome, at least in respect to the beauty of the Maison Carrée. Significant in his letters is not, however, the identity of specific monuments, large or small, but his reaction to them. His letters to his “carrissimo amico,” his dearest friend, express his longing for Duchesne's presence: Natoire wanted to face the sights with Duchesne; more importantly, he seems to have wanted Duchesne to experience Natoire's own response to them, to witness it as authentic and as coming from within. That response was not unequivocal, like we assume Bouchardon's to have been from Drouais's portrayal; rather, it was ambivalent. Natoire's line about his pleasure in hunting *antiquailles* was followed in the very next sentence of his letter by distress at news of a death: “here we are,” he cried, “back among the dead.”[25] The juxtaposition of topics, and the adverb “back,” suggest that numbered among them are also the dead of antiquity. In response, months later, to the unexpected death of De Troy on the eve of his return to Paris, Natoire observed that "the most brilliant things" are almost always accompanied by shadow. At one level he was no more than repeating the Christian trope of the vanities. However, by articulating it metaphorically using "a phrase from painting," as he acknowledged, he also suggested that death wastes not just individuals but civilizations.[26] The countervailing force of death in the letters shades Natoire's references to the antique with nostalgia. In Drouais's portrait and Mariette's *Traité*, antique gems are represented as a medium, the means by which the masterpieces of sculpture and paintings of antiquity had unintentionally been perfectly preserved for the present in order to be renewed. For Natoire, antiquities, perhaps including his gems, were the battered material survivals of a past from which he felt separated but for which, desiring, he searched. Finding souvenirs in and around Rome and appropriating these *antiquailles* for his villa (fig. 85), he set his treasures in niches, on sconces, on pedestals, and on entablatures in the garden, at once safe from and united with the ruins beyond its walls. Past and present came together by his art. §

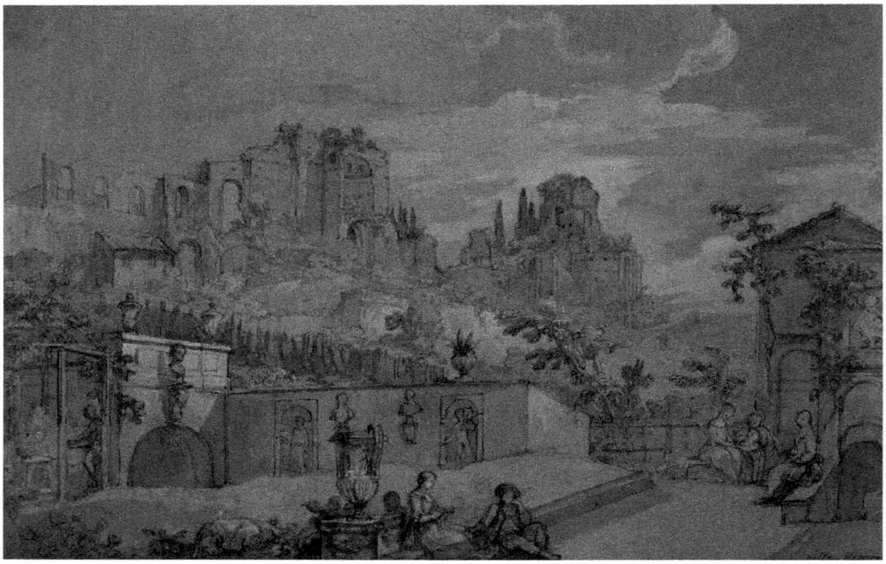

FIG. 85 Charles Natoire (French, 1700–1777), *Villa Natoire*, ca. 1760–62. Pencil, pen, ink, and gray wash with white gouache and watercolor, 29.7 × 45.2 cm. Frankfurt am Main, Städel Museum, 16733. (bpk Bildagentur / Städel Museum/ Ursula Edelmann / Art Resource, NY.)

1. Some things were sold in Italy before shipment. See *CDR*, 13:327–28.

2. [Alexandre-Joseph Paillet], *Catalogue des tableaux et dessins originaux des plus grands maîtres . . . qui composoient le cabinet de feu Charles Natoire* (Paris: Chariot & Paillet, 1778). See also JoLynn Edwards, *Alexandre Paillet: Expert et marchand de tableaux au XVIIIe siècle* (Paris: Arthena, 1996), 233–34.

3. Paillet, *Catalogue*: 24 lots out of a total of 377.

4. On Natoire's collection excepting the gems, see George Brunel, "Charles-Joseph Natoire collectionneur," in *Charles-*

Joseph Natoire, exh. cat. (Troyes: Musée des Beaux-Arts, 1977), 34–38.

5. See Pierre-Jean Mariette, *Traité des pierres gravées* (Paris: Mariette, 1750), 1:3–4, 49, 55.

6. Krzysztof Pomian, "Medals/Shells = Erudition/Philosophy," in *Collectors and Curiosities, Paris and Venice, 1500–1800* (Oxford: Polity, 1990), 121–38.

7. Brunel, "Natoire collectionneur," 37. Boucher's collection included gems, classed as "jewels" and mostly polished semi-precious stones "engraved" by nature's hand, not man's—tree agates and an amber ring with a fly inclusion. Exceptions were an agate portrait cameo, and a white agate intaglio engraved with "the god Priapus and a satyr," which may have been antique. See *Catalogue raisonné des tableaux, desseins, estampes . . . de feu M. Boucher* (Paris: Musier, 1771), lots 1083, 1085, 1086, 1088, 1091, 1092, 1098.

8. See Paillet, *Catalogue*, lots 354–57 (*Pierres antiques*); 358–61 (*Pierres modernes: Pickler*); and 362–77 (*Pierres modernes: Alexandre Cadès*).

9. Paillet, *Catalogue*, lots 375, 358; lots 362, 366; lot 362.

10. Paillet, *Catalogue*, lots 355, 356.

11. See Kristel Smentek, *Mariette and the Science of Connoisseurship in Eighteenth-Century Europe* (London: Routledge, 2014), 191–227.

12. The first attempt to publish the king's gems was initiated by the comte de Caylus in the 1720s. By 1730 he had enrolled the services of Coypel and De Troy. Sometime between 1733 and 1737 Bouchardon became involved. See Smentek, *Mariette*, 195–96 and 296n22.

13. *Catalogue de la vente des desseins, estampes et tableaux de M. Natoire, fait avant son départ pour Rome* (6 September 1751), lots: 143 (volume of prints of *Ruines de Rome* published by Justus Sadeler); 151 (volume of *Figures antiques de Rome,* etched by François Perrier); 153, 161 (Two volumes of prints after the Column of Trajan), INHA, Ms. VP1763/1f.

14. See Mariette, *Traité*, 36. On Natoire and Mariette, see Perrin Stein, "Copies and Retouched Drawings by Charles-Joseph Natoire," *Master Drawings* 38, no. 2 (2000): 167–86.

15. Charles-Joseph Natoire to Antoine Duchesne, 6 October 1751, in "Charles Natoire: Correspondance avec Antoine Duchesne, prévôt des Bâtiments du roi," ed. Paul Mantz, *AAF* 2 (1852): 261.

16. Natoire to Duchesne, 1 March 1752, in "Charles Natoire: Correspondance," 272.

17. [Pierre-Jean Mariette], *Catalogue des tableaux, dessins, marbres, bronzes, modèles, estampes et planches gravées . . . du cabinet de feu M. Coypel* (Paris: n.p., 1753), lot 202.

18. See Antoine Furetière, *Dictionnaire universelle* (The Hague: Husson, Johnson & Swart, 1727), 1: s.v. "Antiquaille"; *Dictionnaire de l'Académie Françoise*, 4th ed. (Paris: Brunet, 1762), 1: s.v. "Antiquaille."

19. Pierre Remy, *Catalogue d'une collection des très beaux tableaux, desseins, et estampes . . . de la succession de feu M. J.B de Troy* (Paris: Didot, 1764), lots 330, 336. As an executor of De Troy's will, Natoire was familiar with his gems and arranged their dispatch to Paris after De Troy's death in 1752.

20. On the excavations, see Caroline Millot, "Les jardins de la Fontaine à Nîmes et l'oeuvre de Jacques-Philippe Mareschal (1689–1778): Un patrimoine aux multiples facettes," *Patrimoines du Sud* 8 (2018), http://journals.openedition.org/pds/372.

21. Natoire to Duchesne, 9 November 1751, in "Charles Natoire: Correspondance," 264.

22. Natoire to Duchesne, 22 September and 6 October 1751, in "Charles Natoire: Correspondance," 258–63.

23. See Susan Stewart, *On Longing* (Durham and London: Duke University Press, 1993), 132–50.

24. See Charles-Joseph Natoire, "Inventaire après décès," 18 August 1762, AN, MC/ET/LXXVI/334.

25. Natoire to Duchesne, 1 March 1752, in "Charles Natoire: Correspondance," 272.

26. Natoire to Duchesne, 19 January 1752, in "Charles Natoire: Correspondance," 269.

Journal

Johann Georg Wille (1715–1808)

TYPE OF OBJECT	THEME	MATERIAL
Companion, Souvenir	Community, Death, Everyday, Memory, Money	Animal | Leather/Parchment, Synthetic Materials | Ink, Synthetic Materials | Paper

For four decades Johann Georg Wille, the German-born, Paris-based engraver, kept a journal.[1] From 1759 to 1793, regular entries record his quotidian doings from when he was a forty-something *agréé* (provisional member) at the Académie until a few months after his seventy-eighth birthday. In our search for things through which to retrieve their owners' lives, an artist's journal presents the ultimate biographical metaobject: a thing that exists entirely in order to record that person's experiences in firsthand accounts. Usually, the biographical value of a journal comes from considering it as a text. Indeed, ever since the publication of Wille's journal by the art historian Georges Duplessis in 1857 (forty-nine years after the artist's death), it has been read as a crucial source of insights, most of which can be gleaned by merely consulting Duplessis's transcription.[2] Wille's writings grant access to his professional activities, international social networks, and personal relationships, and as a whole the text offers a fascinating encounter with a singular moment of French history. Inadvertently chronicling the final chapter of the ancien régime, Wille's journal takes its reader on a journey from the seeming immutability of Louis XV's reign, through the escalating uncertainty of the Revolution, to the chaotic dismantling of an entire social order as the new Republic emerged. But what if Wille's journal is encountered not just as a text but as a "thing"? What stories emerge not from the meaning of the words but from the materiality of the notebooks that contain them? When it is the biography of the object itself—rather than the autobiographical text inscribed in it—what else might Wille's journal reveal about the engraver's habitual quirks, lived rhythms, and unexpected disruptions?

As a material thing, Wille's journal survives as a set of five bound notebooks (fig. 86), dispersed today between the Bibliothèque Nationale de France (the four volumes that Duplessis published, all donated to the library by Wille's son, Pierre-Alexandre, in 1834) and the Frits Lugt Collection (a volume that had been thought lost but which reemerged in 2005).[3] Even from a first glance at these notebooks, there are patterns of consistency and deviation in their materiality that reveal histories of use—habits and departures—suggesting Wille was a man who enjoyed routine without being beholden to it.

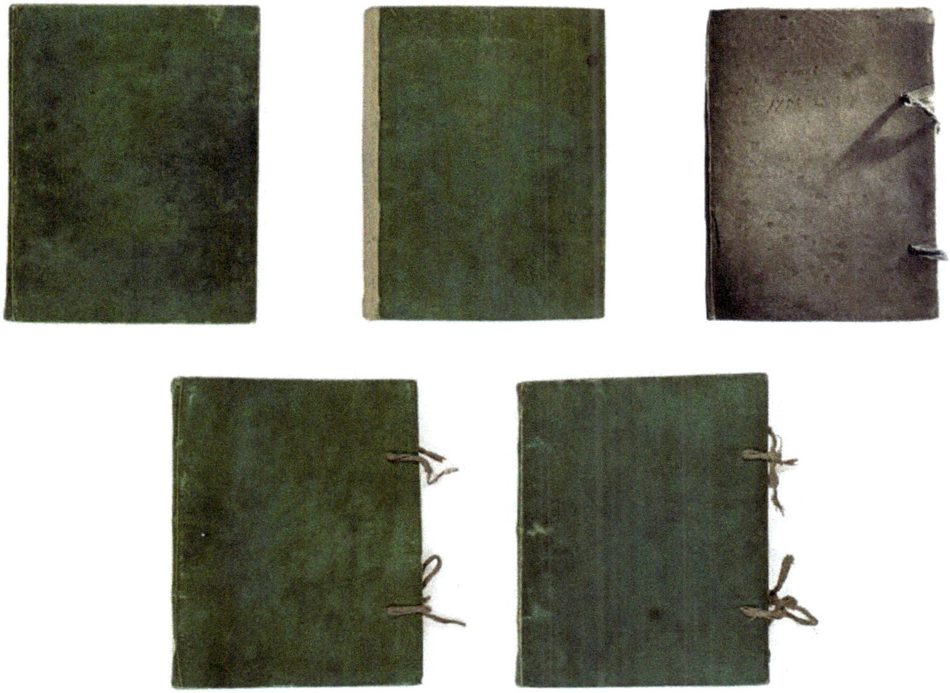

FIG. 86 Covers of the five surviving volumes of Johann Georg Wille's journal. Top row, left to right: BnF vol. 1 (1759–68), BnF vol. 2 (1768–76), Frits Lugt volume (1777–83); bottom row, left to right: BnF vol. 3 (1783–89); BnF vol. 4 (1789–93). Paris, Bibliothèque Nationale de France, images courtesy of Gallica; and Paris, Frits Lugt Collection, Fondation Custodia.

Anyone who keeps a diary or notebook for random jottings will understand the importance of its physical characteristics for determining aspects of use and storage, both during its active life and in retirement. All Wille's notebooks were the same size and format: octavo *carnets* of around 22 by 17 centimeters. Too large to be easily carried in a pocket, Wille's journal was probably a homebound object, likely a denizen of his "*cabinet de travail*" (workroom), given the prominence of work-related matters in the entries: business activities, correspondence, and other professional affairs.[4] It is not difficult to envisage the evenly sized volumes of his journal stored together, somewhere readily accessible for reference, gradually accumulating over the years into a set, albeit a mismatched one. For, despite their prevailing physical similarities, there are also minor differences: four of the notebooks are covered in green parchment and one in natural parchment; three have integrated ribbons to tie them shut, and two have none. Given the stash of notes, letters, and random slips of paper (lists, calculations of prices, business cards, etc.) still tucked into the inside cover of the Frits Lugt volume (fig. 87), the ribbon ties were no doubt a practical solution for this "temporary" filing system, keeping every scrap safely contained. It certainly seems as though Wille developed a preference for ribbons, as only the earliest volumes are without this handy feature. Wille's color choices, meanwhile, reveal an interruption rather than a change of habit, with the anomalous natural-covered notebook disrupting Wille's evident aesthetic preference for green covers. Perhaps this was an experimental switch that did not stick, or perhaps green notebooks were just temporarily out of stock in December 1776, when Wille had filled his previous notebook and was on the hunt for a new one.

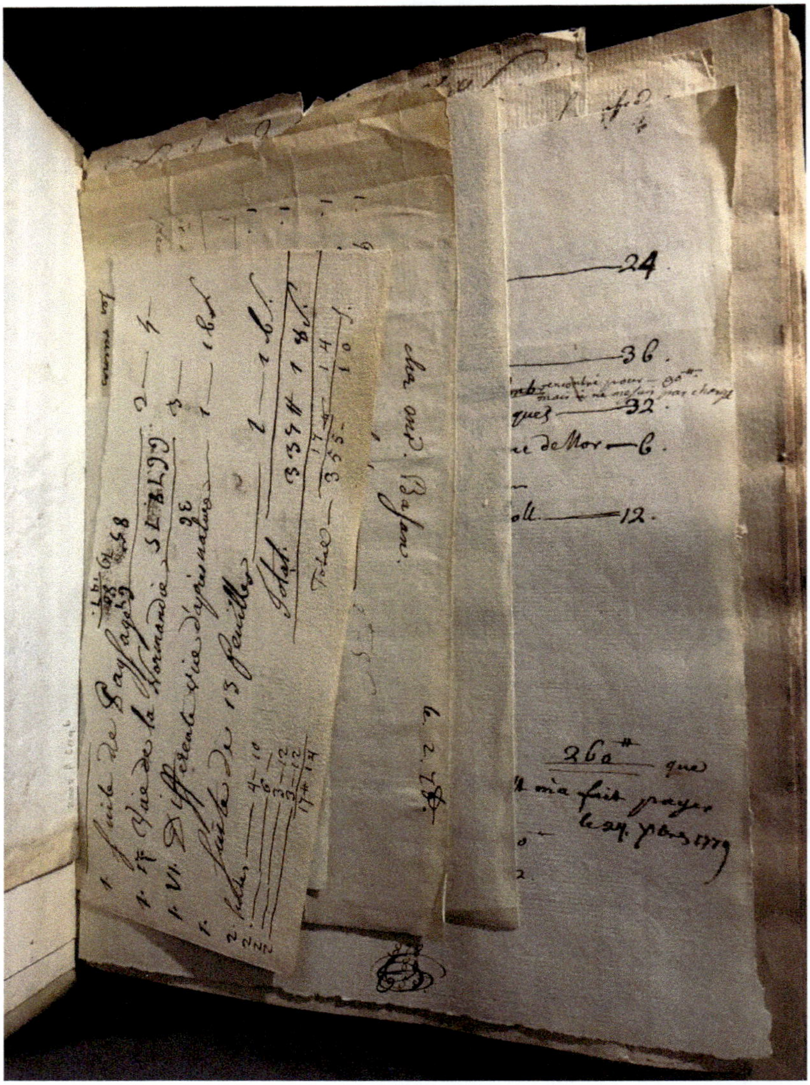

FIG. 87 Loose papers tucked inside the front cover of the Frits Lugt volume of Johann Georg Wille's journal (1777–83). Paris, Frits Lugt Collection, Fondation Custodia. (Photo: Hannah Williams.)

The question of where Wille purchased his notebooks can be answered with remarkable specificity. Unlike most of the commodities in this book, whose precise point of retail can only be guessed, three of Wille notebooks still bear the small trade cards that stationery merchants often pasted inside the cover of *carnets* and ledgers (fig. 88). Each seller's label is from a different shop, suggesting that whatever preferences Wille formed regarding his notebooks, those habits did not extend to the act of procuring them. One came from "A La Sagesse," a *marchand mercier* on Quai des Augustins that specialized in paper, sealing wax, and writing **quills**; another was bought at "L'Image de Notre Dame," a *marchand papetier* (stationer) on Rue de Buci selling office supplies, drawing paper, and writing equipment; and another was from "Au Portefeuille Anglais" on Rue Dauphine, run by an ink manufacturer, who sold paper and wax but specialized in stationery wallets and portable writing desks. These ephemeral vestiges of commerce draw attention to the ready availability of consumable items like notebooks, stamping each of these strikingly similar objects as an item sold in three different kinds of shop. But as all these shops were located within a few streets of each other, the trade cards also evocatively locate Wille's journal in a particular Parisian neighborhood.

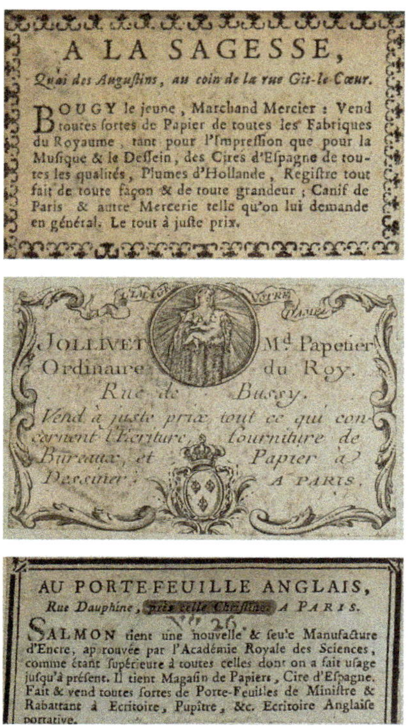

FIG. 88 Sellers' labels inside the covers of Johann Georg Wille's journal notebooks. Top: BnF vol. 1 (1759–68); middle: BnF vol. 3 (1783–89); bottom: BnF vol. 4 (1789–93). Paris, Bibliothèque Nationale de France.

Most artists would not have had quite so many stationery options on their doorstep, but Wille's Left Bank quarter of Saint-André-des-Arts was in the heart of Paris's printmaking and bookselling districts, so paper—bound, loose leaf, printed, or plain—was the specialty of the area. Not surprisingly, this was the neighborhood that Wille (along with many of his engraver colleagues) lived throughout his career, in the same house on Quai des Augustins, overlooking the Seine and the Île de la Cité.[5] As the journal of a German émigré who settled in Paris in 1736 but maintained active international business connections, Wille's writings have often been used as a source for thinking about quite global ideas, from Franco-German cultural transfer to European art markets.[6] But the trade cards in these notebooks are a material reminder of Wille's more local experiences in the streets of Paris. Indeed, in the pages of his diaries, international art deals are frequently recorded alongside quieter observations of life in the city, like the time in February 1764 when the Seine flooded so badly he had to use a boat to leave his house, or his encounter in July 1784 in the Jardin du Luxembourg with the latest aeronautical technology (as described in this book's entry on Janinet's **hot-air balloon**).[7] As "lived" objects that themselves once resided in that Quai des Augustins home, Wille's notebooks have a particular poignancy when recording things experienced in those very spaces, whether crises of family life (like in 1762, when both his sons caught chicken pox at the same time), or frustrations of artistic practice (like in 1773, when he had to abandon months of work on an uncooperative plate, causing him to bemoan "the maliciousness of copper").[8] Most striking of all, however, are the accounts of dramatic historic events that happened on his doorstep and that Wille witnessed from his home. From the vantage of his window onto the Seine, for instance, Wille watched all night on 8 June 1781 as the Paris Opera burned to the ground, and he stood there again eleven years later, on 12 August 1792, to watch the revolutionaries topple the statue of Henri IV on Pont-Neuf.[9]

Kept regularly for decades, Wille's journal was both a record and a practice. Over time it became a useful chronicle of everyday minutiae and extraordinary events; but in its making, it was a routine of writing that became habitual. This makes us wonder when Wille began his diary, how his rhythms developed, and why he eventually stopped. While there is likely a missing first volume, which, if ever found, might shed light on Wille's initial intentions, the surviving material evidence suggests that Wille may have originally planned to keep an **order book** (like Lagrenée's, discussed elsewhere in this book).[10] The notebooks' red-ruled pages reveal a stationery selection oriented to accounting (fig. 89). Their five columns of different widths are designed to accommodate bookkeeping records of date, item, and price in livres (pounds), sols (shillings), and deniers (pence). Every volume of Wille's journal is thus an account book, distinguished as such by these prominent red lines, and yet in none of the surviving notebooks did he ever use the columns as they were intended. Writing against the affordances of the page, Wille always wrote his entries in prose, even when noting sums of money spent or received. But whatever the rationale behind Wille's original choice, his continued preference for account books might be explained in the habits of practice he developed around those red lines. As evident on a sample page from July 1760 (see fig. 89), for instance, Wille tended to deploy the first column as it was intended, to record the date, and then the last two narrow columns to serve as a page margin, only occasionally letting a misjudged word trail over the lines.

Over the years, certain patterns of use became fixed, but Wille's relationship with the journal and its role in his life were far from static. There were, for instance, annual rhythms. Wille made his entries frequently, usually several times a month, though not always with predictable regularity, except for his habitual entry on 1 January to mark the new year. His longest entry of the year, meanwhile, tended to come in September, when he usually traveled to the countryside for a drawing holiday and so interrupted the quotidian flow of city life. But over the decades, there were also changing practices. Most notable is the gradual shift in form and content: from short, succinct, businesslike entries recording almost exclusively professional matters, to longer, more anecdotal entries interweaving the professional and the personal and including more observations and narrative accounts. Indeed, as time went by, each notebook served him fewer and fewer years as his longer entries filled them more quickly: the first lasted nearly ten years (1759–68), the next just over eight years (1768–76), then six and a half (1777–83), then six exactly (1783–89), and finally four (1789–93), although the last notebook did not get filled.

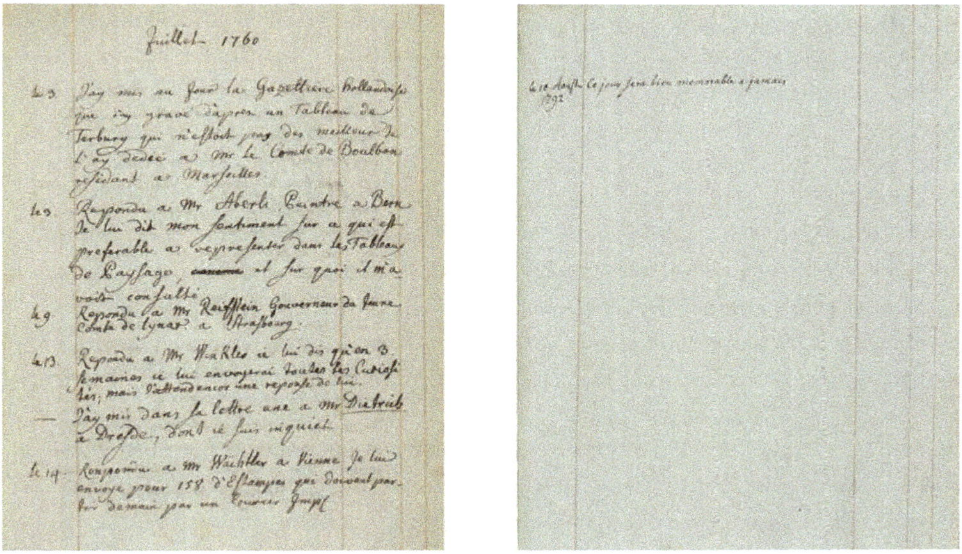

FIG. 89 Pages from Johann Georg Wille's journals. Left: July 1760 (page 24), BnF vol. 1 (1759–68); right: August 1792 (page 86), BnF vol. 4 (1789–93). Paris, Bibliothèque Nationale de France. (Images courtesy of Gallica.)

Along with gradual changes, there were also sudden ruptures, when Wille's habitual rhythms and evolving patterns were halted completely. Like any life, Wille's was occasionally interrupted by unanticipated events, some of which were so disruptive that they left their mark in the journal as either physical or temporal gaps. On 15 October 1778, for instance, Wille's younger son, Louis-François, died unexpectedly at twenty years of age.[11] Describing it as "the saddest day of my life," Wille recorded the tragic incident in his journal and then left five unexplained blank pages after the entry. Perhaps, when Wille made his fragile return to the journal three weeks later, it was simply too difficult to carry on as before without creating some distance from that fateful day. A handful of blank pages provided a material buffer—like a physical passage of mourning—creating respectful and emotional space before an attempt to return to everyday life. A few years later, Wille experienced another death that left a different kind of gap. On 29 October 1785, Wille's wife of nearly forty years, Marie-Louise Deforge, died after a period of worsening ill health. So overwhelmed was the engraver by this loss that, for the first time in his life, he stopped writing in his journal completely. For over a year, he wrote nothing, as though in a kind of hiatus, unable to reconnect with the routines and rhythms of his previous existence when nothing around him was the same. Then, at the beginning of 1787, he came back to the notebook to make a tentative reprisal of his old journaling habits. In this moment of re-engagement, he made a rare self-reflexive mention of the diary itself, writing: "Since the month of December 1785, I have written almost nothing in this journal, having had such sadness in my heart from the death of my dear wife, who I will never forget—and here we are in the month of March 1787." Somehow, in order to overcome the gap, Wille first needed to articulate it, but even then it took him many months to reestablish former rhythms and create new habits.

Despite disruptions and detours, Wille maintained a relationship with his journal for four decades. What compelled him, it is difficult to say. As the essayist Joan Didion notes, sometimes the impulse to write things down is peculiarly compulsive: "inexplicable to those who do not share it, useful only accidentally, only secondarily, in the way that compulsion tries to justify itself."[12] This certainly seems to have been the case for Wille. In 1792 he reflected on his journaling practice in an act of retrospective repurposing. A German printseller had asked him for "the story of his life," and Wille noted that, while he was not vain enough to have produced such a thing, if, after he was gone, anyone should want to write his story, they would find what they needed in these pages.[13] Though not intended as such from the outset, this was the function Wille started envisaging for his journal, perhaps as a result of the self-conscious turns it took during the Revolutionary years. As the world transformed around him, and ordinary life became a constant source of extraordinary experience, Wille's entries developed a new historicizing tone and sometimes paralyzing self-awareness. On 10 August 1792, for instance, the day the new Republic was declared, Wille began his entry grandly, proclaiming, "This day will be remembered forever" (see fig. 89). But there he ran out of steam and he wrote nothing more. Perhaps feeling unable to do the account justice that day, he left three pages, presumably planning to return when he could find the words it deserved. But he never did. And the following year, Wille stopped writing his journal altogether, though the notebook was only half full and he would go on to live for fifteen more years.[14] Whether it was the impending weight of posterity or something else that disrupted Wille's journaling habits, it is no surprise really that Wille should end his old routines in 1793, that year of endings and new beginnings for the entire nation.[15] It was, in many ways, a fitting time to finish. ‡

---

1. It is possible that Wille began keeping the journal before 1759. If so, the earlier volume is currently untraced.

2. *Mémoires et journal de J.-G. Wille, graveur du roi*, ed. Georges Duplessis, 2 vols. (Paris: Veuve Jules Renouard, 1857). Some of the most comprehensive explorations of Wille's journal are to be found Élisabeth Décultot, Michel Espagne, and François-René Martin, eds., *Johann Georg Wille (1715–1808) et son milieu: Un réseau européen de l'art au XVIII*[e] *siècle* (Paris: École du Louvre, 2009). On the journal as a source for understanding Wille's friendship with Greuze, see Hannah Williams, "Academic Intimacies: Portraits of Family, Friendship, and Rivalry at the Académie Royale," *Art History* 36, no. 2 (April 2013): 338–65.

3. For a detailed analysis of the Frits Lugt volume, see Peter Fuhring and Hans Buijs, "Quelques relations de Wille en Hollande: Lecture préliminaire d'un volume du Journal récemment apparu," in Décultot, Espagne, and Martin, *Johann Georg Wille*, 223–46.

4. *Cabinet de travail* is the term Wille uses to refer to his studio.

5. On the geography of Paris's engraver communities, see Marianne Grivel, *Le commerce de l'estampe au XVII*[e] *siècle* (Geneva: Droz, 1986); and Hannah Williams, "Artists and the City: Mapping the Art Worlds of Eighteenth-Century Paris," *Urban History* 46, no. 1 (2019): 106–31.

6. See several of the essays in Décultot, Espagne, and Martin, *Johann Georg Wille*, and the introductory sections to Elisabeth Decultot, Michel Espagne, and Michael Werner, *Johann Georg Wille (1715–1808): Briefwechsel* (Tübingen: Max Niemeyer, 1999).

7. Johann Georg Wille, *Journal*, BnF, 1:102v; BnF, 3:27v.

8. Wille, *Journal*, BnF, 1:73; and BnF, 2:116v.

9. Wille, *Journal*, Frits Lugt volume, n.p.; and Wille *Journal*, BnF, 4:58.

10. In 1792 Wille claims to have been keeping his journal for "more than forty years," but the surviving volumes cover a total of only thirty-four years. Wille, *Journal*, BnF, 4:86. On the likelihood of another volume, see also Fuhring and Buijs, "Quelques relations de Wille," 224.

11. Wille, *Journal*, Frits Lugt volume, n.p.

12. Joan Didion, "On Keeping a Notebook," *Slouching towards Bethlehem* (London: Fourth Estate, 2017), 132.

13. Wille, *Journal*, BnF, 4:85v, 86. Duplessis cites this justification in his preface, *Mémoires et journal de J-G Wille*, xv–xvi. Ironically, Wille did write a biographical account, known as his "mémoires," which was published by Duplessis in 1857 in the first volume of the journal.

14. On Wille's reasons for stopping this and his other writing activities during his later years, see Fuhring and Buijs, "Quelques relations de Wille," 224.

15. The year 1793 began with the execution of the king, Louis XVI, in January and continued with the dismantling of former state structures, including, in August, the Académie Royale de Peinture et de Sculpture.

Key

Pierre Peyron (1744–1814)

TYPE OF OBJECT	THEME	MATERIAL
Instrument	Community, Louvre	Metal | Gold/Gilding, Metal | Steel

Returning to Paris from Rome in February 1783, the history painter Pierre Peyron was handed the key to a studio on the first floor of the Cour Carré at the "old" Louvre. He must have been aglow with pleasure from the exceptional privilege. He was officially still a student, having yet to be admitted to the Académie.[1] His neighbors at the Louvre, by contrast, were all academicians of established distinction.[2] Only later was he made aware of the fracas his preferment provoked.

The studio key, a thing almost invisible to history as a material object and personal possession, in this instance leaves a trace in the correspondence between the *directeur des bâtiments du roi*, the comte d'Angiviller, and the painters Claude-Joseph Vernet and Jean-Baptiste-Marie Pierre. Pierre was the king's *premier peintre* (first painter) and responsible as such for the execution of d'Angiviller's orders with regards to the artists employed by the king, and resident in his palaces; Vernet was the injured party in the reallocation of studio space. In early February it was Vernet who had had the key to the studio whose title belonged neither to him nor to Peyron but to the painter Louis-Jean-François Lagrenée, who was temporarily in Rome, discharging his duty as director of the French school.[3] Vernet had been given use of the studio to paint six large landscapes for Carlos, prince of Asturias, pictures that had been despatched to the Escorial in Spain at the end of the previous year.[4] But in a letter of 15 February, d'Angiviller accused Vernet of having refused to return the key though he had finished the work for which enjoyment ("jouissance") of it had been granted.[5] Affronted and indignant, Vernet replied via Pierre that he had uttered no such refusal, and indeed, that no one had asked him for return of the key. Four days later he moved out of the Cour Carré and proposed a compromise: division of the studio between Peyron and himself, because he too had commissions of scale in the pipeline.[6] By February 23 he had withdrawn the requested concession and resigned himself to working in the cramped quarters of his *logement* (lodgings) at the Galerie du Louvre beside the Seine.[7] Pierre noted, at the very end of the month, that the key had been returned, and that Peyron had called on Vernet. The men apparently kissed and made up, following Peyron's explanation that he had been unaware that his arrival entailed Vernet's departure.

What more can we learn from this anecdote, this microhistory of a key? To progress, we need to know why, and to what effect, the key became the focus of debate, rather than the *brevet*, or certificate, which formally established a title of residency, and which was, in the ancien régime, the paradigmatic administrative instrument of royal housing for the arts. A *brevet*, legally speaking, was a royal act expedited by a secretary of state, and by which the king conferred the gift of a title, office, property, pension, or other gratuity.[8] In the case of the Louvre *logements*, these certificates granted named artists exclusive and lifetime residency rights to a studio-cum-living space in exchange for royal service. Issued first under Henri IV, during whose reign the system of *logements* was established, and on parchment, the official medium of legal acts, by the time of d'Angiviller's administration, the brevet-as-thing involved standardized paperwork, a partially printed form (fig. 90), to which the personal details of the individual recipient, in this example the sculptor Jean-Jacques Caffieri, were inserted by hand.[9] To us this degraded paperwork seems dull, dreary, and even fragile next to the heavy and enduring significance we imaginatively project onto a royal, fleur-de-lis key (fig. 91), forged with a bow at one end and with a notched bit for the lock at the other, the parts united by a circular iron shank. But this would be a mistake. The key on its own afforded no security of tenure, though in the technical discourse on locksmithing, keys and locks were the instruments, *par excellence*, for enclosing and safeguarding private property.[10] It functioned, in fact, more like a hinge or a handle, the furniture that opened the door and kept it moving and to which Henri-Louis Duhamel de Monceau categorically opposed lock and key in *L'art du serrurier* (1767).[11]

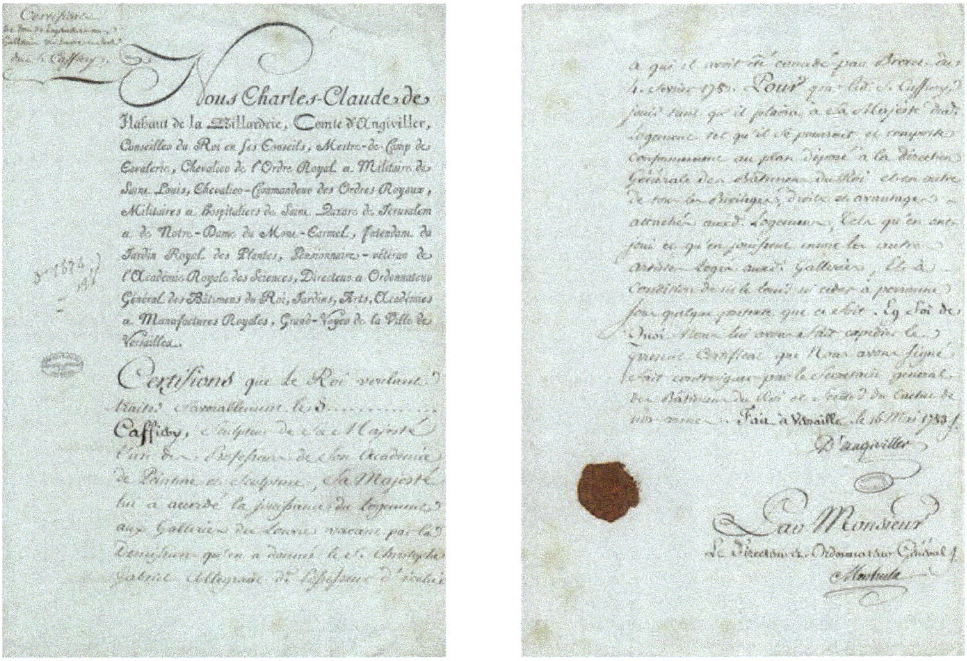
Nous Charles-Claude de Flahaut de la Billarderie, Comte d'Angiviller, Conseiller du Roi en ses Conseils, Mestre-de-Camp de Cavalerie, Chevalier de l'Ordre Royal et Militaire de Saint Louis, Chevalier-Commandeur des Ordres Royaux, Militaires et Hospitaliers de Saint Lazare de Jerusalem et de Notre-Dame du Mont-Carmel, Intendant du Jardin Royal des Plantes, Pensionnaire-vétéran de l'Académie Royale des Sciences, Directeur et Ordonnateur Général des Bâtimens du Roi, Jardins, Arts, Académies et Manufactures Royales, Grand-Voyer de la Ville de Versailles.

Certifions que le Roi voulant traiter favorablement le S. Caffiery, [illegible]

[illegible] Pour [illegible]

[illegible] Fait à Versailles le 16 Mai 1783 [illegible]

D'angiviller

A Monsieur

Le Directeur et Ordonnateur Général [illegible]

FIG. 90 *Brevêt de logement for Jean-Jacques Caffieri*, 1783. Printed form with pen and ink. Paris, Archives Nationales.

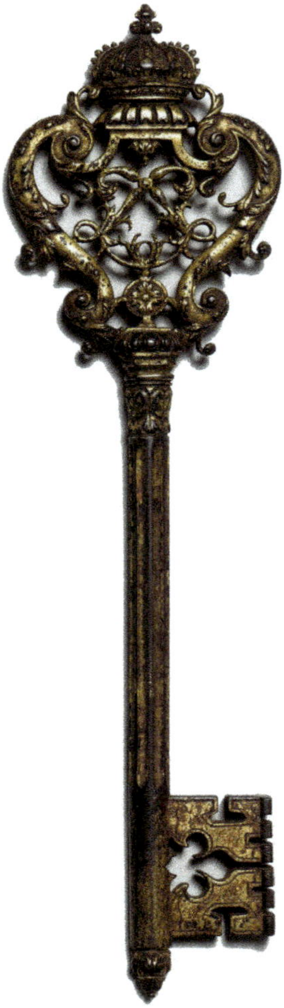

FIG. 91 Attributed to Grettepin (sculptor) and Jacques Desjardins (bronze caster), Key for the chapel at the Château de Versailles, ca. 1710. Gilt bronze and steel, 31 × 8.5 cm, 510g. Châteaux de Versailles et de Trianon, V6295. (© RMN-Grand Palais / photo: Gérard Blot / Art Resource, NY.)

Getting the key to a royal studio was, arguably, an easier challenge than securing a *brevet*, because entry by key was always conditional. The *directeur des bâtiments* was, therefore, less constrained in his choice by precedent and succession planning. When requesting such temporary studio space, how then did artists attempt to unlock d'Angiviller's favor? In Vernet's case, he reiterated his need, post loss of the Lagrenée/Peyron studio, on the grounds of the prestige of his patrons and the size of their commissions: specifically, in November 1783, he informed the *directeur des bâtiments* that the "Grand duc of Russia" had ordered from him "*grands tableaux*" (big pictures), repeat uses of the adjective "great" that he underscored in his letter with capital Gs.[12] Only when d'Angiviller turned him down did he make a spectacle of his age, rank, and years of royal service.[13] Several years earlier, the young genre painter Étienne Aubry, a d'Angiviller protégé, had requested a temporary Louvre studio, not this time for its size but for its better light: the direct brightness of the midday sun.[14] Here again, the painter stressed both practical needs and the contingencies of the moment; his search for appropriate accommodation in Paris had yet to yield fruit. Both Aubry and Vernet framed their applications in terms of production, the execution moreover of specific painting projects. Neither refers to invention, or to the mind's need for personal space and solitary retirement, that is, to those spatial tropes of the artist that, since the renaissance, have been associated with genius. They appealed to the *directeur des bâtiments*'s reason, not his values.[15] Neither, however, was successful.

In d'Angiviller's hands the studio became a pivotal tool of reform, one by which he turned prime working space over to key artists in pursuit of his proclaimed goal to reorient and regenerate the French School.[16] For d'Angiviller, "grand" denoted the genre of history painting and the values of public art; the Louvre studios were to produce works for the king and the Salon public, not subsidize artists' commissions in lesser genres for private clients, however distinguished. Peyron returned to Paris to take his place at the Louvre, bringing with him his large *Funeral of Miltiades* (fig. 92), a scene of heroic filial self-sacrifice in ancient Athens that is informed by the study of classical sculpture and Italian old masters. It was commissioned privately by d'Angiviller but served also as Peyron's diploma piece and was exhibited at the Salon in 1783 after his election as an *agréé* (provisional member) of the Académie.[17] The agency of the diploma piece, its unlocking not just of Académie membership but also of studio space at the Louvre, finds its parallel coincidentally in the masterpieces of the Paris guild of *serruriers*, makers of miscellaneous metal things: the lock and key traditionally earned locksmiths the title of master.[18] The studio at the Cour Carré was, however, not so much a reward as a goad. D'Angiviller intended it to expand Peyron's creative vision, talent, and ideas, and to inspire him to realise ever larger and more consequential works for the king.[19]

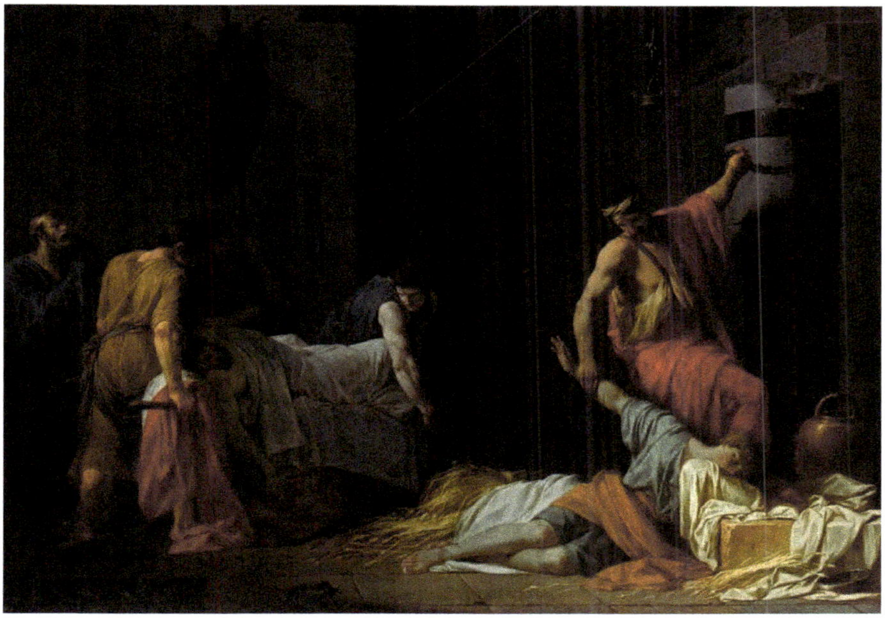

FIG. 92 Pierre Peyron, *Funeral of Miltiades*, 1782. Oil on canvas, 98 × 136 cm. Paris, Musée du Louvre, 7179. (© RMN-Grand Palais / photo: Michel Urtado / Art Resource, NY.)

At the Louvre's Cour Carré, d'Angiviller had a freer hand because, as Jules Guiffrey observed in his inaugural study of the royal studios, the convention of lifetime tenure as a form of virtual property was less entrenched there than at the gallery *logements* by the river.[20] D'Angiviller not only assigned space in the "old" Louvre on shorter terms, he also rescinded longer arrangements. In 1784 the sculptor Jean-Baptiste Cyprien d'Huez was given three months' notice to quit his studio. In reply to his angry objections, d'Angiviller reminded him that a *brevet* was a contract, not a deed—that is, an exchange, not a gift. He added, bluntly, that had he another studio to offer him by way of alternative, but "justice" would compel him to assign it elsewhere, to an academician "who by assiduous work endeavors to merit the king's grace."[21] The year before, Caffieri had been given a studio, not before time, to continue his work on d'Angiviller's *grands hommes* (illustrious men) series.[22] D'Angiviller's *logement* policy was, you could say, one of "key," not *brevet*, insofar as he successfully allocated studios to those with talent, instead of by "succession," that is, by descent from father to son, as had often been the practice in the administrations of previous directors.[23] Use of keys, which in the discourse of the Bâtiments department had formerly denoted illegitimate circulation, came to represent a dynamic exercise of administrative power.

We can never know how Peyron felt as he took the key from his pocket, slipped it into the lock, turned it, and opened the door into his room looking out to the river. The records of the Bâtiments du Roi, rich though they are in information about the emotions that motivated artists to ask for a studio—pride, ambition, entitlement, love, desperation, etc.—tell us nothing about the experience of taking possession of one. The history painter Louis Galloche was an exception: he wrote to Philibert Orry in January 1744 of his joy on learning that the king had granted him a *logement*, and he fully expected to blossom from "the great advantage" of occupying "one of the most beautiful vantage points in the universe" from which to view and reflect upon Nature's "tout ensemble."[24] Peyron's joy, if such it was, was short-lived. In 1785 he was moved to the Gobelins. §

---

1. Peyron was *agréé* on 27 September 1783. See *PV*, 9:168.

2. At the Cour Carré in 1783 were Nicolas Brenet, Gabriel-François Doyen, Joseph-Siffred Duplessis, Jean-Baptiste Le Prince, and Hubert Robert.

3. It was Lagrenée's idea initially that Peyron, one of his pupils, be assigned his studio, thereby safeguarding its return to Lagrenée when he returned to Paris. See *CDR*, 14:96, 97, 265, 266.

4. The six paintings sent in October arrived in Madrid in January 1783. Three (*Landscape with a Sunset*, *Landscape with a Waterfall*, and *The Kite*) are at the Prado, Madrid, and a fourth is in the Duke of Westminster's collection. The remaining two are lost.

5. Jules Guiffrey, "Correspondance de Joseph Vernet avec le Directeur des Bâtiments du roi sur la collection des *Ports de France*, 1756–1787," *Revue de l'art ancien et moderne* 9 (1893): 85.

6. Guiffrey, "Correspondance," 85. Vernet's letter does not survive, but its contents were communicated by d'Angiviller's to Pierre on 19 February 1782.

7. Guiffrey, "Correspondance," 86–87.

8. "Brevet," *Encyclopédie*, http://encyclopedie.uchicago.edu/, 2:414; and *Dictionnaire de l'Académie française*, 2 vols, 4th ed. (Paris: Brunet, 1762), 1: s.v. "Brevet." Secretary of State of the *Maison du roi* was at that time Louis Charles Auguste Le Tonnelier, baron de Breteuil.

9. "Papier et parchemin timbré," *Encyclopédie*, http://encyclopedie.uchicago.edu/, 11:862–72.

10. "Serrurie," *Encyclopédie*, http://encyclopedie.uchicago.edu/, 17:811–31, at 821–22.

11. Henri-Louis Duhamel de Monceau, *L'art du serrurier* (Paris: Saillant & Desaint, 1767), 109, 119–20.

12. AN, O^1/1674/158: Vernet to the comte d'Angiviller, 4 November 1783.

13. Guiffrey, "Correspondance," 90: Vernet to the comte d'Angiviller, 2 December 1783.

14. AN, O^1/1673/504: Aubry to the comte d'Angiviller, 1 March 1777.

15. Both also said they had found it impossible to find alternative studio space in the immediate environs of the Louvre.

16. As classically retold by Thomas Crow in *Painters and Public Life in Eighteenth-Century Paris* (New Haven: Yale University Press, 1985), 175–209. In October 1784 David was granted a studio at the Louvre to return to after completing *The Oath of the Horatii* (1785) in Rome.

17. Crow, *Painters and Public Life*, 201–3.

18. See Duhamel de Monceau, *L'art du serrurier*, 203–4.

19. D'Angiviller's commissioned the *Death of Alcestes* (1785) for himself, and the *Death of Socrates* (1787) for the king.

20. Jules-Joseph Guiffrey, "Logements d'artistes au Louvre," *NAAF*, 1873, 15, 18.

21. AN, O^1/1674/240, Jean-Baptiste Huez to the comte d'Angiviller, 27 November 1784; and AN, O^1/1674/240bis, d'Angiviller to Huez, 15 December 1784. D'Angiviller took much more care in choosing his words to Vernet. The repeated crossed-out words in a draft of a letter to Vernet, 21 February 1782 (AN, O^1/1674/104) indicate that he was keen to spare Vernet's pride.

22. AN, O^1/1674/117.

23. See Guiffrey, "Logements d'artistes au Louvre," 14, 127–35.

24. AN, O^1/1672/81.

Lantern

Jean-Siméon Chardin (1699–1779)
Charles-Nicolas Cochin (1715–90)
Claude-François Desportes (1695–1774)
Pierre-André Jacquemin (1720–73)
Jean-Baptiste Lemoyne (1704–78)
Jean-Baptiste Pigalle (1714–85)
Claude-Joseph Vernet (1714–89)
Joseph-Marie Vien (1716–1809)

TYPE OF OBJECT	THEME	MATERIAL
Instrument	Community, Gender, Louvre	Synthetic Materials | Glass

The lantern is exceptional in this book. A utensil, to paraphrase the *Dictionnaire de l'Académie française* (1762), made of glass, horn, oilcloth, or other translucent material to protect the flame of an enclosed tallow or wax candle from the wind and rain, the lantern was generally thought to be a public utility for outdoor use in the eighteenth century, not a personal thing privately owned.[1] These particular lanterns were ones used to light the public or semipublic passageways between artists' *logements* (lodgings) at the Louvre. They belonged, insofar as the cost of fueling and maintaining them was borne collectively, to the group of artists granted rights of residency at the Louvre by royal patent (*brevet*) and listed above. The lanterns count as "artists' things" because they served, on the one hand, to create an internal sense of community and personal belonging, distinguishing *brevetaires* from the master craftsmen of the town, and on the other, as an instrument of internal discipline.

Bought from glaziers and supplied with fuel by chandlers, lanterns generally fall below the threshold of notice in personal records and communication. Notaries did not itemize and value stocks of candles. Candles were classed for the purposes of probate with perishable goods like food, and not stores or supplies like wood or coal.[2] Lanterns went largely unnoticed, too, in diaries and letters. They are, in short, difficult to connect historically to particular persons. Those at the Louvre become visible and knowable only because in November 1769 a number of unnamed artists at the palace threatened not to pay the dues collected annually at New Year to cover the cost of keeping the lanterns in good repair and supplied with the wicks and fuel needed to light them.[3] This mini rebellion, which pitted the interests and concerns of the community of *brevetaires* against those of particular individuals, prompted the sculptor Jean-Baptiste Lemoyne to write to the *directeur des bâtiments du roi*, the marquis de Marigny, forwarding a petition signed by fellow sculptor Jean-Baptiste Pigalle; the painters Jean-Siméon Chardin, Claude-François Desportes, Joseph-Marie Vien, and Claude-Joseph Vernet; the draftsman and printmaker Charles-Nicolas Cochin; and the king's jeweler, Pierre-André Jacquemin, and to ask him to intervene in the matter.[4]

The petitioners justified their case principally on grounds of custom. The public passages had, they said, always been lit at night. "Decency requires it, and the good of all is united in it."[5] The Louvre was a community as well as a legally protected enclave. The king's artists living there were, by an act of Henri IV in 1608, distinguished from the city's ordinary painters and sculptors by privileges that included the freedom to practice their arts without let or hindrance from the Paris guilds and by exemptions from certain municipal taxes and duties, including taxes levied to pay for the lighting and cleaning of the city's streets.[6] At one level the passageway lanterns represented a sign of exceptionalism: royal lighting, we might say, as opposed to city lights. At another level, and more importantly, the practice of lighting the passages played a part in fostering and sustaining a sense and style of community among the denizens of the Louvre.

Though not mentioned directly in the memorandum, the circumstances of the Desportes household was a likely factor in the affair. At the time of writing, Mme Desportes, wife of still-life painter Claude-François Desportes, was responsible for collecting the lantern dues.[7] Lemoyne alludes to the desire to spare her humiliation. Claude-François was the son of the "great" Alexandre-François Desportes, painter of Louis XIV's hunts. He had inherited his father's *logement* in 1743 and continued to perpetuate the family business in animal and still-life painting as best he could but without his father's flair.[8] Claude-François was keen, it seems, to preserve his wife's income from lantern tending. His warm commendation of his mother's contribution in her time to the domestic economy—she had worked as a linen draper and lace seller to afford his father the leisure to perfect his studies after nature—suggests he actively approved his wife's occupation.[9]

Care and supply of lanterns at the Louvre represented unofficially, one could say, an office, a poor relation of the governor of Versailles's office to supply the *grands appartements* with beeswax candles or equivalent in the visual arts to the posts of keeper of the king's cabinet and drawing master to the royal household; less distinguished and less remunerative certainly, but significant nevertheless to the modest artist's income.[10] That the community at the Louvre took action in part to support its more vulnerable members is strongly suggested by the fact that most of the signatories of the lantern petition, signed another in 1774 to second Nicolas Desportes's begging request to Marigny to be allowed keep the family *logement* after his cousin Claude-François's death.[11] Nicolas Desportes had lived with and worked for, first, Alexandre-François, his uncle, and then Claude-François; the *logement* had been his only home and its free accommodation was crucial to his prospects of supporting himself independently by painting.[12] "The good of all" highlighted in the lantern petition entailed safeguarding the little jobs, like the tending of lanterns, in order to keep modest artistic livelihoods afloat in precarious times, and the corps at the Louvre united.

More obviously, of course, the lanterns lit the communal areas of the Louvre. The kind of lanterns used is not made clear in the memorandum. Not lanterns with wax candles certainly. Candles made of beeswax were prohibitively expensive.[13] More likely, they would have been either oil lamps, that is, an enclosed ceiling version of the one depicted by Cochin at the Académie's drawing school (fig. 93), the reservoir for oil plain to see, or lanterns supplied with tallow candles. Either could have provided, more or less unattended, a source of continuous light for between five and a half to twelve hours, or from dusk to dawn, according to the season.[14]

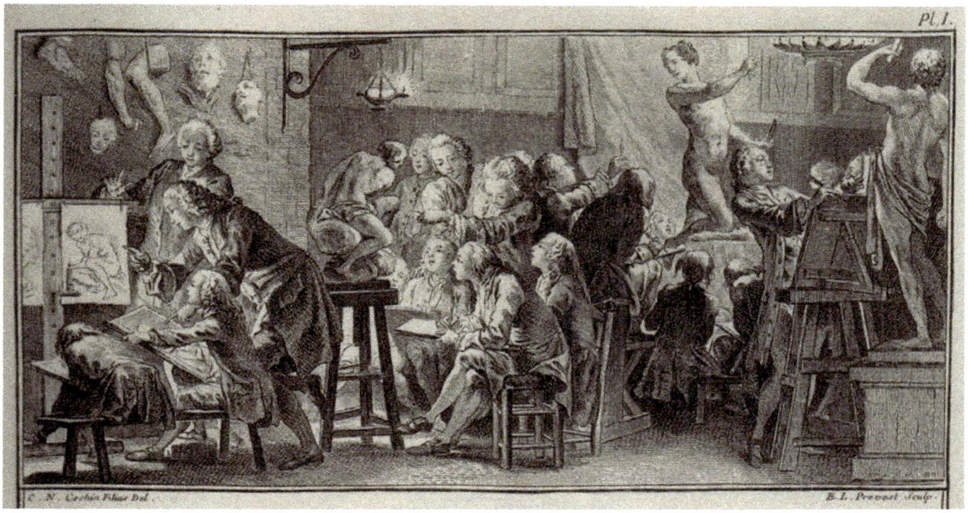

FIG. 93 Drawing school, detail from *Recueil de planches sur les sciences, les arts libéraux et les arts mécanique* (1765), plate I. (Image courtesy of the ARTFL Encyclopédie Project, University of Chicago.)

The light shed would not have been as intense as that afforded by wax candles, but it was sufficient to vouchsafe "decency" in what the petitioners called their "gallery," the passage connecting the *logements* at mezzanine level. By "*décence*" they meant that "exterior" or public expression of polite bearing appropriate to spaces of prestige.[15] By naming the mezzanine passageway the "small gallery," they implicitly invited comparison of it to the celebrated Grande Galerie above, and invoked an interior space of habitation and belonging as well as of convenient transit.[16] In this passage-cum-gallery, the private space of individual studios and the public space of the palace and the greater world beyond collided. Hubert Robert's gray-washed black-chalk drawing of a corridor (fig. 94), once thought to represent the entrance to his studio, affords a vivid picture of the flows in and out of this transitional space: pictures being moved out from studios or stores, a woman poised on the threshold of the private, about to step in. In the depths, a group of loiterers take up residence. Light reaches the space from a distance, through contiguous spaces. Momentarily brightened by the opening of a door, its natural state is half shadow even in the daylight hours.

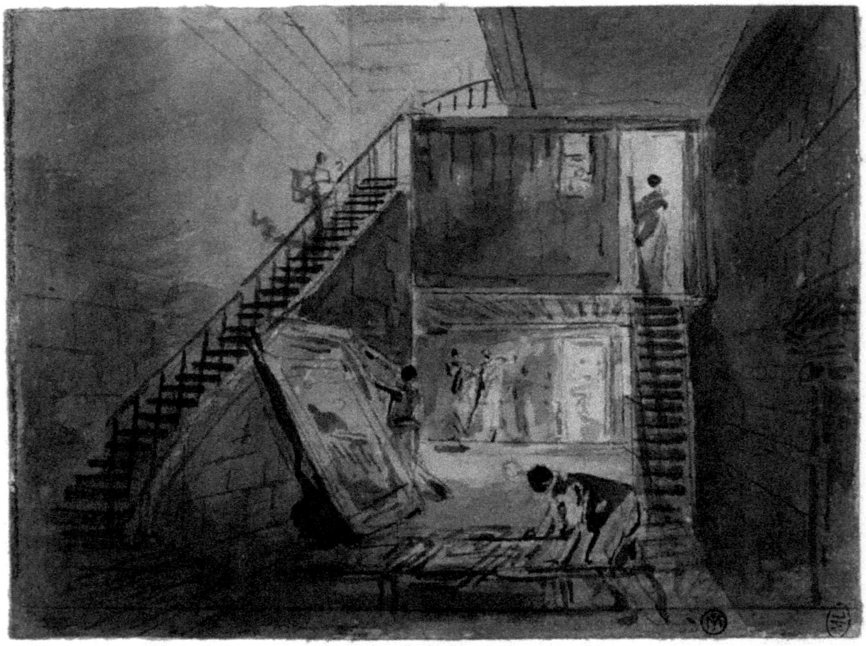

FIG. 94 Hubert Robert, *View of a Corridor in the Louvre*, ca. 1780. Black chalk and gray wash, 10.2 × 13.4 cm. Paris, Musée du Louvre, RF28940-recto. (© RMN-Grand Palais / photo: Thierry Le Mage / Art Resource, NY.)

According to the Bâtiments' archives, the propriety of the passages at the Louvre was regularly under threat. In December 1777, the cleanliness, rather than the lighting, of the passages led to the intervention of the comte d'Angiviller, Marigny's successor as director, into the trivialities of the everyday.[17] The now so-called corridors were supposed to be swept once every two weeks and sprinkled with water to settle the dust, but notwithstanding the conscientiousness of the cleaner, the place was, reported Jean-Baptiste-Marie Pierre, the king's first painter, unacceptably filthy.[18] D'Angiviller took up the matter with Barthouil, Inspecteur du Louvre, from whom he learned that art students habitually used the corridors as latrines and, moreover, that when Barthouil had instructed the Swiss guard to stop them defecating, he had been treated to a generous portion of their wastes on his doorstep in retaliation.[19] Lighting was an important weapon in repressing such behavior. If it did not shame the student cohort, it did enable the identification of individual culprits.[20]

Tensions arose not only between young and old for definition of the culture of the public space at the Louvre—wild or civilized, dark or light—but also between bachelors and married academicians. D'Angiviller touched on the inconveniences caused by absent single artists, because there was no wife to open the door to receive messages, no one to answer for and to them.[21] This suggests that bachelor households were potentially dangerous to order and decency too. Were bachelors perhaps the ones who threated not to pay the lantern charge? It is a point to note that the majority of the signatories of the petition were married men: Chardin, Desportes, Lemoyne, Pigalle, Vernet, and Vien. That the Louvre was no place for a woman is intimated by the case of Anne Vallayer-Coster, the only woman artist to have been granted a *logement* at the *galerie du Louvre*, a grace she appears to have hesitated in accepting.[22] When in April 1779 she came for a site visit to inspect the rooms that d'Angiviller had assigned her and to establish whether she could in fact live there "honorably" and "comfortably," she came "in the greatest . . . incognito" that a large "*calèche bonnet*" could afford, one so profound, according to the architect Maximilian Brébion, not a little impressed, that it "left the curious in some doubt as to whether the wearer possessed a face at all."[23] The passage-cum-gallery ideal that Lemoyne and company were bent upon preserving as a reality in 1769 was one in which riotous and sometimes rebellious masculinity was tamed by lantern light, and women like Mme Desportes and Vallayer-Coster were free to circulate and pursue their domestic and working lives without cover and without risking mockery and shame.

The later context of the Bâtiments' role under d'Angiviller in disciplining behavior at the Louvre could suggest, reading back, that the lanterns of 1769 were in practice Marigny's things, though they belonged to Lemoyne and his *logement* neighbors. Marigny's regime was notably less oppressive that d'Angiviller's. Even so, the petitioners' concern for decency certainly suggests that the artists at the Louvre were subjects of what Michel Foucault has called "biopower," unconsciously internalizing norms of behavior and self-control useful to the state and which, by use of lanterns, they themselves intended to perpetuate.[24] Yet their attachment to the lanterns exceeded the merely instrumental. In calling the mezzanine corridor a "gallery" and by invoking custom, their petition indicates that they valued lantern light also for its symbolic meaning. It styled their manner of existence "privileged" in contrast to the artisanal neighborhoods of Paris, where lanterns oriented passage at night rather than illuminating it.[25] Privilege lived entailed responsibilities as well as representation. The Louvre artists, the petition has suggested, were a community conscious of its interdependence. Defending the custom of lighting was also defending the right of the lesser artists to little jobs. It articulated a concern to mitigate the social and cultural differences within privilege between the haves and the have-nots, between students and elders, between men and women, between bachelors and married men, and ensure thereby the better security for all. If we would be mistaken in raising the coincidental connection here between lanterns, light, and social solidarity to the metaphorical level of Enlightenment it is, perhaps, no coincidence that the phalanstery imagined by Charles Fourier and other utopians in the nineteenth century was informed, as Roger Luckhurst has recently shown, by the "corridic" (his word) spaces of the Louvre and other royal palaces.[26] The collectively owned lantern in the public corridor embodies a different strand of modernity's myth of artistic genius, one rooted not in the isolated individual studio but in community, and manifest in such housing projects as La Ruche, the artist community established by the sculptor Alfred Boucher at Montparnasse in the wake of the Great Exhibition of 1900, and which is still home to around fifty artists today. §

1. *Dictionnaire de l'Académie française* 4th ed. (Paris: Brunet, 1762), 2: s.v. "Lanterne."

2. The point is more fully made by Stephane Castelluccio in *L'Éclairage, le chauffage, et l'eau au XVIIe et XVIIIe siècles* (Montreuil: Gourcuff gradenigo, 2016), 34.

3. It is unclear whether Mme Desportes actually lit the lanterns or simply administered their use. The Swiss guard was responsible for the public spaces of the Louvre.

4. Jean-Baptiste Lemoyne to the marquis de Marigny, 4 November 1769. AN, O^{1}/1673/152.

5. Jean-Siméon Chardin, Charles-Nicolas Cochin, Pierre-André Jacquemin, Jean-Baptiste Lemoyne, Jean-Baptise Pigalle, Claude-Joseph Vernet, and Joseph-Marie Vien, "Memorandum," AN, O^{1}/1673/153.

6. For the letters patent of Henri IV (1608), confirmed and elaborated by Louis XIV (1673), see Jules-Joseph Guiffrey, "Logements d'artistes au Louvre," *NAAF*, 1873, 40, 73. On the *logements* more generally, see Yvonne Singer-Lecocq, *Un Louvre inconnu: Quand l'état logeait ses artistes, 1608–1806* (Paris: Perrin, 1986); and Elena Palacios Carral, "The Freelancer: The Individuation of the Artist's Work in Paris, 1608–1805," *AA Files* 77 (2020): 103–12.

7. Mme Desportes is identified in Claude-Joseph Vernet's accounts as the person in charge of the lanterns. See Léon Lagrange, *Joseph Vernet et la peinture du XVIIIe siècle* (Paris: Didier, 1864).

8. Claude François had moved in with his father in 1739.

9. See Claude-François Desportes, "Vie de M. Desportes, peintre d'animaux" (1748) in *Mémoires inédits*, 2: 101.

10. On the supply of candles to the royal palaces, see Castelluccio, *L'Éclairage*, 63–76.

11. AN, O^{1}/1673/345: Resubmission of a *placet* originally tendered by Claude-François Desportes (AN, O^{1}/1673/330) before his death. The resubmission is signed by Chardin, Vernet, Loriot, Bailly, Lagrenée, Restout, Roettiers, Duviver, Lemoyne, Vien, and La Tour among others. See also AN, O^{1}/1673/329.

12. Nicolas Desportes had lived at the family *logement* for forty-three years. An independent report on the matter (AN, O^{1}/1673/344) by Bâtiments personnel noted that the Desportes "has for a long time been a loved and regarded family" ("est une famille aimée et considérée depuis longtemps dans les galleries.")

13. On prices of oil, tallow, and wax, see Castelluccio, *L'Éclairage*, 19–20, 32–33. Beeswax candles were roughly three times as expensive as tallow.

14. Castelluccio, *L'Éclairage*, 40.

15. See *Dictionnaire de l'Académie française*, 1: s.v. "Décence."

16. "Memorandum," AN, O^{1}/1673/153. On the early history of corridors, see Reed Benhamou, "Parallel Walls, Parallel Worlds: The Place of Masters and Servants in the 'Maisons de Plaisance' of Jacques-François Blondel," *Journal of Design History* 7, no. 1 (1994): 1–11.

17. See Marc Furcy-Raynaud, ed., "Correspondance de M. d'Angiviller avec Pierre," *NAAF*, 1905, 152–54, Jean-Baptiste Marie Pierre to the comte d'Angiviller, 4 December 1777.

18. On the "*ballayeurs*" resident in the palace, see Guiffrey, "Logements d'artistes au Louvre," 150–51.

19. See Furcy-Raynaud, "Correspondance," 156–57, d'Angiviller to Pierre, 16 December 1777. Barthouil's *logement* was on the first floor of the Cour Carré. See Guiffrey, "Logements d'artistes au Louvre," 148.

20. The students of the painters Hugues Taraval, Pierre-Antoine De Machy, Charles-Louis Clérisseau, and Louis Jean-Jacques Durameau were identified.

21. Furcy-Raynaud, "Correspondance," 157.

22. See AN, O^{1}/1673/571: d'Angiviller to Vallayer-Coster, 9 April 1779.

23. AN, O^{1}/1673/574: Brébion to d'Angiviller, 12 April 1779.

24. Michel Foucault, *A History of Sexuality: Volume 1, An Introduction* (New York: Vintage, 1980), esp. 94, 139.

25. See Wolfgang Schivelbusch, "The Policing of Street Lighting," *Yale French Studies* 73 (1987): 61–74.

26. Roger Luckhurst, *Corridors: Passages of Modernity* (London: Reaktion, 2019), 43–69.

Letters

Hyacinthe Rigaud (1659–1743)

TYPE OF OBJECT	THEME	MATERIAL
Document, Ritual Thing, Symbolic Thing	Administration, Identity	Animal | Wax, Synthetic Materials | Ink, Synthetic Materials | Paper

Becoming a member of the Académie—the preeminent institution of the Paris art world—was a process transacted through a ritual exchange of "things." The artist's side of this material interaction was a reception piece: an artwork that demonstrated the candidate's requisite skill in their chosen media or genre (thus sculptors submitted sculptures, landscapists submitted landscapes, portraitists submitted portraits, and so on).[1] If a reception piece was deemed worthy, the artist would be admitted directly into the Académie and the object would be accessioned into the institution's collection, to be hung on a wall or displayed on a plinth somewhere within the Louvre apartments. From the Académie's side, the counter offering in this ritual exchange was paper: a set of official letters—known as *lettres de réception* or *lettres de provision*—customarily given to the artist before or during their first meeting as a member. Though materially far less substantial than the artist's contribution, the letters were just as consequential when it came to their ritual and legal significance, as objects that both embodied and declared the artist's new status as an academician and *peintre du roi* (painter to the king).

A copy of Hyacinthe Rigaud's reception letters (fig. 95), now in the archives of the École Nationale Supérieure des Beaux-Arts, reveal an object whose contemporary equivalent might lie somewhere between a membership card and an employment contract. Beginning with a clear indication of institutional identity ("Letters of the Académie Royale"), the document went on to designate the holder ("Hyacinthe Rigaud") and the date of issue ("2 January 1700"), marking the point of validity of this non-transferable title.[2] Crucially, the letters also established the precise nature of Rigaud's membership, designating him not only as an academician but, more specifically, as a history painter. This was key in an institution where medium and genre functioned as a class system, in which only history painters and sculptors were allowed to hold the highest ranks and were thus the only artists with any real administrative power. The remaining text of the letters then proceeded to celebrate the ideological mission of the Académie ("to raise the arts . . . to the highest degree of perfection possible"), to establish the duties of Rigaud as a member ("to see that its lessons, lectures, and other public and private activities are undertaken attentively to the complete satisfaction of His Majesty"), and to note the benefits due to the painter in his new capacity (including all the "privileges, honors, pensions, and rights" attributed to academicians). Finally, before the Académie's wax seal and the signatures of its current director (Charles de La Fosse) and other officers, the letters recorded the genre in which the new member was received and gave specific details about the correlating reception piece accepted by the Académie.[3] In Rigaud's case, this is where things got complicated.

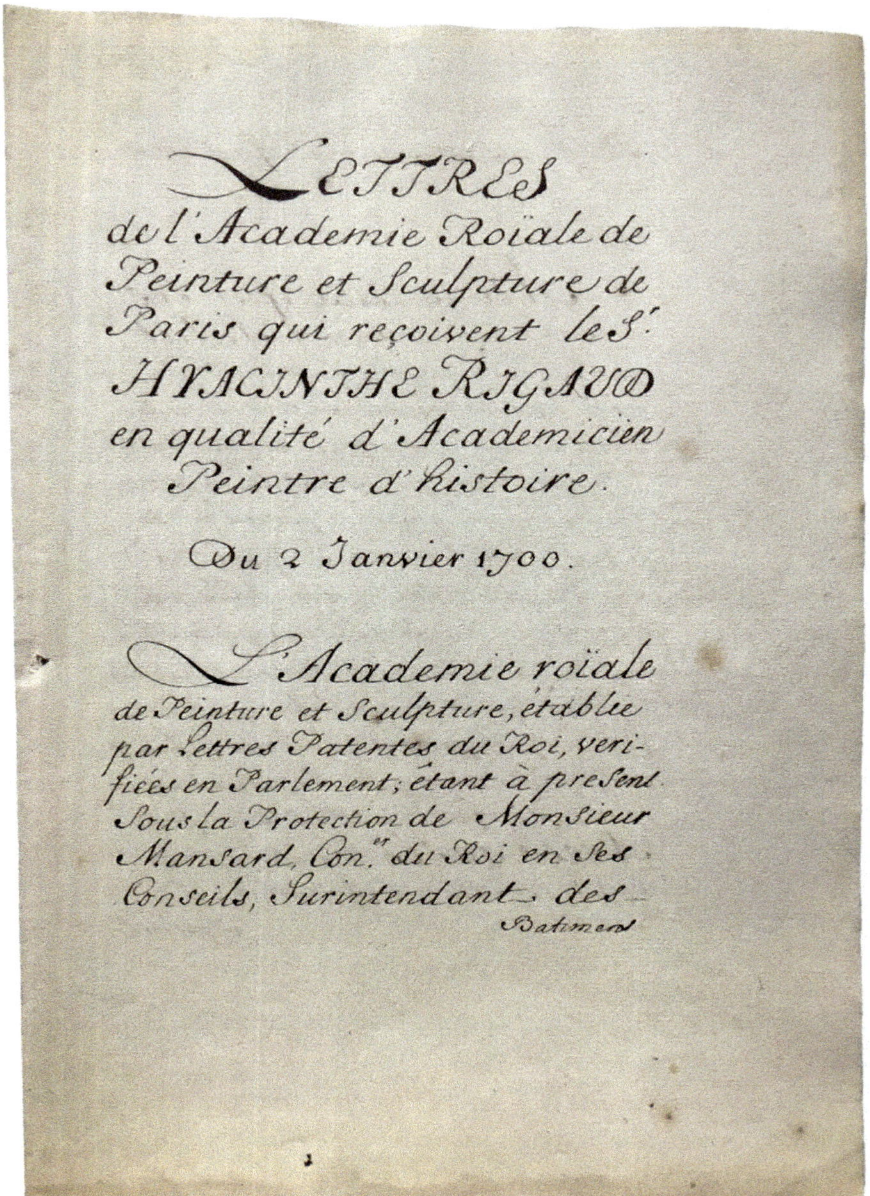

Lettres
de l'Academie Roïale de
Peinture et Sculpture de
Paris qui reçoivent le S.r
HYACINTHE RIGAUD
en qualité d'Academicien
Peintre d'histoire.

Du 2 Janvier 1700.

L'Academie roïale
de Peinture et Sculpture, établie
par Lettres Patentes du Roi, veri-
fiées en Parlement; étant à present
Sous la Protection de Monsieur
Mansard, Con.er du Roi en ses
Conseils, Surintendant des
Batimens

FIG. 95 Front page of the copy of Hyacinthe Rigaud's *lettres de réception* (1700), transcribed by Henri van Hulst (1685–1754). Paris, École Nationale Supérieure des Beaux-Arts, Ms 117. (Courtesy of École Nationale Supérieure des Beaux-Arts, Paris. Photo: Hannah Williams.)

Though Rigaud's letters were categorically those of a history painter (declared in the words "Peintre d'histoire" emblazoned across the first page), the reception piece he had submitted was *only* (as the Académie might have considered it) a portrait, representing the sculptor Martin Desjardins (fig. 96). Rigaud's letters attempted to camouflage this imbalance through some clever wording, registering his talents in both genres and describing this painting as a "*portrait historié*" (historicized portrait), a term conventionally used for allegorical portraits in which the sitter appears in a historical or mythological guise.[4] Yet even *if* a historicized portrait could be envisaged as a history painting, Rigaud's reception piece was no such thing. Desjardins appeared as himself, uncostumed, with the sculptor's chisel and a bronze sculpture as his only attributes, no different, in fact, from any other portraitist's reception piece in the Académie's collection (a later example being Duplessis's portrait of Joseph-Marie Vien (see fig. 36). Thus, in the composition of Rigaud's letters, the Académie seems to have fiddled the paperwork, bureaucratically obscuring a moment when it had collectively acted against its own theoretical principles.

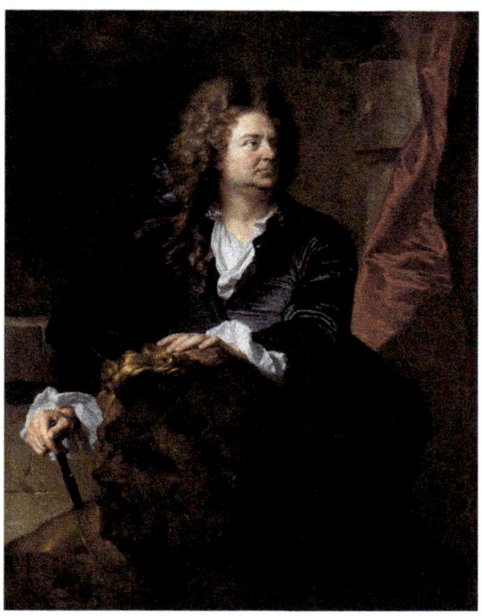

FIG. 96 Hyacinthe Rigaud (French, 1659–1743), *Martin Desjardins*, 1700. Oil on canvas, 141 × 106 cm. Paris, Musée du Louvre, Inv. 7511. (© RMN-Grand Palais / photo: Franck Raux / Art Resource, NY.)

One of the things that precipitated this situation was that, by 1700, Rigaud had proved himself a far more impressive artist than academician. He had actually been *agréé* (provisionally admitted) in 1684 at the age of twenty-five and, as per the custom, given six months to complete his reception pieces (portraits of Desjardins and an honorary member, Henri de La Chapelle-Bessé).[5] But missing the deadline spectacularly, he ended up taking sixteen years and only managed half the task.[6] In the interim, however, Rigaud had made a name for himself in Paris and beyond as an exceptional artist with an elite list of clients (from the Archbishop of Paris to Louis XIV) and had become, for the Académie, both a respected colleague and a figure whose reputation would raise the prestige of the institution.[7] So when, at forty-one, Rigaud eventually sought to complete his admission, there was no question that this was an artist who was worthy (artistically and socially) of joining the institution's highest ranks. But there remained that problem of his genre. Rigaud's particular talent for portraiture was at odds with the Académie's entrenched theoretical privileging of history painting, and so the only way to reward him with the career he deserved was to make him, on paper at least, something he was not.[8]

Rigaud's reception letters make it seem that his status as a history painter was a done deal. But in fact, the minutes of his reception stipulate that Rigaud had only been admitted in that capacity on "the promise" that he would furnish the Académie "as soon as possible"

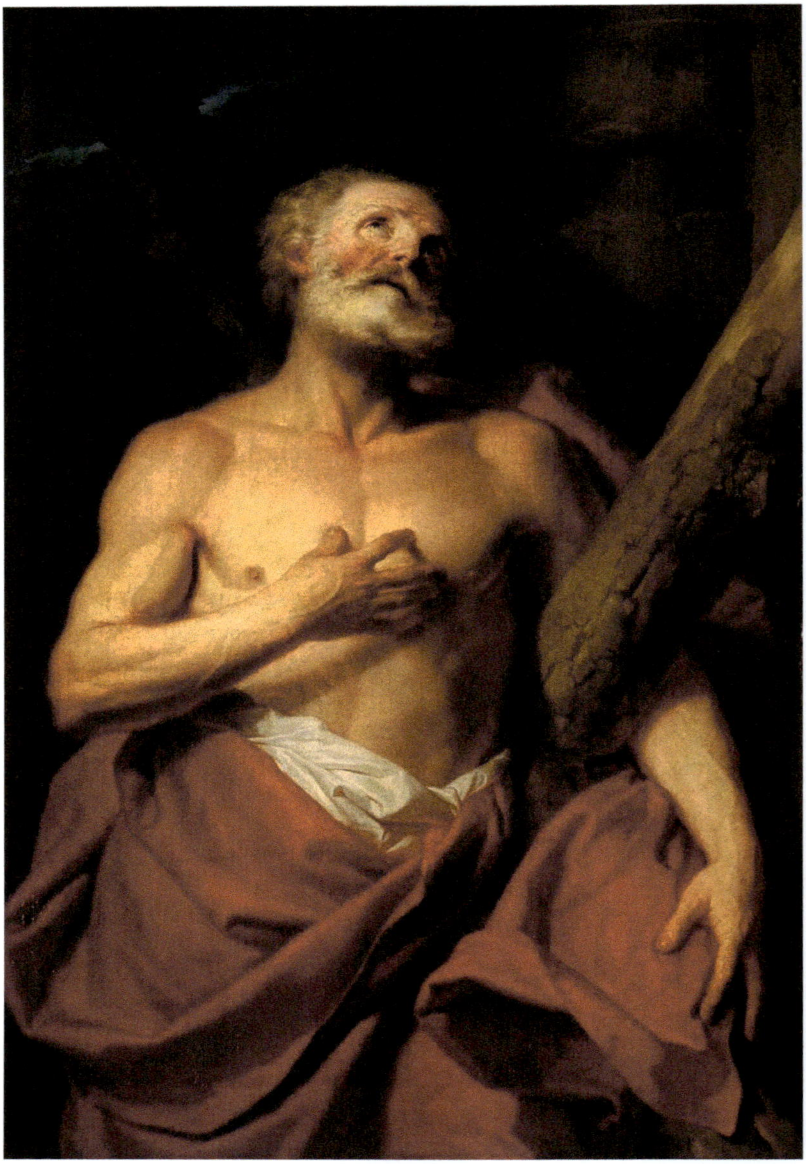

FIG. 97 Hyacinthe Rigaud (French, 1659–1743), *Saint Andrew*, 1742. Oil on canvas, 153 × 106 cm. Paris, École Nationale Supérieure des Beaux-Arts, MRA 103. (© Beaux-Arts de Paris, Dist. RMN-Grand Palais / Art Resource, NY.)

with a history painting.[9] In other words, this was to be a reversal of the conventional exchange—artwork-for-letters became letters-for-artwork—but in this order of things, the Académie had no leverage to exact its tribute. Armed with the status embodied in his letters, Rigaud steadily climbed the ranks of the Académie becoming *recteur* and *directeur* in the 1730s, but year after year he failed to submit his history painting. The Académie did not forget this ritual debt, issuing occasional reminders, and, eventually, the year before he died, Rigaud made good on his promise.[10] Whether an elderly man's effort to settle accounts and safeguard his legacy, or a gesture of acknowledgment for his career as a "history painter" (despite an oeuvre consisting overwhelmingly of portraits), in 1742, Rigaud presented the Académie with a painting of Saint Andrew (fig. 97), explaining its forty-two-year delay (somewhat unconvincingly) by noting how frustrating it had been that "a constant series of affairs had prevented him from keeping his word any sooner."[11] Rigaud's *Saint Andrew* stayed true to the painter's real talents, presenting a historical subject in the form and composition of a portrait—a single three-quarter-length figure with identifying attributes and minimal setting—not so different after all from the "portrait historié" alluded to in his letters. Whatever its accomplishments as a history painting, this object was at least a retrospective fulfillment of that ritual exchange and a belated ratification—at the age of eighty-four—of the status Rigaud had held throughout his career.

Though Rigaud received his letters in that ritual exchange in 1700, the copy that survives in the Académie's archives (see fig. 95) was not the set owned by Rigaud during his lifetime. Instead, this was a version created not long after his death in 1743 to serve a very different purpose. They were copied word for word from the originals by Henri van Hulst, an amateur at the Académie and Rigaud's friend and first biographer, who created an archive of duplicate documents to preserve the details of Rigaud's career: from his letters of ennoblement from the consuls of Perpignan (his hometown) in 1709, to the letters declaring his nomination to the Order of Saint Michel in 1727, to extracts of his **order book** recording all the artworks he produced.[12] In a book of object biographies, this particular version of Rigaud's letters thus shares something of the self-reflexivity of Wille's **journal**: a material thing destined from its inception to record the life of an artist. ‡

---

1. On the rituals of the admission process, see Hannah Williams, *Académie Royale: A History in Portraits* (New York: Routledge, 2015), 82–98. On reception pieces submitted by painters, see *Les peintres du roi*, exh. cat. (Paris: Réunion des Musées Nationaux, 2000).

2. Copy of Hyacinthe Rigaud's *lettres de réception* (1700), ENSBA, Ms. 117, n.p.

3. The text of Rigaud's *lettres de réception* was, as per the custom at the time, transcribed into a register so that the Académie also had a copy of its contractual contents: *Registre de toutes les expeditions emenées de l'Académie Royalle de Peinture et de Sculpture—commencé le dixième octobre 1681*. ENSBA, Ms. 40.

4. *Encyclopédie méthodique: Beaux-Arts* (Paris: Panckoucke, 1788), 1:415–16.

5. Rigaud was *agréé* in August 1684: *PV*, 2:281–83.

6. Rigaud struggled to get La Chapelle-Bessé to sit, so in 1687 the Académie agreed that his reception could proceed with the portrait of Desjardins alone: *PV*, 2:347. Rigaud was still supposed to paint the other portrait, but this presumably became more difficult after La Chapelle-Bessé died in 1694.

7. Between his *agrément* and his *réception*, Rigaud's studio produced more than six hundred portraits. See Ariane James-Sarazin, *Hyacinthe Rigaud, 1659–1743* (Dijon: Faton, 2016), 2:37–231.

8. Most artists of other genres who wanted the status of a history painter were initially given letters in the "lesser" genre and then had to reapply with a history painting for a second reception. For instance, Jean-Jacques Bachelier was admitted as a still-life painter in 1752 but submitted a new reception piece of *Roman Charity* and was reissued the letters of a history painter in 1763: *PV*, 7:231.

9. 2 January 1700: *PV*, 3:285.

10. One such reminder was issued in January 1712, *PV*, 4:139–40.

11. 26 May 1742, *PV*, 5:320.

12. ENSBA, Ms. 117.

Mannequin

Jean-Baptiste Le Prince (1734–81)

TYPE OF OBJECT	THEME	MATERIAL
Prop, Tool	Making, Studio, Travel	Animal | Hair, Plant Matter | Cork, Plant Matter | Wood, Textile | Silk

Four lifeless figures once stood in Jean-Baptiste Le Prince's studio. One was a life-size model of an adult man; the other three (one male, two female) were of a smaller scale but still stood at three feet, or around the height of a small child.[1] These four anthropomorphic objects served the painter as mannequins, mechanical devices to aid the artist in the representation of the human form. Made and deployed in idiosyncratic ways in European artistic practice from at least the Renaissance, the mannequin became, during the eighteenth century, a more standardized machine with distinctly formulated functions.[2] Establishing themselves firmly as familiar denizens of the atelier, these lifelike bodies were a valuable if uncanny presence that both facilitated and threatened art's relationship with the natural and the artificial.

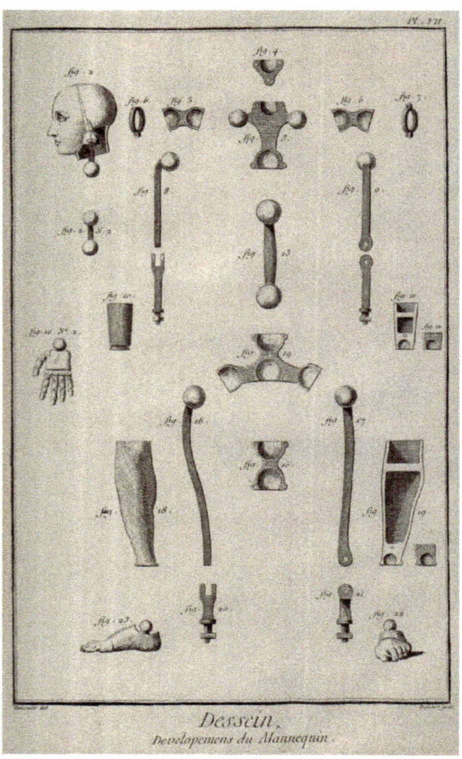

FIG. 98 The constituent parts of a mannequin, "Dessein" from *Recueil de planches sur les sciences, les arts libéraux et les arts mécaniques* (1765), plate VII. (Image courtesy of the ARTFL Encyclopédie Project, University of Chicago.)

Signaling its status as part of the artist's habitual apparatus, the mannequin features several times in the *Encyclopédie*'s suite of plates for "Drawing." Plate VII provides a schematic breakdown of the constituent parts of the mannequin's internal mechanics (fig. 98): a metal structure (referred to as the "carcass") whose individual pieces tended to derive their names from osteological terminology ("shoulder blade," "clavicle," "spine," "humerus," "femur").[3] The mannequin's debt to biology also extended to its mode of assembly, borrowing the skeleton's efficient ball-and-socket joints to enable the multidirectional movement and rotation of its generally copper or iron members. With the exception of a carved wooden head, the flesh of the mannequin would consist of a filler substance (like cork or hair), which was molded over the metal carcass and covered with a skin, usually of chamois leather or silk stockings cut and stitched to size.[4] A notable example of this kind of mannequin survives in the Museum of London in an item once owned by the London-based French sculptor Louis-François Roubiliac (fig. 99). Made of a copper-alloy skeleton, fleshed out with cork and horsehair, and covered in silk stockinette, it was topped with a delicately carved and painted wooden head, which, as Jane Munro suggests, was likely the work of the sculptor himself.[5] Like Le Prince's smaller mannequins, Roubiliac's was a scaled-down model (measuring only 68 centimeters in height), but unlike Le Prince's gendered mannequins (itemized as "men" and "women" in the sale of his estate), Roubiliac's was androgynous and still has its range of doll-like clothing and wigs that allowed the figure to appear male or female as required.

Neither in the case of Le Prince nor Roubiliac is it known where these artists acquired their studio companions, but Paris was certainly the major production center for mannequins during the eighteenth century. By the end of this period, mannequin making had begun to develop as a specialized trade, but at midcentury many of the best-known suppliers were in fact artists (usually members of the guild rather than the Académie) with a commercial sideline in producing mannequins, among them the sculptor Jean-Jacques Perrot, the pastel portraitist Nicolas Anseaume, and the pastellist and flower painter Michel Rabillon.[6] Later in the century, more specialist makers emerged, like Paul Huot, whose mannequins became sought after across Europe.[7] Another was François-Pierre Guillois, a mechanical engineer who made it his mission to improve mobility in mannequin design, creating machines that could mimic the body's specific actions, like the pronation and supination of the hand and forearm: the more human its movements, the more proficiently the mannequin could fulfil its role as stand-in for the human body.[8]

Mannequins were just one of several kinds of inanimate object called to perform this role of stand-in for actual people, sometimes proving better adapted for the task than the original. Drawing from living models in the Académie's *école du modèle* (life drawing classes) was the pinnacle of the eighteenth-century curriculum, training artists to understand and represent the corporeality of the male nude in the production of *académies* (see fig. 34). (Women's bodies could also serve as models, but only in the relative privacy of the studio.)[9] The vitality of those living bodies, however, posed their own challenges (not least, the need to move), which made artificial replacements indispensable

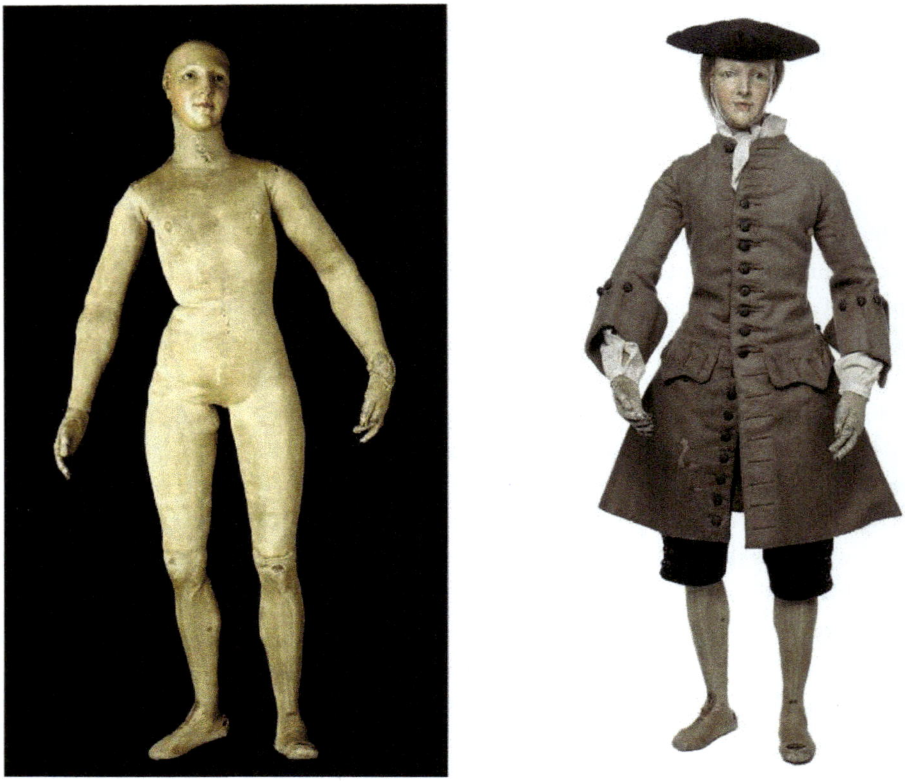

FIG. 99 Mannequin once owned by Louis-François Roubiliac (French, worked in England, 1702–62), undressed (left) and dressed in men's attire (right), ca. 1750–62. Bronze, iron, hair, cork, wool, wood, leather, and silk, height 68 cm. Museum of London. (Photos: © Museum of London.)

tools in certain circumstances. For the beginner, plaster casts of body parts provided students with immobile transitional objects to study before graduating to the trickier mobile versions; while for the expert, **écorchés** provided a privileged pedagogic insight into the underlying anatomy that a living model's skin otherwise denied. Mannequins, meanwhile, were perhaps the furthest of all these objects from the corporeality of the human body, for despite the biological language and structures deployed in their assembly, their job was to stand in not for flesh but for form.

As a studio tool, the mannequin was a compositional device. According to eighteenth-century handbooks, it performed two principal services, both of which are modeled in another of the *Encyclopédie*'s "Drawing" plates showing the object in use (fig. 100).[10] First, it was a vehicle for drapery. Thanks to the mannequin's anthropomorphic shape, fabrics fell over it as they would over a person—folding, gathering, hitching, floating, or hanging—allowing artists to observe the behavior of textiles across the body's various parts and to capture their distinctive formal qualities. The art of "throwing and styling" drapery to look naturalistic was so associated with the object that it later adopted its name—*mannequiner* (to mannequinize)—and was an important technique to master to avoid rigid-looking folds and overly labored effects.[11] Second, the mannequin was a posable structure (unlike the static **écorché**) that could stay in formation for any length of time (unlike a live model). This made it an invaluable instrument for modeling all kinds of postures, but particularly those actions that the human body found challenging (posing with arms raised overhead) or even impossible (flying through the air).[12] To assist with the assemblage of such figural compositions, an artist's studio might be equipped with all manner of paraphernalia, from ropes and pulleys to raise items overhead, to grills and boards upon which to stage a mannequin at the required angles, elevations, and perspectives.[13]

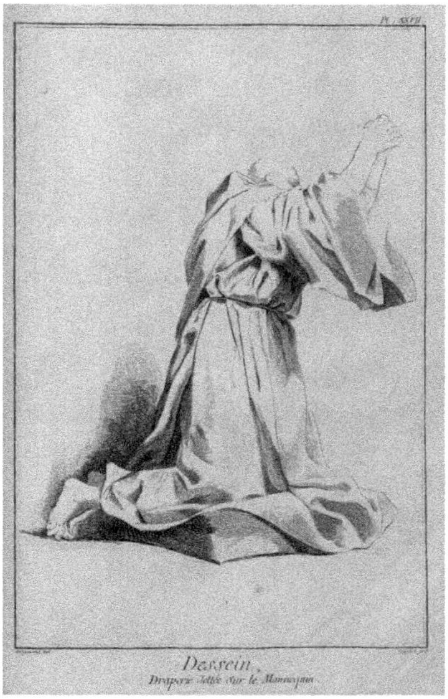

FIG. 100 A mannequin posed and draped, "Dessein" from *Recueil de planches sur les sciences, les arts libéraux et les arts mécanique* (1765), plate XXVII. (Image courtesy of the ARTFL Encyclopédie Project, University of Chicago.)

Le Prince was certainly among the artists who made liberal use of such props and mechanics. In both the inventory of his Louvre apartments and the catalog of his estate sale, his mannequins were part of a plethora of studio equipment.[14] Along with the numerous tools a painter and engraver might use for representing a subject (easels, a **color box**, a ***porte-crayon***, a pair of compasses, and a **camera obscura**), Le Prince also owned a profusion of things for staging those subjects. This studio collection included, for instance, an extensive range of apparel, comprising both a large number of garments made especially for his mannequins, and a substantial assortment of foreign clothing, including sets of Chinese, Russian, Circassian, and "primitive" garments, and even the complete costume of a Mandarin. Some of these were no doubt souvenirs acquired on Le Prince's European travels (he spent several years in Russia and eastern Europe, visiting Saint Petersburg, Moscow, the Kamchatka Peninsula, Livonia, Finland, and Siberia), but others were presumably imported, as he never traveled as far as China.[15] Kept in a large *armoire* (a far larger receptacle than Watteau's **dressing-up box**), Le Prince's studio wardrobe also extended to a collection of armor and weaponry: helmets, a shield, a sabre, a pike, a halberd, a dagger, a **sword**, pipes, a club, a bow, arrows, and a quiver. Finally, Le Prince also possessed several items that could be used to orchestrate all his mannequins, props, and costumed models into scenes. Among these staging instruments he had a "table for the model," a set of stairs, two large wooden columns painted in faux marble, a Chinese table, and a model Russian carriage.

For an artist who made his name painting foreign genre scenes—where "exotically" attired figures engaged in everyday yet curiously othered activities—Le Prince's studio collections were, like David's **table**, things that existed between the real and the fictional:

functional items (clothing and weapons) that operated as theatrical agents (costumes and props). The crucial role that these performative inanimate objects played in Le Prince's practice is evident in a work like *The Russian Cradle* (fig. 101). Having once encountered the material trappings of his studio, it is difficult not to envisage Le Prince's painting as a staged tableau of "things." The slumped physique of the old man on the right recalls the lifeless noncorporeality of a stuffed mannequin; the old woman on the left wears the costume of a Russian peasant but seems incongruously overdressed, as though festival apparel was the only option; the woman pulling the rope to raise the cradle occupies precisely the pose at which a mannequin would excel; and the cloth hanging incongruously between tree and hut starts to look like a length of studio drapery. Almost a still-life genre scene, Le Prince's painting comes close to exposing the artifice that exists behind any figural composition, which, for the period's art theorists, was often decried as the mannequin's greatest risk.

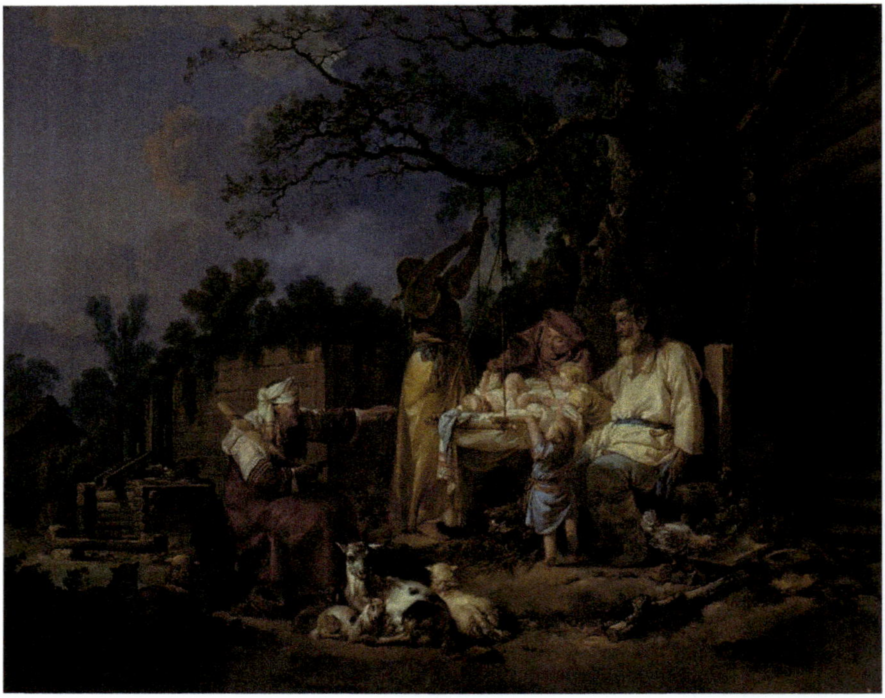

FIG. 101 Jean-Baptiste Le Prince (French, 1734–81), *The Russian Cradle*, 1764–65. Oil on canvas, 59.1 × 72.7 cm. Los Angeles, The J. Paul Getty Museum.

Though the object's use was sanctioned thanks to its deployment by the old masters (Tintoretto, Veronese, Poussin), there were constant warnings about the dangers of dependence or overuse.[16] De Piles cautioned that a mannequin should never be a replacement for nature, only called upon "like a witness" for confirmation.[17] Claude-Henri Watelet, meanwhile, was more wary, seeing mannequins as "traps" for the painter, with their "ridiculous forms" threatening to "slip imperceptibly into the painting" and render it "incorrect, cold, or inanimate."[18] This may indeed have been the root of Denis Diderot's concerns with *The Russian Cradle* and several other paintings that Le Prince exhibited at his first Salon appearance in 1765. For while Diderot appreciated Le Prince's skill with drapery, he criticized the painter for his "cold compositions" enlivened only by "picturesque clothing," and for the troubling "amphibology" of *The Russian Cradle* in particular, with its ambiguously disjunctive elements.[19] Yet given Le Prince's artistic engagement with the human body, it is difficult to say whether this was error or intention. Though he had trained in François Boucher's studio, presumably with aspirations of history painting, when Le Prince was eventually admitted to the Académie it was in the genre of "views and landscapes adorned with figures."[20] Thus for Le Prince, technically a landscapist, the human body was not the anatomical corporeal presence it was for the history painter, but instead figural staffage: a shape to structure the composition and ornament the scene. That was a role the mannequin was born to play. ‡

---

1. *Notice des principaux articles de tableaux, dessins, estampes, terres cuites, plâtres, planches gravées, habillemens étrangers, armes curieuses, manequins, & autres objets, provenans de la succession de feu M. Le Prince, peintre du Roi* (Paris: n.p., 1781), 19.

2. The most comprehensive history of the mannequin's form and use is to be found in Jane Munro, *Silent Partners: Artist and Mannequin from Function to Fetish*, exh. cat. (Cambridge: Fitzwilliam Museum, 2014).

3. Description of Plate VII, "Développements du Mannequin," *Encyclopédie*, https://encyclopedie.uchicago.edu/, 20:21:8.

4. Description of Plate VI, "Le Mannequin," *Encyclopédie*, https://encyclopedie.uchicago.edu/, 20:21:7–8.

5. Munro, *Silent Partners*, 43.

6. On mannequin makers in Paris, see E. J. J. Barillet, *Sur le mannequin* (Paris: Annales du Musée, 1809), 14–18; and Munro, *Silent Partners*, 43–51.

7. Jane Munro, "Perfected Thing: A Lay Figure by Paul Huot," in *The Material Cultures of Enlightenment Arts and Sciences*, ed. Adriana Craciun and Simon Schaffer (London: Palgrave Macmillan, 2016), 165–67.

8. Barillet, *Sur le mannequin*, 16.

9. On drawing from female models, see Candace Clements, "The Academy and the Other: Les Grâces and Le Genre Galant," *ECS* 25, no. 4 (Summer 1992), especially 472–82.

10. Antoine-Joseph Pernéty, *Dictionnaire portatif de peinture, sculpture et gravure* (Paris: Bauche, 1757), 403–4; and Jacques Lacombe, *Dictionnaire portatif des beaux-arts* (Paris: La Veuve Estienne & Fils, 1752), 384–85.

11. Entry for "Mannequin," *Encyclopédie*, https://encyclopedie.uchicago.edu/, 10:17; and Lacombe, *Dictionnaire*, 385. On "mannequinizing," see Munro, *Silent Partners*, 28–29.

12. Live models could pose with arms raised—as Germain Drouais's *académie* demonstrates (see fig. 34)—but usually only where ceiling ropes had been installed for the model to hold.

13. Roger de Piles discusses this use of the mannequin in his remarks in Charles-Alphonse Dufresnoy, *L'art de peinture* (Paris: Nicolas L'Anglois, 1668), 109–11.

14. The following items are mentioned in *Notice des principaux articles* (1781), 19–20; and in Le Prince's estate inventory (10 October 1781), transcribed in Jules Hédou, *Jean Le Prince et son oeuvre* (Paris: Baur, 1879), 250–51.

15. On Le Prince's travels, see Hédou, *Jean Le Prince*, 22–24.

16. De Piles in Dufresnoy, *L'art de peinture*, 109–10; Pernéty, *Dictionnaire*, 403; "Dessein," *Encyclopédie*, https://encyclopedie.uchicago.edu/, 4:890; and Claude-Henri Watelet, *Encyclopédie méthodique: Beaux-Arts*, 2 vols. (Paris: Pancoucke, 1788), 1:203.

17. De Piles in Dufresnoy, *L'art de peinture*, 110.

18. Watelet, *Encyclopédie méthodique*, 1:203.

19. Denis Diderot, "Salon de 1765," *Oeuvres de Denis Diderot: Salons* (Paris: Brière, 1821), 1:293, 302–3.

20. Le Prince was received in 1765; his genre was described during his *agrément* in 1764: *PV*, 7:243.

Marriage Contract

Jean-Baptiste Greuze (1725–1805)

TYPE OF OBJECT	THEME	MATERIAL
Document	Family, Gender, Identity, Money, Religion	Synthetic Materials | Ink, Synthetic Materials | Paper

There were many happily married artists in eighteenth-century France. But Jean-Baptiste Greuze was not among them. According to their marriage contract (fig. 102), Greuze and Anne-Gabrielle Babuty (1732–1811), the daughter of a Paris bookseller, were married on 31 January 1759, when the groom was thirty-three, the bride twenty-six.[1] Greuze had supposedly been struck by her beauty when he walked into her father's shop one day on Rue Saint-Jacques, but he would later claim that he was tricked into the union, and that their relationship started to fall apart a few years later.[2] After many years of escalating domestic discontent, acts of betrayal, cruelty, and rage, the marriage eventually ended thirty-four years after it began. In light of these unfortunate circumstances, it may appear a little sensationalist to select Greuze's marriage contract for this book, given how many other contracts from happier artists' marriages are likewise preserved in the notarial records of the Archives Nationales in Paris. But it is the very demise of Greuze's marriage that makes the contract—as a thing—more intriguing, not least because the ensuing events gave the document a more active role than usual.

In ancien régime France, marriage involved a combination of religious and civil acts: a holy sacrament received from a priest and a legal agreement drawn up by a notary. There is no surviving trace of the wedding that Greuze and Babuty celebrated in the parish church of Saint-Médard on 3 February, but the civil procedures from four days earlier are preserved in this marriage contract. When encountering a document produced during such an important life event, it is tempting to envisage the marriage contract as an embodiment of the relationship—a material thing representing the union of two people. But the reality is far less romantic. On closer perusal, the language and contents of the document make clear its actual purpose, namely the legal arrangements of not a loving union of persons but a fiscal union of properties. In Greuze and Babuty's case, the contract established a *communauté de biens* (joint estate), consolidating all their finances and possessions, and recorded the contractual provisions made by each party, including: a *dot* (dowry) of 10,000 livres paid by Babuty's parents and a *douaire* (dower) from Greuze of a lifetime pension of 1,000 livres.[3] Once the terms had been agreed to, the contract was signed and witnessed, like any other legal or financial arrangement, by all the relevant parties: groom, bride, parents of the bride, witnesses for both sides, and the notary, Alexandre Fortier.

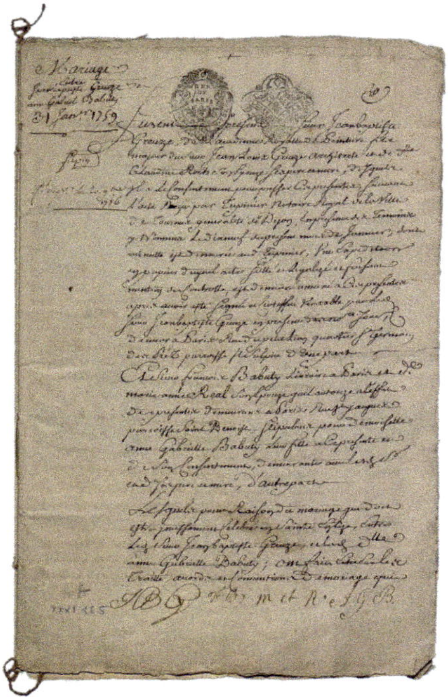

FIG. 102 Front page of the marriage contract of Jean-Baptiste Greuze and Anne-Gabrielle Babuty, 31 January 1759. Paris, Archives Nationales, MC/ET/XXXI/165.

Coincidentally (or not), within two years of this contractual act, Greuze became the artist responsible for the eighteenth century's most celebrated visualization of a marriage contract. *The Village Bride* (fig. 103), exhibited at the Salon of 1761, originally appeared under a longer title describing the action as a precise stage of the civil proceedings: *Un marriage, & l'instant où le père de l'Accordée délivre la dot à son Gendre* (A marriage, & the moment the father of the bride hands the dowry to his son-in-law).[4] The contract itself is also present, on the table at the right, shown at its moment of creation by the notary. Greuze's painting has been the subject of much art-historical interpretation, with compelling readings seeing it alternatively as depicting a patriarchal transaction between two men, with the woman as commodified object, or a reformist model of marriage as a civil consensual exchange.[5] Whether or not this painting was informed by the artist's own experience (connections have certainly been drawn),[6] Greuze and Babuty's contract provides documentary evidence for both of these visions of eighteenth-century marriage. Babuty was indeed traded for the price of 10,000 livres paid by her father, but her signature demonstrates her independent agency in this agreement (fig. 104). Meanwhile, the *douaire* promised by Greuze indicates the mutual financial commitment involved in this two-way exchange, and the legal outcome of this contract, that *communauté de biens*, meant that whatever belonged to Greuze now also belonged to Babuty. Marriage made the bride property, but the contract, at least in this case, also made the wife joint holder of the estate.

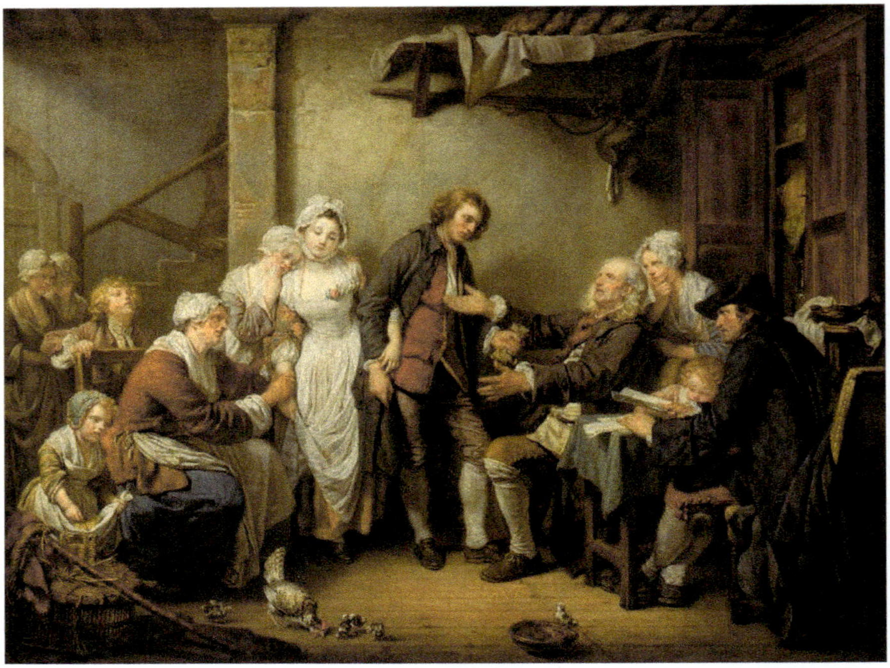

FIG. 103 Jean-Baptiste Greuze (French, 1725–1805), *The Village Bride*, ca. 1761. Oil on canvas, 120 × 117 cm. Paris, Musée du Louvre, INV5037. (© RMN-Grand Palais / photo: Franck Raux / Art Resource, NY.)

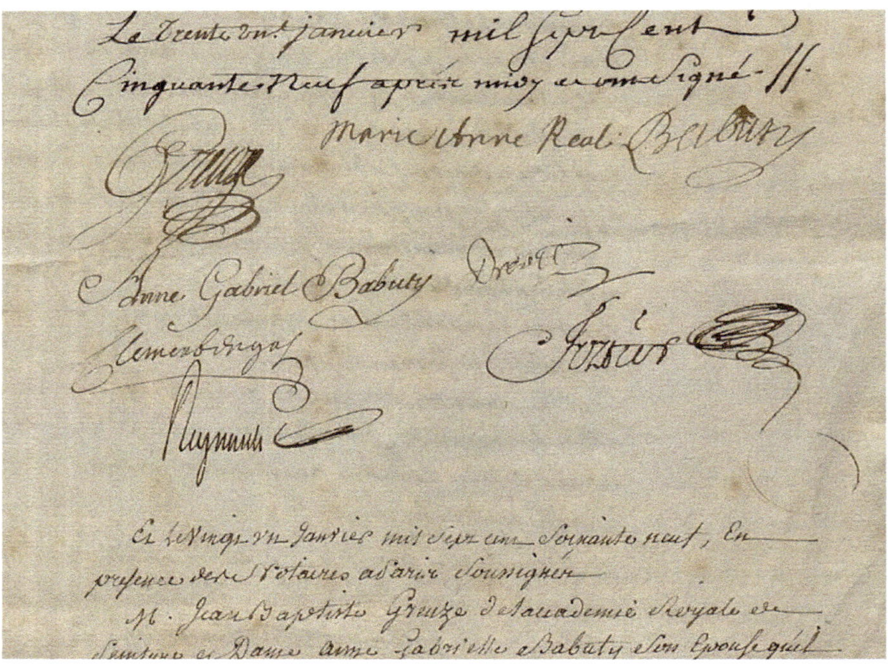

FIG. 104 Detail of signatures in the marriage contract of Jean-Baptiste Greuze and Anne-Gabrielle Babuty, 31 January 1759. Paris, Archives Nationales, MC/ET/XXXI/165. (Photo: Hannah Williams.)

In a twist of conjugal fate, this contractual consolidation of wealth and property, which in 1759 had symbolized their nuptial union, would eventually become a contributing factor in its rupture. Among the many accusations leveled by Greuze against his wife during the process of separation—including numerous extramarital affairs, acts of physical violence, and efforts to destroy his professional reputation—he also charged her with financial fraud.[7] Greuze claimed that Babuty, who (like many artists' wives) had been in charge of the couple's fiscal affairs, had embezzled the proceeds of his lucrative artistic practice (to the enormous tune of 120,000 livres, by Greuze's calculation) and then destroyed the account books to cover up the deception.[8] While not a criminal act per se, thanks to their *communauté de biens*, it became a compelling part of the grounds for separation as their relationship broke down irreparably and they sought to extricate themselves from their contractual marital bind.

Greuze's unhappy marriage is now a well-known saga precisely because of the documents that were produced to enable the dissolution of that original contract. During the religiously observant ancien régime, divorce was not permitted, so in 1786 the contractual obligations of the marriage were instead ended with a *séparation de biens* (separation of assets). To achieve this, Greuze lodged a *plainte* (complaint) at the Châtelet colorfully describing his wife's misconduct.[9] While the couple lived separately from that point, their civil contract disbanded, their marriage continued in the eyes of the Church. After the Revolution, as the new regime sought to separate French law from the tenets of Church law, Greuze and Babuty were quick to take advantage of the nation's first divorce law—introduced in 1792—permitting the dissolution of marriages on numerous grounds (including incompatibility, madness, mistreatment, moral misconduct, and abandonment).[10] Greuze had ensured an evidentiary record of several of these grounds in a *mémoire* detailing more of Babuty's misdemeanors, which eventually brought the ratification of their divorce in 1793.[11] There is, unfortunately, no comparable set of documents to relate Babuty's side of the story.

After these legal proceedings, Greuze and Babuty's marriage contract would make one final appearance, in another notarial document that forms its resonant counterpart: an *inventaire après divorce* (post-divorce inventory) taken in 1793.[12] Following a detailed description of the possessions in Greuze's home (furniture, linen, **books**, jewelry, silverware, artworks, etc.), the notary reached a commode where important papers were kept in a drawer. Right at the top was the marriage contract.[13] Beyond merely itemizing its presence, the notary proceeded to read it, recording salient details about the couple's property and its legal entailment in that erstwhile *communauté de biens* that had been dissolved in the divorce. Both the contract and this inventory were, after all, things that organized the redistribution of things. Thus, in some ways, although separation was never the intended outcome of the marriage, the contract had been created for precisely this kind of moment, when a new distribution of property was necessary.

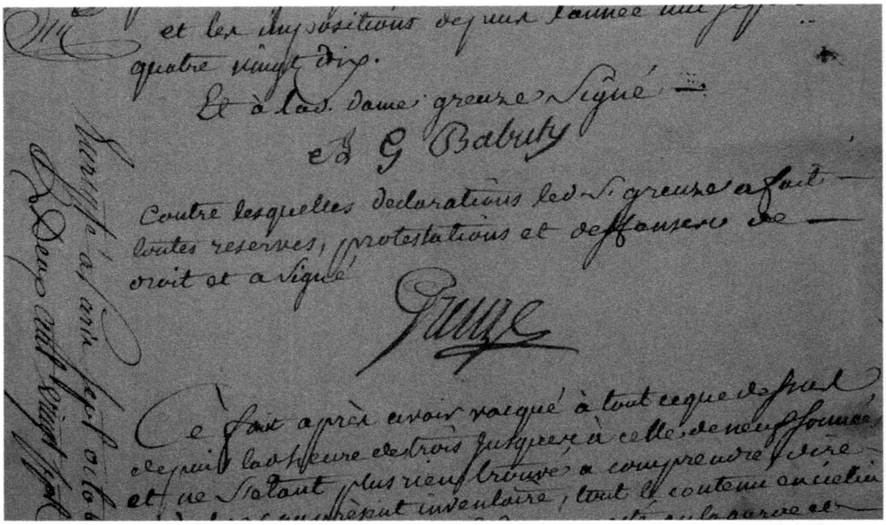

FIG. 105 Detail of signatures in the *inventaire après divorce* (post-divorce inventory) of Jean-Baptiste Greuze and Anne-Gabrielle Babuty, 30 August 1793. Paris, Archives Nationales, MC/ET/XLVIII/375.

As detached as notarial documents may seem as sources, the marriage contract and the post-divorce inventory remain the material vestiges of two civic rituals that marked the beginning and end of a relationship. As such, these things also bear a trace of the human experience. This emerges perhaps most strikingly in the couple's signatures and the poignant contrast between their confident ebullience at the marriage of 1759 (see fig. 104) (Babuty's elegant and calligraphic; Greuze's complete with flourishing underwhirl) and their austere pragmatism at the divorce of 1793 (fig. 105) (Babuty's reduced version written in a tremulous hand; and Greuze's perfunctory in its lack of ornament). Indeed, in the latter, the names are not even signed in the same ink, suggesting either they refused to share a **quill** or, more likely, they signed on separate occasions. In one document, a bride and groom are standing together surrounded by friends and family; in the other, an acrimoniously divorced couple is unwilling to share the same space. ‡

---

1. Marriage contract, Jean-Baptiste Greuze and Anne-Gabrielle Babuty, 31 January 1759. AN, MC/ET/XXXI/165.

2. "Mémoire de Greuze contre sa femme," (ca. 1791), transcribed in *AAF* (1852–53), 154–60.

3. Marriage contract, Jean-Baptiste Greuze and Anne-Gabrielle Babuty.

4. *Explication des peintures, sculptures, et gravures de Messieurs de l'Académie royale* (Paris: Collombat, 1761), 26.

5. On these debates, see especially Bernadette Fort, "Framing the Wife: Jean-Baptiste Greuze's Sexual Contract," in *Framing Women: Changing Frames of Representation from the Enlightenment to Postmodernism*, ed. Sandra Carroll, Birgit Pretzsch, and Peter Wagner (Tübingen: Max Niemeyer, 2003), 93–99; and Emma Barker, *Greuze and the Painting of Sentiment* (Cambridge: Cambridge University Press, 2005), 46–64.

6. For an autobiographical interpretation, see Edgar Munhall, *Diderot et l'art de Boucher à David*, exh. cat. (Paris: Hôtel de la Monnaie, 1984), 225. Without going so far, Fort also points to compelling resonances between life and art, not least the physiognomic similarities between Babuty and the bride, and between Babuty's father and the father of the bride: Fort, "Framing the Wife," 97–98.

7. For Greuze's account of the marriage, see Edmond and Jules de Goncourt, *L'art du XVIII*[e] *siècle* (Paris: Charpentier, 1881–82), 32–49; and, more recently, Fort, "Framing the Wife," especially 92–93.

8. "Mémoire de Greuze contre sa femme," 163.

9. "Plainte de Greuze au sujet de l'inconduite de sa femme" (1785), in *BSHAF* (1877): 164–66.

10. Roderick G. Phillips, "Le divorce en France à la fin du XVIIIe siècle," *Annales: Economies, sociétés, civilisations* 34, no. 2 (1979): 385.

11. "Mémoire de Greuze contre sa femme," 153–64.

12. Jean-Baptiste Greuze et Anne-Gabrielle Babuty, "Inventaire après divorce," 30 August 1793, AN, MC/ET/XLVIII/375.

13. One copy of Greuze and Babuty's marriage contract was kept in their home, the other (the one that survives today) was kept by the notary.

Model

Edme Bouchardon (1698–1762)

TYPE OF OBJECT	THEME	MATERIAL
Instrument, Tool	Education, Making, Studio	Animal | Wax, Mineral | Clay, Synthetic Materials | Plaster

The word *model* (*modèle*) meant a number of different things according to the dictionary compiler Antoine Furetière. In life it meant the "original"—person or thing—selected for emulation; in industry it denoted the "template" used to direct operations; and in the arts it referred to a sketch medium: the sculptor's equivalent to a drawing.[1] This is not to say that sculptors didn't draw. The sculptor Edme Bouchardon was regarded by his contemporaries as sculptor and draftsman in equal measure.[2] Inventoried in his "*cabinet d'études*," or studio, after his death were many and various models (one of them in mid-process on a four-legged **modeling stand**), a drawerful of assorted brass ***porte-crayons*** and compasses, and a range of drawing surfaces (pine tables and boards) used to make some, possibly all, of the four hundred–plus drawings related to his last project, the equestrian statue of Louis XV.[3] However, of the three hundred drawings of the horse and rider, most were studies "after nature," which is to say drawings that declare their orientation to the object depicted (the flesh-and-blood stallion and king), not the monument commissioned.[4] By contrast, sculptors' models were more like Furetière's "originals" and "templates," that is, targeted by emulation at inventions yet to be realized. Models were tools made by the sculptor for doing sculpture. As such, they were the product of a contract of work and belonged to the studio; they were not made for the market, though some of Bouchardon's models found their way into collectors' hands during his lifetime.[5]

Bouchardon made models in a variety of media: wax, clay, and plaster. To model the figures of the Four Seasons Fountain, built on the Rue de Grenelle between 1739 and 1745 (fig. 106)—our "thing" for this book—Bouchardon used all three: wax in a model (now lost) of the central portion of the monument,[6] clay in a terracotta model of the River Marne at the Louvre (fig. 107), and plaster in the model, exhibited at the Salon in 1740 and recently acquired by the Musée Carnavalet (fig. 108).[7] Plasticity was the characteristic these media shared. Choice between them was determined by the structural resilience of each, or each substance's ability to hold form without distortion or breakage, from weakest (wax) to strongest (plaster). By relating model size proportionately to material strength, the *Encyclopédie*'s description of modeling established not only a typology of models, from smallest (wax) to largest (plaster), it also suggested a chain of operations from first to last.[8]

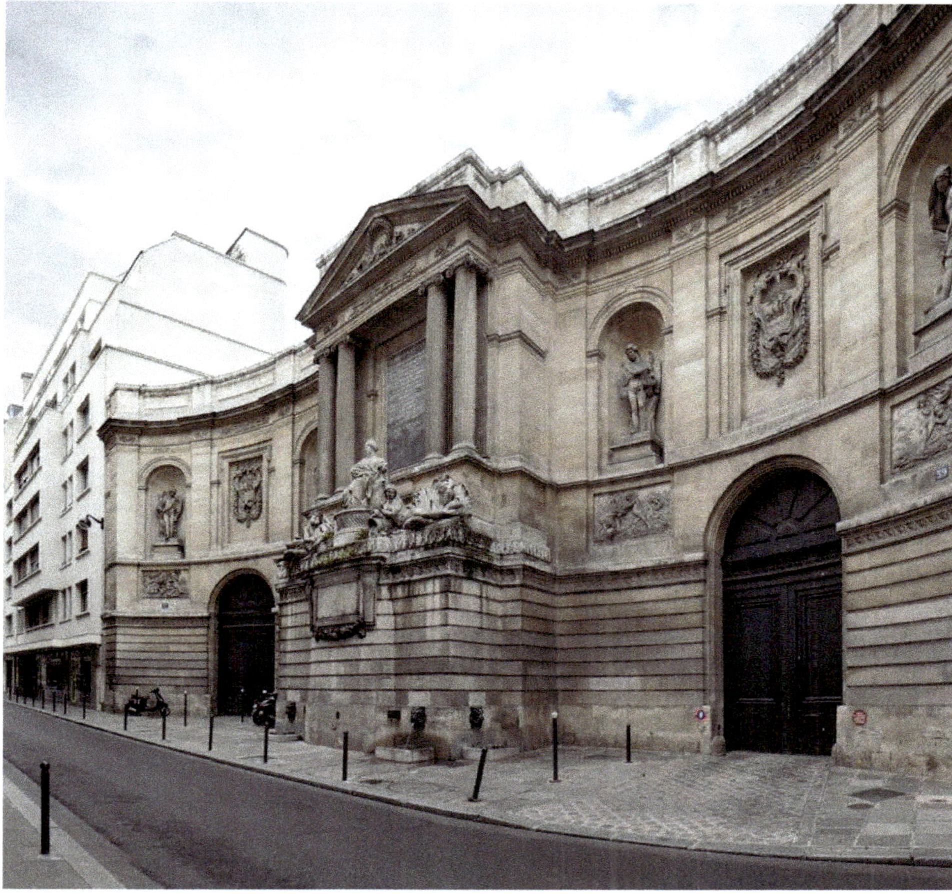

FIG. 106 Edme Bouchardon (French, 1698–1762), Four Seasons Fountain, 1739–45.
Marble. Paris, Rue de Grenelle. (© Kim Young Tae/Bridgeman Images.)

The physical property of pliability was thus crucial not only in the practice of sculpture but also, at a metaphysical level, to eighteenth-century ideas of creativity as the outflow of genius.[9] Implicit in the comte de Caylus's comparison of drawing and modeling as creative acts inserted in his *Life of Bouchardon* (1762) is the notion of unmediated artistic expression, or matter's absolute passivity, its utter subsumption to the thrust of the artist's thinking hand.[10] He envisaged the ***porte-crayon*** and the *ébauchoir* (modeling tool) as instruments for giving immediate form to inner states. Bouchardon shared his view, to judge by the invoice he submitted to the *directeur des bâtiments du roi* in 1743 for a project that never progressed beyond the model stage.[11] In justification of his claim of 210,000 livres in remuneration, a vast sum, Bouchardon enumerated his costs: (1) eight days of thought in preparation to meet the king's order; (2) thirty-five years of study in France and Italy to satisfy the king's standards of taste; (3) three months of working on "different ideas, both in chalk and modeled in wax, ideas made and remade a number of times, and vigorously subjected to artistic critique by the author."[12] Making was conceptualized as a

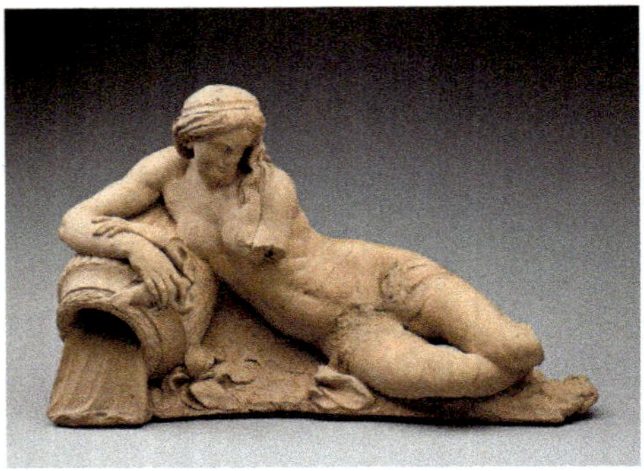

FIG. 107 Edme Bouchardon (French, 1698–1762), Maquette for the figure of the River Marne for the Four Seasons Fountain, ca. 1739. Terracotta, 50 × 48 × 24 cm. Paris, Musée du Louvre, RF2313. (© RMN-Grand Palais / photo: Adrien Didierjean / Art Resource, NY.)

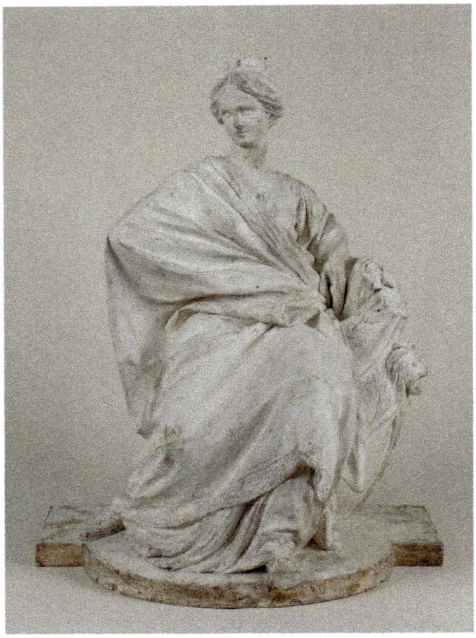

FIG. 108 Edme Bouchardon (French, 1698–1762), Model for the figure of Paris for the Four Seasons Fountain, ca. 1739–43. Plaster, 50 × 42 cm. Paris, Musée Carnavalet.

movement outward from mind to world in the conduct of which the ideal model served as a transparent interface between conception and realization.

Gerold Weber, who inaugurated study of Bouchardon's models, understood his task as one of reconstructing the linear sequence of the modeling operations. He naturalizes the trajectory from interior to exterior, imagination to world, by analogy to gestation. Like Caylus, he explains Bouchardon's models as iterations of an idea, a progress of representation, in which the "first thought," called a maquette, is superseded and surpassed by the second and more finished model, and so on, increasing in size and development until the end work becomes.[13] Although Weber's classification of the models depends on sequence, the models do not represent discrete stages of operation: rather, they are construed as a continuum of things, models all *of* an equestrian monument, or a fountain, or a tomb. However, models, in their difference from representations, are also models *for*, or things capable of intervening in the world.

What are the properties and merits specific to Bouchardon's models, and how is their functionality manifest? To return to materials, Bouchardon used wax and clay not only because they are cheap, tractable, and easy and quick to work but also because of the potential of each to anticipate the appearance of the medium selected for the finished work. The consistency of beeswax could be varied by addition of plasticizers (turpentine, olive oil) to maximize ductility, or hardeners (rosin) to increase resistance.[14] A stiffer consistency enabled the modeling of carved detail and surface polish prized in marble.[15] Comparing the maquette (see fig. 107) and the model of the River Marne (fig. 109), we immediately note that matter is more assertive in the maquette. *La Marne* emerges from the loaf of clay: an outcrop of the riverbank, she is united yet with her vase source.[16] The condensed forms of her shoulder and neck betray clay's softer structure. The sensuality of her body's surface suggests sensitive fingers have been at work. By contrast, in the Lille model, figure, riverbank, and urn are clearly distinguished by undercutting. *La Marne*'s arm, shoulder, and neck lift in expectation of the greater rigidity afforded by marble. A gap opens up between body and urn, the neck disengages from the mass of the upper chest, and the silhouette of the figure becomes more emphatically linear and hardens. Meanwhile, the seemingly open, sensitive surface of the maquette closes; it is sealed in the model.[17] By artificial manipulation and alteration of clay and wax matter, Bouchardon successfully modeled the otherness of the material proposed for the commissioned sculptures: marble.

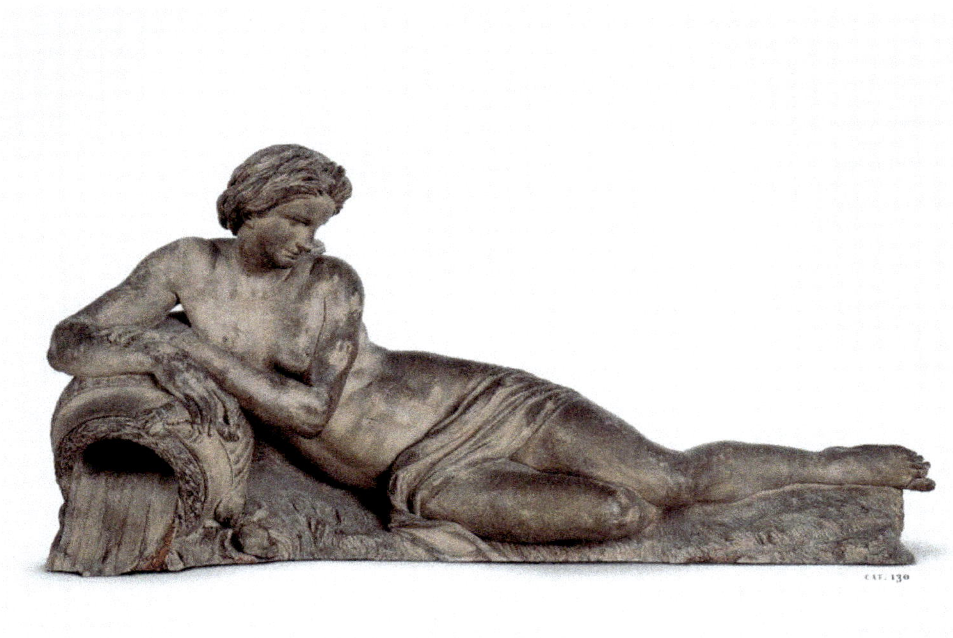

FIG. 109 Edme Bouchardon (French, 1698–1762), Model for the figure of the River Marne for the Four Seasons Fountain, ca. 1739–43. Terracotta, 29 × 61 cm. Private collection.

Plasticity was not the model's only property of convenience. Size was another. Bouchardon's models for the Four Seasons Fountain are between a quarter and a third of the size of the executed marbles. The reduced dimensions scaled Bouchardon's gestures of grasping, experimenting with, and evaluating forms for the monument comfortably to the distance between his two hands.[18] At the same time, the conventions of the colossal—that is, prioritization of volume and weight over surface and detail—were imported into the model such that, smallness notwithstanding, the models of Paris (see fig. 108) and the River Marne (see fig. 109) rehearse holding the viewer at a respectful distance, the response that public monuments demand as appropriate.[19] Charles-Nicolas Cochin called this "the art of working for the site."[20] The models, in short, have not the allure of the small bronzes avidly collected in the early eighteenth century for intimate contact with the precious and the ornamental.[21] They make no virtue of smallness as an aesthetic property; smallness in them is a condition for success on a large scale.[22]

Analysis of the properties of models demonstrates that making models, like making in general, according to the philosopher Vilém Flusser, was dialectical, not linear.[23] Bouchardon's hands modeled not only what he thought his fountain monument ought to be, externalizing his idea, but also the physical conditions and social settings with which the realized monument would have to contend, thus internalizing relevant aspects of the external world. In recounting the genesis of another fountain, the Neptune fountain at Versailles (1737–40), the comte de Caylus described how Bouchardon abridged his initial idea for a complex and rich group of two figures to a single, "simple, real, and fully formed" Triton, because it was more fitting for the setting. Caylus made a point (without explanation) of emphasizing that the Neptune maquette had not been made after nature. According to Weber, the purpose of nature was not to inspire but—and as seen in Bouchardon's life drawings for the Grenelle fountain's river gods and seasons—to provide a testing ground for the *dessein* (in the dual sense of design and intention), to check form against objects in the real world.[24] Models, in this sense, were fictions.

Once the experimental stage of modeling was complete and the design established, the model as a physical thing required stabilization in order to be put to work. Clay models could be rendered immutable by firing. However, firing involved risks. The broken arm, legs, and terrace of the Louvre *Marne* (see fig. 107) was damage sustained either when the maquette dried out and shrank, or when water trapped in the clay (due to poor preparatory kneading) turned to steam and expanded in the kiln, breaking the model apart.[25] In the eighteenth century, sculptors increasingly chose the safer option of casting their models in plaster (see fig. 108). At Bouchardon's studio on the Rue du Roule, the plaster workshop, or *gachoir*, was one of the largest, consisting of two rooms in which gypsum was calcinated, broken up in mortars (forty were inventoried in 1762), mixed with water, and stored as plaster in barrels (ten wood barrels were itemized in the *gachoir*).[26] The molds for the models were made by specialist cast makers, and the models cast were made by studio hands.[27] Stabilization was achieved not just materially, by the greater durability of plaster, but also temporally: an infinity of casts could be made from the molds.

The plaster model was a "transitional" object, transitional not only in the sense that it functioned to mediate between all the models and drawings networked by the production process but also in the sense in which it is defined by knowledge visualization theory as an object for sharing knowledge and collaboration. With the plaster model, our viewpoint shifts from Bouchardon's *cabinet d'études*, his private work space, to the workshop, where the finished model on its stand serves as a fixed reference point for collective work on the sculpture proper. In the vignette on working in marble (fig. 110), one of the plates illustrating sculpture in Diderot and d'Alembert's *Encyclopédie* (1765), a roughly shaped block of marble with an uncanny resemblance to Bouchardon's *Paris* is depicted in the foreground, with the plaster model next to it, slightly set back.[28] Hanging from the ceiling above both block and model is a measuring device, called an *equerre*, consisting of a chassis, its edges notched in units of length, from which plumb lines drop. The geometric principle informing the device is triangulation. What it afforded was measurement not only of the distance between two points but the relationships of those points to one another in space—so, not just the distance between the fall of the drapery from Paris's waist to her hem but the depth of the synch relative to the projection of the fold over her knee.[29] The text keyed to the plate explains that the figure standing before the block of marble is not carving but taking depth soundings to set points on the block. The *equerre* enables sharing exact knowledge about the design in all relevant parameters, and thus the faithful replication of the model in marble in its essential points by the studio hands.

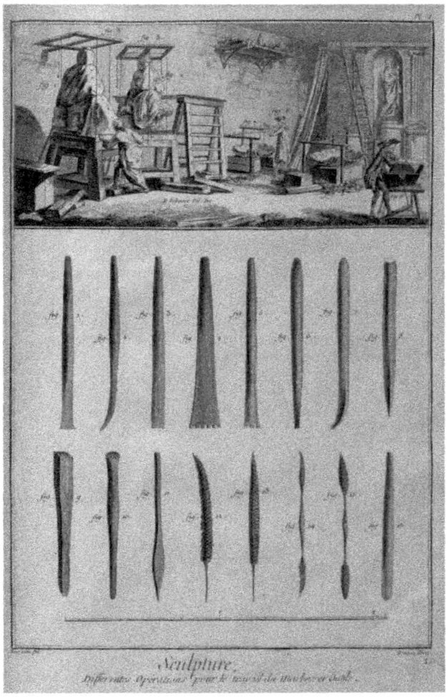

FIG. 110 Sculpture, work in marble, from *Recueil de planches sur les sciences, les arts libéraux et les arts mécaniques* (1765), plate I. (Image courtesy of the ARTFL Encyclopédie Project, University of Chicago.)

Bouchardon was thorough in setting points, and excessively so according to Cochin.[30] Cochin supposed that the points were to guide Bouchardon's own work and was astounded that so "skilled" an artist should feel obliged to copy himself so "slavishly." The draftsman thought he was observing an absurd instrumentalization of the model, or the model as template. Such a template *does* rather than *makes* sculpture, in the sense in which we understand the difference between doing and making as actions respectively commensurate and incommensurate with their ends.[31] Making models, as we have seen, involves techniques of modeling distinct from the model produced, but when the model becomes the instrument of its own duplication, means and ends are identical and sculpture becomes a performance. The points Bouchardon set rigidly orchestrated reproduction of the work. Cochin claimed that Bouchardon had set more points than would the greenest journeyman, but it was almost certainly to obtain compliance from his studio hands that Bouchardon multiplied them beyond conventional practice.[32] Of the motivations for Bourchardon's idiosyncrasy considered by Cochin—"precaution" and "supererogation"—precaution seems the more likely.[33] The focus of Bouchardon's anxiety was deviation from the model.

Cochin's anecdotes on Bouchardon's life were written after the sculptor's death and revised circa 1780.[34] They appear to paint a picture of the early-stage mechanization of the sculptural process and the quasi-alienated sculptural labor that are usually associated with late eighteenth-century studios, such as Jean-Antoine Houdon's, where casts were used routinely to reproduce sculpture as commodities for the market. But such a reading of Bouchardon's models seems inappropriate. He was attached to his models not as means to extract surplus profit by merchandising his artistic estate but, according to Cochin, emotionally. He insisted on keeping his models, even though convention held that the finished model belonged to the patron. He kept and cared for them as both originals and as tools whose value to him endured even when their utility was spent.[35] Other sculptors, such as Claude-Philippe Cayeux, who worked with him on the Rue de Grenelle fountain, treasured his models as embodiments of right principles to emulate.[36] §

---

1. Antoine Furetière, *Dictionnaire universel*, 2 vols. (Paris: Husson, Johnson & Swart, 1727), 2: s.v. "Modèle."

2. See Juliette Trey, "'Ils veulent tous l'imiter, et aucun n'en approche': Bouchardon et les dessinateurs de son temps," in *Edme Bouchardon (1698–1762): Une idée du beau*, exh. cat. (Paris: Musée du Louvre, 2016), 24–33.

3. Edme Bouchardon, "Inventaire après décès," 18 August 1762, AN, MC/ET/LXXVI/384.

4. See Édouard Kopp, *Edme Bouchardon: The Learned Draftsman* (Los Angeles: J. Paul Getty Museum, 2017), 193–234.

5. For Pierre-Jean Mariette, see Édouard Kopp, "Les Collectionneurs de Bouchardon," in *Edme Bouchardon (1698–1762)*, 44–53. For the comte de Caylus, see Anne-Claude-Philippe de Tubières, comte de Caylus, *Vie de d'Edme Bouchardon, sculpteur du roi* (Paris: n.p., 1762).

6. See François Basan, *Catalogue des tableaux, desseins, estampes . . . modèles en cire et en plâtre laissés après le décès de M. Bouchardon* (Paris: de Lormel, 1762), lot 16.

7. This is a representative sample of the models actually produced. For a wider canvas, see Guilhem Scherf, "La Fontaine de Grenelle," in *Edme Bouchardon (1698–1762)*, 228–34.

8. *Encyclopédie*, http://encyclopedie.uchicago.edu/, s.v. "Modeler," 10:600.

9. On fountain as metaphor, see Isabelle Trivisani-Moreau, "L'Ultime métamorphose: Enjeux et difficultés de la représentation et de l'utilisation de l'eau dans les romans de 1660 à 1680," in *Sources et fontaines du Moyen Âge à l'âge baroque* (Paris: Classiques Garnier, 1998), 415–35.

10. Caylus, *Vie*, 16–17.

11. See *Edme Bouchardon (1698–1762)*, cat. 212, model for the Cardinal Fleury monument.

12. AN, AB/XIX/4228, dossier 10, *Mémoire des frais fait par E.B. . . . pour le mausolée de Son Em^{ce} le Cardinal de Fleury*, 24 May 1743. He gave four months' anxiety and worry as his fourth and last reason. He received 4,000 livres for the work and kept the model.

13. Gerold Weber, "Dessins et maquettes d'Edme Bouchardon," *Revue de l'art* 6 (1969): 39–50.

14. *Encyclopédie*, http://encyclopedie.uchicago.edu/, s.v. "Modeler," 10:599. See also Nicolas Penny, *The Materials of Sculpture* (New Haven: Yale University Press, 1993), 215–18.

15. Caylus conflates softness of medium and quietness of sorrow when describing the "impressions douces" of the model of the Fleury monument; see *Vie*, 75. In its stiffer consistency, wax was also used for portraiture.

16. See Nicolas de Largillière's *Portrait of René Frémin* (ca. 1713, Berlin, Gemäldegalerie) for a juxtaposition of unformed matter and full-formed models.

17. On Bouchardon's balance of hardness and softness, see Pierre-Jean Mariette, "Lettre de M. M*** à un ami de province, au sujet de la nouvelle Fontaine de la rue de Grenelle" (1746), reprinted in Caylus, *Vie*, 93.

18. On the gesture of making, see Vilém Flusser, *Gestures* (Minneapolis: University of Minnesota Press, 2014), 32–71.

19. Mariette uses "colossal" to describe and commend the fountain's forms. See Mariette, "Lettre de M. M***," in Caylus, *Vie*, 90.

20. Charles-Nicolas Cochin, *Mémoires inédits de Charles-Nicolas Cochin*, ed. Charles Henry (Paris: Baur, 1880), 86. Cochin thought Bouchardon's models failed to reach perfection in this regard.

21. See, for instance, the small bronzes of the antique Nile and the Tiber by Buirette in the sculptor François Girardon's collection.

22. On smallness, see John Mack, *The Art of Small Things* (London: The Trustees of the British Museum, 2007), esp. 49–60.

23. Flusser, *Gestures*, 32–71.

24. Weber, "Dessins et maquettes."

25. See *Bernini: Sculpture in Clay*, exh. cat. (New York: Metropolitan Museum of Art, 2012), 89–93.

26. Pierre-Jean Mariette, *Description des travaux qui ont précédé, accompagné et suivi la fonte en bronze . . . de la statue équestre de Louis XV* (Paris: P. G. Le Mercier, 1768), plate 1. See also Geneviève Bresc-Bautier, "Fonderie et ateliers du Roule," in *Rue du Faubourg Saint-Honoré* (Paris: DAAVP, 1997), 372–77.

27. See AN, MC/ET/LXXVI/384, 18 August 1762, for models stored in the principal atelier.

28. *Encyclopédie*, http://encyclopedie.uchicago.edu/, 25:22:1.

29. For a description and history of setting points, see *On Sculpture by Leon Battista Alberti*, ed. Jason Arkels (Morrisville, NC: Lulu, 2013), 39–53.

30. Cochin, *Mémoires*, 98.

31. On making and doing, see Giorgio Agamben, "Poiesis and Praxis," in *The Mass without Content* (Stanford: Stanford University Press, 1999), 68–94.

32. The context was the model of the Louis XV monument. See Guilhem Scherf, "Le Monument à Louis XV," in *Edme Bouchardon (1698–1762)*, 371.

33. Cochin, *Mémoires*, 98.

34. Christian Michel, *Charles-Nicolas Cochin et l'art des lumières* (Rome: École française de Rome, 1993), 614.

35. Gilbert Simondon, *The Mode of Existence of Technological Objects* (Minneapolis: University of Minnesota Press, 2016).

36. Pierre Remy, *Catalogue raisonné des tableaux, bronzes, terres cuites, figures et bustes de plâtre . . . qui composent le cabinet de feu M. Cayeux* (Paris: Vente, 1769), lot 87.

Modeling Stand

Jean-Antoine Houdon (1741–1828)

TYPE OF OBJECT	THEME	MATERIAL
Tool	Making, Studio	Mineral | Clay, Plant Matter | Wood

One of the more mundane objects on display at the Musée Carnavalet, the museum of the history of Paris, is an eighteenth-century *selle* (modeling stand) (fig. 111) that once belonged to the sculptor Jean-Antoine Houdon. Mundane as it is in the context of the Carnavalet's collections, and also as an item of the sculptor's equipment, this stand is, however, rare as a tool that survives from an eighteenth-century studio. There are few such others, and certainly none to compare to Jean Bourdelle's at his house-museum near Montparnasse, or to the contents of Constantin Brancusi's atelier reconstructed at place Georges Pompidou. Both Bourdelle and Brancusi bequeathed their tools to the public in the belief that these objects were uniquely placed to promote a better understanding of their work. That conviction was not shared by sculptors in the eighteenth century. Their tools, if not passed on to sons, pupils, or assistants, were sold in job lots in estate sales and have been lost to history. This object, like the **palette** and the **color box** in the case of painting, stands, therefore, as an example of a larger category of artists' things: their tools—whose purpose was to assist, develop, and improve skills of making, and to make artists smarter and cannier.

As an instance of stands more generally, Houdon's *selle* is mundane, too, in the sense that the French anthropologist Pierre Lemmonier gives to the word: "not much to look at," yet crucially important to the sculptor who used it, and a material anchor, potentially, for his conceptual thinking.[1] Stands belong, in this sense, to that category of object whose origin is unknown and that appear timeless, part of culture, unlike novel or specialist sculptural tools such as the lathe and the well-tempered chisel, whose historicity is the more usual subject of art-historical inquiry: to understand both the creation of new forms and the materials whose working they newly made possible.[2] Lemonnier characterizes "mundane objects" as a form of nonverbal communication, sometimes, indeed, the unique and only available expression of the structure and values of a social order. In the eighteenth century, however, language, and specifically technical discourse, was foregrounded as the new and progressive tool that exteriorized the embodied know-hows of the arts and trades and replaced craft secrets with rational knowledge and information. In 1765 the theorist and academician Michel-François Dandré-Bardon lamented that no author had yet taken up the task of describing the mechanics of sculpture.[3] The same year also saw the publication of volume 14 of the *Encyclopédie*, which contained entries on "sculpture of all kinds," but Diderot and d'Alembert's commitment to making known the arts and trades notwithstanding, the tools and processes of modeling and carving were

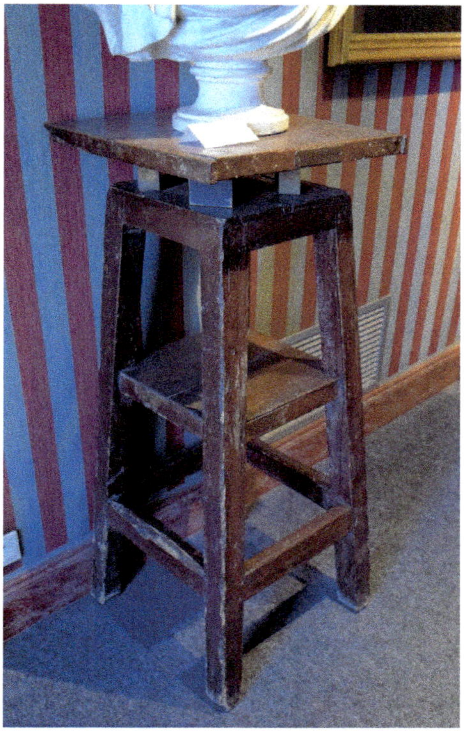

FIG. 111 Jean-Antoine Houdon's *selle* (modeling stand), second half of the eighteenth century. Wood. Paris, Musée Carnavalet. (Photo: Hannah Williams.)

not, in fact, the primary concern of Étienne-Maurice Falconet's definition in the text.[4] It was only with the publication of the *Encyclopédie*'s plates in 1771 that enumeration and description of them was finally made fully known.[5] These plates will help us understand Houdon's modeling stand, but in the spirit of Lemonnier they will be read both with and against the grain of its technical discourse.

Houdon's stand rests firmly on four square legs braced by stretchers at the bottom and gathered at midpoint by a shelf. The top afforded the sculptor a secure work surface. In the plates of the *Encyclopédie*, such stands are subdivided into two kinds (fig. 112): first, the tall tripod stand for modeling (wax, clay, plaster); and secondly, the lower, squatter, four-legged stand for carving (wood, stone, and especially marble).[6] They were rudimentary machines insofar as they contained moving parts set in motion by muscle power.[7] In the case of the modeling stand, a screw system or, alternatively, a hole-and-peg system, transformed the stand into a lever that by relaying force through the parts, raised or lowered the upper platform and the matter on it. A ball-bearing mechanism, in the case of the carver's stand, likewise enabled through a lateral movement of force the sideways displacement of its surface and the block of stone in work.[8] Sculptors' stands thus performed a double function: they held fast the material the sculptor wished to fashion (a function enhanced in the case of the modeler's stand by addition of a brace to support the stuff on the vertical) and they performed its removal: upward, downward, and side to side.

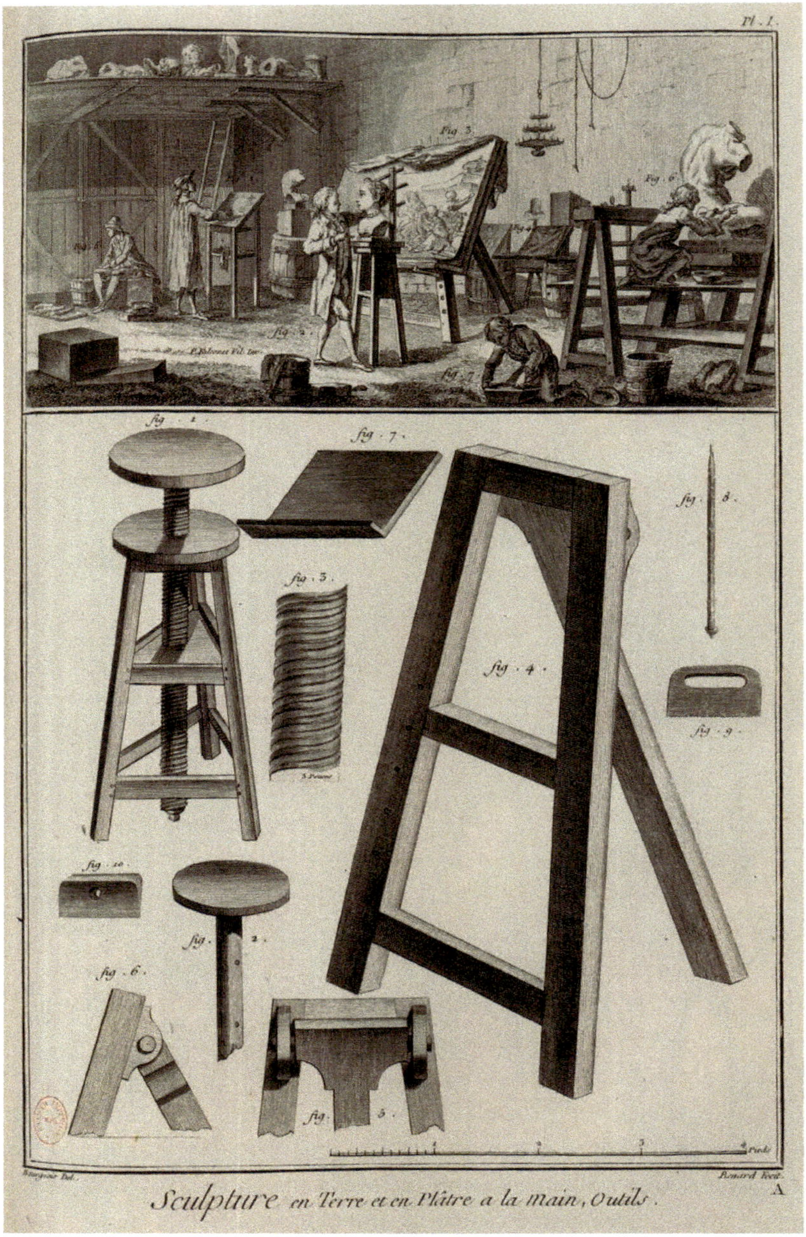

FIG. 112 Sculpture in clay and plaster, from *Recueil de planches sur les sciences, les arts libéraux et les arts mécaniques* (1765), plate I. Paris, Bibliothèque Nationale de France. (HIP / Art Resource, NY.)

In the vignette above the selection of tools (see fig. 112), the stand is depicted in real rather than abstract space. According to Tony Vidler, this spatial transposition, rather than introducing a different pictorial mode, in fact merely extends and completes the technological discourse of the tools and machines, representing the studio workshop as "a kind of machine in its own terms."[9] Another way to put it might be to say that "tools" and "vignette" perform an analogy between machine and (scientific) method: the successive turns of the screw that relay force rigorously through the stand, raising the platform by degrees, correspond to links in the chain of reasoning that transport evidence, strictly and without deviation, along a line from premise to conclusion. Geometry, according to Vidler, articulates this analogy by superimposing temporal sequence onto spatial order. In this instance, the diagonal of the studio wall that runs from the background to the right foreground becomes a line of trajectory that causally links the preparation of the clay by the studio hand over there to the modeling of the prepared loaf by the sculptor in the middle, and, finally, to the tempering of plaster to cast the clay model produced over here. The tools (kneading trough, modeling stand, trowel, and pan) function in the image as discrete landmarks in this technical discourse that enables the gaze of the unenlightened, nonprofessional viewer to run through the spatial structure grasping, understanding, and remembering production as ordered sequence, not skill. The depicted human agents, as William Sewell has noted, are little more than "appendages" to the technology, appearing almost alienated from their tools and environment.[10]

The stand itself (see fig. 111), in contrast to the *Encyclopédie*'s image, is not generic, nor manifestly a standard stand. Rather, it was made by a joiner to a specification scaled to the user, the sculptor Houdon. It afforded him a work surface. Any steady, rigid, flat, and level surface could have served his modeling, but this stand, which Houdon could tune minutely, limited the risk of accident, unforeseen displacements of the clay, or slips of the hand. If the abbé Louis Gougenot recounted with relish Robert Le Lorrain's lack of precautions when sculpting, and his insouciant improvisation of a **wine** cask in lieu of a stand,[11] the scuff marks on the stretchers of the Carnavalet stand made by Houdon's shoes indicate that he was careful to balance and brace his body while working. The shelf below the work surface provided Houdon, in addition, with a convenient storage surface within arm's length for his hand tools: the round- and tooth-ended spatulas, and the leaf and spear tools variously used for cutting, piercing, scoring, and smoothing clay.[12] Its surface also presented a handy resting place for a bowl of water into which Houdon could dip a sponge to moisten his work, and a place across which to drape a damp cloth to cover the model at the end of the modeling session and thereby prevent it from drying out before the next. In short, the stand's virtue was that of a lodestone rather than a landmark—that is, not a signpost of discrete stages of production but a source of attraction that drew things and agents together in a "sphere of activity."[13]

That sphere of activity was not limited to the immediate vicinity of the stand, and attraction is not the only virtue of the loadstone; it also affords direction. The plinthlike shape of Houdon's stand, and its capacity figuratively as well as practically to elevate, invokes the pedestal and points to a destination; the end of the work is present from the beginning. At Carnavalet today, Houdon's *selle* is repurposed just so: to display a plaster cast of his bust of "le beau Barnave."[14] Similarly, the tools on the shelf, immediately in Houdon's line of vision and ready to hand, were prompts to potential action. Latent in them were solutions to modeling problems that the primary, forming gestures of the hand could not solve alone.[15] Such tools were ingrained with the memory of the knacks found by the tool and the hand together in the past; touch of the tool brought that experience alive.[16] When we open up the site of the stand to encompass Houdon's studio, known from Louis-Léopold Boilly's genre portraits of 1804 and 1808 (fig. 113), we can imagine how Houdon may have jigged his whole workspace to direct and support his creative choices in analogous ways.

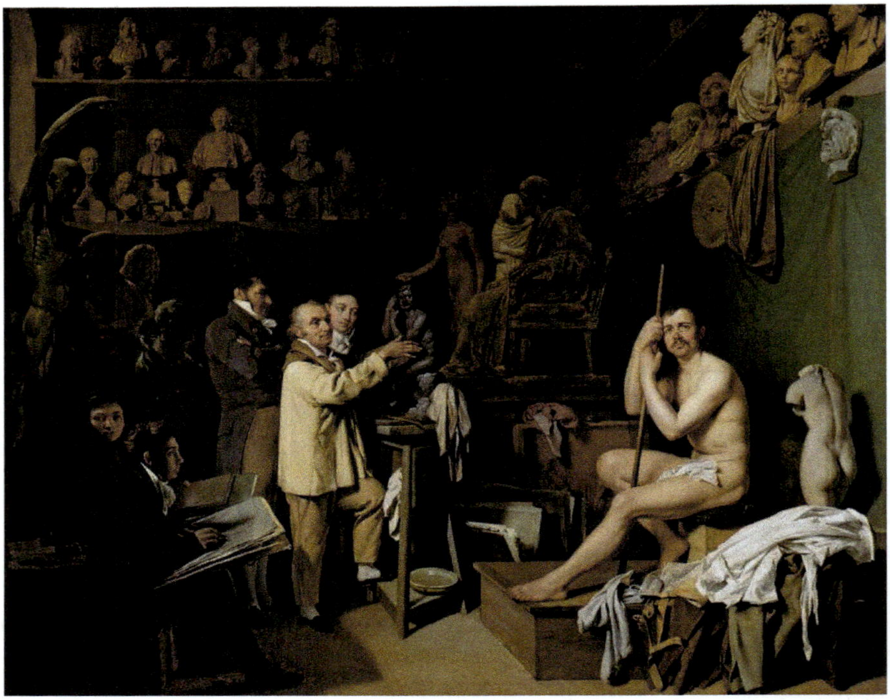

FIG. 113 Louis-Léopold Boilly (French, 1761–1845), *Studio of the Sculptor Jean-Antoine Houdon*, 1808. Oil on canvas, 87 × 105 cm. Cherbourg-en-Cotentin, Musée Thomas Henry.

Art historians have tended to interpret Boilly's paintings in terms of sociability—Houdon's studio as a space open to family, students, amateurs, the public—or in light of the sculptor's energetic commercialization of replicas of his works cast from the "originals" depicted on the shelves in the background.[17] Considered instead as a portrayal of a space of creative work, we can note that Boilly organized around the stand an encompassing field of force that includes not only manual tools but also other objects that his composition encourages us to interpret as resources of invention, and as guides and goads to Houdon's choices, judgments, and adjustments of his work in the flow of execution. Thus, the cast of *Voltaire Seated* (ca. 1780–90, Montpellier, Musée Fabre) appears to triangulate the relation between the life models and the clay models, cueing Houdon's earlier rendition of a "seated figure" as the potential solution to the pose of his present project after life.[18] Likewise, the models of the **écorché** and a female nude with which Boilly brackets the scene suggest themselves as triggers for Houdon's embodied knowledge of anatomical and ideal forms, to be drawn on in the realization of his work. In short, in this version of *Studio of the Sculptor*,

Houdon is represented taking his bearing from his stand, and Boilly's organization of the scene suggests some of Houdon's leading lines of passage to the safe delivery of his task.

The detail and precision of Boilly's depiction notwithstanding, *Studio of the Sculptor* brings us little news of the practical gestures of eighteenth-century modeling as such; it is not in that sense informational.[19] Its narrative is that of the storyteller rather than the encyclopedist. Time is condensed so that tradition, present making, and its future accomplishment appear to overlap. A heterogeneity of seemingly conflicting discourses about modeling—as practice and as idea, from the life and after the ideal, after the flayed model and from the antique fragment—are successfully drawn together. The rules that define the spatial organization of modeling depicted in the painting do not form a clear and continuous linear sequence of measures; they form a pattern that endows the posing, the modeling, and the witnessing with meaning by identifying them as part of the whole. What, then, is the meaning of the stand and of modeling in *Studio of the Sculptor*? And why is a stand, not a spatula, or a chisel, or a rasp, the sculptor's tool that history has chanced to save?

Before the 1770s, modeling was not a sign for the art of sculpture as a whole, at least not on the evidence of the portraits of sculptor academicians painted as *morceaux de réception* for admission to the Académie.[20] This was because it was associated with trial work. *Ébauchoir*, the French word for the spatula used in modeling, appears in the *Encyclopédie* as a term of reference in the legend to plate 1 of "Dessein" (see fig. 93). The viewer is directed to notice in Charles-Nicolas Cochin's vignette of a drawing class, a young student using an *ébauchoir* to model in clay after the antique.[21] The abbé Pernéty tells us that students habitually destroyed these trials at the end of every class, no doubt recycling the material.[22] Clay was cheap and messy, a base material used in elementary and preparatory work.[23] It was neither enduring as a material prior to firing nor sure in its statements. Michel-Ange's Slodtz's indecisiveness was figured by reference to his compulsive model making in Cochin's memoirs.[24] The verb *ébaucher* means to begin. From the midcentury, however, it was identified increasingly with the sculptor's *première pensée*, his first creative thought, analogous, therefore, to the painter's sketch. Some have connected the rise in the status of terracotta as a sculptural medium to rival marble and bronze to the taste of amateurs and connoisseurs for artists' sketches in which they discovered material evidence of the immediacy and verve of genius.[25]

Houdon, however, did not use clay for rough work, or, to be more exact, he buried his beginning in the finished work, rather than leaving it standing. Moreover, his exacting commitment to the perfect imitation of his sitters—in the busts that made his reputation and dominated his output—precluded the expression of his self on the surface of his forms through traces of his touch. However, his commissions did always begin with clay. Sometimes they also ended in terracotta. At others, the clay model led to a marble, or more rarely to a bronze, and almost invariably generated multiple plaster casts. In all cases he reserved the right to the "original."[26] The modeling stand thus anchored that point of origin of his *oeuvre*, in the formal sense of all the work he acknowledged, and in which he formally recognized himself as author. It speaks, therefore, to the social and ideological investments that artists had in this modern notion of authorship. Purchased after his death in 1828, a brass plaque was screwed to it that reads "SELLE DE HOUDON": the stand had become an icon. §

---

1. Pierre Lemonnier, *Mundane Objects: Materiality and Non-Verbal Communication* (London: Routledge, 2012), 13.

2. See Joseph Connors, "Ars Tornandi: Baroque Architecture and the Lathe," *Journal of the Warburg and Courtauld Institutes* 53 (1990): 217–36; and *Porphyre: La pierre pourpre des Ptolémées aux Bonapartes*, exh. cat. (Paris: Musée du Louvre, 2003).

3. Michel-François Dandré-Bardon, *Essai sur la sculpture* (Paris: Desaint, 1765), 60. Consequently, he recommended observation of the moderns as the best means to understand the techniques of the ancients (p. 61). See also Louis Guy Henri de Valori, "Vie de M. Frémin," in *Mémoires inédits*, 2:202, who regarded this "veil of ignorance" as a point in sculpture's favor.

4. "Sculpture," *Encyclopédie*, http://encyclopedie.uchicago.edu/, 14:834–37; and Juan A. Calatrava, "Idées sur la sculpture dans l'*Encyclopédie*," *Dix-huitième siècle* 24 (1992): 397–410.

5. "Sculpture," *Encyclopédie, Recueil des planches*, http://encyclopedie.uchicago.edu/, 25:22/1–2, 12 plates.

6. *Encyclopédie, Recueil*, http://encyclopedie.uchicago.edu/, 25:22/1. André Félibien, *Principes de l'architecture, de la sculpture et de la peinture et des arts qui en dépendent* (1676) represents both stands on the same page, making comparison easier.

7. In Antoine-Joseph Pernéty, *Dictionnaire portatif de peinture, sculpture et gravure* (Paris: Bauche, 1757), s.v. "Selle," the stand is defined precisely as a "machine de bois."

8. *Encyclopédie, Recueil*, http://encyclopedie.uchicago.edu/, 25:22/2.

9. Antony Vidler, "Spaces of Production: Factories and workshops in the *Encyclopédie*," *The Writing of the Walls* (Princeton: Princeton Architectural Press, 1987), 23–24.

10. William H. Sewell Jr., "Visions of Labour: Illustrations of the Mechanical Arts before, in, and after Diderot's *Encyclopédie*," in *Work in France: Representation, Meaning, Organization and Practice*, ed. Steven Kaplan and Cynthia Koepp (Ithaca, NY: Cornell University Press, 1986), 258.

11. Louis Gougenot, "Robert Le Lorrain," in *Mémoires inédits*, 2:219.

12. See the definitions of "Ébauchoir," "Lance," and "Lancette" in Pernéty, *Dictionnaire portatif*, and also his description of the actions "Bretter," "Bretteller," and "Ébaucher."

13. *Encyclopédie*, http://encyclopedie.uchicago.edu/, s.v. "Aimant," 1:214

14. Antoine Barnave (1761–93), elected to the Estates general by the third estate of the Dauphiné, and renowned orator at the Assemblée Nationale.

15. *Encyclopédie*, http://encyclopedie.uchicago.edu/, s.v. "Modeler," 10:600; and Gougenot, "Le Lorrain," 219.

16. See David Esterly, *The Lost Carving* (New York: Penguin, 2012), 196. Esterly recounts his experience of restoring and reconstituting carvings at Hampton Court Palace badly damaged by fire in 1988.

17. Heather Belnap Jensen, "Picturing Paternity: The artist and father-daughter portraiture in post-revolutionary France," in *Interior Portraiture and Masculine Identity in France, 1789–1914*, ed. Balducci et al. (London: Routledge, 2009), 36–37; and Ronit Milano, *The Portrait Bust and French Cultural Politics in the Eighteenth Century* (Leiden: Brill, 2015), 56–57.

18. The cast has been identified with the one now at Musée Fabre, Montpellier.

19. See Walter Benjamin's "The Storyteller: Reflections on the Works of Nikolai Leskov," in Dorothy Hale, ed., *The Novel: An Anthology of Criticism and Theory 1900–2000* (Redwood City: Stanford University Press, 2006), 262–378, on the difference between information and narrative.

20. The portraits of Jean-Baptiste Lemoyne (1734) and Christophe-Gabriel Allegrain (1774) by Louis Tocqué and Joseph-Siffred Duplessis, respectively, represent the sculptors with chisel in hand, marble at the ready, and with monumental marble figures on massive low stands in the background.

21. "Dessein," *Encyclopédie, Recueil*, http://encyclopedie.uchicago.edu/, 20:21/4

22. Pernéty, *Dicionnaire portatif*, s.v. "Éreinter" ("to scrap"). In the context of sculpture competitions in ancient Rome, Dandré-Bardon noted that the losing models were always destroyed; they were thrown into the Tiber. See Dandré-Bardon, *Essai sur la sculpture*, 62.

23. Louis-Jean-Marie Daubenton defines clay (*argille*) as the most plentiful and useful material known to man ("Argile," *Encyclopédie*, http://encyclopedie.uchicago.edu/), 1:645; sculptor's clay was sourced in Normandy, according to Pernéty (*Dictionaire portatif*, s.v. "Glaise"). Étienne Aubry's *Portrait of Louis-Claude Vassé* (1771, Musée et Château de Versailles) is a remarkable pictorial attempt to obscure the dirt of working with clay by hand.

24. See Charles Henry, ed., *Mémoires inédits de Charles-Nicolas Cochin sur le comte de Caylus, Bouchardon, les Slodtz* (Paris: Baur, 1880), 113–14.

25. Notable collectors included La Live de Jully and Crozat de Tugny. See Maria Giulia Barberini, "Base or Noble Material? Clay Sculpture in Seventeenth and Eighteenth-Century Italy," in *Earth and Fire: Italian Terracotta Sculpture from Donatello to Canova*, exh. cat., Museum of Fine Arts, Houston (New Haven: Yale University Press, 2001), 43–59.

26. Guilhem Scherf, "Houdon 'Above All Modern Artists,'" in *Jean-Antoine Houdon: Sculptor of the Enlightenment*, exh. cat. (Washington: National Gallery of Art, 2003), 16–27, esp. 22–23.

Nightingale

Marie-Anne Collot (1748–1821)

TYPE OF OBJECT	THEME	MATERIAL
Gift	Animal, Gender, Identity, Money	Animal

On 15 May 1769 a nightingale arrived at the residence of the French sculptor Marie-Anne Collot in Saint Petersburg, together with the following note from the empress Catherine II to Étienne-Maurice Falconet, Collot's master, whom she had accompanied to Russia: "Beg Mlle Collot to be kind to this little wild thing (*petit sauvage*)."[1] Collot was in a state of heightened anticipation and anxiety apparently, the bird having been announced for some time.[2] Five days earlier the gift had suddenly seemed in doubt. Catherine had written to say that not one bird in song could be found in the city, though the feast day of Saints Peter and Paul, ordinarily the time when nightingales fall silent, had yet to pass.[3] Collot's wholehearted joy at the nightingale's eventual arrival did not, however, suspend Catherine's caution to hang cage and bird outside her palace lodgings, because "no one can long endure his song indoors."[4] What are we to make of this thing, a thing that proved both so difficult to give, because of the unpredictability of the creature's performance, and a challenge to receive, because it was wild and excessive in song? Our knowledge of Collot's life and career is largely indirect, refracted through Falconet's correspondence with the empress and with the *philosophe* Denis Diderot (see **quill**). Does the nightingale, her very own thing, speak to us more directly about her?

Catherine's gift was, most likely, a thrush nightingale (*Luscinia luscinia*), not the common nightingale (*Luscinia megarhynchos*) familiar to France, which does not venture so far north.[5] Small, brown, and plain, the thrush nightingale differs in appearance from its common or garden relative only in added drabness. Nightingales of neither sort were kept for their looks.[6] In this, they bucked the trend for strange and highly colorful imported species such as canaries, parrots, and mynahs that had taken hold of bird keeping in Europe from the late seventeenth century.[7] Neither expensive nor rare—that is, not an expression of the depth and scope of Catherine's power—nor yet a thing connected, like a portrait, to her person, Collot's nightingale was quite unlike the conventional gifts the empress made to courtiers, ambassadors,[8] and other visitors to her court.[9] It was, in this regard, an especially recipient-focused present. To understand it, we need to know what singled Collot out for a gift, and what made a bird seemingly appropriate for this "prodigy,"[10] a woman apparently unique in her talent in the eighteenth century.[11]

In 1766 Catherine II had formally invited Falconet to Saint Petersburg to create a colossal equestrian monument to Peter the Great in bronze.[12] Falconet accepted on condition that Collot was included in the contract as a sculptor in her own right, independent of him, though eighteen and as yet virtually untested.[13] However, by 1769, the time of the nightingale, Collot had successfully completed two different marble busts of Catherine, one in Russian dress, wearing a *kokochnik* and veil, the other crowned with laurel, together with a bust of count Orlov, Catherine's favorite.[14] Moreover, in progress in Collot's studio were a further marble bust of Catherine, intended by the empress as a gift to Voltaire, and one of Falconet, also commissioned by Catherine. Meanwhile, on 10 January 1767, Collot had been elected a foreign associate member of the Russian Académie of Fine Arts. Thus, in little more than two years Collot's status had risen from that of unknown student of Falconet to that of a premier court artist and academician, if not exactly Falconet's equal then at least first among all the other sculptors at the Russian court and certainly worthy of imperial note.

For each of her works Collot was paid in addition to the royal pension she received from Catherine. Having arrived at Saint Petersburg without a penny, her fortune on her marriage in 1777, was estimated at an impressive 110,000 livres, over twice that of the groom's.[15] Evidently, the nightingale was not an alternative form of recompense, like Coypel's **watch**. But nor does it resemble Falconet's silver **snuffbox** with repoussé relief of Peter the Great's victory at the battle of Poltava, or his miniature of Aleksander Menshikov, hero of Poltava, both gifts from Catherine that directly related to the monument for Saint Petersburg on which he was working.[16] Was gender perhaps a factor?

Although the literature on bird keeping that emerged in tandem with the proliferation of avian pets in middle-class urban households in the first half of the eighteenth century was often addressed to *curieux*, or amateur men of science, the "soft and innocent pleasures" of rearing, domesticating, and training birds described in these manuals drew conspicuously on a feminine discourse about household management and child care.[17] As Julia Breittruck has noted, careful consideration was given to the layout of the bird's cage as a living space (and not a trap), with a ground floor long enough for hopping and an upper level sufficiently high for flight to a perch.[18] In Jean-Siméon Chardin's genre painting *La serinette* (fig. 114), the equivalence of the bars of the birdcage and those of the window render cage and interior, bird and woman, uncomfortably alike. Chardin's bird is a *serin*, or canary, the eighteenth-century pet of choice: pretty, easy to raise, and, above all, rewarding to train.[19] Among the effects listed in the inventory of the painter's friend and neighbor, the portraitist Jacques-André Joseph Aved, is a *serinette*, a mechanical barrel organ that, at the crank of a handle (the action Chardin depicts) plays single-octave tunes for the canary to imitate.[20] Aved's *serinette* completed the furnishings of a small cabinet upholstered in red calamanco and appointed with seat furniture and porcelain tea sets. It very likely served as his wife's private room.[21]

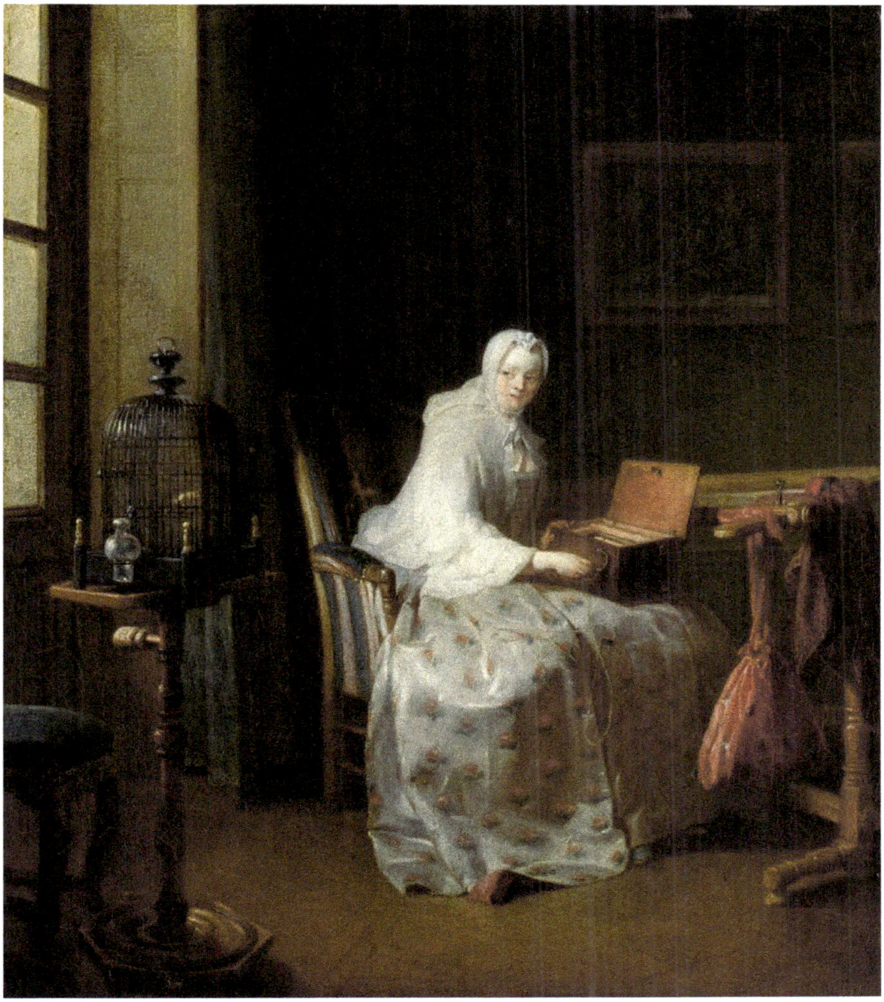

FIG. 114 Jean-Siméon Chardin (French, 1699–1779), *La serinette*, 1750–51. Oil on canvas, 50 × 43 cm. Paris, Musée du Louvre. Inv. RF1985-10. (© RMN-Grand Palais / Photo: René-Gabriel Ojéda / Art Resource, NY.)

The comparison is not, however, enlightening, first because Collot was not the mature, poised, and confidant Mme Aved, née Anne-Charlotte Gauthier de Loiserolles, daughter of a military officer, whom we know from Aved's portrait of his wife, engraved by Jean-Joseph Balechou.[22] She was young and unmarried, without, that is, a household of her own. Moreover, her relationship with her master, the fifty-year-old Falconet, whom she followed unchaperoned to Russia, was the subject of unwanted and malicious gossip.[23] It is unlikely that the gift of a "pet" was intended by Catherine to remind Collot of what she had not and all that she was not.

Secondly, nightingales are not canaries. Indeed, the naturalist Georges-Louis Leclerc, comte de Buffon, made a point of contrasting them. In his audit of their respective characteristics, Buffon determined that for every trait that denoted the canary as tame and social, thus eradicating the ordinary distinctions between human and animal, the nightingale exhibited qualities that marked it as essentially animal and utterly other.[24] Not only are nightingales difficult to keep because, as insectivores, they require live prey, they are also difficult to domesticate and train.[25] Where the canary is an "open learner" (it listens, it remembers, it imitates), the nightingale is "closed."[26] It despises all song but its own, says Buffon.[27]

Finally, where canaries have a heart and form human attachments, nightingales are proud and solitary.[28] So secretive are they, claimed Arnoult de Nobleville, that illustration of the bird in his treatise was justified, because its appearance, though lackluster, was virtually unknown.[29] The bird is portrayed in the wild (fig. 115), the bloomy spray of its foliated perch serving as a synecdoche for nature, specifically silvan nature, the bird's preferred habitat. Of human civilization there is no trace. We can infer from Catherine's recommendation that Collot hang the nightingale outside her window, rather than inside her casement, and that the empress was aware of the limits to this songbird's taming. The gift was an addition to Collot's *logement*, not her household.

Collot was not, however, without feeling for her songbird—"joy" at his arrival, "pity" for his injured wing—but hers (unlike Duplessis's for his **dog**) were emotions that emanated, according to Enlightenment thinking, from the soul and thus set her and humanity apart from the animal kingdom.[30] If not a love object, what was the nightingale's purpose and meaning? For an answer we should perhaps consider the recipient's professional rather than her personal and domestic life. Catherine's gift punctuated a stream of commissions issued with avowed impatience and at escalating pace. In her exchanges with Falconet on the subject of Collot's work, nightingale and marble almost serve as counterpoints. Catherine cannot wait to see "a good and large body of marble between Collot's hands," begs her in July 1768 to take a "block" from the royal reserve, "marble" Collot quits carving in May the following year only "to jump for joy" at the prospect of the nightingale's arrival.[31] Catherine thus openly acknowledges the manual labor of carving, refuses to disguise sculpture's rude materiality, and, contrary to convention, does not, on these grounds, deny the chisel to this woman, Collot.[32] Instead she sends her a bird: not a canary to occupy her leisure, but a nightingale to afford her rest.

Birdsong was closely associated with repose. A commonplace, or "topic," in French chamber music and opera, birdsong invoked pastoral's idyll: at Delos in, for example, one of Elizabeth Jacquet de La Guerre's "French" cantatas (ca. 1710), or at Diana's grove, in Jean-Philippe Rameau's opera *Hippolyte et Aricie* (1733).[33] In Collot's case, the nightingale's song may have opened her casement magically onto more recent, but no less ideal, times and spaces, onto recollections of the garden, Rue d'Anjou, where she and Falconet had shared a studio, and of times spent there among friends, memories stoked by Diderot's reminiscences of their "cottage" in his letters to them.[34] However, to interpret the nightingale as an instrument only of Catherine's hospitality doesn't seem fully yet to account for the choice and time of it as a gift for Collot.

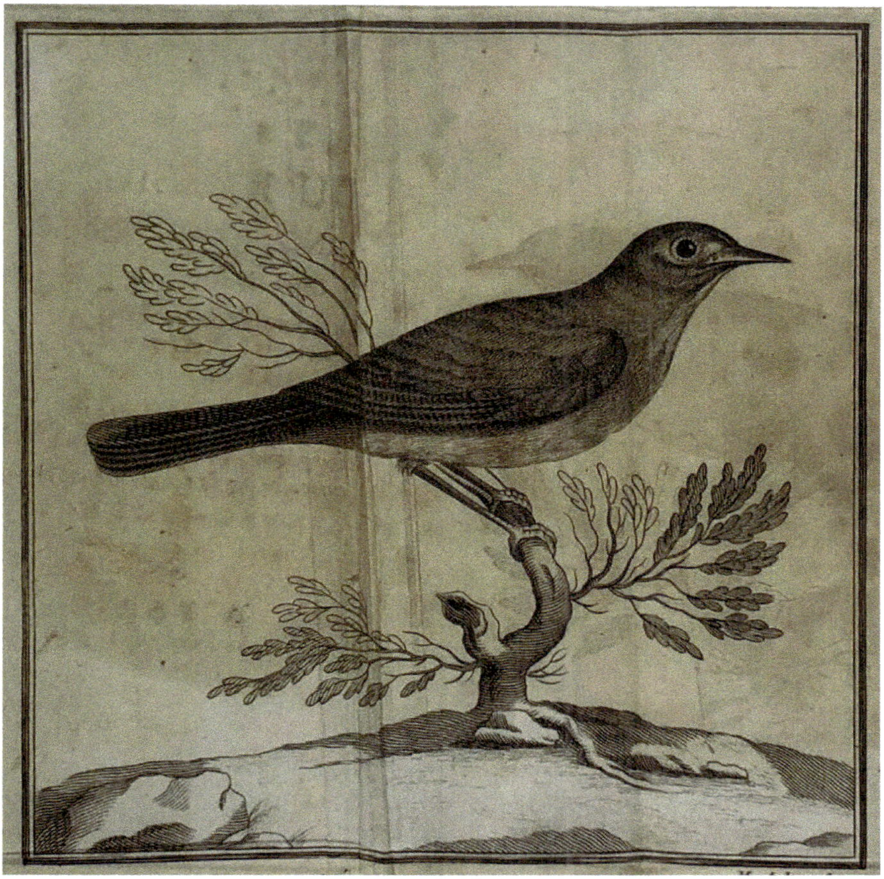

FIG. 115 Michel-Guillaume Aubert (French, ca. 1704–57), *Nightingale*, from Arnoult de Nobleville, *Aëdologie, ou Traité du rossignol franc ou chanteur* (Paris: Debure, 1751). Etching. Paris, Bibliothèque Nationale de France. (Image courtesy of Librairie Jean-Baptiste de Proyart.)

Regarded as the origin of music, birdsong symbolized freedom and imitation of nature as foundational principles of the fine arts.[35] Such was the nightingale's passion for liberty that it often broke its wings against the cage in its efforts to escape.[36] Such was its pride in its song that its melodies were originals, the product of a creative or virile, and not a servile, imitation.[37] It seems significant that Catherine chose to recognize Collot's talent with a nightingale soon after gaining her consent to produce a pair of historical effigies. Portraits of the dead called, arguably, for genius that making a portrait from life did not. In May 1768 Catherine had asked Falconet whether Collot had ever "seen" Henri IV and Sully "en rêve," that is, in her imagination.[38] Falconet hastened to confirm that Collot was indeed "very dreamy," that the idea of these Bourbon heroes would in fact probably prevent her from waking for some three or four days, and that the outcome would in fact be very happy.[39] In the busts (fig. 116) Collot deftly combined naturalism (the sideways glance, the fleeting expression of animation) and historicism (the regal calm and seventeenth-century costume), elevating portraiture above mere likeness and demonstrating that the scope of a woman's artistry extended beyond mere copying to invention. In recognizing the

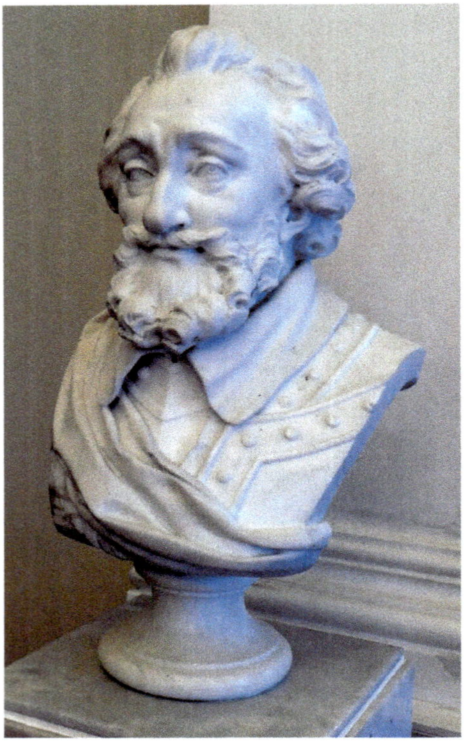

FIG. 116 Marie-Anne Collot (French, 1748–1821), *Henri IV*, 1770. Marble, 55 cm. Saint Petersburg, State Hermitage Museum.

nightingale in Collot, in attending to his or her needs, and in thus favoring one "who dares to raise herself above her sex," Catherine secured for herself not only Collot's talents but the reputation of a patron and sovereign who, rather than oppressing genius, sets it free.[40]

§

---

1. Catherine II to Falconet, 15 May 1769, in Louis Réau, ed., *Correspondance de Falconet avec Catherine II, 1767–1779* (Paris: Édouard Champion, 1921), 81. See also Christiane Dellac, *Marie-Anne Collot: Une sculptrice française à la cour de Catherine II, 1748–1821* (Paris: L'Harmattan, 2005), 45. Warmest thanks to Melissa Hyde for her brilliant suggestion of Collot's nightingale for this book.

2. Falconet to Catherine II, 14 May 1749, in Réau, *Correspondance*, 79.

3. Falconet to Catherine II, 14 May 1749, 77.

4. Falconet to Catherine II, 14 May 1749, 79. On Collot's lodgings, first on Nevsky Prospect and, by 1769, in Millonnaya Street, see Alexander Schenker, *The Bronze Horseman: Falconet's Monument to Peter the Great* (New Haven: Yale University Press, 2003), 95–98.

5. Today, nightingales are more closely associated with Moscow than Saint Petersburg. Mospriroda counts returning nightingales every year as part of its environmental program. See the map at https://www.google.com/maps/d/viewer?mid=11TgYCIPoMRNnRtbsqHvE50anCdWu0jrv&hl=ru&ll=55.74903519084849%2C37.543251199999986&z=9.

6. See Arnoult de Nobleville, *Aëdologie, ou Traité du rossignol franc ou chanteur* (Paris: Debure aîné, 1751), 2.

7. See Louise E. Robbins, *Elephant Slaves and Pampered Parrots: Exotic Animals in Eighteenth-Century Paris* (Baltimore: Johns Hopkins Press, 2002), 110–13. For contrast with the seventeenth century, see "Rossignol, linotte, pinson: l'inventaire d'un oiselier en 1665," *Archives minutes*, 28 August 2017, https://archivesminutes.wordpress.com/2017/08/28/le-contraire-dune-tete-de-linotte-linventaire-dun-oiselier-en-1665/. For an example of a parrot-owning eighteenth-century artist, see the inventory of the printmaker Gilles Demarteau (6 September 1776), according to which he kept a parrot at the printing shop on the Île de la Cité. See partial transcript of the inventory at the Musée Carnavalet library (Yb^3 337), 7. Warm thanks to Carole Nataf for drawing our attention to this.

8. In 1763 Catherine had given a set of Russian-made hunting weapons to Louis Charles Auguste Le Tonnelier, baron de

Breteuil, the French ambassador. The flintlock fowling piece from the set is now at the Art Institute of Chicago.

9. In 1768 Catherine had given an Imperial porcelain tea and coffee set to the English physician Thomas Dimsdale in thanks for inoculating her against smallpox. It was acquired by the Hermitage Museum, Saint Petersburg, in 2013.

10. "Prodigy" was Prince Gallitzin's word for Collot when describing her to Nikita Ivanovitch Panine, secretary of state for foreign affairs in 1766. See Marie-Louise Becker, "Marie-Anne Collot (1748–1821), l'art de la terre-cuite au féminin," *L'objet d'art* 325 (1998): 73.

11. She may have been alone in her profession in France, but not in Europe. See Marjan Sterckx, "Pride and Prejudice: Eighteenth-Century Women Sculptors and Their Material Practices," in *Women and Material Culture, 1660–1830*, ed. Jennie Batchelor and Cora Kaplan (New York: Palgrave, 2007), 86–102. The number of women sculptors rose markedly by the turn of the nineteenth century. See Anastasia Easterday, "*Labeur, Honneur, Douleur*: Sculptors Julie Charpentier, Félicie de Fauveau and Marie d'Orléans," *Women's Art Journal* 18, no. 2 (1997–98): 11–16.

12. On the commission, see Louis Réau, *Étienne-Maurice Falconet* (Paris: Demotte, 1922), 1:81–89, and most recently Schenker, *The Bronze Horseman*.

13. This distinguished Collot from the studio hands that Falconet also contracted to take with him. On Collot's works before her departure to Russia, see Becker, "Marie-Anne Collot (1748–1821)," 72–82.

14. On Catherine's commissions, see Réau, *Falconet*, 2:429–48; and Marie-Liesse Pierre-Dulau, "Trois artistes à Saint-Petersburg au XVIIIe siècle," in *L'Influence française au XVIIIe siècle*, ed. Jean-Pierre Poussou, Anne Mézin, and Yves Perret-Gentil (Paris: Presses de l'Université de Paris-Sorbonne, 2004), 148–56.

15. See Louis Réau, "Contrat de marriage de Pierre-Étienne Falconet et de Marie-Anne Collot, 27 juillet 1777," *BSHAF* (1918–19): 157–61. Collot did not enter into a "communauté de biens" with her husband, as was then the custom (see **marriage contract** and **burin**), but expressly retained control of her own money.

16. See Louis Réau, "Inventaire après décès de M. Falconet, 31 janvier, 1791," *BSHAF* (1918–19): 163–68.

17. See [Nicolas Venette], *Traité du rossignol qui enseigne la manière de les connoître et de les élever* (Paris: Claude Prudhomme, 1707), preface (unpaginated); and Nobleville, *Aëdologie*, i. Jean-Claude Hervieux de Chanteloup's *Nouveau traité des serins de canarie* (Paris: Claude Prudhomme, 1713) was dedicated, however, to the princesse de Condé. Hervieux was the keeper of her aviary. On the visual discourse, see René Démoris, "L'oiseau et sa cage en peinture," *Lumières* 5 (2005): 29–48.

18. Julia Breittruck, "Pet Birds: Cages and Practices of Domestication in Eighteenth-Century Paris," *Interdisciplines* 1 (2012): 6–23. See also, for example, Hervieux de Chanteloup, *Nouveau traité des serins*, 14–25, esp. 22; and Nobleville, *Aëdologie*, 58.

19. See Olga Petri and Philip Howell, "From the Dawn Chorus to the Canary Choir: Notes on the Unnatural History of Birdsong," *Humanimalia* 11, no. 2 (2020): 163–92.

20. See Georges Wildenstein, *Le peintre Aved: Sa vie et son oeuvre (1702–1766)* (Paris: Les Beaux-Arts, Edition d'Études et de Documents, 1923), 2:205. The instrument's maker was the famous Jean Richard, whose shop was on the Rue de Richelieu. The collection of the Philharmonie de Paris includes a late eighteenth-century *serinette* by Ferry. It plays a mixture of "airs," often marches, such as "Malbroug s'en va en guerre," intended to render the bird's song comic. To hear a *serinette* played, see Audrey Defrasne's performance at Musée de la musique mécanique, Les Gets: https://www.youtube.com/watch?v=1RF4P3kRuJ0. The Aved barrel organ raises the possibility that Mme Aved may have served as a model for Chardin's picture; it is unlikely to have been a portrait, since the painting was a royal commission.

21. Described as a "*salle*" and the penultimate room in an enfilade of four, giving onto the Rue de Bourbon (now Rue de Lille). The theme of birds was picked up in the decoration: a pair of gilt bronze girandoles decorated with Meissen birds provided some of the lighting of the room. See Wildenstein, *Aved*, 205.

22. The portrait (current whereabouts unknown) was exhibited at the Salon of 1740. Balechou's print was advertised in the *Mercure de France*, October 1743, 2243.

23. See Réau, *Falconet*, 1:100–101.

24. On pets in the human/animal debate, see Marc Shell, "The Family Pet," *Representations* 15 (1986): 121–53.

25. Georges Louis Leclerc, comte de Buffon, called nightingales "carnivors," in contrast to grain-eating, and by implication, tamer canaries. See Buffon, *Histoire naturelle des oiseaux* [1770–83] (Dordrecht: Blusse, 1796), 4 2. Venette called nightingales "birds of prey" in *Traité*, 56.

26. Buffon, *Histoire naturelle*, 4:2. Nobleville disagreed: see *Aëdologie*, 83–93. See also Marc Shell, "Animals That Talk," *Differences: A Journal of Feminist Cultural Studies* 15, no. 1 (2004): 93–95.

27. Buffon, *Histoire* naturelle, 4:1–2. According to the ornithologist Tim Birkhead, the failure of nightingales to learn songs other than their own may in fact have been consequent on the lack of incentive to persuade them to do so. See T. R. Birkhead and S. van Balen, "Bird-Keeping and the Development of Ornithological Science," *Archives of Natural History* 35, no. 2 (2008): 283.

28. Buffon, *Histoire naturelle*, 4:2. See also [Venette], *Traité*, 13, 34; and Nobleville, *Aëdologie*, 8. Both Venette and Nobleville insist that nightingales do not flock together, even when migrating. The English language does, however, possess a collective noun for nightingales: a watch.

29. Nobleville, *Aëdologie*, 2. The nightingale's Latin name, *Luscinia*, can be translated as "little-seen songster," from the Latin "luscus," meaning "half-blind" or "half-understood," and "cano," "to sing."

30. See the essays by Richard Nash ("Joy and Pity: Reading Animal Bodies in Late Eighteenth-Century Culture") and Jonathan Lamb ("Sympathy with Animals and Salvation of the Soul") in a special issue of *The Eighteenth Century: Theory and Interpretation* 52, no. 1 (2011).

31. Réau, *Correspondance*, 52, 56, 83.

32. In contrast, see Diderot's letter to Ivan Ivanovitch Betsky, 28–31 August 1766. In it, Diderot cannot stop himself from drawing attention to the contrast between Collot's "delicate hands" and the materials (clay and stone) that her art gave her to work. Denis Diderot, *Correspondance*, ed. Laurent Versini (Paris: Robert Lafont, 1997), 688. The unsuitability of carving for women was a prejudice perpetuated by academic theory until the end of the nineteenth century; see Karl Robert, *Traité pratique du modelage et de la sculpture* (Paris: Henri Laurens, 1889), 7.

33. See Charles Blainville, *Histoire générale, critique et philologique de la musique* (Paris: Pissot, 1767) v, 1–3.

34. See, in Diderot, *Correspondance*: Diderot to Falconet, 10 September 1766, 698; Diderot to Falconet, 12 November 1766, 704; and Diderot to Falconet, 15 May 1767, 737. The nightingale's haunting song was, of course, used by Diderot as a metaphor for posterity in his debate on that subject with Falconet. Falconet drew on birdsong heard daily in his garden at Rue d'Anjou to counter Diderot's arguments. See **quill**.

35. See Matthew Head, "Birdsong and the Origins of Music," *Journal of the Royal Musical Association* 122 (1997): 1–23.

36. [Venette], *Traité*, 44.

37. Nobleville, *Aëdologie*, 7–8.

38. Catherine II to Falconet, 16 May 1767, in Réau, *Correspondance*, 42–43. See also Réau, *Falconet*, 2:435–36.

39. Falconet to Catherine II, 23 May 1768, in Réau, *Correspondance*, 44.

40. Diderot to Ivan Ivanovich Betzki, 28–31 August 1766, in Diderot, *Correspondance,* 688. On the relations between *salonnières* and men of letters as relations between bird-keepers and birds, see Jean Starobinski, "Diderot: A Geography of Chatter," *Hudson Review* 65, no. 3 (2012): 368–80.

Order Book

Louis-Jean-François Lagrenée (1724–1805)

TYPE OF OBJECT	THEME	MATERIAL
Tool	Administration, Antiquity, Everyday, Identity, Louvre, Money, Studio, Travel	Synthetic Materials | Ink, Synthetic Materials | Paper

"This book was written by Lagrenée, History Painter, Director of the Académie in Rome" (fig. 117). Inscribed on the first page of a large notebook, roughly 23 by 17 centimeters, these handwritten words serve as the makeshift title page to Louis-Jean-François Lagrenée's order book.[1] Yet from page one, the order promised by this document is disrupted by the disorder in its making. For while Lagrenée served as director of the Académie de France in Rome from October 1781 until September 1787, the book's contents suggest that he started keeping the record much earlier, about a decade before he could have styled himself with this particular institutional moniker.[2] Like many other pages in this book, then, the title page was written out of order, either added in its entirety at a later date or updated with a new title when its author was too.

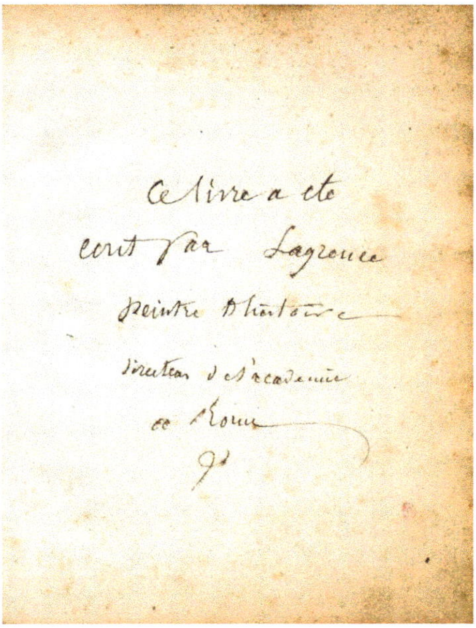

FIG. 117 Louis-Jean-François Lagrenée's order book (*livre de raison*), ca. 1770–1805, main title page. Paris, Bibliothèque de l'Institut National d'Histoire de l'Art, Ms. 50. (Photo: Bibliothèque de l'Institut National d'Histoire de l'Art.)

An order book was a common object in eighteenth-century France. A kind of register kept by every commercial agent, it was updated regularly to keep track of accounts and details of business. Despite their ubiquity, their organizational functions, and their often official status (merchants were required to keep them by statutory regulation), order books tended not to adhere to prescribed forms. Instead, like Lagrenée's, they took shape with the idiosyncrasies of their makers.[3] Indeed, according to the *Encyclopédie*, the principal job of the order book, or *livre de raison*, was to establish order for its owner out of their affairs ("il rend raison à celui qui le tient de toutes ses affaires").[4] How, then, did this book create order for Lagrenée? Which aspects of his business were rendered orderly in its pages? And what does the book's internal order and disorder reveal about the life of the object and its owner?

Inside, the contents of Lagrenée's 311-page book are composed of two main parts (fig. 118). The first is the more unexpected. Beginning on a recto numbered "1," under the title "Recueil de sujets d'histoire" (Compendium of history subjects), Lagrenée neatly copied out over fifty stories to serve as potential themes for paintings, like the "Death of Cleopatra" or the "Battle of Alexander against Darius." Separating his selections thematically—ancient history, Roman history, mythology, sacred subjects—Lagrenée also recorded his sources, for instance, his most frequent citation, Charles Rollin's *Histoire ancienne* (1730–38), referenced impeccably with volume and page numbers. About two-thirds of the way through the book, on page 217, that compendium comes to an end, on a recto numbered 218 (he accidentally left out page 186, upsetting the numbers). A new title marks the beginning of the second part, more expected for an order book: "État des tableaux faits par Monsieur Lagrenée" (Register of paintings made by Monsieur Lagrenée).

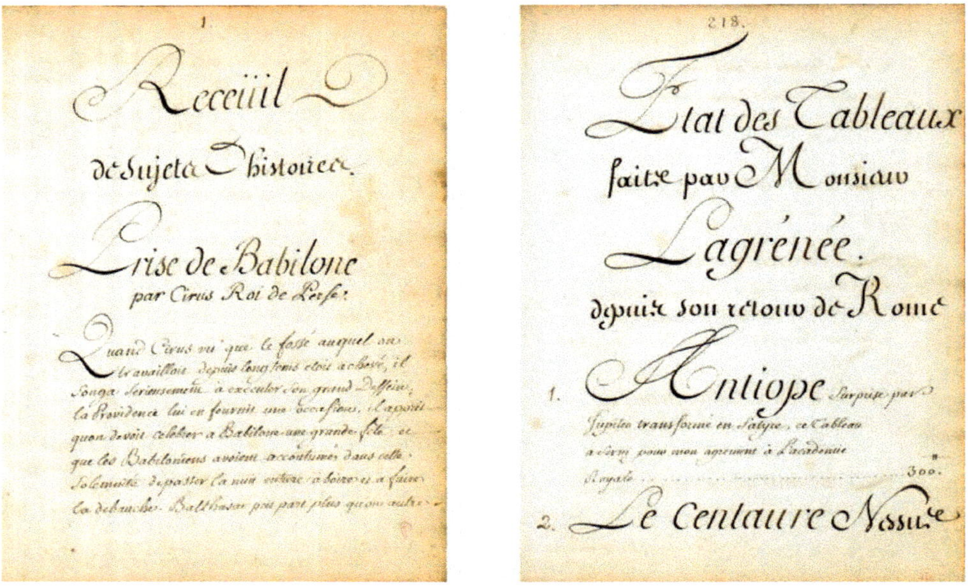
1
Receüil de Sujets historiques.
Prise de Babilone
par Cirus Roi de Perse:

218.
État des Tableaux
faits par Monsieur
Lagrenée.
depuis son retour de Rome
1. Antiope surprise par Jupiter transformé en Satyre, ce Tableau a servi pour mon agrément à l'Académie Royale ... 300.
2. Le Centaure Nessus

FIG. 118 Title pages to the two main parts, "Recueil de sujets d'histoire" (Compendium of history subjects) and "État des tableaux faits par Monsieur Lagrenée" (Register of paintings made by Monsieur Lagrenée), in Louis-Jean-François Lagrenée's order book (*livre de raison*), ca. 1770–1805. Paris, Bibliothèque de l'Institut National d'Histoire de l'Art, Ms. 50. (Photos: Bibliothèque de l'Institut National d'Histoire de l'Art.)

This register was a comprehensive record of the artist's output. In a continuously numbered list, Lagrenée itemized every painting he produced: from no. 1, *Antiope Surprised by Jupiter*, the *agrément* piece he presented to the Académie in 1754; right up to no. 457, *Bellona Dragging Mars from the Arms of Venus*, painted toward the end of his life.[5] With subheadings to structure the content, his productions were organized by time and place: first, "since his return from Rome," meaning back in Paris after being a *pensionnaire* and joining the Académie (1754–60); next, "in Saint Petersburg," where he served as imperial court painter (1760–62); then, "since my return from Saint Petersburg," a long section that actually includes his directorate in Rome (1762–87); and finally, "Return from Rome," which runs to the end (1787–1805). The register ends on page 298, with only a few pages left in the book, most of which are blank, apart from a four-page description of a "Subject of a Painting for the King," and, on the final page, a small pencil outline of an antique urn—the only image in the entire book.

Lagrenée's order book was a thing whose purpose was to reduce. To create order by making compact. Its two parts denote two distinct efforts in this vein: first, an attempt to scale down history; and second, a system to condense his own artistic practice. History, that vast textual discourse, was the stock-in-trade for any history painter, the raw material from which the artistic product was created. Thanks to Lagrenée's meticulous scholarly citations, we know that the sources he was using were already compilations. Rollin's histories offered summaries of stories drawn from a range of ancient texts, but clearly these multivolume editions with their lengthy accounts—like *Histoire ancienne* at thirteen volumes or *Histoire romaine* (1738–48) at seven volumes—were too much for Lagrenée and needed further paring down to suit his specific needs. Discarding the tedious or superfluous, Lagrenée created for himself a bespoke edited selection, extracting only the parts of stories he might want to paint, along with details to aid visualization (like the clothing worn by Persians, or the attributes of gods). From the calligraphic quality of his headings and writing, he clearly intended his abridged history to serve as a long-term reference—perhaps even a "traveler's edition" for an artist planning to voyage—obviating the need for constant consultation of a large library.

With the order book's transition from historical compendium to register, its functionality became multipurpose: from product guide to stock list and accounting system. Each page of Lagrenée's register followed a methodical layout (fig. 119). At the left margin, an item number; in the middle, title of the work and salient details (short descriptions, commissioners, locations); and at the right margin, price. At the top of each page, Lagrenée noted the total of prices from all previous pages, and at the bottom he added those from the current page, thus keeping a running calculation of the value of his production to date. He stopped including prices toward the end (from page 282, soon after his return from Rome as *directeur*), at which point his career total stood at 283,120 livres. This systematic register molded Lagrenée's studio output into a neat chronological and financial record, organizing his career into chapters and keeping track of his income along the way. Yet as its title page has already revealed, the book's apparent order belies the disorder of its making, with temporal disjunctions, retrospective fabrications, and nonsequential interventions.

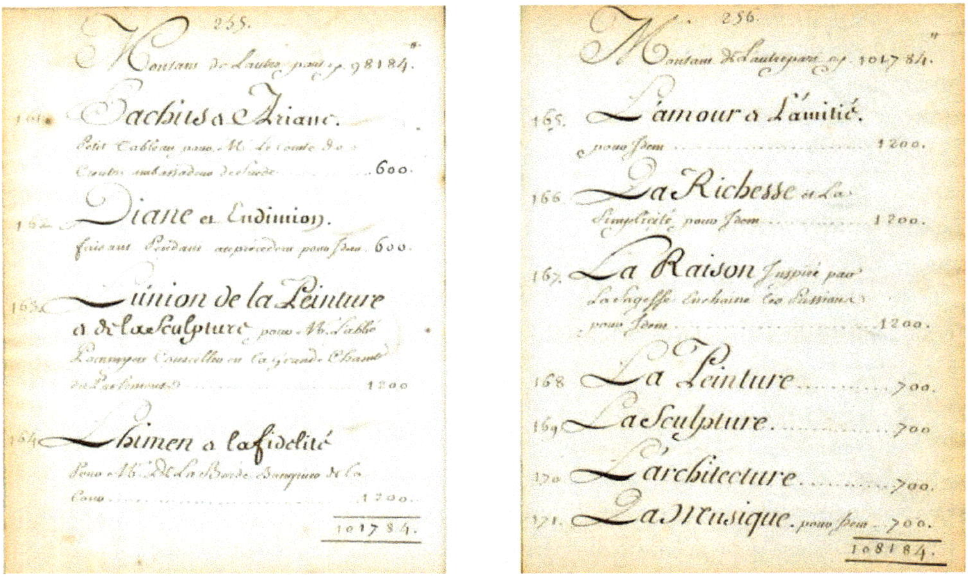

FIG. 119 "État des tableaux faits par Monsieur Lagrenée" (Register of paintings made by Monsieur Lagrenée), from Louis-Jean-François Lagrenée's order book (*livre de raison*), ca. 1770–1805, 255–56. Paris, Bibliothèque de l'Institut National d'Histoire de l'Art, Ms. 50. (Photos: Bibliothèque de l'Institut National d'Histoire de l'Art.) (Photos: Bibliothèque de l'Institut National d'Histoire de l'Art.)

What, then, do the pages divulge about the book's life as an object? Based on medium and facture, it appears to be the product of two stages of making, but, intriguingly, not ones that align with its two parts. The first stage—and the book's creation—took place all at once, during which Lagrenée composed the historical compendium and over a third of the register. Covering pages 1 to 256, this stage is characterized by remarkable consistency in the book's production, not least in the calligraphic headings/painting titles and stylized handwriting (see figs. 118, 119). Then, from page 257, the inconsistencies and variations begin: first an ink change from brown to black; then page totals start appearing in pencil rather than ink; then come small lapses in style, until eventually the calligraphic features are abandoned entirely and the writing becomes quicker and messier (fig. 120). Clearly, somewhere around this point the book entered a second and much longer stage of making, which, unlike the first (contained at a single moment, with the register reconstituted retrospectively), unfolded in real time over the rest of his career.

Once being formed in real time, the book also started to require corrections, from marks crossing out canceled items, to annotations noting changes and updates. On page 259, for instance, under the entry for *Diana and Acteon*, a succession of additional lines indicates the painting's turbulent life: initially painted for the duc de Praslin, his exile prevented him from taking it; next, the work was sold to the comtesse du Barry for 720

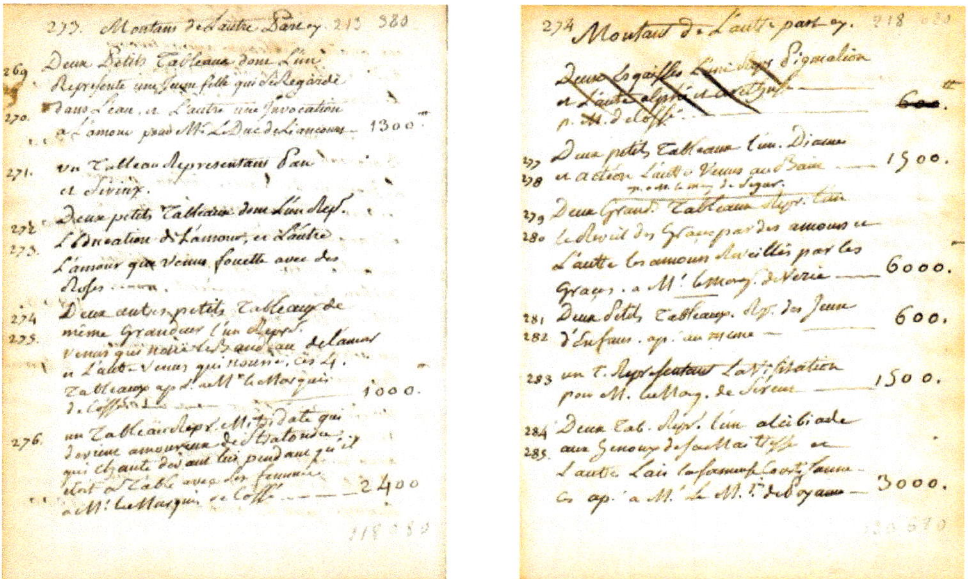

FIG. 120 "État des tableaux faits par Monsieur Lagrenée" (Register of paintings made by Monsieur Lagrenée), from Louis-Jean-François Lagrenée's order book (*livre de raison*), ca. 1770–1805, 273–74. Paris, Bibliothèque de l'Institut National d'Histoire de l'Art, Ms. 50. (Photos: Bibliothèque de l'Institut National d'Histoire de l'Art.)

livres, but she returned it; then, eventually, it went to Monsieur de la Borde. This sense of the book's constant use and reuse is not limited to the register. Traces of revisits also punctuate the pages of the compendium, where Lagrenée would jot notes after painting the subjects described. On page 8, for instance, following the story of two widows vying to join their late husband on his funeral pyre (from a chapter on the successors of Alexander), Lagrenée noted, "I executed this subject in a drawing," then later in a different ink and more tremulous hand "since as a large painting for the king in Rome in 1782." The painting in question, *Two Widows of an Indian Officer* (1782, Dijon, Musée des Beaux-Arts), was exhibited at the Salon of 1783, and the explanatory text in the exhibition *livret* reads as though derived from the version in Lagrenée's order book, suggesting yet another instance of reuse.[6]

The order of the book's making invites speculation about Lagrenée's motivations. Why start it, and why then? Based on the dates of the paintings itemized around the transitional point (pages 255–60), Lagrenée decided to create his book sometime between 1769 and 1771.[7] Given the timing, it is tempting to imagine that the painter's desire to order his affairs at this moment was prompted by the mundane practicalities of moving home. Lagrenée had been living for a few years on Rue de l'Arbre-Sec near the church of Saint-Germain-l'Auxerrois, having earlier lived at various other addresses in the neighborhood. But in May 1771, Lagrenée was finally granted a *logement* in the Louvre after years of trying to acquire that privilege, ever since his return from Saint Petersburg.[8] Perhaps creating a new order book was an effort to consolidate disorderly papers before the move, or perhaps it was part of that desire (familiar to many) to want to start afresh after unpacking: to create a new order for a new life. Either way, Lagrenée's order book looks like the product of that natural inclination, when faced with material excess or systematic chaos, to seek to reduce, condense, and simplify.

Lagrenée was certainly not alone among his colleagues in keeping an order book, but the considerable variations among the handful that still survive suggest they were often driven by different ends. Hyacinthe Rigaud's order book was a list of portraits with prices, including sums paid to studio assistants, which indicates a prevailing concern with financial matters.[9] Jean-Baptiste Oudry's order book was also a record of portrait subjects, but this time in illustrated form, each entered into the book as a small sketch of the composition.[10] This might suggest an inclination to catalog visually, or that the book served an additional purpose as a presentation album for clients. Meanwhile, Joseph Vernet's order books were effectively **journals** chronicling nearly everything—from commissions received, to useful addresses, and household happenings and expenses—revealing the landscapist's general proclivity to archive.[11] By comparison with his colleagues, Lagrenée's register of prices and patrons suggests, like Rigaud, an interest in commercial affairs (both economic and social). But his decision to combine that with a historical compendium draws an unusually direct connection between the business of history painting and the intellectual activities of his practice, not least in those numerous cross references between the book's two parts. Despite the Académie's privileging of scholarly pursuits and its conflicted relationship with commerce, Lagrenée's order book makes it an easy cohabitation.

It seems fitting to end by returning to the beginning, back on Lagrenée's title page, where, on its verso, we find the final annotation ever made in the book, and the most out of order of all. Made not by its original owner but by a subsequent one, the words were written by one of the Goncourt brothers, those celebrated nineteenth-century collectors and historians of the eighteenth-century art world. Having purchased the order book as an item of interest, the brothers accessioned it into their collection, getting it rebound with a monogrammed cover and inscribing it on the back of the title page with a cataloging description. Highlighting its historical significance, they described it as a "document without which it would be impossible to write the life of this likeable French painter." Like the metal plaque added to Jacques-Louis David's **table** by his heirs, this inscription pulls the object into its future afterlife—recalling its passage from everyday item in an eighteenth-century studio, to documentary evidence in the historiographical narratives of French art—a trajectory that would surely have delighted the self-historicizing Lagrenée.

‡

---

1. The manuscript is now in the collection of the INHA in Paris. It has recently been digitized: https://bibliotheque-numerique.inha.fr/viewer/32482.

2. Lagrenée's appointment had been determined by 14 February 1781, so that seems the earliest possible moment for the inscription of the words "directeur de l'Académie à Rome."

Letter from comte d'Angiviller to Jean-Baptiste-Marie Pierre (14 February 1781), in *CDR*, 14:82.

3. "Livres (commerce)," *Encyclopédie*, https://encyclopedie.uchicago.edu/, 9:613. On the legal role of the *livre de raison*, see Michel Cassan and Christine Nougaret, "Une typologie des écrits du for privé," in *Les Écrits du for privé en France de la fin du Moyen Âge à 1914*, ed. Jean-Pierre Bardet and François-Joseph Ruggiu (Paris: Éditions de Comité des travaux historiques et scientifiques, 2014), 76–77.

4. "Livre grand," *Encyclopédie*, https://encyclopedie.uchicago.edu/, 9:613.

5. *Bellona* is dated to ca. 1804 in Marc Sandoz, *Les Lagrenée: I. Louis-Jean-François Lagrenée, 1725–1805* (Paris: Éditart-Les Quatre Chemins, 1983), 308.

6. "Exposition de 1783," *Collection des livrets des anciennes expositions depuis 1673 jusqu'en 1800* (Paris: Liepmannssohn, 1870), 14–15.

7. The dating of Lagrenée's oeuvre here follows Marc Sandoz's catalogue raisonnée. It is another fascinating sign of the potential disorder of Lagrenée's inventory that Sandoz felt the need to reorder it in accordance with his own cataloging system. See Sandoz, *Les Lagrenée*, 359–73.

8. Jules Guiffrey, "Brevet de logement dans la Galerie du Louvre," *NAAF* (Paris: Charavay Frères, 1873), 95, 97.

9. Rigaud's *livres de raison* are held in the libraries of the Institut de France and ENSBA, Paris. The most comprehensive study is Joseph Roman, *Le livre de raison du peintre Hyacinthe Rigaud* (Paris: Laurens, 1919).

10. Oudry's albums are held in the Musée du Louvre. They were analyzed as "liber veritatis" in Hal Opperman, *Jean-Baptiste Oudry (1686–1755)*, PhD diss., University of Chicago, 1972, 2 vols. (New York: Garland, 1977), 2:608–40.

11. Vernet's *livres de raison* are held in the Bibliothèque Municipale, Avignon; they were partially transcribed in Léon Lagrange, *Joseph Vernet et la peinture au XVIIIe siècle* (Paris: Didier, 1864). For a sensitive analysis of their contents and materiality, see Charlotte Guichard, "Les écritures ordinaires de Claude-Joseph Vernet: Commandes et sociabilité d'un peintre au XVIIIe siècle," in *Les Écrits du for privé*, 231–44.

Palette

Elisabeth Vigée-Lebrun (1755–1842)

TYPE OF OBJECT	THEME	MATERIAL
Symbolic Thing, Tool	Education, Identity, Making, Memory, Studio	Plant Matter | Wood, Synthetic Materials | Paint/Pigment

On one memorable occasion early in her career, Elisabeth Vigée-Lebrun had her social plans unexpectedly disrupted by her palette. She had received an invitation to dine with the Princess Rohan-Rochefort and was readying herself for this high-society occasion, dressing fashionably in a brand-new white satin gown.[1] Just on the point of calling her **carriage**, the painter found herself momentarily distracted by the portrait she had begun that morning. Absorbed in that feeling of creative intensity at the start of a new project, she was "seized by a sudden desire" to revisit the canvas, so she sat down in front of her easel to contemplate what she had achieved so far.[2] To her utter dismay, however, she discovered she had left her palette face-up on the chair. With the morning's wet oil paint now smeared all over her new white dress, she was forced to abandon her dinner invitation, and she resolved there and then never to accept another.

Palettes, it would seem, were not always the innocuous objects they might first appear. Recalled decades later in her memoirs, Vigée-Lebrun's anecdote about her palette is striking for several reasons, not least for the relatable nature of that quotidian crisis caused by a momentary lapse of concentration. But it also offers a glimpse into the place of tools in the working practices of an eighteenth-century painter. Few artists had the luxury of a studio separate from the home, so art making—with all its technical processes and messy procedures—often had to take place alongside domestic activities, sometimes in the very same rooms.[3] The workspace of a portraitist like Vigée-Lebrun was especially complex, needing to accommodate the competing social and practical demands of sittings. These required a space commodious enough for elite clients to visit, yet utilitarian enough to cope with the paraphernalia of tools and activities, be it preparing paint, cleaning brushes, or mixing colors. For a woman artist, the difficulties of carving out a working space in the home could be even more difficult, depending on the claims already made on the domestic environment by her husband's or father's profession. A painting like Marie-Victoire Lemoine's *Studio of a Woman Painter* (fig. 121) articulates the sometimes uncomfortable juxtapositions of such multiuse spaces, the studio in question being simultaneously a finely appointed *cabinet*. The room's ornate carpet, upholstered **armchair**, and embroidered tablecloth all seem dangerously at risk from the equipment of the studio: its open **color box**, an easel with wet canvas, dust from a chalk drawing, and, above all, the heavily charged palette in the center, tilting perilously with gleaming globules of paint, held against the artist's pristine white dress. Lemoine's painting may have been an artistic construction of studio space, but Vigée-Lebrun's anecdote underscores its realities, as the mess of art making could clearly become a domestic hazard. Both of these encounters, moreover, remind us that artists' studios were spaces defined as such by things—tools, supports, and media that demarcated the room's transition to professional functionality. And for a painter, no thing was as definitive as the palette, whether practically, symbolically, or self-reflexively.

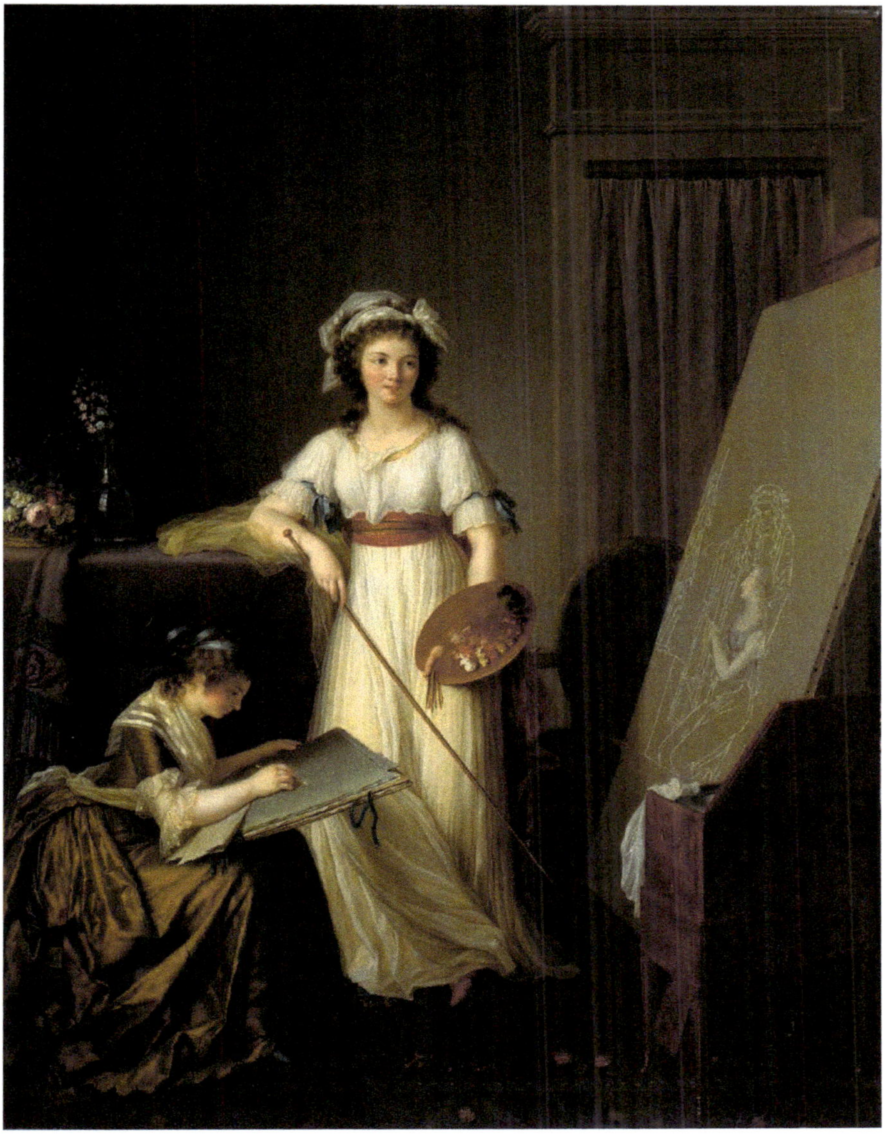

FIG. 121 Marie-Victoire Lemoine (French, 1754–1820), *Studio of a Woman Painter*, 1789. Oil on canvas, 116.5 × 88.9 cm. New York, Metropolitan Museum of Art, Gift of Mrs. Thorneycroft Ryle, 1957. (Image copyright © The Metropolitan Museum of Art / Art Resource, NY.)

As a tool, the palette was fundamental to the painter's craft. Though extremely simple (a flat plank of wood), if made and maintained properly a palette was also an incredibly effective item of art-world technology. In terms of material, woods of choice for eighteenth-century palettes were apple or walnut, both hardwoods with tight grains that could be polished to a smooth finish, creating an ideal surface for mixing colors and for cleaning afterward.[4] New palettes had to be prepared before they could be used, by coating the top numerous times with walnut oil until the wood could absorb no more.[5] Without this preparation, the binder in mixed oil paints (usually linseed or walnut oil) would seep into the wood, leaving the paint to dry out and stain the palette's surface.[6] Designwise, there was a selection of shapes available, as illustrated in the plates of painters' tools in the *Encyclopédie* (fig. 122). Most eighteenth-century painters, like Vigée-Lebrun, preferred an oval palette—certainly the most ubiquitous in artists' portraits—but a minority opted for rectangular (among them, Louis-Michel Van Loo and Nicolas Bertin).[7] No matter the shape, all palettes were engineered in a similar way to ensure the ergonomics of use. A bevel-edged thumbhole and a cutaway section on the palette edge (to accommodate a bunch of brushes and sometimes a *godet* (pot) for oil) permitted the painter to hold everything at the ready in their left hand, while the active right hand undertook the dexterous work of mixing and applying colors. For the minority of left-handed painters (among them, Nicolas Mignard), the configuration was reversed.[8] Palettes were also designed to be thicker at the thumbhole side and thinner toward the "tail," ensuring an efficient distribution of weight and a more commodious experience when working for lengthy periods.[9]

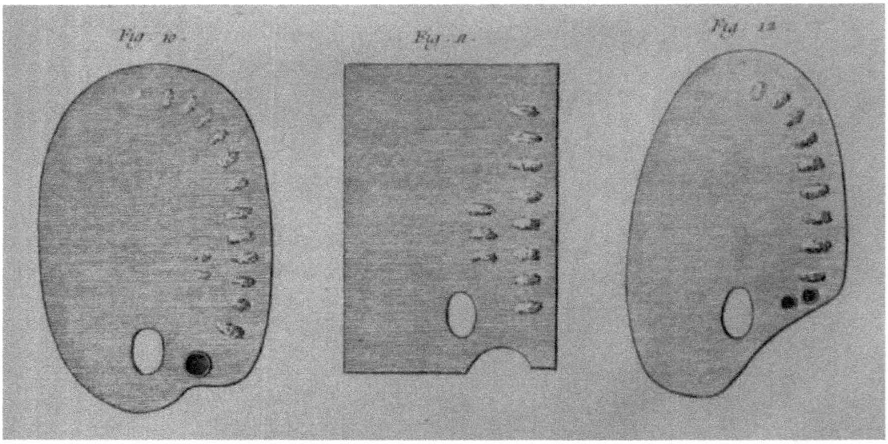

FIG. 122 "Painting" from *Recueil de planches sur les sciences, les arts libéraux et les arts mécanique* (1765), plate I, detail. (Image courtesy of the ARTFL Encyclopédie Project, University of Chicago.)

Along with its physical optimization for being comfortably held, the palette's design as a tool also supported its principal function as a "color laboratory," to invoke Charlotte Guichard's term for a space where scientific color theories were transformed into practical painterly substances.[10] Though little more than a flat, unmarked piece of wood, for the trained painter a palette was far from a mere undifferentiated surface. Instead, it was divided invisibly into distinct zones, where colors were distributed in fixed patterns or one-off concoctions. At the top, a register of raw colors was arranged in a set scheme; then in the middle and bottom of the palette, those raw colors could be progressively mixed to achieve the range of tones and shades required for a particular artwork.[11] Describing this practice in *Les premiers éléments de la peinture pratique* (1684), Roger de Piles included a diagram for the following top register of *couleurs capitales* (principal colors) (fig. 123): (1) lead white, (2) yellow ocher, (3) brown red, (4) **red lake**, (5) stil de grain, (6) green earth, (7) umber, (8) bone black. In a second diagram, he included additional pigments that might be added below (e.g., vermillion (A), massicot (B), or ultramarine (D), and he showed how the artist used the palette surface systematically to create a spectrum of mixed tonal variations (fig. 124). Judging by the palettes represented in artists' portraits, it would appear that the method de Piles described was largely adhered to throughout the eighteenth century, at least as a shared theoretical starting point. Most portrait palettes show a top register of whites, yellows, reds, browns, and blacks, arranged roughly lightest to darkest from thumbhole to tail. But painters also developed their own idiosyncratic palette habits to suit their style and subject matter. Thus, when it came to the number of principal colors and the actual pigments selected, there were as many variations as there were artists: Vien, for instance, began with a restricted set of seven principals (see fig. 36), while Vernet preferred a lavish array of eleven (see fig. 183).

Palettes in artists' portraits prove intriguing evidence for exploring their use, but their presence in these artworks also draws attention to their roles beyond utility. So ubiquitous was the palette as a studio tool, so synonymous with the trade, and so personal to the artist, that, not surprisingly, this piece of wood also became the artform's defining attribute. As a symbol, the palette performed both self-fashioning and allegorical services, whether as that traditional prop held in so many professional portraits, or in decorative allegories or still lifes, like Jean-Siméon Chardin's *Attributes of the Arts* (1766, Minneapolis Institute of Art). More than any other material thing, the palette came to stand for both painting, as an art, and the painter, as its agent.

It is in this performative guise that we come face to face with the palette of Vigée-Lebrun in her celebrated *Self-Portrait in a Straw Hat* (fig. 125). Set unconventionally outdoors, the portrait places Vigée-Lebrun beyond any of those material markers of the studio described in Lemoine's portrait (see fig. 121). In the absence of other signs, her palette deftly assumes full visual responsibility for signifying its bearer's professional identity. Tilted forward to face the viewer and lit brightly from above, the palette's indexical value is immediate, indicating categorically who Vigée-Lebrun is and what she does. Held so naturally on her thumb that it is practically worn over her arm, it becomes a corporeal extension, as much part of Vigée-Lebrun as the rest of her clothing. Yet it is the blobs of paint *on* the palette that make it such a potent "site of self-declaration," to use Philip Sohm's expression for when the portrayed palette serves as metacommentary on the image containing it.[12] Emerging as the artwork's captivating punctum, those blobs of paint

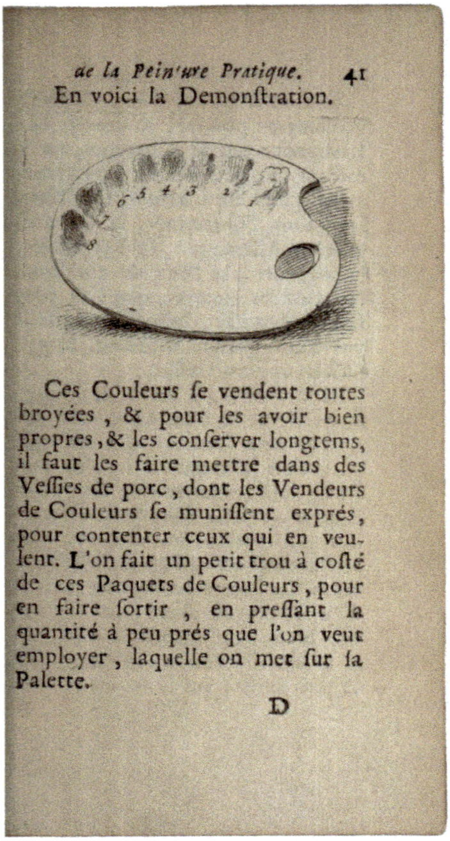
de la Peinture Pratique. 41

En voici la Demonſtration.

Ces Couleurs ſe vendent toutes broyées, & pour les avoir bien propres, & les conſerver longtems, il faut les faire mettre dans des Veſſies de porc, dont les Vendeurs de Couleurs ſe muniſſent exprés, pour contenter ceux qui en veulent. L'on fait un petit trou à coſté de ces Paquets de Couleurs, pour en faire ſortir, en preſſant la quantité à peu prés que l'on veut employer, laquelle on met ſur ſa Palette.

D

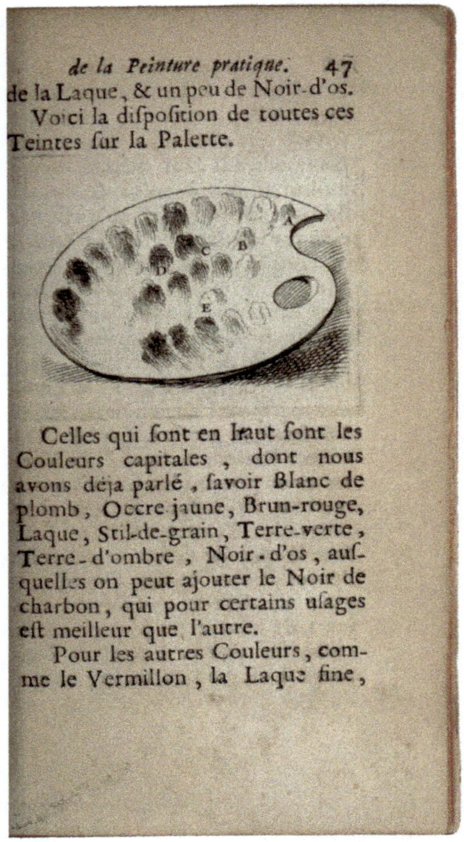
de la Peinture pratique. 47

de la Laque, & un peu de Noir-d'os.

Voici la diſpoſition de toutes ces Teintes ſur la Palette.

Celles qui ſont en haut ſont les Couleurs capitales, dont nous avons déja parlé, ſavoir Blanc de plomb, Ocre jaune, Brun-rouge, Laque, Stil-de-grain, Terre-verte, Terre-d'ombre, Noir-d'os, auſquelles on peut ajouter le Noir de charbon, qui pour certains uſages eſt meilleur que l'autre.

Pour les autres Couleurs, comme le Vermillon, la Laque fine,

FIG. 123 Jean-Baptiste Corneille (French, 1649–95), Illustration of a charged palette showing the top register of *couleurs capitales*, from Roger de Piles, *Les premiers éléments de la peinture pratique* (Paris: Langlois, 1684), 41. Paris, Bibliothèque Nationale de France.

FIG. 124 Jean-Baptiste Corneille (French, 1649–95), Illustration of a charged palette showing additional colors added on lower registers, from Roger de Piles, *Les premiers éléments de la peinture pratique* (Paris: Langlois, 1684), 47. Paris:, Bibliothèque Nationale de France.

pierce the divide between the fiction of the canvas and the reality of its making. For if the painted Vigée-Lebrun is a self-portrait of the maker, then the painted palette is likewise: a self-image of the surface bearing the principal colors that created it all, from the white collar to the black shawl, via the blue sky, soft pink dress, bright red flower, and even the warm brown of its own polished wood.

Vigée-Lebrun's self-reflexive engagement with her palette in her self-portrait underscores its complex role in the painter's working life. As an intermediary surface in the stages of painterly creation—the space where color was workshopped before being applied to its next and final surface—the palette was different from most tools in the artist's studio. Some tools, like easels or **modeling stands**, were valuable mechanical aids, but not exactly indispensable; things intentionally designed to make easier, speed up, or simplify the practices of the studio. Others, like brushes or **burins**, were more imperative to the actions and gestures of art making; things that served as extensions of the artist's hand, enhancing its dexterity, precision, or facility. The palette, meanwhile, was both and more: a useful

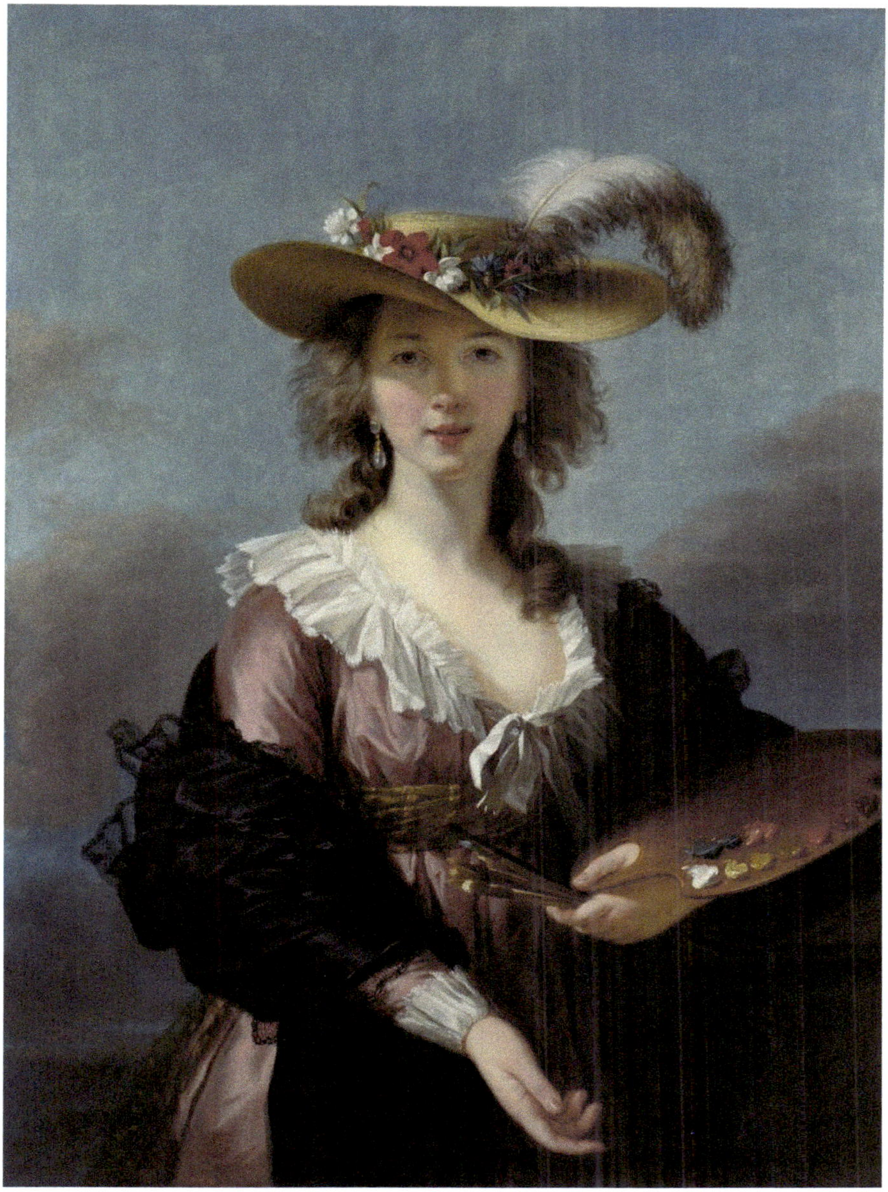

FIG. 125 Elisabeth Vigée-Lebrun (French, 1755–1842), *Self-Portrait in a Straw Hat*, 1782. Oil on canvas, 97.8 × 70.5 cm. London, National Gallery, NG1653. (© National Gallery, London / Art Resource, NY.)

mechanical aid, an extension of the hand, and also an extension of the mind—an experimental space where ideas could be rehearsed and refined into material form. In this respect it was perhaps closer to the **sketchbook**, though instead of investigating form and subject matter for future use, the palette concocted color in the moment, to be wiped clean afterward, ready for the next the experiment.

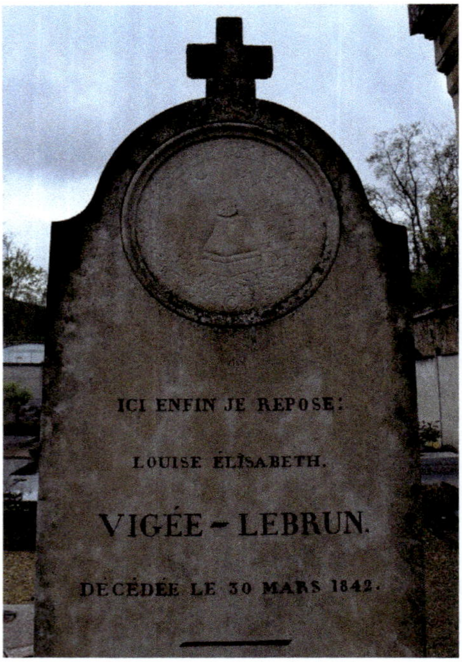

FIG. 126 Palette on a plinth adorning the grave of Elisabeth Vigée-Lebrun, ca. 1842. Cimetière de Louveciennes. (Photo: Hannah Williams.)

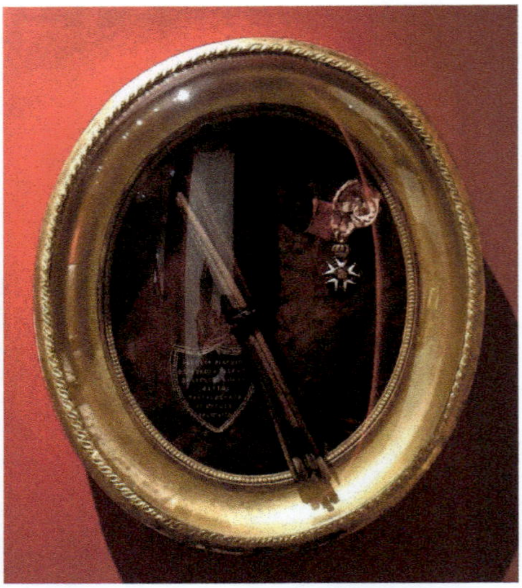

FIG. 127 Palette and assembled items of Jacques-Louis David (French, 1748–1825), 50 × 42.5 cm. Collection Alexandre Moura, on long-term loan to Paris, Musée de la Légion d'Honneur.

As a color laboratory, site of self-definition, and embodied extension of the creative agent, Vigée-Lebrun's palette was, like that of every painter, perhaps the most representative possession in her working life. No surprise, then, that in death the palette became her commemorative marker. Her gravestone in the cemetery of Louveciennes is adorned with a tombstone maker's crude line carving showing a palette resting atop a plinth: a memorial to the painter engraved into this memorial to the painter (fig. 126). This monumentalizing of the painter's palette in death reaches its zenith in a very different commemorative object for one of Vigée-Lebrun's contemporaries, Jacques-Louis David. Few eighteenth-century palettes have survived still attached in provenance to their owners, but, at the Musée de la Légion d'Honneur in Paris, David's is now preserved in a quasi reliquary (fig. 127). Framed and encased under a glass dome, his palette is the centerpiece of an arrangement of items: a double *godet* clipped to its edge; a bunch of brushes and utensils suspended over the cutaway; and David's **decoration** as *commandeur* of the Légion d'Honneur (awarded by Napoleon in 1815) hanging through the thumbhole. An inscription affixed on a leather shield serves as tombstone, in both senses, a museum label with elegiac shades: "Palette, brushes, and palette knife of Jacques-Louis David, restorer of the French School."[13] Assembled sometime after his death in 1825, this object is a testament to David's renown, and also to the cults of artistic celebrity that began emerging in the nineteenth century. Like Vigée-Lebrun's grave, this was an honorific act of memorialization by an anonymous maker, but rather than remaining in the symbolic realm, this one transformed the palette itself into a **relic**—a precious physical remnant of the great painter. ‡

1. This anecdote is recounted in Elisabeth Vigée-Lebrun, *Memoirs of Vigée Lebrun*, trans. Lionel Strachey (New York: Doubleday, Page & Company, 1903), 18.

2. Vigée-Lebrun, *Memoirs*, 18.

3. Charles-Antoine Coypel and Jacques-Louis David are examples of artists who had multiple working and living spaces, as discussed in **bed** and **table**.

4. *Encyclopédie*, https://encyclopedie.uchicago.edu/, s.v. "Palette," 11:781.

5. "Palette," *Encyclopédie*.

6. Jean-Felix Watin, *L'art du peintre, doreur, vernisseur* (Paris: Grangé, 1773), 54; and Roger de Piles, *Les premiers éléments de la peinture pratique* (Paris: Nicolas Langlois, 1684), 61.

7. Bertin holds a rectangular palette in his portrait by Jacques-François Delyen (1725, Château de Versailles), while Van Loo holds one in his *Self-Portrait with His Sister* (see fig. 141).

8. Mignard's "left-handed" palette designed for his right hand is depicted in his portrait by Paul Mignard (1672, Musée des Beaux-Arts, Lyon).

9. De Piles, *Les premiers éléments*, 59.

10. Charlotte Guichard, "Palettes et tableaux: Des laboratoires de la couleur?," *Dix-huitième siècle* 51, no. 1 (2019): 187–204.

11. "Palette," *Encyclopédie*.

12. Philip Sohm, "Palettes as Signatures and Encoded Identities in Early Modern Self-Portraits," *Art History* 40, no. 5 (2017): 995.

13. "Palette pinceaux / & couteau à palette / de Jacque [*sic*] Louis/ (David) / restaurateur / de l'école / française."

Pastels

Marie-Suzanne Giroust (1734–72)

TYPE OF OBJECT	THEME	MATERIAL
Tool	Making, Studio	Mineral | Chalk, Synthetic Materials | Paint/ Pigment

Clutching a tray of vibrantly colored pastel sticks, Suzanne Giroust appears to have been searching for the right one (fig. 128). Seated before her easel, in the company of her husband, she is painting a pastel portrait of a family friend.[1] Her **color box** is open beside her, a white **handkerchief** lies at the ready to wipe the constant chalky dust from her hands, and a knife rests nearby to sharpen a stick should finer lines be required. From her cluttered assortment of colors, Giroust has made her selection—a deep blue—now held lightly in her fingers and about to be deployed. But first she looks up, casting a final glance at her sitter to confirm her choice by scrutinizing his garment once more. As a representation of the studio setting, this portrait of Giroust by her husband, Alexander Roslin, offers some sense of the processes and substances of pastel painting: from the equipment and media required, to the patterns and activities of their employment. But there is a pervasive incongruity in this encounter. As a material experience, the art of pastel is presented to us here not actually *in* pastel, but in Roslin's own preferred medium of oil.[2] We find ourselves thus witness to an awkward moment of artistic tension, invited (ostensibly) to marvel at a celebration of pastel but instead facing an implicit declaration of oil's superiority. While it plays out here in the domestic context of Roslin and Giroust's relationship, pastel was a medium that, in the artistic hierarchies of eighteenth-century France, was quite habituated to underestimation, latent or otherwise.

Pastel's ambiguous position as a medium may have been due in part to the odd disjunction between its form and function; it looked like one thing but performed the artistic activities of another. As physical objects, pastels appear so similar to ***crayons*** (chalks) that one might wonder why this book needs an entry on the thingness of Giroust's pastels when it already has one on Huët's *crayons*. But in use, gesture, and even materiality, pastel was something else entirely. While *crayon* was the Académie's medium of choice for drawing, pastel was a medium for painting, categorized and defined as such by Roger de Piles: a method by which "visible objects are rendered *through color* on a flat surface" (our italics).[3] As Roslin's portrait of Giroust suggests, this also made the actions and processes of pastel quite different from *crayon*. Rather than used horizontally on a drawing board, pastels were used upright at an easel, borrowing the apparatus of oil painting, and even to an extent simulating its support, as the paper was often pasted onto fabric stretched over a wooden strainer, making it easier to frame and glaze afterward.[4] In general, however, the studio paraphernalia of a pastellist like Giroust was less extensive than for many of her

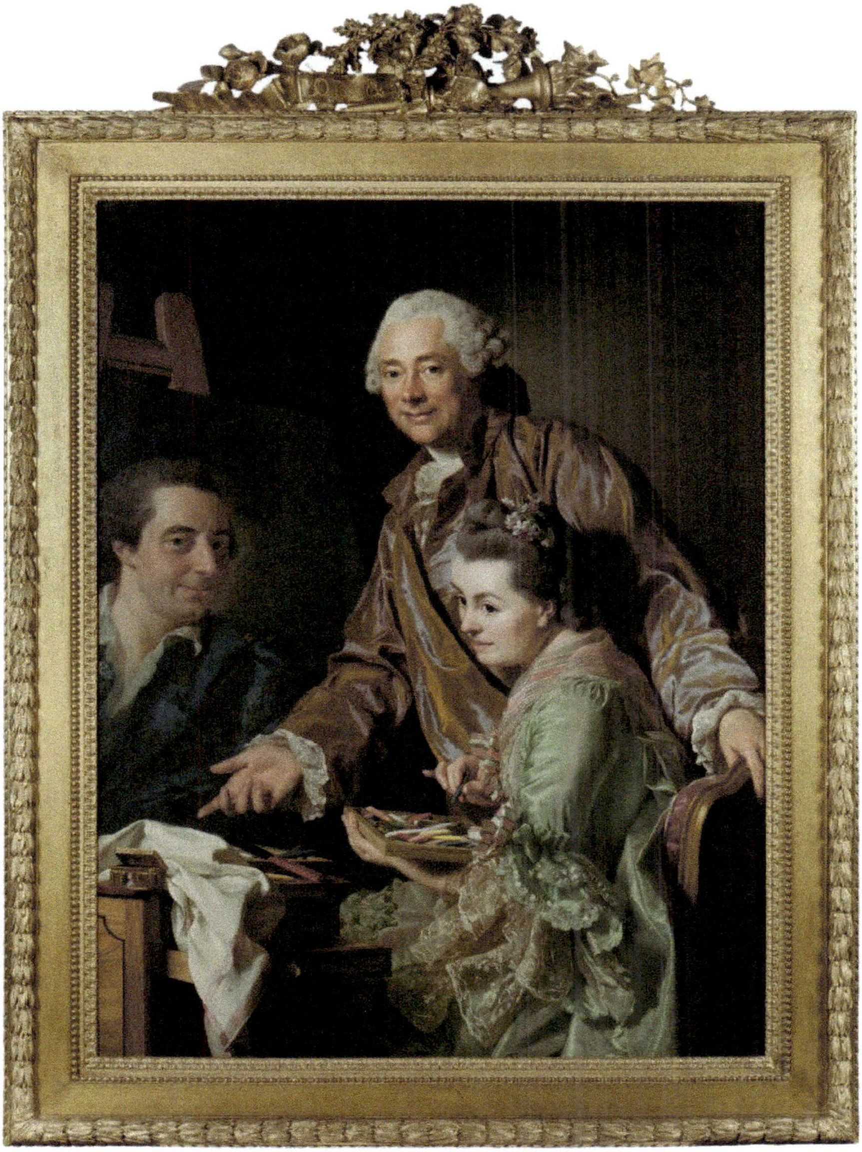

FIG. 128 Alexander Roslin (Swedish, 1718–93), *Self-Portrait with the Artist's Wife, Suzanne Giroust, Painting a Portrait of Henrik Wilhelm Peill*, 1767. Oil on canvas, 131 × 98.5 cm. Stockholm, Nationalmuseum, NM 7141. (incamerastock / Alamy Stock Photo.)

painter colleagues, because as "things," pastels were both medium and tool—an all-in-one device requiring no mechanical holder or applicator. Pastellists eschewed the draftsman's ***porte-crayon***, with all its promises of linear control, and had no use for the oil painter's brush and **palette**, because pastel colors could not be mixed in advance, their tonal nuances being achieved only in situ. Instead, pastel sticks were held directly in the hand, and fingers—embedded with dust—became an extension for blending color on the paper's surface. While practical (if messy), a pastel's very thingness thus made it something of a renegade. With its dependence on manual engagement and its emphasis on the representational force of color, pastel posed an inherent challenge to those entrenched academic hierarchies that privileged line over color and mind over hand.

Sharing the physical form of *crayon* but the functionality of paint, pastels also found themselves as neither-nor when it came to their materiality. While there was little consistency in the composition of pastels—and different colors required different ingredients and recipes—each stick was essentially a combination of three substances: a pigment to give it a specific color; a white extender (chalk, gypsum, talc, starch, tobacco pipe clay, alabaster) to give that color bulk and opacity; and a binder (natural resins, gum tragacanth, drying oils, egg, whey) to hold everything together.[5] Perfecting the balance was key, according to Robert Dossie's handbook on artists' materials: too much binder and the pastels would not cast; but too little and they would not adhere to the paper.[6] Pastel was thus very much a manufactured substance, a contrast to the usually natural materials of *crayons*—charcoal, quarried chalk, etc. (notwithstanding Nadaux's improvements)—and actually had much in common materially with oil paint. Despite their vastly different forms, the colors of pastels and oils were derived from the same organic and inorganic pigments (like yellow ocher, stil de grain, vermillion, or umber).[7] But the different binders of pastel and oil paint meant that sometimes the most successful colors in one were trickier in the other. Dossie, for instance, advised caution with **red lake** and Prussian blue, which in pastel were "apt to turn pale, and sometimes entirely lose their hue," unless prepared in exactly the right manner.[8] Given the complexity of knowledge and know-how required for their production, it is not surprising that, by the time Giroust was practicing, most pastellists tended to procure their sticks from commercial manufacturers rather than routinely making their own in the studio.[9]

Giroust's preferred pastel-maker is not known, but she would have had many options with Paris's emergent specialist trade in artists' materials. Commercial production of pastels had been limited in the seventeenth century, but as Majorie Shelley notes, the trade in ready-made pastels proliferated considerably in the eighteenth century.[10] One of the Parisian suppliers with connections to Académie circles was Jean-Nicolas Vernezobre, a guild painter who worked principally as a pastel merchant (a professional combination of art making and art supplies that was not uncommon for artists outside the Académie). Vernezobre was directly connected with Giroust's teacher, Maurice-Quentin de La Tour, who painted Vernezobre's portrait in the 1760s (Musée Antoine Lécuyer, Saint-Quentin), and he certainly supplied Alexis Loir, whose name appears in a list of outstanding debts (he owed 6 livres, 19 sols, 6 deniers) in an inventory taken after the death of Vernezobre's wife in 1760.[11] That same document also recorded the extent of Vernezobre's stock, including 6,534 pastel sticks of various colors, which were valued at a total of 330 livres, 14 sols, suggesting that on average each stick cost just over 1 sol. A box of pastels supplied by Vernezobre remarkably survives in a private collection (fig. 129), offering an extremely rare encounter with this eighteenth-century artistic medium. Some sticks are still at their original size; others are worn with use or broken to stumps, perhaps for use on their side.

All of them are arranged in compartments to form a loose chromatic spectrum of color families—blues, pinks, browns, yellows, and so on—which both optimized the artist's selection process and protected each stick from the taint of differently colored neighbors.[12] The drawers of Giroust's **color-box** presumably functioned in a similar way (see fig. 128), storing like colors together, while the small tray in her hand is instead a practical improvization for work in progress—like a palette—not for mixing colors, but for gathering those currently in use.[13]

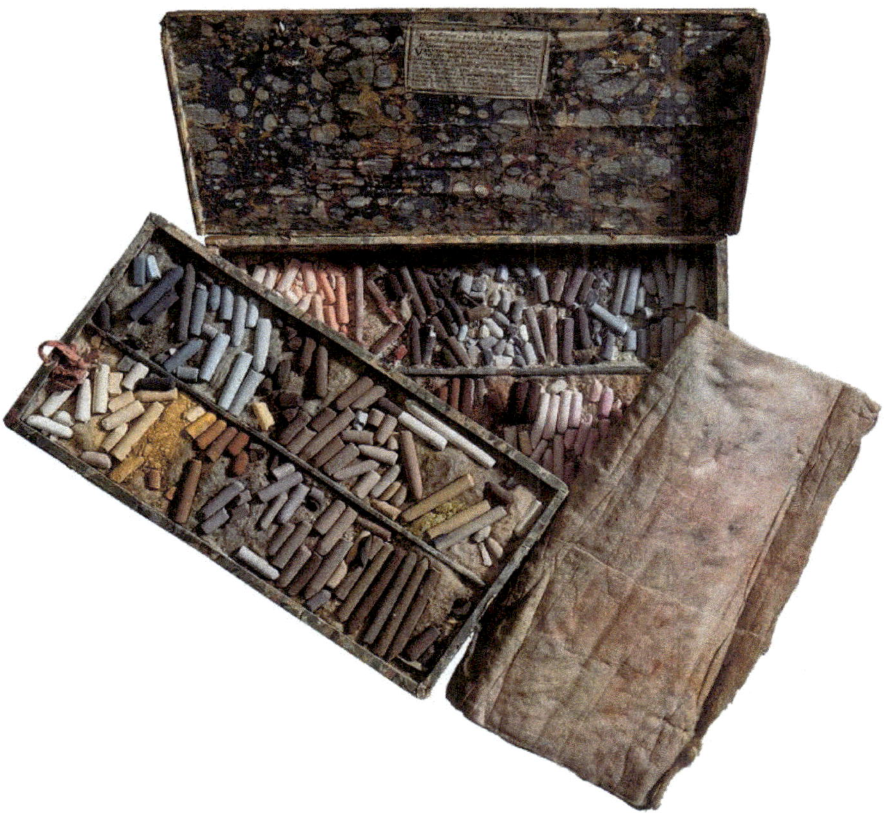

FIG. 129 Wooden box of pastels supplied by Jean-Nicolas Vernezobre in 1772. 6 × 34 × 18.5 cm. Private collection. (© Masson & Ritter, Restaurierungsatelier für Kunst auf Papier, Zürich. Photo: Peter Schälchli, Zurich.)

Another quality of pastel's thingness, evident in the thick, dusty residue lining every compartment of the Vernezobre box, was its extreme friability. Created from ground pigments and extenders, pastels were essentially powder, bound together but constantly threatening to revert to their powdery origins. As soon as the rolled stick was used or handled, it began to disintegrate with every stroke, some of it transferring to the paper's surface, but much of it becoming particles of chalky waste. Aside from the incessant dust, the most pressing problem arising from this fragility was that the artworks themselves were as volatile as the sticks. The images formed through that colored layer left on the paper were so vulnerable that, as Paul-Romain Chaperon noted in his treatise on pastel, with "the least jolt" or "the lightest rub" the whole thing could be gone for good.[14] Efforts to overcome this volatility inspired technological innovation with chemical fixatives (like isinglass or fish glue), which the Académie became keen to support as pastel's wider popularity progressively established the medium in the institutional consciousness.[15] In 1753 the inventor Antoine-Joseph Loriot presented his "secret" for fixing pastel without ruining the work's finish or marring the brilliance of its colors.[16] Though it was acclaimed, Loriot did not publish his secret and in 1772 (two years after Giroust's admission to the Académie) a new method was proposed by a Sardinian painter, Joseph Saint-Michel, which was supposed to make pastels "as solid and as durable as oil paintings."[17] Giroust's husband, Roslin, was one of the academicians given the task of testing Saint-Michel's method for the Académie, and it is difficult to imagine that Giroust (the more proficient pastellist of the couple) was not involved—or at least invested—in that testing process.[18]

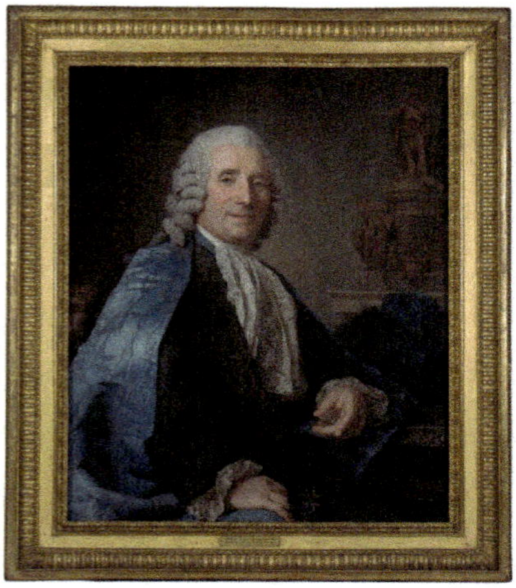

FIG. 130 Marie-Suzanne Giroust (French, 1734–72), *Portrait of Jean-Baptiste Pigalle*, 1770. Pastel on paper, 90 × 73 cm. Paris, Musée du Louvre, Département des Arts Graphiques, INV30860-recto. (© RMN-Grand Palais / photo: Michel Urtado / Art Resource, NY.)

Despite inventive fixing technologies, pastel's fragile materiality did restrict its artistic reach, both in terms of who used it and how. According to Chaperon, the "great" painters tended to avoid it, preferring oil to ensure their works were preserved for "posterity."[19] Rarely deployed for the Académie's prized genre of history painting, pastel instead found its raison d'être in portraiture, the genre in which Giroust excelled.[20] Her stunning portrayal of her sculptor colleague Jean-Baptiste Pigalle (fig. 130) exemplifies the qualities of pastel that Antoine-Joseph Pernéty found so felicitous for portraiture, especially the "velvetiness" created by its powdery dust, which in his opinion made it the best medium for capturing the softness and liveliness of skin and the texture of fabrics.[21] In Giroust's exceptional handling, we encounter those representational possibilities in the lifelike articulation of Pigalle's face, with his pronounced stubble, the glowing capillaries in his cheeks, and the sweaty shine on his forehead contrasting almost viscerally with the dryness of his powdered **wig**. Beyond the fleshtones of his face, Giroust deftly mobilized a limited chromatic range of blues, blacks, whites, and earth tones to differentiate an exquisite array of textures and materials, from the hard bronze of the sculpture behind, to the delicate patterns of his lace cuffs and *jabot*, and the dazzling shimmer of the blue watered silk robe and the tantalizing floaty tactility of his feathered hat. Giroust's exemplary portrait, submitted as her reception piece at the Académie, not only showcases the representational potential of pastel but also reveals the payoff to its material vulnerability. Pastel paintings may be dust held perilously on the paper's surface, but the counter to the medium's fragility was its chromatic longevity. Pigments suspended in oil and covered in layers of varnish could be prone to discolor, fade, or darken over time, but in pastel those same pigments maintained a vibrancy and "éclat" that would pique the envy of any oil painter.[22] ‡

---

1. On the sitters, see Magnus Olausson, "Roslin's Self-Portrait with His Wife Marie Suzanne Giroust Painting a Portrait of Henrik Wilhem Peill," *Art Bulletin of Nationalmuseum Stockholm* 20 (2013): 17–18. An in-depth study of Giroust is being undertaken by Melissa Hyde and is forthcoming under the title Painted by Herself: Marie-Suzanne Giroust, the Forgotten Académicienne.

2. Roslin did practice in pastel but was better known for his oils. For both artists' work in pastel, see Neil Jeffares, *Dictionary of Pastellists before 1800*, http://www.pastellists.com/Articles/RoslinMS.pdf and http://www.pastellists.com/Articles/RoslinA.pdf.

3. Along with pastel, he included oil, fresco, distemper, miniature, enamel, and mosaic. Roger de Piles, *Cours de peinture par principes* (Paris: Jacques Estienne, 1708), 313–14.

4. On pastel supports see Majorie Shelley, "Pastelists at Work: Two Portraits at the Metropolitan Museum by Maurice-Quentin de La Tour and Jean-Baptiste Perronneau," *Metropolitan Museum Journal* 40 (2005): 105.

5. Joyce H. Townsend, "Analysis of Pastel and Chalk Materials," *The Paper Conservator* 22, no. 1 (1998): 21; and Marjorie Shelley, "Joseph Wright's Pastel *Portrait of a Woman*: Part III: Technique and Aesthetics," *Metropolitan Museum Journal* 44 (2009): 113.

6. Robert Dossie, *The Handmaid to the Arts* (London: J. Nourse, 1758), 181–82.

7. On common pigments in pastel making, see Paul-Romain Chaperon, *Traité de la peinture au pastel* (Paris: Defer de Maisonneuve, 1788), 28–29.

8. Dossie, *The Handmaid to the Arts*, 183–84.

9. By contrast, in the 1710s and 1720s, Rosalba Carriera did both. Her correspondence indicates efforts to procure commercial pastels as well as approaches to making her own, including using tailor's chalk and ground **shell**. See the entry on Rosalba in Jeffares, *Dictionary*, http://www.pastellists.com/Articles/Carriera.pdf.

10. Majorie Shelley, "Painting in the Dry Manner: The Flourishing of Pastel in 18th-Century Europe," *Metropolitan Museum of Art Bulletin* 68, no. 4 (Spring 2011): 5–8.

11. Françoise-Marguerite Desbois (wife of Jean-Nicolas Vernezobre), "Inventaire après décès," 11 March 1760, AN, MC/ET/CXXII/711.

12. On storing pastels, see Chaperon, *Traité*, 26.

13. Another instance of a pastellist using a "tray-palette" can be found in Georg-Anton Urlaub's *Self-Portrait* (1735, Würzburg, Lower Franconian Museum).

14. Chaperon, *Traité*, 10.

15. On fixing methods and substances, see Chaperon, *Traité*, 307–29.

16. Entry for 6 October 1753, *PV*, 6:367.

17. Charles-Nicolas Cochin, "Arts utiles et agréables," *Journal encyclopédique* 6, no. 2 (September 1772): 476.

18. Jean-Jacques Bachelier was the other tester: 6 June 1772, *PV*, 8:101. Giroust would die prematurely of breast cancer only a few months later on 31 August 1772.

19. Chaperon, *Traité*, 10–11.

20. Some attempts (often unsuccessful) were made to use pastel for history subjects, such as Jean-Étienne Liotard's *Apollo and Daphne*, 1736 (Rijksmuseum, Amsterdam).

21. Antoine-Joseph Pernéty, *Dictionnaire portatif de peinture, sculpture et gravure* (Paris: Bauche, 1757), cxxviii.

22. This dichotomy of fragility and "éclat" is observed in Claude-Henri Watelet, *L'art de peindre* (Paris: Guérin & Delatour, 1760), 52.

Picture

Nicolas de Largillière (1656–1746)

TYPE OF OBJECT	THEME	MATERIAL
Artwork	Identity, Religion	Metal | Gold/Gilding, Synthetic Materials | Paint/Pigment, Textile | Canvas

Virtually all eighteenth-century artists owned pictures. At his death in 1746, the ninety-year-old portrait painter and director of the Académie, Nicolas de Largillière, owned five hundred.[1] His assemblage of pictures far exceeded that which is accounted for by the stock, **models**, unfinished projects, and wastes of the busy studio. The sale in 1765 of the "cabinet of Monsieur de Largillière" might suggest that he combined painting with collecting, even, perhaps, picture dealing, were it not the case that, of the one hundred and fifty or so works to which attributions can confidently be made, the majority are to the artist himself.[2] They consist of both pictures directly related to his portrait practice, and pictures not. Of the latter, a significant few were decorative, among them *Trompe l'Oeil with a Curtain, a Parrot, and a Cat* (fig. 131), today at the Louvre. It was painted to decorate a specific room and remained in place after Largillière's death at the house built for him ca. 1713–16 at 7 Rue Geoffroy Langevin, and into which he removed with his family in the first year of the Regency.[3] The picture thus asks to be understood in the context of the domestic interior and in relation to the host of things (**armchair**, **bed**, **gaming set**, **lantern**, etc., as well as pictures) by which space was experienced as privately owned, if not private per se. The question is: did this picture distinguish Largillière's house as the house of the artist?

Trompe l'Oeil with a Curtain provides no easy answers. Largillière, as a native of Antwerp, would likely have known and admired the trompe-l'oeil grisailles of antique masterpieces that Rubens recreated on the exterior of his house in that city, to designate it the home of Mercury and Minerva, and he may have aspired similarly to mark his house as a locus of the liberal arts.[4] But as a genre, still life spoke only indirectly to Largillière's professional priorities.[5] The technique of trompe l'oeil was marginal to portraiture and also to all the forms of painting taught at the Académie, notwithstanding the growing interest in optics and optical devices (see **camera obscura**) at the turn of the seventeenth century. *Trompe l'Oeil with a Curtain* was, thus, at one level an incongruous thing. Tellingly, perhaps, it occupied a place in Largillière's house not in or adjacent to the studio but rather in the space dedicated to sociability and private life.

Trompe l'Oeil with a Curtain, along with its two companion wall paintings (now lost) and four overdoors—two depicting fruit and flowers, the other two *Painting* and *Music* (also lost)—invoked an interior that Largillière could not, as a painter, have aspired to own.[6]

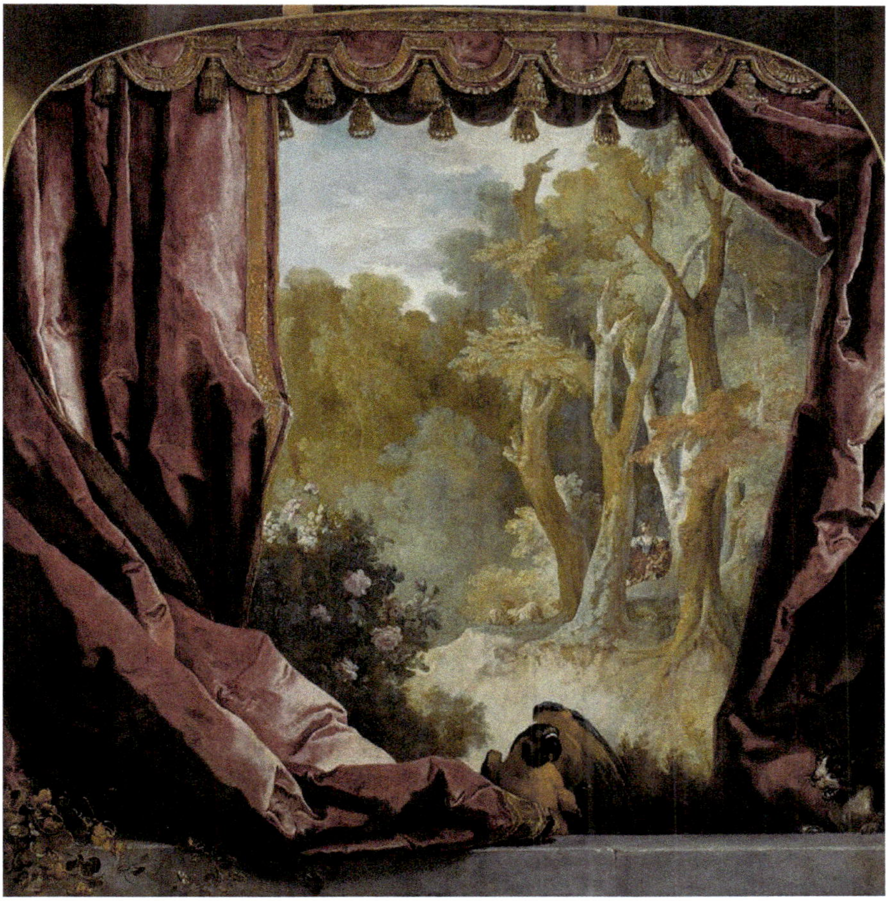

FIG. 131 Nicolas de Largillière (French, 1656–1746), *Trompe l'Oeil with a Curtain, a Parrot, and a Cat*, ca. 1715. Oil on canvas, 261 × 251 cm. Paris, Musée du Louvre, RF1979-59. (© RMN-Grand Palais / photo: Franck Raux / Art Resource, NY.)

His house was built on land giving onto the elite quarter of the Marais but actually trapped in the densely parceled urban tissue of the commercial and largely working-class neighborhood of Les Halles.[7] Admittance from the street was via a porte cochère (carriage entrance), but the house was L shaped—not U shaped, as befitted an *hôtel* so grandly announced from the street.[8] The main living space was distributed on the second floor; the first and best floor was rented out. This second floor consisted of two apartments: one in front, along the street, and the other leading back from the road at a forty-five-degree angle, flanking the courtyard.

Trompe l'Oeil with a Curtain was set into the paneling of a room belonging to this second apartment. It decorated the middle room in an enfilade of three, preceded by an antechamber and followed by Largillière's bedroom. To reach it the visitor would have had to have entered from the street, traversed the courtyard, mounted the stairs, crossed the sparsely furnished antechamber with its lone piece of furniture, a kneehole desk that advertised the room's purpose for business, before reaching the decorated room. The surprise must have been considerable at then finding oneself on the threshold of enchantment: that of gracious and leisured piano nobile living cultivated at *maisons de plaisance* in the capital's environs.[9] The manifest contradiction between the picture's airy and open fictional vista and the cramped and obscure urban reality upon which the actual windows, curtained in plain white cotton, looked out, could only have amplified the experience of giddy, almost comedic disorientation created by the mingle and contrast of different levels of representation in the pictures. In our painting, folds of madder-red curtain and tumbles of nasturtium reach across the frame to claim existence in our third dimension, and the rustic idyll recedes from it, like a picture within a picture, its framing doubled and contradicted within the picture by the illusion of the parapet. As a device, trompe l'oeil oversteps the conventional function of the picture frame; in this picture it does so in both directions.

The "why?" of *Trompe l'Oeil with a Curtain* seems obvious: to hijack by force of illusion the aristocratic discourse on the pastoral, and the associated ornaments of a noble rank to which Largillière was excluded by birth, though not by fortune.[10] He had himself once painted a nearly identical trompe l'oeil at the country estate for one of his exalted patrons.[11] This appropriation of genre and fictional things was seemingly multiplied in the overdoors, notably in *Music*, in which Largillière extended luxury's scope from gold-trimmed curtains and richly tasseled lambrequin, to elaborately chased gold and silver vessels, blue-and-white Chinese porcelain, gold-tooled leather-bound books, and a string of pearls. Known from a studio copy (fig. 132), these things push forward in the painting and overwhelm the violin that gives the picture its ostensible emblematic meaning. They are painted, moreover, with an attention to texture and shine that belies the symbolic and bespeaks care and pride in possession.

During Louis XIV's reign, nonnobles were prevented from buying many such luxury items not only by cost but by sumptuary law, which in March 1700 proscribed, for instance, the production and consumption of gold and silver vessels.[12] In April that year, and when living in the Rue Saint-Avoye, Largillière had had to surrender those of his things that contravened the act.[13] They included a **harpsichord** on a gilded stand, two marquetry pedestals (*guéridons*) with gilded ornament, a marble-topped table on a gilt console, four armchairs, six chairs and four stools, all with frames of gilded wood, and an assortment of hearth furniture with gilt-bronze handles and ornaments. In the wake of this experience, and notwithstanding the eventual return of at least some of his costly furniture, Largillière appears to have chosen for the new Rue Geoffroy Langevin house decoration that, with the exception of the pictures, was comparatively plain and sober.[14] Rooms were either simply paneled or dressed in plain fabrics (green and red damask, or yellow satin). The furniture was mainly ungilded. Ormolu was absent from the fire irons. Only the frames of the mirrors and easel paintings were edged with gold, a license admitted by the 1700 edict.[15] By recourse to trompe l'oeil, Largillière apparently enjoyed that which he was denied by law.

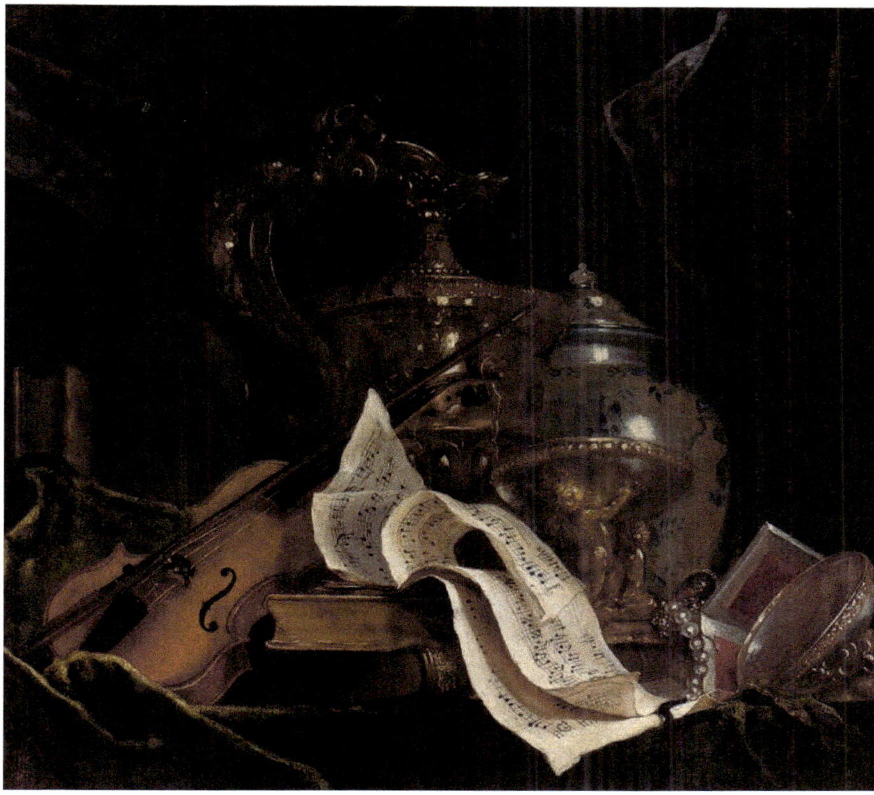

FIG. 132 Nicolas de Largillière (French, 1656–1746), *Still Life with a Violin*, ca. 1715. Oil on canvas, 79 × 87.3 cm. Quimper, Musée des Beaux-Arts, Inv873-1-169. (© RMN-Grand Palais / photo: Mathieu Rabeau / Art Resource, NY.)

However, to classify trompe l'oeil painting with other imitations (mock marble, simulated wood, or the faux gilt-leather wallpaper decorating Largillière's dining room), stuffs that were produced in volume and shaped into "populuxe" goods by the decorative trades for the bourgeois consumer, is to miss an important distinction between these various forms of illusion.[16] Where ersatz luxury goods depended for their success on so-called secret arts and on absolute deception for the consumer's satisfaction, the claim of Largillière's painted curtain that it is Venice velvet trimmed with gold, and that it will shut, is an open lie. The viewer's pleasure is one of surprise when the spell shatters and the image is beheld as exactly that: an illusion or artifice.[17] Thought, quickened by the eye's surprise that what it sees is a flat surface, asks how the painter transformed inert, gross matter, or the substance of painting, into this lively picture of the world.[18] The impossibility of possessing the picture intellectually though having it materially within touch cast a "halo effect" around the work.[19] The exchange between picture and beholder is phenomenological. The undeceived viewer saw not the referent, and nobility honored by gleam of gold, but painting, and the artist's parade of his own skill.

Trompe l'oeil has a long, storied history in the life of the artist, beginning with Zeuxis's grapes, so lifelike that birds attempted to eat them.[20] Largillière may have hoped that the *amateurs* who, according to Germain Brice, beat a path to his door to admire his works, saw echoed in his trompe l'oeil Parhassius's famous curtain, so seductively real that Zeuxis was said to have lifted his hand to draw it away from the picture "behind."[21] The left-lit pastoral scene revealed beyond Largillière's curtain appears formally and thematically detached from the right-lit drapes and the balustrade of the extravagant interior "before," so much so that it does invite analogy with the ancient Greek painter's devise of the picture-within-a-picture. In the odes and obituaries published after his death, Largillière was praised for his singular ability to capture a likeness—in one elegy, the gods vie to inherit his tools[22]—but the trompe-l'oeil decorations at his house attracted no sustained comment in the art literature of the time. Nothing to make us think that the trompe l'oeil of the picture succeeded in marking the house as the house of an artist.

In Antoine-Joseph Dézallier d'Argenville's life of Largillière, the decorated room helps define the house as "beautiful," or a place where beauty abides, but both d'Argenville and Pierre-Jean Mariette were more profoundly struck by the quantity and quality of the artist's religious painting (fig. 133).[23] Mariette noted that Largillière had "left his heirs" twelve paintings depicting scenes from the lives of Christ and the Virgin, of which a set of four depicting moments from the Passion warranted "particular attention" by their considerable size, complexity, and "surprising effects." He singled them out as evidence of the "fecundity" of Largillière's "genius"; they were proof of his "universal talent."[24] To the extent that Mariette and Dézallier d'Argenville measured Largillière's achievements, they did so with reference, it would seem, to the hierarchy of genres rather than the ancien régime's order of estates; they located nobility in history painting, not in the elite's taste for decorative painting.

The performance of identity through and with things real and depicted was risky. There was a special risk in the gesture of trompe l'oeil. It depends on the readiness of the beholder to overlook contradictory contextual evidence, to stand still and transfixed and be willingly deceived. Largillière doubled that risk when he yoked his apparent desire for status and luxury to his self-reflexive performance of imitation, because the artistry of trompe l'oeil rests ultimately on knowing and valuing the gap between reality and illusion, between legitimate status and a play with—or is it for?—it. For the trompe-l'oeil project to succeed, other observers have to be enrolled in its performance and be persuaded that the illusion of luxe is equal to, if not better than, the stuff of status itself.

What of the religious pictures that weighed so heavily with Mariette and Dézallier d'Argenville? The random hang of the works at Rue Geoffroy Langevin, not in sets as Mariette implied but mixed in with other things and genres, undermines reading them as alternative reputational things. It might be more productive to think of them as counterweights to the materiality of the furnishings, and counter values. Like the decorative paintings, Largillière's religious works were, with few exceptions, painted for himself and not for public exhibition or for sale. But unlike the decorative works, his devotional painting had no fixed purpose or setting. His practice in religious painting was,

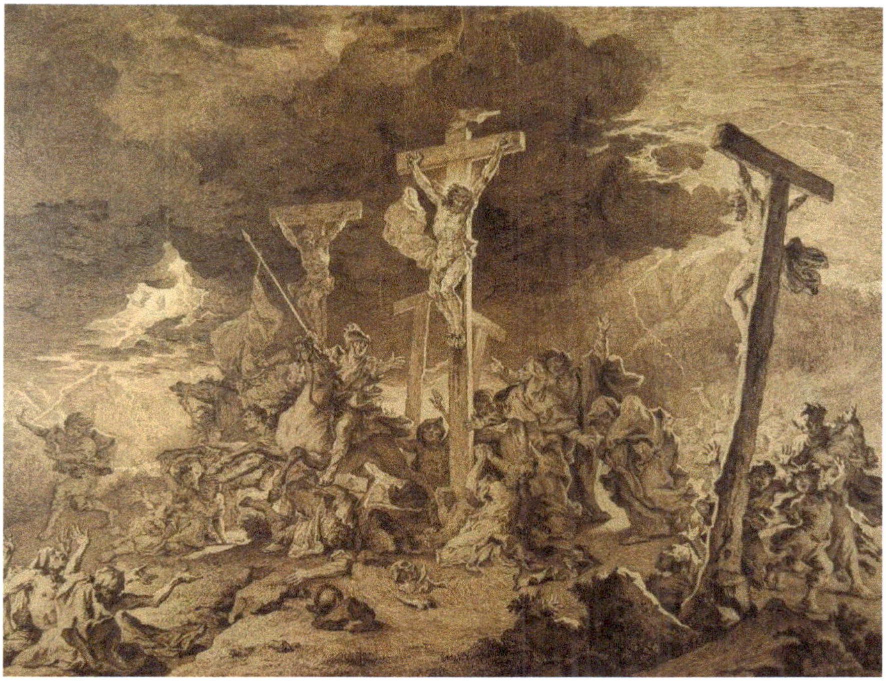

FIG. 133 François Roettiers (Flemish, 1685–1742), after Nicolas de Largillière (French, 1656–1746), *Crucifixion*, ca. 1719. Black chalk. Nouveau Musée National de Monaco, n° 1984.13. (Photo : NMNM / Marcel Loli.)

apparently, open and ongoing. Myra Rosenfeld dates *Christ's Entry into Jerusalem* at the Louvre, one of Largillière's earliest devotional works, to circa 1690.[25] It was a picture he brought with him to his new house, not one he painted for it. The Louvre's *Moses in the Bulrushes* is signed and dated 1728 and is among his last.[26] Largillière was, in short, busy with religious painting over thirty years or more. To paint such works was for him not a circumstantial interlude but a repetitive, meditative exercise whose makings hung in rooms throughout his house. Both the practice and the products of his devotional work were always on his horizon, not in the background, that is, not decoration. The social discourse of devotion preached reduction of the self, contra market culture's ideology of infinite extension and upward trajectory. The geometry of devotional work was one of point, not plane, and required focus on the self within the frame chosen by God: "humility does not take up much space."[27]

Trompe l'Oeil with a Curtain and the *Crucifixion* (see figs. 131, 133), painted at around the same time, seem to propose contradictory versions of the artist.[28] On the one hand: the would-be gentleman and aristocrat, recognized for the talent of his handiwork whose illusions bested nature's best and the finest weaver's and goldsmith's work. On the other: the devout and self-effacing painter whose representations of the Passion were, according to Pellegrino Antonio Orlandi, "lifelike"—that is, vibrant not surprising; vibrant in the telling of their stories, not in their illusionism. The life force of the *Crucifixion* derives, according to Orlandi, from the handling of light, which illuminates the scene such that the expressive reaction to Christ's "*consummatum est*" is easily read in the ghastly gloom.[29] The sacred subject engrosses all the image's pictorial effects; none is left to draw attention to the author or to art in the narrowly material and technical sense of trompe l'oeil. The possibility remains, however, that decoration and icon made greater sense together, that the fantasy of bourgeois illusions in the inner space of the anteroom was framed by an outer ideal of Christian virtue filling the house. Such a reading suggests that Largillière's house in the early eighteenth century was a theatrical and semipublic space in which he created illusions in order to prick them, blew bubbles to watch them burst. §

---

1. Georges de Lastic, "Nicolas de Largillière: Documents notariés inédits," *GBA* 98 (1981): 7, 23–27.

2. See *Catalogue de tableaux, estampes, desseins, bronzes, figures de marbre . . . provenant du cabinet de M. de Largillière* (Paris: Merigot, 1765).

3. On the provenance of the picture, see *Largillière (1656–1746)*, exh. cat. (Paris: Musée Jacquemart-André, 2003), no. 7. On the house, built on the site of a former tennis court, see Michel and Fabrice Faré, *La vie silencieuse en France: La nature morte au XVIIIe siècle* (Fribourg: Office du Livre, 1976), 58–60. From a *constitution de rente* between the Largillière and François Chaban-Delafosse we know that the Largillière family was living at the house by February 1716. See Mireille Rambaud, *Documents du Minutier central concernant l'histoire de l'art (1700–1750)* (Paris: Imprimerie Nationale, 1964–71), 1:179.

4. On Rubens's house in Antwerp, see Elizabeth MacGrath, "The Painted Decoration of Rubens's House," *Journal of the Warburg and Courtauld Institutes* 41 (1978): 245–72. Largillière, the son of French parents, grew up in Antwerp and received his early training there. At eighteen he left the city, arriving in Paris for the first time in 1679 and settling there in 1686.

5. On his still-life practice, see Faré and Faré, *La vie silencieuse*, 48–62; and Pontus Grate, "Largillière et les natures mortes de Grenoble," *Revue du Louvre* 11 (1961): 23–30.

6. For the valuers' summary descriptions of the lost paintings, see de Lastic, "Largillière," 17 (no. 13), 25 (nos. 59, 60).

7. Anne Lombard-Jourdan, *Les Halles de Paris et leur quartier (1137–1969)* (Geneva: Droz, 2009), 83–111.

8. Largillière did not own a carriage but his sitters did, hence the need for a porte cochère and a forecourt.

9. See Charles Le Brun's Gobelins tapestry series, the *Maisons royales* (1668), with which Largillière's composition bears comparison.

10. On Largillière's fortune, see Pierre-Jean Mariette, *Abecedario*, ed. Antoine de Montaiglon (Paris: Dumoulin, 1853–62), 3:61, 62; and de Lastic, "Largillière," 4, 12–14.

11. See Antoine-Joseph Dézallier d'Argenville, *Abrégé de la vie des plus fameux peintres*, 2nd ed. (Paris: De Bure, 1762), 4:300–301.

12. *Edit du Roy pour retrenchement du luxe des meubles, habits, vaisselle, équipages et bâtiments*, March 1700; see Nicolas de La Mare, *Traité de police* (Paris: Brunet, 1705–38), 1:419–22.

13. AN, Y3583 (17 April 1700), in Emile Compardon in *NAAF*, 1874–75, 223–24. See also *Largilliere*, 42. Among other artists to face similar charges were Jacques Van Schuppen (Largillière's pupil) and Jacques Oudry (father of another). See "Catalogue des noms et demeures de ceux qui ont faits leurs déclarations en execution de l'Édit de Sa Majesté du mois de mars 1700," BnF, Ms. f.f. 21627.

14. They are identifiable from his estate inventory. See de Lastic, "Largillière," 15–18.

15. La Mare, *Traité de police*, 1:422.

16. See Reed Benhamou, "Imitation in the Decorative Arts of the Eighteenth Century," *Journal of Design History* 4, no. 1 (1991): 1–13; and Cissie Fairchilds, "The Production and Marketing of Populuxe Goods in Eighteenth-Century Paris," in *Consumption and the World of Goods*, ed. John Brewer and Roy Porter (London: Routledge, 1994), 228–48.

17. On the aesthetics of surprise, see Roger de Piles, *Cours de peinture* [1709] (Paris: Gallimard, 1989), 7–19, esp. 8, 11, 14.

18. For a firsthand account of the experience of trompe l'oeil, see Charles de Brosses, *Lettres d'Italie*, 2 vols. (Var: Editions d'Aujourd'hui, 1976), 1:15–16.

19. The phrase "halo effect" is Alfred Gell's. See Gell, "The Enchantment of Technology and the Technology of Enchantment," in *The Art of Anthropology: Essays and Diagrams* (London: Athlone, 1999), 159–86.

20. Largillière's still lifes include the trompe l'oeil *Two Bunches of Grapes*, signed (1677, Paris, Fondation Custodia).

21. Germain Brice, *Nouvelle description de la ville de Paris* (Paris: Gandouin, 1725), 2:68–69.

22. "Ode en strophes libres à Titon du Tillet sur la mort de M. de l'Argillière [*sic*] chancellier et ancien directeur de l'Académie," in *Mercure de France*, May 1746, 134.

23. Dézallier d'Argenville, *Abrégé*, 302.

24. Mariette, *Abecedario*, 3:62.

25. In *Largillière and the Eighteenth-Century Portrait*, exh. cat. (Montreal: Museum of Fine Arts, 1981), 56–59.

26. See Françoise Maison and Pierre Rosenberg, "Largillière, peintre d'histoire et paysagist," *Revue du Louvre* 23, no. 2 (1973): 89–94; and Myra Rosenfeld, "La culture de Largillière," *Revue de l'art* 98 (1992): 48–49.

27. Jean Puget de La Serre, *La vie heureuse, ou l'homme content* (Paris: 1709), 119.

28. The painting is lost.

29. Pierre Rosenberg, "Un nouveau tableau à sujet religieux de Nicolas de Largillière," *Revue du Louvre* 39, no 4 (1989): 245–48.

Porte-Crayon

Jean-Baptiste Perronneau (ca. 1715–83)

TYPE OF OBJECT	THEME	MATERIAL
Companion, Tool	Identity, Studio	Animal | Leather/Parchment, Metal | Silver, Mineral | Chalk

On 9 April 1767, the following ad appeared in the French newspaper *Annonces, affiches et avis divers*: "Lost on the 25th March between the Stock Exchange and Château Trompette, *an emerald shagreen-covered* CASE [ÉTUI] *containing a pair of compasses, a porte-crayon and a set-square in silver, on which is inscribed "by Butterfield."* The person who finds it is begged to return it to the hand of M. Perronneau, Peintre du Roi, Place du Marché Royal, at M. Lagarde's. . . . [The finder] will receive a reward of 12 livres."[1] Never, arguably, had the *porte-crayon* (chalk holder) been more present to Perronneau than in its absence and more consciously tangible than in this moment of loss.[2] Though translated above idiomatically as "to the hand of M. Perronneau," literally, he begged for its return to "his grasp," that he might hold it again. Perronneau, a Paris portrait painter in **pastel** and in oil, was on a working tour to Bordeaux when his pencil case went missing. It was not his first trip to this thriving inland Atlantic city and port on the river Garonne in the southwestern province of Guyenne and Gascony. The port was second only to Nantes in the volume and importance of its trade in sugar, tobacco, and slaves with Saint-Domingue (present-day Haiti). The city had grown rapidly in the early eighteenth century, and the neighborhood between the medieval castle Trompette and Ange-Jacques Gabriel's new Stock Exchange, where Perronneau lost his pencil case, was fashionable and home to the mansions of the city's premier merchants. On the other side of the Exchange was the Place du Marché Royale, where Perronneau lodged; built in 1760, it was the focus of the similarly well-to-do *quartier* Saint-Pierre. The prosperity and salubriousness of the city notwithstanding, Perronneau was nevertheless perhaps more vulnerable to misadventure away from home, and certainly more sensitive to the pain of it.

Although highly conventionalized forms of writing, lost-property ads are nevertheless first-person narratives. In this sense, they resemble the personal avowals of possession found in letters, **journals**, and holograph **wills**, rather than public statements of ownership made by notaries and dealers in inventories and sale catalogs. However, in contrast to Charles-Nicolas Cochin's invocation of the ideal **handkerchief** in his letters to a friend, Perronneau's description is *d'après nature*, an immediate, detailed account of the salient features of that which was and was already his. Unlike Jean-Baptiste Massé's **will**, it frames his thing in a narrative of dispossession rather than voluntary separation or giving. He tells where and when he lost it but reveals nothing of the object's biography and how the *porte-crayon* came to be his. A paradoxical genre, the lost-property ad combines anguished expression of displaced ownership with objective description of surface appearance. To reconnect the two, we first need to know more about this thing before, in a second move, reconstructing its value via the text's discourse of possession and the particular circumstances of Perronneau's life.

According to Patrick Rocca and Françoise Launay, silver drawing instruments were relatively rare. They are recorded in only 1 to 5 percent of probate inventories in the period between 1680 and 1780, the golden age of silver drawing sets.[3] Brass was standard for such things.[4] The form of the *porte-crayon*, however, did not vary significantly with the material. It consisted of a hollow cylinder with two rings. The cylinder was slit at either end in order to render it sufficiently flexible to receive the sticks of chalk inserted into it. These were held tightly in place by the grip of the rings, once slid down over the cylinder and chalk.[5] The only observable difference between silver and brass *porte-crayons* was that silver ones tend to be smaller and were generally fashioned to hold chalk at one end only.[6] The precious metal added nothing to the functionality of the tool.[7]

Inherently valuable, Perronneau's set was also expertly made. "Butterfield" was Michael Butterfield, an Englishman who had moved to Paris in the mid-1660s to become, according to Anthony Turner, one of the most important scientific instrument makers in Paris in the last quarter of the seventeenth century.[8] Inventor of the so-called Butterfield dial (a pocket sun dial) and supplier of astronomical instruments to the Royal Observatory, drawing instruments were the bread-and-butter business of his workshop (fig. 134).[9] Since Butterfield died in 1724, Perronneau must have acquired his instruments second-hand.[10] By contrast, the case in which he kept them was very likely new. Shagreen, or fish leather, scraped and dyed to reveal its characteristically dotted dermal pattern, only became fashionable in the 1750s, when developed and marketed by the Paris glover Jean-Claude Galluchat.[11] Shagreen was pretty but valued also for its practicality. Tougher than animal leather and waterproof, it provided an ideal outer skin for containers of all kinds. Perronneau's green speckled case may have been stock, but it was more likely bespoke because his instruments were few and the set incomplete; even the smallest sets included a ruler.[12] In sum, though drawing sets were standardized commodities by the end of the seventeenth century, there was little that was standard about Perronneau's.

The painter put a price on its return. What did 12 livres represent? Not the cost of replacement, to judge by the silver drawing sets made and sold by the Paris instrument maker Jacques Canivet on the Quai de l'École. The stock inventoried at his death in 1773 included sets of silver drawing instruments valued at half the price of Perronneau's reward.[13] Not its exchange value either, since used goods generally sold for less than new.[14] What 12 livres represented had less to do with the market than with the material form of the currency. Rewards were paid in cash, and values were therefore determined by the denominations of coin. Twelve livres represented the account value of a demi-louis, the smallest of the gold coins in circulation in the eighteenth century. According to the *Affiches*, it potentially bought back pocketbooks, seals, walking sticks, and handbags.[15] If

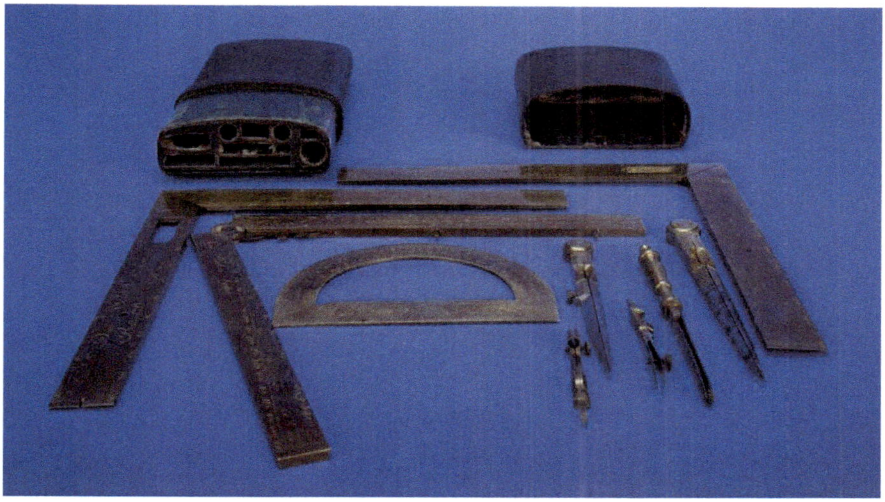

FIG. 134 Michael Butterfield, *Porte-crayon* and other drawing instruments with their case, ca. 1700. Brass instruments and leather case. Washington, Division of Medicine and Science, National Museum of American History, Smithsonian Institution.

the reward appears roughly commensurate with the value of things lost, it is, however, an illusion because, as Jonathan Lamb points out, "reward" is by definition excessive.[16] Loss does not alienate property, and buying it back is a legal and commercial nonsense since ownership is not transferred. The value of the reward Perronneau promised the one who returned his pencil case thus indexed not its exchange value but the feelings he had for his drawing instruments, their sentimental value, and the desire he had for their restoration that he might enjoy holding them once again.

That Perronneau treasured his *porte-crayon* might seem surprising. He was not an artist reputed as a draftsman. Few autonomous drawings by his hand survive, and unlike his rival, Maurice-Quentin de La Tour, he does not appear routinely to have made preparatory drawings for his **pastel** portraits.[17] Rather, he did the preliminary line work for his pastels directly on the support. Sketched lines mapping the relative positions of Olivier Journu's temple, hairline, and chin are just discernible under infrared light in the 1756 portrait (fig. 135) of this sugar and slave trader, which Perronneau had painted on an earlier visit to Bordeaux.[18] Merchant families in the sugar business feature prominently in Perronneau's patronage circle, the Journu among others.[19] The painter may have used his *porte-crayon* on Journu, but the lines of underdrawing are broad, their application seemingly rapid and sweeping, consistent with chalk gripped, like sticks of **pastel**, directly between the fingers rather than mediated by a holder.

The pencil case and loss of it in the street suggest that the *porte-crayon* was for drawing *en pleine société* (to adapt the phrase *en plein air*), not in the studio. It was, in this sense, part of the paraphernalia of sociability and social representation that made up the bulk of the lost property that owners sought to entice home by reward: medals, pocket **watches**, fancy bags, and **snuffboxes**.[20] A rare portrait drawing by Perronneau of the Dutch collector Louis Metayer Phzn (fig. 136), dated circa 1767–68, at the time the painter visited Amsterdam, represents the kind of refined and detailed portrait drawing that Charles-Nicolas Cochin had made fashionable as a social pastime among friends at Mme Geoffrin's salon in the 1750s.[21] The control and refinement of the lines indicate that the *porte-crayon* has been active. Attentiveness and delicacy, attributes of Perronneau's graphic gesture, found their correlates in polite social intercourse, thereby commending drawing as a polite art.

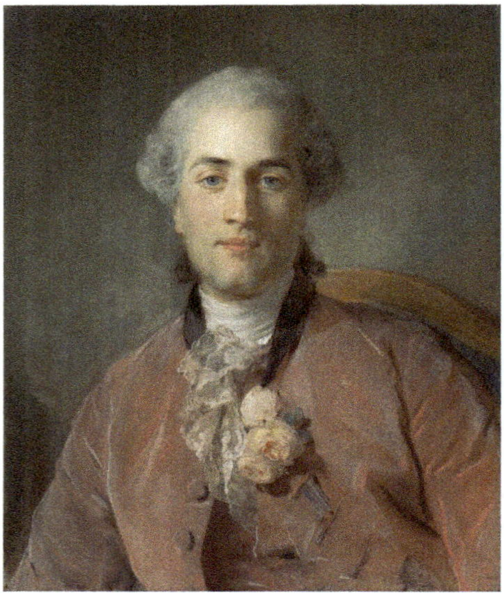

FIG. 135 Jean-Baptiste Perronneau (French, ca. 1715–83), *Olivier Journu*, 1756. Pastel on blue-gray laid paper, laid down on canvas, 58.1 × 47 cm. New York, Metropolitan Museum of Art, Wrightsman Fund, 2003 (2003.26). (Image copyright © The Metropolitan Museum of Art. Image source: Art Resource, NY.)

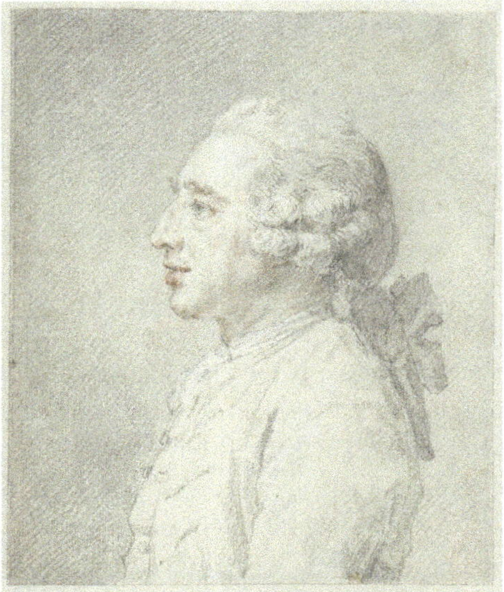

FIG. 136 Jean-Baptiste Perronneau (French, ca. 1715–83), *Louis Metayer Phzn*, ca. 1767–68. Trois crayons and graphite on paper, 23.2 × 19 cm. Amsterdam, Rijksmuseum. On loan from the Koninklijk Oudheidkundig Genootschap.

Where does that leave the *porte-crayon*? Answer: as only indirectly the subject of this inquiry? Its thingly claims to our attention having been drowned out by the voice of the subject? Reducing the *porte-crayon* to the status of object sign of Perronneau's artistic ego does not, however, account fully for the painter's distress at losing it. Steven Fowles has noted that things obtrude in consciousness not only when they break or malfunction but also when they disappear.[22] Lost things prey on our minds. They have material effects, leaving painful holes in our selves.[23] The announcement to the world in the newspaper of the depleted subject, self minus thing, was a cry for restoration of not only lost property but also the unity of self. If Perronneau selected chalk only occasionally as a medium for his art, he more regularly seems to have signed his pastels using graphite, very possibly manipulated into elegant cursive lines by his silver *porte-crayon*.[24] The artist Perronneau minus *porte-crayon* was, in his mind, and perhaps in the opinion of others, not just an artist with an incomplete tool set but, simply and more significantly, not quite an artist at all.[25] §

1. *Annonces, affiches et avis divers,* 9 April 1767, 58. Quoted from Francesca Whitlum-Cooper, "Itinerant Pastellists: Circuits of Movement in Eighteenth-Century Europe," PhD diss., Courtauld Institute of Art (London, 2015), 230.

2. On the paradoxical dependence of immateriality on materiality for its expression, see Daniel Miller, "Materiality: An Introduction," in *Materiality*, ed. Daniel Miller (Durham, NC: Duke University Press, 2005), 20–29.

3. Patrick Rocca and Françoise Launay, "La dynastie Langlois-Lordelle-Canivet-Lennel, 'fabricateurs' d'instruments de mathématiques à Paris au XVIIIe siècle," *Artefact: Techniques, histoire et sciences sociales* 7 (2018): 151–86. See also Patrick Rocca, "French Silver Drawing Instruments," *Bulletin of the Scientific Instrument Society* 114 (2012): 30–38.

4. See "Porte-crayon," *Encyclopédie*, http://encyclopedie.uchicago.edu/, 13:139.

5. Plate I, fig. 1, "Dessein," *Encyclopédie*, http://encyclopedie.uchicago.edu/, 20:21:1, see fig. 93, above. In Perronneau's portraits of artists holding *porte-crayons*, for example, his portraits of Laurent Cars (1759, Paris, Musée du Louvre), and Charles-Nicolas Cochin (1759, Louisville, KY, Speed Art Museum), the chalk holders are invariably brass ones, although Cochin certainly also owned a silver one.

6. "Porte-crayon," *Encyclopédie*, http://encyclopedie.uchicago.edu/, 13:139.

7. Alain Manesson noted that in the case of a ruler, silver was a positive disadvantage because it tarnished and marked the paper on which one was drawing a line. Manesson, *La géométrie pratique, divisée en quatre livres* (Paris: Anisson, 1702), 1:152.

8. Anthony Turner, "Mathematical Instrument-Making in Early Modern Paris," in *Luxury Trades and Consumerism in Ancien Régime Paris*, ed. Robert Fox and Anthony Turner (London: Routledge, 1998), 79.

9. See Mike Cowhan, "The Butterfield Dial," *Bulletin of the Scientific Instrument Society*, 113 (2017): 25–28. The sculptor Edme Bouchardon owned a Butterfield dial in a shagreen case.

10. On the second-hand market in Paris, see Natacha Coquery, "The Social Circulation of Luxury and Second-hand Goods in Eighteenth-Century Parisian Shops," in *The Afterlife of Used Things*, ed. Ariane Fennetaux, Amélie Junqua, and Sophie Vasset (London: Routledge, 2015), 13–24.

11. See Christine Gut, "Towards a Global History of Shagreen," in *The Global Lives of Things*, ed. Anne Gerritsen and Giorgio Riello (London: Routledge, 2016), 62–80.

12. According to Manesson, a drawing set comprised a pair of compasses, a *porte-crayon*, a ruler, a setsquare, and a protractor. See Manesson, *La géométrie pratique*, 1:152.

13. See Rocca and Launay, "La dynastie Langlois-Lordelle-Canivet-Lennel," appendix 2, "Inventaire après décès de Jacques Canivet," item 316, also items 302, 303, 317, 318.

14. See Laurence Fontaine, "The Exchange of Second-hand Goods: Between Survival Strategies and 'Business' in Eighteenth-Century Paris," in *Alternative Exchanges: Second-hand Circulation from the Sixteenth Century to the Present* (Oxford: Berghahn, 2008), 97–114.

15. *Annonces, affiches et avis divers*: "Porte-feuille," 14 January 1765, 30; "Cachet de crystal," 21 January 1765, 59; "Sac," 31 January 1765, 83; and "Canne," 17 March 1766, 211.

16. Jonathan Lamb, "The Crying of Lost Things," *English Literary History* 71, no. 4 (2004): 949–67.

17. See Marjorie Shelley, "Pastelists at Work: Two Portraits at the Metropolitan Museum of Art by Maurice-Quentin de La Tour and Jean-Baptiste Perronneau," *Metropolitan Museum of Art Journal* 40 (2005): 105–17.

18. Shelley, "Pastelists at Work," 110. On Perronneau's portrait of the Journu family, see Neil Jeffares, "The Pastels of the Journu family by Perronneau," http://www.pastellists.com/Essays/Perronneau_Journu.pdf.

19. Aignan Thomas Desfriches, another patron, was in the sugar refinery business at Orléans. See Patrick Villiers, "Quelques exemples d'influence du commerce atlantiques à Orléans au XVIIIe siècle," in *Villes atlantiques dans l'Europe occidentale du Moyen Âge au XXe siècle*, ed. Guy Saupin (Rennes: Presses Universitaires de Rennes, 2006), 89–100.

20. The drawing set in a shagreen case lost in the pit of the Comédie Française and the gold crayon holder in a Galluchat case found in the Tuilleries gardens were almost certainly the paraphernalia of amateurs, not professional artists. See *Annonces, affiches et avis divers*, 7 February 1765, 99; and 13 June 1766, 539.

21. On the Portrait of Metayer, see *De Watteau à Ingres: Dessins français du XVIIIe siècle du Rijksmuseum Amsterdam*, exh. cat. (Paris: Fondation Custodia, 2003), no. 73. On Cochin's portraits and Mme Geoffrin's salon, see Christian Michel, *Charles-Nicolas Cochin et l'art des lumières* (Rome: École Française de Rome, 1993), 121–22, 172.

22. Steven Fowles, "People without Things," in *An Anthropology of Absence: Materializations of Transcendence and Loss*, ed. Mikkel Bille, Frida Hastrup, and Tom Sørensen (New York: Springer, 2010), 23–41.

23. See Lamb, "The Crying of Lost Things."

24. See Perronneau's signatures on his portraits of Mme Antoine Molles and Jean Jourdan, Maisonneuve painted during his 1756–57 trip to Bordeaux and reproduced by Neil Jeffares in "Two Pastels."

25. See Fowles, "People without Things."

Quill

Étienne-Maurice Falconet (1716–91)

TYPE OF OBJECT	THEME	MATERIAL
Commodity, Tool	Friendship, Identity	Animal | Feather, Synthetic Materials | Ink, Synthetic Materials | Paper

The goose, observed Georges Louis Leclerc, comte de Buffon, in his *Histoire naturelle* (1749–88), is unjustly overshadowed by the swan; not only does she provide meat, she also affords "the delicate duvet feather on which idleness likes to repose, and that other flight feather, quill of our thoughts, with which," he added, "I here write her eulogy."[1] To put figures on the goose's utility: in March and September she molts a maximum of ten feathers fit for quills.[2] In the eighteenth century, the best such feathers were imported from the Netherlands at 16 sous per thousand and 8 sous per hundred.[3] Guyenne, Normandy, and the environs of Nevers supplied the rest of the capital's less exacting middle market.[4] Customers bought their quills from stationers, individually and in packets, rough or dressed, cut or uncut.[5]

If, as Buffon suggests, farmyard familiarity had bread contempt of the bird, the ubiquity of her non-singularized quills may explain blindness to pens in the historical record of artists' things. ***Porte-crayons*** were routinely itemized in postmortem inventories; quills, however, were not, though they were common enough instruments for drawing, and essential implements for writing.[6] Oppenord's penwork on his copy of Cesare Ripa's *Iconologie* (**book**) combines the two practices: lines of letters share the page with figures and ornament.[7] Penmanship is responsible also for other things indexed in this book: the **journal** and the **order book**, and legal documents such as the **marriage contract** and the **will**. Moreover, data on **handkerchiefs** and **swords** and more generally about timekeeping and memory, taste, and shopping habits, social ties and legal claims, were secured by the formal practices of writing.[8]

Why chose the sculptor Étienne-Maurice Falconet's quill out of all the thousands of lost pens that once belonged to eighteenth-century artists? Because Falconet, unlike Wille (**journal**), Lagrenée (**order book**) and Massé (**will**), was one of the few eighteenth-century artists, other than the secretaries and historiographers of the Académie, to take up the pen self-consciously.[9] On 27 March 1772 he sent Voltaire a copy of his translation of books 34, 35, and 36 of Pliny's *Natural History* (77–ca. 79).[10] "If you find my work absolutely awful, have the goodness to tell me," he begged in the accompanying note, "and I will throw my pen on the fire; I don't, however, promise to do the same with my chisel."[11] Writing was more than a technology to Falconet; pen and ink, more than a medium. His letters suggest that for him the pen was an alluring object. Its qualities, unlike the chisel's, were out of reach.

Falconet started writing around 1760. The lecture on sculpture he gave at the Académie in June 1760 was published as a pamphlet the following year.[12] Five years later, in December 1765, it was republished in edited form as articles in the *Encyclopédie*, cementing both Falconet's membership of the *philosophes*' clan and his friendship with Denis Diderot.[13] In the same month, Falconet and Diderot began an exchange of philosophical letters on the subject of posterity.[14] Louis-Michel Van Loo's portrait of Diderot (fig. 137), completed in 1767, is perhaps not coincidentally an epistolary one. Diderot sits at his desk replying to letters (recognizable among the papers by their characteristic folds),[15] fictions, perhaps, of those missives actually sent by Falconet from Saint Petersburg in February and April that year.[16] The portrait depicts not just letter writing; it also describes the paraphernalia necessary to it: ink, sealing wax, bell to summon the messenger, and, of course, (Diderot's) pen.

Thin bodied and black tongued, it appears to have submitted unreservedly to the flaying, cropping, lopping, picking, and splitting by which, as Jonathan Swift mockingly described, the gracefully fringed feather was brutally reduced to a writing implement.[17] The goose's reality, her personal stories of flight and float invoked in Buffon's "eulogy," were voided in Van Loo's visual record. The once sensuous and multipurpose feather had been turned, by the "dutching" of industry[18] and the cut of the user's penknife, into a single-purpose thing, interchangeable with others of its kind: Van Loo depicted a second, virgin quill waiting on Diderot's silver inkstand, ready should the first fur and fail to force forth his words. The implement of the professional writer is, as Van Loo depicts it, pure functionality.[19] It lacks substance, body: a short white line tapering into translucency, it points to the black lines of writing and draws attention not to itself but to the ink held in reserve at its point for imminent notation.[20]

It is tempting to paint a mirror image: Falconet sitting, writing at a desk at his house, Rue d'Anjou, in the northwest of Paris, diagonally opposite Diderot at his apartment, Rue Taranne, in the southeast of the city. Falconet reading letters and writing replies at one of the two desks listed in the inventory of his furniture drawn up in August 1766, shortly before his departure to Saint Petersburg.[21] Falconet pressing Diderot to respond to his arguments, not selectively but point for point, and drafting his own replies, apparently, in between the lines Diderot had written to him.[22] But this effort at dialogue notwithstanding, Falconet felt outmatched by Diderot's literariness.[23] In one of his letters he lamented the "dryness" and the "heaviness" of his own hand.[24] Though it was his style not his handwriting, his phrasing not his pen, to which Falconet was ostensibly referring, fluidity and lightness—that is, the binary opposites of heavy and dry—were the very qualities that writing masters extolled in a good pen and a good hand, and that Van Loo attributed to Diderot: the point of Diderot's pen hovers above the letter paper momentarily paused in flow.[25]

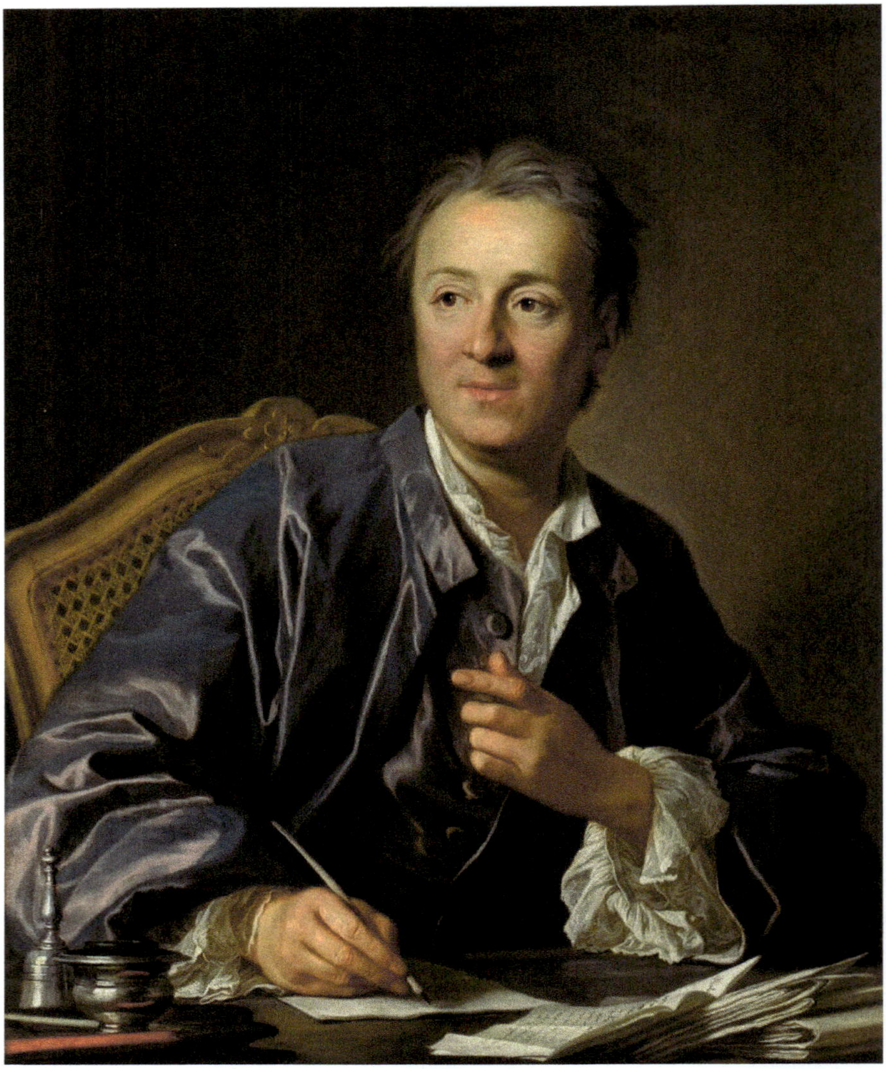

FIG. 137 Louis-Michel Van Loo (French, 1707–71), *Denis Diderot*, 1767. Oil on canvas, 81 × 65 cm. Paris, Musée du Louvre, Inv. RF1958. (© RMN-Grand Palais / Art Resource, NY. Photo: Stéphane Maréchalle.)

In Diderot's view, Falconet's writing was not heavy in the sense of crabbed, awkward or clumsy, but he did concur that Falconet landed points like blows. With some admiration he noted, "You turn with the wind, you make arrows from any wood. . . .Sometimes, facing forward, you loose your arrow with force; sometimes appearing to run away, you turn your bow back."[26] Diderot's arrow metaphor draws on "graphien," the Greek word meaning "to write," or literally to pierce, score, or inscribe a surface. It confirms, rather than contradicts, Falconet's perception of his writing as weighty, even penetrative, an intermittent jabbing characterized by lifts of the hand rather than fluid joins between marks. Diderot observed that Falconet's writing was incoherent, the points scattered instead of arranged in constructive argument or pleasing digression.[27]

In an earlier letter, Falconet had named his talent "Pegasus,"[28] after the divine winged horse of Greek mythology whose attributes of boldness and grace were commonly confounded with those of the genius writer. Falconet was being ironic. "My Pegasus," he confided to Diderot, "is not bold." He was "solid," a "carthorse" (*lourdier*), who, rather than deviating from the common track in Pegasus-like leaps of imagination, traveled "straight" and arrived at his mark by right reason.[29] Like the self-deprecating description of his writing hand, the target of Falconet's irony was himself, not the metaphor. Falconet set great store by his reason and by his historical and technical knowledge, resources with which he fully intended to win the debate with Diderot. Nevertheless, Pegasus stands for all that he found other and alluring in the pen.

The philosopher Graham Harman defines "allure" as an enlightenment of the object, a moment when objects cease to be fused with their defining qualities and functions and become more fully visible.[30] We can examine the difference between use and allure in the diverse ways in which Falconet spoke about his chisel and his quill. When addressing Diderot's claim that posterity inspires great works, Falconet countered that art comes into being unmotivated, through the mechanical emulation of praxis.[31] In practice, the chisel is its instrumental value, or the sum total of its carving potentialities. Falconet's description of inspiration ("enthousiasme") in full flood is one where tools perform their functions so utterly that they become invisible agents, obscured by the arc of the artist's intention. If the tool fails, an equivalent is improvised: "in the absence of ink, one would write with a burning coal."[32]

By contrast, Falconet did not extend his being and doing through the pen. He did not identify with it, as far as we can see, and his pen did not denote his writing gesture in the way that, according to the dictionary of the Académie française, the expression "avoir une excellente plume" (to have a good quill) commended an individual's personal literary style.[33] It was rather a thing apart. The metaphorical name Pegasus attributed to the quill values—freedom, innovation, spirit—not ordinarily listed in the description of its technological function or calculated in its exchange value. Moreover, these mythological allusions did not exhaust all the possible points of likeness between pens and horses, winged or otherwise.[34] In Buffon's *Natural History*, a book Falconet read, the horse is exalted for sharing as well as embodying mankind's ideals of courage and glory as well as for its noble bearing and beauty, its obedience to the hand.[35] Buffon likens mankind's empire over animals to that of spirit over matter. In naming his horse Pegasus, even mockingly, Falconet tacitly recognized in the pen a richer, less circumscribed, and therefore more alluring reality, one that perhaps quickened in him dreams of mastery.

This is not to say that Falconet aspired to the status of man of letters. On the contrary, he repeatedly declared himself an artist and writer, not an author.[36] His opposition to posterity was entangled with his conviction that, in matters of art, the works themselves and the judgment of artists are the only reliable sources of reputation. He thus conspicuously avoided oratorical appeals to sentiment and the virtues of ancient texts in setting out his case against posterity.[37] He introduced specific examples to anchor the debate in the concrete. He countered Diderot's poetic comparison of posterity to a sweet, distant melody overheard with his prosaic claim that the only praise worth having, now and in the future, was that which he could hear with the same two ears as those attuned to the birds singing in his garden as he wrote.[38] He argued that for every Diderot who rose each morning and begged posterity to inspire and not to abandon him, another found in a cup of coffee the more effective motivation to excel.[39] Self-consciously adopting ordinary language and common sense, yet also giving his pen a figurative name, suggests that Falconet's relationship with his quill was ambivalent. He was enthralled by its rhetorical promise yet committed to write materially grounded and banally truthful statements with it. §

---

1. Georges-Louis Leclerc, comte de Buffon, *Histoire naturelle et particulière*, 36 vols. (Paris: Imprimerie Royale, 1749–1804), 17:36–39. Swan, raven, and crow feathers were also used to make quills; the best for writing were goose feathers. Crow feathers were used for drawing and to make plectra for **harpsichords**.

2. Jacques Savary des Bruslons, *Dictionnaire universel de commerce* (Paris: n.p., 1741), 3: s.v. "Oye."

3. Savary des Bruslons, *Dictionnaire*, 3: s.v. "Plume." In the late 1760s a six-pound loaf of bread cost approximately 12 to 14 sous.

4. Savary des Bruslons, *Dictionnaire*, 3: s.v. "Plume à écrire."

5. See "Plume à écrire," *Encyclopédie*, http://encyclopedie.uchicago.edu/, 12:800. For examples of stationers selling quills in the 1750s to 1770s, see, for example, the trade cards of Basan (*À la Justice*), Cabaret (*Au Griffon*), and Cheron (*Au Temple du Goût*) at Waddesdon Manor (invs. 3686.1.80.160; 3686.1.101.210; and 3686.2.3.4).

6. See Charles-Antoine Jombert, *Méthode pour apprendre le dessein* (Paris: Jombert, 1755), 74–75. See Carbonnel's trade card (*Aux Armes de la Princess de Conti*), Waddesdon Manor (inv. 3686.1.60.109).

7. See Oppenord's two frontispieces, cartouche, and monogram reproduced in Jean-François Bédard's facsimile *Decorative Games: Ornament, Rhetoric and Noble Culture in the Work of Gilles-Marie Oppenord (1672–1742)* (Newark: University of Delaware Press, 2011), 43, 45, 47. On the creative interdependency of writing and drawing, see David Rosand, *Drawing Acts* (Cambridge, England: Cambridge University Press, 2002), 139–44.

8. Savary des Bruslons, *Dictionnaire*, 3, s.v. "Plumes à écrire." Handwriting in the eighteenth century was not primarily a personal matter. The different hands (*ronde*, *batarde*, and *coulée*) were suited to different purposes. See for examples Louis Rossignol, *L'art d'écrire* (1756).

9. For a comparison with Charles-Nicolas Cochin, secretary of the Académie between 1755 and 1773, see Anne Betty Weinshenker, *Falconet: His Writings and His Friend Diderot* (Geneva: Droz, 1966), 118–24.

10. Étienne Maurice Falconet, *Traduction des XXXIVe, XXXVe, et XXXVIe livres de Pline* (Amsterdam: Rey, 1772).

11. See Jules Guiffrey, "Correspondance des artistes français travaillant à l'étranger," *NAAF*, 1878, 81–82.

12. Étienne-Maurice Falconet, *Réflexions sur la sculpture* (n.p.: n.p., 1761). See Falconet, "Reflections on Sculpture," in *Lectures on Art: Selected Conférences from the Académie Royale de Peinture et de Sculpture, 1667–1772*, ed. Christian Michel and Jacqueline Lichtenstein, trans. Chris Miller (Los Angeles: Getty Research Institute, 2020), 408–27.

13. See the entries "Sculpture" and "Relief," *Encyclopédie*, http://encyclopedie.uchicago.edu/, 14:834–37 and 14:107–9.

14. The correspondence was first published by Yves Benot in 1958 under the title *Diderot et Falconet—Le pour et le contre* (Paris: Éditeurs Français Réunis, 1958). For the most recent critical edition with a material history of the letters, see Emita Hill's *Le pour et le contre*, vol. 15 of Diderot's *Oeuvres complètes* (Paris: Hermann, 1986).

15. On letters and their folds, hear Peter Stallybrass, "What Is a Letter?," Wing Foundation Lecture on the History of the Book, The Newberry, Chicago (12 October 2017), https://soundcloud.com/newberrylibrary/what-is-a-letter.

16. Letters XXII, XXIII, and XXV, in Benot, *Le pour et le contre*, 233–41, 243.

17. Jonathan Swift, "On a Pen," in *The Poems of Jonathan Swift*, ed. William Browning (London: Bell, 1910), 62.

18. So-called "dutching" or "dressing" enhanced the strength, durability, and flexibility of the quill. See, *Encyclopédie*, http://encyclopedie.uchicago.edu/, 12:800.

19. Compare the quills in Jacques Aved's *Portrait of Jean-Gabriel du Theil*, 1738–40 (Cleveland Museum of Art) or Maurice-Quentin de La Tour, *Portrait of President des Rieux*, 1739–41 (Los Angeles, J. Paul Getty Museum) with Van Loo's portrait. The seal, not the quill, identifies the sitter.

20. On ink, see Adrian Johns, "Ink," in *Materials and Experience in Early Modern Europe: Between Market and Laboratory*, ed. Ursula Klein and E. C. Spary (Chicago: University of Chicago Press, 2010), 101–24.

21. AN, MC/XCI/1036, 21 August 1766. The inventory was drawn up in the name of Falconet's wife Anne Suzanne Moulin, who had died in 1748. Falconet bought the property in 1756 from the heirs of the sculptor Jules Martin Desjardins (AN, MC/ET/LXXVII/251, vente 2 June 1756). There was a desk in the antechamber and another, of walnut, in the *cabinet* on the first floor.

22. See Letters IV and VI in Benot, *Le pour et le contre*, 60, 67, 71. Falconet took two letters from Diderot with him when he left for Russia, and he inserted a draft of his responses between Diderot's lines. See Emita Hill, "Diderot's Letter to Falconet, Summer 1767," *Diderot Studies* 20 (1981): 125–41. None of the original letters of the correspondence survive, only fair copies. See Biblithèque Nationale de France, Département des Manuscrits, n.a.f. 24983.

23. Letter IX, in Benot, *Le pour et le contre*, 101.

24. Letter VI, in Benot, *Le pour et le contre*, 71.

25. Smoothness and flow were recurrent points of concern in the writing manuals of the period. See, in relation to the gesture of writing, Honoré-Sébastien Roillet, *Les Nouveaux principes de l'art de l'écriture* (Paris: Mesnier, 1731), 14–17; and Nicolas Duval, *Pratique universelle des sciences les plus nécéssaires dans le commerce et en la vie civile* (Paris: Mesnier, 1735), 1:10, 12–13, 16–18, 19–24.

26. Letter VIII, in Benot, *Le pour et le contre;* and Diderot, *Oeuvres completes*, 89.

27. Letter VIII, in Benot, *Le pour et le contre;* and Diderot, *Oeuvres completes*, 89.

28. Letter IV, in Benot, *Le pour et le contre*, 60–61.

29. Falconet was no doubt thinking about the kind of carts used to shift stone; see **Carriage**.

30. Graham Harman, *Guerrilla Metaphysics: Phenomenology and the Carpentry of Things* (Chicago: Open Court, 2005), 141–43; and Graham Harman, "A Larger Sense of Beauty," *Dialogica Fantastica* (2011), www.dialogicafantastica.wordpress.com/2011/02/01=a-larger-sense-of-beauty/.

31. Letter II, in Benot, *Le pour et le contre*, 52. "Mechanical" is implicitly opposed to "moral" in the context of critique. In writing manuals, on the contrary, manual and moral emulation are combined in the writing samples. See, for example, Louis Rossignol, *L'art d'écrire* (1756).

32. Letter X, in Benot, *Le pour et le contre*, 131.

33. *Dictionnaire de l'Académie française*, 4th ed. (Paris: Brunet, 1762), 2: s.v. "Plume."

34. Mythology is used in the Barthian sense here, although Roland Barthes argues that to discuss writing instruments is generally an "anti-mythological" action. See Roland Barthes, "An Almost Obsessive Relation to Writing Instruments," in *The Grain of the Voice* (Berkeley: University of California Press, 1991), 17–82.

35. Buffon, *Histoire naturelle*, s.v. "Cheval," 4:174–77, 197. See Falconet's extended critique of Pliny the naturalist by comparison to Buffon in *Traduction des XXXIVe, XXXVe, et XXXVIe livres de Pline*, 2nd ed. (The Hague: Monnier, 1773), 2:33–45.

36. Letter X and Letter XIX, in Benot, *Le pour et le contre*, 135, 212. See also Falconet, *Réflexions sur la sculpture*, "Avertissement"; *Traduction de . . .Pline*, 2:109; and Weinshenker, *Falconet*, 58–82. Falconet was contributing to a broader quarrel between artists and men of letters on who had the better claim to judge art. See Stéphane Peltier, "'Les Misotechnites aux enfers,' ou l'imposture de la critique selon Charles-Nicolas Cochin," in *L'Invention de la critique de l'art*, ed. Pierre-Henry Frange and Jean-Marc Poinsot (Rennes: Presses Universaires de Rennes, 2002), 107–20.

37. See Letters XV, XVII, XIX, in Benot, *Le pour et le contre*, in which Falconet sets the writings of the ancients, notably Pliny, against critique and example.

38. Letter IV, in Benot, *Le pour et le contre*, 64.

39. Letter X, in Benot, *Le pour et le contre*, 130.

Red Lake

Joseph-Siffred Duplessis (1725–1802)

TYPE OF OBJECT	THEME	MATERIAL
Tool	Invention, Making, Studio	Plant Matter, Synthetic Materials | Paint/ Pigment

On 2 December 1786, a four-page memorandum on red lake written by the portraitist Joseph-Siffred Duplessis was read to members of the Académie by the secretary, Antoine Renou.[1] The designation *mémoire*, or memorandum, indicates that the discourse had not been solicited by the Académie, unlike a *conférence*, which was a public lecture on art that an academician was invited to give.[2] *Mémoires* were, rather, projects submitted by individuals soliciting the Académie's approval and imprimatur. Rare in the first half of the eighteenth century, the number of such memoranda by artists, inventors, and amateurs rose significantly after 1750, in spite of the fact that the Académie as professional body and as school did not formally concern itself with the materiality and craft of art. Thus, when "couleur" was discussed in the *conférences*, it was in the context-specific sense of "coloris," that is, in relation to its aesthetic value and with regard to questions of color distribution and pictorial harmony.[3] The making, mixture, and manipulation of colors were the know-how, or secrets, of the studio transmitted by apprenticeship, not discourse. Duplessis tipped his hat at the distinction and readily admitted that pigments do not, of themselves, make good pictures. But he argued that much of a picture's "freshness," "brilliance," and therefore beauty depended on them, and as such the Académie had, he implied, a very proper though as yet formally unacknowledged interest in them. By his memorandum he sought to break with the tradition of artisanal secrecy and overcome academic hauteur. He offered his stock of personal and private knowledge of red, acquired through lengthy research and experimentation, as a gift to his fellow academicians, opening up a public road between studio and Académie.

His subject was red lake.[4] Not a mineral pigment like vermillion or ultramarine, ground from cinnabar and lapis lazuli, red lake is an organic pigment precipitated from a dye such as madder or cochineal by means of an inert binder, in this case alum.[5] It is translucent and strongly colored and was often used as a glaze over other paint layers, notably in the depiction of drapery and dress.[6] It was not new. On the contrary, it was an old and established artist's pigment: *Rubia tinctorum*, or madder, was brought to Europe from Asia in the fourteenth century and widely grown as a crop thereafter, especially in Zealand in the Netherlands, but also in France; cochineal was imported from Mexico, beginning in the sixteenth century. A Spanish monopoly, it reached France via the port of Cadiz.[7] Although historians argue that red was declining sharply in importance in the eighteenth century, eclipsed by blue, red lake was, with other reds, an important component, with other reds, of Duplessis's **palette**—perhaps even, of his artistic identity.[8] In 1781 he had exhibited a portrait of himself in a red coat (fig. 138). Tradition has it that he wore it during regular visits to the Salon so that Salon goers might compare the original and the copy.[9] Hanging thereafter at his lodgings at the Louvre, it is possible that the gradually fading color of the depicted satin spurred him to review his materials and processes. The fugitive nature of red lake was, he assumed, a modern ill and the inevitable hazard of commercially produced pigments.[10] As he relates in his memorandum, he decided to fix the problem by making his own lake.

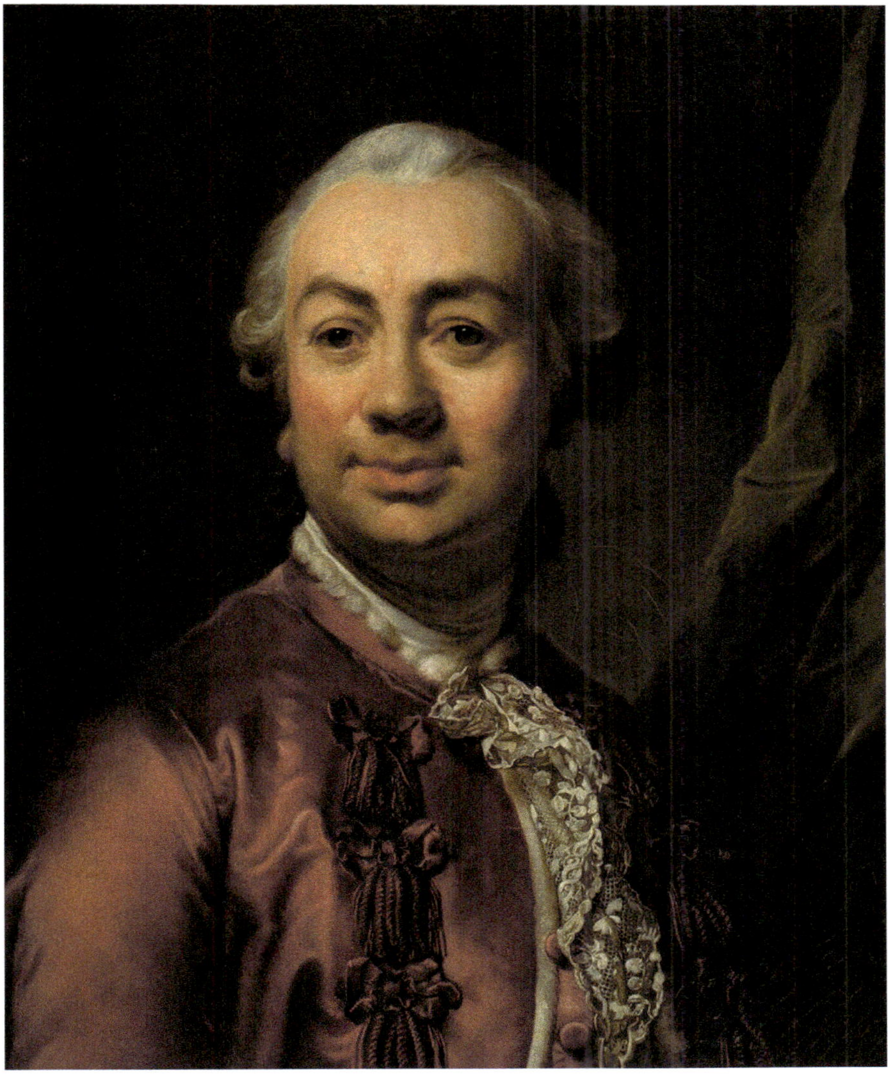

FIG. 138 Joseph-Siffred Duplessis (French, 1725–1802), *Self-Portrait,* 1780. Oil on canvas, 60 × 50 cm. Carpentras, Bibliothèque Inguimbertine. (HIP / Art Resource, NY.)

On the surface, Duplessis's insourcing of color production to the studio looks like a return to early modern craft practices in which the making as well as the application of pigments was conducted in-house. It implies purchase of the cochineal virtually unprocessed, or of ground madder in one of the three grades (from expensive, fine, and light, to cheap, coarse, and dark). And it implies that, once in the studio, the stuffs were dispersed in water (hot for cochineal, cold for madder) and mixed with the binder before the water was evaporated off and the residue ground to a fine powder ready to make into paint. The memorandum contradicts such an interpretation, however. Having experimented with a "pure" and "solid" carmine lake of his own manufacture that proved no more enduring than those he had bought ready-made, Duplessis looked for enlightenment outside the studio, to the most recent and relevant published sources and to chemists. He proceeded, moreover, by formulating clear and distinct hypotheses rather than operating blindly by the chance of trial and error.[11] First he conjectured that animal colorants are intrinsically superior in brightness and solidity to vegetal ones; second, he theorized from a passage in the abbé Raynal's *Histoire des deux Indes* (1780) (which described indigenous practices of extracting colorant from gastropods in the gulf of Guayaquil) that obtaining such a bright and solid purple red was a question of method not matter;[12] and third, he hypothesized that the solidity of pigments was determined by their adhesiveness. In short, he took a quotidian pigment of the studio, a real red, and constructed it anew as a "scientific object," to use Lorraine Daston's terminology, an object of intellectual inquiry, and target also of his cognitive experimentations.[13]

To confirm and prosecute his theories he contacted the chemist Jean Darcet, recently appointed to succeed Pierre-Joseph Macquer at the *Jardin des plantes* and advisor at the Gobelins and at Sèvres.[14] Darcet challenged Duplessis's ideas and persuaded him to experiment instead with madder, the growing of which the government had been working to encourage with tax breaks since the 1750s, and which had been the subject of the Mignot de Montigny prize in applied chemistry at the Académie Royale des Sciences in 1783–85.[15] Duplessis was very likely familiar with the plant because it was an important crop for Carpentras (Duplessis's place of birth) and the surrounding region.[16] Darcet referred Duplessis to the recent trials on madder published by the Berlin chemist Andreas Margraff in the *Journal Polytipe* and also described in the article "Garance" in the *Encyclopédie méthodique* (1784).[17] Having agreed on the hue they wanted to create—at the purple rather than the orange end of the red spectrum—Duplessis and Darcet separately produced madder lakes, achieving comparable, and therefore valid, results. Duplessis then exposed samples of his new madder lake and his original carmine lake to the weather and to sunlight. Within a short time, the cochineal in the carmine lake sample had "evaporated"; the madder sample was, meanwhile, unchanged.[18] Against expectations, madder outperformed cochineal in relation to solidity: the dyestuff, not the technology of pigment generation, confounded both Duplessis's first and his second premises. His ideal red was vegetable. Use of the verb "to evaporate" indicates that in relation to method, Duplessis was led, under Darcet's tutelage, to abandon his earlier "mechanical" theory of colorfastness and replace it with an organic one. The coloring properties of his red were reimagined or invented as chemical.[19]

Thus far our account of Duplessis's memorandum has stressed the scientific nature of its discourse and of the painter's thinking and experimenting: his division of natural objects into animal, vegetal, and, by implication, mineral realms; his problematization of the "goodness" of pigments in terms of common variables (brightness and solidity); and his recourse to repeat trials to establish chemical "facts." However, this recipe for red lake, his gift to the Académie, was traditionally wrapped. Duplessis framed his "discovery" of a conceptually stable and enduring red lake by reference to the ancient dyestuff murex, source of the prestigious Tyrian purple praised by Pliny.[20] He did not subscribe to the chevalier de Jaucourt's contentions that the imperial purple of the ancient world had been no more beautiful that its modern manifestation, and that murex had ceased to be used simply because cheaper and better alternatives (cochineal and Brazil wood) had been sourced in the New World; rather he thus accepted the importance of history in determining the value and meaning of color.[21] "Pourpre" was, according to Duplessis, a lost art, a holy grail, toward whose recovery all his spare energies were bent.[22] The objectivity with which he seemingly treated the "facts" about colorants from Europe and the Americas may have stripped red of the local knowledge and meaning that it had for farmers in Zealand, or peasants in Oaxaca, but in doing so it also enabled the better translation and embedding of red lake into the semiotics of European art.[23] Duplessis, as portrait painter to the king and the court, was acutely aware of the symbolic value of pigments and hues: the silky shimmer of purple for aristocrats, dull woolen scarlet for the untitled.[24] It is surely significant that his only other intervention on matters of color should have concerned ultramarine, an old pigment, first imported from Afghanistan and at times worth more than its weight in gold.[25] Though "Prussian" blue had generally been accepted as a cheaper synthetic alternative of equal stability and strength, Duplessis lobbied the *directeur des bâtiments du roi* to pursue measures at an international and diplomatic level to secure a readier supply and consequently a fall in price.[26] Duplessis's sympathies were thus entirely with the Académie, whose secretary, harassed apparently by the increasing number of new art products submitted by inventors to the Académie for examination, argued that what was needed was not new pigments but a better understanding of the old ones. In this the Académie was sometimes at odds with the Bâtiments. While the comte d'Angiviller made concerted efforts to secure ultramarine for the king's artists from Turkey and Russia through diplomatic channels, he chided academicians as reactionary, resistant to progress, specifically to the introduction of new, commercially invented alternatives to traditional compounds.[27] §

---

1. *PV*, 9:300.

2. See Christian Michel and Jacqueline Lichtenstein, eds., *Lectures on Art: Selected* Conférences *from the Académie Royale de Peinture et de Sculpture, 1667–1772*, trans. Chris Miller (Los Angeles: Getty Research Institute, 2020).

3. The distinction between *couleur* and *coloris* was one made by Roger de Piles in *Dialogue sur la couleur* (Paris: Langlois,

1673). See also his "Termes de peinture" at the end of *Conversation sur la connoissance de la peinture* (Paris: Langlois, 1677). Thomas Puttfarken, *Roger de Piles's Theory of Art* (New Haven: Yale University Press, 1985), 59–63.

4. ENSBA, Ms. 237.15, fol. 4.

5. See Jo Kirby and Raymond White, "Identification of Red Lake Pigment Dyestuffs and a Discussion of Their Use," *National Gallery Technical Bulletin* 17 (1996): 56–80; and Jo Kirby, Marika Spring, and Catherine Higgit, "The Technology of Eighteenth- and Nineteenth-Century Red Lake Pigments," *National Gallery Technical Bulletin* 28 (2007): 69–81.

6. It seems to have been used only sparingly in the representation of flesh, mostly to enrich shadows.

7. See Georges Roque, *La Cochenille, de la teinture à la peinture: Une histoire matérielle de la couleur* (Paris: Gallimard, 2021), 52, 126. See also *A Red Like No Other: How Cochineal Colored the World: An Epic Story of Art, Culture, Science and Trade*, ed. Carmelle Padilla and Barbara Anderson (New York: Skira-Rizzoli, 2015).

8. See Michel Pastoureau, *Red: The History of a Color*, trans. Jody Glading (Princeton: Princeton University Press, 2016), 142–93.

9. Jules Belleudy, *Joseph-Siffred Duplessis (1725–1802)* (Chartres: Durand, 1913), 95. What is being suggested here is that Duplessis was more concerned with registering his abilities as a colorist and painter of stuffs than his skill at capturing a likeness, which did not depend on the clothes he was wearing.

10. We know little about colormen in eighteenth-century Paris. See, as precursor to the nineteenth-century trade, Séverine Sofio, "Colourmen in the Nineteenth Century, Artisans or Experts (Paris, Tours)," *Ethnologie française* 165, no. 1 (2017): 75–86.

11. Prussian blue was a chance product of attempts to make cochineal red lake. See Jo Kirby and David Saunders, "Fading and Colour Change of Prussian Blue: Methods of Manufacture and the Influence of Extender," *National Gallery Technical Bulletin* 25 (2004): 73.

12. In 1768 the chemist Pierre-Joseph Macquer had demonstrated similarly that a change in the sequence of operations used to dye wool with cochineal resulted in the successful dyeing of silk with the same dyestuff. See Macquer, "Sur un nouveau moyen de teindre la soie en un rouge vif de cochenille," *Mémoires de l'Académie royale des science* (1768): 82–90.

13. See Lorraine Daston, ed., *Biographies of Scientific Objects* (Chicago: University of Chicago Press, 2000).

14. On Darcet, see Michel Jean Jérôme Dizé, *Précis historique sur la vie et les travaux de Jean d'Arcet* (Paris: Gillé, 1802); and Jaime Wisniak, "Jean Darcet," *Revista CENIC* 35, no. 2 (2004): 105–10. Concurrently, or possibly prompted by Duplessis's investigations, Darcet conducted experiments on cochineal.

15. For the Arrêt du Conseil d'État, 24 February 1757, see Henri-Louis Duhamel de Monceau, *Mémoire sur la garance et sa culture* (Paris: Imprimerie royale, 1757), written specifically for farmers in order to promote madder as a crop, 78–79. The Montigny prize was not awarded because the single project submitted was judged insufficiently original by the Académie. See Christine Lehman, "L'art de la teinture à l'Académie royale des sciences au XVIIIe siècle," *Methodos: Savoirs et textes* 12 (2012).

16. Robert Chencier, *Madder Red: A History of Luxury and Trade* (London: Routledge, 2000), 10, 202–51.

17. *Encyclopédie méthodique, ou par ordre de matières*, 3 (Medicine) (Paris: 1784): s.v. "Garance." See also Kirby, "The Technology," 76.

18. In his memorandum Duplessis offered to bring the samples to the Académie for academicians to see for themselves.

19. On mechanical and chemical models of dye process, see Alan E. Shapiro, *Fits, Passions and Paroxysms* (Cambridge, England: Cambridge University Press, 1993), 242–67.

20. Pliny the Elder, *Natural History*, trans. W. H. S. Jones, Loeb Classical Library 10 (Cambridge: Harvard University Press, 1951), 6:296–97.

21. "Pourpre," *Encyclopédie*, https://encyclopedie.uchicago.edu/, 13:245.

22. ENSBA, Ms. 237.15, fol. 3–4.

23. On the discourse of science in France as "objective" or "neutral," see Camille Frémontier-Murphy, "La construction monarchique d'un lieu neutre: L'Académie royale des sciences au palais du Louvre," in *Règlements, usage et science dans la France de l'absolutisme*, ed. Christiane Demeulenaere-Douyère and Éric Brion (Paris: Tec & Doc, 2002), 170–203.

24. Compare Duplessis's *Portrait of comte d'Angiviller,* 1778, Musée et Château de Versailles, with his *Portrait of Benjamin Franklin,* 1778, New York, Metropolitan Museum of Art.

25. In Charles Parrocel's Inventaire après décès, 3 June 1752, lapis lazuli, or ultramarine in solid form, was itemized with the painter's "jewels," not his studio equipment. See AN, MC/ET/CXXII/684.

26. See AN, O^{1}/1918/237.

27. On d'Angiviller's efforts in 1786 to obtain ultramarine from Turkey and Russia through the intermediary of Auguste de Choiseul Gouffier, ambassador to Constantinople, see AN, O^{1}/1918/ 313, 316; and O^{1}/1919/99, 107, 146. D'Angiviller's frustration boiled over in the case of zinc white, proposed by the chemist De Morveau in 1781 as an alternative to the carcinogenic lead white traditionally used by painters. See d'Angiviller to Jean-Baptiste-Marie Pierre, 19 January 1783 (AN, O^{1}/1916/123).

Relic

Hyacinthe Rigaud (1659–1743)

TYPE OF OBJECT	THEME	MATERIAL
Apparel, Commodity, Companion, Container, Devotional Thing, Gift, Heirloom, Ritual Thing, Symbolic Thing	Family, Luxury, Religion	Metal | Gold/ Gilding, Plant Matter | Wood

A relic—the physical remnants of a saint or holy figure—is something one might expect to find in a church, rather than in the home of an artist. Fragments of bodies (bones, hair, teeth, or vials of blood) and material things that once touched those bodies (clothing, belongings, instruments of death or torture) are readily accommodated in sacred sites where their ritual purpose is evident, but we do not often imagine the domestic environment of an eighteenth-century artist as a space for that kind of activity. Yet among the possessions of Hyacinthe Rigaud was an item that would suggest otherwise. Indeed, the history painter was the devoted owner of one of the most sacred types of relic worshiped within the Catholic Church: a small piece of the True Cross upon which Jesus Christ was crucified.[1]

Perhaps the first question posed by Rigaud's relic is how a fragment of Christ's cross, from the first-century Holy Land, got into the hands of an eighteenth-century French painter. This is not actually as unlikely as it might seem, for while traces of the True Cross were among the most venerated of relics (due to their direct connection to the body of Christ), they were also fairly common.[2] Following its legendary discovery in fourth-century Jerusalem, the cross was supposedly broken up and parts of it taken to Rome and Constantinople before being fragmented and dispersed further, until alleged pieces proliferated to quite impossible extents.[3] While the Catholic Church accepted and even facilitated this proliferation through a system of relic regeneration (in which new, lesser relics could be created by touching an original), it became a point of contention during the Protestant Reformation, prompting John Calvin's mocking quip that if all the relics of the True Cross were collected together, there would be enough wood "to fill the hold of a very large ship."[4] This abundance does, however, suggest how a Parisian painter might have found himself in possession of such a precious sliver of wood. During Rigaud's lifetime, Paris was home to a particularly celebrated relic of the True Cross, acquired by the medieval king and saint Louis IX, kept in Sainte-Chapelle, and later destroyed during the Revolution.[5] But there would also have been a profusion of smaller or "lesser" versions, like Rigaud's tiny fragment, circulating through more recent Counter-Reformation economies of religious material culture.

For Rigaud, this holy object was one of his most treasured possessions, evident in both how he kept it during his life and what he planned to do with it after his death. Like most relics, Rigaud's was preserved in a reliquary, a bespoke container designed to protect the precious and often physically fragile remnants inside. Rigaud's wooden fragments had been shaped into a cross (recalling their sacred origins in the True Cross) and then encased within a gold cross-shaped reliquary, fashioned as a pendant, and hung on a gold chain.[6] During his life, the painter wore the cross at all times around his neck (so he claimed in his **will**), and upon his death he wanted it to pass to his beloved wife, Elisabeth de Gouy, and for her to do the same. In several versions of his will, Rigaud included these special instructions regarding the relic, noting that the bequest was made as a mark of his consideration for and friendship with his wife, and that he could not conceive of "a more precious gift," nor one better suited to "her virtue and her piety."[7] In the end, however, Elisabeth de Gouy died a few months before her husband and, as Rigaud had not made a new will before his own death, the relic presumably passed to one of his other heirs. Having no children, Rigaud divided most of his estate between his three nieces, among whom the universal legatee was Marguerite-Elisabeth Rigaud, the wife of Rigaud's former student and fellow academician Jean Ranc.[8]

Although they represent but a few lines in a notarial document, this trace of Rigaud's relic in his will offers an intriguing insight into the way that devotional objects were treated in eighteenth-century France. On one hand, it suggests there was something distinct about the relic that made it different from other things: we glean how special it was to Rigaud, venerated for its sacred value, worn on his person at all times, and considered the most precious gift imaginable for his pious and virtuous wife. But on the other hand, despite its sacred status, the relic was also like many other things that belonged to the painter: an item of property that was treasured during his life and bestowed as a sign of affection on his death. While in a religious sense Rigaud's relic was unique among his possessions (the only thing he owned that had touched Christ), in a legal sense it was not so different from, for instance, his gold medal from the king of Poland, which, a couple of paragraphs earlier in his will, Rigaud bequeathed to his godson, the history painter Hyacinthe Collin de Vermont.[9]

Yet the fact that an ordinary individual like Rigaud could *own* a relic, as though it were any other consumable product, did not make that object any less holy. Indeed, this was characteristic of a broader shift in the circulation and ritual use of religious material culture during the early modern period. As Cissie Fairchilds has observed, this was a moment when devotional objects evolved from public things worshiped collectively in sacred spaces to personal possessions that could be worshiped privately in the domestic sphere.[10] In eighteenth-century Paris, where the heightened ritualization of Counter-Reformation religiosity combined with the emergence of consumer markets, religious objects like relics had, in other words, become luxurious commodities. Whether Rigaud bought his relic himself (perhaps from one of the merchants selling devotional objects on the Pont Notre-Dame) or acquired it some other way (a gift or bequest), his ownership of this sacred item was part of the commercialized circulation of such objects and the increasingly individualized religious practices around them.[11] It would, after all, be difficult to envisage a devotional object intended for more personal use than a reliquary designed as a pendant necklace. Hanging constantly at his chest, Rigaud's relic was not a fashionable accessory (like Charles-Antoine Coypel's **watch** or Charles-Nicolas Cochin's **handkerchiefs**), not an adornment for display (never visible in any of his numerous portraits), but a sacred item kept close to the body in an act of permanent private devotion.

Aside from Rigaud's revelation about wearing his relic, however, there is little to indicate precisely how he used it in his devotional life. Certainly there were particular feasts throughout the liturgical calendar in which Christ's cross became a focus of veneration, not least Good Friday, the feast of Christ's crucifixion, which was marked by an adoration of the Cross. There were also special feasts devoted to the True Cross, such as the Invention of the Cross, celebrated on 3 May, and the Exaltation of the Cross, celebrated on 14 September (both of them listed annually in the royal **almanac**). But given its constant presence around his neck, Rigaud's relic likely featured much more frequently in the artist's private religious practices, which, based on the other items in his home, probably took place in his bedroom. According to his after-death inventory, all the objects in this room served a devotional purpose. Hanging on the wall, there was a small painting of the Virgin and Child, and a framed crucifix mounted on black velvet. Along with these, Rigaud also kept another crucifix: a gilded copper figure of Christ, mounted on a wooden cross, "with neither stand nor frame."[12] Comparable from its description to the handheld crucifix in Jean Restout's portrait of the Jansenist Abbé Tournus (fig. 139), this was an object, like the relic pendant, intended for personal devotions and in particular for meditations on Christ's suffering. Rigaud may indeed have used both objects together—the sculptural representation of the cross and the actual fragment of it—signifier and signified united, held in different hands, each intensifying the spiritual resonance of the other and creating a powerful material vehicle for daily prayers and devotional rites.

Retrieving a sense of artists' inner spiritual lives is an elusive challenge with a dearth of textual sources to explore them. But as Rigaud's relic suggests, their material possessions can often fill in the gaps. Every artist at the Académie, according to the institution's statutes, was supposed to be a professed Catholic (unless a foreigner granted exception by the king), and it is clear from Rigaud's will that he dutifully performed the religious responsibilities of a devout believer, leaving money to his parish church for the poor, and requesting a requiem mass to be sung for the repose of his soul.[13] But in a less public sense, the objects in his home grant insights into Rigaud's more personal religious inclinations. His books, such as Louis-Isaac Lemaistre de Sacy's translation of the Bible (1667–96) and Nicolas Letourneux's *Année chrétienne* (1686), point compellingly to sympathies with Jansenism, a controversial doctrinal thread considered heretical in the Catholic Church, which nevertheless became a strong current of belief in France and especially in Paris.[14] Among his artistic colleagues, Rigaud was not alone in sharing these theological inclinations. While declarations of Jansenist tendencies were seldom made overtly, many artists of the Académie were connected with the movement, most

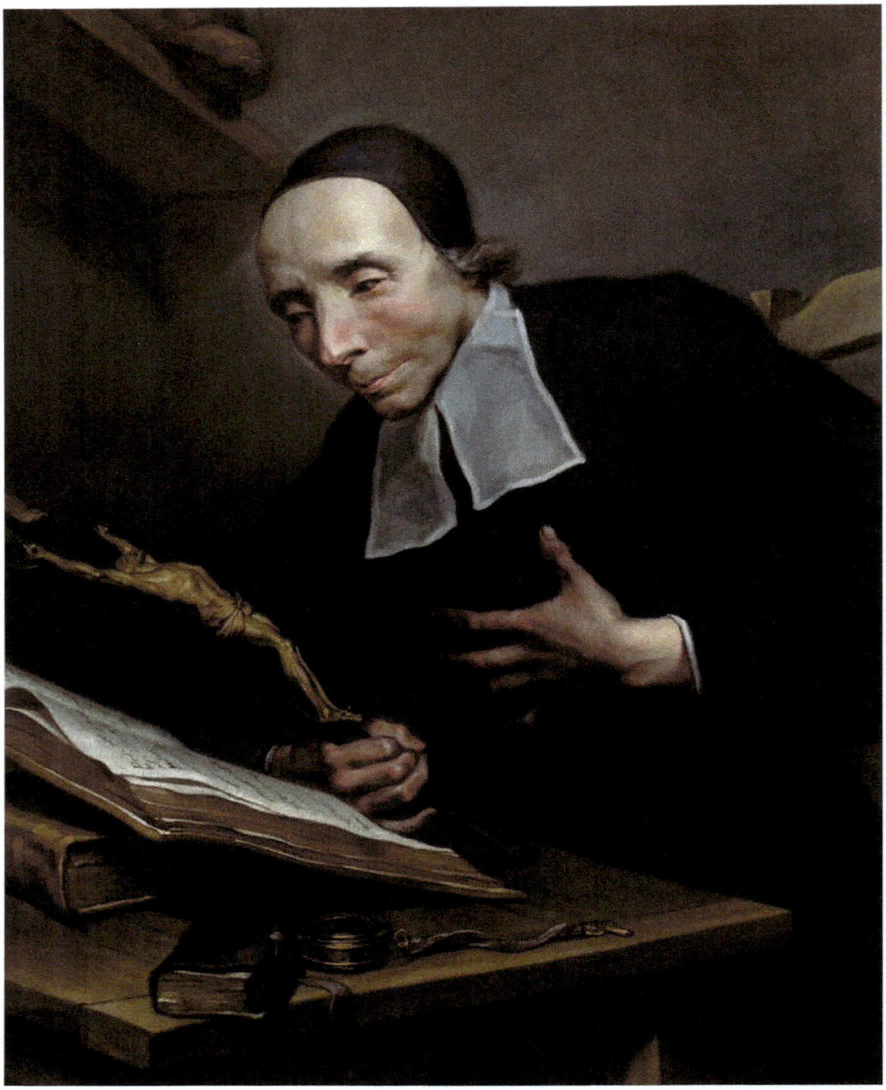

FIG. 139 Jean Restout (French, 1692–1768), *Portrait of Abbé Tournus*, ca. 1720–30. Oil on canvas, 92 × 73 cm. Paris, Musée Carnavalet.

prominently the history painters Philippe and Jean-Baptiste de Champaigne, Jean Restout, and the engraver Charles-Nicolas Cochin.[15] A doctrinal interest in Jansenism would certainly chime with Rigaud's possession of the relic and his crucifixes, and with their Christocentric focus and their devotional functionality. In the absence of writings articulating his beliefs, contentious or otherwise, the material things in Rigaud's life thus offer a tantalizing glimpse of the painter's religiosity, in terms of both his ideas and their embodied practices: a sense of the theological tenets underlying his faith, and the ritual acts he may have performed to fulfil them. ‡

1. Rigaud's relic is described in several of his wills, including those of 16 June 1726, AN, MC/ET/LIII/237; 11 February 1731, AN, MC/ET/LII/256; and 29 September 1735, AN, MC/ET/LIII/275. It is mentioned in Ariane James-Sarazin, *Hyacinthe Rigaud* (Dijon: Faton, 2016), 1:247.

2. Theologically, Christ is said to have ascended bodily into heaven, and so, unlike saints, there are very few corporeal relics related to Christ. Passion relics (like the True Cross) are thus among the most venerated.

3. Joe Nickell, *Relics of the Christ* (Lexington: University of Kentucky Press, 2007), 77–95. On the history of relics of the True Cross, see also Anatole Frolow, *Les reliquaries de la Vraie Croix* (Paris: Institut Français d'Études Byzantines, 1965); and Barbara Baert, *A Heritage of Holy Wood: The Legend of the True Cross in Text and Image*, trans. Lee Preedy (Leiden and Boston: Brill, 2004).

4. Jean Calvin, *Traité des reliques* (1543) (Paris: Bossard, 1921), 113.

5. On Sainte-Chapelle's relic in eighteenth-century Paris, see Jérôme Morand, *Histoire de la Sainte-Chapelle royale du Palais* (Paris: Clousier, 1790). On the medieval cult of the True Cross, see Cynthia Hahn, *Passion Relics and the Medieval Imagination: Art, Architecture, and Society* (Los Angeles: University of California Press, 2020). Thanks to Emily Guerry for directing me to scholarship on Sainte-Chapelle and medieval relics.

6. These details are recorded in the relic's description in Rigaud's wills; see note 1.

7. Will, Hyacinthe Rigaud, 29 September 1735, AN, MC/ET/LIII/275. The relic is mentioned in the three wills listed in note 1.

8. The terms of inheritance of Rigaud's estate are outlined at the beginning of his estate inventory: 6 March 1744, AN, MC/ET/XLIII/383. The relic is not mentioned in this inventory.

9. Will, Hyacinthe Rigaud, 29 September 1735, AN, MC/ET/LIII/275.

10. Cissie Fairchilds, "Marketing the Counter-Reformation: Religious Objects and Consumerism in Early Modern France," in *Visions and Revisions of Eighteenth-Century France*, ed. Christine Adams, Jack R. Mason, and Lisa Jane Graham (University Park: Pennsylvania State University Press, 1997), 33–34. On the presence of devotional objects in Parisian homes, see Annik Pardailhé-Galabrun, *The Birth of Intimacy: Privacy and Domestic Life in Early Modern Paris*, trans. Jocelyn Phelps (Cambridge: Polity, 1991), 202–12.

11. On the location of dealers in religious material culture, see Jeffry Kaplow, *The Names of Kings: The Parisian Laboring Poor in the Eighteenth Century* (New York: Basic Books, 1972), 6.

12. Hyacinthe Rigaud, "Inventaire après décès," 6 March 1744, AN, MC/ET/XLIII/383.

13. Will, Hyacinthe Rigaud, 29 September 1735, AN, MC/ET/LIII/275. In practice, if not in theory, some of the Académie's French artists were actually Protestants, such as Jean-Baptiste Massé and François-André Vincent.

14. "Inventaire après décès." James-Sarazin has explored the Jansenist tone of Rigaud's library in more detail: James-Sarazin, *Hyacinthe Rigaud*, 1:247–54. On the history of Jansenism, see William Doyle, *Jansenism: Catholic Resistance to Authority from the Reformation to the French Revolution* (London: Macmillan, 2000).

15. On artists associated with Jansenism, see Christine Gouzi, *L'art et le jansénisme au XVIIIe siècle* (Paris: Nolin, 2007).

Robe de Chambre

Louis-Michel Van Loo (1707–71)

TYPE OF OBJECT	THEME	MATERIAL
Apparel	Gender, Identity, Luxury, Studio	Textile | Silk, Textile | Wool

"*Robe de chambre*" (dressing gown), "*robe de nuit*" (nightgown), "*Indienne*" (India gown), "*robe interieur*" (house coat): these are just some of the words used in the eighteenth century to denote the garment depicted by Louis-Michel Van Loo in two self-portraits, the first in 1762, the second a year later (figs. 140, 141). The portraits describe a kimono-style *robe de chambre*. It has no arm or shoulder seams, and no revered collar. Instead, two widths of shot *bleu céleste* silk taffeta, joined, we infer, by a central seam at the back, fall over Van Loo's shoulders and down the front. A small and simple upright band of silk inserted into slits on the shoulder line builds up the neck, and prevented the back seam from splitting.[1] The detail of the visual record of cut, color and styling, the reproduction of the gown from different angles in the two self-portraits, and its reappearance in 1767 in Van Loo's celebrated *Portrait of Diderot* (see fig. 137), leads Lesley Miller to propose the existence of a model object, an actual dressing gown, one belonging to Van Loo and later lent to the *philosophe*.[2] The self-portraits thus raise specific questions about Van Loo's wardrobe and about how he wished to be seen and remembered. They also prompt general reflection on the practices and meaning of artists' clothing before the emergence of self-consciously styled artistic dress in the nineteenth century.[3]

The only source of information about Van Loo's wardrobe, other than the self-portraits, is the inventory taken after his death in 1771, or nearly a decade after his essays in self-portrayal.[4] Obviously, it must be used with caution to reconstruct and interpret Van Loo's earlier dressing habits. According to the inventory, his wardrobe was substantial and expensive. He owned nine three-piece suits (*habits complets*), two coats (*habits*), three coats with matching breeches (*culottes*), two coats with matching waistcoats (*vestes*), three frocks (*fracs*), two of them with matching waistcoats, two overcoats (*surtouts*), one of them with matching waistcoat and breeches, and five waistcoats, valued all together, with assorted hats, wigs, gloves, and shoes, at 1,816 livres, a consequential sum, roughly comparable in value to the wardrobes of the lesser court nobility.[5]

Nothing in the inventory corresponds to the depicted dressing gown exactly; indeed, no *robe de chambre* of any kind is listed, although record is made of a pair of slippers. Among Van Loo's suits, however, is one described as of shot camlet (*camelot*), a stuff of mixed animal fibers (originally including camel hair, hence the name) that was produced domestically, often as imitation silk.[6] It seems possible that the breeches and waistcoat depicted in the portraits are idealized versions of this set of clothes, which may originally

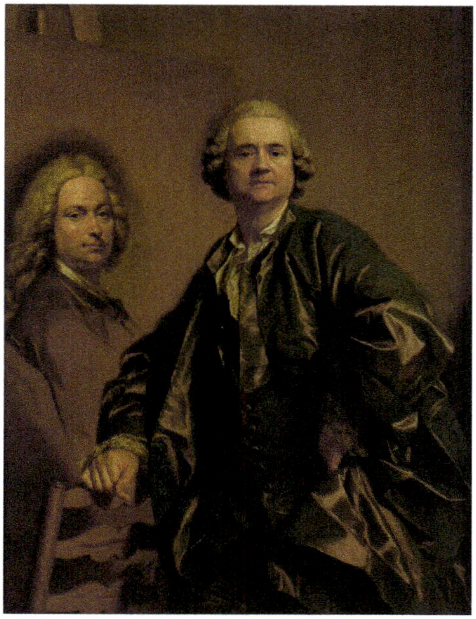

FIG. 140 Louis-Michel Van Loo (French, 1707–71), *Self-Portrait Painting the Portrait of His Father, Jean-Baptiste Van Loo*, 1762. Oil on canvas, 129.5 × 98 cm. Châteaux de Versailles et de Trianon, MV5827. (© RMN-Grand Palais / photo: Christophe Fouin / Art Resource, NY.)

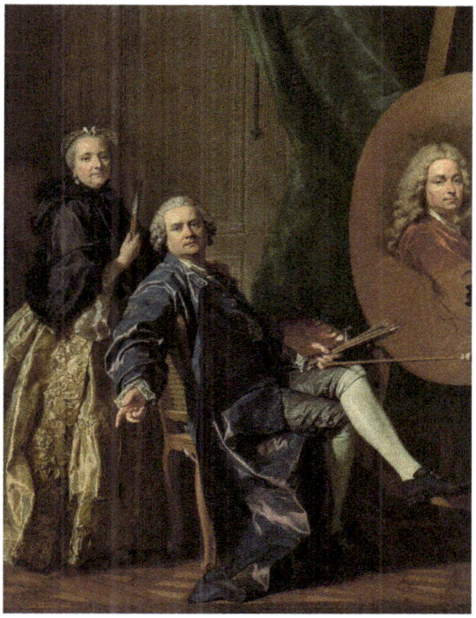

FIG. 141 Louis-Michel Van Loo (French, 1707–71), *Self-Portrait with His Sister*, 1763. Oil on canvas, 230.5 × 162 cm. Châteaux de Versailles et de Trianon, MV6774. (© RMN-Grand Palais / photo: Christophe Fouin / Art Resource, NY.)

have included a matching *robe de chambre*. Unlike Diderot, who famously regretted the loss of his "old dressing gown," Van Loo seems to have had no moral or sentimental attachment to his old clothes.[7] None is described in the inventory as old or worn. On the contrary, Van Loo appears to have updated his wardrobe regularly. His outfits were fashionable, as befitted a man who had been directly involved in the silk industry.[8] At his death, two widths of silk embroidered with silver purl thread and sequins were found in a chest of drawers, ready for making into a waistcoat. He recycled only old linings: "different colored," "old silk" ones.[9] The inventory appears, in summary, to support the compelling evidence of the paintings—or it does not absolutely contradict it: that in the 1760s Van Loo had owned a *robe de chambre* of blue shot stuff that, spoiled or shabby, he had later abandoned.

What was a *robe de chambre*? And why, of all items of clothing, select it for this book? The dressing gown was introduced to the European wardrobe in the seventeenth century, a garment imported at first from India, the Levant, and also Japan via the Netherlands.[10] By the eighteenth century both the cloth and the needlework were generally of European origin. We know, for instance, that in the 1740s, when Jean-Étienne Liotard, the so-called Turkish painter, was in Paris he had gowns of the more fitted variety, listed later in his inventory as "Greek," with "Turkish" sashes, made by a seamstress on the Pont Notre-Dame.[11] However, its association with the rare, the curious, and with luxury persisted.

Though called dressing gowns, *robes de chambre* were not specifically for bed but for indoors generally. Liotard earned his soubriquet not simply for possessing one but for his idiosyncratic custom of wearing his "Turkish" gown abroad, in public places.[12] We adopted the eighteenth-century French term *robe de chambre* for our book in order to defamiliarize a little the thing we now call a "dressing gown" and invariably associate with **bed**. Not only was it not specifically connected to bedtime, it was also not necessarily a private and personal piece of clothing like linen. It could be dressed up with a wig and shoes for receiving guests or dressed down with cap and slippers when alone.[13] It was, however, linked to intimacy. In the 1738 seduction scandal involving the ornamental bronze sculptor Philippe Caffieri and the daughter of landscape painter Louis Silvestre, testimony that Caffieri had been seen on the steps of the Silvestre house in a *robe de chambre* served as compelling evidence that the sculptor was no casual visitor to the house on Rue du Mail, but residing, in fact, cohabiting.[14] Caffieri, contended his father, had been diverted from the life class at the Académie, his proper path and his filial duty, by Mlle Silvestre, whose seduction of him the dressing gown embodied: originally hers, it had been altered to fit him.[15]

We picked the *robe de chambre* for *Artists' Things* because, although symptomatic of deviancy in Caffieri's case, historians today have proposed a connection between the gown and the eighteenth-century artist so close and so general that it virtually assumes the condition of normative occupational dress.[16] Liotard, who adopted the gown on his trip to Constantinople in 1738 and thereafter wore it to the exclusion of conventional dress, seems to confirm the contention. Arguably, however, his "exotic" dress served him in lieu of recognition by the Académie, and of the legal status of *peintre du roi* enjoyed by the likes of Louis-Michel Van Loo.[17] To judge by the *morceaux de réception* at the Académie, the high point of artist portraits *en robe de chambre* was not the eighteenth century but the last quarter of the seventeenth century: in the seventy-five years after 1700, the proportion of artists depicted gowned dropped from 56 percent to just 18 percent.[18] The overwhelming majority (83 percent) of portraits-*morceaux* executed between 1700 and 1775 depicted academicians in coats and three-piece suits, that is, formally, as public persons. The *robe de chambre* was not, it seems, artists' dress in the iconic manner, say, of the artisan and the apron. The relationship between nightgown, body, and identity was rather more complex and unstable.

Claudia Denk relates developments in costume in eighteenth-century artist portraiture—specifically the **handkerchief** (as scarf and headdress), and less categorically the dressing gown—directly to changes in modes of consumption: from luxury spending and the semiotics of appearance to being and ordinary living.[19] She illustrates her case with a comparison of Van Loo's 1762 self-portrait (see fig. 140), a conventional *portrait d'apparat* apparently, and Jean-Siméon Chardin's unprecedented pastel self-portraits (see fig. 67), in which the aged still-life painter reveals himself unwigged and at work in the studio. We are led to understand that Chardin's portrayal is at one with his occupation (unlike Van Loo's) and to infer the cause of the fit in the actuality of Chardin's dress practice. Chardin, Denk implies, dressed not to communicate something about his self but in order to paint; he picked clothes unconsciously, comfortable clothes because they were right for his task.[20]

Comfort was certainly the alibi that Liotard gave for preferring a Turkish gown to the formal French *habit*.[21] The warm folds of the *robe de chambre en chemise*, which encompasses some seven plus yards of cloth, generously drapes the body and can be gathered close and tethered with a sash or left loose.[22] Pace Denk, Van Loo, not Chardin, is the painter so dressed in the pictures. In the 1762 *Self-portrait*, the gown visibly takes the mold of Van Loo's left arm and shoulder and rises curved over his breast. Folds are lifted and tucked in at the waist by the painter's hand in one self-portrait; trusted to move aside for the gesture of painting in the other (see fig. 140). The dressing gown thus responds dynamically, both to and independently of the body, a freedom represented in painting by loosened collars and unbuttoned coats and waistcoats. Gores in the side seams flared the gown, releasing the arms for liberal movement, and the simple shirt-styled cuffs vouchsafed spoiling a detail of dress that fashion reserved on the coat for decoration: simple bands of braid or more elaborate embroidery.[23] Among the practical conveniences of the *robe de chambre*, additional to cover and wrap, Diderot noted that its surplus stuff at front and hem afforded the writer a "third hand" to unclog pens, mop messes, and dust surfaces.[24] To the painter, the prosthesis provided an extra hand with the potential to clean brushes and wipe palettes, blend pigments and erase lines.[25]

Describing the feel and agency of stuff runs the risk of assuming that the comfort, free movement, and multiple utilities afforded by nightgowns are natural bodily satisfactions common to all and self-evidently desirable, too, as conditions for work. However, in his life of Carle Van Loo (1765), Michel-François Dandré-Bardon described his subject (Louis-Michel's uncle) as, on the contrary, intentionally *un*easy in his practice, hard on himself. Carle eschewed comfort, apparently; he always worked standing and refused a fire even in the coldest weather.[26] Though Dandré-Bardon does not specifically mention Carle's clothes, the character he and others gave the great history painter suggests that Carle dressed formally to paint, that he submitted mind and body to the molding of the clothes he wore because the noble ideal embodied in gentleman's dress was the one he wished to instill in his figurative work.[27] The *morceaux de réception* portraits of artists in coats, not gowns—coats that by virtue of the narrow cut at back and sleeve forced an upright bearing on the wearer, shoulders back—may likewise represent the "reality" of other artists' vocation, if not the actual daily goading provided by the clothes that wore them.[28]

By this account, being an artist was accomplished differently in a *robe de chambre* and in a coat. However, Louis-Michel's wardrobe complicates matters. It indicates a sensitivity to the feel of cloth that extended beyond the body's subconscious desire for comfort to a sophisticated appreciation of surfaces. The wool of his woolens was dense and soft (*drap*), loose and nubby (*ratine*), woven and knitted. The silk of his silks was "coarse grained" (*gourgouran*), thick ribbed (*gros de Naples*), close piled (velvet), and smoothly glossy (satin). Stuffs were both robust and delicately sheer (*voile*). Ornament was feather trimmed and embroidered with metal braid and spangles, not flat (woven or printed). To his expert's knowledge of texture, Van Loo added an amateur's eye, filling his wardrobe with stuffs that attracted light's play upon them:[29] the silk lining of one suit interplayed with the *voile* facing, shimmering forth shades of black and gray with every movement of light and every adjustment of the body. The calendared finish of another suit produced, when worn, fleeting swells of brightness and shadow, like the fall of light on water.[30] The iridescence created by the different colors of warp and weft of his shot camlet suit (depicted with the matching silk nightgown) drew attention to the endless mutability of color in binary combination. The vibrant matter of his various stuffs, especially conspicuous in the generous folds of the *robe de chambre*, called out to Van Loo and drew him into conscious reflection on the sensuousness of surfaces perhaps every bit as inspiring to the painter of portraits as austerity was, apparently, to the painter of ancient history.

What, finally, of the *robe de chambre*? In *Self-Portrait with His Sister* (see fig. 141), its bright, almost metallic radiance unfolds and breaks against the steady glow of white stockings and the long lines of shadow twisting across the green drapery. More importantly, it tells of the difference between things with and without a sealed surface, between the open, inviting, almost hungry-looking primed canvas on the easel, willing its under-wear overpainted, and the tight, sealed surfaces of the waxed or varnished parquet floor, chair frame, and **palette**. But if on the one hand, the *robe de chambre* tells of painting as a process, on the other, it spoke also of the painter.

At the time Louis-Michel painted his self-portraits, he was seeking appointment to the directorship of the French School in Rome. Promotion to such high academic office favored ennobled candidates—to be exact, *chevaliers* of the Order of Saint Michel, the highest civil order of the ancien régime.[31] Both Carle and Louis-Michel Van Loo had been knighted in the early 1750s, and in 1753 Carle exhibited a portrait of himself wearing the **decoration**. The portrait was scorned for its ostentatious parade of *noblesse*, shockingly misplaced, according to one Salon critic, in a man of talent.[32] Humiliated, Carle destroyed the work.[33] When Louis-Michel turned to portraiture to promote himself a decade later, he was more circumspect (see fig. 140). He avoided symbols and resorted to body language. So convincing is his Van-Dyckian swagger that Claudia Denk sees the Maltese cross and black sash at his elbow, though neither is actually present in the picture.[34] The order's regalia included a ceremonial cape, which was closely comparable in its cut to the *robe de chambre*.[35] By substituting the *robe de chambre* for the cape in the self-portraits, Van Loo discovered in this robe of Bourbon blue not only a cover to veil merit in modesty but also a visual metaphor with which to ground and naturalize artistic distinction in the everyday, locating its field of honor in the studio. §

---

1. See François-Alexandre-Pierre de Garsault, *L'art du tailleur* (Paris: Latour, 1769), 21 and plate 11; and Margaret Swan, "Nightgown into Dressing Gown," *Costume* 6 (1972): 10–21.

2. Lesley Ellis Miller, "A Portrait of the 'Raphael of Silk Design,'" *V&A Online Journal* 4 (2012) http://www.vam.ac.uk/content/journals/research-journal/issue-no.-4-summer-2012/a

-portrait-of-the-raphael-of-silk-design/. For other instances of clothes sharing by sitter and artist, see Jean-Marc Nattier's *Portrait of His Wife* (1760, private collection). Mme Nattier wears the dress in which her husband had depicted queen Marie Lescinska in 1748. Guillaume Faroult and Catherine Voiriot, "De Chardin à Voiriot: Destinée du 'merveilleux portrait de femme à la brochure' du Louvre," *Revue du Louvre* 58, no. 3 (2008): 60–68, fig. 9.

3. See Colin Cruise, "Artists' Clothes," in *The Gendered Object*, ed. Pat Kirkham (Manchester: Manchester University Press, 1996), 112–19; Elizabeth Wilson, "Bohemian Dress and the Heroism of Everyday Life," *Fashion Theory* 2, no. 3 (1998): 225–44; and Robyne Calvert, "Manly Modes: Artistic Dress and the Styling of Masculine Identity," *Visual Culture in Britain* 16, no. 2 (2015): 225–42.

4. Louis-Michel Van Loo, "Inventaire après décès," AN, MC/ET/LVI/166, 22 April 1771. The sections of the inventory relating to clothes are published in *Autour des Vanloo: Peinture, commerce de tissus et espionage en Europe (1250–1830)*, ed. Christine Rolland (Rouen: Publications des Universités de Rouen et du Havre, 2012), 56–57.

5. On court dress, see Daniel Roche, *The Culture of Clothing*, trans. Jean Birrell (Cambridge, England: Cambridge University Press, 1989), 184–220, 429–30.

6. See Jacques Savary des Bruslons, *Dictionnaire universel du commerce*, 3 vols. (Paris: Estienne, 1723–30), s.v. 1: "Camelot."

7. See Denis Diderot, "Regrets on Parting with My Old Dressing Gown," trans. Kate Tunstall and Katie Scott, *Oxford Art Journal* 39, no. 2 (2016): 175–84.

8. His frocks—coats with turn-down collars (*fracs*)—were of a style imported from England in the 1760s, one of many fashions associated with Anglomania. On Van Loo's partnership in the Lyon silk firm Berger, Vanloo et Cie, see Christine Rolland, "Louis-Michel Van Loo, Premier Peintre to the King of Spain," in *Spanien und Portugal im Zeitlater der Aufklärung*, ed. Christoph Frank and Sylvaine Hänsel (Frankfurt am Main: Vervuert, 2002), 295–311. For comparison, see the wardrobe of Bonnaventure Carret, traveling salesman for the Lyon silk industry, in Lesley Ellis Miller, "Dressing Down in Eighteenth-Century Lyon: The Clothing of Silk Designers from Their Inventories," *Costume* 29 (1995): 25–39.

9. "Inventaire après décès," in *Autour des Vanloo*, 56. On recycling, see *The Afterlife of Used Things*, ed. Ariane Fennetaux et al. (London: Routledge, 2015), especially the essays by Natacha Coquery, 13–24, and Fennetaux, 122–41.

10. See Martha Hollander, "Vermeer's Robe: Costume, Commerce and Fantasy in the Early Modern Netherlands," *Dutch Crossing* 35, no. 2 (2011): 177–95; and, most recently, Susan North, "Indian Gowns and Banyans—New Evidence and Perspectives," *Costume* 54, no. 1 (2020): 30–55. Warm thanks to Lesley Miller for these references.

11. See Marcel Roethlisberger and Renée Loche, *Liotard: Catalogue, sources et correspondence* (Beukenlaan: Davaco, 2008), 1:68.

12. See Étienne Liotard's 1753 enamel self-portrait (London: Royal Collection, Windsor Castle) for detailed visual record of his dress. Roethlisberger and Loche, *Liotard*, 2: no. 262.

13. See *Gallerie des Modes* (1780), cahier 31: "Robe de chambre à manche en pagoda"; discussed in Anne de Thoisy-Dallem, "La vieille robe de chambre de Diderot et les vêtements d'intérieur masculins au siècle des lumières," *Revue du Louvre*, 2016, no. 1, 69.

14. See Jules Guiffrey, *Les Caffiéri sculpteurs et fondeurs ciseleurs* (Paris: Morgand & Fatout, 1887), 101–8.

15. Guiffrey, *Les Caffiéri*, 106.

16. See Ariane Fennetaux, "Men in Gowns: Nightgowns and the Construction of Masculinity in Eighteenth-Century England," *Immediations* 1 (2004): 83–84; and Thoisy-Dallem, "La vieille robe de chambre."

17. See Roethlisberger and Loche, *Liotard*, 1:66. According to his eldest son, Liotard always twinned his gown with a **wig** and hat, "because it was these that distinguished the French from others."

18. The figures are calculated from the catalog of *morceaux de réception* in *Les peintres du roi 1648–1793*, exh. cat. (Tours: Musée des Beaux-Arts, 2000), 221–83.

19. Claudia Denk, "'Chardin n'est pas un peintre d'histoire mais c'est un grand homme': Les auto-portraits tardifs de Jean-Siméon Chardin," in *L'art et les normes sociales*, ed. Thomas Gaehtgens et al. (Paris: Editions de la Maison des Sciences de l'Homme, 2001), 279–97.

20. Denk, "Chardin," 288–97.

21. Roethlisberger and Loche, *Liotard*, 1:66. On eighteenth-century comfort, see John E. Crowley, "The Sensibility of Comfort," *American Historical Review* 104, no. 3 (1999): 749–82.

22. Garsault, *L'art du tailleur*, 21.

23. Garsault, *L'art du tailleur*, 30–31; and Sarah North, *18th-Century Fashion in Detail* (London: V&A, 2018), 66–67.

24. On the prosthetics of dress, see Daniel Miller, *Stuff* (Oxford: Polity, 2010), 23–31.

25. On the importance of cleanliness in the studio, see Elisabeth Lavezzi, "La peinture au supplice," *Cycnos* 11/1 (2008), http://revel.unice.fr/cycnos/index.html?id=1358.

26. Michel Dandré Bardon, *La vie de Carle Van Loo* (Paris: Desaint, 1765), 51.

27. See Johann Christian Mannlich's account of the formalities attending entry to Carle Van Loo's studio, in *Histoire de ma vie* (Trier: Spee, 1993), 2:50–51.

28. See Jessica Munns and Penny Richards, *The Clothes that Wear Us* (Newark: University of Delaware Press, 1999), 9–32.

29. See *Jouer la lumière*, exh. cat. (Paris: Paris de la Mode et du Textile, 2001), 109–23.

30. Warm thanks to Lesley Miller for information and interpretation of the stuffs and clothing listed in Van Loo's inventory.

31. See **Decoration**. Also Benoît de Faucompret, *Les chevaliers de Saint-Michel 1665–1790: Le premier ordre de mérite sociale* (Paris: Patrice du Puy, 2007).

32. See Étienne de La Font de Saint-Yenne, "Sentiments sur quelques ouvrages de peinture, sculpture et gravure," in *La Font de Saint-Yenne: Oeuvre critique*, ed. Étienne Jollet (Paris: ENSBA, 2001), 286. Charles-Nicolas Cochin's official reply on behalf of the Académie's painters did not contradict the critique of the self-portrait. For a contrary view, see abbé Charles Le Blanc, *Observations sur les ouvrages de MM. de l'Académie* (n.p., 1753), 11.

33. See Dandré Bardon, *La vie de Carle Van Loo*, 34.

34. Denk, "Chardin," 282.

35. See Garsault, *L'art du tailleur*, 21–23, pls 10–11. Van Loo owned two: one silk; the other wool, see "Inventaire après décès," in *Autour des Vanloo*, 56.

Shell

François Boucher (1703–70)

TYPE OF OBJECT	THEME	MATERIAL
Collectible, Commodity, Tool	Global Commerce, Luxury	Animal | Shell

The name and reputation of the painter and academician François Boucher is, for many, synonymous with the shell. The **wig** he wore for his portrait by the Swedish artist Gustaf Lundberg (Paris, Musée du Louvre), painted in 1741, at the time he had started to collect, falls down his back in a cascade of curls that against the background of blue look almost like ropes of white and silver scallops. Shells were not, however, the only things that Boucher collected. Neither were they things greatest in number or highest in value in Boucher's cabinet sold at his death in 1770. A handwritten note at the back of a copy of the painter's sale catalog gives a breakdown of the sums raised by the different kinds of thing in order of sale.[1] Rearranging the subtotals by value puts shells sixth: first among the categories of natural history, certainly, but significantly below the records fetched by painting, drawing, furniture, and porcelain.[2] Yet "shell" was and is often promoted as the synecdoche for Boucher's art and collection, both by reason of novelty—he was one of a few artists in his taste for natural history[3]—*and* because the shell, a signature motif of the rococo, came to signify the excess, the luxe, of that style's reign, a style of which Boucher's work is a defining instance.[4] That said, recent discussions of Boucher's shells have mostly ignored the awe and fear spelled by the temptation of his shells;[5] they have focused less on obvious questions of consumption and critique, appetite and idiom, and have opted instead to interrogate the "science" of his conchyliology.[6] Collection, as opposed to accumulation, puts things under cover of the charge of luxury because it consecrates the value of collected things as real, innate, not simply determined by exchange.

What happens if we address Boucher's things as goods, not ideas? First, we refuse to treat shells as found, discovered, or given, and acknowledge that they entered the collection having been traded like any other thing. Second, we reject naturalizing the relationship between Boucher and his collection, that is, we stop treating his taste as idiosyncratic and self-explanatory. Third, while acknowledging the vestigial part still played by the discourse of curiosity in the reception of the collection, we note the ascendency of the language of taste and fashion.[7]

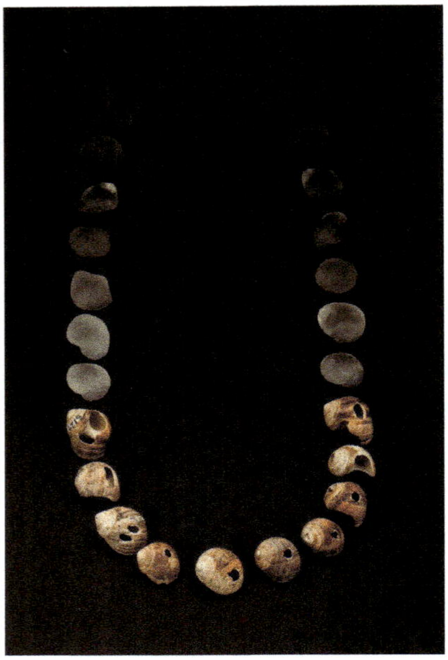

FIG. 142 Reconstructed Cro-Magnon shell bead necklace, 28,000 BCE. Shells. Washington, Smithsonian National Museum of Natural History, A8129, Department of Anthropology, Smithsonian Institution. (Photo by Chip Clark.)

The market for shells was emergent in the eighteenth century. According to Krzysztof Pomian, natural history rose as the market for medals fell:[8] a symptom not of changing taste among the privileged, apparently, but rather evidence of a structural transformation of that elite—of its penetration by money. Pomian's argument is one to which we will return, so conspicuously does it address the ethical problem of consumption, of luxury, but first let us consider Boucher's specimens in the *moment* of exchange and at the *places* it occurred in order to advance their historical candidacy as commodities. In not being made, the minerals, corals, and shells were obviously not exactly like other luxury goods: **snuffboxes**, **teacups**, **watches**, lacquer, furniture, and so forth. In fact, in a process that exactly reversed the mounting of Chinese and Japanese ceramic in gilt bronze, the better to fit it for European consumption,[9] shells imported from the West Indies were stripped of useful fastenings; holes remained where craft had once made nature into "primitive" jewelry (fig. 142).[10] Specimens of agate, jaspe, and other hard stone that had been sized, shaped, polished, and fitted for **snuffboxes** were likewise uncaged.[11] For nature to appear natural often required creative labor;[12] the distinction between natural history and luxury goods was not as distinct as we sometimes suppose.

More a "phase" than a property of things, commodity or exchange value was, according to the dealer Pierre Rémy, most conspicuous at auction.[13] To quote from the catalog of his first natural history sale in 1757, "more reliable knowledge about the rarity and value of shells is to be got at an auction than by looking at [*par la vue*] collections," because the collector is invariably in the habit "of boasting about his belongings, and of valuing the preciousness of a thing, either by what he paid for it, or by the price his fantasy has set on it," whereas auctions do not lie.[14] Boucher certainly attended such sales: in 1745 he bought two drawers of shells and several individual specimens for 108 livres at Antoine de La Roque's sale[15] (he paid 100 livres for twenty-three drawings from Charles-Antoine Coypel's sale in 1753), and in 1766, at the important natural history sale of Mme Dubois-Jourdain, he bid on more than two hundred lots, spending a total of 1,254 livres,[16] or more than twice the annual rent for his apartment on Rue de Richelieu.[17]

Like Rémy, modern scholars contrast the auction and the *cabinet*, identifying the first with the commodity and the second with the gift. One of Boucher's pupils recorded the pleasure and excitement his master experienced on receipt of a "gift" of minerals.[18] Boucher "was delighted like a child," apparently. That pleasure was, however, more calculating than the simile allows. Boucher reserved only two items from the consignment for his own collection; he set the rest aside as swaps. Auctions accentuated the commodity dimension of objects but it was by no means absent from shells in the *cabinet*. Boucher's swaps functioned not unlike shells in the so-called cowrie zone of West Africa (fig. 143), a medium of exchange in the eighteenth-century slave trade, or wampum beads (made from the quahog clam shell) in North America, used in the same period by European coastal settlers to trade with the Iroquois, that is to say, they functioned *like* money, but as a limited, not a generalized, medium of exchange.[19] To argue thus that Boucher sometimes mobilized the abstract exchange value of his natural things as the means of acquiring others is not to imply that he was insensible to their concrete form. Boucher's thirty-five cowries (*porcelaines*) were, according to Rémy, each unique in size ("very big" to "small"), shape ("egg-shaped," "shuttle-like," "hump-backed," etc.), color ("olive," "mole," "mouse gray," "snow white," etc.), and surface pattern ("tiger-skin," "mottled," etc.), each individual therefore capable of accumulating histories of where it had been, to whom it had belonged, to what purpose it had served. Each was the material object of Boucher's desire.[20] However, in the catalog, taxonomy serves to index value in lieu of history and provenance. Just one of Boucher's cowries is credited with an origin: "from Panama." Stripped in the discourse and practices of collecting and trade of their cultural fastenings, of traces of the social relations that constituted them as valuables or commodities, and often even of geographical knowledge, the shell's exterior sign of visuality becomes generic glitter.[21] Far from the *cabinet* having been a haven from trade, it was a place of greater market risk.

After his death, Boucher's collection was sold at auction. The sum raised, 70 percent of the value of his estate, represented the bulk of the inheritance later divided among Boucher's heirs.[22] There had been no inventory, a remarkable omission considering the value of the estate and the number of parts into which it was to be divided. That omission is perhaps explained by the fact that Boucher had no landed property, no *rentes*, no securities, only *meubles* (movable property, things), the estimation and realization of the value of which required an expert and a dealer, but not a notary. That he should have sought to protect his fortune by collecting, rather than investing, suggests that although scientifically the shells, corals, and minerals were, as Pomian notes, comparatively "young"—had yet to earn themselves settled names and secure taxonomic classification—they were commercially mature in the sense that their exchange-value was known and relatively stable. In general, the arc of Boucher's collecting, from modest beginnings in the early 1740s to important purchases in 1760s, mirrors the steady upward trajectory in shell values.[23] To be more precise, the prices fetched indicate a marked correlation between size and price. His many spiny bivalves fetched sums between 9 and 18 livres, with a concentration at 12 to 15 livres.[24] Notwithstanding Rémy's prefatory claim that the painter was willful and impulsive, unable to deny himself the least thing beautiful, Boucher was not

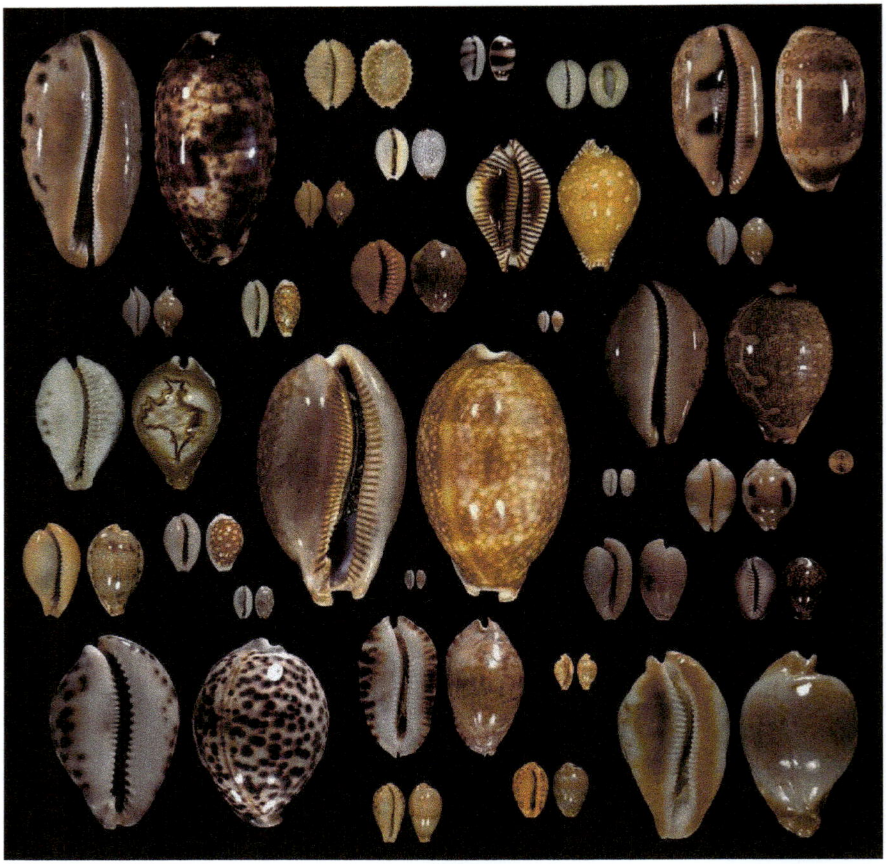

FIG. 143 Selection of cowries. Washington, Smithsonian National Museum of Natural History. (Photo: Chris Meyer.)

reckless. He calculated carefully and shrewdly.[25] The 120,000 livres realized by his sale left his widow and children comfortable.

The importance of the Boucher sale warranted the expense of a frontispiece.[26] Two putti hold attributes of Painting and Glory, two others trumpet the painter's fame. The **palette**, brushes, portfolio, and loose drawings, like the putti, direct the viewer to the artist's studio; ironically, no reference is made to the *cabinet*. Boucher's sale, like that of other artists, included work, tools, and studio equipment, but these accounted for no more than 34 out of the sale's total 1,865 lots. Rémy establishes no causal connection between Boucher the painter and Boucher the collector, but he does promote for praise formal parallels between the fecundity of the artist's imagination and the immense size and richness of his collection, between the amiability of the owner and the attraction of his possessions. Others were not so approving. Bret de Dijon found that the painter had compromised his talents for the sake of his collection, not as the seventeenth-century art theorist Alphonse Dufresnoy had supposed it possible, by painting too fast, but by accepting tasks beneath a true artist's calling.[27] Lempereur too discovered that Boucher had been led by profit to corrupt his talent, though in condemning the painter he spared the collection.[28]

Such contemporary response to Boucher's collection dates from the period after he had taken up lodgings at the Louvre, and more especially after he became *premier peintre*. Following the death of Charles-Antoine Coypel, Boucher was given the latter's grand set of rooms on the first floor of the north wing, overlooking the Rue Saint-Honoré. His immediate neighbors were not other artists but courtiers and members of the king's household. At the end of the century, Sébastien Mercier would mock the culture of favor that had had the elite, or would-be elite, compete for and traffic in such lodgings, notwithstanding the gross discomfort occasioned by their lack of proper amenities.[29] In such an elite social setting it is perhaps not surprising that the architect Jacques-François Blondel should have chosen to draw attention to Boucher's *cabinet*—"very beautiful"—rather than his adjacent studio.[30] Boucher had spent over 9,000 livres, a significant sum of money, on improvements necessitated, it is generally supposed, by the installation of his collection.[31] Two visitors recorded their impressions. In 1766 Horace Walpole was struck by the "*quantities* of shells, mosses, ores, Japan, China, vases, Indian arms and music etc."[32] A year later, those same quantities impressed the Polish tourist count André Mniszech not at all. He mocked Boucher's *cabinet* as "a vast curiosity shop,"[33] sly allusion, perhaps, to the trade card the painter had once designed for Gersaint in which, coincidentally, the very assortment of things Walpole listed is depicted.

Bret and Mniszech faulted Boucher's collecting not because they detected in it conspicuous imitation of signs of noble rank but because they thought they recognized simple consumerism: a gross bourgeois accumulation of stuff like so much stock or a commodity of natural history objects. Visitors were offered neither a narrative of God's creation nor a lesson in nature's wondrous order, just the mundane store of Boucher's possessions, all show and no tell. Collecting was traditionally justified in the case of artists by use. And for collecting to serve art it must precede and inspire creation, not succeed it and reward artistic labor. In a very literal sense, shells provided that support to genius (fig. 144). They were his everyday objects of the studio, his tools for holding water-based paints, their white, nacreous interiors, allowing the painter to anticipate the effect of the pigment on paper.[34]

In criticizing Boucher, Lempereur remarked the contrast in the lives and manners of Boucher and Bouchardon.[35] According to François Basan, Bouchardon's collection was a spur to emulation.[36] The sculptor had bought pictures, drawings, books, and prints in order to succeed better in the greatness of his art. Boucher bought only for pleasure. Bouchardon's virtue and Boucher's vice is not explained by subject matter; the difference lies, rather, in ordering and arrangement. Certainly Bouchardon's collection consisted predominantly in items directly connected to sculpture (see **model**), but the sculptor also owned shells: there were four on the marble chimneypiece in his salon, along with a garniture of porcelain.[37] In the studio, he had copies of the entomologist Maria Sibylla

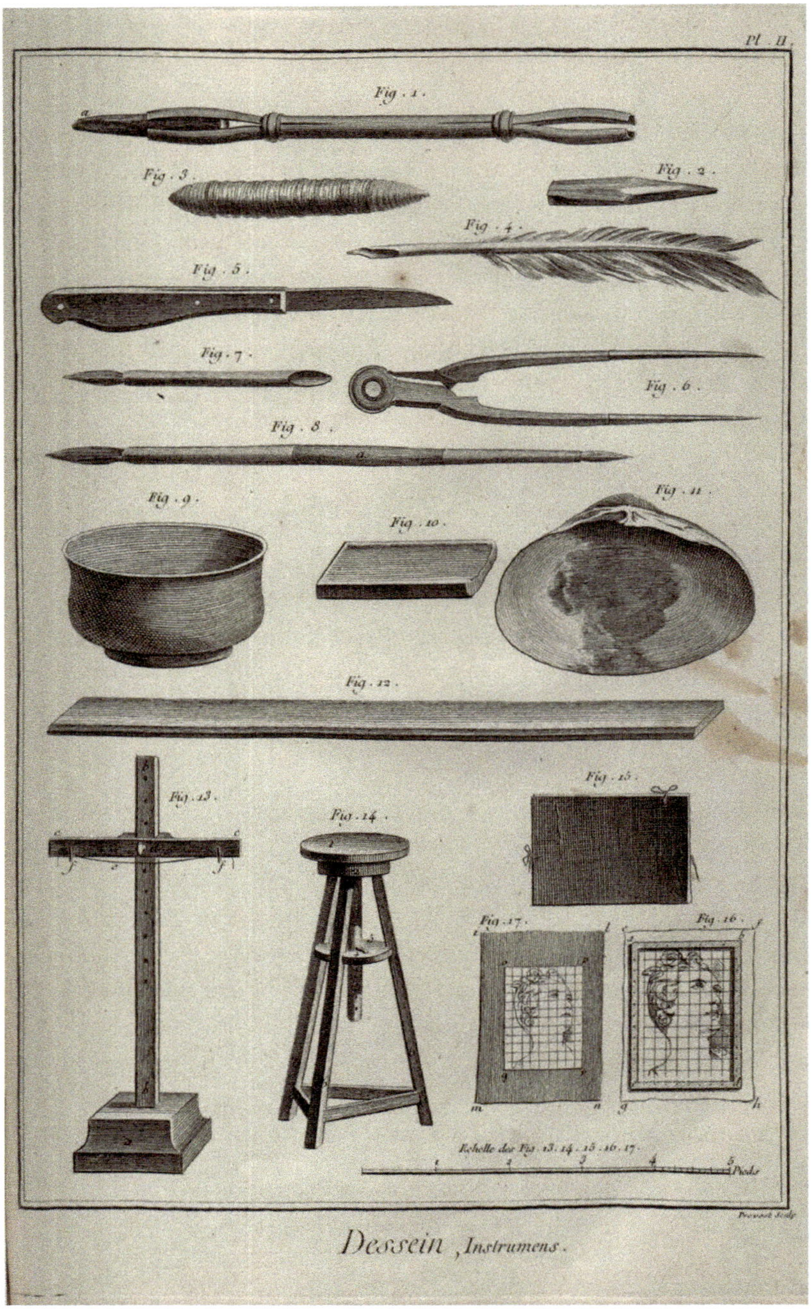

FIG. 144 Instruments, "Dessein," from *Recueil de planches sur les sciences, les arts libéraux et les arts mécaniques* (1765), plate II. (Image courtesy of the ARTFL Encyclopédie Project, University of Chicago.)

Marian's publications, vellums by botanist Nicolas Robert, and a copy of the 1711 edition of Rumphius's *Ambonese Curiosity Cabinet.*[38] Bouchardon's objects did not form a collection as such, insofar as they were not displayed for or visited by others. Boucher's, on the other hand, were conspicuously staged. Sixteen glass-topped tables housed some of the shells; others were sheltered in a *coquiller* made by the *ébéniste* François Oeben and the *bronzier* Philippe Caffieri, and yet more were displayed under glass bells.[39] Jessica Priebe has suggested that in Boucher's frontispiece for Edmé Gersaint's 1736 natural history sale we see something of the effect later created at the Louvre (fig. 145).[40] The "mélanges," or lots of mixed specimens in Boucher's sale, were disposed, she argues, to form exactly this kind of confection of shells, corals, and sponges loosely piled around a vertical axis.

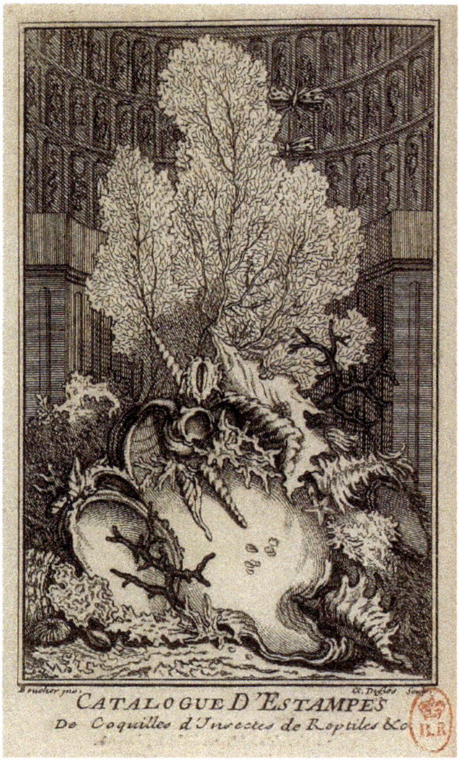

FIG. 145 Edmé Gersaint (French, 1694–1750), *Catalogue raisonné de coquilles et autres curiosités naturelles* (1736), frontispiece. Paris, Bibliothèque Nationale de France.

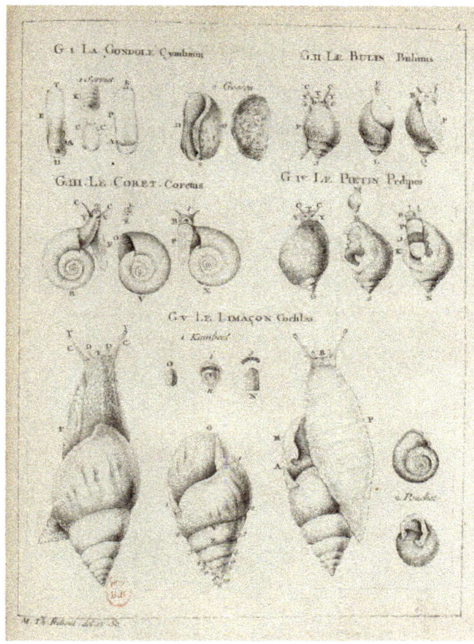

FIG. 146 Marie-Thérèse Reboul-Vien (French, 1738–1805), Illustrations of shells from Michel Adanson, *Histoire naturelle du Sénégal: Coquillage* (1757), plate 1. Paris, Bibliothèque Nationale de France.

However, the interlacing of amateur and professional natural history, of luxury and learning, of the aesthetic and the scientific that such displays secured and celebrated in the 1740s was beginning to come undone by the 1760s. "Mixture" in Rémy's catalog of Savalette de Buchelay's collection qualifies not the display but denotes instead the relation of the mineral specimens to the jars of chemical preparations arising from them.[41] Thus color, the distinguishing effect of Boucher's *cabinet* by grace of scope and visual surprise,[42] was the utility of Savalette's: copper produced copper acetate or verdigris, iron generated the hydrated oxides red and yellow ochre, ferrous ferro-cyanide salts precipitated Prussian blue, from lead came the compound lead carbonate or flake white, and from mercury, apparently, orpiment—red, yellow, and orange.[43] Meanwhile, in the case of shells, long before Rémy sharpened his **quill** to describe Boucher's *cabinet* in the terms in which it had been formed, those of exterior appearance—shape, color, pattern, and surface texture—other amateurs, such as Gabriel Bernard des Rieux, had begun to acknowledge the importance of the animal inside. Des Rieux had acquired anatomical preparations of shellfish by the scientist and academician Jean Méry to exhibit alongside his shells, and it was these, Dézallier d'Argenville admitted, that constituted proof that shells were not entirely "without purpose" ("*inutiles*").[44]

In 1757 Michel Adanson published a powerful critique of the aesthetic that informed contemporary collection and display of shells: "this very beauty," he wrote, "which attracts the eye to shells, has become a huge obstacle to the progress of science. . . . Up until now, molluscs have only been appreciated for their dress, their exterior envelope, the shell, and not the creatures that live inside them."[45] The result was a profound misunderstanding of the order of this branch of nature, which Adanson proposed to rectify with the help of illustration by the academician Marie-Thérèse Reboul-Vien (fig. 146). Drawing could enter the shell by section, could reinstate the lost animal. Bouchardon's preference for illustrated books over specimens, and his own practice of drawing animals from life (fig. 147), bore witness to the kind of productive—and not consumerist—engagement with knowledge that was deemed proper to the artist.[46]

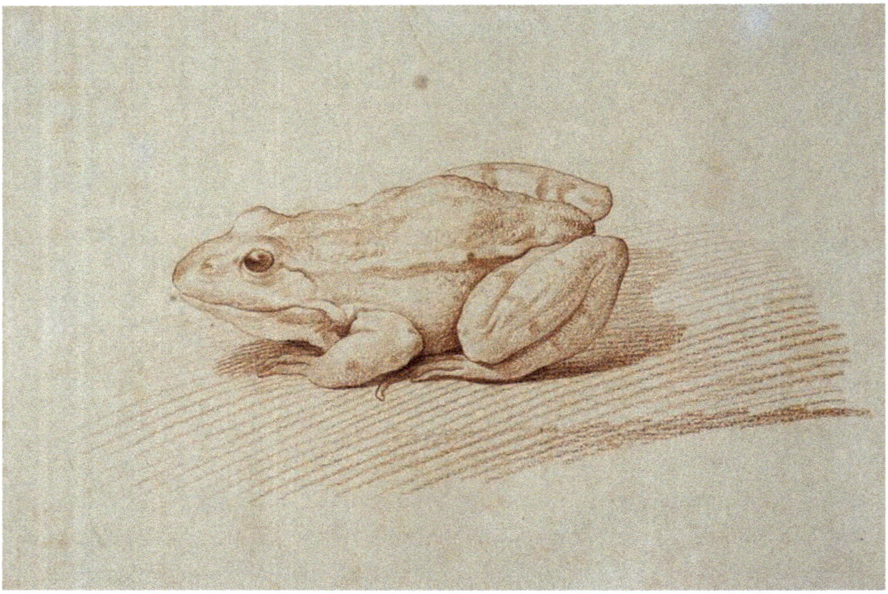

FIG. 147 Edme Bouchardon (French, 1698–1762), *Frog*, ca. 1745. Red chalk on paper, 15 × 20 cm. Paris, Musée du Louvre, Département des Arts Graphiques, INV24311-Bis-recto. (© RMN-Grand Palais / photo:Suzanne Nagy / Art Resource, NY.)

Boucher's shells may or may not have informed his artistic practice. Generic and specific shelly objects certainly feature in many of his designs for fountains, urns, and other decorative objects in the 1730s and 1740s, but their forms owe at least as much to ornament as to nature. Moreover, on the evidence of Boucher's sale, the style denoted by shells, the *rocaille*, was not conspicuously present at his Louvre interior. The keynote there was struck by minerals, not shells: the gilt bronze of Caffieri's "antique" lights, the marble tops of classic cabinets and consoles. It was, perhaps, the disconnection between Boucher's art and his things that led Mniszech to describe his *cabinet* as a shop, as if, that is, the objects had no reason for permanent residence. They were "arranged only to catch the eye" and offered "no further thought," for either the visitor or the artist.[47] The themes of superfluity, appearance, and disorder encountered in the critique of amateur conchology were ones also present in the luxury debate at the midcentury.[48] §

---

1. Pierre Rémy, *Catalogue raisonné des tableaux, desseins, estampes, . . . minéraux, cristallisations, mandrepores, coquilles & autres curiositées, qui composent le cabinet de feu M. Boucher, premier Peintre du Roi* (Paris: Musier, 1771); annotated copy at the INHA library, Paris.

2. "Tableaux: 41,965"; "Dessins: 16,047"; "Meubles: 15,003"; "Porcelaines: 14,557"; "Coquilles/polipines: 10,838"; "Minéraux/pierres: 9,856"; "Bronzes/lacques: 9,701"; "Estampes: 2,873."

3. René-Antoine Houasse and Jean-Baptiste Slodtz are among the very few other painters known to have bought shells in the 1730s. See Jessica S. Priebe, "Conchyliologie and Conchyliomanie: The Cabinet of François Boucher, 1703–1770," PhD diss., University of Sydney, 2011, 113.

4. See most recently Jamie Mulheron, "François Boucher and the Art of Conchology," *BM* 158 (2016): 254–63.

5. See Françoise Joulie's fuller discussion of Charles-Antoine Jombert's comments in Joulie, "La collection de François Boucher," in *L'artiste collectionneur de dessins*, ed. Catherine Monbeig-Gognel and Cordelia Hattori (Milan: 5 Continents, 2006), 129–219. See also Ewa Lajer-Burcharth, *The Painter's Touch* (Princeton: Princeton University Press, 2018), 73–80.

6. Bettina Dietz and Thomas Nutz, "Collections Curieuses: The Aesthetics of Curiosity and Elite Life in Eighteenth-Century Paris," *ECL* 29, no. 3 (2005): 44–75.

7. Fashion was a significant point of reference in specimen description (e.g., fanlike, lacelike, cufflike, pleated, *découpé*, fringed).

8. Krzysztof Pomian, "Médailles/coquilles = erudition/philosophie," Transactions of the IVth International Congress on the Enlightenment, *SVEC* 4 (1976): 1677–1703.

9. See Kristel Smentek, *Rococo Exotic: French Mounted Porcelains and the Allure of the East*, exh. cat., The Frick Collection (New York: Antique Collectors' Club, 2007); and Smentek, "Objects of Encounter: Mounting Asian Porcelain in Eighteenth-Century France," in *The Challenge of the Object*, ed. Ulrich Grossmann and Petra Krutish (Nuremberg: Germanischen Nationalmuseums, 2014).

10. For instances of such use or possible use in Boucher's collection, see Rémy, *Catalogue Boucher*, lots 1608, 1610. See also Antoine-Joseph Dézallier d'Argenville, *L'Histoire naturelle éclaircie* (Paris: De Bure, 1742), 95–96.

11. Rémy, *Catalogue Boucher*, lots 1350, 1354, 1359, 1363, 1369, and 1375.

12. On cleaning and polishing shells for display, see Dézallier d'Argenville, *L'histoire naturelle*, 98–101.

13. The notion that commodity is a phase in the biography of a thing is Igor Kopytoff's. See Kopytoff, "The Cultural Biography of Things: Commoditization as Process," in *The Social Life of Things: Commodities in Cultural Perspective*, ed. Arjun Appadurai (Cambridge, England: Cambridge University Press, 1986), 64–91.

14. Pierre Charles Alexandre Helle and Pierre Rémy, *Catalogue raisonné d'une collection considérable de coquilles rares et choisies du Cabinet de M Le **** (Paris: Didot, 1757), vii.

15. See Guillaume Glorieux, *À l'enseigne de Gersaint* (Seyssel: Champ Vallon, 2002), 562–76.

16. See Priebe, *Conchyliologie*, 123–25.

17. See Colin B. Bailey, "Marie-Jeanne Buzeau, Madame Boucher (1716–96)," *BM* 1047 (2005): 224–34.

18. Johann Christian von Mannlich, *Histoire de ma vie* (Trier: Spee, 1989), 2:156; Jo Hedley, *François Boucher: Seductive Visions* (London: Wallace Collection, 2004), 53–54; and Priebe, *Conchyliologie*, 131–40.

19. The definition of "*peak*," or wampum, and "*Porcelaine*," or cowrie, in *Encyclopédie*, http://encyclopedie.uchicago.edu/, 12:214; 13:106 indicates awareness that shells were currency in West Africa and the Americas. See also Marc Shell, *Wampum and the Origin of American Money* (Champaign: University of Illinois Press, 2013); and Toby Green, *A Fistful of Shells. West Africa from the Rise of the Slave Trade to the Age of Revolution* (London: Penguin, 2020).

20. Rémy, *Catalogue Boucher*, 235: lots 1695–97.

21. On the role of visuality in theories of value, see David Graeber, "Beads and Money: Notes towards a Theory of Wealth and Power," *American Ethnologist* 23, no. 1 (1996): 4–24.

22. See Georges Brunel, *Boucher* (London: Trefoil, 1986), 36; and Bailey, "Mme Boucher," 233.

23. On the market value of shells, see Bettina Dietz, "Mobile Objects: The Space of Shells in Eighteenth-Century France," *BJHS* 39, no. 3 (2006): 363–82.

24. See Rémy, *Catalogue Boucher*, lots 1698–1738.

25. Rémy, *Catalogue Boucher*, "Avant-propos."

26. See Rémy, *Catalogue Boucher*, frontispiece.

27. Antoine Bret de Dijon, "Nécrologe," reprinted in Alexandre Ananoff and Daniel Wildenstein, *François Boucher* (Lausanne: Bibliothèque des Arts, 1983), 1:136.

28. J. B. D. Lempereur, *Dictionnaire des artistes . . .* (1795), reprinted in Ananoff and Wildenstein, *Boucher*, 1:147–48.

29. Louis-Sébastien Mercier, *Tableau de Paris* (Amsterdam, 1781–88), 6:208–9.

30. Jacques-François Blondel, *L'architecture françoise* (Paris: Jombert, 1754–56), 4:36, and note (d).

31. Brunel, *Boucher*, 51–52; Hedley, *Boucher*, 54; Bailey, "Mme Boucher," 226; and Priebe, *Conchyliologie*, 145–76.

32. Bailey, "Mme Boucher," 227.

33. Bailey, "Mme Boucher," 227.

34. See Henri Gautier, *L'art de laver* (Lyon: Amaulry, 1687), 66–67; and "Dessein," *Encyclopédie, Recueil*, https://encyclopedie.uchicago.edu/, 2: plate II.

35. Lempereur, *Dictionnaire*, 147.

36. François Basan, *Catalogue des tableaux, desseins, estampes, livres d'histoire, sciences & arts de Bouchardon* (Paris: de Lormel, 1762), 3–8.

37. François Boucher, "Inventaire après décès," AN, MC/ET/LXXVI/384, 18 August 1762.

38. AN, MC/ET/LXXXVI/384, 18 August 1762; and Basan, *Catalogue . . . Bouchardon*, lots 163–64, 169, 171.

39. See Rosemarie Stratmann-Dohler, *Jean-François Oeben, 1721–1763* (Paris: Amateur, 2002), 38, 134. For specimens under glass, see Rémy, *Catalogue Boucher*, lots 1716, 1785.

40. Priebe, *Conchyliologie*, 174–75.

41. See Pierre Rémy, *Catalogue raisonné . . . de la succession M. de Savalette de Buchelay* (Paris: Didot, 1764).

42. Rémy, *Catalogue Boucher*, "Avant-propos."

43. Rémy, *Catalogue... de Savalette de Buchelay*, 14, 16–17, 21–22, and 25.

44. Antoine-Joseph Dézallier d'Argenville, *Conchyliologie* (Paris: De Bure, 1780), 1:231.

45. Michel Adanson, *Histoire naturelle du Sénégal: Coquillages* (Paris: Bauche, 1757), vi. Adanson's collection was given by his heirs to the Musée National d'Histoire Naturelle in 1939. See E. Fisher-Piette, "Les mollusques d'Adanson," *Journal de Conchyliologie* 85, nos. 2–4 (1942): 101–377.

46. This is obviously not to say that Boucher did not draw animals, but it is to note that he did not, like Bouchardon, adopt the conventions of depiction particular to natural history.

47. André Mniszech, "Un gentilhomme polonais à Paris en 1767: Notes de voyage," *Revue rétrospective* 61 (1887): 108. Mniszech praised Mme la présidente de Bandeville's collection instead, noting that she *knew* her collection and showed it to visitors with "intelligence."

48. See, for example, Victor de Riquetti, marquis de Mirabeau, *L'ami des hommes* (Paris: Guillaumin, 1883), 275–315.

Sketchbook

Jean-Michel Moreau the Younger (1741–1814)

TYPE OF OBJECT	THEME	MATERIAL
Artwork, Companion, Souvenir, Tool	Education, Everyday, Family, Making, Studio, Travel	Animal | Leather/Parchment, Metal | Gold/Gilding, Mineral | Chalk, Synthetic Materials | Paper

Jean-Michel Moreau's sketchbook does not really look like a sketchbook (fig. 148).[1] A small, leather-bound, hard-covered volume, with decorative tooling and gilding, and even its own title—"ETU/DES" (studies)—inscribed in a panel on the spine. Moreau's sketchbook appears far more like a **book** that might be at home on a shelf amid plays, poetry, treatises, and histories. More commonly in the eighteenth century, artists' sketchbooks took the form of *carnets*, a kind of notebook (not unlike Johann Georg Wille's **journal** (see fig. 86), though with different paper) with fairly workaday binding that could be purchased from stationers' shops or suppliers of artists' materials. Jacques-Louis David, for instance, tended to shop for his sketchbooks near the Louvre, buying at least one from a color merchant on Rue du Coq Saint-Honoré and another from a paper merchant on Rue des Prêtres Saint-Germain-l'Auxerrois.[2] By contrast, Moreau's sketchbook was an object that seemed to owe its materiality to the largely Left Bank world of bookbinders and booksellers, in which Moreau had been immersed since 1765, when he married the niece of a bookseller and printer.[3] From the outside, Moreau's sketchbook thus pulls us into the public spaces of the Paris book trade. But on the inside, its drawings evoke a far more private sphere of personal encounters and intimate sociability. Made in a period when the lines between professional and domestic were less distinctly drawn, this was a thing that embodied and navigated those mutable boundaries.

Moreau's choice of word for the contents of his book, reiterated again in handwriting on the flyleaf ("Etudes de M. Moreau"), is also different from that selected by David or Hubert Robert, who used croquis (quick sketches) to describe the contents of their sketchbooks.[4] One such *carnet*, kept by Robert in Rome, contains page after page of monuments, architectural spaces, antiquities, and figures—some hasty, some partial, some crammed together on shared sheets. Perhaps exactly what we might imagine an artist's sketchbook to resemble, Robert's *carnet* served as something between an album, storing images for reuse in future artworks (like the bound books of figure studies kept by Antoine Watteau to populate his fêtes galantes), and a travelogue, recording the encounters and experiences of his European voyage.[5] Moreau's sketchbook, meanwhile, contained a record of more local travels through the homes and spaces he frequented in Paris—salons, sitting rooms, parlors, studios, workshops, churches, and very occasionally a street or park. The drawings he made in these spaces were not sketches of sites but carefully composed

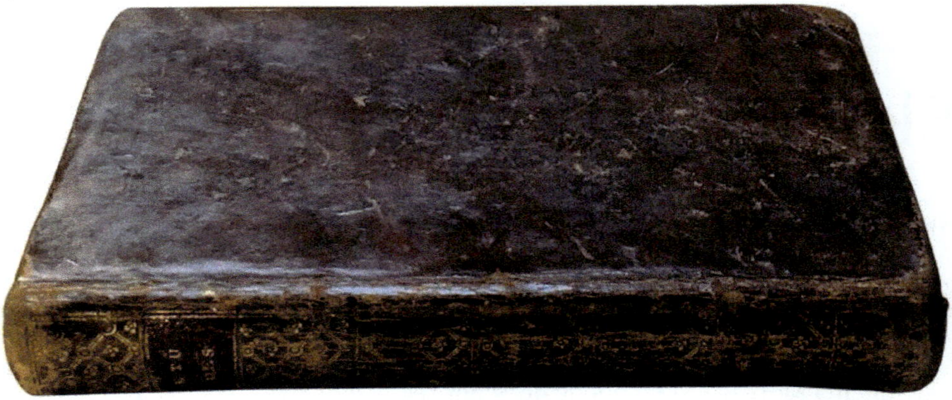

FIG. 148 Cover and binding of Jean-Michel Moreau the Younger's sketchbook, ca. 1770s. Brown leather with gilding, 18.2 × 11.1 cm. Paris, Musée du Louvre, Département des Arts Graphiques, Album Moreau Jean-Michel, RF1656. (© Musée du Louvre, dist. RMN-Grand Palais.)

studies of people, far more consistent in their form and subject matter than Robert's random croquis, but far more ambiguous in their purpose than Watteau's albums.

With only a handful of exceptions, every drawing in the book records an encounter with a person. Each figure, sketched invariably in pencil or black ***crayon***, fits a loose set of criteria: they nearly always appear on their own; they are usually absorbed in a moment of domestic or sociable activity; and they seldom acknowledge the draftsman's gaze, indeed they often seem thoroughly unaware of it.[6] Moreau evidently chose his opportunities deliberately, preferring subjects whose attention was protractedly caught elsewhere—reading, chatting, sewing, playing guitar, looking the other way, or even fast asleep. One young woman, for instance, is entirely focused on her needlework (fig. 149), looking down at her hands and concentrating on her stitches, while even the **dog** under her chair stares calmly off in the other direction. Another figure is completely beyond consciousness, having fallen asleep in his **armchair** (fig. 150). Named on the back of the page as Moreau's colleague Étienne Jeaurat, he is captured in a state of utter ease, dressed casually in shirtsleeves and cap with no **wig**, his legs comfortably outstretched on a stool, as though having drifted off during a casual visit or a session in the studio.[7] Despite the consistency of Moreau's interests in these drawings, it is difficult to pin down his motivations. Was he employing sketching as a diversion in these moments, occupying himself while those around him were otherwise engaged? Or was he taking advantage of his companions' stillness, using the extended time it afforded to linger over each observation? Whatever the case, "study" is certainly the most apt word for these drawings. Less rough and more composed than Robert's croquis, Moreau's *études* are efforts to consider, analyze, and contemplate each person in that moment.

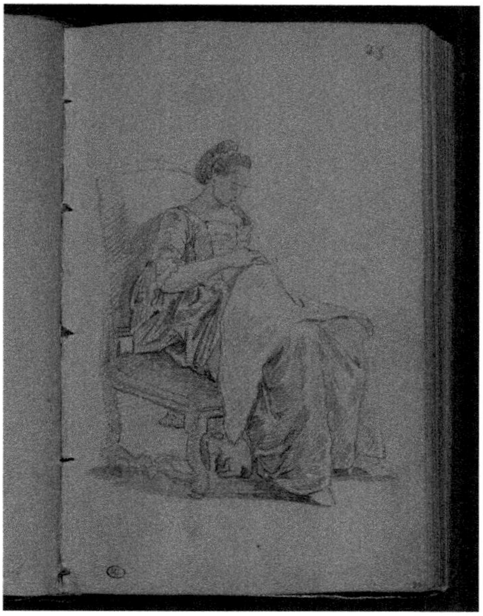

FIG. 149 Jean-Michel Moreau the Younger (French, 1741–1814), *Woman Sewing,* Album Moreau Jean-Michel, folio 23. Pencil on paper, 18.2 × 11.1 cm. Paris, Musée du Louvre, Département des Arts Graphiques, RF1640, 24. (© Musée du Louvre, Dist. RMN-Grand Palais / Marc Jeanneteau./ Art Resource, NY.)

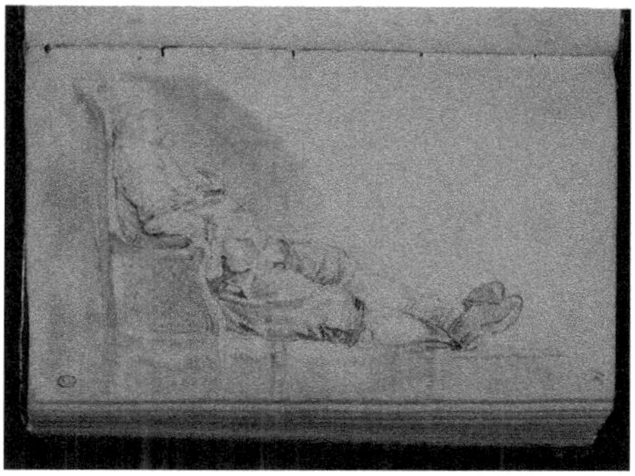

FIG. 150 Jean-Michel Moreau the Younger (French, 1741–1814), *Étienne Jeaurat Sleeping,* Album Moreau Jean-Michel, folio 14. Pencil with stumping on paper, 18.2 × 11.1 cm. Paris, Musée du Louvre, Département des Arts Graphiques, RF1631, 15. (© Musée du Louvre, Dist. RMN-Grand Palais / Marc Jeanneteau./ Art Resource, NY.)

Turning the pages of Moreau's sketchbook often feels like an intrusion into a private world. Whether or not his subjects were cognizant of their capturing, the images give the impression of covert glances and domestic informality. Taken together they are an intimate record of friends, family, and chance encounters, a collection seemingly made more for personal interest than professional purpose. But, as ever in the eighteenth century, that was an ambiguous distinction. Professionally, Moreau was a draftsman and engraver whose highest accolade was his appointment as *dessinateur du cabinet du roi* in 1775 (a title he used on the sketchbook's flyleaf). But from the 1770s onward, much of his practice was devoted to book illustration. According to his obituary from 1814, Moreau produced over 2,400 drawings destined to become engraved prints in books, including editions of ancient texts by Homer, Virgil, Ovid, and Thucydides; modern classics by Racine, Molière, Corneille, and La Fontaine; and contemporary works by Montesquieu, Crébillon, Marmontel, Rousseau, and Voltaire.[8] Creating images to complement and enhance the printed words of such diverse books, Moreau's subject matter was necessarily varied and quite different from his sketchbook drawings, from mythological stories and ancient histories to theatrical scenes and pastoral vignettes.

Yet for much of the contemporary literature, Moreau's studies of domestic encounters may have been as informative to his professional practice as Robert's buildings and monuments were to the landscapist. Among Moreau's most celebrated scenes of everyday life were, for instance, the illustrations he produced in the 1770s for a publishing project initiated by his uncle-in-law, Laurent Prault, which later became the *Monument du costume* (1789).[9] Relating quotidian events and contemporary tastes, the series included drawings like *Have No Fear, My Good Friend* (fig. 151), in which a woman pregnant with her first child lies in a daybed, conversing for reassurance with friends and a visiting priest. As they depict figures occupied with ordinary activities in the home, there is certainly something reminiscent of Moreau's sketchbook encounters, and yet their animation and theatricality could not be further from the sketchbook's moments of quiet absorption.[10] If Moreau's book illustrations were the staged performance of everyday life, then his sketchbook drawings were like the private view, the real observations that would be edited later into fictionalized worlds.

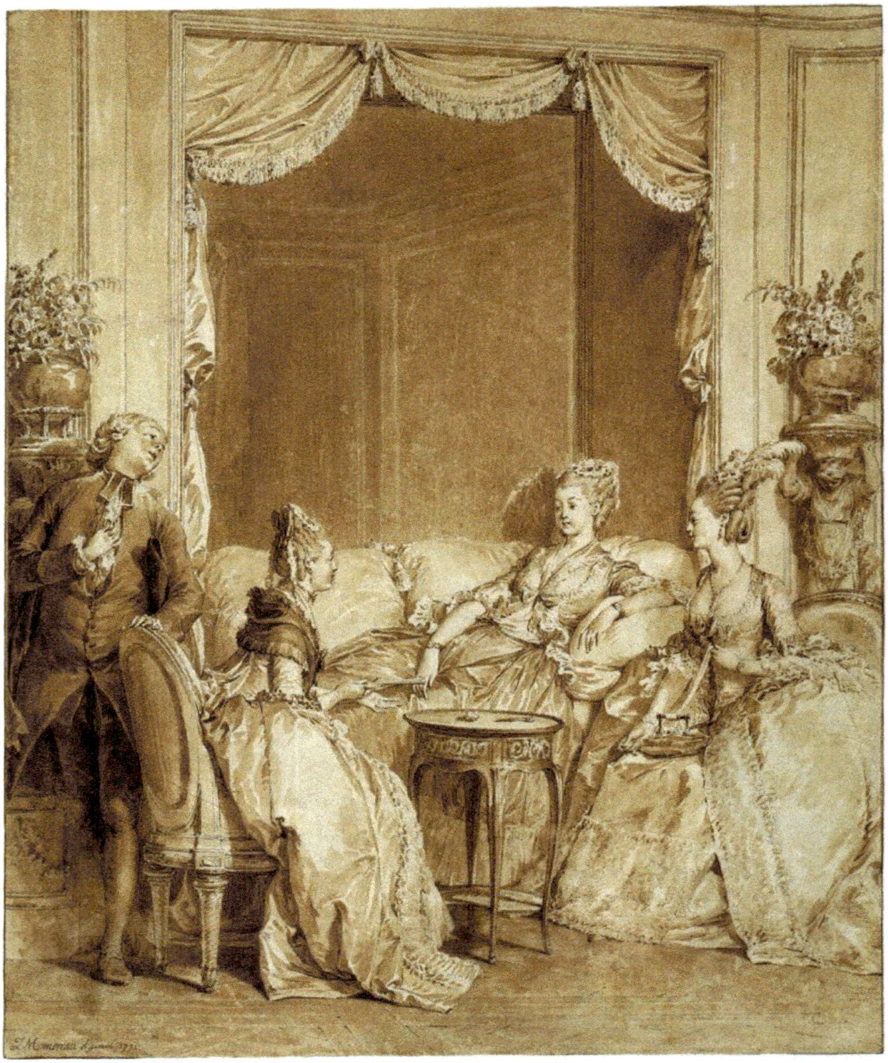

FIG. 151 Jean-Michel Moreau the Younger (French, 1741–1814), *Have No Fear, My Good Friend*, 1775. Pen and brown ink and brush and brown wash, 26.7 × 21.6 cm. Los Angeles, The J. Paul Getty Museum, 85.GG.416.

As a material thing and a used thing, Moreau's sketchbook sits somewhere in between the categories of objects in this book. In some ways, it fits most neatly with tools, things that artists used to enable the practical and technical aspects of their work. Alongside **burins**, ***crayons***, chalk holders, **shells**, brushes, and **camera obscuras**, Moreau's sketchbook formed part of the arsenal of studio equipment that the draftsman-engraver needed to make and create—a tool for recording ideas, practicing techniques, or seeking inspiration. In other ways, however, as an artwork in its own right, the sketchbook might align more closely with things like Largillière's **picture** or Drevet's **votive**: art objects that were called upon to serve functional as well as aesthetic purposes. But in quite different ways, the sketchbook might have more in common with the written books that artists kept to manage their affairs—things like **journals** and **order books**. With these, the sketchbook shared not only their physical form of bound pages but also that particular quality of their contents, where professional matters became inextricably entwined with domestic life. Despite the near total absence of words, the sketchbook certainly reads like a diary of mingled recollections: a sleepy afternoon in the workshop, when a student dozed off against the wall mid-sketch; a lighthearted episode playing with the dog on the floor; a time when his former master, Jacques-Philippe Le Bas, pontificated from a chair with cane in hand; a moment witnessing two gossiping ladies in church; or the numerous occasions (twice at least) when Jeaurat nodded off for a nap.[11] With his working world embodied in its binding, and the private sociability navigated through its pages, Moreau's sketchbook was surely the most personal of all the books he illustrated. ‡

---

1. Album Moreau Jean-Michel, Musée du Louvre, RF1656. Thanks to David Pullins for discussions about this object.

2. Sellers labels appear inside the covers of Album David Jacques-Louis 2, Musée du Louvre D.A.G., RF6071; and Album David Jacques-Louis 3, Musée du Louvre D.A.G., RF9136.

3. Moreau's wife was Françoise Pineau, daughter of the sculptor François Pineau and Jeanne-Marie Prault, whose brother was Laurent Prault, the *libraire-imprimeur*. On Moreau's biography and family, see Adrien Moureau, *Les Moreau* (Paris: G. Pierson, 1893).

4. The word *croquis* is written on the title page, cover, or flyleaf of numerous sketchbooks including: Hubert Robert Roman Sketchbook (1760), The Morgan Library & Museum, New York, inv. 1958.5; Album Robert Hubert 2, Musée du Louvre D.A.G., RF55311; and Album David Jacques-Louis 3, Musée du Louvre D.A.G., RF9136.

5. Hubert Robert Roman Sketchbook (1760), The Morgan Library & Museum, New York, inv. 1958.5. On the nomenclature of different kinds of bound repositories for drawings and their uses, see David Pullins, "Albums and Sketchbooks," *Drawing: The Invention of a Medium*, exh. cat. (Cambridge: Harvard Art Museums, 2017), 135–43; and Christian Michel, "Le goût pour le dessin en France aux XVIIe et XVIIIe siècles: De l'utilisation à l'étude désintéressé," *Revue de l'art* 143 (2004): 27–34. On Watteau's drawings and albums, see Alan Wintermute, ed., *Watteau and His World: French Drawing from 1700 to 1750*, exh. cat. (New York: American Federation of Arts, 2000).

6. Of the fifty-eight drawings in the book, only five are not figure studies.

7. Moreau almost never named his sketchbook figures or annotated the drawings in any way. Only three include names, all of them depicting artists (two of Jeaurat and one of Jacques-Philippe Le Bas).

8. "Notice sur M. Moreau" (excerpt from *Moniteur*, no. 355, 1814, [2–3]. See also Linda Gil, "Les illustrations des *Contes* et *Satires* de Voltaire par Moreau le Jeune, pour la première édition des *Oeuvres complètes* de Voltaire (1784–1789)," *Féeries* 11 (2014): 221–43.

9. Moreau's drawings first appeared in the *Seconde suite d'estampes pour servir à l'histoire des moeurs et du costume française dans le dix-huitième siècle* (1777). They were re-published in the *Monument du costume* (1789). On this publication, see Colette Bertrand, "Le 'Monument du costume' de Rétif de la Bretonne," *Dix-huitième siècle* 15 (1983): 389–406.

10. This is to invoke Michael Fried's theory of the contrasting dynamics of theatrical and absorptive relations to the beholder in eighteenth-century French art. Michael Fried, *Absorption and Theatricality: Painting and Beholder in the Age of Diderot* (Chicago: University of Chicago Press, 1980).

11. The drawings referred to are on folios 14, 16, 24, 28, 35, and 39 of Album Moreau Jean-Michel, Musée du Louvre, RF1656.

Snuffbox

Jean-Baptiste Oudry (1686–1755)

TYPE OF OBJECT	THEME	MATERIAL
Apparel, Collectible, Commodity, Container, Intoxicant	Global Commerce, Identity, Leisure, Luxury	Metal | Gold/Gilding, Plant Matter, Synthetic Materials | Lacquer, Synthetic Materials | Paint/Pigment

The still-life painter Jean-Baptiste Oudry took snuff. The evidence for his habit is circumstantial. In the portrait of the artist painted by Jean-Baptiste Perronneau in 1753 (fig. 152), a red, white, and blue striped **handkerchief** blooms from the sitter's unbuttoned pocket. It is the kind of large, dark-colored utilitarian handkerchief that was known as a *mouchoir de tabac*, or snuff napkin (see fig. 70). The painted handkerchief therefore implies the presence of a snuffbox, if not in the same pocket then perhaps in the pocket of his white silk under-waistcoat, closer to the body for safer keeping. It could have been any one of the twenty different snuffboxes inventoried two years later at Oudry's lodgings at the Galerie du Louvre, Rue des Orties.[1] Given the studio context of the portrait's fiction and the silhouette of the dog outlined in white on the canvas ready for work, the gold-lined, lacquered box (*boëte de vernis*) listed in the inventory and described as decorated on all sides with animals and hunting scenes, "painted by the late Mr. Oudry," would have been particularly appropriate. It is this lost thing that our book aims to know better in order to understand how and why a snuffbox became an artist's thing in the eighteenth century, precious (valued at 240 livres in the inventory) and doubly personal to Oudry for having been made for and, in part, by him.

Inventory and portrait point to contexts for the interpretation of Oudry's snuffbox. The dominant piece of case furniture inventoried in Oudry's mezzanine *cabinet*, where the snuffboxes were found, was an "English" oak bureau-bookcase with multiple drawers and compartments in which the snuffbox was possibly kept when not on his person.[2] Pockets and drawers have this in common: in them things are recessed and removed from view. In other ways, however, drawers and pockets differ. The sequestered world of the drawer created by new techniques of cabinetmaking that transformed old forms of case furniture like the coffer into new varieties, such as the chest of drawers and the bureau, reorganized domestic belongings by imposing on them systems of classification and valuation detached from use.[3] Snuffboxes came under the category of *bijoux*, or jewels. As such, they were grouped with other luxuries, such as **watches**, and were separated from clothes, on the one hand, and from papers and writing equipment (the things typically brought to order by the desk), on the other.[4] In the space of the desk, each of Oudry's snuffboxes would have assumed an identity in relation to all the others: as the round, oval, square, or oblong box; as the gold, turtle-shell, wood, lacquer, or porcelain box; as the snuffbox covered in shagreen, or decorated with rhinestone; as the portrait box, or the box with the medal on

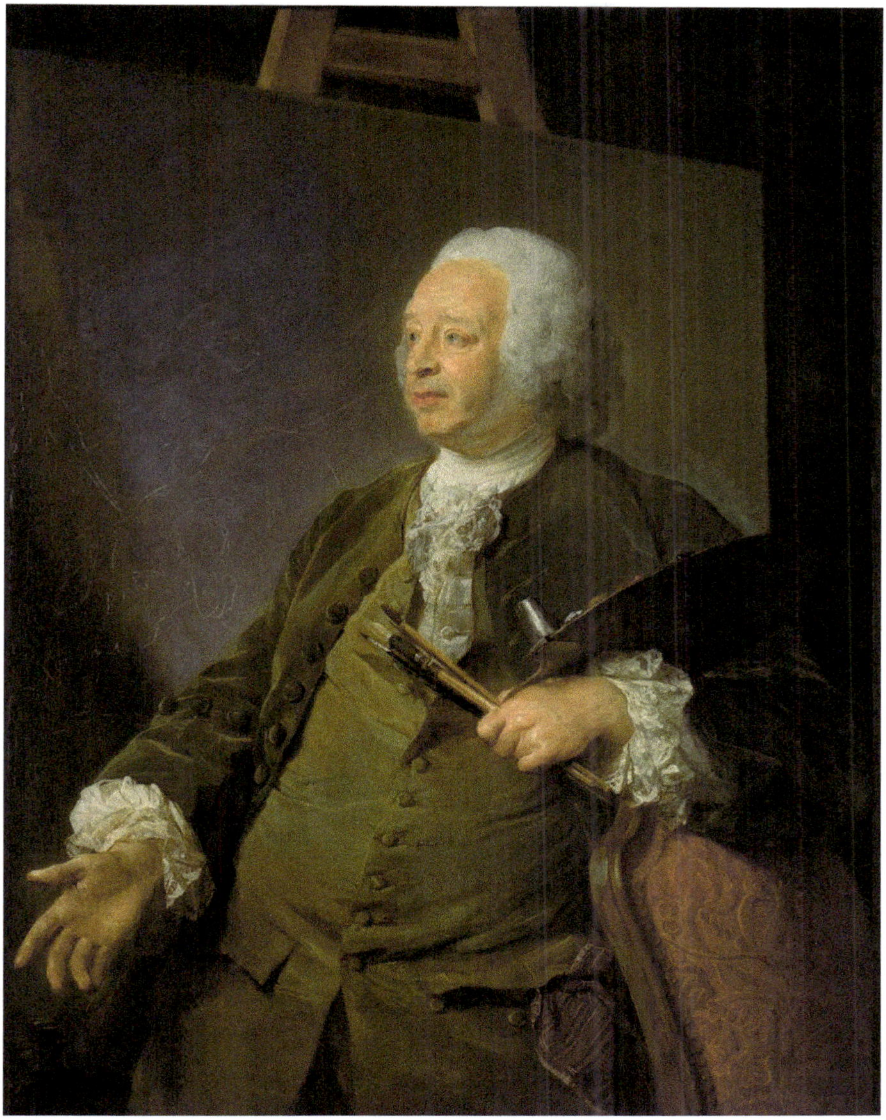

FIG. 152 Jean-Baptiste Perronneau (French, 1686–1755), *Jean-Baptiste Oudry*, 1753. Oil on canvas, 131 × 105 cm. Paris, Musée du Louvre, INV7158. (© RMN-Grand Palais /Photo: Franck Raux / Art Resource, NY.)

its lid, struck to commemorate the marriage in 1745 of the dauphin to the infanta of Spain.[5] Their functionality was secondary to their variety—variety fostered by expansion of the overseas trade in tobacco. By the 1740s, the volume and value of France's importation of Virginian tobacco via Britain exceeded that of every other nation.[6] Completely indigenized as a commodity by travel literature, natural history texts, newspaper articles, and consumer literature, tobacco was, by 1700, poised to spread as a consumer item to all social classes and to stimulate in turn growth and diversity in the snuffbox.[7]

The contents of a pocket, in contrast, is seemingly random and without singular cause. When the history painter Jean-Marc Nattier was arrested for sodomy in 1725, the inventory of his pockets itemized the following: a desk key, a toothpick holder, two ***porte-crayons***, a lorgnette, and a microscope.[8] These objects make sense not as a category or collection of thing but in relation to the body. The pocketed things variously enhanced, by prosthetics, the pocket-coat wearer's skills: to access, to clean, to draw, and to see, in Nattier's case. Things in pockets are always, therefore, connected to actions and gestures. The pocket is the starting point of a highly stylized gesture by which the snuffbox is drawn from the pocket with the right hand, placed in the left, tapped, opened, a pinch of snuff removed with the right thumb and index finger, the box closed, the snuff inhaled from the thumb or the back of the left hand, and the box returned with the right hand to the pocket, only for the performance to begin again.[9] Significant here is the technology of the box, not its style: first, precision in the working of its moving parts to ease opening and closing while preserving tightness in the seal to prevent spillage of snuff when the box is stored, and second, balance when the box is open so that the weight of the lid does not upend the mess of contents.

Snuff-taking as a two-handed gesture is an occupation that necessarily interrupts others, such as drawing and painting. That Perronneau did not depict a snuffbox in his portrait of Oudry at work (see fig. 152), that he, in fact, painted its absence by rhyming the colors of the handkerchief with the paint charged on the palette, disavowing snuff's power to suspend painting, is perhaps not surprising, given that as a *morceau de récéption* the portrait was to hang in the rooms of the Académie and to inspire future generations of painters and sculptors. The image of the studio that the Académie sought to perpetuate through its member portraits was, predictably perhaps, of the studio as a place of art, not sociability, though we know the practices of both were in fact tightly enmeshed. Why, then, did Oudry decorate one of his snuffboxes, and in so doing underscore his relation to a substance, habit, and thing apparently contrary to his vocation?

Eighteenth-century painters were active in the luxury trades, which from the 1760s included the production of gold boxes mounted *à cage*.[10] In snuffboxes of this kind only the armature (*cage*), rather than the whole body of the box, was made of gold. Plaques of lacquer, or mother-of-pearl, or semi-precious hardstone, or miniatures painted on card, ivory, or vellum were inserted into the cagework to create a complex and "curious" visual effect.[11] Some artists, such as the Van Blarenberghe family, specialized in such commercial painting. For academicians it provided some others with an occasional outlet: Claude-Joseph Vernet supplied his friend and neighbor at the Louvre, the court jeweler Ange-Joseph Aubert, with miniature landscapes for the purpose.[12] We will probably never know exactly what kind of landscapes Vernet supplied—whether, for instance, scenes from his Atlantic seaports, such as the *Port of Bordeaux*, or the *Port of La Rochelle*, ports at which the colonial commodities he depicted on the quayside—tobacco, sugar, cotton—were actually landed. We do know for certain, however, that Oudry eschewed drawing on his repertoire of imagery of the Four Continents to match the decoration of his snuffbox to its contents. In the center foreground of *America* (fig. 153), one of four overdoors he painted in 1724, he depicted the hogsheads in which tobacco was traded and transported to Europe. Omitted here is any direct reference to plantations and enslaved labor.[13] Such failures to connect slavery and the things produced from it were, according to historians of colonialism, commonplace before the beginning of the abolitionist movements in the 1770s.[14] Oudry's occlusions in the overdoor were perpetuated, even amplified, in his decoration of his snuffbox, on the surfaces of which America in any of her discursive forms is nowhere to be seen.

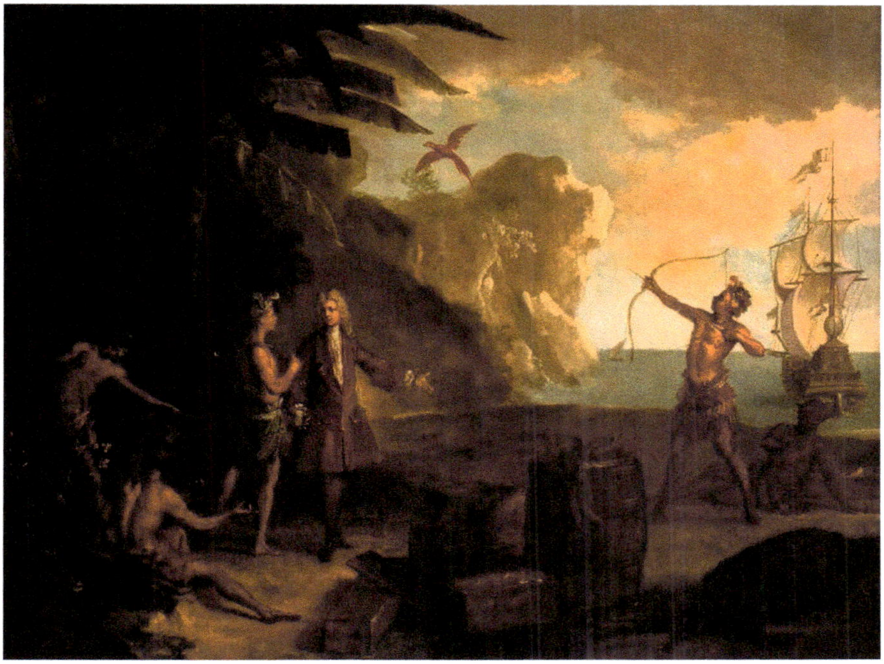

FIG. 153 Jean-Baptiste Oudry (French, 1686–1755), *America*, from *The Four Continents*, 1724. Oil on canvas. Current location unknown. (Photo © Christie's Images/Bridgeman Images.)

The notary's description of the craftsmanship of Oudry's snuffbox is short on the kind of detail that would enable us to know it fully as a material thing, and, in particular, to understand how it integrated different materials and media: (Oudry's) painting in gouache and lacquer. Consumers had been infatuated by lacquer since its arrival from Asia in significant quantity at the end of the seventeenth century, infatuated sufficiently to give rise, in the eighteenth, to a market for imitation domestic lacquer combining surface shine with chinoiserie or *pittoresque* ornament.[15] Oudry's snuffbox may have resembled one of the *papier maché tabatières*, with hunting-dog, exhibited at *Les Secrets de la laque française* at the Musée des Arts Décoratifs in 2014 (fig. 154), which featured an Oudry hunting-dog on its lid.[16] Were this so, it might on the one hand indicate the painter's openness to exploiting his talent to decorative ends, and a related interest in new uses for art materials (varnish) in the luxury trades.[17] On the other hand, choice of lacquer and the exotic, orientalist glow it affords can also propose Oudry's snuffbox as a candidate of Madeleine Dobie's "displacement," whereby representation of the colonial is relocated on the veneered surfaces of the "oriental."[18] By bringing together materials, techniques and representation in this way, even hypothetically, we can entertain the possibility of tension in the surfaces and voids of Oudry's snuffbox, not so much in the making as in the meaning of the making. Though Oudry assumed a position at either end of the commodity chain, as simultaneously both producer and consumer of the snuffbox, it was, however, in his place as consumer that this particular snuffbox served as a foundation of the subjectivity that he projected through his possession of it.

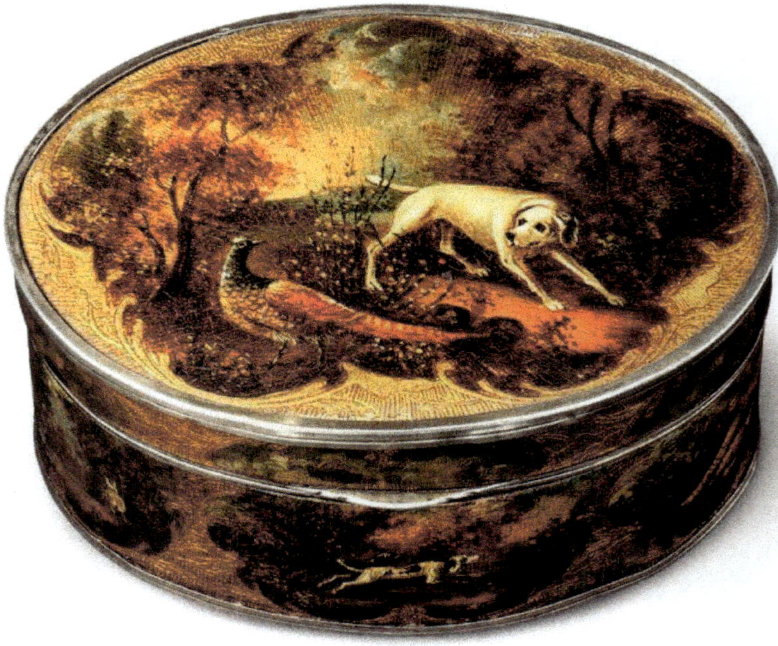

FIG. 154 Snuffbox, ca. 1740. *Papier maché*. Private collection.

Louis-Nicolas van Blarenberge signed his snuffboxes; arguably, Oudry's snuffbox was his signature. In his desk along with his snuffboxes and **watches** was a seal emblazoned with a **dog**—the seal with which, presumably, he closed his letters and announced himself to addressees in advance of those letters being opened.[19] The dog figures in the abbé Louis Gougenot's life of Oudry likewise as the sign and agent of the painter's artistic identity.[20] Oudry had first trained as a portrait painter under Nicolas de Largillière; it was, according to Gougenot, Largillière's praise of Oudry's portrayal of the dog, not the sitter, in Oudry's inaugural portrait of a *chasseur*, that instituted his calling to animal painting and set him on the road to independent artistic recognition. The simple, single, and explicit function of biography and seal to name is not, however, shared by the snuffbox, which characterizes rather than denotes its subject, and does so by association with the ideology of snuff.

The work performed by the snuffbox in the visual discourse of eighteenth-century male portraiture was to signify status through leisure, not luxury. In Quentin de La Tour's portraits of the 1740s, for example, it either recalibrated the active, standing body around a decentered axis, delicately swaying the pose to the right to counter the weight of the box in the left hand, or, when the sitter was depicted seated, it silenced the fiction of speech acts by monopolizing both hands in the gesture of snuff taking, their withdrawal from meaningful bodily communication marked by analogy with the knot of gracefully crossed legs. In neither of the portrait by La Tour of Étienne Perrinet de Jars (1740, Baltimore Museum of Art) nor Louis Duval d'Épinay (1745, Lisbon, Museu Calouste Gulbenkian), evoked here, was the snuffbox itself the fetishized object of attention. Virtually hidden by the hands, it was a prop in the ritualized performance of a social practice.[21] In the literary discourse of the eighteenth century, meanwhile, the snuffbox was often paired with the **watch**, not on grounds of difference but on principle of likeness. Leisure time is for watching, not regulating and filling.[22] In *Jacques le fataliste* (ca. 1765–80), Denis Diderot assigned play with snuffbox *and* watch to Jacques's master as his defining tic. His tap to gather snuff in advance of the *prisé*, and his snap to follow and close the box, echo the tick-tock of his watch, and afforded time a daily measure for the tedium of leisure by the quantity of snuff remaining unconsumed at nightfall.[23] Diderot appropriated the elite commodity box, and its image of benign gentility, and freighted it anew as an iconic object of bad luxe, or waste, in this his late comic fable of aristocratic idleness.

The snuffbox's lack of semiotic fixity, its standing as a metasymbol for luxury goods, and the debates for and against the materiality of modern culture suggests that acting out the self through gestures of snuff taking was not without risk. The refinement of snuff, its dark natural color lightened by addition of yellow ocher, its acrid taste and smell when raw, softened by blending with orange blossom, jasmine, or rose, raised the snuff taker above the vulgar smoker;[24] yet inactivity—idleness—potentially also shamed the nicotine-addicted artist.[25] For Oudry it was a risk apparently worth taking. The aristocracy of his clientele, his extensive employment by the crown, and his lodgings at the Louvre had not conferred upon him the reputation of a gentleman. He was known rather for his exceptional industry: Gougenot describes him as a workaholic, straining to build a family enterprise, exploiting his artistic capital by efficient production of lines of copies—in short, as commercially orientated and successful in business.[26] Was the attraction of snuff its promise to offset this bourgeois artisanal image by integrating gentlemanly leisure as the also, not the other, of the entrepreneurial artist? Not according to Gougenot. He selected the guitar as the sign of Oudry's affective life away from the studio, no doubt because of the sisterhood attributed to music and painting in humanist art theory, and also, more importantly, because sociability is necessarily entailed by musical performance.[27] Oudry the guitarist was gay, cheerful, amusing, or good company, defining characteristics in the eighteenth century of the good artist or happy genius. The consumption of snuff, though a companionable habit, did not resonate with painting in the same way, even though the practices involved in its preparation and consumption required many of the substances, tools, and skills familiar to painting.[28] It was the immateriality of smoke and the association of smoking with dreaming that revolutionized relations between tobacco and art and led to the representation of smoking as a condition of creativity.[29] §

---

1. Jean-Baptiste Oudry, "Inventaire après décès," AN, MC/ET/LIII/345, 7 May 1755.

2. The cabinet was situated on the mezzanine floor, next to the dining room. The bureau is described as "an English oak secretaire with two large and two small drawers below and several compartments and drawers above enclosed behind a pair of doors (un secrétaire anglois de bois de chêne à deux grands et deux petits tiroires par bas, à deux volets par haut avec plusieurs compartimens et tiroirs)." It was valued at 84 livres.

3. Glenn Adamson, "The Labor of Division: Cabinetmaking and the Production of Knowledge," in *Ways of Making and Knowing: The Material Culture of Empirical Knowledge*, ed. Pamela Smith, Amy Meyers, and Harold Cook (Chicago: University of Chicago Press, 2014), 243–79.

4. Inventoried were two Paris-made **watches** *à répétition* in their gold cases.

5. The argument that the snuffboxes in the desk address themselves to sight more than use is supported by the lack of other snuff-taking paraphernalia (tobacco jars and rasps) inventoried in the room.

6. See Jacob M. Price, *France and the Chesapeake: A History of the French Tobacco Monopoly 1674–1791* (Ann Arbor: University of Michigan Press, 1973); and also Jacob M. Price, "The Economic Growth of the Chesapeake and the European Market, 1697–1775," *Journal of Economic History* 24, no. 4 (1964): 796–511.

7. On the role of books in the indigenization of tobacco in the West, see Peter C. Mancall, "Tales Tobacco Told in Sixteenth-Century Europe," *Environmental History* 9, no. 4 (2004): 648–78. Oudry's modest collection of books included only one example of such literature: *Nouvelle relation contenant les voyages de Thomas Gage dans la nouvelle Espagne* (1648, Paris, Marret, 1699). While Gage describes a number of foods and products from the Americas and West Indies, notably chocolate, these do not include tobacco. On demiluxury goods, including snuffboxes, see Cissie Fairchilds, "The Production and Marketing of Populuxe in Eighteenth-Century Paris," in *Consumption and the World of Goods*, ed. John Brewer and Roy Porter (London: Routledge, 1994), 228–48.

8. Philippe Renard, *Jean-Marc Nattier (1685–1766)* (Saint-Rémy-en-l'Eau: Monelle Hayot, 1999), 52.

9. See *Mercure galant*, December 1693, 176–80; and Tessa Murdoch, "Snuff-taking, Fashion and Accessories," in *Going for Gold: Craftsmanship and Collecting of Gold Boxes*, ed. Tessa Murdoch and Heike Zeik (Brighton: Sussex Academic Press, 2014), 1–16.

10. See Charles Truman, "From the Boîte à Portrait to the Tabatière: The Production of Gold Boxes in Paris," in *Going for Gold*, 17–28, esp. 25–26. Some illegally produced boxes began to appear on the market in the 1740s, but production *à cage* only accelerated after 1756, when it became legal by an *arrêt du Conseil* of May 4.

11. None of Oudry's boxes were described as *à cage*, but along with them the notary inventoried two "petites plaques de Caillou d'Egypte en forme ovale" for mounting in that manner.

12. On Aubert, see Vincent Bastien, "L'orfèvre-joailler, Ange-Joseph Aubert, fournisseur de la reine Marie-Antoinette," *Versalia* 16 (2013): 31–46. On Vernet's work for him, see Léon Lagrange, *Joseph Vernet et la penture au XVIIIe siècle* (Paris: Didier, 1864), 1:188, 270–71.

13. Enslaved labor is depicted in the overdoor *Africa*. For viewers of the set, connections were there to be made between *Africa*, *America*, and *Europe* through colonial trade.

14. Exceptions in the case of Britain include Elizabeth Kim, "Race Sells: Racialized Trade Cards in Eighteenth-Century Britain," *Journal of Material Culture* 7, no. 2 (2012): 137–65; and Catherine Molineux, "Pleasures of the Smoke: 'Black Virginians' in Georgian London's Tobacco Shops," *The William and Mary Quarterly* 64, no. 2 (2007): 327–76.

15. See Thibaut Wolvesperges, *Le meuble français en lacque* (Paris: Édition de l'Amateur, 2000).

16. *Les Secrets de la laque française*, Paris, Musée des Arts Décoratifs (2014), 161, cat. 104. On the making of papier-maché boxes, see also "Tabatière de carton," *Encyclopédie*, http://encyclopedie.uchicago.edu/, 15:793–94.

17. Inventoried among Oudry's drawings were volumes of unattributed ornament (nos. 30, 37), containing designs by Gilles-Marie Oppenord (no. 25), Claude Gillot (no. 77), prints after Juste-Aurèle Meissonnier (no. 94), and a volume of his own ornamental work (no. 34), not to mention many items of chinoiserie. There can be little doubt of his interest in design.

18. Madeleine Dobie, *Trading Places: Colonization and Slavery in Eighteenth-Century French Culture* (Ithaca, NY: Cornell University Press, 2010), esp. 61–88.

19. "Un cachet garni d'un petit chien avec une cornaline" (a seal with a carnelian decorated with a little dog), valued with one of his watches at 100 livres. According to Pierre-Jean Mariette, seals were understood to have had biographical significance since antiquity; see Mariette, *Traité des pierres gravées* (Paris: Mariette, 1751), 20–25.

20. Abbé Louis Gougenot, "Vie de M. Oudry," in *Mémoires inédits*, 2:367.

21. When snuffboxes are visible in portraits (e.g., fig. 71), they are not in the hands but rest on a surface.

22. On the late emergence of accuracy as a measure of value for watches in the eighteenth century, see Marie-Agnès Dequidt, "La qualité de l'horlogerie commune à Paris, à la fin du dix-huitième siècle," *Histoire et mesure* 27, no. 2 (2012): 137–64.

23. Denis Diderot, *Jacques le fataliste* (Paris: Folio Classique, 1970), 59–60, 75, 77, 82, 138, 141, 143, 167, 169, 176–77, 202, 262, 286.

24. Gougenot, "Vie de M. Oudry," 377.

25. See the anecdote the painter Jacques-Charles Dutillieu tells about his grandfather's spoiled career at court owing to his having allowed a snuff-stained "roupie" (drop of snot) to fall on and ruin work destined for the duc de Bourgogne. *Livre de raison* *de Jacques-Charles Dutillieu*, ed. F Breghot du Lut (Lyon: Mougin-Rusand, 1886), 10–11.

26. Gougenot, "Vie de M. Oudry," 379.

27. Four guitars "de différentes marqueterie" were listed in Oudry's cabinet (along with the gold boxes) and valued together at 100 livres.

28. See Edme Ballard, *Discours sur le tabac* (Paris: Jombert, 1693), 88–89; and [J. Brunet], *Le bon usage du tabac en poudre* (Paris: Quinet, 1700), 46–48.

29. Marc-Antoine Girard de Saint-Amand's sonnet "Le fumeur" (1629) is an early example; Tacita Dean's *Portrait of David Hockney Smoking* (2016) is a recent one.

Sugar Spoon

François-Hubert Drouais (1727–75)

TYPE OF OBJECT	THEME	MATERIAL
Commodity, Intoxicant, Tableware	Food and Drink, Global Commerce	Metal | Silver

Did Drouais have a sweet tooth? Determining the culinary inclinations of an eighteenth-century artist is hampered by the omission of foodstuffs from the household contents generally itemized in estate inventories (with the notable exception of **wine**).[1] What Drouais preferred to eat and drink can, however, be surmised from the less perishable objects that he owned—the utensils, gadgets, and vessels used to prepare, cook, serve, and consume the family's meals and beverages. Given the period's proclivity to specialize when it came to the functionality of kitchenware and tableware, many of these items were differentiated for quite specific uses, so that a glance even at their assortment of spoons inadvertently reveals something of the Drouais family's dietary predilections. Via Drouais's *cuillères à bouche* (tablespoons), *cuillères à potage* (soup spoons), *cuillères à ragout* (gravy spoons), *cuillères à café* (teaspoons), a *cuillère à olive* (olive spoon), a *cuillère à moutarde* (mustard spoon), and a *cuillière à sucre* (sugar spoon), we encounter a palate for hot soups and stews, fiery condiments, salty bites, caffeinated beverages, and indulgent sweet treats.[2] There may be no trace of sugar itself in the records of Drouais's home, but its erstwhile presence is betrayed by that silver sugar spoon, and with it the artist's place in a global economy stretching from his Paris dining table to the plantations of the Caribbean and the slave trading ports of West Africa.

By the mid-eighteenth century, when Drouais was at the height of his career as a court and society portraitist, sugar had become a ubiquitous staple in the Parisian diet. Though still an extravagance for many, it was far from the elite luxury it had been before the expansion of French colonial territories—in particular Saint-Domingue (present-day Haiti) in 1664—and the development of an international trade network worth millions to French investors. Across the eighteenth century, according to Robert Stein, the economic value of French colonial sugar production increased fivefold (from 15 million livres in 1713, to 75 million in 1789) and by the end of the century, Parisians like Drouais consumed an average of ten pounds of sugar per person every year.[3] As supply increased demand, and demand increased supply, sugar's uses proliferated across "larder, kitchen, and pharmacy."[4] It had medicinal value as an ingredient in numerous remedies, particularly against coughs and colds, either as a syrup or as solid candies like *sucres d'orge* (barley sugars).[5] But its primary use was in cooking, both as an addictive sweetener and a powerful preservative, two modes of employment that were certainly in evidence in the Drouais household.[6]

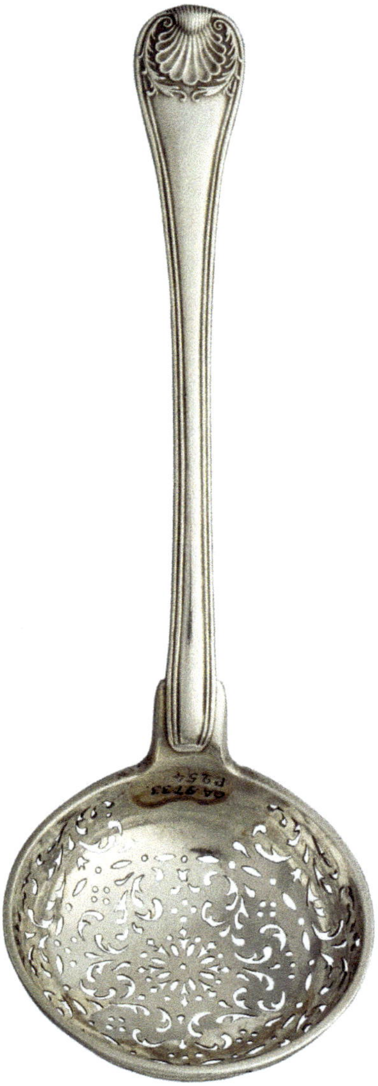

FIG. 155 Éloi Guérin (French, ca. 1714–65), Sugar spoon, 1757–58. Silver, Length 21.6 cm. Paris, Musée du Louvre, Inv. OA9733. (© RMN-Grand Palais / Art Resource, NY.)

Drouais's home on Rue Saint-Honoré, right next to the parish church of Saint-Roch, had not one but two kitchens: one on the ground floor backing onto a garden, the other upstairs on the fourth floor near the room that served as Drouais's painting studio. Each contained a variety of common European domestic items that, like his sugar spoon, owed their existence to a global trade of colonial commodities and reveal the quotidian ways in which the Drouais family participated—consciously or unconsciously—in those consumer economies. The sugar spoon in question was most likely a sifter spoon, used for casting sugar over dishes of fruit, desserts, or cakes. Made of silver by an unknown Parisian *orfèvre* (goldsmith), it may have resembled one in the Louvre produced by Éloi Guérin (fig. 155), with a perforated head designed to be dipped into a sugar bowl, then shaken gently to sprinkle sugar through the holes.[7] The specific foods that Drouais's spoon may have sweetened are harder to discern, but the family certainly seem to have been partial to a waffle, keeping no fewer than three sets of waffle irons in the upstairs kitchen. Waffles themselves required a substantial amount of sugar in the batter (half a pound per batch according to one midcentury recipe), but this could be supplemented with an extra sprinkle from the silver spoon when served hot at the table.[8] More sugar would have been required to sweeten coffee, which was clearly a beverage of choice for a family with seventeen cafetières distributed around the house and a coffee mill in the downstairs kitchen for grinding the roasted beans. The same kitchen was also equipped with a copper *poêle à confiture* (jam saucepan) for cooking fruits and vegetables into jams and preserves in recipes that required even larger quantities of sugar to act as a humectant, prolonging the life of condiments by fending off bacteria and mold.

A hearty consumer of sugar, Drouais was a small link in the global economic chain of this commodity, and yet his experience of sugar—as he enjoyed his coffee, waffles, and jam—would rarely have required much recognition of the realities of its production. From local acts of purchase to domestic rituals of use, Drouais's encounters with sugar were demonstrably detached from those colonial contexts, and indeed, following Elizabeth Heath, may have actively contributed to the increasing abstraction of colonial labor during this period.[9] This is not to say that Drouais would have been unaware of sugar's Caribbean origins or the slave labor that drove plantations. Sugar's farming and refinement were well documented in early modern texts, both general and specific, from Diderot's *Encyclopédie* to Jean-Baptiste du Tertre's *Histoire générale des Antilles*, both of which included descriptions and illustrations of enslaved workers.[10] Sébastien Leclerc's *Sucrerie* (fig. 156), for instance, a plate from Tertre's book, visualized the stages of sugar's production set in a Caribbean landscape, where Black plantation laborers gather cane and work the machinery at gunpoint. But, like the refining process that transformed raw sugar into the fine white powder sprinkled at Parisian tables, the sugar that reached Drouais had been semantically distilled from the violence of its production by layers of commerce and ritual.[11] For Drouais, shopping for sugar involved a simple walk down the street to one of his neighborhood's numerous *épiciers* (grocers) or apothecaries, the two trades permitted to retail sugar in eighteenth-century Paris.[12] By the 1770s, on Drouais's street alone, the lengthy Rue Saint-Honoré, there were at least eighteen *épiciers*, two of them—Monsieur Carrey-Villiers and Monsieur Travers—specialist *confiseurs* (confectioners) or purveyors of sugary products.[13] Consuming his purchased sugar was then facilitated through that paraphernalia of common household objects—spoons, casters, **teacups**, bowls, tongs—all of which created habits of practice that made sugar native to the Parisian home, a familiar component of daily routines.[14]

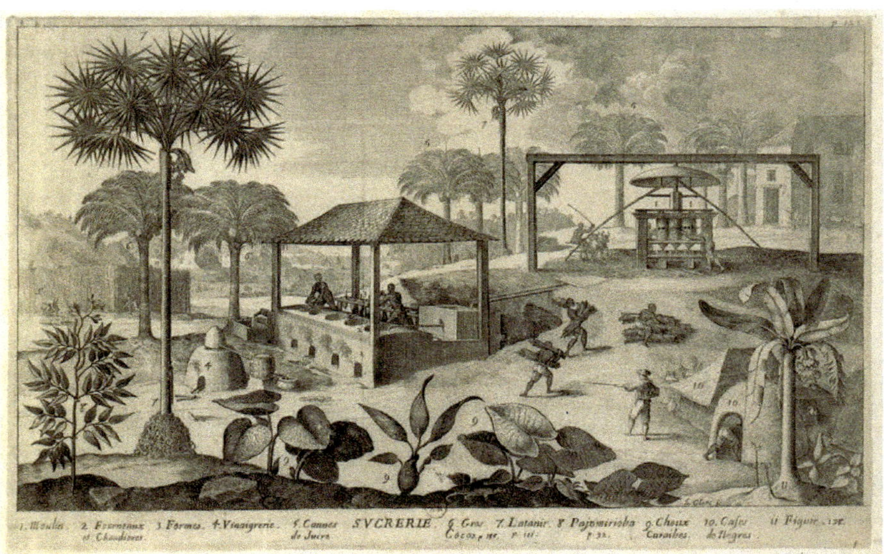

FIG. 156 Sébastien Leclerc (French, 1637–1714), *Sucrerie* (Stages of sugar production), from Jean-Baptiste du Tertre, *Histoire générale des Antilles habitées par les François* (Paris: Thomas Jolly, 1667), ED-59(A)-FOL Folio 28. Vol. 2, plate 9. (© RMN-Grand Palais / Art Resource, NY. Photo: BnF, Dist. RMN-Grand Palais / image BnF.)

Drouais's sugar spoon was, like Oudry's tobacco-filled **snuffbox**, a European thing that existed with and because of a colonial commodity. These luxury objects were symbiotically linked to the substances they served, each depending on the other for purpose and enhancing the market together for both. Yet, in their design, both spoon and snuffbox actively abstracted those colonial economies to which they were inextricably tied.[15] In the case of Drouais's spoon, this is an assumption, for there is no description of its decoration beyond the *poinçon* (mark) of its Parisian maker.[16] Most midcentury sifter spoons, however, adopted the kind of ornamentation found in Guérin's (see fig. 155): common rococo motifs (like scallop shell ends and C-scroll foliage perforations) that cast no allusions to a colonial connection. While this was the norm, not all tableware maintained such decorative detachment. Though rarer, some objects did explicitly call attention not only to the colonial commodity they held but to the oppressive colonial labor that produced it.

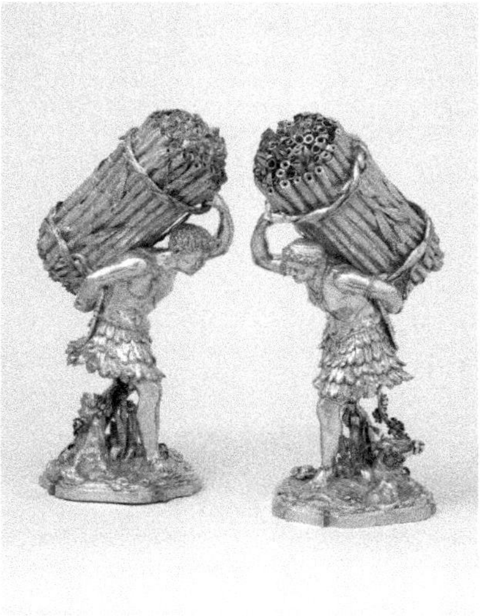

FIG. 157 Unknown maker, Pair of sugar casters in the form of enslaved plantation workers, ca. 1730–40. Silver, 28.2 × 11 × 15 cm. Paris, Musée du Louvre, Inv. OA 11749, 11750. (© RMN-Grand Palais / Photo: Martine Beck Coppola / Art Resource, NY.)

A pair of silver *sucriers* (sugar casters), once in the collection of Louis-Henri, duc de Bourbon, are a case in point (fig. 157).[17] Taking the form of two enslaved plantation workers—a man and a woman—the figures stoop under the weight of enormous bundles of harvested sugar cane, which, in the logic of the instrument, served as the receptacles for the powdered sugar to be poured through pierced holes at the ends. At the time of their making, these enslaved figures circulated through the same decorative discourses as playful peasants or exotic *chinoiseries*, bodies other to the elite French consumers who owned them.[18] To the modern viewer, however, these are far more difficult objects than Drouais's spoon. Not only does their form grossly trivialize the suffering of the enslaved bodies, turning them into playthings for the aristocratic table, but as functional instruments that serve, the objects become a disturbing stand-in for their represented human subjects who, under France's *Code noir*, were likewise items of property serving a master.[19] By comparison, a spoon innocuously decorated with organic motifs seems far less problematic. And yet, considered differently, might not the decorative detachment of a spoon like Drouais's actually be just as troubling? The enslaved figures that form the *sucriers* are, after all, at least an acknowledgment of some kind (however indifferent) of the trafficked bodies and slave labor that produced the sugar they cast. The spoon, meanwhile, so similar in function, innocently dissociates itself from any colonial connections, placing itself instead at a resolutely European remove: just a piece of Parisian silverware, like any other item of cutlery on the table.

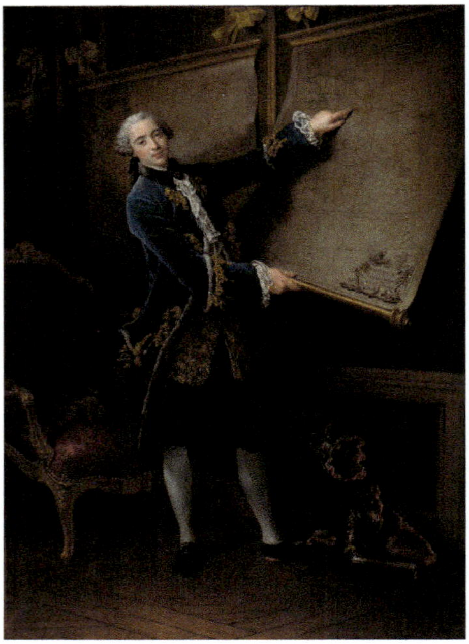

FIG. 158 François-Hubert Drouais (French, 1727–75), *Portrait of Joseph-Hyacinthe-François de Paule de Rigaud, comte de Vaudreuil*, 1758. Oil on canvas, 225 × 161.1 cm. London, National Gallery, Presented by Barons Emile-Beaumont d'Erlanger, Frédéric d'Erlanger and Rodolphe d'Erlanger, in memory of their parents, 1927, NG4253 (© National Gallery, London / Art Resource, NY.)

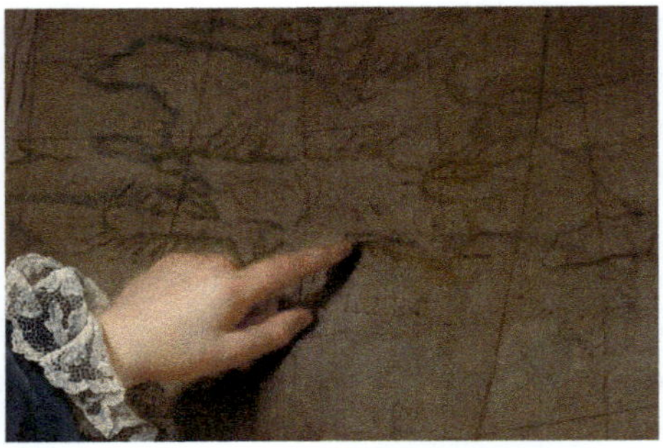

FIG. 159 François-Hubert Drouais (French, 1727–75), *Portrait of Joseph-Hyacinthe-François de Paule de Rigaud, comte de Vaudreuil*, detail, with a map showing the French colony of Saint-Domingue (present-day Haiti), 1758. Oil on canvas, 225 × 161.1 cm. London, National Gallery, Presented by Barons Emile-Beaumont d'Erlanger, Frédéric d'Erlanger and Rodolphe d'Erlanger, in memory of their parents, 1927, NG4253 (© National Gallery, London / Art Resource, NY.)

In using his sugar spoon, it is unlikely that Drouais was ever prompted to reflect upon his place within the global colonial economy, not least because that spoon made no demand upon him to do so. But the painter's place was in fact more complicated than one of mere consumer, as detached in the European metropole as his spoon's decoration was from the realities on the other side of the world. There is no evidence that Drouais had any direct role in the sugar trade, but as a society portraitist in a fashionable neighborhood of Paris, he was certainly drawn into the social milieu of those who did. Perhaps most notable in this regard was Drouais's connection to the comte de Vaudreuil (1740–1817), a member of the colonial aristocracy whose portrait he painted in 1758 (fig. 158). Born in Saint-Domingue, Vaudreuil was son of the island's governor general and owner of several sugar plantations, along with the hundreds of enslaved people who worked them.[20] Vaudreuil's connection to Saint-Domingue, the largest producer of sugar among France's colonies, was emphasized by Drouais through the setting of the portrait in a map room, where the comte turns his back on a map of European territories and holds one of Caribbean islands.[21] In this rhetorical gesture, Vaudreuil makes an embodied claim for France's colonial interests, their bright future promised in the fall of light, but he also indicates his own interests with a possessive index finger pointing to the words "S. Domingue" (fig. 159), where his family's plantations were located and their fortunes made. By the 1790s, Vaudreuil estimated that the annual income from his Saint-Domingue property would reach £15,000 sterling (equivalent to over £1 million today).[22] Drouais, as the maker of Vaudreuil's portrait, thus assumed an indirect part in this nexus, profiting from these colonial holdings while devising the visual argument that staked the colonizer's possessive claim. His sugar spoon may not have prompted the connection, but Drouais certainly had occasion to consider the colonial economies of the sugar that sweetened his coffee and his waffles. ‡

---

1. This was in part due to food's short-lived commercial value (given its perishable nature), and also because food tended to be bought fresh for imminent consumption, rather than stocked for future use. Annik Pardailhé-Galabrun, *The Birth of Intimacy: Privacy and Domestic Life in Early Modern Paris* (Cambridge: Polity, 1991), 87.

2. François-Hubert Drouais, "Inventaire après décès," 12 December 1775, AN, MC/ET/LIII/521.

3. Robert Louis Stein, *The French Sugar Business in the Eighteenth Century* (Baton Rouge: Louisiana State University Press, 1988), 10.

4. "Sucre," *Encyclopédie*, https://encyclopedie.uchicago.edu/, 15:608.

5. "Sucre," *Dictionnaire de l'Académie Française*, 3rd edition (Paris: Jean-Bapiste Coignard, 1740), 2:710.

6. Stein, *French Sugar Business*, 12–13.

7. In the inventory it is described simply as being made of silver "poinçon de Paris." AN, MC/ET/LIII/521.

8. François Marin, *Les dons de Comus, ou l'Art de la cuisine, réduit en pratique* (Paris: Pissot, 1758), vol. 3, 131–33.

9. Elizabeth Heath, "Sugarcoated Slavery: Colonial Commodities and the Education of the Senses in Early Modern France," *Critical Historical Studies* 5, no. 2 (2018): 171–74.

10. The *Encyclopédie*'s entry "Sucrerie" explains in detail the types of slave labor involved in the production of sugar. *Encyclopédie*, https://encyclopedie.uchicago.edu/, 15:618. Jean-Baptiste du Tertre, *Histoire générale des Antilles habitées par les François*, 2 vols. (Paris: Thomas Jolly, 1667).

11. On the full commercial circuit of sugar in this period, see Maud Villeret, *Le gout de l'or blanc: Le sucre en France au XVIIIe siècle* (Rennes: Presses Universitaires de Rennes, 2017).

12. In 1777, sugar's trade was ceded entirely to the *épiciers*. Christian Warolin, "La vente du sucre par les apothicaires et les épiciers parisiens au XVIIe siècle," *Revue de l'histoire de la Pharmacie*, 1999, 217–26.

13. *Almanach Dauphin, ou Tablettes royales du vrai mérite des artistes célèbres et d'indication générale des principaux marchands, banquiers, négocians, artistes et fabricans des six-corps, arts et métiers de la ville de Paris* (Paris: Lacombe, 1777), n.p.

14. On the transformation of tastes, habits, and rituals associated with the rise of the sugar trade see Sidney W. Mintz, *Sweetness and Power: The Place of Sugar in Modern History* (New York: Penguin, 1985). On the cultural legacy of slavery in everyday objects, including sugar bowls, see James Walvin, *Slavery in Small Things: Slavery and Modern Cultural Habits* (Chichester: Wiley Blackwell, 2017).

15. On material culture and colonial economies, see Anne Gerritsen and Giorgio Riello, eds., *The Global Lives of Things: The Material Culture of Connections in the Early Modern World* (London: Routledge, 2015).

16. François-Hubert Drouais, "Inventaire après décès."

17. On the provenance of the *sucriers*, see Jannic Durrand, Michèle Bimbenet-Privat, and Frédéric Dassas, *Décors, mobilier et objets d'art du musée du Louvre de Louis XIV à Marie-Antoinette* (Paris: Somogy, 2014), 344–46.

18. On the kind of European material culture described as "africaneries" by Anne Lafont, see Lafont, "Géographie du gout ou manufacture des africaneries," *L'art et la race: l'Africain (tout) contre l'oeil des Lumières* (Dijon: Les presses du reel, 2019), 253–316.

19. First decreed by Louis XIV in 1685, the *Code noir* defined legal conditions in France's colonies. *Code noir, ou recueil d'édits, déclarations et arrêts concernant les esclaves nègres de l'Amérique, avec un recueil de règlemens concernant la police des Isles Françoises de l'Amérique et les Engagés* (Paris: Libraires Associez, 1743).

20. The comte de Vaudreuil's father was Joseph-Hyacinthe de Rigaud de Vaudreuil (1706–64), born in Quebec to Philippe de Rigaud de Vaudreuil (1650–1725), the governor-general of all New France. On Vaudreuil's Haitian holdings at the end of the century, see Carl Ludwig Lokke, "London Merchant Interest in the St Domingue Plantations of the Émigrés, 1793–1798," *American Historical Review* 43, no. 4 (1938): 796.

21. Humphrey Wine, *The Eighteenth-Century French Paintings: National Gallery Catalogues* (London: Yale University Press, 2018), 181–83.

22. Lokke, "London Merchant Interest," 796. Currency calculations based on the National Archives Currency Converter, https://www.nationalarchives.gov.uk/currency-converter.

Sword

François Lemoyne (1688–1737)

TYPE OF OBJECT	THEME	MATERIAL
Apparel, Commodity, Symbolic Thing, Weapon	Antiquity, Death, Gender, Health/ Medicine, Identity, Louvre	Metal | Gold/Gilding, Metal | Steel

Many of the things in this book were present when their owners died, but this is the only one that was responsible for its owner's death. On 4 June 1737, François Lemoyne committed suicide by stabbing himself nine times with his own sword. Professionally, at this moment, Lemoyne appeared to be at an all-time career high, having just been appointed *premier peintre du roi* (first painter to the king) after completing his enormous ceiling painting at Versailles of the *Apotheosis of Hercules* (1731–36, Château de Versailles). But at the same time, personally, he was experiencing his deepest low. After losing his wife a few years earlier, Lemoyne had plunged himself into excessive work and then gradually descended into a relentless psychological state of anxiety and paranoia, convinced that his colleagues at the Académie were plotting to bring him down.[1] It was in this state that, at 11 o'clock on a Saturday morning, following an ordinary session in the studio with his students, and just before a meeting with a patron about a commissioned painting, Lemoyne locked himself in his bedroom, took up his sword, and ended his life with that painful and violent act.

Lemoyne's sword no longer survives, but because of the task the painter gave it in those final minutes of his life, the object left an archival trace in a series of police reports.[2] It makes its most detailed appearance in the police *commissaire*'s account of the crime scene (suicide still being a crime in eighteenth-century France), where his methodical description of the sword in situ gives a vivid sense of the last act it performed for its owner. Upon entering Lemoyne's bedroom, the *commissaire* described encountering the painter's blood-soaked body lying in the doorway, and then, casting his eye around the room, he noted first "the brown **wig** of the deceased" flung on the floor near a **table**, under which he then observed "the deceased's sword," where it had fallen after the deadly ordeal was over. Along with suggesting its recent actions, the report also indicated some of the sword's physical characteristics, distinguishing it as "an *olinde* with guard and grip of gilt steel," which, the *commissaire* noted with grisly accuracy, was at that point "almost entirely covered in blood, as was its naked blade."[3]

From the few lines describing Lemoyne's sword in the police reports it is possible to extract a substantial amount of information. First, not surprisingly, we discover that Lemoyne's sword was an *épée* or smallsword (similar to that in fig. 160), a light sword designed for dueling and thrusting and that was the most prevalent bladed weapon in

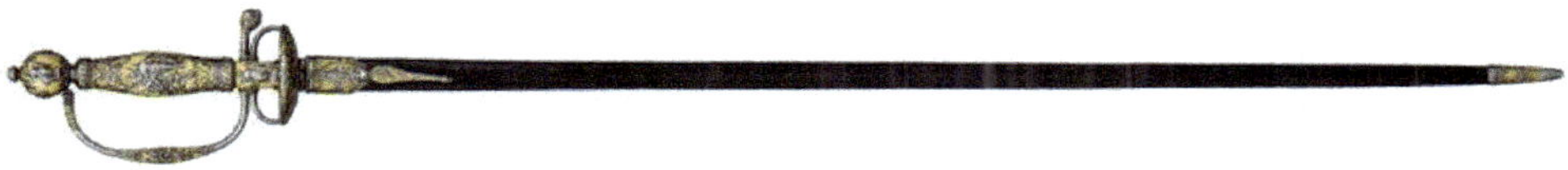

FIG. 160 French smallsword (with scabbard) with Solingen blade, ca. 1730. Steel, gilding, 69 × 1.8 cm. London, Wallace Collection, inv. A688. (© Wallace Collection, London, UK/Bridgeman Images.)

eighteenth-century France. Next, more specifically, the *commissaire* provides some details about the sword's two main parts: the hilt and the blade. The hilt of an *épée* was composed of several elements (guard, grip, and pommel) and was conventionally the most decorated area of the sword. Worn prominently at the front of the body (as modeled by Jean-Jacques Caffieri in his portrait; see fig. 175), the hilt could be an eminently fashionable commodity, made from precious metals by an *orfèvre* (goldsmith) and signifying wealth and status like other accessories (jewelry, shoe buckles, **watches**, etc.). Lemoyne's hilt, however, made from gilt steel rather than gold, was not such a high-end item and had likely been made by and acquired from a *fourbisseur* (swordsmith). The blade, meanwhile, was top of the line. The *commissaire* describes it as an "*olinde*," a francophone corruption of the German town of Solingen (Solingue in French), which had a reputation for producing the finest-quality blades in Europe. (The sword in fig. 160 is also a Solingen blade mounted on a French hilt). The blade of Lemoyne's sword features again in the autopsy report, written by the police surgeon, who observed that the cadaver's wounds appeared to have been inflicted by a "*trois carré*" blade.[4] This triangular-shaped blade—flat on one side and with two faces on the other, like those at the bottom of a plate from the *Encyplopédie* (fig. 161)—was the lightest and swiftest of the regular blade types. Thus, on the scale from lethal weapon to luxurious accessory, Lemoyne's sword—with its top-quality blade on a mid-range hilt—certainly came closer to the weapon side. While it is extremely unlikely that Lemoyne purchased his *épée* with any real intent to kill (himself or anyone else), the sword was, nevertheless, ideally suited to the deadly task it was given.

Yet as lethal as Lemoyne's sword was as a weapon, it was not an efficient tool for suicide. An *épée* was, after all, designed for dueling. Optimized to keep an opponent at a distance, the smallsword's blade was intentionally longer than a human arm, making it a difficult instrument with which to self-inflict a stab wound. As a method of suicide, the sword therefore resulted in a death that was both extremely violent and logistically onerous, as Lemoyne repeatedly engineered the blade to pierce his body nine times—three times into his throat, then six times into his chest around and through his heart (five with enough vigor to drive right through his torso).[5] While Lemoyne's actions were, by this point, far from rational, the painful and protracted manner of his death calls into question the significance of the sword as the object chosen for the task. What did Lemoyne's sword mean to its owner in life that he would select it as the instrument of his death?

In ancien régime France, a sword was the mark of a gentleman. As a signifier of nobility, it was far less specific than regalia identifying ranks or roles (like Joseph-Marie Vien's **decoration** as a *chevalier* of the Order of Saint-Michel), but its elite connotations stemmed

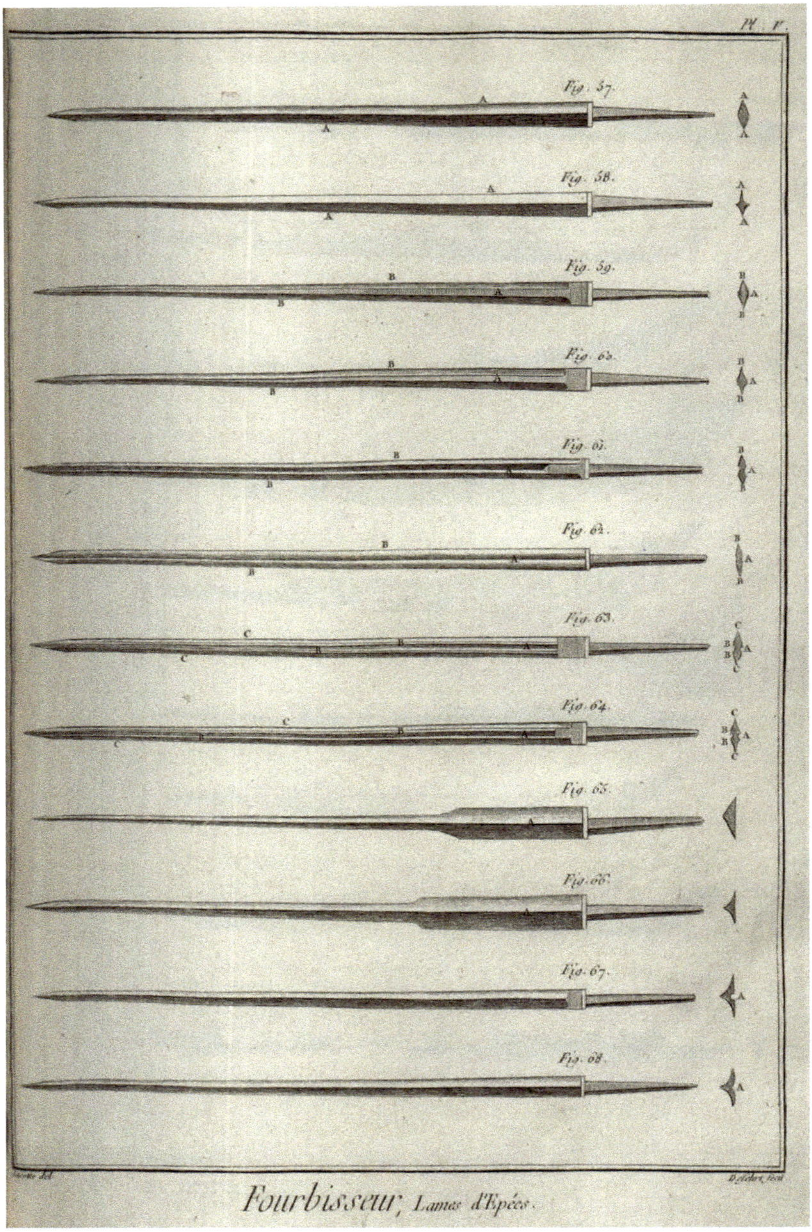

FIG. 161 "Fourbisseur: épée blades," from *Recueil de planches sur les sciences, les arts libéraux et les arts mécaniques* (1765), plate V. Image courtesy of the ARTFL Encyclopédie Project, University of Chicago.

from sixteenth-century sumptuary laws restricting the right to carry a sword to those of noble status.[6] By the eighteenth century, however, the regulations were not as strictly enforced. While some artists (like Vien) were ennobled and legitimately entitled to wear a sword, the sartorial practice was much more widespread. Indeed, it became customary for academicians (ennobled or not) to wear an *épée* as an indication of the gentlemanly status they held as members of a royal institution. For academicians, this commonly owned item also became a problematic one, not least because swords were dangerous objects to accommodate in a professional space. In a gesture toward control, the Académie banned the wearing of swords on the premises, but it was a rule that required regular reinforcement due to its consistent flouting, especially by the students.[7] In fact, during his own student days Lemoyne's artistic career had nearly been even more prematurely derailed by his sword, though in a very different way. In 1708 he was temporarily expelled, along with the painter Nicolas Lancret and the engraver Joseph-Charles Roettiers, for wearing his sword in the Académie and using it in a fight with another student.[8]

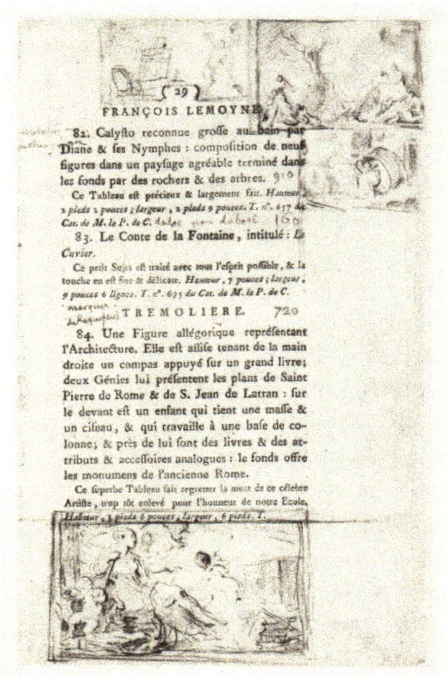
(29)

FRANÇOIS LEMOYNE.

82. Calyſto reconnue groſſe au bain par Diane & ſes Nymphes : compoſition de neuf figures dans un payſage agréable terminé dans les fonds par des rochers & des arbres.

Ce Tableau eſt précieux & largement fait. *Hauteur, 2 pieds 2 pouces; largeur, 2 pieds 9 pouces. T. n°. 657 du Cat. de M. le P. de C.*

83. Le Conte de la Fontaine, intitulé : *Le Cuvier.*

Ce petit Sujet eſt traité avec tout l'eſprit poſſible, & la touche en eſt fine & délicate. *Hauteur, 7 pouces; largeur, 9 pouces 6 lignes. T. n°. 675 du Cat. de M. le P. de C.*

TREMOLIERE.

84. Une Figure allégorique repréſentant l'Architecture. Elle eſt aſſiſe tenant de la main droite un compas appuyé ſur un grand livre; deux Génies lui préſentent les plans de Saint Pierre de Rome & de S. Jean de Latran : ſur le devant eſt un enfant qui tient une maſſe & un ciſeau, & qui travaille à une baſe de colonne; & près de lui ſont des livres & des attributs & acceſſoires analogues : le fonds offre les monumens de l'ancienne Rome.

Ce ſuperbe Tableau fait regretter la mort de ce célebre Artiſte, trop tôt enlevé pour l'honneur de notre Ecole. *Hauteur, 3 pieds 6 pouces, largeur, 6 pieds. T.*

FIG. 162 Gabriel de Saint-Aubin's marginal sketches in *Catalogue de la deuxième vente du prince de Conti* (1779). Location unknown. Image after Emile Dacier, *Catalogue de ventes et livrets de salons illustrés par Gabriel de Saint-Aubin* (Paris: Au Siège de la Société, 1909).

Dying by the sword was, like wearing it, evocative of noble ideals. The classical connotations of valor and heroism associated with suicide by sword—whether historical (like Cato the Younger) or fictional (like Sophocles's Ajax)—would eventually provide Lemoyne's colleagues and contemporaries with a means of mythologizing his violent death. In his Life of Lemoyne, Antoine-Joseph Dézallier d'Argenville claimed that, in the weeks before his death, Lemoyne had found solace in having friends read aloud to him from the histories and "whenever some Roman killed himself with great honor, Lemoyne had them re-read the passage, exclaiming *now there is a beautiful death!*"[9] The relative horror of Lemoyne's own far-from-beautiful death was glossed over at the time in most official death announcements, from which the sword (and the suicide) were generally absented.[10] But over time, Lemoyne's tragic end became the stuff of art-world legend, and the sword returned to center stage. This was certainly how Gabriel de Saint-Aubin recalled it, though he was barely a teenager at the time of Lemoyne's death. Forty years later, however, while attending a sale at which some of Lemoyne's paintings were being sold, the suicide came to mind. Ever the annotator of **books**, Saint-Aubin sketched some of the works in the margins, among them Lemoyne's *Diana and Callisto* (1725–28, Los Angeles County Museum of Art). But in a separate vignette around Lemoyne's printed name, he imagined a sensationalized scene of the painter's death (fig. 162). Rushing from the easel with arms dramatically outstretched, Lemoyne throws himself upon a sword rising up to meet him in the corner of the studio. In this romanticized vision, Lemoyne becomes a tortured genius, driven from his canvas, and his sword becomes the instrument that enabled his honorable death. Over the intervening years, Lemoyne's painful, desperate, and violent suicide had been reinvented to almost mythic proportions, a tale like any other represented on that page. ‡

---

1. For a full investigation of Lemoyne's death and the circumstances around it, see Hannah Williams, "The Mysterious Suicide of François Lemoyne," *Oxford Art Journal* 38, no. 2 (2015): 225–45. Parts of this entry have been drawn from that article.

2. Suicide was still a crime in eighteenth-century France, so Lemoyne's death was treated as a criminal investigation. On suicide in this period, see Jeffrey Merrick, "Death and Life in the Archives: Patterns and Attitudes to Suicide in Eighteenth-Century Paris," in *Histories of Suicide: International Perspectives on Self-Destruction in the Modern World*, ed. John Weaver and David Wright (Toronto: University of Toronto Press, 2009), 73–90; and Dominique Godineau, *S'abréger les jours: Le suicide en France au XVIIIe^ siècle* (Paris: Armand Colin, 2012).

3. "Procès-verbal d'apposition de scellés après le décès de François Lemoyne, premier peintre du roi," in Jules Guiffrey, *Scellés et inventaires d'artistes français du XVIIe et XVIIIe siècle* (Paris: Charavay, 1884), 1:341–42.

4. "Rapport du chirurgien du Châtelet sur l'état du cadaver du sieur Lemoyne," *NAAF*, 1877, 196–97.

5. "Rapport du chirurgien," 196–97.

6. Ellery Schalk, *From Valor to Pedigree: Ideas of Nobility in the Sixteenth and Seventeenth Centuries* (Princeton: Princeton University Press, 1986), 148–49.

7. See, for instance, Charles-Nicolas Cochin's letter to the marquis de Marigny, 5 September 1768, in Marc Furcy-Raynaud, *Correspondance de M. de Marigny*, *NAAF*, 1904, 155–56.

8. *PV*, 4:69–70, 76.

9. Antoine-Joseph Dézallier d'Argenville, *Abrégé de la vie des plus fameux peintres* (Paris: 1762), 425.

10. The Académie's minutes recorded only "the death" of the history painter (28 June 1737, *PV*, 5:207), while his obituary in the *Mercure* noted simply that "he died" (*Mercure de France*, June 1737, 1410), with no further details in either case.

Table

Jacques-Louis David (1748–1825)

TYPE OF OBJECT	THEME	MATERIAL
Furniture, Heirloom, Prop, Symbolic Thing	Antiquity, Family, Louvre, Making, Studio	Metal | Bronze, Metal | Gold/Gilding, Plant Matter | Wood

In August 1789, Jacques-Louis David exhibited at the Salon his celebrated painting of *The Lictors Returning to Brutus the Bodies of His Sons* (fig. 163). At this decisive moment, just weeks after the storming of the Bastille, the painting became an instant icon of revolutionary politics, a celebration of Republican ideals encapsulated in Brutus's heroic self-sacrifice of having his own sons murdered when they conspired to restore the corrupt Tarquin monarchy and overthrow the new Roman Republic.[1] Art historians have written at length about the significance of this now canonical painting, but generally overlooked in these political narratives is a seemingly inconsequential detail at the center of the composition. Almost completely hidden by a red cloth, but recognizable by its distinctive feet, is a table that David commissioned from the *menuisier* (cabinetmaker) Georges Jacob (fig. 164).

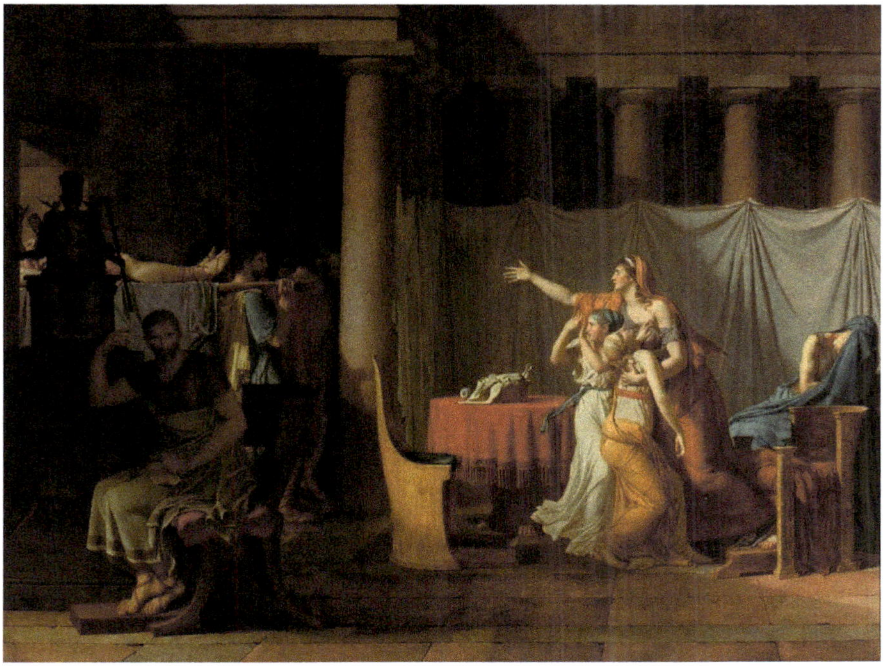

FIG. 163 Jacques-Louis David (French, 1748–1825), *The Lictors Returning to Brutus the Bodies of His Sons*, 1789. Oil on canvas, 323 × 422 cm. Paris, Musée du Louvre, INV3693. (© RMN-Grand Palais / photo: Thierry Ollivier / Art Resource, NY.)

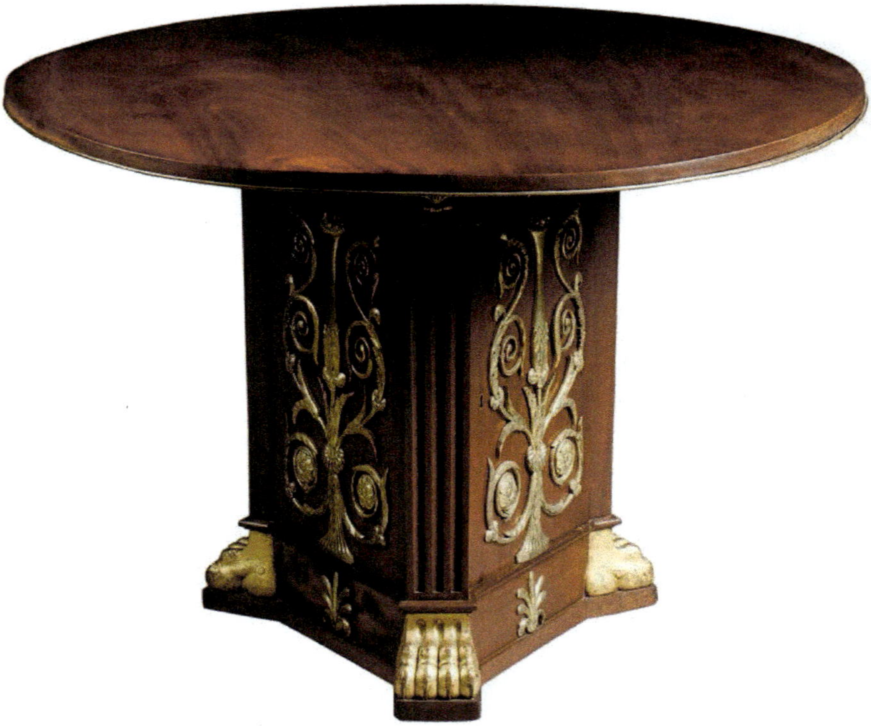

FIG. 164 Georges Jacob (French, 1739–1814) and Jacques-Louis David (French, 1748–1825), Table, ca. 1787–89. Gilt-bronze mounted mahogany. Private collection. (© Sotheby's Picture Library.)

After its starring role as Brutus's table, this elegant object lived on for many years in David's studio, and then for even longer in the homes of his heirs. In fact, it did not leave the family's possession until as recently as 1955.[2] The lives and afterlives of this table offer significant insights into David's artistic practice, but they also lead to some uncanny mediations between real and unreal spaces, and between past and present temporalities. A prop for a painting, a piece of furniture, an inherited heirloom: David's table is one of those things that sits in the ambiguous space between the professional fabric of an artist's working life (like Vigée-Lebrun's **palette** or Houdon's **modeling stand**) and the material culture of a personal life (like Cochin's **handkerchiefs** or Nattier's **harpsichord**). The lines between these realms of experience were frequently blurred in the eighteenth century, but in the particular case of David's table, tensions emerged between those various states it came to inhabit. Its aesthetic role as a designed object was, for instance, frustrated by its theatrical role as a studio prop; and its pervasive fictional life as Brutus's table complicated its functional role as a piece of furniture, turning it into a quasi **relic** that would haunt David's studio and the domestic interiors of his descendants.

As an aesthetic object, David's table was a round mahogany pedestal table, decorated with gilt-bronze mounts, measuring 77 centimeters high and 107 centimeters across the top. Its triform plinth has three fluted canted corners, each with a stylized anthemion at the top and a griffin foot at the base. The three panels bear flaming torches flanked by scrolling acanthus, and one is a lockable cupboard door, still with its original **key**.[3] Designed by David, the leading history painter of the day, and executed by Jacob, the leading *menuisier* of the day, this strikingly modern neoclassical interpretation of the antique was stylistically of its moment. Extensive research by decorative arts historian Alvar Gonzalez-Palacios has unearthed classical sources for some of its elements, such as the torch and acanthus motif derived from a fragment of the *Ara Pacis Augustae* in Rome (Museo Nazionale Romano), where David spent formative years as a *pensionnaire* at the Académie de France in Rome (1775–80).[4] This table was part of the neoclassicizing wave that began in the 1760s but took firm hold in the 1780s and during the Revolution, when it became a politicized stylistic rejection of courtly taste: a new style for the new Republican regime. David's table was in fact so fashionable as to be ahead of the curve, heralded in retrospect as the dawn of the luxurious Empire style, which came to define Napoleon's imperial reign (1804–15) and of which both David and Jacob were key designers.[5]

David's table was not, however, designed with the explicit intent of revolutionizing aesthetic taste. Rather, it was an object purpose built for pictorial composition—an accessory for a painting—not unlike the **mannequins**, armor, and faux-marble columns kept in Jean-Baptiste Le Prince's studio for constructing his scenes. David began planning *Brutus* around 1785, laboring (as was his practice) over the setting, distribution of objects, and pose of figures.[6] Through a series of preliminary compositional sketches, he settled on the structure of his interior—a spatial demarcation of public and private marked by fabric partitions and domestic furniture (fig. 165).[7] At this stage, the table found its position within the scene, but not its final stylistic form. David next started working through the details, experimenting with the furniture's size, shape, and decoration. In his hunt for archaeological accuracy, David's earliest design for the table was a spindlier three-legged affair, taken from a **sketchbook** probably made in Rome (Paris, Musée du Louvre, album 11, folio 21), and rehearsed in the Getty drawing. But in the end he found his model in an engraving of antiquities in the abbé de Saint-Non's *Voyage pittoresque de Naples et de Sicile*.[8] David sketched the table (fig. 166) and Jacob created it, the two working together to create a "modern pastiche" (as Gonzalez-Palacios puts it) of classical Rome.[9]

David and Jacob worked successfully to create several such pieces of "stage" furniture, including the **bed** upon which Madame Récamier would later recline in her portrait (1800, Paris, Musée du Louvre). But while Récamier's bed is almost as central to the composition as the sitter herself, what is perplexing about the table is the minimal role it eventually played. Indeed, it raises more questions about David's practice than it answers. If, for instance, it was so important for David to have a quintessentially antique table for his image of Republican Rome, why invent a modern pastiche instead of replicating an original? Having taken such time, care, and expense in the design and production of the table, why cover all but its feet with a plain red cloth? And why did David even need an actual table, given that he had already designed it in the two-dimensional form required for his composition?

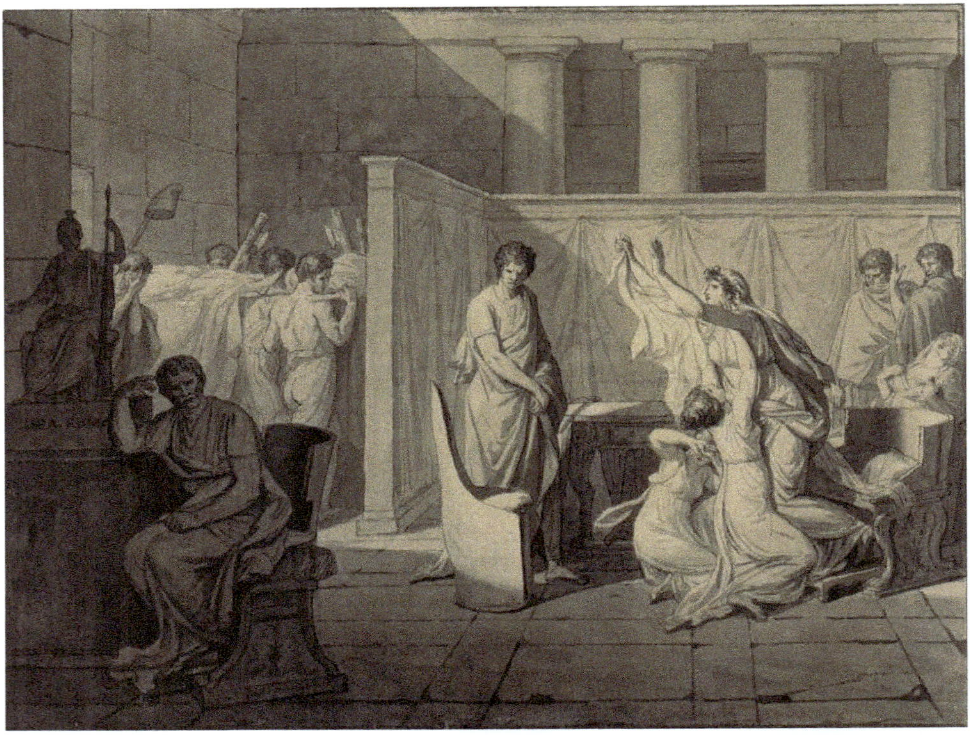

FIG. 165 Jacques-Louis David (French, 1748–1825), *The Lictors Returning to Brutus the Bodies of His Sons*, 1787. Pen and black ink and gray wash, 37.2 × 42.1 cm. Los Angeles, The J. Paul Getty Museum.

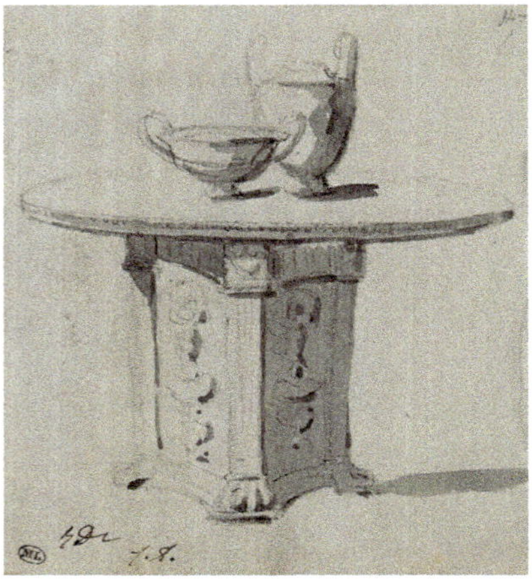

FIG. 166 Jacques-Louis David (French, 1748–1825), *Table with Two Vases*, n.d. Wash and chalk, 12.3 × 11.4 cm. Album 11, folio 13r. Paris, Musée du Louvre, Inv. 26156. (© RMN-Grand Palais / photo: Laurent Chastel / Art Resource, NY.)

As a prop in the staging of *Brutus*, the table inhabited a very different role from that of aesthetic object. Through placement and use, props on stage define space and create narratives.[10] Their material qualities enhance the realism of a fictional place, but they also exert what performance theorist Gay McAuley calls a "gestural force," contributing to the dynamics of the play by determining the actions that take place around them.[11] Like an actor in character, props are material things playing fictional roles; thus, unlike other objects, they have the unique quality of being simultaneously real and unreal.[12]

The setting for the table's theatrical début was Brutus's palace. In David's static tableau, the table becomes one of three key points in this emotional climax as its red costume resonates with two further chromatic notes: Brutus's chair cushion and the sandal straps of his dead son. This tonal connection between Brutus and the dead body emphasizes the agonizing import of the father's decision, the pain suffered in placing civic duty before personal feeling. Linked to the table, spotlit at center stage, the red echo then turns this political drama into a domestic drama. The anguished outpouring of grief by mother and sisters is heightened by this still center, where the life-altering event contrasts poignantly with the quotidian calm of a sewing basket. An ordinary habitual activity is paused—the needle poked through the cloth—to be resumed later, "afterward," when going back to it will inevitably and painfully recall the cause of interruption. The table's concealing costume now makes sense as a directorial choice to sacrifice continuity for affect. In David's sketch of Saint-Non's engraving (see fig. 166), his original model is an archaeological artifact, displayed with two antique vessels that perfectly evoke the look of Republican Rome. But these unlived archaeological specimens lack the emotional connection of domestic things. Covering his antique table with that incongruous but homey red cloth, and replacing the cold ancient vases with a modern sewing basket, David let historical accuracy give way to dramatic intensity.[13] His domestication through textiles extended to the palace itself, where the space of home was demarcated by blue sheets pinned to stark Doric columns. This stagey partition creates a crucial subspace, setting the women apart as agents who respond rather than act, while creating that necessary juxtaposition of civic and familial realms.

Theatrical analogies are only pertinent because this table existed in real life. Most objects in history paintings only have a fictional life; they do not need to be accommodated, adjusted, or costumed for performance, because they are created for and within the pictorial space. But David's table existed in both real and unreal states, physically and fictionally. The German painter Johann Heinrich Wilhelm Tischbein claimed that David had accessories made for his compositions because he could only paint objects if they existed in three dimensions.[14] Gonzalez-Palacios argues that this was so David could accurately represent the effects of perspective and depth.[15] But this explanation glosses over the issue. After all, imagining three-dimensional worlds in two dimensions was the very business of a history painter. Scaled models, **mannequins**, or tools like a **camera obscura** might be used to aid the translation process (Charles-Antoine Coypel even owned miniaturized theater sets for this purpose), but a history painter as skilled as David did not need to create life-size replicas to represent a historical or fictional scene. David's interest in fabricating objects like his table instead looks like a vested aesthetic interest. During the Revolution and the decades that followed, David became the nation's tastemaker because his modern incarnations of classical forms were not mere representations of Republican or Imperial Rome, but fresh re-creations for a Republican or Imperial France. In terms of his artistic practice, David's desire for these objects seems more in the vein of a method actor—a "method artist," if you will—seeking verisimilitude through immersive techniques. Through material things, David could access the experience of his characters, entering into shared phenomenological encounters, sitting in their chairs or standing at their tables.

David's props tended to perform only once, rather than being reused in other fictional worlds. So after its starring role in Brutus's dramatic narrative, the table retired from theatrical life. But it did not retire from the studio. Continuing to reside in the spaces of David's daily life, the table commenced its afterlife as **relic**, a role it has inhabited ever since. Literally remnants or remains, relics are objects that hold significance as traces; things instilled with the power to embody and even to connect with lost individuals via a differed bodily encounter—touching something they once touched. While more commonly used to describe the sacred traces of holy figures (like Rigaud's **relic** of the True Cross), it is a term that might be applied figuratively to any of the things in this book. As items once owned by eighteenth-century artists—used, misused, held, played, worn, and handled—all these things are relics of a sort, mediating between past and present, between their world and ours. But as an object both real and unreal, the relichood of David's table is twofold.

Initially, for David and for visitors to his studio, the table became a relic of its fictional owner, Brutus. One of David's students, Étienne Delécluze, recalled years later his first experience of entering his master's studio in 1796, when following David's release from prison he had returned to official favor with lavish lodgings in the Louvre.[16] In the north wing of the colonnade, David had set up his "atelier des Horaces" (studio of the Horatii), so named because it contained David's two great quasi-pendant masterpieces: *Brutus* and *The Oath of the Horatii* (1784, Paris, Musée du Louvre).[17] Delécluze's memoirs provide an evocative account of this space. Climbing a narrow creaking staircase, he emerged into a dark and slightly unnerving space full of stacked canvases and draped **mannequins**, before passing through a tiny doorway into the enormous "atelier des Horaces."[18] About 45 by 30 feet, the room had olive-gray walls and a single window at one end, and the two famous paintings were hung on the long lateral walls: *The Oath* on the left upon entering, *Brutus* on the right.[19] But despite their brilliance, it was the furniture that most drew Delécluze's attention, for the room was also home to all those period pastiches made by Georges Jacob: the tables, **beds**, and chairs that once starred in those paintings on the walls and in other well-known works, like *Madame Récamier* or *Paris and Helen* (1788, Paris, Musée du Louvre).[20]

Delécluze tellingly describes this room as a "vessel," evoking a space consciously conceived as a container, a reliquary for David's past productions.[21] Displayed here, the table was unequivocally "Brutus's table," a pervasive trace of its one-off performance. But standing alongside that performance (that is, next to the painting itself), the table's studio installation effected a palpable blurring of real and unreal worlds, dissolving the metaphysical divide between the painting-as-object in the room and the painting-as-representation within the frame. There is no doubt that this was David's intention. At the other end of the studio, David had dramatized it even further, setting in place some partitioning that recalled *Brutus* by hanging green sheets pinned precisely in the manner of the domestic quarters in his painting.[22] Like an eighteenth-century prefiguration of Hollywood's Universal Studios, where visitors walk through movie sets, Brutus's table in David's studio invited visitors into uncanny encounters with actual things from imaginary places. In this strange performative studio space, the table made the fictional world of Brutus's palace seem real, while the painting made that piece of furniture into a memento from an unreal world.

Starting its afterlife in this near-sacred diorama perhaps explains why the table led such an inactive existence thereafter. Over 220 years since its making, David's table is now in a remarkable state of preservation. Apart from a crack in the cupboard panel and some thin-wearing gilding on the feet, it shows few blemishes and minimal scars of use. Inside, the shelves have been replaced, suggesting it may have been used for storage, but that is unlikely given the awkward size of the cavity and the difficulty of access. There are a few scratches underneath the table-top from turning on its pedestal, but hardly enough to suggest daily activity. Even after David's death, the table seems to have remained a relic: an object for veneration rather than a piece of furniture to be used. But passing into the hands of its subsequent owners, it transformed from a relic of the *Brutus* painting into a relic of David himself.

Inside the cupboard, a brass plaque attached toward the end of the nineteenth century records the object's history: "This table belonged to the painter Louis David. It was left to Madame Bianchi, great-granddaughter of David, by Monsieur Jules David-Chassagnol, grandson of David."[23] In this account of its significance, *Brutus* rates no mention. What matters now is that this table once belonged to David, its authenticity as a relic secured in a firm provenance via heirs whose relationships to the great man are clearly marked.[24] While most of the things in this book that survive in physical form did so in museums or archives as historical artifacts, David's table survived as a family heirloom. But apart from its journey through hands, it is difficult to know the life the table had with David's descendants. Was it a cherished souvenir of a beloved forebear; a prized possession that showed off distinguished bloodlines? Or was it an annoying thing looming awkwardly around their homes; too "special" to be used as a piece of furniture, but with too much sentimental value to be given away?

Whatever its subsequent owners' attachment (or lack thereof), David's table survived because it was never just a table but rather a material object with layers of significance from the outset. Its performances, exchanges, and interactions passed from a fictional Roman palace and an eighteenth-century Paris studio, to nineteenth-century domestic interiors and, more recently, the back room of a London auction house. Through its experiences, we witness the political drama of the Brutus clan, the family dynamics of the David line, and the working practices of an artist who designed the decorative look of two successive French regimes. Throughout its lives and afterlives, its gestural force continued to determine the dynamics of the play, whether as aesthetic object, theatrical prop, symbolic relic, sewing table, memorabilia, antique, heirloom, commodity (lot 28 in a Sotheby's sale), or even here in this book as "research object." One thing, one life, but countless roles. ‡

1. Thomas Crow, *Painters and Public Life in Eighteenth-Century Paris* (New Haven: Yale University Press, 1985), 247–54; and Antoine Schnapper, *David, témoin de son temps* (Paris: Bibliothèque des Arts, 1980), 89–93.

2. This provenance was established when the table came up for sale at Sotheby's in London in 2012. "Princely Treasures," Sotheby's sale catalog, 4 July 2012, 184. With thanks to Mia Jackson for alerting us to the presence of David's table in this sale.

3. "Princely Treasures," 184.

4. Alvar Gonzalez-Palacios, "Jacques-Louis David: Le décor de l'antiquité," in *David contre David,* ed. Régis Michel (Paris: Documentation Française, 1993), 2:948–950.

5. Gonzalez-Palacios, "Jacques-Louis David," 949. On David's engagement with the antique during the First Empire, see Philippe Bordes, *Jacques-Louis David: Empire to Exile* (London and New Haven: Yale University Press, 2005), 183–97.

6. On David's working methods, see Perrin Stein, "Crafting the Neoclassical: Two New Drawings for Jacques-Louis David's *The Lictors Bringing Brutus the Bodies of His Sons,*" *Master Drawings* 47, no. 2 (2009): 221–36; and Thomas Crow, *Emulation: David, Drouais, and Girodet in the Art of Revolutionary France*, rev. ed. (New Haven: Yale University Press, 2006), 102–11.

7. Most of the drawings related to *Brutus* are cataloged in Pierre Rosenberg and Louis-Antoine Prat, *Jacques-Louis David (1748–1825): Catalogue raisonné des dessins*, 2 vols. (Milan: 2002). Two works discovered later are discussed in Stein, "Crafting the Neoclassical," 221–36.

8. Abbé de Saint-Non, *Voyage pittoresque de Naples et de Sicile* (Paris: 1781–86), 2:225.

9. Gonzalez-Palacios, "Jacques-Louis David," 946.

10. Andrew Sojer, *The Stage Life of Props* (Ann Arbor: University of Michigan Press, 2003), 2.

11. Gay McAuley, *Space in Performance* (Ann Arbor: University of Michigan Press, 1999), 175.

12. McAuley, *Space in Performance*, 171.

13. For an alternative interpretation of the sewing basket as a historicized element of the scene, see Yvonne Korshak, "*Paris and Helen* by Jacques-Louis David: Choice and Judgment on the Eve of the French Revolution," *Art Bulletin* 69, no. 1 (1987): 106.

14. Louis Hautecoeur, *Louis David* (Paris: Table Ronde 1954), 304, cited in Gonzalez-Palacios, "Jacques-Louis David," 937.

15. Gonzalez-Palacios, "Jacques-Louis David," 937.

16. David was in prison following Robespierre's fall, first from 2 August to 28 December 1794, then from 29 May to 3 August 1795. On David in prison, see Anita Brookner, *Jacques-Louis David* (London: Thames & Hudson, 1980), 121–35.

17. Étienne Delécluze, *Louis David: Son école et son temps* (Paris: Didier 1855), 14–16.

18. Delécluze, *Louis David*, 17.

19. Delécluze, *Louis David*, 19.

20. Delécluze, *Louis David*, 20–21.

21. Delécluze, *Louis David*, 19.

22. Delécluze, *Louis David*, 21.

23. "Cette table a appartenu au peintre Louis David. Elle a été léguée à Madame Bianchi, arrière petite fille de David, par Monsieur Jules David-Chassagnol, petit fils de David."

24. When David died, the table was bequeathed to his second son, Eugène, who left it to his son, Jacques-Louis-Jules David (the "Jules David-Chassagnol" of the plaque). Without children of his own, Jules bequeathed the table to his cousin's daughter, Mathilde Jeanin, who became "Madame Bianchi." She left it to her daughter and only then, after Thérèse Bianchi's death in the mid-twentieth century, was the table sold out of the family. "Princely Treasures," 184; and Gonzalez-Palacios, "Jacques-Louis David," 950.

Teacup

Jean-Marc Nattier (1685–1766)

TYPE OF OBJECT	THEME	MATERIAL
Collectible, Commodity, Intoxicant, Tableware	Food and Drink, Global Commerce, Leisure, Luxury, Studio	Metal | Silver, Mineral | Clay

The court portrait painter Jean-Marc Nattier owned multiple teacups. To be exact, five sets in all: a set of six Japanese porcelain cups and saucers with a sugar bowl, a pair of "old Japan" covered cups mounted in ormolu, a set of six Meissen cups and saucers, and two sets of uncertain origin, one "Asian" and consisting of twelve cups and saucers, a teapot, and a sugar bowl, and the remaining four cups and saucers described merely as of "red and white" china.[1] Most, and perhaps even all, of these cups were marked by travel. Having survived undamaged over sometimes vast distances and always against considerable odds, they partook of the marvelous and exotic.

Description of the items in the catalog of Nattier's sale in 1763 is so summary that we can only imagine what they may have looked like: possibly Kakiemon-style (fig. 167), since it was these white-bodied Japanese wares, typically decorated with vegetal ornament in bright enamel colors, that were most admired by Western consumers and were widely copied in Europe, especially by Meissen. They were sold with the rest of Nattier's collection, which included Oriental vases, urns, jars, potpourris, and figurines, begs the question: What were the teacups for? Did a passion for porcelain lead Nattier to collect them for themselves, or did a taste for tea entail purchase of a tea set? To put it another way, was Nattier oriented toward his teacups as a functional part of his everyday life, or as an aesthetic diversion from it? How does the answer to this question inform, moreover, our understanding of Nattier's encounter with cultures different from his own? Finally, how might the answer also explain the conspicuous lack of visual reference to porcelain in his paintings?

By the beginning of the eighteenth century, Chinese and Japanese porcelain was being imported to France in quantity. It was retailed in Paris by luxury-goods merchants (*marchands merciers*) and was sold at auction.[2] Nattier's first purchases were made in the early 1720s. Sometime before 1722, he bought a garniture of Japanese porcelain for one of the chimneypieces at his lodgings, on Rue de Hasard.[3] He was admiring and acquiring Asian porcelain, we can thus note, long before his contemporary François Boucher, with whom it is today more famously connected.[4] If the name "Nattier," inscribed in 1756 against lot 1043—a pair of ewers with blue painted flowers—in a copy of the catalog of the duc de Tallard's sale, refers to Jean-Marc, he was, moreover, still augmenting his collection more than thirty years later.[5] Between these dates, the painter was appointed artist in residence

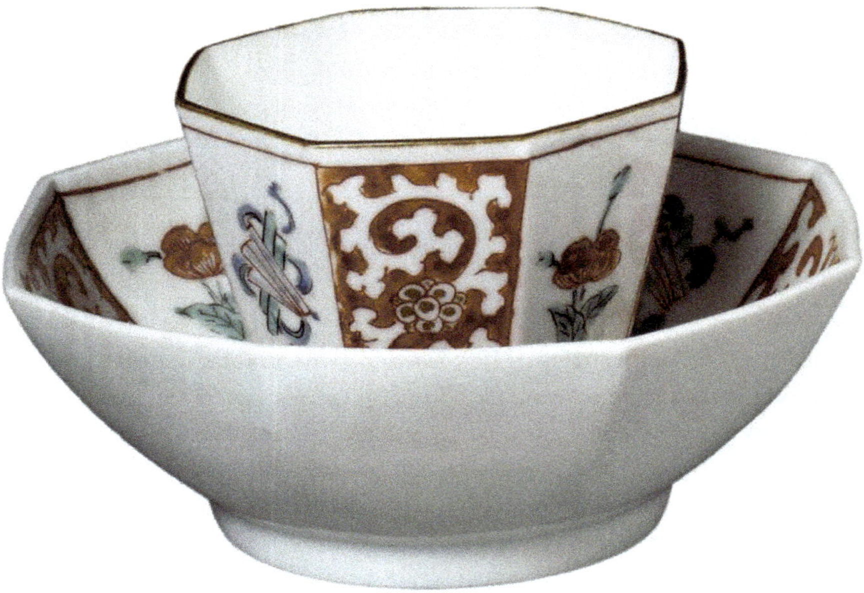

FIG. 167 Maker unknown, Cup and saucer, ca. 1700. Porcelain from Arita, Japan. London, Victoria & Albert Museum, Given by Lt. Col. Kenneth Dingwall DSO. (© Victoria & Albert Museum, London.)

to the Grand Prieur of the Order of Malta and in 1735 moved into a suite of rooms at the Temple, an enclave of houses, workshops, and shops clustered around the Grand Prieur's palace in Paris.[6] It was there that Nattier assembled his collection and also, perhaps, there that he was introduced to the rituals of tea. The prince de Conti, who acceded to the office of Grand Prieur in 1748, and his mistress, the salonnière Marie-Charlotte, comtesse de Boufflers, were renowned for their tea parties, depicted by Michel-Barthélemy Ollivier (fig. 168), though not in sufficient detail to be absolutely certain whether the teacups are Asian or European.

Nattier's encounter with Japan and China via cups and tea was mediated by institutions of trade and sociability. In the literature of the sales rooms, "Japanese" denoted not an object's place of origin but its excellence.[7] "Japanese" teacups were of high quality, "old Japanese" teacups of the highest. When dealers like Pierre Rémy, who cataloged the Tallard sale, or François Joullain, who auctioned Nattier's cabinet, qualified Japanese porcelain as "old," they were unaware that porcelain was actually a modern art in Japan, introduced from China in the seventeenth century. Age for them was a synonym of rare—rare sometimes to the point of rendering an object virtually unique.[8] "Old Japan" was thus a name, not a narrative. No scholarly discourse on porcelain equivalent to that on the history and theory of Western art and antiquities existed outside the trade. No Pierre-Jean Mariette wrote for porcelain the like of his treatise on engraved gems (see **intaglio**). History in the case of the porcelain object only began when it arrived in Europe and acquired a biography in the form of provenance.[9]

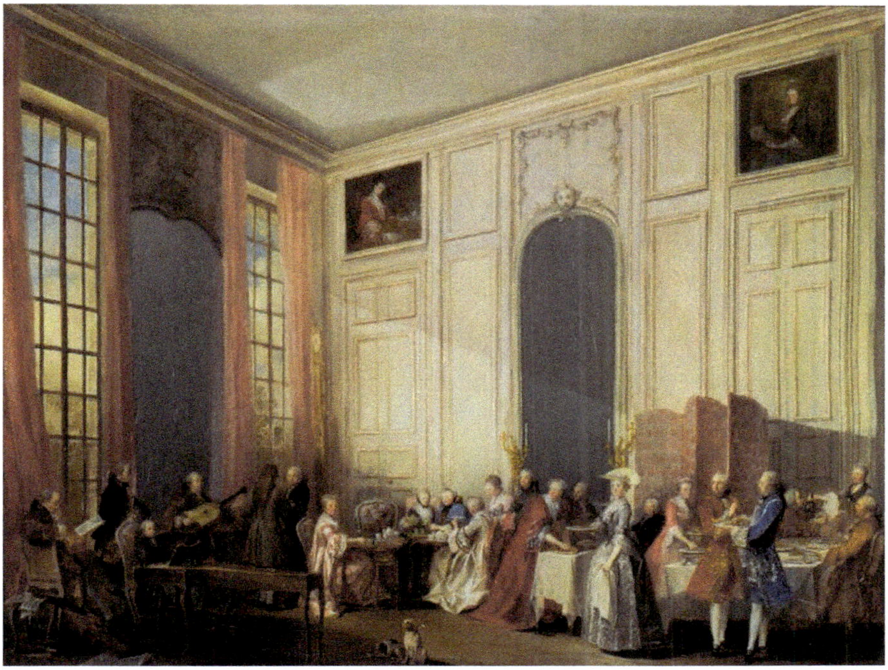

FIG. 168 Michel-Barthélemy Ollivier (French, 1712–84), *English Tea in the Salon des Quatres Glaces at the Temple*, 1766. Oil on canvas, 53 × 68 cm. Châteaux de Versailles et de Trianon. (© RMN-Grand Palais / Art Resource, NY.)

The temporal shift that occurred through the recontextualization of the object as it moved from East to West and was removed from its original context of use to begin a new, shelf life in a *cabinet* stripped it of its pre-collection histories. According to Rémy, porcelain was not a collector's item as such; rather, it ornamented the nobleman's collection proper by providing a light counterpoint to his European bronzes and a fragile foil to his antique vases.[10] As ornament and counterpoint, oriental porcelain was, in the discourse of collecting, always after, later than, an addition or supplement to the real (classic and classical) objects of curiosity, its own antiquity and cultural autonomy disavowed by European taste and epistemology.

We can't know whether Nattier's porcelain was a decorative supplement to his sculptures, whether novelty cups introduced accent by offsetting his sanctioned art works—small bronzes of *The Gladiator*, *Venus and Cupid*, *Louis XIV on Horseback*—because Nattier sold his collection in 1763, shortly before retiring from the Temple to live with his youngest daughter.[11] Without an inventory, there is no way to tell whether his things were gathered and arranged together, or whether the "*cabinet*" sold by Joullain comprised possessions scattered throughout his rooms, the tea sets perhaps stored in a cupboard until needed. That Nattier's teacups were arranged in sets does not of itself indicate use; Rémy described one of Tallard's tea sets as a mini collection within the ducal cabinet, carefully assembled from disparate things, set on a tray, and circumscribed by it.[12] European collectors were compelled by circumstance so to act—to act Japanese, in fact, partly because the matching tea set was unknown, foreign to Japan. Tea bowls were unique, individually precious, often named, and chosen by the tea master for each performance of the tea ceremony (茶道) according to the particular occasion and specific guests.[13] In France, by contrast, the sameness of sets was a visual metaphor of the social whole and of the nonhierarchical ideal of politeness that characterized salon sociability chez Mme Boufflers and her sisters (see fig. 168).[14] French users of teacups—of which, given the number of his sets, Nattier was probably one—bought, therefore, against the grain of Japanese culture and also that of European supply: they bought to match, in order to make sets out of single cups.

Tea was introduced to France in the early seventeenth century and was taken initially as a medicinal remedy, but by the eighteenth century it had become an elite recreational drink.[15] We could perhaps imagine that using a teacup and drinking tea afforded Nattier the illusion of a more intimate experience of Japan than merely admiring his china; that the experience and objectives of collecting and using could and did coincide for him. However, according to Anne Eatwell, the fashion for tea at midcentury and notably at the Temple was mediated by anglomania and a desire not for contact with Japan but with England. To drink tea was to ape English manners and to consume porcelain was, arguably, to poach its tea things—Japan in translation, so to speak.[16] Thus the cultural dichotomies of East and West that structured the discourse on collecting were present also in the discourse and language of use. According to the dictionary of the Académie française, *tasse* (cup) is related to *goblet* (beaker), by implication an earlier word for an older vessel.[17] Goblets were made of silver or gold. Cups could be of porcelain, faience, or glass. The height of the beaker was reduced in the cup, but the rim of the cup expanded the perimeter of the beaker to expose a larger surface of liquid for cooling. Cups, unlike beakers, were synonymous with their exotic contents (teacups, coffee cups, chocolate cups), thus doubly different. To use a teacup, in sum, was to handle something familiar *and* different, something translated: both like a beaker and like no other cup, in substance, form, and purpose.

Porcelain resembled French earthenware but exceeded it in refinement, producing notably thinner vessels of finer, whiter ceramic, lighter in the hand, more brilliant and lively to the eye (see fig. 167).[18] From the beginning of the century, attempts were made across Europe to rival imported porcelain, but it was not until the 1770s that the royal manufactory at Sèvres succeeded in reproducing "true," or hard-paste porcelain, chemically identical to that of China.[19] In Nattier's lifetime, porcelain was a mystery still. Although in 1712 the Jesuit missionary François Xavier d'Entrecolles chose the cup as a simple, familiar, model object to illustrate the production process at Jingdezhen, porcelain teacups nevertheless remained unknown to French consumers;[20] they were experienced rather in metonymic relation to what they resembled in form (beakers), and what they bettered in stuff (everyday faience). Was the painter's pleasure in his intensely material cups made uncanny by this mix of the familiar and the strange and by the animation of porcelain's uniquely high-gloss surface, described by another French Jesuit, Louis Le

Comte,[21] as alive with the infolded reflection of things around it? Nattier's mixed feelings about his collection are certainly on record. At the end of his life, he confessed to his eldest daughter that, in the balance sheet of his worldly achievements, he counted his cabinet among his regrets.[22]

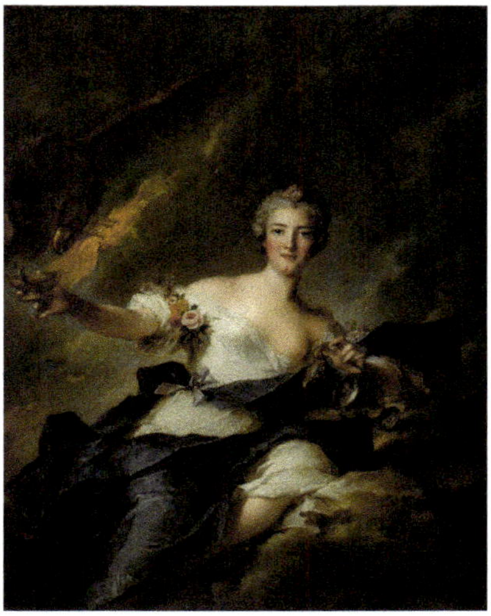

FIG. 169 Jean-Marc Nattier, *The Duchesse de Chaulnes as Hebe*, 1744. Oil on canvas, 144 × 110 cm. Paris, Musée du Louvre, RF1942-32. (© RMN-Grand Palais / photo: Franck Raux / Art Resource, NY.)

Were we able to attribute Nattier's ambivalence specifically to his porcelain, would it explain his decision not to incorporate porcelain in his work? The duchesse de Chaulnes, in Nattier's portrait of her serving Jupiter with elixir (fig. 169), does so from a cup of gold and silver, not a porcelain one, notwithstanding the fact that both Chaulnes's brother, Joseph Bonnier de la Mosson, and her husband, Michel-Ferdinand d'Albert d'Ailly, were keen collectors of china.[23] It would, of course, have been anachronistic to have depicted the Hebed *duchesse* holding an exotic modern thing, but even in Nattier's portraits of sitters in contemporary dress, porcelain is absent, in contrast to the bourgeois portraits by his contemporary Jacques-André-Joseph Aved.[24] The obvious explanation is not, however, in patterns of class consumption, since according to Daniel Roche, it was the nobility, not the bourgeoisie, who drove the boom in porcelain vending.[25] It was they who rushed to supplement, update, or replace their silverware with china tea and dinner services, while the bourgeoisie cautiously accumulated silver, teaspoon by teaspoon, hallmarked things of guaranteed value that served as both ornament and safeguard, because easily converted back into specie when circumstance necessitated. Nattier conforms to this pattern: he had silver, to a value nearly four times that of his china.[26]

Roche argues that in its passion for porcelain, the nobility sought to express its intellectual curiosity and appetite for cultural risk. That sitters had Nattier portray them with silver indicates, however, the limited semantic resonance of the china object in the public discourse on distinction, perhaps because in representation its materiality is overshadowed by form. We can note that the ewer and cup depicted in Mme de Caumartin's hands in Nattier's portrait of her (1753, Washington, National Gallery of Art) are decorated with graceful and flowing patterns of elegant figures, precisely the human motifs that Europeans scorned as grotesque and ill-proportioned "magots" in Chinese painting and ornament.[27] Orientalism is not, however, completely repressed. It returns in gesture: Chaulnes holds her golden kylix (see fig. 169) as if it were a Japanese tea bowl; she ignores the handles, and delicately balances the cup between finger and thumb as tea etiquette demanded, according to the king's physician Nicolas de Blegny.[28]

If we have come to know Nattier's teacups better by this microhistory of their "lives" it has been not by the dictionary's function to define but by history's tracking of their movement across geographical, epistemological, social, and aesthetic spaces. For Nattier, entanglement with these and other things was, as for his patrons, both exciting and disturbing. That he returned his teacups to the market in 1763 suggests that, in the end, he failed to make them truly his own. §

---

1. [Nattier], *Catalogue des desseins, tableaux, estampes, bronzes, porcelaines et livres du cabinet de M. D**** [Nattier] (Paris: Joullain & Prault, 1763), 14–15.

2. See Carolyn Sargentson, *Merchants and Luxury Markets* (London: V&A, 1996); and Stéphane Castelluccio, "Le goût pour l'Asie: Le commerce des objets chinois et japonais à Paris dans la première moitié du XVIIIe siècle," in *Une des provinces du rococo: La Chine rêvée de François Boucher*, exh. cat. (Besançon: Musée des Beaux-Arts et d'Archéologie, 2019), 26–39.

3. Philippe Renard, *Jean-Marc Nattier (1685–1766)* (Saint-Rémy-en l'Eau: Hayot, 1999), 186–87.

4. See Yohan Rimaud, "Les couleurs célèstes de la terre: La collection d'objets orientaux de François Boucher," in *Une des provinces du rococo*, 62–75.

5. Pierre Rémy and Jean-Baptiste Glomy, *Catalogue raisonné des tableaux, sculptures . . . desseins et estampes, porcelains anciennes . . .qui composent le cabinet de feu M. le duc de Tallard* (Paris: Didot, 1756) (copy at INHA, Paris), lot 1043. There was a copy of the sale catalog in Nattier's library, see [Nattier], *Catalogue*, 22: lot 44.

6. Renard, *Nattier*, 58.

7. Stéphane Castelluccio, *Collecting Chinese and Japanese Porcelain in Pre-Revolutionary Paris* (Los Angeles: J. Paul Getty Museum, 2013), 114–81, esp. 136.

8. Rémy and Glomy, *Catalogue Tallard*, lot 1050.

9. See Rémy and Glomy, *Catalogue Tallard*, 257–58, on the grand dauphin as the origin of collecting porcelain.

10. Rémy and Glomy, *Catalogue Tallard*, 256–57.

11. On Nattier's sculpture, see [Nattier], *Catalogue*, 9.

12. Rémy and Glomy, *Catalogue Tallard*, lot 1089. Tea sets were not produced in Japan because the Japanese tea ceremony entailed selecting utensils specific to the occasion and the particular guests.

13. See Sadako Ohki and Takeshi Watanabe, *Tea Culture of Japan*, exh. cat. (New Haven: Yale University Art Gallery, 2009).

14. On self-same sets for decoration, not use, see Mimi Hellman, "The Joy of Sets: The Uses of Seriality in the French Interior," in *Furnishing France*, ed. Dena Goodman and Kathryn Norberg (London: Routledge, 2006), 129–53.

15. According to Antoine Furetière, by the end of the seventeenth century coffee had prevailed over tea as the everyday drink of choice. Furetière, *Dictionnaire universel* (The Hague: Husson, Johnson & Swart, 1727), 2: s.v. "thé."

16. Anne Eatwell, "Tea à la Mode: The Fashion for Tea and Tea Equipage in London and Paris," in *Boucher and Chardin: Masters of Modern Manners*, exh. cat. (London: Wallace Collection, 2008), 50–76.

17. *Dictionnaire de l'Académie française*, 3rd ed. (Paris: Coignard, 1740), 1: s.v. "gobelet," 2: s.v. "tasse." Edmé Gersaint used *gobelet* (beaker) to denote the cups in the Bonnier de la Mosson sale. See Gersaint, *Catalogue d'une collection considérable de diverses curiosités . . . contenües dans les cabinets de feu Monsieur Bonnier de la Mosson* (Paris: Barois & Simon, 1744), lots 907, 908, 912, 916, 917.

18. In Oudry's *Still Life with Grapes, Celery, and Porcelain* (1725), porcelain is juxtaposed with celery, the blanching, or whitening, of celery perhaps a metaphor for the whitening of earthenware in porcelain.

19. Antoine d'Albis, *The Creation of Hard-Paste Porcelain at Sèvres* (London: French Porcelain Society, 1998).

20. François Xavier d'Entrecolles, *Lettres édifiantes et curieuses sur l'état présent de la Chine*, ed. Louis Aimé-Martin (Paris: Société du Panthéon Littéraires, 1843), "Lettre de père d'Entrecolles au père Orry, sur la fabrication de la porcelain," 12 September 1712, 3:473–74.

21. Louis Le Comte, *Nouveaux mémoires sur l'état present de la Chine* (Paris, 1697), 1:258–59.

22. See Marie-Catherine Pauline Tocqué, "Vie de Jean-Marc Nattier," in Jacqueline Lichtenstein and Christian Michel, *Conférences de l'Académie royale de peinture et de sculpture* (Paris: ENSBA, 2015), tome 6, vol. 2:919–33, at 932–33. Nattier was not alone in turning against his collection. According to Gougenot, Jean-Baptiste Oudry formed a collection "de vases, de figures, de porcelaines et de curiosités de la Chine," but "il s'en dégoûta," and he sold it for 9,000 livres. See Louis Gougenot, "Vie de M. Oudry," *Mémoires inédits*, 2:371.

23. On Nattier's portrait, see *Jean-Marc Nattier 1685–1766*, exh. cat. (Paris: Musée National des Chateaux de Versailles et de Trianon, 1999–2000), no. 39. In the British Museum, see a famille rose teapot with the d'Ailly coat of arms (Franks 808+), Jingdezhen, which belonged to the duc de Chaulnes's father.

24. For example, see Aved's portraits of *Mme Crozat* (1741, Musée Fabre) and *Madame Brion, Seated, Taking Tea* (1750, Seattle Art Museum).

25. Daniel Roche, *France in the Enlightenment* (Cambridge: Harvard University Press, 2000), 632–34.

26. Renard, *Nattier*, 159.

27. On French scorn for Chinese "magots," see Kate Tunstall, "*Le Neveu de Rameau*, règne des magots et des pagodes," *Diderot Studies* 35 (2015): 329–48.

28. Nicolas de Blegny, *Le Bon usage du thé, du café et du chocolat* (Lyon: Amaulry, 1687), 11.

Umbrella

Jacques-Philippe Le Bas (1707–83)

TYPE OF OBJECT	THEME	MATERIAL
Commodity, Instrument	Community, Everyday	Plant Matter | Wood, Textile | Canvas, Textile | Silk

A rare green silk umbrella (fig. 170) is one of the eighteenth-century treasures of the Palais Galliera, the Paris museum of fashion. It has a turned oak handle, an eight-rib hinged metal frame, and a retracting and divisible central pole to enable the close and collapse of the umbrella into a pocketable thing (fig. 171). Although the framework of the umbrella was sometimes made of other materials (wood, baleen), the structure of this type of umbrella was generic to both umbrellas and parasols, which differed, when they did, only in the stuff of the canopy.[1] A close taffeta weave was the choice treatment for resistance to sun and rain and for pliable stiffness. The cloth was sometimes given additional proofing by a coat of gum, oil, or wax, though eighteenth-century dictionary definitions suggest that a distinction was not thereby routinely made between umbrellas (*parapluies*) and parasols.[2]

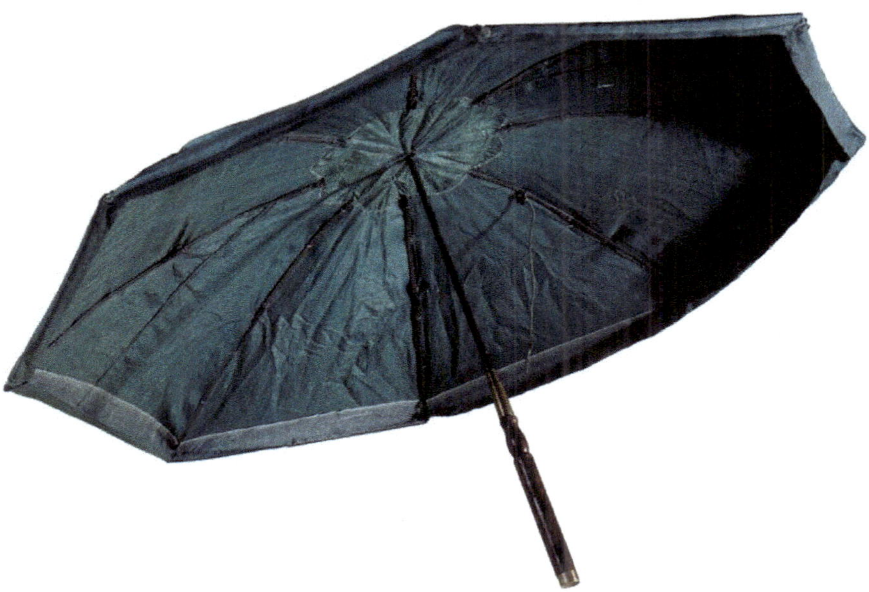

FIG. 170 Umbrella, after 1715. Green silk, oak handle, metal frame. Paris, Palais Galliera, Musée de la Mode de la Ville de Paris.

The telescopic mechanism of the Galliera umbrella was of a type invented and patented by purse maker Jean Marius at the beginning of the eighteenth century, for the umbrella-parasols he sold at his shop, The Three Funnels, on Rue des Fossés Saint-Germain.[3] It transformed the parasol from a heavy and cumbersome object, permanently open and used by the elite on ceremonial occasions, into an every-rainy-day consumer item.[4] Competition for control of the rapidly expanding market for collapsible umbrellas after Marius's patent expired in 1715 was vigorously conducted by members of three guilds: the turners, licensed by statute to make the wooden handles; the purse makers, who, as depicted in the *Encyclopédie* (see fig. 171), cut wire for the ribs and sewed gores of stuff to the frame for the canopy; and the petty mercers of incidentals and accessories, or *peigneurs-tabletiers*, who enjoyed the legal right to sell them. The ultimate victors were the *peigneurs-tabletiers*, some of whom began in the 1760s to specialize in umbrella vending, becoming *marchands de parasols*. Their stock continued to be supplied by turners and purse makers for the sticks and canopies, but the petty mercers were able to organize their subcontracting on a scale large enough to drive down unit cost and thereby the price of umbrellas. According to Cissie Fairchilds's calculations, by 1785 over 30 percent of lower- and middle-income households in Paris owned an umbrella or parasol.[5] The engraver and highly successful printseller and publisher Jacques-Philippe Le Bas was among them.[6] A "green parasol," very possibly resembling the one at Galliera, was listed at his death in his probate inventory; it was in a cupboard in his bedroom, on the first floor of a house he rented on Rue du Foin-Saint-Jacques.[7]

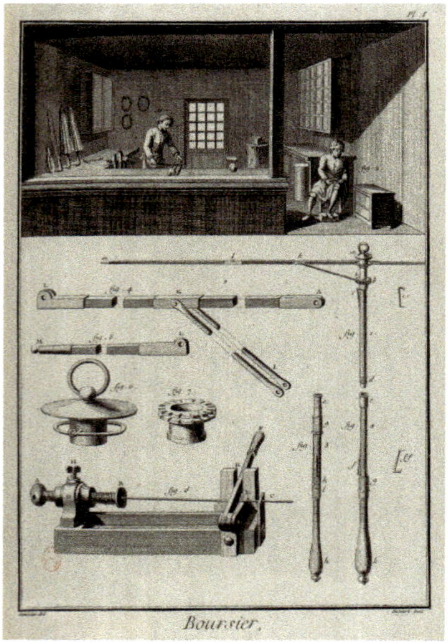

FIG. 171 "Boursier" from *Recueil de planches sur les sciences, les arts libéraux et les arts mécaniques* (1765), plate I. Paris, Bibliothèque Nationale de France.

For Fairchilds, the significance of the umbrella is the part it played in the consumer revolution that transformed the urban economy and, in turn, destabilized the social hierarchy of the ancien régime. She brackets umbrellas with fans, **snuffboxes**, stockings, **teacups**, and gold **watches** under the heading of "populuxe" goods—cheap copies of aristocratic luxury items, desired, she argues, not for their utility but rather for the touch of class they added to working-class and bourgeois lives. Le Bas's things, as inventoried in 1783, seem to confirm her findings. Among them were a porcelain **snuffbox**, a London-made gold **watch**, and a china tea set. Moreover, his wardrobe was exceptionally fashionable; it included fine linen, cotton and silk stockings, lace cuffs, silver buckles, gold buttons, and a gold-knobbed cane (perhaps the one depicted by Moreau the Younger in his **sketchbook**).[8] However, the fashionable picture this acquisitiveness appears to paint of Le Bas does not entirely chime with the contemporary biographies of the engraver, or rather his lives challenge the presumption of many histories of consumption: that rises in luxury spending were inspired by social ambition and personal pleasure and expressed a modern kind of individualism.

Though Le Bas was an academician, indeed elected one of the Académie's councilors in 1771, the authors of his lives belonged to the print trade and were not "amateur" members of the Académie or professional men of letters, as was usually the case with the biographers of painters and sculptors. François-Charles Joullain, a printmaker and art dealer, wrote two lives of Le Bas: a formal historical biography published with the sale catalog of Le Bas's collection and stock in 1783, and an informal and unpublished life inserted at the beginning of the Oeuvre of Le Bas that he compiled and donated in 1789 to the royal library.[9]

What sets these texts apart from those written for the Académie's *conférences* is the license Joullain took, on the basis of his direct and close knowledge of his subject, to multiply the number of personal "anecdotes."[10] When such miscellaneous facts (*faits divers*) feature in academic lives, they exemplify and endorse the ideal image of the artist as learned, naturally gifted, or, in private life, modest and disinterested.[11] In Joullain's lives, however, things are not in the service of such literary tropes, but nor are they things in themselves. Rather, they serve as the occasion and stuff of social relationships, often structuring the brief narratives of the anecdotes: the set of clothes given him by his mother, an impoverished widow, the moment he leaves home on life's adventure, the jewels he bestowed on Elisabeth Duret to secure her hand and which he sold in a crisis shortly after the wedding day.[12] Even seemingly trivial and inconsequential transactions embody enduring social bonds: Le Bas's offer of his coat for Chardin's *Still Life with a Hare* (1728–29, New York, Metropolitan Museum of Art) is vividly reported as a favor, mutually felt, cementing a lifelong friendship.[13]

When Joullain does invoke the semantic value of objects as signs of distinction, they challenge the official history of the noble order of academic artists with their "low history" (*petite histoire*) of unpretending talent. Dress illustrates Le Bas's refusal to stand on ceremony. Apparently, on memorable occasions the engraver served at the counter in his shop, greeting his elite customers in shirtsleeves and cap.[14] In fact, Joullain reserved his most colorful and surprising anecdotes to illustrate Le Bas's radical egalitarianism, his insistence on engaging with the world on terms of equality, grounded in talent, not rank or birth.[15]

What bearing does this have on Le Bas's umbrella? It suggests that although the low cost of its materials and manufacture and the cheap market price qualified it as "populuxe" by Fairchilds's criteria, its attraction for Le Bas was not necessarily its agency as an index of status. If the umbrella signified class, it is not clear that it did so unequivocally: Louis-Antoine, the marquis de Caraccioli, remarked in 1768 that in Paris the umbrella was "the sign of having *no* **carriage**" and of having to walk on foot. Consequently, it was shunned by those of rank and title, who willingly took the risk of getting wet rather than be "confounded with the vulgar."[16] Joullain does not directly connect Le Bas and the umbrella, but he does associate him with the urban street, the prime location, as Le Bas's own etching of a peddler (fig. 172) in François Boucher's *Cris de Paris* indicates, of their sale and

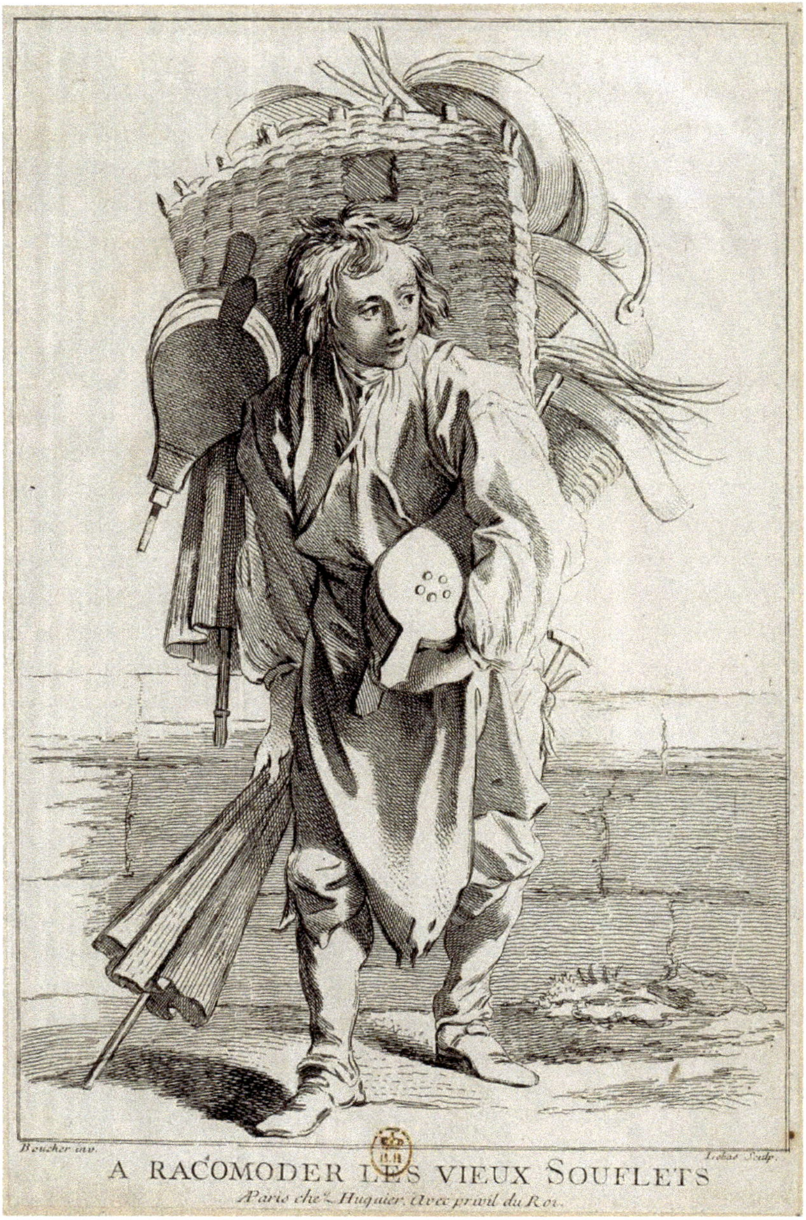

FIG. 172 Jacques-Philippe Le Bas (French, 1707–83), after François Boucher (French, 1703–70), *Le racomodeur de vieux soufflets*, 1737. Etching. Paris, Bibliothèque Nationale de France. (© BnF, Dist. RMN-Grand Palais / Art Resource, NY.)

use.[17] In one anecdote, Le Bas plays the jealous husband, pursuing his wife, whom he wrongly suspects of infidelity, in a taxi (*fiacre*); disillusioned and humiliated, he returns home in the rain, sopping and mud-spattered, presumably having left his umbrella in the cab, or forgotten it in his haste.[18] Le Bas's identity was, according to Joullain, grounded in the neighborhood street, specifically Rue de La Harpe, where he lived for forty-seven years, the address inscribed on the vast majority of the prints he published.[19] "I have seen him," writes Joullain, "magnificently dressed, stopping at the shop of a craftsman, or waylaying common folk in the middle of the road, either to buy from them things he did not need, and which he later gave away to others, or to ask them about themselves, their circumstances, their family, and their needs. [The street] provided him with manifold opportunities for benevolence."[20] Silver buckles, gold buttons, and a collapsible umbrella were not, in Joullain's discourse, the glittery trappings of upward social mobility but symptoms of the generosity he extended to himself and to others.

Joullain's biographies of Le Bas manifestly draw on tropes and themes from the literature of *sensibilité*, and some of the things mentioned in the lives function as sentimental objects whose personal meaning transcends their material and economic value: the portrait of Le Bas's mother, for example, before which, according to Joullain, Le Bas regularly shed the tears of a dutiful son throughout his life.[21] However, what distinguishes Le Bas's umbrella from things recorded and valued as commodities in his inventory, and also from those objects that manifestly serve as touchstones of private emotion in the biographies, is the umbrella's materiality and dependence on the energy and interaction of the human body to bring it to life. Umbrellas require skill and dexterity. Once opened up, they invite the freedom to venture forth in all weather, the opportunity to extend relief and hospitality to others under the intimate circumference of their cover. Human and thing become entangled in networks of material and social relations.

It is of course possible that the confinement of the green parasol in Le Bas's bedroom cupboard indicates a forgotten or discarded thing, not one kept handy, or, that it had originally belonged to Mme Le Bas and that the engraver cherished it as a keepsake. But Joullain's relentless focus on the externalities of Le Bas's life, on what connected him to the collective—family, friends, workshop, neighborhood—supports the argument made here that the shape and rhythm of Le Bas's life depended on the things that he took out into the world, his umbrella perhaps especially. It entrapped him into keeping his responsibilities and commitments and fulfilling his duties come rain or shine. §

---

1. On the fabrication of umbrellas, see Jeremy Farrell, *Umbrellas and Parasols* (London: Batsford, 1985), 9–17.

2. See Antoine Furetière, *Dictionnaire universel*, 2nd ed. (The Hague: Arnould & Reinier Leers, 1701), 2: s.vv. "Parasol," "Parapluie," *Encyclopédie*, http://encyclopedie.uchicago.edu/, 11:922. The *Dictionnaire de l'Académie française*, 4th ed. (Paris: Brunet, 1762), does, however, carefully distinguish the two with separate, not overlapping entries for "Parapluie" and "Parasol."

3. On Jean Marius, see Joan De Jean, *The Essence of Style* (New York: Free Press, 2005), 217–30.

4. As in, for example, Charles Le Brun's *Portrait of Chancellor Séguier at the Entry of Louis XIV to Paris in 1660* (Paris, Musée du Louvre).

5. Cissie Fairchilds, "The Production and Marketing of Populuxe Goods in Eighteenth-Century Paris," in *Consumption and the World of Goods*, ed. John Brewer and Roy Porter (London: Routledge, 1994), 239. According to De Jean, the cost of a collapsible umbrella in 1754 was between 15 and 22 livres (compared to 9 livres for a fixed one). This is expensive, and the price must have dropped to achieve the level of market penetration calculated by Fairchilds.

6. On Le Bas, see Roger Portalis and Henri Beraldi, *Les graveurs du XVIIIe siècle* (Paris: Morgand & Fatout, 1880–82), 2:564–90.

7. Jacques-Philippe Le Bas, "Inventaire après décès," AN, MC/ET/XLV/582, 23 April 1783; the street disappeared with the opening of the Boulevard Saint-Germain in 1855.

8. Le Bas, "Inventaire après décès." Canes and especially stockings are identified by Fairchilds as "populuxe."

9. See Hayot de Longpré, *Catalogue de tableaux, sculpture, desseins, estampes . . . provenant de la succession de feu M. Le Bas* (Paris: Clousier, 1783); and François-Charles Joullain, *L'oeuvre de*

Jacques-Philippe Le Bas, Graveur, 5 vols. (1789), BnF, Département des Estampes et de la Photographie: (Ee11–Ee11d in-fol. See also Charles-Étienne Gaucher, "Nécrologie [de M. Le Bas]," *Journal de Paris*, 12 May 1783, 554–55.

10. Joullain, "L'oeuvre," "Avertissement," n.p. See Lionel Gossman, "Anecdote and History," *History and Theory* 42, no. 2 (2003): 143–68.

11. An exception is the chevalier de Valory's life of Jean-François De Troy; see *Mémoires inédits*, 2:255–88.

12. Hayot de Longpré, *Catalogue*, v (clothes); and Joullain, *L'oeuvre* (Ee 11), iv–v (wedding jewels).

13. Joullain, *L'oeuvre* (Ee 11a), 7. On the picture and the question of its provenance, see *Chardin (1699–1779)*, exh. cat. (Paris: Grand Palais, 1979), no 21. A similar anecdote involving a **wig**, not a coat, was told by Caylus about Watteau, but in that instance the anecdote served emblematically to illustrate Watteau's modesty. See **Dressing-Up Box**.

14. Hayot de Longpré, *Catalogue*, xxi.

15. See Hayot de Longpré, *Catalogue*, xxi–xxiii: Le Bas invited a "président à mortier du Parlement d'une des premières Villes du Royaume" to dinner with other artists in the summer of 1782. When the president took his leave, Le Bas remarked: "You see, Sir, that although I did not place you among your equals in rank and birth, I took care to include with you (in this dinner) only Men of talent, and Talents Equalize Men [Vous voyez, Monsieur, que si je ne vous ai pas mis avec vos égaux pour le rang et la naissance, j'ai eu soin de ne rassembler avec vous que des Gens à talents, et LES TALENS RAPPROCHENT LES HOMMES]." On surprise being a defining feature of "*faits divers*," see Roland Barthes, "Structure du fait divers," in *Essais critiques* (Paris: Seuil, 1964), 188–97.

16. Quoted in Farrell, *Umbrellas*, 23. Robinson Crusoe made himself an umbrella as a basic necessity; see Irene Fizer, "The Fur Parasol: Masculine Dress, Prosthetic Skins, and the Making of the English Umbrella in Robinson Crusoe," in *Eighteenth-Century Thing Theory in a Global Context*, ed. Ileana Baird and Christina Ionescu (London: Routledge, 2013), 209–26.

17. That Le Bas identified himself with the street is suggested by his claim, reported by Joullain, that he had learned to read on the street, from the shop signs of Paris (*L'oeuvre* [Ee 11], iii) and that the memorial he cherished for himself was a series of distance markers on the road from Paris to Bicêtre with his prints posted upon them "so that passers-by are entertained and that they regret (the passing) of their author [afin que les Passans s'en amusent et plaignent leur auteur]." (*L'oeuvre* [Ee 11] xi). Moreover, Le Bas owned Chardin's shop sign for a barber-surgeon (now lost), a street-scene, which hung in his salon. See *Chardin*, no 1.

18. Joullain, *L'oeuvre* (Ee 11), ix–x.

19. See Hayot de Longpré, *Catalogue*, xiii, on Le Bas's change of address.

20. Joullain, *L'oeuvre* (Ee 11), ix.

21. Hayot de Longpré, *Catalogue*, vi. On sentimental objects, see Lynn Festa, *Sentimental Figures of the Empire in Eighteenth-Century Britain and France* (Baltimore: Johns Hopkins University Press, 2006), esp. 67–110.

Votive

Pierre-Imbert Drevet (1697–1739)

TYPE OF OBJECT	THEME	MATERIAL
Artwork, Devotional Thing, Ritual Thing, Symbolic Thing	Death, Family, Health/Medicine, Making, Religion, Studio	Synthetic Materials | Ink, Synthetic Materials | Paper

"Pray to God for him." The words are easy to miss at first, nestled under a plant within the loose cross-hatched lines in the lower-right foreground of Pierre-Imbert Drevet's engraving of *Christ's Agony in the Garden* (fig. 173). From afar, they might be mistaken for an accident on the plate, an inconsistency in the engraver's otherwise crisp, controlled handling delineating the varied textures, substances, and gestures of his subject. Upon closer inspection, though, the seemingly misplaced marks resolve into their intentionally lettered forms: "Gravé Par Pierre Drevet fils / Priez Dieu Pour Luy" (engraved by Pierre Drevet son / Pray to God for him) (fig. 174). Yet even once read, the words remain somewhat elusive in their legibility—never really clear, from no matter how close or what angle they are viewed. There is a persistent uncertainty about their place here. Discrete, but not hidden. Legible, but only just. Intentional, but somehow hesitant. Present, but out of place. Much like Drevet himself at the time he engraved this plate—the final artwork he would ever make—these words recall, in their meaning and their materiality, the desperate disquiet and spiritual suffering of their maker.[1]

In 1739, the year Drevet finished engraving *Christ's Agony*, he was experiencing his own anguishing torment in the form of a relapsing mental instability. For around ten years, Drevet had suffered intermittently from psychological episodes, difficult to diagnose retrospectively according to modern psychopathologies, but described variously by his contemporaries as: "*la démence*" (insanity); "*une faiblesse d'esprit*" (a weakness of the mind); "*le dérangement de son esprit*" (mental disturbance); and "*une maladie [qui l'empêche] de se gouverner*" (an illness that prevents him from controlling himself).[2] Drevet was far from the only eighteenth-century artist who experienced such episodes, as attested, among others, by the tragic demises of his colleagues François Lemoyne (who committed suicide by his **sword** in 1737) and later of André Rouquet (who died in an asylum in 1758).[3] Artists' lapses in mental stability were often attributed to "excessive work" (as some of Drevet's relatives suggested), but Drevet believed his ill health was an act of God.[4]

Writing to the *directeur général des bâtiments* in August 1738 after his father's death (afraid that he might lose the Louvre *logement* they had shared), Drevet described his ongoing mental problems as "la maladie dont Dieu m'a affligé" (the illness with which God has afflicted me).[5] His father, the engraver Pierre Drevet, had also considered his son's psychological complaints to be a divine operation—"ayant plus à Dieu [de] l'affliger d'une

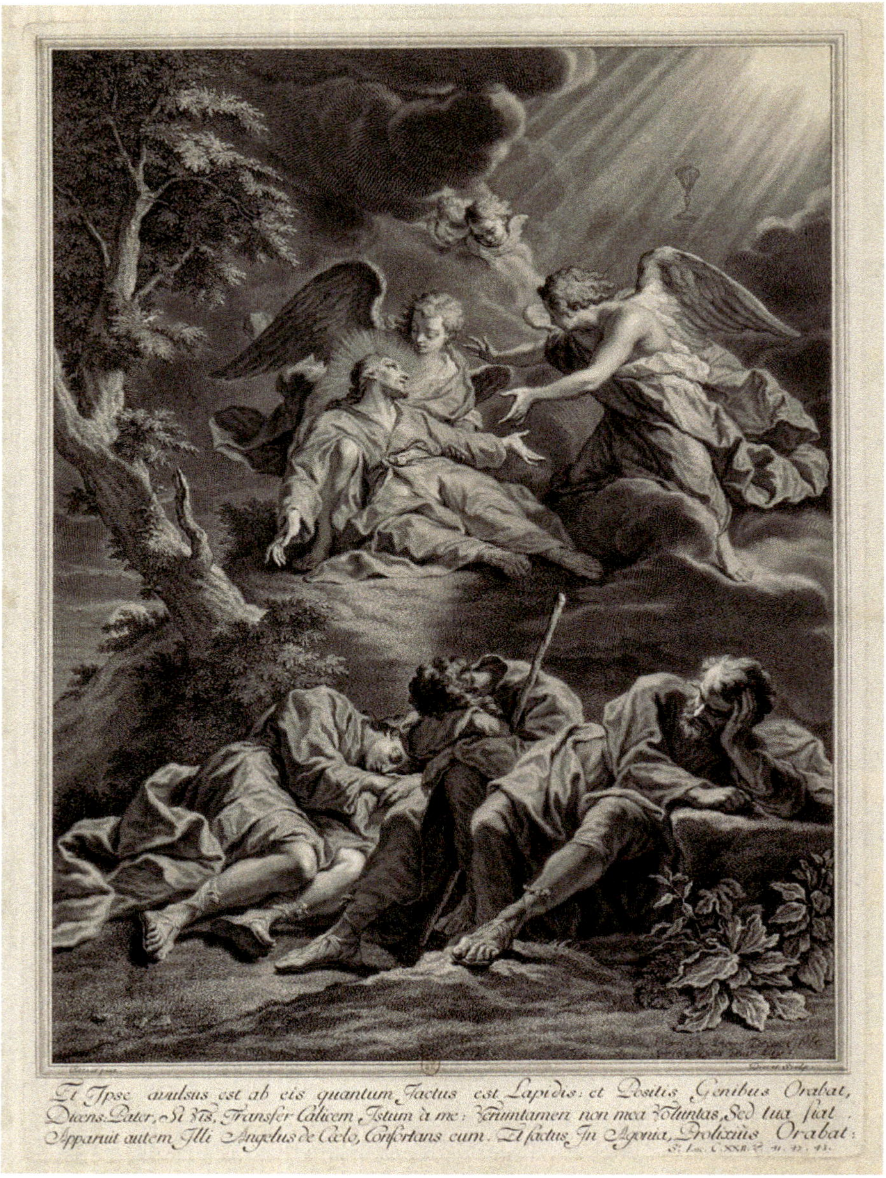

FIG. 173 Pierre-Imbert Drevet (French, 1697–1739), after Jean Restout (French, 1692–1768), *Christ's Agony in the Garden*, 1739. Engraving, first state, 53.1 × 40 cm. Paris, Bibliothèque Nationale de France.

faiblesse d'esprit" (having pleased God to afflict him with a mental weakness)—and made allowances in his will in case "le Seigneur" (the Lord) chose to strike him again. It was during one of these subsequent strikes predicted by his father that Drevet executed *Christ's Agony*, channeling his faith and skill to create an exquisite votive—an object that might help bring an end to his suffering.

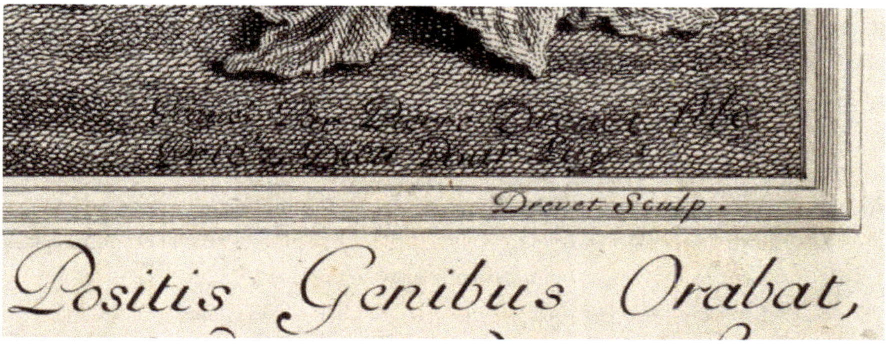

FIG. 174 Pierre-Imbert Drevet (French, 1697–1739), after Jean Restout (French, 1692–1768), *Christ's Agony in the Garden*, detail of inscription, 1739. Engraving, first state, 53.1 × 40 cm. Paris, Bibliothèque Nationale de France.

If God was responsible for Drevet's pain, then God alone had the power to relieve it. That was the reasoning behind any votive, or material offering made in a moment of crisis by or for a person seeking deliverance.[6] Materially, Drevet's engraving of *Christ's Agony* was like any other print; but spiritually, it was an entirely different category of object. Invested with religious purpose as a physical sign of the artist's supplication, this was an artwork made to do, rather than merely to be. Comparable in that respect to Largillière's painted **picture** or Houdon's sculpted **écorché**, this was yet another artwork that can be thought of usefully as a "thing," finding its place in this book because of its functionality rather than for its aesthetic qualities.

As its inscription reveals, the object's votive task was twofold. The first line—"Engraved by Pierre Drevet son"—underscores the artist's act of making the print itself as an offering, an object of devotion given in exchange, as it were, for the request tendered. The second line—"Pray to God for him"—switches from a description of the print to an imperative entreaty to its beholder, turning future viewers into potential agents of prayer to perpetuate Drevet's supplication. Yet poignantly, it is the print, not Drevet, who makes this plea (pray for *him*) in this rare instance of an inanimate thing given direct speech to compel its beholders to do something. For Drevet, this degree of detachment no doubt made the request easier to make, but it also suggests the role he envisaged for his engraving as an object of intercession: a thing that might speak and act on his behalf.

For a man descending into a state of despair and suffering, Drevet could not have chosen a more appropriate subject for his votive. Recounted in the Gospel verses that Drevet included below the image, Christ's Agony in the Garden takes place at Gethsemane just before his crucifixion, when, in a moment of fear and sorrow at the pain of his imminent sacrifice, Christ prays to his Father to relieve him of the burden: "Then he withdrew from them about a stone's throw, knelt down, and prayed, "Father, if you are willing, remove this cup from me; yet, not my will but yours be done." Then an angel from heaven appeared to him and gave him strength."[7]

As the New Testament's ultimate story of overwhelming mental anguish, and the power of prayer to overcome it, Christ's agony must have presented a source of solace for Drevet. His meditations on this subject—as a focus during his own moments of torment—were no doubt aided by the painting of the scene by Jean Restout (now lost), which hung in Drevet's home and was almost certainly the version that served as the engraving's model.[8] Drevet's personal connection to Restout's original makes it seem all the more likely that the creation of the print was a devotional exercise, rather than a commercial commission. In due course, the engraving would become a marketable commodity: its second state included the address for sale ("chez L. Surugue . . . rue des Noyers"), and an advertising notice was published in the *Mercure de France* a few years after Drevet's death.[9] But for Drevet, the original motivations were religious—an act of art making in which creative energy, time, and labor were all dedicated to the votive cause.

Contemplating the artwork instigated by Drevet's mental instability and created through his faith, it is impossible to discern any impairment in his abilities or detriment to its aesthetic qualities. Even the *Mercure* described it as "un de ses plus beaux ouvrages" (one of his most beautiful works).[10] Thus for the beholder of this votive print, there is a profound contrast between the mastery and competence of Drevet the engraver and the desperation and vulnerability of Drevet the man. This juxtaposition is most striking in the lower-right corner, at the intersection of his two signatures on either side of the frame (see fig. 174). While the sign of the engraver's authorship—"Drevet Sculp."—is precisely where it should be, his votive inscription is unsettlingly astray. It is set within the image, but it is not part of its pictorial space; the words are not written into the earth or onto some other surface in the scene but, rather, through the engraved lines of the plate, hovering liminally inside and outside. In their contrasting positionality and presence, these two inscriptions seem to represent the two Drevets: the artist who confidently knows his place and the disoriented man who has lost his way in the margins.

Drevet's psychological condition was certainly deteriorating quickly as he worked on the engraving through the early months of 1739.[11] On 24 January the Lieutenant Civil of the Châtelet was called to Drevet's *logement* at the Louvre to assess his mental capacity. In his bedroom, wearing **robe de chambre** and cap, Drevet received his visitor in a barely responsive state. Having stood, he ignored all entreaties to sit; in the face of numerous questions, he remained completely silent; and when asked to sign the assessment, he turned his head and bowed his body in refusal.[12] Several weeks later, his cousin, the engraver Claude Drevet, reported that the pitiful situation had escalated and that Pierre-Imbert was now "dans une imbécillité totale" (in a state of total insanity).[13] Accordingly, on 9 April the Châtelet issued a *Sentence d'interdiction*, legally prohibiting Pierre-Imbert from any longer managing his own affairs, and officially appointing Claude Drevet as his *curateur*, with power of attorney over his property and guardianship over his person.[14] Pierre-Imbert did not suffer the indignity for long, dying three weeks later on 27 April at the age of forty-one. Somewhere in all this suffering, Drevet finished his votive engraving, carving those tentative, elusive words in a final effort to come back from the margins of his mind and retrieve his place in this world, or find a new one in the next. ‡

---

1. The engraving is considered Drevet's final work according to Ambroise Firmin-Didot, *Les Drevet: Pierre, Pierre-Imbert et Claude* (Paris: Firmin-Didot, 1876), 95.

2. [Hendrick van Hulst], "État général des portraits et autres tableaux sortis du pinceau de l'illustre M. Rigaud," in *Mémoires inédits*, 2:197; Will, Pierre Drevet, 23 April 1736, AN, MC/ET/LX/257; *Mercure de France,* June 1742, 1416; and *Plaidoyer pour les héritiers paternels de Pierre-Imbert Drevet, intervenants, contre Claude Drevet, graveur du roi, appellant* (Paris: d'Houry, 1742), 2, 3.

3. On Lemoyne's suicide, see **Sword** and Hannah Williams, "The Mysterious Suicide of François Lemoyne," *Oxford Art Journal* 38, no. 2 (2015): 225–45. On Rouquet, see David Maskill, "The Neighbor from Hell: André Rouquet's Eviction from the Louvre," *Journal18* 2, "Louvre Local" (Fall 2016), http://www.journal18.org/822.

4. *Plaidoyer pour les héritiers*, 1.

5. Letter from Pierre-Imbert Drevet to Philibert Orry, 12 August 1738, transcribed in Cécile Perroud-Christophle, *Les graveurs Drevet, XVIIe–XVIIIe siècle* (Lyon: Selbstverlag, 1985), 84.

6. Votives or *ex votos* can also be given after deliverance has been granted as offerings of gratitude for divine intervention.

7. Luke 22:41–43.

8. The painting *Christ au jardin des Oliviers* by Jean Restout is recorded in Drevet's "Inventiare après décès," 26 June 1739, AN, MC/ET/LX/266. On Restout's painting, see Christine Gouzi, *Jean Restout: 1692–1768* (Paris: Arthena, 2000), 237–38.

9. *Mercure de France,* June 1742, 1415–16.

10. *Mercure de France,* June 1742, 1416.

11. This engraving of *Christ's Agony* seems to be the "ouvrage regardé aujourd'hui comme un Chef-d'oeuvre de l'Art" that Drevet was working on at the start of April 1739, described in the *Plaidoyer pour les héritiers*, 3.

12. Perroud-Christophle, *Les graveurs Drevet*, 88.

13. "Sentence d'Interdiction," Pierre-Imbert Drevet, 9 April 1739, AN, Y/4562.

14. "Sentence d'Interdiction." On legal proceedings concerning the mentally incapacitated in ancien régime France, see Fayçal El Ghoul, "Enfermer et interdire les fous à Paris au XVIIIe siècle: Une forme d'exclusion," *Cahiers de la Méditerranée* 69 (2004): 175–87.

Watch

Charles-Antoine Coypel (1694–1752)

TYPE OF OBJECT	THEME	MATERIAL
Apparel, Collectible, Commodity, Gift, Instrument, Symbolic Thing	Community, Invention, Louvre, Luxury, Money, Religion	Metal | Gold/Gilding, Mineral | Gem

Amid the extensive collection of *bijoux* (jewelry) itemized in the inventory of Charles-Antoine Coypel's possessions after his death, a luxurious watch was described in some detail: "[A] repeater watch, made in Paris by Julien Le Roy, in a gold casing adorned with a gold chain, comprising two seals mounted on rings, one of agate the other of carnelian, and with two rows of brilliants on the hour hand and on the minute hand, all in a green case garnished with gold."[1] One of at least three watches that Coypel owned, this was, according to the notary who priced it, the most elaborate and the most expensive.[2] It may also have been the most valuable to Coypel in another sense, not due to its cost, per se, but because of how it came to be in his possession.

In terms of its price, the watch's value came in part from its materials and design: precious metals and semiprecious stones worked by an *orfèvre* (goldsmith) into an elegant item of apparel. Conventionally worn hanging off the breeches beneath the waistcoat, a watch was an ostentatious sartorial accessory, but not one that could always be seen in its entirety.[3] The watch's tentative visibility is evident in Adolf-Ulric Wertmüller's portrait of the sculptor Jean-Jacques Caffieri (figs. 175, 176), where all that can be glimpsed of his watch is one of its *cachets* (seals) peeping out from behind the waistcoat. When hidden temporarily by clothing, there was still the sound of the chain and its hanging seals, jangling with the wearer's movements, to indicate the extent of the covered adornment. In the case of Coypel's watch, a different kind of sound was the other source of its value as a luxury. Described as a "repeater watch," this was the latest in pocket-watch technology, its mechanism comprising a whole separate set of cogs that activated a striking instrument to chime on the hour (fig. 177).[4] Though the *orfèvre* responsible for the decorative design of Coypel's watch is now anonymous, the *horloger* (clockmaker) responsible for its engineering was recorded in the signature on its face—Julien Le Roy—one of Paris's most renowned *horlogers*, appointed clockmaker to Louis XV in 1739.[5]

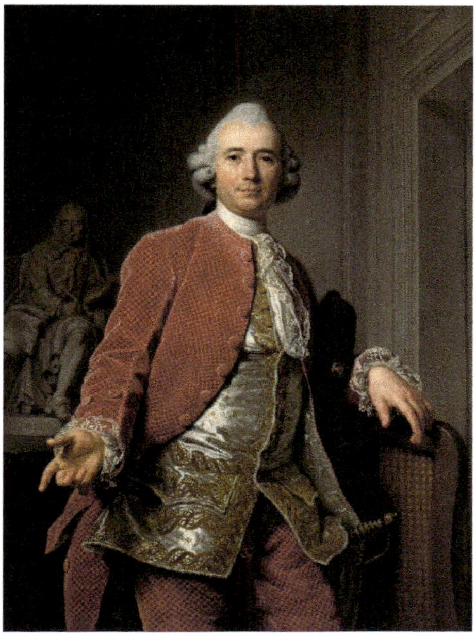

FIG. 175 Adolf-Ulric Wertmüllller (Swedish, 1751–1811), *Jean-Jacques Caffieri,* 1784. Oil on canvas, 129 × 96 cm. Museum of Fine Arts, Boston, Ernest Wadsworth Longfellow Fund. (Photograph © 2024 Museum of Fine Arts, Boston.)

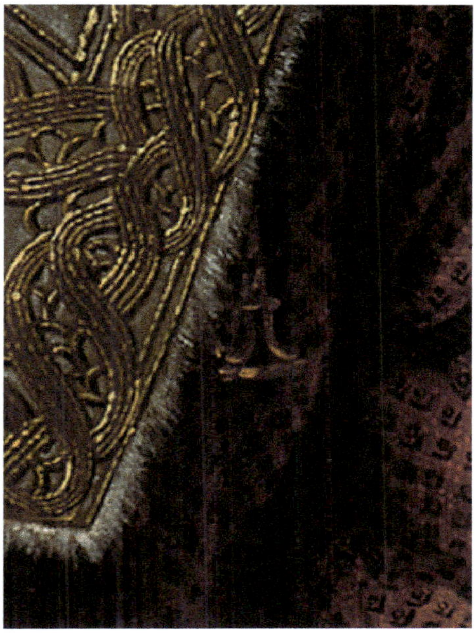

FIG. 176 Adolf-Ulric Wertmüllller (Swedish, 1751–1811), *Jean-Jacques Caffieri,* detail of watch, 1784. Oil on canvas, 129 × 96 cm. Museum of Fine Arts, Boston, Ernest Wadsworth Longfellow Fund. (Photograph © 2024 Museum of Fine Arts, Boston.)

Coypel's fancy piece of modern technology was a desirable commodity. Such a high-end luxury was certainly not out of place among Coypel's possessions, for the wealth of material things in his after-death inventory and sale catalog suggest a life lived in opulent surrounds.[6] His apartments in the Louvre (those Boucher would later inherit and adapt to accommodate his **shell** collection) were filled with luxury objects, among them porcelain vases, lamps, and potpourris; gold boxes; ornate mirrors; lacquered furniture; musical instruments; **snuffboxes**; a Meissonnier clock and barometer; his elaborate **bed**; and a gilt-bronze Boulle chandelier. His person was also luxuriously adorned, his wardrobes filled with velvet suits, lace shirts, cotton **handkerchiefs**, diamond-encrusted shoe buckles, gold-hilted **swords**, and rings with precious jewels. Artists in eighteenth-century France came from a variety of backgrounds and achieved varying degrees of financial success throughout their careers, which, as this book demonstrates, was often reflected in the material environments they inhabited. As the lavish exteriorization of wealth in his lodgings attests, Coypel was certainly one of the richer ones. *Premier peintre* (first painter) to the king and the duc d'Orléans, and director of the Académie, Coypel was part of a successful dynasty of similarly high-status artists, inheritor of his father and grandfather's collections, and he remained unmarried and without dependents, except for his four servants.[7]

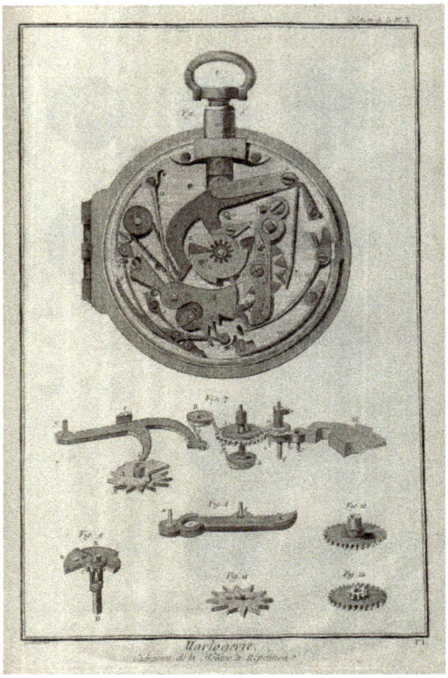

FIG. 177 "Horlogerie" from *Recueil de planches sur les sciences, les arts libéraux et les arts mécaniques* (1765), plate X, detail. (Image courtesy of the ARTFL Encyclopédie Project, University of Chicago.)

Coypel's watch was thus a luxury owned by a man who indulged readily in the delights of material extravagance. But as we know, the value of things cannot always be attributed to their market price. Being expensive might make an object desirable, but it is not the only reason a person may own it, nor the only quality that makes it valuable. Coypel's watch is a case in point, for the story of its acquisition does not take us into Paris's boutiques and commodity markets, but rather into a church, to meet not *orfèvres* and *horlogers* but a parish priest. Indeed, Coypel's watch reveals as much about the artist's faith, his charitable acts, and the social relations formed in his local neighborhood as it does about his penchant for beautiful expensive things.

In 1749 Coypel was commissioned to paint an enormous *Supper at Emmaus* to serve as altarpiece for the new Communion chapel in the church of Saint-Merry (fig. 178). As a resident of the Louvre, Coypel was not a parishioner of Saint-Merry, but he had a personal relationship with the *curé* (parish priest), Antoine Artaud, established years earlier when Artaud had worked at the church of Saint-Nicolas-du-Louvre.[8] Back in 1734, artist and clergyman had made their acquaintance when Coypel donated a large altarpiece of *Christ's Entombment* (now lost) for this small church in his neighborhood.[9] Their long-term association was probably behind Saint-Merry's decision to commission Coypel, for, as it turned out, this high-profile artist was actually far beyond the church's budget. According to the parish accounts, Saint-Merry's annual income just covered their running costs, leaving no revenue for additional expenses.[10] Decoration of the new chapel was funded through special collections from parishioners, but these were quickly exhausted when it came time to pay the numerous artists and tradesmen involved. Faced with dwindling coffers and insufficient funds to pay Coypel, the church instead offered him the Le Roy repeater watch as payment for the painting.[11]

Transactions where luxury objects stood in for monetary payments were fairly common in eighteenth-century France. Watches, as Natacha Coquery has shown, were among the most frequently exchanged items in this business of barter.[12] But in this particular exchange, two things stand out. First, the identity of the giver. A watch is not something usually owned by a corporate body, like a parish council, but rather by an individual, suggesting that this was a personal payment coming directly from Artaud, Coypel's friend. Second, the question of value. There is no record of the original commission for the altarpiece, so we do not know how Coypel estimated the cost of the painting, but the parish accounts valued the watch at 1,277 livres.[13] In transactions where luxury goods were used as currency, the items exchanged usually held equivalent values. But that was not the case here. Going by its market value, the watch would have given the *Supper at Emmaus* a price of only around 6 livres per square foot. Compared with Coypel's other paintings from this period—when he was at the peak of his artistic career—this was around ten times less than his usual going rate.[14]

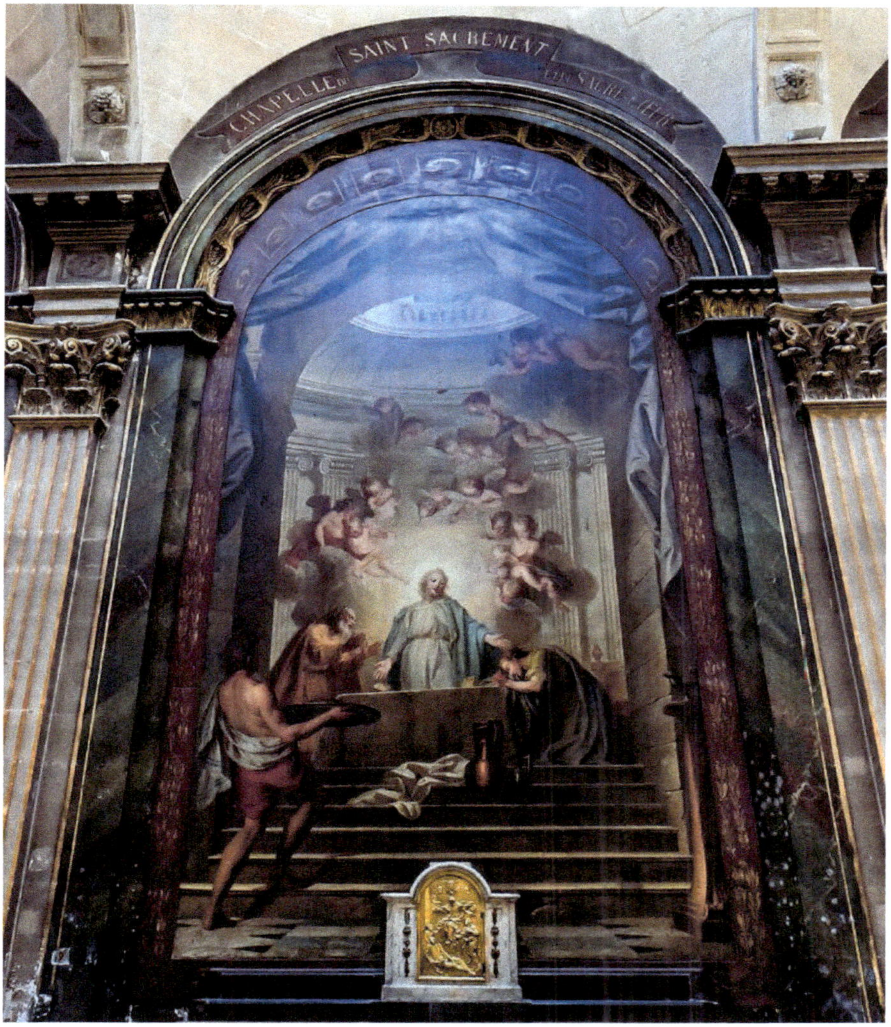

FIG. 178 Charles-Antoine Coypel (French, 1694–1752), *Supper at Emmaus*, 1749. Oil on canvas, 590 × 315 cm. Paris, Communion Chapel, Church of Saint-Merry. (Photo: isogood / Alamy Stock Photo.)

Either the watch was never meant as full payment (though it was the only payment Coypel ever received) or the value of the watch in this exchange was not being defined in purely financial terms. Certainly, both the watch and the painting were commodities, objects whose prices were determined by the materials and labor involved in their production. But when used as currency, objects are different. Unlike abstract sums of money, objects are material things that have lives and relationships; they have a cash value, but they also acquire sentimental value through meanings that become attached to them. Like so many of the objects in this book, Coypel's watch circulated in commercial economies, but also symbolic ones.

In this exchange, the watch's value depended not only on its estimated price but on what it *meant* to the giver and the recipient. Perhaps this meaning was only acquired at the point of exchange, when the watch became a token of thanksgiving for the altarpiece, a memento forever recalling that event. Perhaps its sentimental value was intensified by the personal touch, for presumably Artaud knew of Coypel's penchant for expensive luxury goods, and maybe Coypel even particularly desired a watch of this kind. Or perhaps its meaning was invested by the previous owner, that is, during its time in Artaud's possession and what it already meant to him—a gift, an inheritance, or another significant exchange that somehow intensified the significance of its next exchange. As for the altarpiece, the art market measured value differently from the luxury market, not on cost of materials (paint and canvas) but on skill and labor. A painting's price was dependent on the status of its artist, and as *premier peintre du roi* and *directeur* of the Académie, Coypel's paintings could claim some of the highest prices around. But even here "value" was more ambiguous. After all, *Supper at Emmaus* was not just any painting, but an altarpiece—a sacred object destined to play a devotional role in acts of worship for hundreds of souls—and it is difficult to put a price on that.

Coypel and Artaud's exchange was not a straightforward commercial transaction but an exchange of symbolically resonant objects between two friends, one a priest, the other a member of the faithful. Artaud was not commissioning a painting for a private residence but seeking an object to provide a setting for the distribution of the sacrament to his parishioners. Coypel was not just fulfilling a commission but yet again making a charitable donation, as he had fifteen years earlier for the church of Saint-Nicolas-du-Louvre.[15] This time, however, it seems not to have been intended as a donation from the outset. Instead, when Saint-Merry ran out of money, Coypel performed a face-saving favor for his friend, accepting the watch as "payment" and canceling the rest of the debt as a charitable offering. Coypel's altruistic act depended entirely on the symbolic value of the watch, for it would never have worked if the payment had come in cash. If Artaud had simply given Coypel 1,277 livres, it could only ever have appeared as a partial payment, an embarrassing undervaluing of Coypel's work. The watch, however, was not just a stand-in for money but an enduring sign of this offering, retrospectively transforming Coypel's altarpiece into a donation and Artaud's watch into a gift of gratitude.

The value of Coypel's watch was increased (or at least disguised) in this exchange by its ambiguous position between various economies (commercial, social, and symbolic). And so it continued through the object's life. When the notary itemized the watch in the inventory of Coypel's possessions taken after his death in 1752, it was priced modestly at 1,000 livres, but it appears to have been worth more than that to Coypel. Another of the watches listed by the notary ended up in the sale of the artist's possessions the following year, but this watch did not.[16] Instead, it passed to his brother, Philippe, who inherited most of Coypel's estate, apart from the few special bequests Coypel made in his **will** to family and associates (including 1,000 livres to the *curé* of his own parish of Saint-Germain-l'Auxerrois).[17] This luxury item stood out from many others Coypel had acquired, valued enough to be offered again rather than sold off for revenue. Passing through its varied economies, the object was imbued with new sentimental resonances: changing from the watch that Antoine Artaud gave Coypel for painting *Supper at Emmaus*, to become the watch that Coypel left his brother when he died. ‡

---

1. "Une . . . montre à répétition faite à Paris par Julien Le Roy dans Sa boette d'or garny de Sa chaine d'or, deux cachets montés en Bague l'un d'une agatorin et l'autre de Cornaline, deux Batons de Brillants tant Sur l'eguille des heures que Sur celle des minutes dans Son Etuy de trousset Vert et garny d'or." Charles-Antoine Coypel, "Inventaire après décès," 25 September 1752, AN, MC/LXXVI/337, 11.

2. It was valued in the inventory at 1,000 livres; the other watches were 700 and 200 livres.

3. Genevieve Cummins, *How the Watch Was Worn: A Fashion for 500 Years* (Woodbridge: Antique Collectors' Club, 2010), 19.

4. Repeater mechanisms for watches were patented by David Quare in the 1680s. David Landes, *Revolution in Time: Clocks and the Making of the Modern World* (Cambridge, MA: Belknap, 1983).

5. Jean-Dominique Augarde, *Les ouvriers du temps: La pendule à Paris de Louis XIV à Napoléon 1er* (Geneva: Antiquorum, 1996); and *La dynastie des le Roy, horlogers du roi*, exh. cat. (Tours: Musée des Beaux-Arts, 1987).

6. See Coypel's "Inventaire après décès" and *Catalogue des tableaux, dessins, marbres, bronzes, modeles, estampes, et planches gravées; ainsi que des bijoux, porcelains, et autres curiosités de prix du cabinet de feu M. Coypel, premier peintre du roi & de Monseigneur le duc d'Orléans, & directeur de l'Académie royale de peinture & sculpture* (Paris, 1753).

7. On Charles-Antoine Coypel's professional and personal life, see Thierry Lefrançois, *Charles Coypel, 1694–1752* (Paris: Arthena, 1994), 37–112. On the Coypel dynasty, see Hannah Williams, *Académie Royale: A History in Portraits* (New York: Routledge, 2015), 166–77.

8. Lefrançois, *Charles Coypel*, 360–61.

9. Lefrançois, *Charles Coypel*, 276–79.

10. Abbé Constant Baloche, *Église Saint-Merry de Paris: Histoire de la paroisse et de la collégiale, 700–1910* (Paris: the author, 1911), 568–70. For an analysis of Saint-Merry's finances, see Hannah Williams, *Art and Religion in Enlightenment Paris* (forthcoming).

11. Baloche, *Église Saint-Merry*, 531.

12. Natacha Coquery, "The Language of Success: Marketing and Distributing Semi-Luxury Goods in Eighteenth-Century Paris," *Journal of Design History* 17, no. 1 (2004): 84–86.

13. Baloche, *Église Saint-Merry*, 531.

14. Comparative rates (based on prices recorded by Lefrançois) for Coypel's paintings include: *Sainte Thaïs* and *Garden of Olives* (1736)—each 3 ft. 5 in. by 1 ft. 10 in.—700 livres (58 livres/sq. ft.); *Sainte Landrade* (1747)—3 ft. 8 in. by 2 ft. 5 in.—600 livres (66 livres/sq. ft.); *Cleopatra swallowing poison* (1749)—6 ft. 10 in. by 8 ft. 9 in.—3,500 livres (59 livres/sq. ft.); *L'évanouissement d'Atalide* (1750)—6 ft. 6 in. by 5 ft.—2,500 livres (78 livres/sq. ft.). Soon after, the marquis de Marigny regulated tariffs for history paintings produced for royal commissions. A work of this size (circa 200 square feet) would have fetched at least 5,000 livres (or 10,000 depending on the size of figures). Fernand Engerand, *Inventaire des tableaux commandés et achetés par la direction des bâtiments du roi (1709–1792)* (Paris, 1900), xxii–xxiii.

15. Coypel also donated an *Ecce Homo* for the church of the Oratoire in 1729. Lefrançois, *Charles Coypel*, 222–25.

16. *Catalogue des tableaux . . . de feu M. Coypel*, 100.

17. Will, Charles-Antoine Coypel, 13 June 1752, AN, MC/ET/LXXVI/335.

Water Fountain

Jean-Siméon Chardin (1699–1779)

TYPE OF OBJECT	THEME	MATERIAL
Instrument	Everyday, Family, Gender	Metal | Copper

1731 was an important year for the still-life painter Jean-Siméon Chardin. He married Marguerite Saintard in January and set up his own household in five rooms sublet from his mother and carved out of the family's home, a house on the corner of Rue du Four and Rue Princesse in the parish of Saint-Sulpice.[1] A kitchen was installed on the third floor and furnished with a large copper water fountain (*fontaine de cuivre*) on an oak stand to supply the needs of his household, which included, in addition to his wife, their servant, Marie-Anne Cheneau, and, from November 1731, a son, the newborn Pierre-Jean.[2] A second, "small" copper fountain, of the tabletop variety, illustrated alongside the "large" in volume 3 of the plates of Diderot and d'Alembert's *Encyclopédie* (fig. 179), probably graced either the sideboard or the kitchen table. Both fountains were inventoried in 1737 following the untimely death of Saintard in February 1735. Such mundane things of ordinary consumption are present in countless artists' inventories;[3] only Chardin, however, made the water fountain the subject of his painting (fig. 180), thus providing us with a visual record of its existence.[4] His studio was, according to Georges Wildenstein's reconstruction of the layout of the third floor from land registry records, directly opposite the kitchen, on the other side of the central staircase and at the end of a short corridor.[5] Art historians assume that either the fountain migrated to the studio or that the painter migrated to the kitchen for the realization of the Louvre's small painting, executed on panel circa 1734, which was unsold in 1737 and inventoried in the studio along with two other pictures of kitchen utensils.

What of the copper fountain itself? What kind of a thing was it and in what sense was it Chardin's? It was not a prop or studio tool consciously devised to model for a painting, like Jacques-Louis David's **table**, or the costumes in Watteau's **dressing-up box**, so it cannot, therefore, be read as a mark of the painter's dedication to verisimilar depiction. Nor was it a thing like an **intaglio**, **snuffbox**, or **sword**, a sign more or less consciously acquired to denote personal taste and social distinction. Nor yet was it a novelty, like a **gaming set** or an **umbrella**, or a curiosity like a **shell**, that is, a purchase apparently prompted by desire and the caprices of taste.

Study of Chardin's things has generally focused on the objects depicted in his still lifes of the 1750s and 1760s: the smoking box, the porcelain **teacups**, and the glass.[6] Scholars have argued that these things reflect Chardin's rising standard of living after his second marriage and the consequent enlargement of his taste. Ordinary, mundane, utility wares

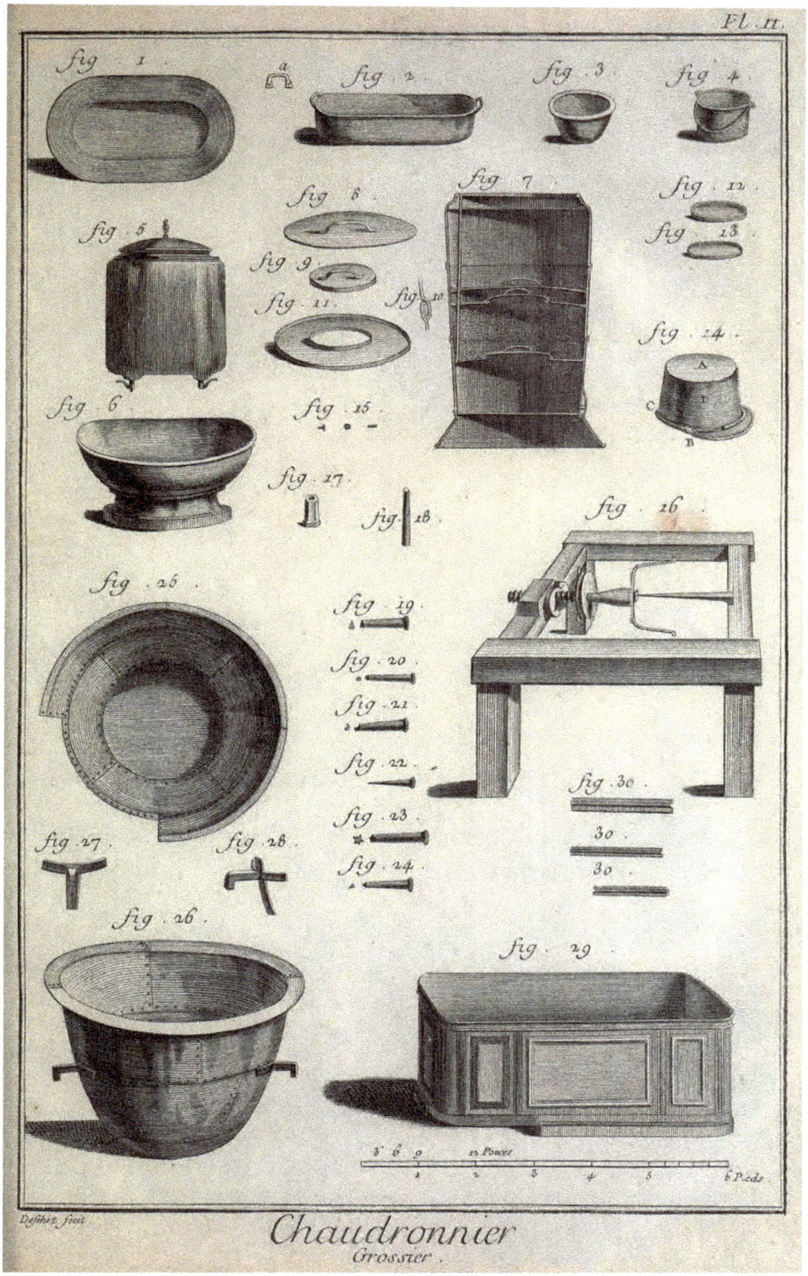

FIG. 179 "Chaudronnier" from *Recueil de planches sur les sciences, les arts libéraux et les arts mécaniques* (1763), vol. 3, plate II. (Image courtesy of the Smithsonian Libraries and Archives.)

like water fountains are, however, poorly captured by such economic and semiotic models of consumption because, as everyday necessities, neither personal choice nor symbolic value seems appropriately to describe ownership of them. They are not the kinds of goods that eighteenth-century Europe, envisaged as birthplace of the consumer society, and site

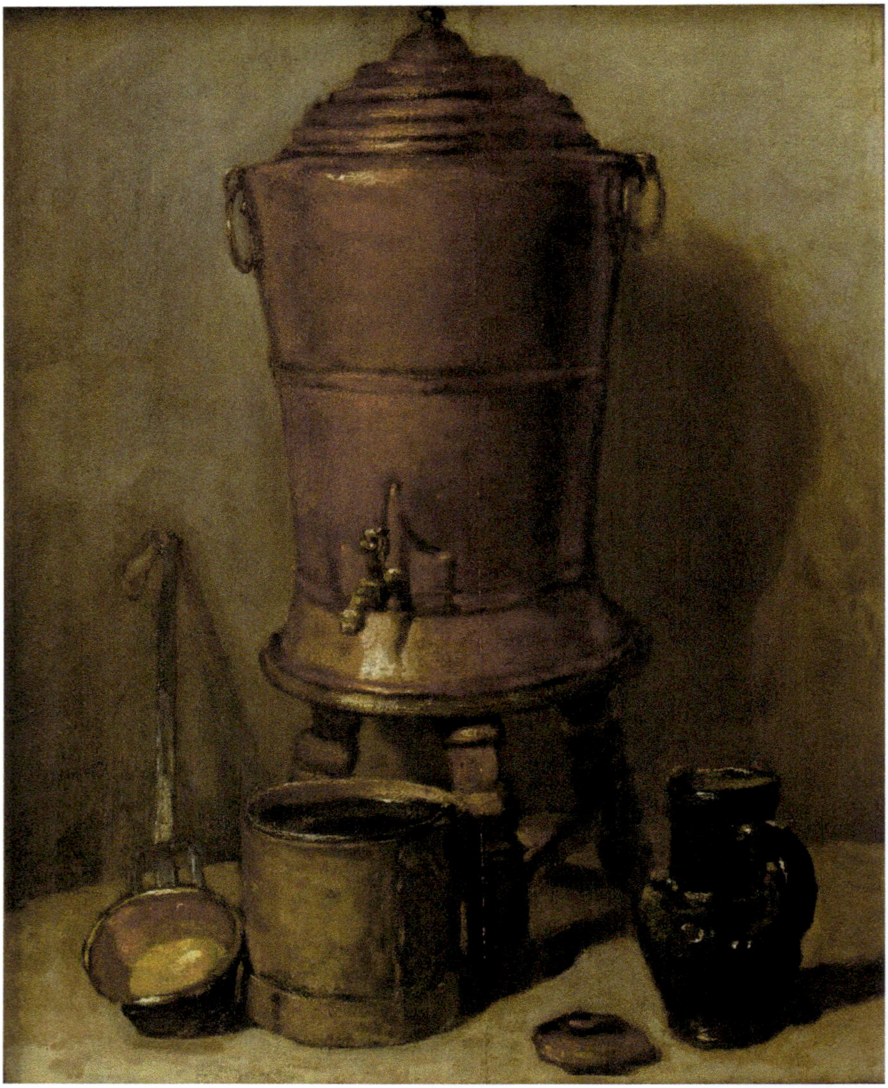

FIG. 180 Jean-Siméon Chardin (French, 1699–1779), *The Copper Cistern*, ca. 1734. Oil on panel, 28.5 × 23 cm. Paris, Musée du Louvre, MI1037. (© RMN-Grand Palais / photo: Stéphane Maréchalle / Art Resource, NY.)

of the industrious revolution, supposes. More promising are theorizations of consumption as practice. Prompted by the material turn, theories of practice focus not on the choice of the sovereign and expressive individual consumer; instead, they trace collective and customary practices of acquiring, appropriating, and using things, and analyze the effect, or doings, of those everyday things.[7]

Ordinary consumption concerns modes of behavior that are routine.[8] Habits such as fetching water, making up fires, lighting candles, and opening doors, severally performed using buckets, pokers, tapers, and handles, are almost entirely lost to history. They were automatic, conventionalized gestures that passed then and pass now largely unnoticed.

Domestic water, and the equipment that enabled its procurement, storage, and use, stands more often than not in the shadow of other more conspicuous and meaningful activities, such as cooking, bathing, and washing. In order to see it we shall have briefly to reconstruct the fountain's existence as a technology.

Chardin's water would have been supplied as a matter of routine by watercarriers.[9] It was probably sourced either from the Fontaine Palatine on Rue Garancière, near the Luxembourg palace or from the Samaritaine on the Pont Neuf over the Seine.[10] Inside the home, water as element was remade by servants for domestic purpose. *The Copper Cistern* (see fig. 180) acknowledges the toil of regular polishing but not care of the fountain's interior, essential to providing water fit for drinking. Copper fountains were tin lined to prevent contamination of the water by verdigris, which forms when water reacts to copper.[11] Fountains, like those illustrated in the section by A. J. Defehrt (see fig. 179), were sometimes also fitted with sand or sponge filters to purify the water. Chardin's is unlikely to have been one of these, however, because they were not widely available until the 1760s.[12] His fountain was simpler and relied on the natural density of matter to separate water from its impurities. The tap was judiciously sited above the filths that sank and gathered at the bottom, and below those that rose floating to the top.[13] Fountains of both kinds required regular maintenance: emptying, cleaning, checking for damage to the tin parts, mending, and refilling. They made temporal as well as spatial demands.

Since owners generally delegated responsibility for those demands to others—servants, wives—kitchenware such as water fountains are rarely considered artists' things. However, Chardin's portrayal of his fountain suggests that his engagement with it ran deeper than mere acquisition and delegation, that he made it, so to speak, his, if not directly through touch and use, then by interpretation and through painting.[14] The still-life objects of *The Copper Cistern* locate Chardin's encounter in the kitchen associating the water fountain specifically with cooking, as opposed, for example, to washing. But his painting is not a cook's picture. The compositional arrangement of pan and pitcher on the ground detaches them from the bodily gestures of cooking. Chardin's portrayal singularized the fountain as his own by presenting it as the fulcrum of a system of collection and distribution. Water has arrived by pail. It awaits to be lifted, poured, and stored in the cistern. When needed, it will run out from the brass tap to fill a copper pot or pitcher. The simple, logical order of the composition distributes the actions (of fetching, lifting, pouring, tap turning, filling) embodied in the objects in time, but the primacy of the vertical axis mutes the impression of operational flow. Chardin interprets the fountain as a container more than a conduit, an instrument not shaped by but shaping time. By storing water, the cistern secured economies of time spent fetching and carrying water up to the third floor. Chardin's fifty-five-liter fountain contained sufficient water for three adults for two and a half days, calculated on the average daily adult consumption of 7.45 liters.[15]

Norman Bryson has argued that Chardin painted ordinary things and the domestic interior from "a native's point of view."[16] He attributes to the male artist a unique sensibility that enabled him to achieve psychological closeness with the domain of his women subjects. Instead of reproducing the household's gender divisions, Bryson argues that Chardin took great pains to disguise painting's intrusiveness.[17] The "informality of his compositions" and the "relaxed focus" of his depictions work, he says, suggest that the painter entered "gently" and "invisibly" into feminine spaces, observing (in senses both of seeing and heeding) the harmonies he discovered there and reproducing them in his painting. In *The Copper Cistern*, however, things do not refer to the ordinary routines of cleaning and cooking performed in domestic space. As we have seen, Chardin's arrangement of the accoutrements of household water articulates a more abstract logic, that of water supply. In the geometry of the composition, the relative positions of the pail, cistern, pot, and pitcher re-trace the circulation of water and money necessary to connect productively coppersmiths, the makers of fountains, water sellers, servants, wives, and Chardin, head of the household and thus master and manager of the system. They represent not the "experience-near" concept of housework but the "experience-far" ideal of household oeconomy, embodied by Chardin's household and understood in the social and moral terms of good order and collective well-being as well as in the more narrowly economic terms of sound stewardship of resources to meet the family's needs.[18]

The fountain became an extraordinary object for Chardin in the 1730s and was consciously appropriated by him, we suggest, because of the responsibilities he assumed on his marriage. Coincidentally, 1731 was also one of the hottest years on record, exceeded in the eighteenth century only in 1733; during both years Paris experienced severe drought.[19] Shortage of water no doubt sharpened further Chardin's awareness of his fountain and of the responsibility for keeping it supplied.

This reading of *The Copper Cistern* suggests that the water fountain as material object engaged Chardin's social and moral self, that it entangled him in a network of sustained and sustaining material, economic, social, and ethical relations with family, servants, coppersmiths, and sundry suppliers of water and household goods: buckets and cookware. To that extent the kitchen and Chardin's water fountain had possibly more in common with the neighborhood fountain and the public street than with the still-life objects the painter imported into the notoriously enclosed personal space of his studio.[20] Indeed, the steep raking light in *The Copper Cistern* and the stone floor and walls that ground the scene invoke a street-level space, internalizing and inverting the corner of corner urban plots (like the one on which Chardin's house stood) as domestic niche.

The Fontaine Palatine, designed by the city's architect Jean Beausire and erected little more than a stone's throw from the Rue Princesse, is simple and ordinary, consisting of a single spout mounted in a shallow recess (fig. 181). The Latin inscription advertised that Anne of Bavaria had ordered its erection, desiring that "water will flow, at her expense, for the citizens" of her neighborhood.[21] Supply and consumption of water are thereby framed in a discourse of civic as well as domestic virtue, and raise questions about how the material culture of containers and conduits, of domestic fountains and cisterns, of pails and pots and pitchers may have served to shape Chardin's subjectivity in the public sphere.[22] His depiction of his fountain does not, to be sure, reproduce the hospitality of the Palatine's. It is portrayed as a cistern, not a fountain. All the other vessels in the picture are lidless, poised either to lose or to gain contents. Only the fountain is sealed. In appearing to hold back and carefully to husband the flow of water, the domestic fountain can, however, be said to mirror the ethics of noble largesse, reproducing it in reverse as private virtue. The virtues of containment are those of temperance, prudence, and, in times of dearth, thrift and fortitude.[23]

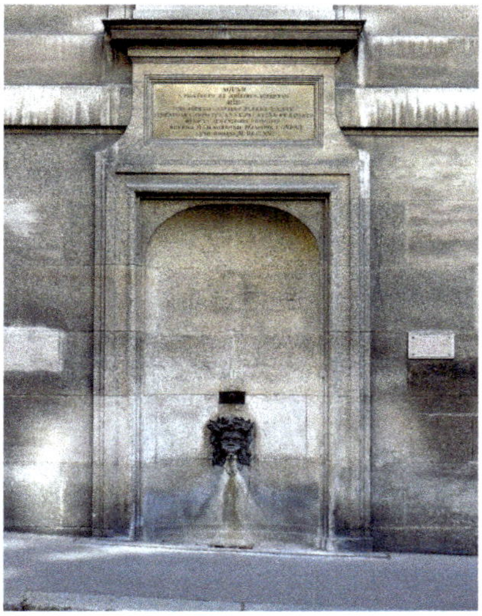

FIG. 181 Jean-Baptiste-Augustin Beausire (French, 1694–1764), Fontaine Palatine, ca. 1715. Paris, Rue Garancière. (Wikimedia, photo: Mbzt.)

Chardin's copper fountain challenges not interpretation of his still-lives as operating on the same plane of existence as the things they depict, but rather the construal of early eighteenth-century domesticity as modern, meaning a separate sphere, distinct from the public, a private realm of women and children. Chardin's attachment to, even identification with, his fountain, as manifest in *The Copper Cistern*, was that of the master of a household in which the practices of consumption, reproduction, and production overlapped. The coexistence of his studio and the kitchen on the same floor speaks eloquently of the interpenetration of the spheres of work, family, and the social. Contemporaries noted as exceptional not the privacy of Chardin's home but the enclosure of his atelier. His door was closed to both students and patrons. In the configuration of his rented rooms, the studio was divided from the communal areas by a lobby that, while scarcely large enough to call a room, nevertheless marked the boundary of the studio, if not guarded the threshold.[24] By contrast, the kitchen was open and busy. Water ascending two or three times a week through the house to fill the copper fountain very likely stamped a background rhythm on Chardin's everyday life. By its cadence the painter may have known the days of the week and times of day.[25] Moreover, this acousmatic signature, overheard in the studio, could also have worked to buttress Chardin's sense of his social self, put at risk when alone, painting. §

---

1. See Félix Herbert, "Les demeures de Jean Siméon Chardin," *Bulletin de la Société historique du VIe arrondissement* 2 (1899): 142–47.

2. For a reconstruction of the third floor, see Georges Wildenstein, "Le décor de la vie de Chardin d'après le tableaux," *GBA* 53 (1959): 97–106. On the inventory of 1737, see André Pascal and Roger Gaucheron, *Documents sur la vie et l'oeuvre de Chardin* (Paris: Éditions de la Galerie Pigalle, 1931).

3. According to Annik Pardailhé-Galabrun, almost 70 percent of Paris houses were equipped with domestic water fountains. See Pardailhé-Galabrun, *La Naissance de l'intime: 3000 foyers* *parisiens XVII–XVIIIe siècles* (Paris: Presses Universitaires de France, 1998), 349.

4. See Humphrey Wine, *National Gallery Catalogues: The Eighteenth-Century French Paintings* (New Haven: Yale University Press, 2018), 89: *The Water Cistern*. Wine provides an in-depth account of water cisterns on which we have been pleased to draw.

5. Wildenstein, "Le décor," 106. The building was pulled down in 1945.

6. See J. Barrelet, "Chardin du point de vue de la verrerie," *GBA* 53 (1959): 305–15; "De quelques objets chez Chardin," in *Chardin, 1699–1779*, exh. cat. (Paris: Grand Palais, 1779), 67–72; and Marie-Laure de Rochebrune, "Ceramics and Glass in Chardin's Paintings," in *Chardin (1699–1779)*, exh. cat. (London: Royal Académie, 2000), 37–52.

7. See Frank Trentmann, "Materiality in the Future of History: Things, Practices, and Politics," *Journal of British Studies* 48, no. 2 (2009): 283–307; and Alan Warde, Daniel Welch, and Jessica Paddock, "Studying Consumption through the Lens of Practice," *Routledge Handbook of Consumption* (London: Routledge, 2017), 25–35.

8. Jukka Groncon and Alan Warde, eds., *Ordinary Consumption* (London: Routledge, 2001).

9. See Roche, *Everyday Things*, 152.

10. See Roche, *Everyday Things*, 143–45; and Daniel Rabreau, *Paris et ses fontaines* (Paris: AAdP, 1997).

11. See Joseph Amy, *Extrait du livre intitulé Nouvelles fontaines domestiques approuvées par l'Académie des sciences* (Paris: Coignard & Boudet, 1752) on attempts to persuade consumers to buy iron rather than copper fountains. Amy dubbed the copper fountain a "masked assassin" because of its potential toxicity. By the 1770s, according to the tradecard of Clément & Cie, quai de la Mégisserie, sale of copper cisterns was prohibited.

12. See Montbruel and Ferrand, *Eau de la Seine filtrée et épurée pour la consummation de Paris* (n.p.: n.p., 1764) on the introduction of commercially filtered water. Servants, they argued, could not be relied upon to manage domestic filtration.

13. Wine, *National Gallery Catalogues*, 90–91.

14. For a discussion of consumption as appropriation, see Alan Warde, *Consumption: A Sociological Analysis* (London: Palgrave Macmillan, 2017), 59–78.

15. Wine, *National Gallery Catalogues*, 90–91. For estimates of average daily water consumption, see Roche, *Everyday Things*, 157.

16. The phrase is Clifford Geertz's. Geertz, "'From the Native's Point of View': On the Nature of Anthropological Understanding," *Bulletin of the Academy of Arts and Sciences* 28, no. 1 (1974): 26–45.

17. Norman Bryson, *Looking at the Overlooked* (London: Reaktion, 1990), 162–68.

18. Geertz, "From the Native's Point of View," 28–29. Antoine Furetière's definition of "oeconomie" in volume 3 of *Dictionnaire universel* (The Hague: Husson, 1727) assigns it a composite moral, social, and economic meaning. "Oeconomie" was also a term in art theory coined by Roger De Piles to denote the good order of a composition's "*tout ensemble.*" See Roger De Piles, *Cours de peinture par principes* (1709; reprint, Paris, 1989), 50, 65–70. On the concept of oeconomy, see Lissa Roberts, "Practicing Oeconomy During the Second Half of the Eighteenth Century: An Introduction," *History and Technology* 30, no. 3 (2014): 133–48; and Keith Tribe, "Oeconomic History: An Essay Review," *Studies in the History and Philosophy of Science* 36 (2005): 586–97.

19. See Fréderic Graber, "Inventing Needs: Expertise and Water Supply in Late Eighteenth- and Early Nineteenth-Century Paris," *British Journal for the History of Science* 40, no. 3 (2015): 318. The drought was such that it gave rise to epidemics. See Bernard de Jussieu, "Examen des causes qui ont altéré l'eau de la Seine, pendant la sécheresse de l'année 1731," *Mémoires de l'Académie royale des sciences, Année 1733* (Paris: 1735), 351–60. Jussieu delayed making the report until 1733, when a repeat of the conditions in 1731 allowed him to verify his findings.

20. On the privacy of Chardin's studio, see Lajer-Burcharth, *The Painter's Touch*, 90–91.

21. The inscription reads: "Aquam a praefecto et aedilibus acceptam hic suis impensis, civibus fluere voluit Serenissima Princeps Anna Palatina, ex Bavarii . . . Anno Domini MD.CC.XV."

22. For a theorization of containers, see Jean-Pierre Warnier, "Inside and Outside: Surfaces and Containers," in *Handbook of Material Culture*, ed. Chris Tilly et al. (Los Angeles: Sage, 2006), 186–95.

23. See Simon Werrett, *Thrifty Science* (Chicago: University of Chicago Press, 2019) on economy as a context for experimental science.

24. One of its two doors was covered in damask and raises the possibility that the studio door was actually masked; the walls of the lobby were decorated with coarse wool-and-hemp hangings into the texture of which the door may have appeared enfolded. See Pascal and Gaucheron, *Documents*.

25. Subscribers to Montbruel's and Ferrand's filtered water, available from 30 January 1764, were required to agree to a fixed amount and time for delivery, which suggests that water supply in Paris was more generally time-regulated. See their notice and advertisement in *Journal Oeuconomique,* February 1764, 54.

Wig

Claude-Joseph Vernet (1714–89)

TYPE OF OBJECT	THEME	MATERIAL
Apparel	Gender, Luxury, Studio	Animal | Hair, Synthetic Materials | Plaster, Textile | Silk

In July 1762 Claude-Joseph Vernet was on the hunt for a new wigmaker. He had just arrived in Paris after nearly ten years traveling around the country—from Marseille to La Rochelle—painting his twenty Ports of France. After this long peripatetic stage of his career, Vernet was keen to settle his family and establish his artistic practice in the capital. His first activities in this endeavor addressed the essentials of Parisian life: wig and wardrobe. According to the purchases he recorded in his **order book**, Vernet began by kitting out the family in the latest fashions: a mantelet and headdress for Madame Vernet, bonnets and collars for the children, and a new silk suit for himself.[1] Shopping for clothes proved straightforward, but the wig situation involved a more assiduous search. After all, this was not just a one-off commercial transaction like buying a hat but, rather, the beginning of a significant new relationship.

In eighteenth-century Paris, one did not so much acquire a wig as a wigmaker. Thing and person came together, the one unmanageable without the other. Wigs were sold as durable products, but ones that, as Mary K. Gayne has shown, required ongoing maintenance, occasional repairs, and frequent refreshments.[2] Vernet eventually settled on a Parisian *perruquier* (wigmaker) in August, but only after an unsuccessful month with the first one he trialed. From the terms of engagement that Vernet reached with his new wigmaker, it is clear why it was so important to find the right person for the job: for a retainer of 10 livres a month, the wigmaker would attend three times a week to the wigs of Vernet and his father-in-law, twice a week to those of his eldest son, plus occasional services for the youngest son, the future painter Carle Vernet.[3] Vernet's wig thus entailed a very personal relationship, not only with the thing itself that would be worn for hours a day on his head, but with a person that he would see more regularly than most colleagues, and with whom he and his family would come into close physical contact several times a week to be shaved, combed, powdered, and plumped.

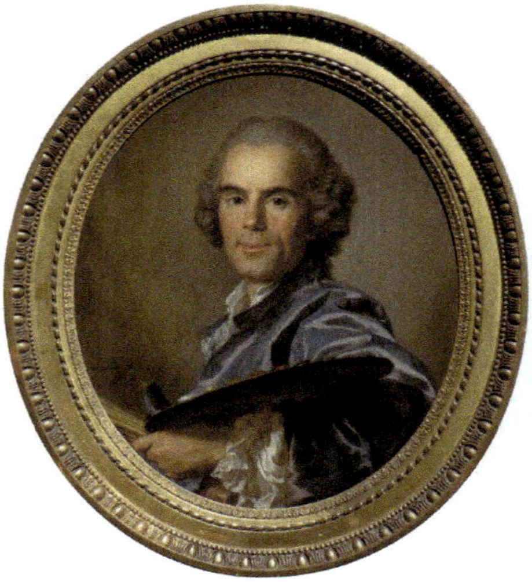

FIG. 182 Louis-Michel Van Loo (French, 1707–71), *Claude-Joseph Vernet*, 1768. Oil on canvas, 65 × 56.5 cm. Avignon, Musée Calvet. (Wikipedia, Photo: Finoskov, CC BY-SA 4.0.)

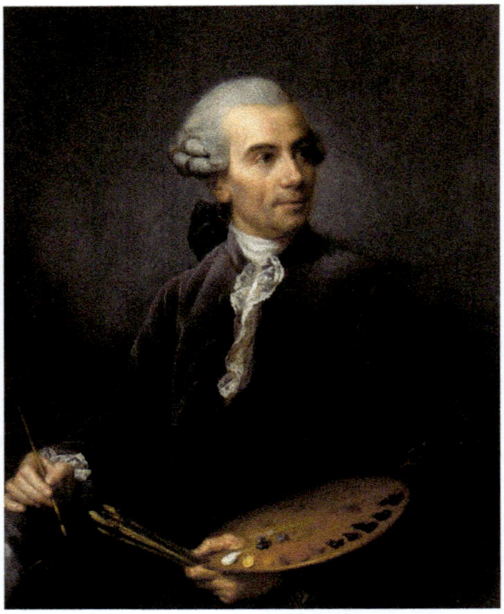

FIG. 183 Elisabeth Vigée-Lebrun, *Claude-Joseph Vernet*, 1778. Oil on canvas, 90 × 70 cm. Paris, Musée du Louvre, 3054. (© RMN-Grand Palais / photo: Jean-Gilles Berizzi / Art Resource, NY.)

When it came to his wig of choice, Vernet's portraits show at least two preferences, possibly changing over the years. In 1768 he sported a looser *perruque en bonnet* (bonnet wig) for his portrait by Louis-Michel Van Loo (fig. 182), while in 1778 he opted for the tightly side-curled *perruque à bourse* (bag wig) when sitting for Elisabeth Vigée-Lebrun (fig. 183). Both styles were at the height of fashion during those decades—*fort à la mode* (strongly on trend)—and appeared at the top of the *Encyclopédie*'s illustrated taxonomy of *perruques* (fig. 184).[4] Shown from front and back, the plate reveals, more than the portraits, the elaborate extent of each wig, whether in the bulk of curls or the additional accessories of bows and bags. Indeed, the weight of the wig was considerable, as was its aroma, due to the materials from which it was made and maintained. Some wigs incorporated horse and other animal hair for strength, but the best were made from human hair (preferably women's, especially from the countryside, and ideally from cooler climates like Normandy or Flanders).[5] Color options varied, with the most sought-after being white, blond, or jet black (brown hair being the most common in France and so the easiest to source), but the eighteenth-century trend for powdering wigs meant that most, like Vernet's, ended up looking gray, whatever the original color.[6] Beyond its chromatic effects, wig powder (a concoction of wheat flour or starch with perfumed additions) also added to the wig's overall smell, as did the pomade (made from lard) with which it was combined for styling purposes.[7] Added regularly to "refresh" the wig, the powder was fine and unruly, often finding its way to the wearer's shoulders and giving that distinctive powdery glow evident in Vernet's portrait by Vigée-Lebrun.

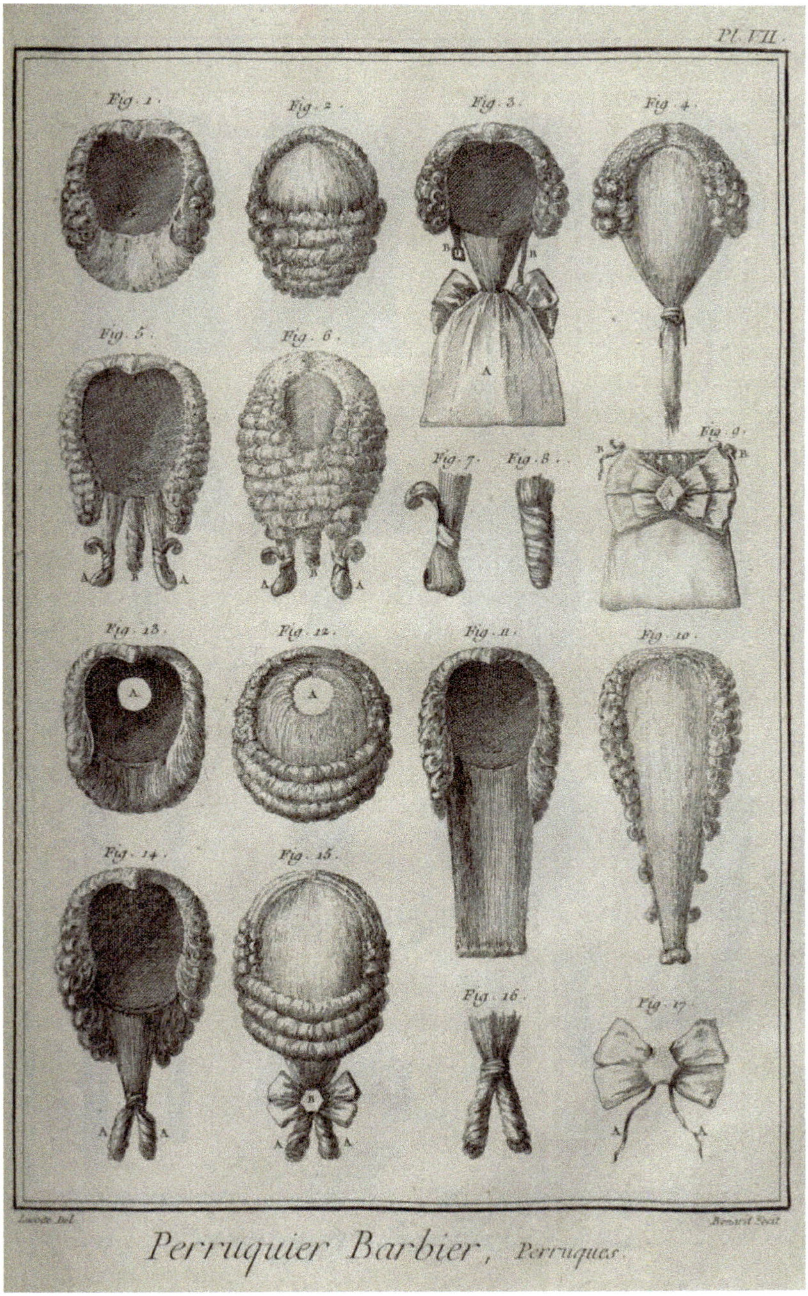

FIG. 184 "Perruquier" from *Recueil de planches sur les sciences, les arts libéraux et les arts mécaniques* (1765), plate VII. (Image courtesy of the ARTFL Encyclopédie Project, University of Chicago.)

For Vernet, owning a wig also meant owning an extensive paraphernalia of products and accessories. Powder and pomade were obviously essential for styling, but Vernet also kept other apparatus required for maintaining, storing, and adorning his wigs, and for preparing his own head to wear them. Among such items, Vernet possessed *houppes* (powder puffs) for applying powder; powder sacks and a special knife for removing the powder; *bourses* (bags) to accessorize his wigs; *têtes à perruques* (wig stands) for storing wigs not in use; combs and *fers pour friser* (curling irons) to service and revolumize the wig; and razors and scissors for cutting his own hair underneath.[8] Indeed, Vernet owned so many of the items that formed the tools of the *perruquier*'s trade that it seems likely he enjoyed home visits, rather than going out to the wigmaker's shop as many did. Moreover, it meant he was well equipped to travel (as he so often had) and maintain his wig on the road, simply employing the services of a *perruquier* en route (something he did twice during voyages to Rochefort in the 1760s).[9]

Vernet's vested interest in wigs may have developed early, when in his twenties he lived in Rome and rented rooms in the home of a wigmaker.[10] For an academician, even a future one, there was a social distinction between the elite circles of the liberal arts and the corporate trade of wigmaking, but Vernet's was not the only intersection between these worlds.[11] In Paris, the engraver Louis I de Silvestre lived for most of his career with a wigmaker on Rue du Mail, and the engraver Jacques-Philippe Le Bas was the son of a master wigmaker, whose corporate status the son was able to surpass thanks to his artistic facility.[12] Even at his professional peak, Vernet chose once again to share his home with a *perruquier*, but this time in a way that indicated the more elevated social status he had attained since his student days in Rome. In 1779, when his royal pension was raised to 1,200 livres a year, Vernet made a financial summary in his order book, which included 300 livres per annum for a *lacquais perruquier* (wig servant).[13] Vernet had several other servants (though none as highly paid) and also allocated 72 livres a year for a wigmaker to attend to Madame Vernet. Thus it seems Vernet was willing to devote a quarter of his royal salary to his own wig requirements.

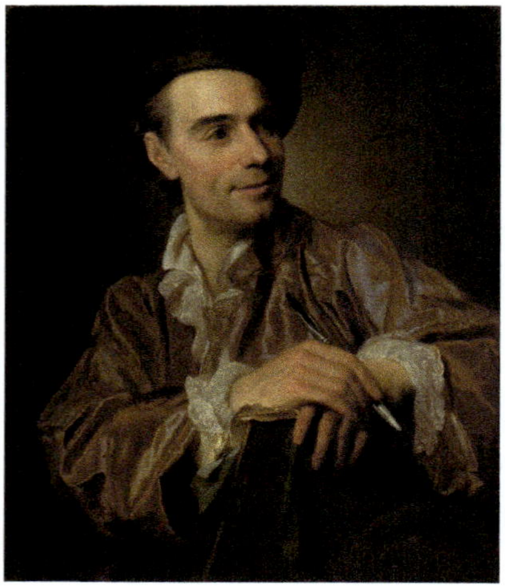

FIG. 185 Alexander Roslin (Swedish, 1718–93), *Claude-Joseph Vernet*, 1767. Oil on canvas, 65 × 54 cm. Stockholm, Nationalmuseum. (HIP / Art Resource, NY.)

From Vernet's financial expenditures, material surroundings, and personal relationships, it is clear that he took his wig very seriously indeed. This may simply have been part of Vernet's general investment in sartorial matters (which was considerable judging by his wardrobe), but the wig was a singular item in this regard—somewhere between clothing and body, yet neither hat nor hair.[14] As such, the wig's significance is perhaps best understood by considering it in moments of presence versus absence: when it was worn and what it meant. Unlike **swords**, customarily worn only by nobility, wigs encompassed a wider social spectrum, reaching from the court to the middling sort. While thus broadly a marker of social class, the wig was more subtly a signifier of sociable formalities. Take, for instance, Alexander Roslin's portrait of Vernet (fig. 185), where the landscapist appears without a wig, his cropped and naturally dark hair tucked under a cap. Though he wears practically the same outfit as in Van Loo's portrait (lace shirt, silk ***robe de chambre***), his unwigged head immediately codes him as more casual, more at ease, as though there is a social boundary in one encounter that does not exist in the other. This boundary is not, however, a straightforward line between public and private spheres; in both portraits, Vernet is professionally "at work" and consciously appearing before an audience. Instead, this is a blurrier scale from semipublic to semiprivate, where the wig connotes respectful formality and its absence suggests intimacy and familiarity. As a man who invested so earnestly in his wigs as material things, we can only imagine that Vernet was equally attuned to the sophisticated social codes that these items of dress, or bodily extensions, could navigate. ‡

---

1. Léon Lagrange, *Joseph Vernet et la peinture au XVIII siècle, avec le texte des livres de raison et un grand nombre de documents inédits* (Paris: Didier et Compagnie, 1864), 119, 388.

2. Mary K. Gayne, "Illicit Wigmaking in Eighteenth-Century Paris," *ECS* 38, no. 1 (2004): 121.

3. Lagrange, *Joseph Vernet*, 388.

4. François-Alexandre-Pierre Garsault, *Art du perruquier, contenant la façon de la barbe, la coupe des cheveux, la construction des perruques d'hommes et de femmes, le perruquier en vieux, et le baigneur-étuviste* (n.p., 1767), 6. On artists and hair trends, see Alden Cavanaugh, "The Coiffure of Jean-Baptiste Greuze," *ECS* 38, no. 1 (2004): 165–81.

5. Garsault, *Art du perruquier*, 7–8.

6. "Perruque," *Encyclopédie*, http://encyclopedie.uchicago.edu/, 12:401–402; and Garsault, *Art du perruquier*, 7–8.

7. "Poudre à cheveaux," *Encyclopédie*, http://encyclopedie.uchicago.edu/, 13:196.

8. Lagrange, *Joseph Vernet*, 252, 387.

9. Lagrange, *Joseph Vernet*, 387.

10. Lagrange, *Joseph Vernet*, 24.

11. Hairdressers (*coiffeurs*), a separate profession, had their own artistic aspirations to break free of the corporate world. See Alicia Caticha, "'Neither Poets, Painters, nor Sculptors': Classical Mimesis and the Art of Female Hairdressing in Eighteenth-Century France," *Eighteenth-Century Fiction* 31, no. 2 (2019): 413–38.

12. Hannah Williams and Chris Sparks, *Artists in Paris: Mapping the 18th-Century Art World*, www.artistsinparis.org; and Roger Portalis and Henri Béraldi, *Les graveurs du dix-huitième siècle* (Paris: Damascène Morgand & Charles Fatout, 1881), 2:565.

13. Lagrange, *Joseph Vernet*, 430.

14. For Vernet's wardrobe, see Claude Joseph Vernet, "Inventaire après décès," 2 March 1790, AN, MC/ET/LVI/369.

Will

Jean-Baptiste Massé (1687–1767)

TYPE OF OBJECT	THEME	MATERIAL
Document	Administration, Death, Family, Friendship, Identity, Money, Religion	Animal | Leather/Parchment, Synthetic Materials | Ink, Synthetic Materials | Paper

On 2 October 1765, the miniature painter Jean-Baptiste Massé signed and dated his will, put his **quill** down on the oval tray of his silver inkstand, depicted in a late red-chalk self-portrait (fig. 186), and stored the document for safe-keeping.[1] He was seventy-eight years old and nearing the end of a successful professional career. The preparation and writing of this, his last will and testament, must have taken days. It runs to thirty-six closely written folio-size pages stitched together with thread. The solemn concluding act of Massé's life was, however, not over. He continued to deliberate on the division of his estate. On 8 September 1766 and 1 May, 20 July, 5 and 17 September 1767, he added a succession of codicils modifying the original will and adding a further twenty-four pages secured at the center of the testament with blue ribbon. Ten days later the will was deposited with his notary, Maître Guillaume-Charles Bioche and is now filed with acts completed in September 1767 by Bioche et Dulion at the Archives Nationales.[2]

Massé is little remarked today and unlikely to become more so because so little of his *oeuvre* as a miniaturist and enameler survives.[3] However, thanks to Émile Compardon's publication of Massé's will in 1880, he continues to be remembered as an exceptional testator.[4] The draftsman and printmaker Charles-Nicolas Cochin had, over a century earlier, cited Massé's will in his eulogy to his dead friend for the evidence it provided of his good character. It was, Cochin recalled, full of the most gratifying expressions of friendship and the most flattering testimony of Massé's attachment.[5] The will interpolates forty-two heirs and legatees, in fact, an extraordinary number, between whom it divided the miniaturist's things, distributing hundreds of objects between them, of which approximately sixty were works of art.

For our book, the will is pertinent not only, therefore, as a thing in itself but also as an agent of transformation. It turned other stuff into hand-me-downs, keepsakes, and heirlooms, things in motion whose trajectories (between testator and beneficiary) enable us to see the human relations that enlivened them with affect and meaning.[6] The will thus enlarges our historical understanding of the emotional response stirred by material culture and embodied in things: emotions of gratitude, friendship, kindness, love, and pity, as well as desire. To the extent that the contents of Massé's will became a matter of public record, when in 1771 Cochin published his eulogy, it revealed the role of wills in the formation and

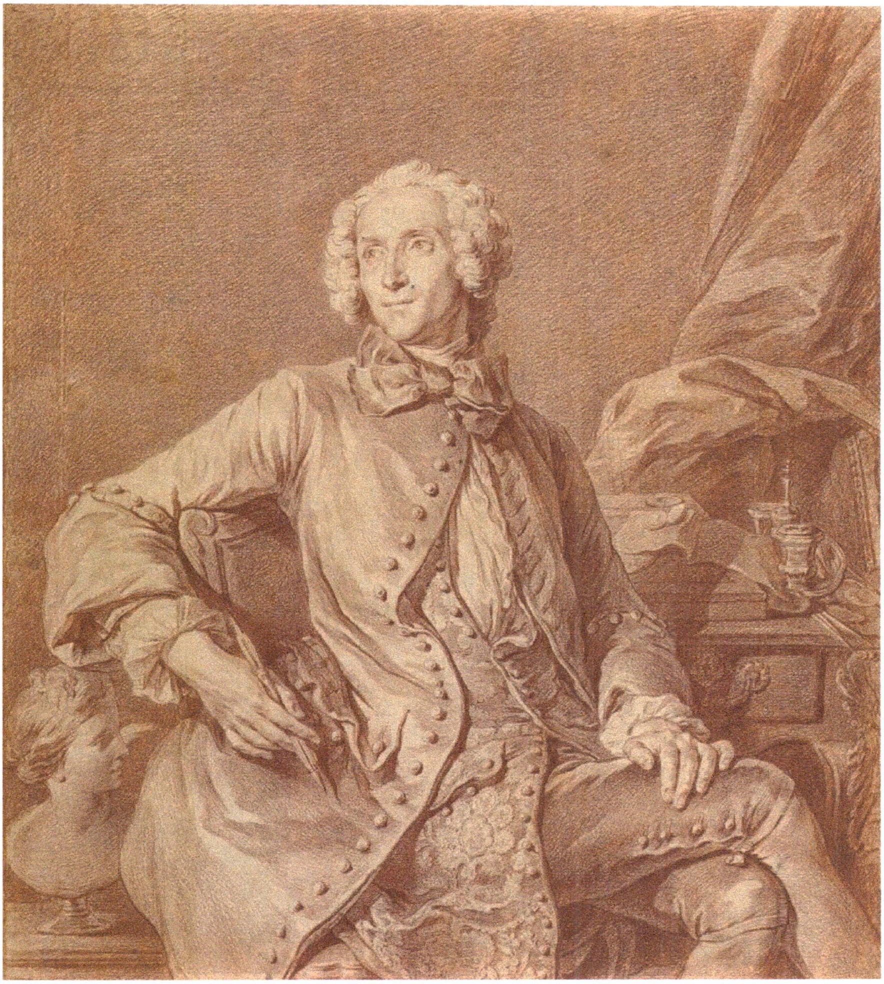

FIG. 186 Jean-Baptiste Massé (French, 1687–1767), *Self-Portrait*, ca. 1740. Red chalk, 41.7 × 37.5 cm. Paris, Musée du Louvre, Département des Arts Graphiques, 30944-r. (RMN-Grand Palais / photo: Tony Querrec / Art Resource, NY.)

reproduction of moral culture, an issue touched upon in conclusion and with regard to the Académie.

Jean-Baptiste Massé was a wealthy man, the descendant of jewelers and goldsmiths.[7] He was also a bachelor and enjoyed as such unrestricted testamentary freedom in disposing of his estate.[8] In writing his will "in his own hand," rather than dictating it to a notary, as was becoming increasingly the norm,[9] he enjoyed the additional freedom to elaborate and explain his wishes, disclosing his personal thoughts and feelings about his stuff and those on whom he intended to bestow it. This is not to say that Massé dispensed with the customary four-part form of the will (1: preamble; 2: instructions for the disposal of his body and the commendation of his soul; 3: division and distribution of the estate; 4: conclusion), but rather to observe that he was forced to hard reflection on his possessions as specific items because he was choosing not to leave them collectively as "effects." Just as he took care in the craft of his will, leveling the script by use of ruled pencil guidelines, precisely forming letters, exactly spacing words, and capitalizing nouns (fig. 187) to forestall misreadings of the stuff indexed for inheritance, he also used pronouns and adjectives with care, clearly to identify the objects of his giving.[10]

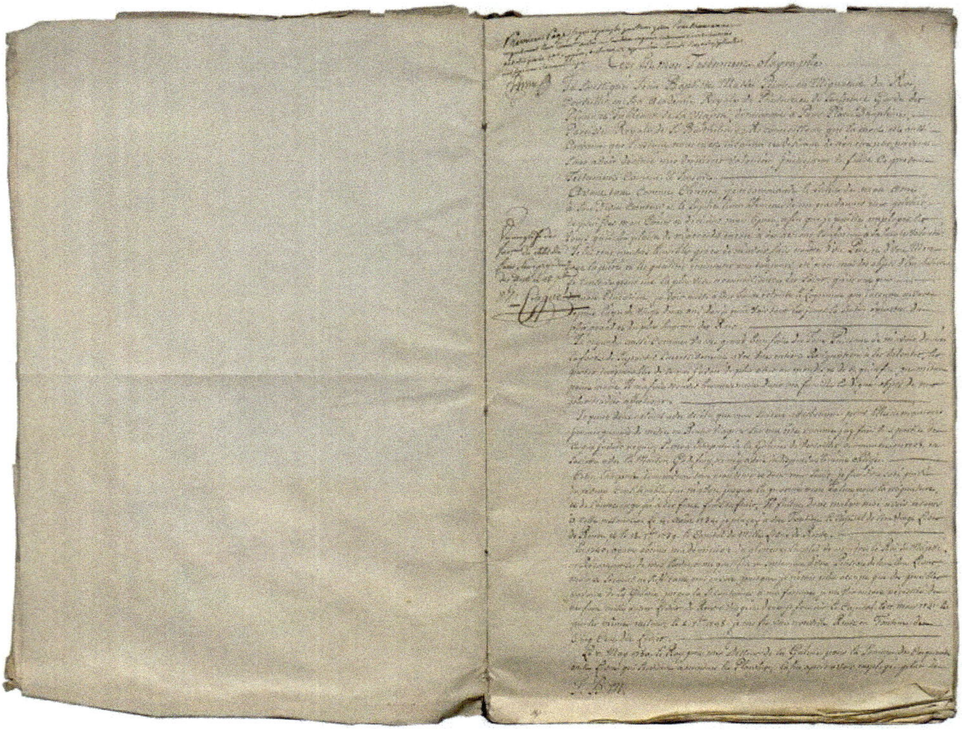

FIG. 187 Will of Jean-Baptiste Massé, 1766–67. Pen on paper. Paris, Archives Nationales.

Attention to the indexical specificity of language is most acute and conspicuous in relation to the bequests Massé made to his four servants, first because as cohabitants the distinction between his things and theirs was not always clear, and secondly because the things being left were mundane, or everyday stuff, which generally passes under the radar of consciousness and was consequently a challenge to describe. Possessive pronouns distinguished between things already "theirs" by virtue of being used in Massé's service (livery) but legally still his; generic things, or chattels, impersonal to Massé (cutlery, furniture); his personal stuff ("my" nightgowns, "my" coat with the gold buttons); and, finally, things in the offing (shirts) that, when made, he intended to pass on.[11] The sustained and intimate nature of Massé's relationship with his servants blurred the difference between gifts *inter vivos* and bequests, and explains the changes Massé made repeatedly to his will concerning them as their relationship evolved.[12] The value of the stuff Massé left them was mostly in its residual utility. He was thus careful to note the condition of things—whether extant or in plan, new or old, used or unused—and to employ physical descriptors to identify them: the "flannel" or "cotton" shirts, the "cotton" or "silk" stockings, the wool "ratine" coat.[13] Effects became candidates for bequests by the intimate knowledge that Massé had not only of his servants' lives but also of his possessions and by his capacity of writing and language to capture them clearly. So good, indeed, was Massé's record of his property that when Me Bioche came to draw up Massé's postmortem inventory he used the will as a template, keying the relevant inventory articles to the bequests described and numbered in the will.[14]

Bequeathing things depended not only on writing; it also required management and maintenance. In order to distribute his possessions appropriately and fairly, Massé needed a vantage from which to survey his stuff.[15] His valet, Courcy, was charged with gathering and readying the contents of the library and cabinet for inclusion in the will.[16] Things like the set of reproductive prints of Charles Le Brun's great ceiling paintings in the Galerie des Glaces at Versailles, to which project Massé had dedicated thirty years of his life and much of his capital, not only needed organizing into sets, but individual impressions also required attention in some cases.[17] For example, those of one set of the total fifteen he gave to family and friends, and which he reserved for his friend Cochin, were not only personally "selected" by him but also "revised" by his hand.[18] Likewise, the bound set destined for the Académie was to have been "repaired," the imperfections of the printing made good, had Massé's health only permitted.[19] Testamentary giving was not so much a "leaving" as an active preparation of property for donation, which in Massé's case, was a task not only scribal, organizational, and legal, but creative. Although, according to Cochin, he had stopped painting some twenty years before his death, the will brought him out of retirement, and in the three years before 1765 he conserved and painted a number of family miniatures for his heirs.[20] The will was, in short, the labor of Massé's last years; he renewed old things, bought and created new ones, and prepared all for their new lives with others.

The work was emotional as well as practical. The portfolios he organized for his prints, the shagreen cases and gold boxes he had made by the glover Jean-Claude Galluchat and the jeweler Pierre-François Drais, to reframe his miniatures, were gestures of love comparable to the loving words that enclose the donations denoted in the will. Massé does not so much describe his miniatures, in the way he did the clothes left to his servants, as enfold them in personal narrative. "To my dear niece Marie-Anne Massé, whose birth I saw and whom I have watched grow in grace and virtue, I give my self-portrait miniature, which I painted when she left for Amsterdam; it was then well received under the sign of love. I hope it will now be under that of friendship."[21] To his lifelong friend and former pupil, the "very worthy and virtuous" Madeleine Basseporte, he gave as "a token of memory," a preparatory drawing by Charles Natoire of the *Apotheosis of Saint-Louis* (fig. 188). "The satisfaction I have in having this work under my eyes makes me wish to afford her . . . the same privilege, and that of feeling as much pleasure as I have always had at looking at this admirable drawing."[22] The emphasis, in both instances, is not on miniature or drawing as such; it is, instead, on the origin and history of the object's association with Massé.[23] Through these histories his niece and his friend were called actively to keep

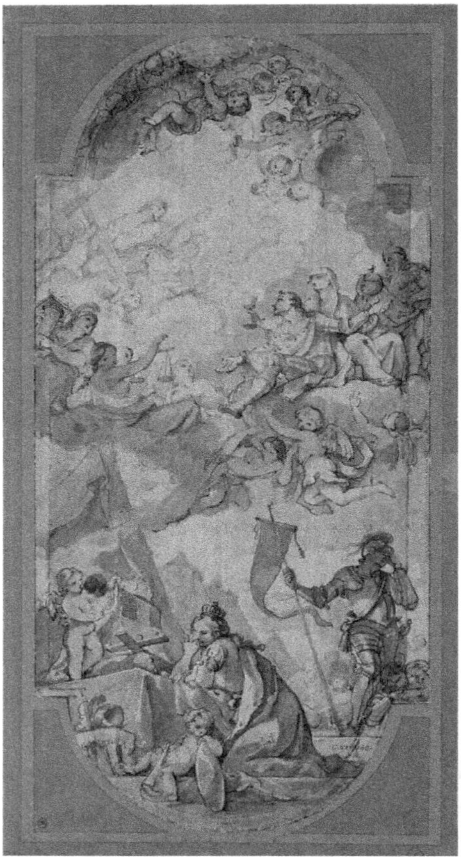

FIG. 188 Charles Natoire (French, 1700–1777), *Apotheosis of Saint Louis*, ca. 1755–56. Pen and brown ink, wash, and black chalk, 49.5 × 24.2 cm. Waddesdon Manor, The Rothschild Collection Trust, inv. 2018. (Waddesdon Image Library.)

Massé's memory alive by holding and looking at his gifts and integrating the story of the objects' former lives into their own.

Massé made and gave such keepsakes inscribed with his memory, mainly to women, as these examples suggest. It was in keeping with his character, apparently; Cochin remembered him as "gallant."[24] His legacies to men were more formal and conventional. He originally left his nephew Renouard, his gold **snuffbox**, shoe buckles, and garters, "wishing with all my heart that these bagatelles will be as useful to him as they have been to me," but he later rescinded the gift, replacing it with a sum of money—the body ornaments, on reflection, too personal and perhaps too frivolous to be judged appropriate.[25]

Sociologists Janet Finch and Jennifer Mason contrast keepsakes with heirlooms.[26] Heirlooms, they suggest, are emotionally cooler because things that testators and beneficiaries feel obliged, rather than want necessarily to exchange. In the eighteenth century, family Bibles, medals, family portraits, and silver were objects of this kind, and as lineal property they circulated primarily between men.[27] Massé's will indicates that by 1765, he was the guardian of the Massé family portraits, his elder brothers Jacob and Étienne having died. He had inherited portraits of his maternal grandfather and his parents, to which small collection he had added new portraits of his parents by Marc Nattier; portraits of his elder brothers, one by Louis Tocqué, the other by Gustav Lundberg; a portrait of Jacob's wife also by Tocqué; and portraits of himself by Jean-Marc Nattier and Tocqué.[28] As a sign of his love, he gave his "very dear" sister a lifetime's right to enjoy the portraits of their mother and their brother Étienne, but he left them entailed to Pierre Massé, his nephew by his eldest brother, whom he also made his principal heir. Were Pierre Massé's own line to fail, the will stipulated that all the portraits should pass to the descendants of the younger brother Étienne, in order "to perpetuate the family's memory of our ancestors and the desire to emulate them."[29]

Massé's will is described above as a legal instrument for the division and distribution of his estate, a document in which the voice of possession rings with enthralling frequency. It appears to confirm the findings of historians, according to whom eighteenth-century testamentary practice was, by contrast to that of earlier generations, conspicuously profane in its concern for family, not Christian fellowship, and for material, not spiritual goods.[30] However, in Massé's case, his sensibility for the stuff and meaning of his things was not developed at the expense of his spiritual aims. As a Huguenot, there was of course no place in his devotions for the kinds of **votive** objects adored by Catholics such as Hyacinthe Rigaud, or for the crucifixes, rosaries, and sacred **pictures** they used to orient their prayers. Nevertheless, it seems likely that Massé's bequests to his servants of clothes, cutlery, beds, and bedlinen were spiritual as well as practical, prompted by a desire to extend God's compassion by Acts of Corporal Mercy, specifically feeding the hungry, clothing the naked, and sheltering the homeless.[31] The *Seven Acts of Mercy* by Sébastien Bourdon, himself a Protestant, was one the few religious works Massé owned (fig. 189). Significantly, he willed the set of prints to nephew Pierre as treasured models of Christian duty, as heirlooms of the faithfulness of his ancestors to the reformed church, and as signs of the family's identity.[32]

In his eulogy, Cochin was conspicuously silent about the state of Massé's soul, though the spiritual portrait was a literary trope of many artists' biographies. Having failed to execute Massé's wish to be buried next to his father at the Catholic church of Saint-Barthélémy,[33] Cochin endeavored in his eulogy to do justice instead to Massé's memory by erecting a secular "monument" to the veteran academician. Gratitude and friendship were, he said, Massé's defining virtues. He related how Massé had had a copy of the Académie's *Portrait of the Marquis de Marigny* by Tocqué made to hang opposite his bed, in the place that is often reserved for the image of Christ, in order to have more frequently before him the likeness of the one to whom so much gratitude was owed by the arts.[34] The virtue of gratitude, not to be mistaken with simple politeness, was, according to moral philosophy, the origin of community and fellowship because it was a freely given response to the personal encounter with human need.[35] It therefore begets charity and friendship.

At the beginning of this entry attention was drawn to Cochin's acknowledgment of Massé's generosity. His liberality, according to Cochin, extended beyond his intimate circle

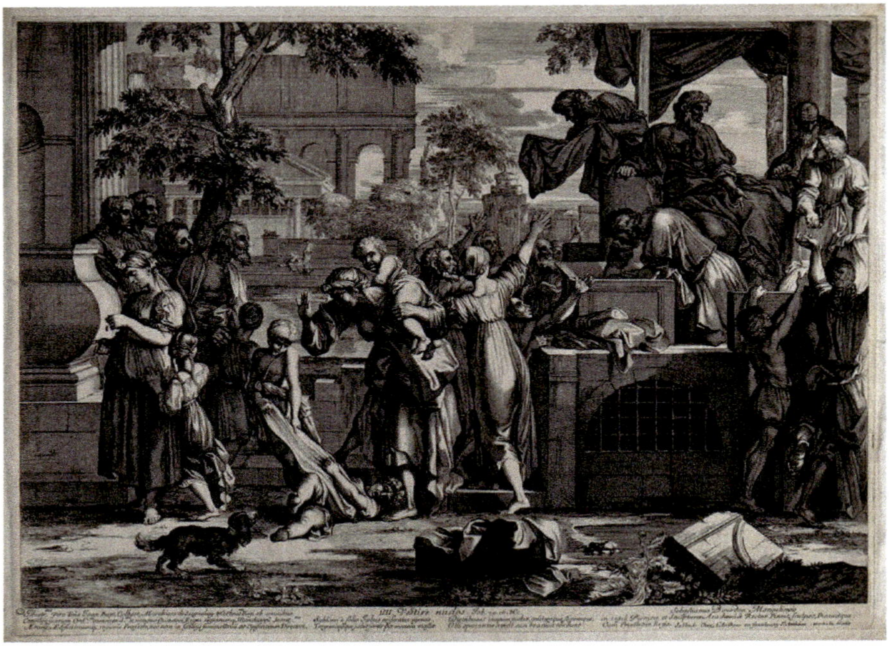

FIG. 189 Sébastien Bourdon (French, 1616–71), *Vestire nudos*, from *The Seven Acts of Mercy*, ca. 1660–70. Engraving. London, Wellcome Collection.

and beyond the bestowal of stuff. Such was his generosity of spirit, says Cochin, that he had sustained friendships with both François Lemoyne and Jean-François de Troy at a time in the 1730s when their professional rivalry had bitterly divided the Académie.[36] The spirit of charitable union that he sought instead always to promote had led him in 1764 to endeavor to level fortunes by establishing an institutional fund for the widows and orphans of impoverished academicians, and it appears also to have informed the pattern of his testamentary giving to individuals.[37] In choosing to leave sets of the same prints of the *Grande Galerie* to all his friends, did he not hope to spare the feelings of those who might have felt wounded by the preference implicit in bequests of different things?[38] Without fear of humiliating others, Cochin publicly acknowledged his inheritance under Massé's will. He ended his eulogy by affirming that the "most precious" gift that Massé had left the Académie was "the example of these his virtues."[39] §

---

1. See Jean-Baptiste Massé, "Inventaire après décès," AN, MC/ET/XCVII/422, 13 October 1767, for a verbal description of the ink stand.

2. "Dépôt de testament," AN, MC/ET/XCVII/ 422, 28 September 1767.

3. Charles-Nicolas Cochin noted in his eulogy that at Massé's death, examples of his work were already hard to find. See Cochin, "Éloge de Jean-Baptiste Massé," in Emile Compardon, *Un artiste oublié: J. B. Massé peintre de Louis XV, dessinateur, et graveur* (Paris: Charavay, 1880), 40.

4. Compardon, *Massé*, 79–191. See Pierre Chaunu, *La mort à Paris* (Paris: Fayard, 1978), 225–30, on the proportion of Parisians who made wills.

5. Cochin, "Éloge," 73. See also Pierre-Jean Mariette, *Abecedario*, ed. Emile Courajod (Paris: J. B. Dumoulin, 1853–62), 3:277–80.

6. On trajectories, see Arjun Appadurai, "Commodities and the Politics of Value," in *The Social Life of Things*, ed. Arjun Appadurai (Cambridge: Cambridge University Press, 1986), 3–63.

7. Massé's will is exceptional in providing a history of his assets prior to donation. See Compardon, *Massé*, 83–91.

8. On French laws of inheritance, see Emmanuel Le Roy Ladurie, "Family Structures and Inheritance Customs in Sixteenth-Century France," in *Families and Inheritance*, ed. Jack Goody et al. (Cambridge, England: Cambridge University Press, 1976), 37–70.

9. See Philippe Ariès, "Du sentiment modern de la famille dans les testaments et les tombeaux," in *Essais sur l'histoire de la mort en Occident du moyen âge à nos jours* (Paris: Seuil, 1975), 132–38; and Serge Briffaud, "La famille, le notaire et le mourant: Testament et mentalité dans la region de Lanchon (1650–1790)," *Annales du Midi* 97 (1985): 389–409.

10. See Louis Rossignol, *L'art d'écrire* (1756), plates 23, 27, for examples of the Italian "batarde" script used by notaries for this purpose.

11. Massé had bought a length of 100 meters (83.5 *aulnes*) of "belle toile" shirting for the purpose. See Compardon, *Massé*, 99, 101–2.

12. See the disinheritance of his servant Le Roux for ingratitude and abandonment, Compardon, *Massé*, 159.

13. Compardon, *Massé*, 99, 100.

14. For marginal references to the will not transcribed in Compardon, see AN, MC/ET/XCVII/422, 13 October 1767.

15. On Massé's sense of his giving, see Compardon, *Massé*, 92–93.

16. For Courcy's "care" and "intelligent attention," Massé left him an additional 500 livres. See codicil, 5 September 1767, in Compardon, *Massé*, 186–87. The engraver Johann Georg Wille is credited (Compardon, *Massé*, 147) with having "bonifier" the prints. *Mémoires et journal de J-G. Wille*, ed. Georges Duplessis, 2 vols. (Paris: Renouard, 1857), 1:366.

17. Jean-Gérard Castex, "Graver Le Brun au siècle des Lumières: Le recueil de la Grande galerie de Versailles de Jean-Baptiste Massé, " 2 vols, PhD diss. (Paris X–Nanterre, 2008).

18. Compardon, *Massé*, 136.

19. Compardon, *Massé*, 175–76.

20. Compardon, *Massé*, 125–28. See Cochin, "Eloge," 40.

21. Compardon, *Massé*, 105.

22. Compardon, *Massé*, 143–44.

23. Massé especially valued his gifts; *The Apotheosis of Saint-Louis* had been given to him by Natoire.

24. Cochin, "Éloge," 35.

25. Compardon, *Massé*, 164–65.

26. Janet Finch and Jennifer Mason, *Passing On: Kinship and Inheritance in England* (London: Routledge, 2000), 139–61.

27. Two medals given to Massé by the king of Denmark are described in the will as a "monument" to the honor of the family. Massé trusted his heirs would not sell them. See Compardon, *Massé*, 115–17.

28. Compardon, *Massé*, 111–13.

29. Compardon, *Massé*, 119–24.

30. See Gaël Rideau, "Pour une relecture globale du testament: L'individualisation religieuse à Orléans au XVIIIe siècle (1667–1787)," *Revue d'histoire moderne et contemporaine* 57 (2010): 97–123.

31. On the material culture of French Protestants, see David Garrioch, "Religious Identities and the Meaning of Things in Eighteenth-Century Paris," *French History and Civilization* 3 (2009): 17–25.

32. See AN, MC/ET/XCVII/422, 13 October 1767.

33. See Compardon, *Massé*, 94–96. Massé was buried in the Protestant cemetery. In 1767 France was emerging from the Callas crisis. Massé owned pamphlets on the torture and wrongful execution of Jean Callas.

34. Cochin, "Éloge," 72–73.

35. Gratitude was a secondary meaning of "reconnaissance," according to the *Dictionnaire de l'Académie française* (Paris: Brunet, 1762), 2: s.v. "Reconnaissance." Its synonym was "bienfaisance," or benevolence. See "reconnaissance" in the moral sense in *Encyclopédie*, 13:860, https://encyclopedie.uchicago.edu/, 13:860.

36. Cochin, "Éloge," 70–72.

37. Cochin, "Éloge," 58–61; and Compardon, *Massé*, 132–33.

38. Massé left his *Grande Galerie* to the following: Madeleine Basseporte, Pierre-Antoine Baudouin, Charles-Nicolas Cochin, Jean-Baptiste Fernex, Étienne Jeaurat, Jean-Baptiste Lemoyne, Jean-Baptiste Pigalle, Joseph-Marie Vien, and Johann Georg Wille. He had originally intended leaving Vien his copy of Bernard de Montfaucon's *L'antiquité expliqué* but changed his mind. See Compardon, *Massé*, 141–42, 182.

39. Cochin, "Éloge," 24–25.

Wine

Alexis Grimou (1678–1733)

TYPE OF OBJECT	THEME	MATERIAL
Intoxicant, Tableware	Community, Death, Everyday, Food and Drink, Global Commerce, Leisure	Plant Matter, Synthetic Materials | Glass

From the historian's perspective, it is fitting that this book of artists' things should end with wine. Not just because of its associations with toasting endings and beginnings but because wine has so often been the first "thing" encountered in our inquiries into the material worlds of eighteenth-century artists. When notaries undertook the lengthy task of an estate inventory, itemizing the contents of a deceased person's home, they usually started their cataloging efforts in the *cave* (cellar), which, if the dwelling had one, was the most common space for storing one's wine. Consequently, wine regularly features in the initial glimpse of an artist's material possessions, offering tantalizing insights into the extent of their wealth, their tastes as a consumer, and, above all, their drinking proclivities.

Jean-Baptiste Greuze, for instance, emerges somewhat against the grain as a strong proponent of white wine, owning sixty bottles of white but not a single bottle of red.[1] Jean-Siméon Chardin leaned more conventionally the other way, with a collection of fifty bottles of red wine but not a single bottle of white.[2] Charles-Antoine Coypel, meanwhile, was more ecumenical in his consumption, keeping in his cellar sixty bottles of red (all Burgundies) and sixty bottles of white wines of various kinds.[3]

Individual tastes in wine evidently varied, but its consumption was almost universal. Wine in eighteenth-century France was a vast commercial industry (one of the state's three largest sources of tax revenue), and its trade was already driven by those familiar dynamics of regional rivalries, consumer preferences, and market trends.[4] While there were some small vineyards in Paris, the enormous amounts of wine needed to supply the capital were imported from the provinces with, according to Daniel Roche, 50 to 60 percent coming from the Orléanais and Blésois regions, 15 percent from Champagne, and 12 percent from Lower Burgundy.[5] The contents of artists' cellars, however, indicate something of an elite art-world preference for Burgundies (both white and red), which, given the region's prized reputation, was indicative of the relative wealth and sociocultural status of many of the Académie's members (including such Burgundy drinkers as Coypel, Jean-Baptiste-Marie Pierre, François-Hubert Drouais, and Claude-Joseph Vernet).[6] Wines from the rival region of Champagne were also enjoyed, though they tended to be kept in smaller quantities and so presumably drunk less frequently, except in the case of Jean-Baptiste Le Prince, who had a country house between Paris and Reims and showed a clear preference for the region.[7] While there was a marked propensity for French wines, some artists' tastes and budgets also extended internationally. Drouais had eight half bottles of Malaga, and Pierre had three half bottles of "Hungarian wine" (probably Tokaji), the small size of the bottles suggesting dessert wines and possibly the indulgence of a sweet tooth (further confirming the assumption made from Drouais's possession of a **sugar spoon**).[8]

Aside from suggesting its contents, the kind of receptacle in which artists stored their wine also gives some insight into their rate of consumption, or at least the size of their collection. Most wine in artists' cellars was kept in *bouteilles* (bottles) or *carafons* (carafes) made from *gros verre* (rough glass) (as in fig. 190), which were vessels that could be brought directly to the table or decanted into finer glassware for more formal occasions (as in fig. 191). Along with the full ones, most also kept numerous empties (sometimes hundreds of them), which could be taken to the *marchand de vin* (wine merchant) for refilling, or, in some cases, refilled on the spot.[9] For, space and budget permitting, some artists also kept much larger quantities of wine stored in various-size barrels or casks: Pierre, for instance, had three *feuillettes* (approximately 137 liters each) of red Burgundy, while Drouais had two larger *demi-queues* (approximately 213 liters each) of "vin rouge cru" from Mâcon.[10] Le Prince, meanwhile, outdid everyone in quantity, though possibly not in quality. From the apparatus in the cellar of his country house (including two grape-picking baskets, a large vat, and a bucket with a funnel), it seems Le Prince engaged in some amateur winemaking activities, the results of which were presumably the substantial quantities (nineteen barrels) of "vin du pays" (local wine) stored in both his property at Lagny-sur-Marne and the cellar of his Louvre *logement*.[11] Not surprisingly, the notaries valuing these artists' wine collections proffered a higher price for Pierre's Burgundy than for Le Prince's countryside "vin du pays."

Wine kept in a cellar, whether homemade or commercially bought, was consumed at meals within the home, even at breakfast (François Lemoyne's servant noted that his master generally took wine, with bread and water, at 9 o'clock after a morning session in the studio with his students).[12] But wine was also bought and consumed in spaces outside the home. Commercially, the wine trade was strictly controlled, divided between *marchands de vin* (some selling wholesale, others retail) who sold wine from shops to stock people's cellars, and *taverniers* or *aubergistes*, who sold wine in taverns and inns for consumption on the premises.[13] Such public establishments were important social spaces for artists, accommodating different kinds of interactions from those taking place in the relative privacy of the home or studio, or within the formalized structures of the Académie. Socializing in taverns and inns could be relatively sedate experiences, like the convivial meals with colleagues and family that Wille occasionally mentions in his **journal**. But wine's intoxicating effects could also lead to dangerous disorder, as during an infamous art-world drunken brawl in 1741. Following an afternoon of boozing at a cabaret near the Louvre called the Galerie d'Avignon, several artists (among them Charles Parrocel, Georges-Frédéric Schmidt, and the cabinetmaker Charles-André Boulle) witnessed an argument escalate to a street scuffle, during which Joseph-Ferdinand Godefroy, a picture dealer and

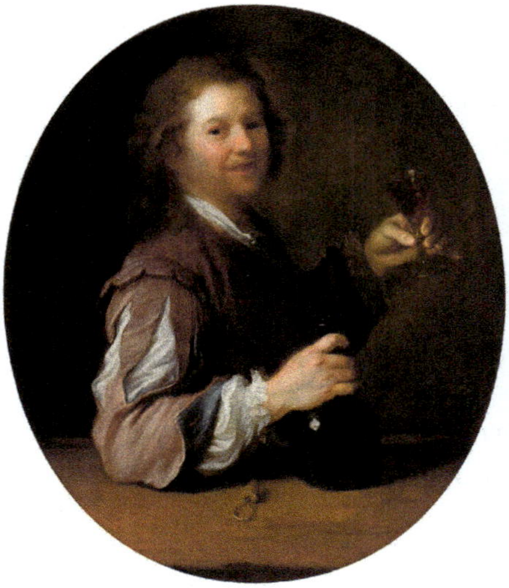

FIG. 190 Alexis Grimou (Swiss, 1678–1733), *Self-Portrait as a Drinker*, 1724. Oil on canvas, 100 × 85 cm. Paris, Musée du Louvre, Inv. 5045. (© Musée du Louvre, Dist. RMN-Grand Palais / Franck Raux / Art Resource, NY.)

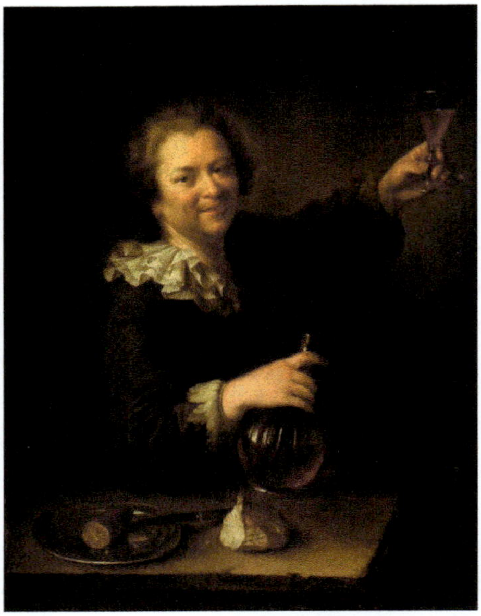

FIG. 191 Alexis Grimou (Swiss, 1678–1733), *Self-Portrait as a Drinker*, ca. 1732. Oil on canvas, 116.3 × 89.7 cm. Edinburgh, Scottish National Gallery, NG664. Presented by William Wright 1881. (Photographer: Antonia Reeve.)

restorer, was stabbed with a **sword** and killed by the painter Jérôme-François Chantereau.[14]

When it comes to drinking in taverns, the artist most associated with this side of the wine trade is without doubt Alexis Grimou. The portraitist had a direct connection to tavern life via his wife, Gabrielle Petit, niece of Francesco Procopio, proprietor of the Left Bank's Café Procope, a renowned meeting place for *philosophes* and now reputedly the oldest Parisian café in continuous operation.[15] More intriguing, however, is the intentional association with wine that Grimou created through his artistic practice, where that liquor flows with conspicuous abundance. Most striking is the unconventional series of self-portraits that Grimou painted throughout his career, including one in the guise of Bacchus, Roman god of wine (1728, Dijon, Musée Magnin), and at least two "as a drinker," presenting himself at a tavern table partaking merrily in the fruits of the vine (see figs. 190, 191).

Yet after the painter's death in 1733, these epicurean images took a less mirthful turn, feeding into a posthumous biographical narrative in which Grimou "the drinker" was recast as Grimou the "utter drunkard" (to quote Pierre-Jean Mariette).[16] Excessive consumption of alcohol and a weakness for the good life became a frame for explaining Grimou's professional path, in particular his unusual decision to abandon his chance at an academic career to instead join the guild. This was a story that neatly tapped into the already ingrained institutional tropes of the elite measured academician versus the bawdy intemperate guildsman.[17] More recently, Melissa Percival has pushed back against this problematic image of Grimou as a dissolute renegade, arguing, among other things, that a nuanced understanding of the cultural and symbolic values of wine in eighteenth-century France actually places Grimou's portraits, and the artist himself, within much more elevated discourses of taste, connoisseurship, and pleasure.[18]

Grimou's self-portraits certainly emphasize the sensory qualities of wine, but in doing so, they also bring us back to its thingness. This is a different sense of thingness from wine's existence as property found in those artists' inventories: contained in bottles and casks; valued for its regional origins and the quality of its vintage; sold, bought, and then stored in a cellar. Instead, Grimou's paintings attend to the feel of wine as a substance: the tactility of the glass vessels that hold it; the viscosity of its liquid form; the resonance of its translucent color; the depth of its taste; and the warm glow of its gently intoxicating effects on the body and mood of the drinker. Here, as often throughout this book, the artist's portraits gesture to the relationship between owner and thing. Where notarized inventories clarify the facts of property (who owned what), these images speak to engagement, connection, and interaction (what it meant to possess that thing). As an act of self-representation, Grimou's portraits draw the artist out of the working space of the studio into the social space of the tavern, constructing a self-image, via things, that lingers in a post-Regency mood of light indulgence, while gently mocking the formal pretensions of his academic colleagues. Grimou adopts the habitual pose of self-portraiture but replaces the "things" conventionally held. Abandoning the tools of **palette** and brush, Grimou instead takes up those vessels of leisure—bottle and glass—and raises a toast with his beholder to the entwined connoisseurial pleasures of art and wine. ‡

---

1. Jean-Baptiste Greuze, "Inventaire après décès," 25 March 1805, AN, MC/ET/XVI/960.

2. Jean-Siméon Chardin, "Inventaire après décès," 18 December 1779, AN, MC/ET/LVI/246.

3. Charles-Antoine Coypel, "Inventaire après décès," 25 September 1752, AN, MC/ET/LXXVI/337.

4. On the wine trade, see Jacques Savary des Bruslons, *Dictionnaire universel de commerce* (Waesberge: Jansons, 1726–32), 1950–63.

5. Daniel Roche, *A History of Everyday Things: The Birth of Consumption in France, 1600–1800*, trans. Brian Pearce (Cambridge: Cambridge University Press, 2000), 232.

6. Charles-Antoine Coypel, "Inventaire après décès," 25 September 1752, AN, MC/ET/LXXVI/337; Jean-Baptiste-Marie Pierre, "Inventaire après décès," 25 May 1789, AN, MC/ET/XXXI/253; François-Hubert Drouais, "Inventaire après décès," 12 December 1775, AN, MC/ET/LIII/521; and Joseph Vernet, "Inventaire après décès," 2 March 1790, AN, MC/ET/LVI/369.

7. Pierre had fifty-five bottles and three large casks of wines from Burgundy, but only three bottles of wine from Champagne. Le Prince had a cask of champagne and sixty bottles of red wine from Champagne in his country house and a smaller cask of red from Champagne in his Louvre apartment. The *scellé* (30 September 1781) and inventory (10 October 1781) of these properties are transcribed in Jules Hédou, *Jean Le Prince et son oeuvre* (Paris: Baur, 1879), 209, 260. On the Burgundy-Champagne rivalry in the eighteenth century, see Jean-Baptiste de Salins, *Défense du vin de Bourgogne contre le vin de Champagne* (Paris: 1702).

8. "Inventaire après décès," of Drouais (1775) and Pierre (1789).

9. For instance, Coypel had 100 empty bottles, Pierre had 150 empty bottles, and Drouais had 80 empty *carafons*.

10. "Inventaire après décès," of Drouais (1775) and Pierre (1789). Cask names and capacities varied enormously by region. For a directory of relative sizes, see *Manuel des propriétaires et des marchands de boissons* (Paris: Garnery & Rondonneau, 1809), 147–48.

11. This included eight *pièces* (approximately 183 liters) and one *demi-pièce* (approximately 91 liters) at Lagny-sur-Marne, and nine *demi-pièces* and a *feuillette* (approximately 137 liters each) at the Louvre. Hédou, *Jean Le Prince*, 209, 260.

12. "Information faite par le commissaire Daminois au sujet de la mort violente du sieur Lemoyne," *NAAF*, 1877, 195.

13. Savary des Bruslons, *Dictionnaire universel*, 1954–55. Étienne Jeaurat's brother, François, was a *marchand de vin* living on the same street as the painter in the 1740s (possibly in the same dwelling), AN, MC/ET/CXV/548.

14. For the case reports, see Jules Guiffrey, *Scellés et inventaires d'artistes français du XVIIe et du XVIIIe siècle* (Paris: Charavay, 1884), 1:394–417. On Godefroy's connections to the neighborhood, see Noémie Étienne, "A Family Business: Picture

Restorers in the Louvre Quarter," *Journal18* 2 (2016), https://www.journal18.org/830.

15. Melissa Percival, "Taste and Trade: The Drinking Portraits of Alexis Grimou (1678–1733)," *Art Bulletin* 101, no. 1 (2019): 19–20.

16. "[U]n franc ivrogne," *Abecedario de P. J. Mariette*, ed. Philippe de Chennevières and Anatole de Montaiglon (Paris: Dumoulin, 1853–1854), 2:335–36. On Grimou's posthumous biographical narrative, see George Levitine, "The Eighteenth-Century Rediscovery of Alexis Grimou and the Emergence of the Proto-Bohemian Image of the French Art," *ECS* 2, no. 1 (1968): 58–76.

17. Grimou was *agréé* in 1705 but never submitted his reception pieces; his provisional status was canceled in 1709. *PV*, 4:78–79. The Académie's vision of the guild as a community of bawdy drinkers was cemented in the institution's first set of Statutes (1648), where Article III banned its members from all "drunkenness, debauchery, and gambling," *PV*, 1:7.

18. Percival, "Taste and Trade," 6–25.

Taxonomies

CHRONOLOGY BY ARTIST

1650–1793	Secretaries of the Académie Royale
1656–1746	Nicolas de Largillière
1659–1743	Hyacinthe Rigaud
1672–1742	Gilles-Marie Oppenord
1678–1733	Alexis Grimou
1684–1721	Jean-Antoine Watteau
1685–1766	Jean-Marc Nattier
1686–1755	Jean-Baptiste Oudry
1687–1767	Jean-Baptiste Massé
1688–1737	François Lemoyne
1688–1752	Charles Parrocel
1694–1752	Charles-Antoine Coypel
1695–1774	Claude-François Desportes
1696–1772	Louis Tocqué
1697–1739	Pierre-Imbert Drevet
1698–1762	Edme Bouchardon
1699–1779	Jean-Siméon Chardin
1700–77	Charles-Joseph Natoire
1702–89	Jean-Étienne Liotard
1703–70	François Boucher
1704–78	Jean-Baptiste Lemoyne
1707–71	Louis-Michel Van Loo
1707–83	Jacques-Philippe Le Bas
1714–73	Renée-Elisabeth Marlié
1714–85	Jean-Baptiste Pigalle
1714–89	Claude-Joseph Vernet
1715–90	Charles-Nicolas Cochin
1715–1808	Johann Georg Wille
ca. 1715–83	Jean-Baptiste Perronneau
1716–91	Étienne-Maurice Falconet
1716–1809	Joseph-Marie Vien
1720–73	Pierre-André Jacquemin
1724–80	Gabriel de Saint-Aubin
1724–1805	Louis-Jean-François Lagrenée
1725–1802	Joseph-Siffred Duplessis
1725–1805	Jean-Baptiste Greuze
1727–75	François-Hubert Drouais
1732–1806	Jean-Honoré Fragonard
1733–1808	Hubert Robert
1734–72	Marie-Suzanne Giroust
1734–81	Jean-Baptiste Le Prince
1741–1814	Jean-Michel Moreau the Younger
1741–1828	Jean-Antoine Houdon
1744–1814	Pierre Peyron
1745–1811	Jean-Baptiste Huët
1746–1816	François-André Vincent
1748–1821	Marie-Anne Collot
1748–1825	Jacques-Louis David
1752–1814	Jean-François Janinet
1755–1842	Elisabeth Vigée-Lebrun

INDEX BY TYPE OF THING

INDEX BY THEME

INDEX BY MATERIAL

Further Reading on Things

Appadurai, Arjun. *The Social Life of Things: Commodities in Cultural Perspective.* Cambridge: Cambridge University Press, 1986.

Bailey, Colin B. *Patriotic Taste: Collecting Modern Art in Pre-Revolutionary Paris.* New Haven: Yale University Press, 2002.

Bourdieu, Pierre. *Distinction: A Social Critique of the Judgement of Taste.* Translated by Richard Nice. Cambridge: Harvard University Press, 1984.

Brewer, John, and Roy Porter, eds. *Consumption and the World of Goods.* New York: Routledge, 1994.

Brown, Bill. *A Sense of Things: The Object Matter of American Literature.* Chicago: University of Chicago Press, 2003.

Brown, Bill, ed. *Things.* Chicago: University of Chicago Press, 2004.

Cavanaugh, Alden, and Michael E. Yonan. *The Cultural Aesthetics of Eighteenth-Century Porcelain.* New York: Routledge, 2016.

Coquery, Natacha, and Alain Bonnet, eds. *Le luxe du commerce et le commerce du luxe.* Paris: Mare et Martin, 2014.

Clunas, Craig. *Superfluous Things: Material Culture and Social Status in Early Modern China.* Honolulu: University of Hawai'i Press, 1991.

Craciun, Adriana, and Simon Schaffer, eds. *The Material Cultures of Enlightenment Arts and Sciences.* London: Palgrave, 2016.

Daston, Lorraine, ed. *Things That Talk: Object Lessons from Art and Science.* New York: Zone, 2004.

Farge, Arlette. *Le peuple et les choses. Paris au* XVIIIe. Paris: Bayard, 2015.

Fennetaux, Ariane, Amélie Junqua, and Sophie Vasset, eds. *The Afterlife of Used Things: Recycling in the Long Eighteenth Century.* New York: Routledge, 2014.

Findlen, Paula, ed. *Early Modern Things: Objects and their Histories, 1500–1800*. London: Routledge, 2012.

Gerritsen, Anne, and Giorgio Riello, eds. *The Global Lives of Things: The Material Culture of Connections in the Early Modern World*. London: Routledge, 2015.

Hamling, Tara, and Catherine Richardson, eds. *Everyday Objects: Medieval and Early Modern Material Culture and Its Meanings*. London: Routledge, 2016.

Harvey, Karen, ed. *History and Material Culture*. London: Routledge, 2009.

Hoskins, Janet. *Biographical Objects: How Things Tell Stories of People's Lives*. London and New York: Routledge, 1998.

La Font, Anne. *L'art et la race: L'Africain (tout) contre l'oeil des Lumières*. Dijon: Presses du Réel, 2019.

Lamb, Jonathan. *The Things Things Say*. Princeton: Princeton University Press, 2016.

Lemonnier, Pierre. *Mundane Objects: Materiality and Non-Verbal Communication*. Walnut Creek: Left Coast, 2012.

Miller, Daniel. *Material Cultures: Why Some Things Matter*. London: Routledge, 1997.

Miller, Daniel. *The Comfort of Things*. Cambridge: Polity, 2008.

Miller, Daniel. *Stuff*. Cambridge: Polity, 2010.

Pardailhé-Galabrun, Annik. *The Birth of Intimacy: Privacy and Domestic Life in Early Modern Paris*. Oxford: Polity Press, 1992.

Pomian, Krzysztof. *Collectors and Curiosities: Paris and Venice, 1500–1800*. Oxford: Polity, 1991.

Roche, Daniel. *A History of Everyday Things: The Birth of Consumption in France, 1600–1800*. Cambridge: Cambridge University Press, 2000.

Stammers, Tom. *The Purchase of the Past: Collecting in Post-Revolutionary Paris c. 1790–1890*. Cambridge: Cambridge University Press, 2020.

Stewart, Susan. *On Longing: Narratives on the Miniature, the Gigantic, the Souvenir, the Collection*. Durham and London: Duke University Press, 1992.

Styles, John, and Amanda Vickery, eds. *Gender, Taste, and Material Culture in Britain and North America, 1700–1830*. New Haven: Yale University Press, 2007.

Thatcher Ulrich, Laurel, Ivan Gaskell, Sara J. Schechner, and Sarah Anne Carter. *Tangible Things: Making History through Objects*. Oxford: Oxford University Press, 2015.

Tilley, Chris, Webb Keane, Susanne Kuechler, Mike Rowlands, and Patricia Spyer, eds. *Handbook of Material Culture*. Los Angeles: Sage, 2006.

Van Horn, Jennifer. *The Power of Objects in Eighteenth-Century British America*. Chapel Hill: University of North Carolina Press, 2017.

Ziskin, Rochelle. *Sheltering Art: Collecting and Social Identity in Early Eighteenth-Century Paris*. University Park: Penn State University Press, 2012.

Acknowledgments

This project owes debts to many kinds of things.

To the pounds and pence and the dollars and cents generously put in our pockets over more than a decade by the academic institutions at which our project emerged, was nurtured, and finally completed. Thank you to the Courtauld Institute of Art, London; St John's College, University of Oxford; the Getty Research Institute, Los Angeles; and Queen Mary University of London.

To Moleskine diaries, wall calendars, and university timetables that enabled us to plan research trips during the academic year and arrange rendezvous with each other. Thank you for fragmenting weeks and months into optimum lengths for writing short and not-so-short entries, and jigging time appropriately to fit those vital trips and meetings into the gaps between teaching and admin.

To trains both regional (Southeastern, First Great Western, SNCF) and international (Eurostar, TGV Lyria) for shrinking the distance between us and our objects of study and making the low-carbon, air-conditioned, clean, and cushioned experience of travel for field trips so enjoyable.

To planes for the flight you provided to far-off places (Germany, USA) to which some few of our chosen objects have migrated since the eighteenth century. Crushed though we were in "economy," and conscious of contributing shamefully to the climate emergency, we acknowledge, nevertheless, that you miraculously brought us into the presence of things otherwise impossibly remote to us.

To our laptops, slick and lightweight, and the software installed on them. You provided files for our things, systems for organizing them, and letters with which to title and fill them with thought, the ridged plastic guide-keys—F(uneral Book) and J(ournal)—keeping us centered and on track.

To all manner of cups: china, Styrofoam, plastic, earthenware, and Thermos. You have been our constant companions in writing and provided the essential coffee and tea that has facilitated our conversations, discussions, and occasional arguments about this book.

To wine and wine glasses. You greeted us at the end of the many rehearsals and presentations of our project and stimulated seminar discussion from which we have benefited hugely.

To a whippet puppy (named Scout) whose cute and persistent calls for attention were a delight, a distraction, and a danger during the final editorial stages of the book.

Things have been vital to this project, but, even more importantly, we acknowledge our debts to the many people who contributed so crucially in different ways to this book's making.

To curators, archivists, and librarians who gave us access to and shared their invaluable knowledge of the objects, documents, and other resources in their care. In particular, we thank Emmanuelle Brugerolles and Alice Thomine-Berrada at the École Nationale Supérieure des Beaux-Arts, Paris; Xavier Salmon at the Musée du Louvre, Paris; David Simonneau at the Musée Carnavalet, Paris; Maud Guichané at Fondation Custodia, Paris; Juliette Trey, then at the Châteaux de Versailles et de Trianon; Marie-Christine Grasse at the Villa-Musée Jean-Honoré Fragonard, Grasse; Antony Griffiths and Kim Sloan at the British Museum, London; Yuriko Jackall at the Wallace Collection, London; Juliet Carey and Mia Jackson at Waddesdon Manor, Aylesbury; Lee Macdonald and Lucy Blaxland at the History of Science Museum, University of Oxford; Bénédicte De Donker and Estelle Fallet at Musée d'Art et d'Histoire, Geneva; Charissa Bremer-David at the J. Paul Getty Museum, Los Angeles; David Pullins and Perrin Stein at the Metropolitan Museum of Art, New York; and the librarians and archivists (whose names we sadly never knew) who hosted and helped us at the Bibliothèque Nationale de France; Bibliothèque de l'Institut National d'Histoire de l'Art; Bibliothèque Historique de la Ville de Paris; British Library; Archives Nationales de France; and Archives de Paris.

To our friends and colleagues who, by suggesting things for inclusion, providing opportunities for us to discuss our work, and challenging our assumptions and conclusions, have helped significantly to shape this book and fruitfully to delay its completion. Among them are: Malcolm Baker, Basile Baudez, Jean-Luc Bédard, Esther Bell, Markus Castor, Jo Cohen, Jeffrey Collins, Stephen Deuchar, Noémie Étienne, Mechthild Fend, Amy Freund, Peter Fuhring, Charlotte Guichard, Keren Hammerschlag, Melissa Hyde, Mia Jackson, Colin Jones, Ewa Lajer-Burcharth, Meredith Martin, David Maskill, Gay McAuley, Lesley Miller, Carole Nataf, Kate Nicholson, Stephanie O'Rourke, Camilla Pietrabissa, David Pullins, Mia Ridge, Julie Anne Sadie Goode, Harvey Shepherd, Perrin Stein, Richard Taws, Kate Tunstall, Francesca Whitlum-Cooper, Sam Williams, Joanna Woodall, and Michael Yonan.

To the great archivists and historians Philippe de Chennevières, Émile Campardon, Louis Courajod, Louis Dimier, Louis-Étienne Dussieux, Jules Guiffrey, Anatole de Montaiglon, and Georges Wildenstein, without whose pioneering work this book would not have been possible.

To Diderot and d'Alembert for inspiration.

To Gail Feigenbaum for being receptive to our project in its final form, to Michele Ciaccio for steering it through to publication, and to Greg Albers and Marci Boudreau for sensitively creating its digital design.

Things and people are united in acts of friendship: in the friendship that has been the bedrock of our own collaboration, and in our dedication of this volume to all those scholars, students, and *compagnons de route* interested in the eighteenth century.

Finally, we offer our heartfelt thanks to Mia Ridge and to Stephen Deuchar: the partners who so generously accommodated this book in the material culture of their own lives for far too long.

—Katie Scott & Hannah Williams

About the Authors

Katie Scott is professor at the Courtauld Institute of Art, London. She is a specialist in French art, architecture, and art theory of the early modern period and is the author of *The Rococo Interior: Decoration and Social Spaces in Early Eighteenth-Century Paris* (Yale University Press, 1996) and *Becoming Property: Art, Theory, and Law in Early Modern France* (Yale University Press, 2019). She is currently working on a cultural and material history of eighteenth-century Paris.

Hannah Williams is senior lecturer in the History of Art in the School of History, Queen Mary University of London. She is a specialist in French visual and material culture from the seventeenth to the nineteenth century. Her research focuses on artistic communities, local and global histories of the Paris art world, and the social lives of objects. She is the author of *Académie Royale: A History in Portraits* (Routledge, 2015), awarded the Prix Marianne Roland Michel. She led the creation of the digital mapping project *Artists in Paris: Mapping the Eighteenth-Century Art World* (www.artistsinparis.org) and is a founding editor of *Journal18*. She is currently writing a book on art and religion in eighteenth-century Paris and researching a project on art-world ties to French colonies in the Caribbean.